Strategic Factors in Nineteenth Century American Economic History

A National Bureau
of Economic Research
Conference Report

Strategic Factors in Nineteenth Century American Economic History

A Volume to Honor Robert W. Fogel

Edited by Claudia Goldin and Hugh Rockoff

The University of Chicago Press

Chicago and London

Claudia Goldin is a professor of economics at Harvard University, and program director and research associate of the National Bureau of Economic Research. Hugh Rockoff is professor of economics at Rutgers University and a research associate of the National Bureau of Economic Research.

The University of Chicago Press, Chicago 60637
The University of Chicago Press, Ltd., London

Printed in the United States of America
01 00 99 98 97 96 95 94 93 92 1 2 3 4 5 6

ISBN (cloth): 0-226-30112-5

Library of Congress Cataloging-in-Publication Data

Strategic factors in nineteenth century American economic history : a volume to honor Robert W. Fogel / edited by Claudia Goldin and Hugh Rockoff.
p. cm. — (A National Bureau of Economic Research conference report)
Papers presented at a conference held Mar. 2–3, 1991 in Cambridge, Mass.
Includes bibliographical references (p.) and indexes.
1. Labor market—United States—History—20th century—Congresses. 2. Capital market—United States—History—20th century—Congresses. 3. United States—Economic conditions—Congresses. I. Fogel, Robert William. II. Goldin, Claudia Dale. III. Rockoff, Hugh. IV. National Bureau of Economic Research. V. Title: Strategic factors in 19th century American economic history. VI. Series: Conference report (National Bureau of Economic Research)
HD5724.S734 1992
330.973′05—dc20 91-38721
CIP

♾ The paper used in this publication meets the minimum requirements of the American National Standard for Information Sciences—Permanence of Paper for Printed Library Materials, ANSI Z39.48-1984.

Since this volume is a record of conference proceedings, it has been exempted from the rules governing critical review of manuscripts by the Board of Directors of the National Bureau (resolution adopted 8 June 1948, as revised 21 November 1949 and 20 April 1968).

National Bureau of Economic Research

[illegible]

Contents

Introduction

Claudia Goldin and Hugh Rockoff

The essays on American economic history that constitute this volume were presented at a National Bureau of Economic Research–Development of the American Economy (NBER-DAE) conference held March 2–3, 1991 in Cambridge, Massachusetts. The conference had two purposes. One was to bring together research on the implications of expanding markets in labor and capital during the nineteenth century. Another was to honor the individual who, in 1978, founded the DAE within the NBER and was mentor to most of the participants. Those he had not advised were the co-authors of his students or are now his grand-students. With few exceptions the authors employ a methodology pioneered by Robert Fogel—the use of large-scale cross-sectional and longitudinal data sets culled from original sources—to answer questions of current policy interest and of historical relevance. The data used include family genealogies, the U.S. federal population census manuscripts, the manufacturing census manuscripts, manumission records, firm accounts, army personnel records for civilian hires, certificates of freedom for ex-slaves, probate records for the thirteen colonies, farmers' account books, bank balance sheets, and a novel qualitative source—the slave narratives from the Work Projects Administration and Fisk University collections.

The topics covered reflect not only the methodology of Robert Fogel but also the subjects that interest him. This may not be surprising since several of the papers come from dissertations written under his supervision. But that is not what accounts for the similarity. Fogel encourages each of his students to find a dissertation topic they can live wih ("a dissertation is like a marriage," he has frequently remarked). He fosters excellence, scholarship, and relevance, never imitation. Rather, the topics often reflect his concerns because of his powerful influence as a scholar. The topics that interest Fogel soon become of interest to those in the profession. Thus the collection includes papers on railroads, slavery, demography, and political economy—the topics that have been, or are soon to be, those for which he is best known. We have borrowed the title for the volume from the graduate course Fogel offered generations of students at Chicago, Rochester, and Harvard.

Collectively the papers address the issues of market integration and its impact on the lives of Americans. Many of the papers consider the extent to which integration was achieved in labor and capital markets during the nineteenth century (Goldin and Margo; Sokoloff and Villaflor; Rothenberg; Bodenhorn and Rockoff; Bordo, Rappoport, and Schwartz). Another group focuses on how the extent and functioning of these markets affected the lives, material existence, fertility, mortality, and nutritional status of Americans, black and white (Pope; Steckel; Wahl; Komlos; Crawford). Several address how non-market collective action, in the form of government and unions, altered the results of the market mechanism (Carlos and Lewis; Friedman; Reid and Kurth). Inequality in economic condition is highlighted in several papers—for example, those on labor markets (Goldin and Margo; Sokoloff and Villaflor; Yang), as well as those on wealth (Galenson and Pope; Jones).

How did the extension of markets affect individuals? Richard H. Steckel's piece explores the intriguing possibility that Americans reduced their fertility as financial markets expanded, and in Jenny Bourne Wahl's we see that fertility declined as couples were more able to produce "higher quality" children. Stephen Crawford finds that the size of a plantation affected the structure of the slave family. Nutritional status and life expectation, according to John Komlos and Clayne L. Pope in separate contributions, decreased sometime during the nineteenth century even as markets were expanding. Komlos argues that it was precisely this market expansion that had negative consequences for certain groups. Migration, according to Pope's genealogical data, diminished the life expectation of women. David W. Galenson and Clayne L. Pope find that early arrival in an area, reinforced by increases in population and thus the extension of markets, enhanced the wealth of individuals. Finally, Winifred B. Rothenberg shows that the expansion of labor markets within the agricultural and manufacturing sectors fostered long-term contracts between farmers and farm laborers. Thus we see that the integration of both capital and labor markets in the nineteenth century had a wide range of effects on Americans.

The ordering of the papers reflects the consideration and development of the theme by the various authors. The evolution of markets in agricultural and manufacturing labor is considered first; that concerning capital and credit is featured next. The impact of markets on individual outcomes is the subject of the third section, and the final group of papers examines the extra-market institutions of governments and unions.

Labor Markets in Manufacturing and Agriculture

Industrialization in the Northeast, from 1820 to 1860, greatly altered the demand for labor, and Kenneth L. Sokoloff and Georgia C. Villaflor assess which laborers gained from market expansion during early industrialization. They find, using various manufacturing census manuscript sources, that all discernable segments of the industrial labor force in the Northeast realized substantial real wage gains over the thirty-year period and that wage differentials between groups (by skill, by firm size, by geographic place) narrowed as markets expanded. Around a rising trend in real wages, however, were occasional downturns attributable primarily to supply-side shocks originating in the agricultural sector and immigration flows. Claudia Goldin and Robert A. Margo examine labor markets during the same period to assess their flexibility by analyzing the persistence of shocks to the real wage. The flexibility of wages determines the distributive consequences of economic upturns and downturns. If nominal wages are somewhat rigid, then deflations will be accompanied by unemployment for some workers but real wage increases for those fortunate enough to retain their jobs. Inflations, however, will involve real wage losses. Shocks, they find, did not have persistent effects on real wages but did take about five years to run their course. Because their source is the civilian payroll of the military, they can assess differences across region and by occupation for laborers, artisans, and clerks. The persistence of shocks differed by occupation (greatest in clerical jobs and least in agriculture) and by region (least in the growing region of the Midwest). The nonagricultural wage laborer in antebellum America, therefore, was likely to have had a greatly enhanced probability of unemployment during economic downturns and price deflations. Thus there may have been important distributive consequences to shocks to the economy before the Civil War.

Winifred B. Rothenberg examines the reasons for, and the consequences of, the rise of contract labor in agriculture during the century preceding the Civil War. Agricultural labor, as revealed in farmers' account books, was once primarily paid by the day. But increasingly over the nineteenth century, laborer and farmer became partners in a mutually beneficial long-term arrangement—an explicit contract binding the two for several months, a season, or a number of seasons. Day labor had often been provided by friends, while contract labor was frequently that of immigrants and other strangers. Increased immigration, the need for room and board, and the less seasonal demand for labor as farmers relied more on livestock and less on grains encouraged the use of contract labor. It was a market response that may have contributed to increased agricultural productivity in the early nineteenth century.

Donghyu Yang also addresses the causes and consequences of contractual form in agriculture. Using data from the manuscripts of the 1860 census of agriculture, he shows that tenants in the North were younger and poorer than owner-operators, suggesting that tenancy was a rung on the agricultural ladder culminating in ownership. But a closer look at the data reveals that this life-cycle depiction is accurate only for the North Central region. In the Northeast, on the other hand, farmers on the lower rung of the ladder were increasingly lured away by rapidly growing industrial labor markets (the development explored in the Sokoloff and Villaflor paper) and the ready availability of land in the West. Yang also explores the productivity of tenant farmers. Economic theory has vacillated on whether tenant farmers are as productive as owner-operators. After holding constant numerous variables that influenced productivity, Yang finds that, in the North Central region, tenant farmers were less efficient than owner-operators, suggesting the existence of traditional Marshallian inefficiencies. In the Northeast, however, tenants were as productive as owner-operators, probably because supervision by owners counteracted any tendency towards inefficiency. The longer period over which agricultural institutions evolved in the Northeast, as brought out in Rothenberg's paper, may help account for regional differences in efficiency by tenure.

Markets in Capital and Credit

Economic historians have assembled considerable evidence that capital markets were not well integrated in the 1870s and 1880s, but they have had scarce knowledge of their functioning in the decades prior to the Civil War. Howard Bodenhorn and Hugh Rockoff explore whether capital markets were as imperfectly integrated before the Civil War as they were in the two decades after. The surprising answer is that short-term interest rates (rates of return to the earning assets of banks) across various regions were more similar to the rate found in New York City before 1860 than they were in the 1870s and 1880s. The Civil War, therefore, must have precipitated a divergence in rates, and various developments during the war—the establishment of the National Banking System, for one—must have impeded the reintegration of a national capital market. While the authors do not discuss in detail the reasons for the initial integration, it seems likely that part of the story concerns the network of correspondent banking relations that fed into the New York call loan market (also explored by Bordo, Rappoport, and Schwartz). The findings in the Bodenhorn and Rockoff paper provide critical evidence for other papers in this volume that hinge on the integration of capital markets in the antebellum period.

In a piece with considerable relevance for current debates among macroeconomists, Michael D. Bordo, Peter Rappoport, and Anna J. Schwartz ask whether bank credit rationing or the supply of money had a larger impact on the vicissitudes of the nineteenth century economy. The central issue is whether monetary phenomena are a key determinant of business cycle fluctuations or whether changes in the composition of bank lending are also important influences. They, therefore, explore reasons for the macroeconomic shocks that are largely treated as exogenous in other papers in this volume (e.g., Goldin and Margo; Sokoloff and Villaflor). The authors find evidence of an integrated national capital market in which excess funds moved through a network of correspondent banks to be invested in the New York call loan market. Fluctuations in bank lending appear to have been due mostly to fluctuations in call loans, with other loans (the most likely channel for bank credit rationing) quite stable over the business cycle. Once the distinction between call loans and other loans is taken into account, the credit rationing effect becomes negligible but monetary factors remain robust.

David W. Galenson and Clayne L. Pope ask how duration in an area affected wealth accumulation and how the "precedence rate" (the persistence rate divided by population growth), as they term it, affected rents to duration. In doing so, they also ask how market growth affected the fortunes of early arrivals as opposed to those who settled later. They find, in an analysis of individuals, that rents to duration were substantial and, in a related county-wide analysis, that these rents were largely due to precedence. Not only were the fortunes of settlers enhanced by their early arrival but they were further magnified by the later arrival of others, thus by expanding markets in labor and capital. The paper by Alice Hanson Jones is based on her unique set of colonial probate records. It was found among her papers which are held at the Columbia University Rare Book and Manuscript Library and was pieced together from various drafts by Boris Simkovich. Jones (with Simkovich) explores the fate of women in the colonial period through the lens of their wealth accumulation. Few women, it appears, held wealth in their own names, and those who did owned on average about half as much as did men. If a woman's husband was wealthy, she was generally provided for after his death. But the limited employment opportunities for women outside the home made it hard for most widows and unmarried women to maintain or increase their wealth.

The Demography of Free and Slave Populations

Five papers on the demography of free and slave populations clearly show the implications of expanding markets in labor and capital for the standard of living of the population. Clayne L. Pope addresses how the mortality experience of Americans changed across the nineteenth century and what levels of life expectation existed for men and women and for migrant and nonmigrant. He finds, using an extensive collection of genealogies, that mortality did not increase during the nineteenth century but, instead, cycled, first up and then down. That life expectation did not increase monotonically during a period of large-scale industrialization, urbanization, and immigration could mean that market expansion and income growth had unexpected consequences for the population. Further, women at age twenty had lower life expectations than did men, and women, but not men, were adversely affected by migration west. Thus, Pope's work clearly addresses how life expectation was affected by the expansion of markets. Not surprisingly for students of Simon Kuznets, market development may initially have made the distribution of labor's rewards more unequal.

In his exploration of the nutritional status of free blacks, John Komlos addresses a related aspect of the impact of market expansion, and his findings add further support to the notion that there were adverse consequences for many in the population. Using anthropometric data (heights by age) from the Maryland Certificates of Freedom (manumission records), he finds that sometime in the early nineteenth century this population of free blacks suffered a decrease in height and thus, by inference, a decline in nutritional status. This work reinforces previous research of Komlos on similar measures for the white population. Because free blacks in Maryland who were positioned closer to food sources were somewhat taller than those who were not, market expansion appears to have had detrimental effects on some individuals. Urbanization and income growth, therefore, may not have had a positive impact on the entire population of Americans in the early nineteenth century.

The family structure of slaves is examined by Stephen Crawford using the remembrances of aged blacks in the 1930s, freed by Emancipation some sixty years before. Two-parent families, on the same or nearby farms, were present for about two-thirds of all children, at least during their early lives, and these unions, perhaps not surprisingly, experienced higher fertility than female-headed families. Larger plantations had a greater percentage of two-parent families, but children in female-headed families do not appear to have been neglected. Ex-slaves who grew up in female-headed families did not recount more deprivation or abuse than did those in two-parent families. Two-parent families, therefore, enhanced the profits of masters through increased births. But the exigencies of market expansion in cotton led them to profit by moving plantations, thus dividing families when husband and wife lived on neighboring farms, and from selling individual children from parents, parents from children, and husbands from wives. Overall the narratives reveal both the strength of the slave family and its vulnerability.

Richard H. Steckel directly addresses how the expansion of the market affected the fertility of rural Americans between 1850 and 1860. Using a linked sample of rural households drawn from the 1850 and 1860 federal population manuscript censuses, he assesses various hypotheses offered to explain the nineteenth century fertility decline. He finds that the model accounting for the largest fraction of cross-sectional variation contains a variable proxying the degree of financial market development. The variable used measures the number of banks per person and could indicate that financial assets substituted for children as old-age security or, more likely, that various aspects of economic development (but not just land density) led parents to have fewer children. A related question—whether parents throughout the nineteenth century progressively substituted higher quality children for more, lower quality children—is posed and answered by Jenny Bourne Wahl. As markets in goods and factors expanded, as schooling costs decreased, and as the opportunities for married women outside the home (but not necessarily in the labor market) expanded, parents had fewer but higher quality children. The paper leans heavily on results that bear on the relationship between wealth and fertility that suggest that the quantity-quality model could have operated in the nineteenth century. The estimation, which nests the well-known bequest model, takes advantage of the richness of a three-generation linked sample from family genealogies.

Political Economy

Three papers look at the role of government in altering the allocation and distribution of resources. Ann M. Carlos and Frank Lewis address whether government subsidies to two Canadian railroads built in the 1850s—the Grand Trunk and the Great Western—made economic sense. The historical literature suggests that these railroads, although privately unprofitable, were socially profitable. The authors, through a careful study of company records, find that the Great Western was socially profitable and that a relatively small additional subsidy would have made it privately profitable as well. But they find that the Grand Trunk was probably socially as well as privately unprofitable. The form of the subsidies offered the railroads—loan guarantees—and the consequences have a depressingly up-to-date ring. While the Great Western received small amounts of limited guarantees, the Grand Trunk received considerable aid. Even though the initial guarantees to the Grand Trunk were limited, the bond offerings convinced many that the government's guarantee might be open-ended. The Grand Trunk was thus encouraged to issue large amounts of heavily discounted debt, contributing to its eventual failure. The government, in turn, felt compelled to bail out the railroad to preserve stability in the market for Canadian debt.

Explanations for the existence of patronage and its decline over time in large cities are examined by Joseph P. Reid, Jr., and Michael M. Kurth. Large-city governments altered their means of gaining votes depending on whether the electorate was heterogeneous or homogeneous, poorer or richer. Thus politically provided goods, individualized and tailored to the needs of a diverse immigrant population, expanded when immigrants were numerically important. As incomes grew and as the citizenry became more homogeneous, public goods flourished and patronage declined. Gerald Friedman provides a somewhat different, but complementary, framework to understand the relationship between market forces and collective action. He asks how governments won over the electorate when labor threatened to organize and become a powerful political force. Large-city governments managed to divide labor, win over a segment of the work force, and reduce the strength of the labor movement. According to Friedman, the building trades became favored by big-city governments and their wages were increased. They, in turn,—it is presumed—supported these governments and weakened the rest of the labor movement. Reid and Kurth would also add that big-city governments directly promoted the building trades through the construction of parks, museums, libraries, and the like. Government, therefore, managed to divide and conquer labor while placating the electorate with public goods.

The volume begins with two appreciations of Robert W. Fogel as co-author, colleague, and scholar by Stanley L. Engerman and Donald N. McCloskey. The essays are more than a collection of revealing, engaging, and humorous remembrances, although they are that too. The appreciations consider the purpose and significance of the methodology innovated by Fogel. The volume concludes with a listing of the dissertations supervised by Fogel and his publications.

Fogel continues to excite students at the University of Chicago to work under his supervision and with him on his projects. He has recently begun a project of enormous complexity and importance on the aging of the American population that may well be his finest. It combines the talents of economic historians, medical doctors, statisticians, and demographers, and is on as grand a scale as any in which he has been involved. He is also finishing a volume, *The Escape from Hunger and Early Death: Europe and America, 1750–2050,* and is writing another (with Enid M. Fogel) on his mentor, Simon Kuznets, and the rise of modern empirical economics. The pace, intensity, and importance of his research have remained undiminished over time.

Two Appreciations

Stanley L. Engerman
Donald N. McCloskey

Stanley L. Engerman

Robert William Fogel: An Appreciation by a Coauthor and Colleague

Sometime in either late 1974 or 1975 I ran across a friend who had just seen a Hollywood musical. It was in the genre of the complications of song-writing partners for whom output required some joint contributions and interactions. This led him to wonder what scholarly work under similar circumstances was like, since both activities were done frequently by individuals but collaborations occurred with sufficient frequency that they were not unusual. In particular, he wondered how Bob and I had begun working together and what was the nature of the input on *Time on the Cross* and our dealing with the related conferences and responses. I doubt if I fully answered his queries—some things are more easily done than described—but, in reflecting on this encounter, certain aspects of our working together did come to mind.

Although Bob and I began collaborating in 1963, we had first begun exchanging ideas at Johns Hopkins soon after I arrived in 1958 to start graduate work in economics. Bob had already been there a year or so, having completed his master's degree at Columbia with Carter Goodrich after leaving his communist past behind in the mid-1950s. When we first met as graduate students, he was completing revisions on his book on the Union Pacific Railroad and starting work on his railroad book, on which I was a research assistant for several weeks, measuring distances of various counties from navigable waterways.

During my first year I had to make a presentation at the Journal Club, a monthly Hopkins graduate-student ritual. The discussion was to be based on a publication in a leading economics journal. After I was talked out of choosing an article on the history of economic thought, I selected the Alfred Conrad and John Meyer article on antebellum slavery in the April 1958 issue of the *Journal of Political Economy.*[1] The ensuing discussions, both at the Journal Club and for weeks after among students and faculty, were lively, with Bob quite heavily involved. Indeed, the arguments led directly to a major publication by a fellow graduate student, Yasukichi Yasuba.[2] Given the impact of the Conrad and Meyer article in history and in economic history, both Bob and I maintained a strong residual interest in the subject, although it did not lead directly to research and publication for a number of years and only after several detours, including Bob's completion of his major work on the railroad.

Bob left Hopkins in 1960 to take a position at the University of Rochester. He soon signed a contract with W. W. Norton to write a text in American economic history. Our next contact came when Bob invited me to work with him on this project. Not soon after, Bob was asked to visit Chicago and, in a related turn of events, I was asked to visit Rochester for a year. Bob stayed at Chicago and I at Rochester. The work on the text moved ahead, but at a rather slow pace. The problem with writing what was meant to be an innovative text was our feeling that, while there was much new in the literature, many issues still seemed open. To get the thing done appropriately (or, rather, as we wanted it) would require much more research and writing, considerably more than we felt we could comfortably accomplish in a reasonable time.

We chose, as an interim step, to publish a collection of articles and papers on the "new economic history," and we called it *The Reinterpretation of American Economic History.* The readings were, for the most part, drawn from the existing literature, but we felt expansions in several areas would be useful. One, in particular, dealt with an analysis of the debates and issues on the economics of slavery that would complement the reprinting of the Conrad and Meyer and Yasuba articles. This, of course, opened up a range of questions and topics that seemed eminently researchable. Thus, when our National Science Foundation grant to study the antebellum iron industry expired, after the collection of primary data from various Pennsylvania archives and the publication of an article in the *Journal of Political Economy,* we decided to shift our research interests to the economics of slavery in the antebellum South, to gather additional data to answer questions posed in the earlier publications and to get at some important historical questions that had not yet received the attention they merited by economic historians.

The actual research and writing on slavery was aided by Bob's appointment to spend each fall semester at the University of Rochester. Rochester at this time was a particularly exciting place to be working on American slavery. Eugene Genovese and Herbert Gutman, in the history department, provided

1. Alfred H. Conrad and John R. Meyer, "The Economics of Slavery in the Ante-Bellum South," *Journal of Political Economy,* 66 (Apr. 1958), pp. 95–122.

2. Yasukichi Yasuba, "The Profitability and Viability of Plantation Slavery in the United States," *The Economic Studies Quarterly,* 12 (Sept. 1961), pp. 60–67.

much in the way of stimulation and interaction, while several members of the economics department, particularly Ronald Jones, Richard Rosett, James Friedman, Sherwin Rosen, and Lionel McKenzie, had interests, for varying reasons, in the application of economics to the study of historical issues. Being together with Bob, even for part of the year, made joint work considerably easier than it had been in our first attempt earlier in the 1960s. We used a then state-of-the-art technology (and one whose use Bob would expand upon)—the tape recorder—and, when not in the same place, exchanged long taped monologues, leaving, at one time, small mountains of tapes in various locales. Being at the same place cut down on the tapes but entailed other costs—including frequent working dinners at the nearest Ponderosa Steak House and a detailed knowledge of various short-order restaurants and diners near the University of Rochester. While we continued to use tapes in future years, we found that the telephone permitted better communicaton, although the bottleneck in exchanging written materials slowed our output in this era before Federal Express, overnight mail, fax, and bitnet. Given Bob's well-known sense of urgency, all this suggests the ability of people to adjust to constraints when necessary but also an eagerness to take advantage of change as it occurs. Bob became one of the earliest users of Federal Express that I am aware of.

Whatever the form of interaction with Bob, the first, and perhaps the most basic, feature was the sense of intellectual excitement. Scholarly work was a cumulative process—there were questions of detail to address, and also the need to discern what the impact would be for broader issues of interpretation and analysis. For example, we had early begun to collect data on slave prices by age and sex from probate inventories at various southern archives. The use of probates was, of course, suggested to us by one of Bob's more remarkable students, Alice Hanson Jones, whose thesis demonstrated their great usefulness in studying many historical problems. Our primary purpose, at first, was to get a set of slave prices by age and sex for use in a refined set of rate of return calculations, as well as to use in making adjustments to the labor force input measure for calculations of southern agricultural productivity. The probate record listings revealed patterns suggesting that slave family units were recognized. These listings often permitted calculations of family size and of differences in age between mothers and children.

Obviously none of this material was as simple to utilize as was initially hoped. But, as some early work indicated, and as the far more extensive collection and analysis of these and related data by Bob's student Richard Steckel have demonstrated, probate listings (and plantation records) have had a larger payoff than originally anticipated. Another example is the use of data on height by age, which were initially found in a source we were made aware of by a graduate student elsewhere. It was suggested that the material on the coastal shipping manifests would be useful in examining the internal slave trade, as they were, but they also opened up to us a line of research with other broad implications. Such a benefit, alas, never accrued from the data on shoe size, another type of anthropometric data found in a number of the plantation records. James Trussell did locate a relevant article on foot length in *Human Biology* in 1944, but that has been the extent of our research on that subject.[3] The plantation records did have other unanticipated uses however. After a lunch conversation with Herbert Gutman we provided him with copies of slave lists from several plantations we found in various archives. These lists grouped slaves in family units or extended for long periods of time and included information on slave births, having the names of both mother and father. These listings were, as Herb generously acknowledged later, important to him in his examination of slave family and naming patterns.

At times the material we uncovered led in a different direction than we anticipated and from the then more widely held view. The next question was to understand why scholars, including ourselves, had looked at the issue differently. What was the basic evidence presented for these views—what sources and tests were undertaken—and how did this all relate to the broader views of the questions under discussion? There was never a sense that evidence would be found that would end debate. Rather, further examination was seen as essential, both to buttress arguments and also to understand, in as much depth as possible, the arguments of those with whom we seemed to be in disagreement (or, at times, agreement). All this involved Bob's considerable imagination and intellectual energy—a work pace of great intensity in order to deal simultaneously with the many facets of any one question, as well as with the many questions that were to be examined.

Working with Bob one understood that just about all questions were, if not answerable, at least approachable with some empirical data. The data need not be restricted to quantitative information, although many of the questions historians discuss are concerned simply with, How many? Data could also be drawn from various sources, given an interest in different questions. But, for Bob, if a question were asked, there must be some way to get an answer. And an answer that, if not fully convincing, at least moved the question (especially if framed and made in particular ways) one step further along—and it was best not to have merely one answer provided by just one approach or data source. As Bob was often reminded by his teacher Simon Kuznets, there should be several different ways to get at a problem. These ways should encompass different sources and methods, and only a multitude of approaches could make one feel confident with any answer. This belief led to a certain view concerning the nature and possibilities of using evidence. Presumably there was always too much potential evidence, and one could only deal with a limited part of it. Yet even if the magnitude of unutilized (and presently unutilizable) evidence was great, what was available meant that a "tentative" an-

3. Howard V. Meredith, "Human Foot Length from Embryo to Adult," *Human Biology,* 16 (Dec. 1944), pp. 207–82.

swer—tentative in that no one had yet utilized all the data that was possible to use—was possible.

This probing of evidence characterized Bob's efforts in at least two different ways. First, whenever a question was asked, he would start by determining the types of evidence that could be brought to bear on it. What was there in primary sources or in the secondary literature? Whom could we call to find out what types of records existed and what information was available? We were fortunate to work in the computer era, permitting extensive use of records that could previously be used only partially by scholars. Second, the collection of data fed on itself, opening up many new questions. In some cases it was the nature of material collected for one purpose that suggested answers to other questions; in others (as Bob describes in the *Cliometrics Newsletter*) there was a feeling that the data might be useful for other questions that could open up new lines of research. An example, as discussed above, was the case of the height data drawn from the coastal manifests of slave shipments, originally used in the study of the slave trade. In other cases, however, the payoff never materialized, but not because questions were left unasked and the potential unexamined.

There are two other characteristics that Bob revealed in this work. First, as a scholar he is truly interdisciplinary, with interests going well beyond those of an economist or historian but encompassing whatever seems relevant for the issues under study. Clearly an economist by training and inclination, as demonstrated in his approach to shaping questions and collecting evidence, he sought to present findings in their broadest interpretive light. Thus all questions were looked at for their relevance to broader themes and, also, whenever other disciplinary areas needed to be pursued to answer questions, this was to be undertaken. Second, Bob has a keen sense of scholarship as a collective discipline. This goes beyond the involvement with collaborative works and large-scale projects. The data collected for *Time on the Cross,* for example, were early made available to all scholars. And with all the criticisms and debates concerning *Time on the Cross*—debates that started early, continued long, and covered just about all issues (sometimes coming from rather opposite directions)—it remained Bob's belief that more evidence, more analysis, and more detailed specification in argument would help to clarify and resolve the disagreements—or at least some of them. The polemical, not just intellectual, tactics of responding to criticism led to problems (interesting, as well as amusing, in retrospect) because of the quite contrasting nature of some of the questions raised, making caution necessary regarding the expected interpretation of any response. But, at the least, it was believed that the questions raised in debate, even in disagreement, were ones that could (and should) be studied and examined, and that it was only by these steps that scholarly knowledge could be advanced.

There was one characteristic in the songwriter movies that remains in mind: that the collaboration, with all its hard work, ultimately was fun for those involved. To ask questions, to search for evidence, to piece things together—all of this can, of course, be done by one person; but, sometimes, a joint effort goes beyond the mere intellectual satisfaction, and the act of collaboration provides its own independent stimulation and enjoyment. Perhaps this is why, over recent years, the magnitude of joint works by economists and also by historians has increased dramatically, although curiously, for those who might have predicted this on the basis of a combining of differing specializations and the division of labor, that explanation seems to account for only a small part of the observed increase. But that is a story, and movie genre, for another time and place.

Donald N. McCloskey

Robert William Fogel: An Appreciation by an Adopted Student

Professors must have had teachers who made a difference. After all, they decided to become teachers themselves rather than movie stars or big-game hunters. Counting from when I began studying economics, the teachers who have mattered most to me were Eric Gustafson, John R. Meyer, Alexander Gerschenkron, and Robert William Fogel. Officially I was not Fogel's student but his colleague, from 1968 when I arrived at Chicago as an assistant professor until 1975, when Fogel left for a sojourn at Cambridge and a new job at Harvard. Being Fogel's colleague, though, felt like being his student (a feeling reinforced by the students he had gathered in 1968, who were about my age but knew a lot more economics than I did). One could not be around the best historical economist since Schumpeter for any length of time without learning a lot, even if such a one were not a great teacher. But Fogel was, and is. Gladly would he learn and gladly teach.

Fogel's personal qualities smoothed the way and taught their own lessons. He is for one thing the soul of wit and warmth. Wit is common enough in academic life, and especially so among economists, irrationally proud of their quickness. William James called it the "Harvard indifference"—"the smoking of cigarettes and living on small sarcasms."[1] Warmth, however, is rare. The average academic applies small sarcasms indiscriminantly to his students and junior colleagues and certainly to his rivals. Fogel refrained from "applying" his wit to anyone. Anyone in Fogel's presence, from the cab driver waiting in front of the Quadrangle Club to the president of the university, gets treated

1. Quoted in Gerald E. Myers, *William James: His Life and Thought* (New Haven, 1986), p. 12.

with the same warmth, a warmth which is spiced—not poisoned—by his ready wit.

Fogel, in other words, is more of a democrat than most of us. He therefore does not commit the characteristic sin of academic life, sneering. In the twenty-odd years I have known him I have not seen him sneer; not once, despite his numerous opportunities. Fogel's personal and intellectual tolerance shames us all. I once complained to him about the rank favoritism that another senior economic historian exhibited in his hiring, disregarding merit in favor of his former students. Fogel laughed tolerantly: it is not the worst of sins, he said, to favor one's own. I once tried to persuade him at lunch that certain activities in mathematical economics, hostile to his empirical values, were not good for economics. No, said he: we cannot tell; the investment in today's existence theorem may pay off in the next century. Fogel can teach because he is willing to learn, from the least of us, ready to see merit in the misled, ready to attribute admirable motives to his enemies.

So the first thing he taught students and colleagues was a simple, democratic, even American openness. Openness is hard to learn. Judith Shklar has described snobbery as "the habit of making inequality hurt."[2] Snobbery and sneering are anti-democratic vices, and American democracy has always been uncomfortable with scholarship. But in Robert Fogel's case, being a superior scholar does not entail making the inequality hurt.

His easy relations with students and junior colleagues were something new for me. Fogel and his wife, Enid, took the social responsibilities of academic leadership seriously. My supervisor, Gerschenkron, had been amusing and courteous in a European way but no drinking buddy with junior faculty and graduate students. At Chicago circa 1968, however, drinking with intellectual buddies was the style, the most serious teachers in this line being Al Harberger, Bob Mundell, Harry Johnson, and Bob Fogel. Fogel would meet the students and faculty after the weekly economic history workshop for beer and too many bowls of potato chips at the Quadrangle Club; he would pick up the bill when the last student tottered home; then he would walk up 57th Street with Harry Johnson to the apartment.

The talk at the table was economics. Students learned economics personally, by discussing real economic institutions with a first-rate economist. We never talked about sports, seldom about public or academic politics. The questions were, What do you make of this or that economic argument? Does it fit the historical evidence? What kind of evidence? How would you get it? How do you know?

The evidence Fogel favored, of course, was quantitative. He approved of the remark by Lord Kelvin, slightly misquoted in the stones of the Social Science Building at Chicago: "When you cannot measure it, when you cannot

2. Judith N. Shklar, *Ordinary Vices* (Cambridge, Mass., 1984), p. 87.

express it in numbers, your knowledge is of a meagre and unsatisfactory kind. . . . It may be the beginning of knowledge, but you have scarcely in your thoughts advanced to the stage of *science*."[3]

Even in conversations outside of class Fogel pursued quantitative science. He pursued it with algebra, not geometry. Fogel believed that when one could not express an economic argument in algebra, your knowledge was of a meagre and unsatisfactory kind. Many lunchtime hours in the solarium of the Quad Club were spent in communal attempts to convert someone's geometrical or verbal argument into algebra, and this for two reasons. First, Fogel thinks algebraically. He will not believe a proposition until it has been put through his algebraic tortures, complete with cunning asterisks, subtle subscripts, and mind-stunning tables of variables.[4]

Second, if one is going to do more than speculate on the direction of effects, you need the algebra, because only then can you use actual measurements. Here was the great principle: measure, then measure again, then measure still again. Fogel is like a carpenter of history, spending as much time in measuring and remeasuring as in sawing or hammering: measure twice, cut once. He agrees with John Clapham, the first holder of a chair of economic history at Cambridge: "every economic historian should . . . have acquired what might be called the statistical sense, the habit of asking in relation to any institution, group or movement the questions: how large? how long? how often? how representative?"[5] Substitute "social scientist" for "economic historian" and add to "institution, group or movement" the phrase "alleged explanation," and you have Fogel's procedure exactly.

The procedure meant that as little as possible was left to blackboard speculation. Other economists might be content to note the *likelihood* that social savings of railroads were small, the *possibility* that economies of scale in sectors served by railroads were large, the *existence* of miscegenation among slaves and masters, the *presence* of nutritional effects in death rates. Fogel insisted on measuring them. As he wrote a few years ago about declining mortality since 1700, "the debate . . . revealed that the critical differences were quantitative rather than qualitative."[6] The "debate," a favorite Fogel word, was always "revealing" to him that the issue was quantitative. One sus-

3. William Thomson, Lord Kelvin, "Electrical Units of Measurement" (1883), reprinted in his *Popular Lectures and Addresses,* vol. 1 (London, 1888–89), first page of this lecture.

4. The mathematician Ian Stewart has said that there are two kinds of mathematicians: "Most work in terms of visual images and mental pictures; a minority thinks in formulas." And so in other fields: "Johannes Müller, a famous biologist, said that his mental picture of a dog was like this: DOG" (*Does God Play Dice? The New Mathematics of Chaos* [New York, 1990], p. 95). Fogel's mental picture of slavery seems to be like this: $P^* = H^* - i^* + X^*$.

5. John H. Clapham, "Economic History as a Discipline," *Encyclopedia of the Social Sciences* (1930), reprinted in F. C. Lane and J. C. Riemersma, eds., *Enterprise and Secular Change* (Homewood, Ill., 1953), p. 416.

6. Robert W. Fogel, "Nutrition and the Decline in Mortality since 1700: Some Additional Preliminary Findings," National Bureau of Economic Research Working Paper no. 1802 (1986), p. 105.

pects that he didn't really need the debate to know that it was. How large? How representative?

Fogel takes fewer shortcuts in measuring things than any student of society I know this side of the medievalists. He even eschews the shortcuts "implied by theory," as the optimistic phrase among economists has it. I have tried repeatedly to persuade him that Harberger's Theorem suffices to show that the static effect of railroads on growth was small: if you multiply together the share of transport in national income, the share of railroads in all transport, and any rough estimate of the cost saving of railroads over canals (noting that all three numbers are well below unity), you are going to get a small number. Fogel was and is unimpressed.[7] He says that to really know you have to scour the records of the industry and write a 296-page book.

Paul David speculated once that railroads induced economies of scale.[8] In Fogel's astonishing presidential address to the Economic History Association, the longest in its history, delivered one September night in a mock-Tudor college hall in Toronto, he actually measured the alleged economies of scale and showed them to be small. The measurement showed the frailties of the qualitative reasoning that David and I and most other economists rely on.[9] He stands with Newton in saying *hypotheses non fingo,* I do not express mere hypotheses, "For what I tell . . . is not Hypothesis but the most rigid consequence, not conjectured . . . but evinced by the meditation of experiments concluded directly and without any suspicion of doubt."[10] Maybe this is why he is so tolerant of the sterile rigor of mathematical economics, seeing in it a shadow of the rigid consequence of fact. The empiricist and rationalist traditions of the West, British and French, meet on the grounds of certitude.

When I first met Fogel's rigid consequence, reading *Railroads and American Economic Growth* in a graduate seminar with Gerschenkron in 1965, I detected a fellow positivist. Since then I have grown critical of the philosophical position that Fogel believes goes along with being quantitative. As most plainly revealed in his little book of 1983 with Geoffrey Elton, Fogel believes that a quantitative science follows the precepts of philosophy of science circa 1950.[11] He has since 1983 shifted ground some, especially in consequence of his work on religious conviction as a force in British and American abolitionism. Yet he is still loyal in his philosophy of science to the older, received view. He would reply: There is no sin in such loyalty. Surely he is right. Fogel

7. His latest restatement is an interview in the *Newsletter of the Cliometric Society,* 5 (July 1990), pp. 3–8, 20–28.

8. Paul A. David, "Transportation Innovations and Economic Growth: Professor Fogel On and Off the Rails," *Economic History Review,* 2d. ser., 22 (Dec. 1969), pp. 506–25.

9. Robert W. Fogel, "Notes on the Social Saving Controversy," *Journal of Economic History,* 39 (March 1979), pp. 1–54, esp. 39–44.

10. *Correspondence,* p. 96f., quoted in Gale E. Christianson, *In the Presence of the Creator: Isaac Newton and His Times* (New York, 1984), p. 94.

11. Robert W. Fogel and G. R. Elton, *Which Road to the Past? Two Views of History* (New Haven, 1983).

keeps the faith. The positivistic faith that inspired Robert Fogel, Milton Friedman, Paul Samuelson, and the rest may not nowadays be persuasive philosophy, but judging from results it served to motivate a lot of good science.

Other features of his personality taught us, too. His convivial but intellectual socializing was presided over by Enid, between her or his airplane voyages to and from Rochester (my wife and I were charmed to hear that Enid and Bob were accustomed to having dates in O'Hare Airport, as their travels crossed; and this before such jet-setting was common). The Fogels together taught that intellectual life was worthy of ceremony. I think Bob was for this reason exceptionally pleased with his year as Pitt Professor of American Institutions at Cambridge: boy from the Bronx sips hundred-year-old port and smokes Havana cigars after dinner with the fellows of Kings.[12]

Fogel's socialist background made a big impression on me and taught me to outgrow my own socialism. Here was a man who had been a paid organizer for one of the principal youth organizations of the Communist Party.[13] And yet he was reasonable. I had heard the Yogi-and-the-Commissar line, that once a radical always a radical, of the right if not of the left. The line is a sort of McCarthyism of the middle (I pause to note the analogy with the anti-Chicago McCarthyism among coastie economists, from which Fogel has suffered, gracefully). Fogel in the flesh, however, was nothing like either the Yogi or the Commissar. He described himself quite accurately as a Scoop Jackson Democrat and argued genially with us about the good sides of Nixon, Vietnam, and Mayor Daley. One learned that people could change their minds on reasonable grounds, and then go on to argue with civility about things that mattered.

One learned also from Fogel the nitty gritty of being a professor. Only my time as a research assistant for John R. Meyer on his projects in history and transportation economics made as much of an impression. Fogel, for example, sends draft papers out for comment on a massive scale. His students have adopted the practice. Invite criticism and take advantage of it. Mail is cheap. "I'd rather be criticized in private by a friend," says Fogel, "than be savaged in public by an enemy." And unlike most of us he actually believes it. He believes deeply in the conversation of scholarship, often starting a new project by writing long, sweetly reasonable letters to other scholars, whether or not he has been introduced.

Fogel does not spurn the nitty gritty of administration, especially if it too is scholarly. He assembled research teams, larger and larger and larger, with the help of Marilyn Coopersmith, administrative genius of the Fogel band and big

12. Enid will, I hope, not mind if I report that she was not so pleased with Cambridge's chauvinistic ceremonies, once flatly refusing a feminine request to break off a conversation and "come out with the other ladies while the gentlemen have their port and cigars."

13. Enid was scornful at the "paid" part. She told me once that being from working-class parents, unlike Bob, she expected the boss to pay the employees on payday, even if the boss was the Revolution.

sister to us all. He has repeatedly created new institutions and taught his students the desirability of doing the same. His workshop in economic history was one of many in the Chicago department of economics. The institution of workshops is Chicago's main contribution to the culture of the field. But Fogel's was suffused with warmth as well as rigor. Some of the other workshops at Chicago seemed to spring more from the dark side of the Force. Fogel did much to advance economic history on a larger stage, from his active service on the Mathematical Social Science Board of the Social Science Research Council down to his creation of the National Bureau of Economic Research's program on the Development of the American Economy. He broadened historical economics by involving scholars from other countries and other disciplines. Chicago had a stream of foreign visitors coming to study with Fogel because Fogel does not view demographers and historians as engaged in some other enterprise, which we economists can safely ignore. Like most economists he believes in intellectual specialization. But unlike most economists he is consistent in his economics: after the specialization he also believes in trade, rather than the piling up of exports unsold in the backyard.

Fogel embraced with enthusiasm the nitty-gritty task of financing all this work. He taught us that a scholarly life was worth paying for. He got fellowships for his visitors, he argued for appointments, and he paid for much of the resulting intellectual activity out of his own pocket. He spent what seemed like enormous sums on cameras and tape recorders and other equipment, using them to record first drafts of papers in seminars and to photograph participants quarreling with each other at conferences. A tape of the departmental skit ran as background music for the famous annual Indoor Picnic at Bob and Enid's.

All these unifications of Fogel's life with his work were corollaries of the Great Nitty Gritty: put scholarship first. Always, always, scholarship came first. Moses Abramowitz, a student of Simon Kuznets as was Fogel, tells how difficult it was for he himself to encounter Kuznets because the older scholar would invariably ask, as though to a graduate student who was not making very good progress on his dissertation, "Well, Moses, what are you working on?" Fogel acted always as though Kuznets was going to show up in a few minutes and pop the overwhelming question, "Well, Robert, what are you working on?" He worked, and works, incessantly, to a plan that Kuznets would recognize as the most serious of scholarly work.

The work is guided by Fogel's Fifty-year Rule, which he taught us all: Will it matter in fifty years? Because he really does believe the rule, Fogel has been calmer in controversy than you or I would have been under similar provocation. He does not worry about short-run defeats, such as the politically poisoned reaction to his book with Stanley Engerman, *Time on the Cross: The Economics of American Negro Slavery.* What matters is the reaction in fifty years. As the driving instructor advises, Fogel aims high in steering.

The Fifty-year Rule entails thinking big, which Fogel does himself and encourages in his students and colleagues. He still has the detailed thesis proposal he presented to Kuznets on 14 January 1959. The seminar participants at Johns Hopkins heard a nineteen-page paper entitled "Notes on the Influence of the Railroads on American Economic Growth, 1830–1890." It begins, "The railroads exercised a decisive influence on the course of American economic growth in the 19th century." There follows a Schumpeterian-Rostovian paean to the iron horse, and a two-page outline of the proposed dissertation. Think big. The outline covers most of the railroad subjects written on since then, such as the economies of scale and the population growth attributable to railroads, capital formation in railroads, and comparisons of social savings in other countries. The long book that finally resulted from this exercise in scholarly chutzpa, it turns out, covered only two of the seventeen proposed subjects. Here was someone building a monument for the ages, more durable than bronze.

But he was always willing to change the plans for the monument as the building proceeded. As a graduate student he changed his mind on American railroads, moving from a pro- to an anti-Rostow position in the face of evidence. As a professor he was enthusiastic when students and junior colleagues (such as Jacob Metzer and John Coatsworth) came to contrary conclusions about the role of railroads in other countries. People who have not been close to Fogel cannot believe that he has a flexible mind. They see only the vigorous advocacy in the short run. Dogmatists interpret advocacy by others as dogmatism like their own. Fogel could say more truthfully than could most of his critics, *dogma non fingo,* I do not express mere dogma. Fogel has changed his mind on railroads, on slavery (he started as a doubter of the Conrad and Meyer view), on abolition (he started as a doubter of the force of religion), and on death rates (he started as a doubter of the importance of nutrition). He has changed his mind more than any scholar I know, although one must admit that the competition in this line is not especially fierce.

It was of course his astounding scholarly productions that most kept our attention as students and colleagues. The man could have been a colorless curmudgeon and still have taught us a great deal.

Fogel is the master of historical economics, taking it to the frontiers of economic and historical study. His works on railways, slavery, abolitionism, and now mortality have carried out in unprecedented detail the program of using modern economics to understand history. No economist or historian combines the scholarly values of economics and of history more thoroughly.

Fogel believes that the example of historical economics will make other parts of history and economics broader. A profession that aims at *histoire totale* can be improved by analytic and computational techniques applied to historical numbers. And as the historical evidence improves (indeed, as the present becomes the past), economic history will take an increasing share of the argument in economics itself. The anti-historical frame of mind in economics cannot last, no more than can the anti-quantitative frame of mind in history.

It would be a strange aberration in the history of astronomy if astronomers resolved to concentrate exclusively on the solar system or to concentrate exclusively on the red side of the spectrum. The stars in all their radiation nonetheless remain and will at last be studied. The interesting but narrow questions of what caused last year's economic downturn or why women participated more in the economy over the past decade will yield to the broader and longer term questions of what causes the business cycle in capitalist economies or what causes the sexual segregation of the work force.

Fogel believes we should study all the evidence with all the techniques. We cannot achieve all things in historical science by scrutinizing the conventional sources, he says, nor all things in economic science by staring hard at a blackboard. We have to look at the evidence hard, as genuine scientists, and then argue the case hard.

Fogel is above all an economic arguer about the evidence, an attorney for the factual prosecution. He takes an empirical idea—such as that one might measure the social savings of railroads—then asks, What conceivable doubts might someone have that the answer is so-and-so? Before the trial gets under way he imagines every move of the opposing attorney. While others build their cases on a rough-and-ready plausibility, such as might persuade their mothers, using observations "consistent with" the hypothesis (and therefore, statistically speaking, ignoring power), Fogel builds his case on excoriating doubt. It is the scholarly standard that Karl Popper and others have held up as the ideal for science. Recent studies of science have shown that even in the physical and biological sciences the standard is seldom achieved. That makes it all the more remarkable that Fogel does achieve it in historical economics.

Fogel meets or exceeds the standard for factual inquiry of, to pick a few comparable scholars in various fields, Simon Kuznets in economics, Louis Namier in British history, V. O. Key in political science, and Ronald Syme in Roman history. That puts him with the great scholars of our century. No stone is left unturned. Repeatedly the ingenuity of critics swarming around him is made to look foolish when their main point turns out to have been anticipated in an obscure footnote by the master himself. Fogel's address to the British Economic History Society in 1976 provides an instance. An English economic historian, well disposed towards him but unable to resist taking advantage of a rumor that Fogel was worried about a certain calculation concerning the slave trade, rose in criticism. Fogel waited until the fellow had finished his apparently devastating remark; then, smiling broadly, he allowed as he was glad the question had been asked: in the month since the news had gone out that he was having difficulty on the point, he and his co-workers had collected observations bearing on it to the number of forty thousand. Fogel then proceeded to re-establish the calculation beyond cavil.

Fogel's opinion, voiced repeatedly since his earliest work, is that "the major obstacle to the resolution of [most of the issues in history and economics] . . . is the absence of data rather than the absence of analytical ingenuity or credible theories." The opinion is worthy of respect for two reasons. First, to repeat, economics has had a long run with blackboard reasoning; perhaps the time has come to take economic observation seriously. Second, Fogel backs his opinion with analytic ingenuity and credible theories in quantity, but most of all by supplying enormous, Tycho-Brahean masses of data. Not *data,* really, which means "things given," but *capta,* "things seized."

Fogel seizes his from every source. He measured the social saving by mastering the engineering literature on railroads. He measured the efficiency of slavery by making use of dozens of southern archives, tens of thousands of prices of slaves, and detailed knowledge of the manuscript censuses. He measured the sources of mortality by using an array of epidemiological and nutritional studies, the records of military recruits, the Mormon family archives, the experiments of biologists, the records of hospitals. He sets a standard of empirical seriousness that no economist in the history of the discipline has matched.

To put it another way, Fogel combines the best of analytic minds in economics with the highest standards of self-doubt in social inquiry and with what historians call "historical imagination." He is a "scientific historian," not in his own sense, recalled from an acquaintance with the positivist philosophies, but in R. G. Collingwood's sense: "scientific historians study problems: they ask questions, and if they are good historians they ask questions which they see their way to answering".[14] Fogel sees the right historical questions to ask and sees his way to answering them. He brings the highest historical standards of factual veracity to economics. He is both the best of economists and the best of historians.

The difficulty of achieving dual excellence late in the twentieth century is worth noting. Scholarly standards in both economics and history have risen since 1950. What would pass for analytic brilliance in an economics article in the 1940s looks routine circa 1990 (consider Samuelson on the multiplier and accelerator). What would be considered impressive breadth of sources from an historian in the 1930s looks now crude and inexplicit (consider Marc Bloch on French agricultural history). Fogel has done it in both fields.

The dual excellence sets a standard that both economics and history might achieve, if they aim high enough in steering. It is peculiar, to pick one, that economics has allowed itself to ignore certain classes of evidence and argument. Ignoring evidence from opinion surveys or arguments from narrative is not a good idea. Yet the official methodology of economics urges this and other narrowings of the evidence. Fogel does not. You cannot read a piece by

14. R. G. Collingwood, *The Idea of History* (London, 1946; New York, edition of 1956), p. 281.

Fogel without bumping against the startling if obvious standard, borrowed from history for the good of economics: examine all the evidence.

The standard has resulted in large scientific advances. His friend and former colleague Richard Rosett is fond of pointing out that few scientists or scholars have the energy or ability to achieve one great scholarly success in the time allotted to them; in twenty-five years Fogel has achieved three:

(1) He discovered that the iron horse, bestriding the economic historiography of the nineteenth century like a colossus, was important but not colossal. He was here testing the theory of Schumpeter and Rostow that modern economic growth has depended on certain great inventions, the analogue in economic history of great men. He tested it with extraordinary thoroughness and began, as I have noted, by believing it to be true. Yet he found it wanting. Transportation strikes the noneconomist as obviously fundamental in some vague fashion—after all, what would happen if we closed down the highways and railroads tomorrow? Fogel noted that the question was one of long-run dispensibility and brought to bear the latest insights of cost/benefit analysis.

The book (really, two books: his master's thesis on the Union Pacific railway was part of the tale) created much controversy. Fogel's argumentative style rubbed some economists the wrong way, and the less self-confident among the historians, frightened by the quantitative history that Fogel was advocating, were pleased to see the historical economists quarreling among themselves. The same story was to be repeated more bitterly ten years later in the controversy over slavery.

In any event, Fogel was right. He was complimented by imitation, in a dozen replications of his study for other countries and other branches of transportation. His argument was scrutinized in a way that only the most important scientific findings are, by the best critical minds in the discipline, inside and outside economic history. It lasts.

(2) He turned then to American slavery, with his colleague at Rochester, Stanley Engerman. (Each successive project of Fogel's has involved more and more work by teams, as his ambitions for *capta* have grown.) Unlike the railroad book the essential plan of the work on slavery was not original with Fogel. The notion that one might view slavery, however vile its moral basis, as an efficient market arrangement had been adumbrated by Kenneth Stampp, Alfred H. Conrad, and John R. Meyer. But adumbration is not the same as painting in oils. Fogel and Engerman in the two volumes of *Time on the Cross* and in their massive subsequent work painted a picture of capitalism gone wrong, of slavery as an economic success that demanded political intervention to kill, and of a black work force that achieved much in bourgeois terms despite the lash.

The uproar occasioned by *Time on the Cross* is hard to understand. Some of the internal criticism, unhappily, arose from personal jealousies, as anyone attending the various conferences about the book could see. The book was favorably reviewed by the doyen of southern historians in the *New York Re-*

view of Books and reviewed at astonishing length and with great respect in numerous technical journals. Then came a reaction to the publicity. Some scholars seem to have been annoyed by the appearances of Fogel and Engerman in *Time* and of Fogel alone on the Today show on television. One is put in mind of the fury that descended on the chemists who had the temerity to announce fusion in a bottle before clearing it with the physicists. Certainly any book that touches the American dilemma incurs the risk of being badly misunderstood, especially in the overheated days of the early 1970s. Fogel was attacked as a racist in some circles and a running dog of capitalism in others. It is hard to imagine labels less apt.

The sober truth is that he and the group of scholars he led greatly increased our understanding of American slavery. They were the first to take seriously the measurement of efficiency, of slave diets and physical conditions, and of the abuse of slaves. On other issues—such as the demography of the slave population—they permanently and substantially raised the level of debate. Any student of the compulsory labor systems that typified the workplace before the twentieth century must use Fogel and Engerman's work, extended by their students and colleagues, and embodied now in the massive volumes of *Without Consent or Contract*.

To put it more broadly, neither the optimistic correlation of capitalism with freedom nor the pessimistic correlation of capitalism with misery make much sense. Fogel has done much additional work on the abolition movement, tracing its roots in political economy and especially in religious conviction. He has found that abolition was a close call, not inevitable, no automatic result of "modernization." Nor was it a self-interested move of the middle class. A quantitative economist has ended by emphasizing the complexities of politics and the saliency of moral freedom. That is scientific integrity.

(3) As if two home runs in a single game were not enough, Fogel pointed to a spot in center field and produced with a mighty swing an explanation of the fall in mortality, 1700 to 1900. The project is less controversial than his other work. It is international in scope (though emphasizing the American experience), undertaken with a still larger team (running into the dozens), and has moved further away from economics strictly defined. It has pioneered entirely new sources of data, especially military recruitment records. In other ways, though, the work is typical of Fogel's earlier performances, especially in the catholicity of literature brought to bear. Fogel has ransacked the literature of human biology, the history of medicine, demography, social history, economic history, nutritional history, pediatrics, clinical nutrition, embryology, historical sociology, tropical medicine, public health, historical geography, epidemiology, agricultural history, physical anthropology, gynecology, international economics, industrial history, toxology, genealogy, and development economics to discover the link between nutrition and life chances. He has concluded that better food accounted for about 40 percent of the decline in mortality, mainly among infants, leaving a considerable unexplained fall in

mortality well before the coming of modern medicine. The work is in progress—another of Fogel's favorite phrases borrowed from careful science is "preliminary results," and he means it: measure twice, cut once. What is clear is that the project is a major contribution to our understanding of how we grew and how we grew rich.

Robert Fogel, in short, has reunified economics and history. Using the best techniques of modern economics and gathering the widest samples of historical data he has reinterpreted American economic growth in brilliant studies of the railroads, slavery, abolition, and death rates. Rather than conjecturing on the causes of growth he has asked persistently "How large?" and seen the way to answer. He has set a new standard for empirical thoroughness in economics and a new standard of logical cogency in history. The quantitative history he advocates has opened new ways to the past. The historical economics he helped create, an economics made wiser by a knowledge of history, brought economics back to the larger questions. It has already reinterpreted the history of American and now other economic lives.

If Fogel had lived at Athens in the late fifth century B.C., he would have been seen daily in the agora with Alcibiades, Crito, Phaedrus, and the rest, trying to persuade Socrates that the slide rule and sampling theory were just what Greek science needed. The historical Socrates was not a writer, a democrat, or a mathematician, but in other ways Fogel resembles the inventor of serious conversation. Both characters have warmth, humor, intelligence, moral courage, singleness of mind, and a genial tenacity in argument, a tenacity that does not endear them to all their compatriots. If the Greek was known to stand stock still for a day to grasp an argument, the American is known to rise at all hours of the night to perfect one. If the Greek was famed for his courage in the imperial wars of Athens, the American is courageous in less bloody but still danger-filled circumstances, from southern hotels under segregation to universities under student siege.

In short, it could be said of Robert William Fogel, as of Socrates, son of Sophroniscus: "to be sure he never professed to teach this; but, by letting his own light shine, he led his disciples to hope that through imitation of him they might attain to such excellence."[15]

15. Xenophon, *Memorabilia*, Josiah Renick Smith, ed. (Boston, 1903), vol. 1, pp. 2, 3 (lines 12–15).

I Labor Markets in Manufacturing and Agriculture

1 The Market for Manufacturing Workers during Early Industrialization

The American Northeast, 1820 to 1860

Kenneth L. Sokoloff and Georgia C. Villaflor

Concern with economic dislocation and associated hardships has long been a familiar theme in histories of the early industrialization of various countries.[1] With the major changes in relative prices, resource allocation, and technology characteristic of this phase of growth, many scholars doubt that workers and institutions could be so flexible in responding to the new conditions that there would be no significant class of losers. Even with competitive markets, those with investments or other interests specific to old ways, or those who bear high costs of adjustment, are likely to be hurt by aspects of progress which would depreciate their assets or compel alterations in behavior. Moreover, these shifts in social behavior, culture, and an individual's circumstance might be especially disturbing because of the lack of previous experience with such an accelerated pace of social change.

Although not devoid of these considerations, the literature on the United States has been something of an exception, with the beginning of economic growth seeming nearly frictionless in some accounts. This traditional assess-

The authors benefited from excellent research assistance by James Lin, Zorina Khan, John Majewski, and Geng Xiao, as well as from comments by Robert Allen, Paul David, Lance Davis, Stanley Engerman, Robert Fogel, Claudia Goldin, Stephen Haber, Carol Heim, Peter Lindert, Robert Margo, Douglass North, William Parker, Hugh Rockoff, Jean-Laurent Rosenthal, Jonathan Skinner, Michael Waldman, David Weir, Jeffrey Williamson, Gavin Wright, and participants in seminars at UC Berkeley, Stanford, UCLA, Columbia, Harvard, Virginia, Illinois, and the D.C. Area Workshop in Economic History. The research was supported by the Center for Advanced Study in the Behavioral Sciences, the California Institute of Technology, and the Institute of Industrial Relations and the Academic Senate at UCLA.

1. Among economic historians, the so-called standard of living debate has focused on the British experience. For example, see Eric J. Hobsbawm, *The Age of Revolution, 1789–1848* (Cleveland, 1962); R. M. Hartwell, "The Rising Standard of Living in England, 1800–1850," *Economic History Review,* 13 (Apr. 1961), pp. 397–416; and Stephen A. Marglin, "What Do Bosses Do?: The Origins and Function of Hierarchy in Capitalist Production," *Review of Radical Political Economics,* 6 (Summer 1974), pp. 33–60.

ment undoubtedly stems from the relatively high standard of living and more equal distribution of income enjoyed by the American population during the colonial and early national periods as compared to their European counterparts.[2] Declining industries, technologies, and districts have certainly been noted, but most studies emphasize the clambering to exploit opportunities and put the extensive geographic and social mobility of the period in a positive light. Indeed, accounts of the classic formative experiences of the Early Republic, such as young women joining the Lowell mills or farmers streaming into midwestern river valleys, often read like textbook descriptions of workers flowing to higher value activities in pursuit of material gain.

This faith in a broad sharing of the benefits appears to be consistent with wage series compiled for the American Northeast in recent years by Donald Adams, Robert Margo and Georgia Villaflor, and Winifred Rothenberg.[3] Their data, which pertain primarily to agriculture, construction, and transportation, concur in suggesting that real wage levels rose markedly during the antebellum period. Relying on different types of evidence, however, other researchers have revived doubts about how the working classes fared. Most prominent among them are the "new labor historians" who have argued that the changes in technology, in the use of alternative pools of labor, and in the degree of commercialization eroded the autonomy and status of many skilled artisans without even providing meaningful improvements in material consumption. These scholars seem to conceive of early labor markets as plagued by persistent problems of oversupply, where competition operated to depress wage rates and prevent workers from capturing much, if any, of the returns to increases in productivity.[4] Although not obviously linked to any particular

2. Daniel J. Boorstin, *The Americans: The National Experience* (New York, 1965); Alice Hanson Jones, *Wealth of a Nation to Be* (New York, 1980); Robert W. Fogel, "Nutrition and the Decline in Mortality Since 1700: Some Preliminary Findings," in Stanley L. Engerman and Robert E. Gallman, eds., *Long-Term Factors in American Economic Growth* (Chicago, 1986); and Kenneth L. Sokoloff and Georgia C. Villaflor, "The Early Achievement of Modern Stature in America," *Social Science History*, 6 (Fall 1982), pp. 453–81.

3. Donald R. Adams, Jr., "Wage Rates in the Early National Period: Philadelphia, 1785–1830," *Journal of Economic History*, 28 (Sept. 1968), pp. 404–26; "Some Evidence on English and American Wage Rates, 1790–1830," *Journal of Economic History*, 30 (Sept. 1970), pp. 499–520; "The Standard of Living During American Industrialization: Evidence from the Brandywine Region, 1800–1860," *Journal of Economic History*, 42 (Dec. 1982), pp. 903–17; and "Prices and Wages in Maryland, 1750–1860," *Journal of Economic History*, 46 (Sept. 1986), pp. 625–45; Robert A. Margo and Georgia C. Villaflor, "The Growth of Wages in Antebellum America: New Evidence," *Journal of Economic History*, 47 (Dec. 1987), pp. 873–95; and Winifred B. Rothenberg, "The Emergence of Farm Labor Markets and the Transformation of the Rural Economy: Massachusetts, 1750–1855," *Journal of Economic History*, 48 (Sept. 1988), pp. 537–66.

4. This school has carried on, and yet broadened, the rich traditions in labor history exemplified by the work of John R. Commons and Associates, *History of Labor in the United States*, 4 vols. (1918–35). Although the "new labor historians" are generally critical of the effect of industrialization on manufacturing workers, there is quite a diversity of views about specifics. Some are accepting of significant increases in productivity as well as in compensation, but the great majority are quite skeptical. For example, Susan E. Hirsch, *Roots of the American Working Class: The Industrialization of Crafts in Newark, 1800–1860* (Philadelphia, 1978). Also see Paul G. Faler, *Mechanics and Manufacturers in the Early Industrial Revolution: Lynn, Massachusetts, 1780–*

sources, a nationwide decline in heights beginning with the birth cohorts of the 1830s and a parallel decrease in life expectancy, uncovered by Robert Fogel and others, have further stimulated interest in the impact of early American industrialization on welfare.[5]

This paper aims to deepen our understanding of these issues by exploring the variation in manufacturing wages across relevant firm characteristics and over time. Wage rates cannot, by themselves, offer a comprehensive index of material welfare. At best, they contain only indirect and incomplete information on fundamental conditions of life such as the nature of work performed, health, and environmental quality. Yet they deserve serious examination because they do provide a useful gauge of purchasing power—a crucial component of the standard of living in early industrial societies—as well as insight into the range of economic possibilities individuals face and the choices they make.

Our focus is on the Northeast, where industrial development was concentrated during the initial stages of the process. The principal bodies of evidence examined are four cross sections of firm data from 1820 to 1860.[6] The central findings are that all discernable segments of the manufacturing labor force realized substantial increases in real wages over the period as a whole, and that those differentials apparent at the beginning narrowed over time, as one would expect with the extension of markets. Workers appear to have benefited almost immediately from the rapid industrial expansion of the 1820s and maintained impressive rates of growth in compensation until the late 1840s or early 1850s, when progress was slowed by heavy immigration and the spread of mechanization to a number of previously labor-intensive industries. Of course, these gains were not continuous, and manufacturing workers suffered

---

1860 (Albany, 1981); Jonathan Prude, *The Coming of Industrial Order: Town and Factory Life in Rural Massachusetts, 1810–1860* (New York, 1983); Howard B. Rock, *Artisans of the New Republic: The Tradesmen of New York City in the Age of Jefferson* (New York, 1979); Stephen J. Ross, *Workers on the Edge: Work, Leisure and Politics in Industrializing Cincinnati, 1788–1890* (New York, 1985); and Sean Wilentz, *Chants Democratic: New York City and the Rise of the American Working Class* (New York, 1984).

5. Robert W. Fogel, "Nutrition and the Decline in Mortality Since 1700: Some Preliminary Findings," in Stanley L. Engerman and Robert E. Gallman, eds., *Long-Term Factors in American Economic Growth* (Chicago, 1986); and Clayne Pope, chap. 9 in this volume.

6. These samples of manufacturing firm data have been described and employed in a number of recent studies. They were drawn from the manuscripts of the 1820, 1850, and 1860 Censuses of Manufactures, and the 1832 Treasury Department survey of manufactures commonly known as the McLane Report (U.S. House of Representatives, *Documents Relative to the Statistics of Manufactures in the U.S.*, 2 vols. [Washington, D.C., 1833]). For details about the samples, see Jeremy Atack, "Economies of Scale and Efficiency Gains in the Rise of the Factory in America, 1820–1900," in Peter Kilby, ed., *Quantity and Quiddity: Essays in U.S. Economic History* (Middletown, 1987); as well as Kenneth L. Sokoloff, "Industrialization and the Growth of the Manufacturing Sector in the Northeast, 1820–1850," (Ph.D. dissertation, Harvard University, 1982); and "Productivity Growth in Manufacturing During Early Industrialization: Evidence from the American Northeast, 1820–1860," in Stanley L. Engerman and Robert E. Gallman, eds., *Long-Term Factors in American Economic Growth* (Chicago, 1986).

through some painful spells. But the evidence bears against notions that the difficult years were due to poorly functioning markets, rapid changes in technology, or other aspects of industrialization. On the contrary, the chief deviations from the upward trend in real wages seem to be attributable to supply-side shocks originating in the agricultural sector or in unusually large immigration flows, rather than to the path of industrial development.

1.1 A Growing Economy

The forty years spanned by the manufacturing censuses used here encompass the early stages of industrialization in the United States and were a period of economic transformation in the Northeast. A formidable modern manufacturing sector began to emerge in that region during the first two decades of the century, spawned by the expansion of domestic commerce associated with state and private efforts to extend the transportation grid, as well as the interruption of foreign trade during the Embargo of 1807 and the War of 1812.[7] Although battered during the postwar contraction, northeastern manufacturing resumed growth at an accelerated pace in the 1820s and maintained it over the next several decades. By 1860, this region was far ahead of others in per capita income and had realized an enormous shift of its resources out of agriculture and into manufacturing and services. Although other regions were moving along similar paths, the Northeast held the lead in manufacturing output, technology, urbanization, the evolution of markets, and other dimensions of industrial development.[8]

The burgeoning manufacturing sector of the Northeast was in constant flux over these years, and the changes concerned composition and technology as well as size. With rising incomes and enhanced opportunities to produce for and consume through the market, more of the population were inclined to indulge tastes for fashionable store-bought merchandise and for material pleasures which had just a generation before been reserved for the genteel, if available at all.[9] Mass-oriented industries such as cotton textiles and boots and shoes quickly grew to become the largest employers in the sector, and in so doing greatly augmented the relative demand for the labor of women and chil-

7. Thomas C. Cochran and William Miller, *The Age of Enterprise: A Social History of Industrial America* (New York, 1961); George Rogers Taylor, *The Transportation Revolution, 1815–1860* (New York, 1962); Diane Lindstrom, *Economic Development in the Philadelphia Region, 1800–1850* (New York, 1978); and Carter Goodrich, *Government Promotion of American Canals and Railroads, 1800–1890* (New York, 1960).

8. Richard A. Easterlin, "Interregional Differences in Per Capita Income, Population, and Total Income, 1840–1950," in Studies in Income and Wealth, vol. 24, *Trends in the American Economy in the Nineteenth Century* (Princeton, 1960); and Viken Tchakerian, "Structure and Performance of Southern and Midwestern Manufacturing, 1850–1860: Evidence from the Manuscript Censuses," (Ph.D. dissertation, University of California, Los Angeles, 1990).

9. Dorothy S. Brady, "Consumption and the Style of Life," in Lance E. Davis et al., *American Economic Growth* (New York, 1972); and Rolla Milton Tryon, *Household Manufactures in the United States, 1640–1860* (New York, 1966).

dren.[10] But these were not the only industries or classes of labor to benefit from economic growth. Ever-increasing levels of consumption bolstered demand for previously exotic items such as musical instruments, fine furniture, window glass, and an array of new products whose manufacture often involved highly skilled workers. The quality and diversity of goods exploded during the antebellum era, with important implications for our understanding of living standards as well as the mobility of factors of production.[11]

Changes in the composition of manufacturing were accompanied by equally impressive advances in organization and methods. Between 1820 and 1860, manufacturing productivity in the Northeast grew at rates approaching those of the late-nineteenth and twentieth centuries. A broad range of industries were able to realize substantial gains in productivity through relatively modest alterations in production processes, that is, without radically new types of equipment or increases in capital intensity.[12] What these alterations consisted of is not entirely clear, but they likely involved many incremental improvements in the design of products and capital, as well as in the coordination of labor and other inputs. For example, even without significant changes in the kinds of tools used, firms raised measured productivity by increasing the division and intensity of labor within their establishments. Small shops with a few skilled artisans were increasingly displaced by so-called non-mechanized factories or manufactories which employed higher proportions of workers lacking in general skills and now responsible for narrowly defined tasks. Those that survived tended to be located in outlying areas or to be specialized in products less suitable for standardized production. It was not until the late 1840s and 1850s that machinery driven by inanimate sources of power came to be widely adopted in many manufacturing industries other than textiles.

10. Claudia Goldin and Kenneth Sokoloff, "Women, Children, and Industrialization in the Early Republic: Evidence from the Manufacturing Censuses," *Journal of Economic History,* 42 (Dec. 1982), pp. 741–74.

11. For discussions of the increases in the quality and range of goods consumed, see Chauncey M. Depew, *One Hundred Years of American Commerce* (New York, 1895); and Jack Larkin, *The Reshaping of Everyday Life, 1790–1840* (New York, 1988). For analysis of how conventional price indices do a poor job in contexts where there are new products or significant improvements in quality, see Robert J. Gordon, *The Measurement of Durable Goods Prices* (Chicago, 1990). The bias is in the direction of understating progress. For the relevance of this problem to the early nineteenth century, see Dorothy S. Brady, "Relative Prices in the Nineteenth Century," *Journal of Economic History,* 24 (June 1964), pp. 145–203. The other point to make about the rise of new industries and the change in the composition of northeastern output is that they indicate that labor must have been quite mobile.

12. Goldin and Sokoloff, "Women, Children, and Industrialization"; and Kenneth L. Sokoloff, "Investment in Fixed and Working Capital During Early Industrialization: Evidence from U.S. Manufacturing Firms," *Journal of Economic History,* 44 (Mar. 1984), pp. 545–56; "Was the Transition from the Artisanal Shop to the Non-Mechanized Factory Associated With Gains in Efficiency?: Evidence from U.S. Manufacturing Censuses of 1820 and 1850," *Explorations in Economic History,* 21 (Oct. 1984), pp. 351–82; and "Productivity Growth in Manufacturing." See Hirsch, *Roots of the American Working Class,* for an industry-by-industry treatment of the record in Newark.

Expanding markets played a major role in promoting the diffusion of such improvements in technology. Whereas most establishments operated in relatively local markets early in the century, these protected circumstances broke down swiftly in the Northeast. Not only did the growing demand for manufactures attract the entrance of additional producers and falling transportation costs increase competition between geographic districts, but the rates of invention and innovation were stimulated as well.[13] Although the speed of this process varied across industry and place, the integration of product markets between urban centers, northern New York, and southern New England was far along by the mid–1820s, with hundreds of roads constructed, navigable rivers extended, and canals such as the Erie in operation. By the late 1840s, there were few pockets in the Northeast beyond the reach of a regional market held together by a network of low-cost transportation.

It is apparent that the impact of industrialization on the market for manufacturing workers involved a variety of mechanisms. On one hand, the rapid growth in industrial output, underway by the 1820s, should have strained the sources of skilled employees, the supply of which must have been somewhat inelastic in the short run. Tending in the other direction, however, were changes in technology that facilitated the substitution of less-skilled classes of workers, including women and children.[14] The net results of these counteracting influences on the demand for manufacturing workers with a traditional artisanal training and on the wage rates for the different classes of labor are unclear but certain to have varied across industries based upon elasticities of substitution and of supply. What can be said, though, is that if workers and firms were responsive to market conditions, as the shift in industrial composition suggests, then increases in productivity and falling transport costs would have led to growth in the return to labor generally and a narrowing of geographic differentials in wages as well as in prices. Trade in products alone could have accomplished this, even without much geographic mobility by workers.[15]

13. For the geographic extension of low-cost transportation and its impact, see Balthasar Meyer, Caroline E. MacGill, et al., *History of Transportation in the United States Before 1860* (Washington, D.C., 1917); Tryon, *Household Manufactures;* Taylor, *Transportation Revolution;* Albert Fishlow, *American Railroads and the Transformation of the Ante-Bellum Economy* (Cambridge, 1965); and Kenneth L. Sokoloff, "Inventive Activity in Early Industrial America: Evidence from Patent Records, 1790–1846," *Journal of Economic History,* 48 (Dec. 1988), pp. 813–50.

14. The substitutability of women for unskilled men in the growing manufacturing sector might be cited as another reason why the elasticity of supply for less-skilled workers would have been greater than for artisans. See Goldin and Sokoloff, "Women, Children, and Industrialization;" and Jeffrey G. Williamson and Peter Lindert, *American Inequality: A Macroeconomic Perspective* (New York, 1980).

15. For a discussion of the conditions necessary for factor-price equalization, see Paul A. Samuelson, "International Factor-Price Equalization Once Again," *Economic Journal,* 59 (June 1949), pp. 181–97.

1.2 The Data on Nominal Wages

We now turn to the estimates of mean nominal annual wages computed from the samples of manufacturing firm data for adult males in the Northeast and presented in Table 1.1. Although such nominal figures are of limited value in gauging the improvement over time in living standards, they help to highlight the patterns of cross-sectional variation and the internal consistency of the data. They were constructed from firm-level reports of mean wage rates on an annual (1820), daily (1832), or monthly (1850 and 1860) basis, and make no allowance for interruptions in employment, other than an effort to exclude part-time establishments from the 1820 sample. The daily and monthly rates were converted to annual figures by assuming 310 days or twelve months of work per year, so as to approximate average annual earnings for full-time employees, not actual average earnings across all manufacturing workers. Little is known about changes over time in the spells of unemployment per worker or in the prevalence of part-time work. But given the evidence of a decrease over time in the length of the average manufacturing workday and that earnings grew more rapidly than daily wage rates, it seems likely that our figures understate the advance in the earnings of year-round manufacturing employees, at least between 1832 and 1860.[16]

Geographic variation in nominal wages appears, by these estimates, to have been quite limited. Wages were somewhat higher in New England than in the Middle Atlantic, and in urban areas relative to rural, but these gaps seem generally modest and to have declined over time. In both parts of the Northeast, wage rates grew most rapidly in rural counties, followed by urban areas, and at the slowest pace in major urban centers such as Boston, New York, and Philadelphia. The only large and persistent deviation from rough equality was that small firms in rural counties of the Middle Atlantic, especially in western Pennsylvania, paid their employees significantly lower wages (20 to 30 percent less than the regional average).[17]

The most straightforward explanation for the convergence of nominal wages is that improvements in transportation served to narrow the range of geographic variation in the returns to workers, both through enhanced labor

16. For the respective findings, see Jeremy Atack and Fred Bateman, "How Long was the Workday in 1880?," NBER-DAE Working Paper no. 15 (1990); and Adams, "Standard of Living." Information collected in the McLane Report indicates that small firms had longer reported workdays than their larger counterparts. This suggests that the difference in the daily wage rate between size classes is due to differences in labor productivity per hour of work and may be related to a need to compensate workers for the greater intensity of labor or other aversive conditions in larger firms. It also supports our claim that the lower average wage in small firms is not an artifact explained by a greater prevalence of part-time operations.

17. The chief source of the discrepancies between the unweighted and weighted means is that wage rates in Pennsylvania, Delaware, and New Jersey vary substantially with the size of firm. There are also a few cases, however, attributable to very large firms with atypically high or low wage rates. The best example of this is a rural New Jersey glass factory which employed several hundred workers at over $450 a year per adult male worker in 1860.

Table 1.1 **Nominal Mean Annual Wage Rates for Adult Males in Northeastern Manufacturing by Geographic Area, Urbanization, and Size of Firm: 1820 to 1860**

	1820		1832		1850		1860	
Unweighted								
Middle Atlantic	$225.4	(430)	$247.6	(300)	$289.1	(485)	$328.3	(419)
Rural	200.8	(297)	241.3	(280)	267.8	(196)	297.7	(148)
Urban	280.2	(133)	336.1	(20)	303.4	(289)	347.8	(271)
Major urban	303.9	(87)	—		327.9	(88)	373.0	(92)
New England	256.4	(196)	291.5	(600)	334.2	(497)	384.1	(440)
Rural	250.1	(145)	292.7	(372)	324.3	(271)	368.8	(170)
Urban	274.2	(51)	289.5	(228)	341.2	(226)	389.4	(270)
Major urban	348.4	(10)	410.4	(14)	376.4	(27)	421.6	(74)
Total	235.1	(626)	267.9	(900)	302.1	(982)	342.2	(859)
Weighted								
Middle Atlantic	265.9	(2,264)	278.0	(4,970)	350.5	(2,713)	354.3	(4,346)
Rural	238.3	(1,171)	270.1	(4,424)	287.2	(466)	374.7	(984)
Urban	295.5	(1,093)	342.0	(546)	362.1	(2,247)	348.8	(3,362)
Major urban	305.8	(896)	—		376.4	(1,428)	340.1	(1,724)
Small	215.7	(689)	213.4	(318)	283.5	(542)	316.8	(441)
Medium	281.7	(698)	293.3	(593)	312.8	(520)	367.8	(517)
Large	292.7	(877)	280.8	(4,059)	375.6	(1,651)	358.4	(3,388)
New England	269.7	(1,489)	299.9	(8,623)	326.9	(3,709)	371.1	(4,587)
Rural	252.2	(875)	303.4	(4,094)	313.5	(1,110)	351.9	(673)
Urban	293.6	(632)	296.8	(4,529)	329.9	(2,599)	372.7	((3,914)
Major urban	325.3	(243)	387.8	(144)	338.0	(772)	411.8	(1,670)
Small	239.5	(359)	285.6	(811)	349.1	(517)	388.0	(440)
Medium	263.0	(506)	290.6	(1,717)	334.4	(814)	368.4	(668)
Large	292.6	(624)	304.4	(6,095)	321.7	(2,378)	370.1	(3,479)
Total	267.4	(3,753)	291.9	(13,593)	341.3	(6,422)	360.1	(8,933)

Notes and Sources: The estimates were computed from the samples of northeastern manufacturing firm data drawn from the schedules of the 1820, 1850, and 1860 Federal Census of Manufactures and from the 1832 McLane Report. The unweighted averages were computed as means of the averages reported by each firm in the category in question. The weighted averages were calculated as means by weighting the firm averages by the number of employees of the relevant type (i.e., number of adult males). In addition, the observations from the 1850 and 1860 samples were weighted for both sets of estimates by state-specific weights that were intended to control for the disproportionate representation of manufacturing firms from the smaller states in those samples. The number of observations, whether of firms or employees, over which the averages were computed are presented in parentheses.

The figures reported for 1832, 1850, and 1860 are based on information that probably pertains to the operations of firms in 1831, 1849, and 1859, respectively. The 1832 estimates were calculated from straightforward reports of average daily, weekly, or monthly wages for adult males, with the annualizations based on assumptions of 12 months, 310 days, or 52 weeks of employment per year. In 1850 and 1860, firms generally did not separately enumerate adult males and boys. Accordingly, the reported numbers of male employees in these years were decomposed into adults and boys by assuming that boys accounted for the same proportions, by industry, of male employees as they had in 1820. In those industries in which boys had accounted for more than 33 percent of male employees in 1820, it was further assumed that the shares had fallen to 33 percent by 1850 and 1860. The average wage for adult males was then estimated from the

Table 1.1 (continued)

average male wage, by assuming that the boy wage was 50 percent of the adult male compensation. The establishments enumerated in the 1820 Census typically recorded their annual wage bill and the number of employees in various classes. Several methods of estimating an adult male wage from this information have been utilized, but the figures presented were computed by assuming that females and children earned 0.35 of the adult male wage. These procedures were selected to bias the 1820 estimates upward relative to the 1850 and 1860 figures.

The estimates have been computed over the firms from eighteen manufacturing industries appearing in the samples: chemicals, cotton textiles, fine work (clocks, jewelry, etc.), furniture, glass, harnesses and wagons, hats, iron and steel, iron products, liquors, flour milling, paper, shoes and boots, tanning, tobacco products, tools and machinery, and wool textiles. All of the observations from these industries in the 1832, 1850, and 1860 samples, with the exception of a small number of outliers, were included in the analysis. As for the 1820 sample, the bottom 30 percent of the establishments in these industries with the relevant information were truncated from the subsample over which the estimates were prepared to control for the likelihood that a number of firms in 1820 were operating only part of the year and would thus lead to understatements of the annual wage rates prevailing at the time.

Urban firms are those located in a county with a city of 10,000 or more, or in a county that borders on such a county. Firm in major urban counties are a subset of urban firms and are those located in counties with cities having a population of 25,000 or more. The estimates are based on a "rolling" classification of urban counties, with the designated group expanding over time. Rural firms are the residual. Small firms are those with five or fewer employees, and large are those with more than fifteen.

mobility and adjustments by employers to changes in their product markets. Wage rates in different areas were driven toward convergence by competition between producers as the radiation of navigable waterways, railroads, and other modes of transport between the cities and hinterlands promoted the extension of markets throughout the Northeast. These developments would be expected to have disproportionately large effects on the opportunities for specialization in outlying districts, and the evidence suggests that these areas did indeed experience a rise in relative wages. Although the minor geographic disparities in nominal wages prevailing in 1860 may not precisely mirror those in real compensation, they are at least consistent with the view that a well-integrated northeastern labor market for manufacturing workers was largely in place by that date.

Another feature of these estimates is that employees of small firms (1 to 5 workers) gained ground on their counterparts in both medium- (6 to 15 workers) and large-sized (16 or more workers) enterprises over the period. In both New England and the Middle Atlantic, workers at small firms received much lower wages in 1820 but closed the gap steadily to pull ahead in the former subregion by 1850, and within 15 percent in the latter by 1860.[18] Exhibiting a similar qualitative pattern, employees of medium-sized establishments overtook their peers in larger firms. This pattern is intriguing, because the shops

18. As is clear from the numbers of firms and employees reported within parentheses in Table 1.1, there was a marked shift over time in the distribution of resources from smaller to larger establishments. This pattern likely reflects the competitive pressures on the former.

with only a few workers tended to rely on artisans with traditional skills, whereas larger establishments used methods involving an extensive division of labor and accordingly hired workers who were on average lacking in general skills.[19]

At first, the likelihood that workers with a comprehensive knowledge of the production processes might be less well remunerated than were those with fewer skills appears remote. However, on reflection, the phenomenon seems feasible in a pre- or early-industrial economy, where many of the skilled workers in small establishments were initially geographically insulated from regional markets. Although not possessing the human capital of an accomplished artisan, adult males who were specialized by task could have achieved greater productivity through fuller integration into a broad market or adapted more easily to advances in production methods. By this logic, larger firms paid higher wages in the short run, because they operated more efficiently by focusing on the manufacture of a standardized product for a mass market instead of customized or diverse outputs at an irregular or below full-capacity rate. But as product and labor markets expanded over time, the small shops that survived had to raise their productivity and wage rates to competitive levels. This interpretation appears borne out by the data. Not only did the relative performance of small firms improve in productivity as well as wages between 1820 and 1860, but the small firms with low productivity and low wages that managed to survive were located in ever more outlying counties.[20]

19. Although there are seldom references to precise firm sizes, there appears to be a clear consensus among economic, labor, and technological historians that the reliance on traditional artisans with a general set of skills typically declined with the number of employees, after adjusting for industry. Blanche E. Hazard, *The Organization of the Boot and Shoe Industry in Massachusetts Before 1875* (Cambridge, 1921); Pearce Davis, *The Development of the American Glass Industry* (Cambridge, 1949); H. J. Habakkuk, *American and British Technology in the Nineteenth Century: The Search for Labour-Saving Inventions* (Cambridge, 1962); Hirsch, *Roots of the American Working Class;* Goldin and Sokoloff, "Women, Children, and Industrialization"; Wilentz, *Chants Democratic;* and Ross, *Workers on the Edge*. The new technologies in manufacturing generally involved extensive division of labor within the firm and required larger scales of production. It is not straightforward, however, to infer from this "stylized fact" that the proportion of adult male employees who were skilled artisans decreased with firm size. Women and children filled many of the unskilled positions, and large enterprises often employed artisans as supervisors or for tasks which could not easily be subdivided or left to others. Nevertheless, the judgment that small (5 or fewer workers) establishments had the highest proportion of adult male employees who were artisans appears sound, because they had little potential for separation of tasks. The literature has generally treated traditional artisans as the model for a skilled worker, partially because of special concern with how they fared as a group. For other purposes, a broader definition might be preferred, and the attributes that allowed one to work productively under the new organizations of labor might reasonably be viewed as a type of skill.

20. In addition to Kenneth L. Sokoloff, "Was the Transition?"; "Productivity Growth in Manufacturing"; and "Manufacturing Productivity Growth During the Antebellum Period," in Robert E. Gallman and John Wallis, eds., *American Economic Growth and the Standard of Living Before the Civil War* (Chicago, 1992, forthcoming), see Tchakerian, "Structure and Performance," for his finding that the difference in productivity between small and large firms was greater in the South than in the Midwest, and much greater in either region than in the Northeast. His results support the interpretation that firms which were insulated from broad markets had markedly lower productivity. The results of the regressions in Tables 1.4 and 1.5 below also indicate declining quantitative significance and concentration in rural districts.

Despite the reasonableness of their patterns of cross-sectional variation, one might still question the levels of our nominal wage estimates. Two of the manufacturing censuses sampled suffer from problems of representativeness, and all may be vulnerable to biases from the inclusion of firms operating less than full-time.[21] Though these are serious concerns, confidence in our figures is strengthened by checks of consistency with alternative wage series. In Figure 1.1, our weighted-average estimates are compared with the series of daily wage rates constructed by Rothenberg for agricultural labor in Massachusetts, and by Margo and Villaflor for civilian workers (artisans and laborers separately) hired by the U.S. Army, expressed on an annual basis. The assumption of 310 days of employment at the specified rates may yield overstatements of yearly compensation, but the basic agreement about the amount of nominal wage growth over the period should be unaffected. There is a particularly close correspondence between our estimates and the Rothenberg series, with the former about 10 to 15 percent higher throughout. Both suggest greater wage increase during the 1820s, and slower advance during the 1830s and 1840s, than do those of Margo and Villaflor.[22] Also of significance is the finding that the 1820 estimate is not unreasonably low, as would be the case if it were biased downward by the inclusion of many part-time establishments in the data.[23]

1.3 Price Indexes and Real Wages

Although nominal figures are useful, real wage estimates provide a richer picture of change over time in living standards. Reliable price indexes are required for their construction. The preparation of such indexes, however, is a formidable problem given the limited number of commodities and places covered by existing price series, our imperfect knowledge of how the composition of expenditures varied over household characteristics, and the incidence of sharp changes in relative prices between commodities and places over the period. Thus, although one in principle would like a set of indexes which

21. Although stringent measures and sensitivity tests have been employed to cope with the possibility of the 1820 wage estimates being contaminated by the inclusion of part-time firms (see the note to Table 1.1), it is conceivable that we did not go far enough with the establishments in the Middle Atlantic. However, the New England estimates for that year seem totally unaffected by this problem, and daily wage rates from the 1832 McLane Report sustain the finding that small firms in the Middle Atlantic offered lower compensation. If the 1850 and 1860 samples were afflicted with this problem, the results would be biased to understate the extent of real wage growth. In general, since the qualitative results hold within both subregions and part-time firms appear unlikely to have affected the New England estimates, the findings seem robust.

22. The discrepancy is puzzling, but may be related to the small number of observations for the 1820s or the disproportionate representation of urban areas in their northeastern sample. Margo and Villaflor, "Growth of Wages."

23. The surprisingly close fit between our estimates and Rothenberg's lends support to the downplaying of the part-time firm problem and strengthens the case for a relatively well integrated labor market in districts close to major product markets. It may be, however, that the percentage gap between our estimates and the others is underestimated because of workers receiving higher wages when paid by the day or because the assumption of 310 days of work per year is too high.

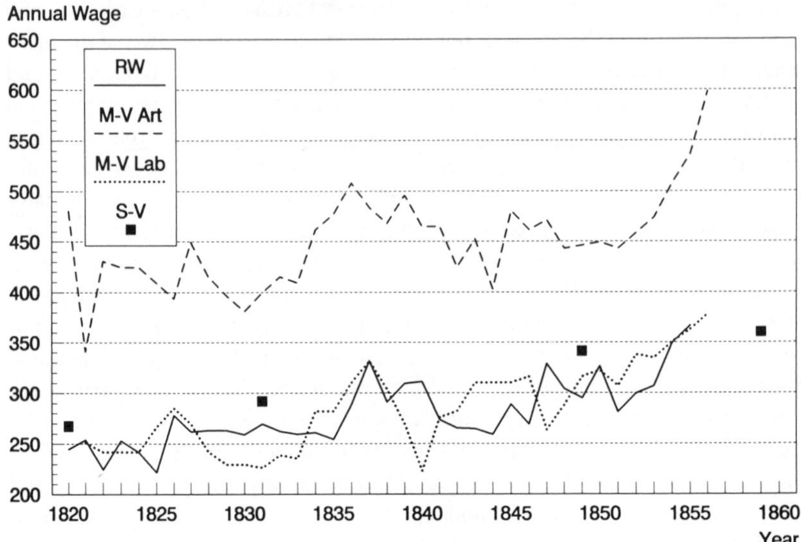

Fig. 1.1 Annual Wage Series in Current Dollars

Notes and Sources: Included are the Rothenberg weighted (RW) series for agricultural labor in Massachusetts; the Margo and Villaflor series for northeastern laborers (M-V Lab) and artisans (M-V Art); and our weighted averages from Table 1.1 for adult males in northeastern manufacturing (S-V). The Margo-Villaflor and Rothenberg daily wage rates were converted to annual estimates by assuming 310 days of work per year. The Rothenberg series estimates for higher paid and lower paid tasks were averaged at 1820 and extended over time by applying the trend from the weighted (RW) series. See Robert A. Margo and Georgia C. Villaflor, "Growth of Wages in Antebellum America: New Evidence," *Journal of Economic History,* 47 (Dec. 1987), pp. 873–95, and Winifred B. Rothenberg, "The Emergence of Farm Labor Markets and the Transformation of the Rural Economy: Massachusetts, 1750–1855," *Journal of Economic History,* (Sept. 1988), pp. 537–66.

would encompass all groups in all places, this goal is not yet attainable.[24] Accordingly, our analysis is based on examination of the sensitivity of results to the choice among an array of indexes assembled from different sources and with disparate methods. Included are several which appear prominently in the

24. In addition to the problems associated with the limited number of commodity price series available and the lack of adequate measures for housing costs, there is also uncertainty about the division of expenditures between general categories of expenses and between commodities within those categories. These seemingly fine points can affect the qualitative results because of the many radical changes in relative prices experienced during this period. For example, if indexes of food prices incorporated Matthew Carey's estimates (Larkin, *Reshaping of Everyday Life,* p. 175) that common laborers in Philadelphia spent more on tea and sugar than meat (at the household level), they would decline much more over time than they do with more conventional weights. Moreover, when relative prices vary substantially across geographic areas, as in the early nineteenth century, it is difficult to make a meaningful comparison of real wages across them without allowing for quite different market baskets being consumed. Studies of how the relative wages for two groups vary over time can be similarly flawed if expenditure patterns differ across the characteristics of interest. For excellent discussions of the issues involved in studying consumer prices during this era, see Dorothy S. Brady, "Price Deflators for Final Product Estimates," in Dorothy S. Brady,

literature as well as some we constructed from retail and wholesale price series for Boston, New York City, Philadelphia, and rural Vermont.

There are salient discrepancies between the alternative consumer price indexes for the years from 1820 to 1860, but they should not be allowed to obscure the impressive similarities. Indeed, many findings concerning the record of real wages are robust to the selection between them. To illustrate this point, four consumer price indexes (CPIs) pertaining to the Northeast are presented in Figure 1.2: the Williamson index for the urban poor, the David-Solar index for the nation as a whole but based on northeastern data, and two others which we have constructed for manufacturing workers in New York City and rural Vermont, respectively. Although they diverge by up to nearly 40 percent for brief intervals, the series move broadly together and within a relatively narrow band. They all show a significant decline in the cost of living over the entire period, with the trend interrupted by two severe cycles of approximately five years' duration. To be specific, all register a marked decline in consumer prices between 1820 and the early 1830s, before spiking to a peak in 1837, and then plunging to nearly the lowest point of the antebellum era at the cyclical trough of 1843. From this point, each rises slowly through the beginning of the 1850s, when living costs again surge upward by 15 to 40 percent for the next five years before falling back sharply. It is only during these extreme episodes of the late 1830s and mid–1850s that major gaps between the indexes are evident.

Since each of the four indexes indicates a significant decline in the cost of living over the period as a whole, our nominal wage figures are consistent with substantial improvement in real wages between 1820 and 1860 in the American Northeast. Estimated real wage growth for the average manufacturing worker ranges from the nearly 60 percent implied by the New York City CPI to the roughly 90 percent yielded by the David-Solar index (see Table 1.2).[25] All classes of employees gained over the period, with rural workers advancing relative to urban, New Englanders doing marginally better than their peers in the Middle Atlantic, and those at small establishments realizing more rapid wage growth than those in medium-sized plants, who in turn gain on their counterparts at larger enterprises. One can speculate about how the

---

ed., *Output, Employment, and Productivity in the United States After 1800* (New York, 1966); "Relative Prices"; and "Consumption and the Style of Life"; Ethel D. Hoover, "Wholesale and Retail Prices in the Nineteenth Century," *Journal of Economic History,* 17 (Sept. 1958), pp. 298–316; and "Retail Prices After 1850," in Studies in Income and Wealth, vol. 24, *Trends in the American Economy in the Nineteenth Century* (Princeton, 1960); Paul A. David and Peter Solar, "A Bicentenary Contribution to the History of the Cost of Living in America," *Research in Economic History,* 2 (1977), pp. 1–80; and Robert A. Margo, "Wages and Prices During the Antebellum Period: A Survey and New Evidence," in Robert E. Gallman and John Wallis, eds., *American Economic Growth and the Standard of Living Before the Civil War* (Chicago, 1992, forthcoming).

25. We adopt these two indexes as "bounds" for the presentation of results, because they represent extremes among the alternatives. Of course, since all of the others suffer from the problems discussed in the Appendix, the "true" index could lie outside of our "bounds."

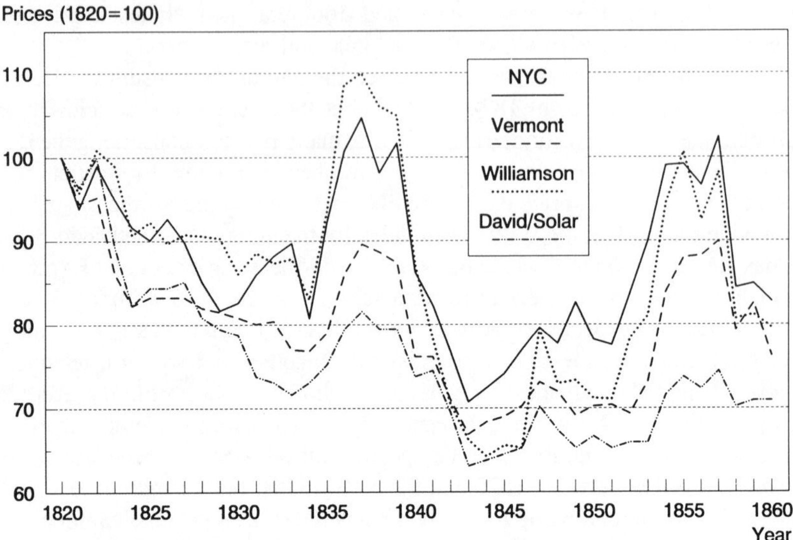

Fig. 1.2 Selected Consumer Price Indexes
Source: See Appendix A.

wage levels would compare or patterns of relative wage movements change if group-specific price indexes were available. For example, given that improvements in transportation led the prices of manufactures and imported (domestic) food products to fall (rise) over time in rural areas relative to urban levels, it seems likely that there were also differences between cities and the countryside in the record of the cost of living.[26] However, without more detail on commodity prices or on how the budget shares of manufacturing workers varied across place, any claims on the issue would be heroic at best. Accordingly, our analysis will apply one index at a time but is tempered with an appreciation of the crude approximations involved in the implicit assumption of the cost of living in the Northeast being everywhere the same.[27]

Since all of the indexes manifest a decline on the order of 15 to 25 percent in consumer prices from 1820 through the early 1830s, the conclusion that

26. The indexes for the prices paid to Vermont farmers for grains, livestock, dairy products, and vegetables rise between 1820 and 1860 relative to those for the wholesale prices of bread/grains, meat/fish, dairy products, and fruit/vegetables in New York City (see Figures 1.6 through 1.9 below). Conversely, the Vermont retail prices for clothing and other manufactures, building materials, and imported foods fall relative to the wholesale prices in New York (T. M. Adams, *Prices Paid By Vermont Farmers for Goods and Services and Received by Them for Farm Products 1790–1940,* Bulletin 507 [Burlington, VT, 1944]). Most of the divergence in movements, or presumed convergence in levels, occurs during the late 1840s and 1850s when railroads were being constructed at an intense pace throughout the Northeast (Fishlow, *American Railroads*).

27. Given that the changes in relative prices referred to in footnote 26 are not all that substantial and tend to offset each other, the implicit assumption may not be far wrong.

Table 1.2 **Indexes of Real Wages for Adult Males in Northeastern Manufacturing by Geographic Area, Urbanization, and Size of Firm: 1820 to 1860**

	1820	1832	1850	1860	Per Annum Growth Rate, 1820–60
Unweighted					
Middle Atlantic	100	128–150	155–197	171–205	1.4–1.9%
Rural	89	125–147	144–182	156–186	1.5–1.9
Urban	124	174–204	163–206	182–218	1.0–1.5
Major urban	135	—	167–223	195–233	1.0–1.4
New England	114	150–177	179–227	201–240	1.5–1.9
Rural	111	151–178	174–221	193–231	1.4–1.9
Urban	122	149–176	183–232	203–244	1.3–1.8
Major urban	155	212–249	202–256	220–264	0.9–1.4
Total	104	143–168	162–206	179–214	1.4–1.9
Weighted					
Middle Atlantic	100	122–143	159–202	157–188	1.2–1.6
Rural	90	118–139	131–166	166–199	1.6–2.1
Urban	111	150–176	165–209	154–185	0.8–1.3
Major urban	115	—	171–217	151–180	0.7–1.2
Small	81	93–108	129–163	140–168	1.4–1.9
Medium	106	128–151	142–180	163–195	1.1–1.6
Large	110	123–144	171–216	159–190	0.9–1.2
New England	101	131–154	149–188	164–197	1.3–1.7
Rural	95	133–156	143–181	156–187	1.3–1.8
Urban	110	130–153	150–190	165–198	1.2–1.5
Major urban	122	170–200	154–195	182–218	1.0–1.5
Small	90	125–147	159–201	172–206	1.7–2.2
Medium	99	127–149	152–193	163–195	1.3–1.8
Large	110	133–157	146–185	164–196	1.0–1.5
Total	101	128–150	155–197	159–191	1.2–1.6

Notes and Sources: See the notes to Table 1.1 and the Appendix. The consumer price indexes applied to convert the current dollar figures to constant dollars were the New York City CPI prepared by the authors and the David-Solar index. The range presented is bounded by the two deflated figures. In each set of estimates, the Middle Atlantic average in 1820 was normalized to 100 and all other estimates expressed relative to that standard.

real wages in manufacturing rose substantially during the intervening decade seems robust. Again using the New York City and David-Solar CPIs for bounds, the estimates indicate growth between the 1820 Census and the 1832 McLane survey of 2.2 to 3.7 percent per annum. This fast pace may reflect the effects of beginning the eleven-year period of rather steady prosperity near a cyclical trough, as well as the strength of the industrial expansion of the 1820s. The rate of advance moderated to a more sustainable 1.1 to 1.5 percent between 1831 and 1849 (the 1832, 1850, and 1860 figures pertain to information for 1831, 1849, and 1859, respectively), despite the wild price fluctuation of the late 1830s and the prolonged downturn following the Panic of 1837. Finally, all of the price indexes imply little if any real wage growth in manufacturing over the 1850s. Average compensation was essentially flat over the decade as a whole, but workers must have suffered greatly during the middle years when consumer prices soared.

The strong underlying positive trend in real wages between 1820 and 1850, followed by a slowdown in the 1850s, extends to most segments of the manufacturing labor force distinguishable in our data. There are some deviations from the central tendency, but overall the experiences of the different groups included in Tables 1.2 and 1.3 are quite similar. Especially striking is the uniformity of dramatic progress between 1820 and 1832, a decade of major increases in patenting and manufacturing productivity, geographic extensions of transportation infrastructure and markets, as well as uninterrupted industrial expansion.[28] The record seems to indicate that virtually all categories of workers in the Northeast shared in an important bidding up of labor compensation during the first three decades of industrialization.

Both the deceleration of real wage growth for the average manufacturing employee and the actual drop in compensation offered by large and urban Middle Atlantic establishments highlight the 1850s as different from the previous thirty years and a genuinely protracted period of hard times for wage labor. Whereas fundamental changes in manufacturing organization, technology, and output were accompanied by substantial increases in real wages between 1820 and 1850, real wages stagnated during this last decade of the antebellum era despite continued, if not accelerated, productivity growth. The surge in immigration of the late 1840s and early 1850s seems to be the most likely explanation of this marked change in pattern. In particular, the coincidence of impressive advance in productivity with roughly constant real wages can readily be accounted for by the highly elastic supply of labor provided by the immigration flows.[29] Moreover, since the new immigrants were on average less skilled than the native born and concentrated in Middle Atlantic urban centers, the argument also seems consistent with the observation that large and urban Middle Atlantic establishments had the worst record of wage growth during the 1850s.[30]

28. There were a number of major transportation improvements, such as the Erie Canal, completed during the 1820s, and the years after the cyclical trough of 1820–21 through 1832 appear to have escaped any significant downturn. See Robert W. Fogel, *Railroads and American Economic Growth* (Baltimore, 1964); Sokoloff, "Productivity Growth in Manufacturing"; and "Inventive Activity"; and Meyer, MacGill, et al., *History of Transportation*.

29. From 1846 through 1857, immigration was extraordinarily heavy, with some of the largest inflows as a proportion of the population on record between 1847 and 1854. For the annual totals, see United States Bureau of the Census, *Historical Statistics of the United States, Colonial Times to 1970* (Washington, D.C., 1975), C-89. Such a vast expansion of the labor supply can account for the coincidence of a roughly constant marginal product of labor (wage) with increases in average labor productivity (Sokoloff, "Productivity Growth in Manufacturing") when there is technical change.

30. Although many had been craftsmen in their home countries, immigrants appear less skilled in manufacturing on average than natives. See Hirsch, *Roots of the American Working Class;* Wilentz, *Chants Democratic;* and Ross, *Workers on the Edge*, for discussions. Moreover, in the

Table 1.3 **Indexes of Real Wages for Adult Males in Selected Manufacturing Industries: 1820 to 1860**

	1820		1832		1850		1860		Per Annum Growth Rate, 1820–60
Unweighted									
Coaches and harnesses	95	(30)	130–153	(60)	154–196	(111)	180–215	(128)	1.7–2.1%
Cotton textiles	100	(71)	147–173	(145)	145–184	(24)	132–158	(22)	0.7–1.2
Furniture and woodwork	75	(28)	124–145	(30)	158–200	(52)	194–232	(49)	2.5–2.9
Grist mills	79	(42)	105–123	(17)	124–158	(135)	134–160	(117)	1.4–1.8
Iron and steel	100	(59)	124–145	(106)	153–194	(38)	164–196	(28)	1.3–1.7
Paper	103	(28)	127–149	(42)	149–189	(22)	171–205	(22)	1.3–1.8
Shoes	100	(19)	99–116	(108)	128–163	(265)	141–168	(178)	0.9–1.3
Tanning	71	(59)	101–118	(130)	139–177	(106)	153–183	(83)	2.0–2.5
Tools and machinery	107	(14)	152–178	(68)	165–209	(71)	155–185	(84)	1.0–1.4
Wool textiles	91	(59)	113–133	(140)	146–185	(46)	149–178	(23)	1.3–1.7
Weighted									
Coaches and harnesses	91	(168)	126–148	(415)	151–192	(438)	168–201	(701)	1.6–2.1
Cotton textiles	100	(487)	136–160	(2,460)	125–159	(504)	125–150	(438)	0.6–1.0
Furniture and woodwork	76	(79)	111–130	(199)	124–157	(279)	202–242	(263)	2.5–3.0
Grist mills	85	(100)	111–130	(111)	113–143	(116)	122–146	(93)	0.9–1.4
Iron and steel	90	(678)	107–126	(3,225)	135–172	(562)	162–194	(1,050)	1.5–2.0
Paper	96	(182)	117–137	(302)	139–176	(105)	145–173	(112)	1.1–1.6
Shoes	101	(236)	94–110	(2,325)	115–146	(1,397)	141–169	(1,992)	0.9–1.3
Tanning	81	(231)	104–122	(489)	140–178	(266)	156–186	(421)	1.7–2.2
Tools and machinery	105	(45)	150–176	(892)	151–192	(1,730)	138–165	(2,136)	0.7–1.2
Wool textiles	88	(395)	116–136	(2,409)	135–171	(301)	126–151	(406)	0.9–1.4

Notes and Sources: See the notes to Tables 1.1 and 1.2. The industries were selected to provide an adequate number of observations in each year. The number of observations is reported in parentheses. The estimates for shoes in 1832 include many firms that relied on putting-out workers. Since they appear to have worked only part-time at manufacturing shoes, their estimated annual wage significantly understates the earnings of a full-time worker.

Alternative explanations that rely on a technologically driven deskilling of the work force are not easily reconciled with the evidence. The principal problem is the strong records of real wage growth between 1820 and 1850, the period of most extensive diffusion of the new organizations of manufacturing production which involved greater division of labor and use of less-skilled workers. Accounts that turn on a failure of labor markets, owing to reduced bargaining power of artisans in the context of increasingly competitive product markets, falter on similar grounds.[31]

Moreover, the observation that the wage rates paid by small firms rose over time relative to those of larger establishments seems inconsistent with the view that the demand for artisanal labor was undercut by technological development. If skilled artisans were indeed disproportionately concentrated in small shops, then this change in the structure of wages would imply that such workers realized an increase in their relative wage. Technological change may indeed have facilitated the substitution of less-skilled workers for artisans in many industries and, in so doing, bolstered the relative demand for the former.[32] What the evidence suggests, however, is that this effect was dominated by countervailing developments which supported the wage for skilled artisans in manufacturing: rapid growth of the industrial sector, with a relatively inelastic short-run supply of artisans; expanding markets which led to more intensive and effective use of skilled labor; and the change in the relative supplies of different classes of workers produced by immigration.

The idea that artisans in traditional labor-intensive industries may have adjusted flexibly to the changes in labor market conditions, and done well, receives further support from the estimates presented in Table 1.3. The largest gains in real wages between 1820 and 1860 were registered in manufacturing industries which had long relied on artisans who worked with simple tools and equipment. For example, of the four industries with the most improvement, three of them—coaches and harnesses, furniture and woodwork, and tanning—are cases where firm sizes had grown significantly to accommodate

sample of Civil War recruits discussed below, the foreign born were disproportionately concentrated in large Middle Atlantic cities and much more likely to be classified as laborers than were the natives.

31. See Faler, *Mechanics and Manufacturers;* Prude, *Coming of Industrial Order;* and Wilentz, *Chants Democratic,* for examples of such arguments. However, the transition from the artisanal shop to the non-mechanized factory, as well as the geographic spread of competitive product markets, was largely over in the Northeast by 1850. See Hirsch, *Roots of the American Working Class;* Lindstrom, *Economic Development;* Sokoloff, "Productivity Growth in Manufacturing" and "Inventive Activity."

32. Two phases of technological change may conceivably have had such effects. The first was marked by changes in the organization of production within a non-mechanized establishment, but appears to have been accompanied by significant increases in real wages. In the second, however, during the late 1840s and 1850s, mechanized technologies spread to many of the previously labor-intensive industries. This development, which is reflected in the acceleration of capital deepening between 1850 and 1860, might have facilitated the substitution of less-skilled workers for artisans and contributed to slowing the growth of real wages generally. See Hirsch, *Roots of the American Working Class,* and Sokoloff, "Productivity Growth in Manufacturing."

a larger number of workers lacking in general skills and division of labor within the firm. By 1860, furniture and woodwork and coaches and harnesses offered the highest wages among the ten industries examined. In contrast, four of the five industries that lagged the manufacturing average in wage growth were highly capital-intensive and are seldom cited as cases of deskilling: cotton textiles, grist mills, tools and machinery, and wool textiles.

1.4 Cyclical Fluctuations

It seems clear that the early stages of industrialization in the Northeast were characterized by a positive secular trend in real wages across a broad range of manufacturing workers. There were, however, severe cycles about that growth path during the late 1830s and mid–1850s, when sharp increases in the cost of living coincided with steep, if transitory, declines in real wages. These events are evident in Figure 1.3, which depicts the annual wage series of Rothenberg and of Margo and Villaflor, as well as our weighted estimates for the years of the four cross sections, deflated by the New York City CPI. Although the reversals stand out more with this deflator, the secular advance with cycles in the late 1830s and 1850s is robust to other price series, as are the drops in non-agricultural wages during the episodes of spikes in the cost of living.

Those who emphasize the detrimental effects of industrialization on the material conditions of workers would probably not be surprised by these intervals of pronounced volatility in real wages. Indeed, some have argued that the growing use of unskilled labor and machinery by manufacturers led to an economy which was more prone to cyclical booms and busts as well as a work force that was less able to resist reductions or obtain increases in wages. Detailed investigation of these bad spells, however, raises questions about the nature of their connections to industrial development.

Perhaps the most striking basis for skepticism about the contribution of industrialization to the difficulties of manufacturing workers during the late 1830s and mid–1850s is the evidence that the sharp increases in consumer prices during the two episodes were primarily driven by movements in food prices. As depicted in Figures 1.4 and 1.5 for New York City and Vermont, the food component of the CPI is the principal source of the major jump in the cost of living between 1834 and 1837. Although the other components also advanced during the middle 1850s, food prices registered the most dramatic gains and were dominant in an accounting sense. This radically unbalanced pattern suggests that it may have been shocks to the economy originating in the agricultural sector that were responsible for the fluctuations in real wages, rather than any structural impediments to wage adjustment or business cycles induced by the process of industrialization.[33]

33. For treatments of cyclicality by labor historians, see Faler, *Mechanics and Manufacturers*, and Wilentz, *Chants Democratic*. Agricultural supply shocks seem to have preceded, and perhaps triggered, macroeconomic downturns in both cases. For a year-by-year chronology, see Willard Thorp, *Business Annals* (New York, 1926). For the macroeconomic theory concerning the effects of supply-side shocks, see Robert J. Barro, *Macroeconomics* (New York, 1984).

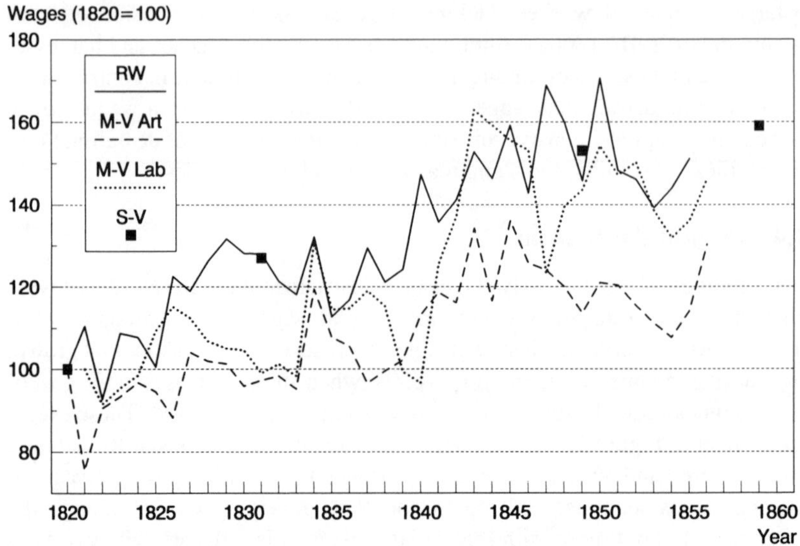

Fig. 1.3 Real Wage Indexes Deflated by the New York City CPI
Notes and Sources: See Appendix A and the notes to Table 1.1 and Figure 1.1.

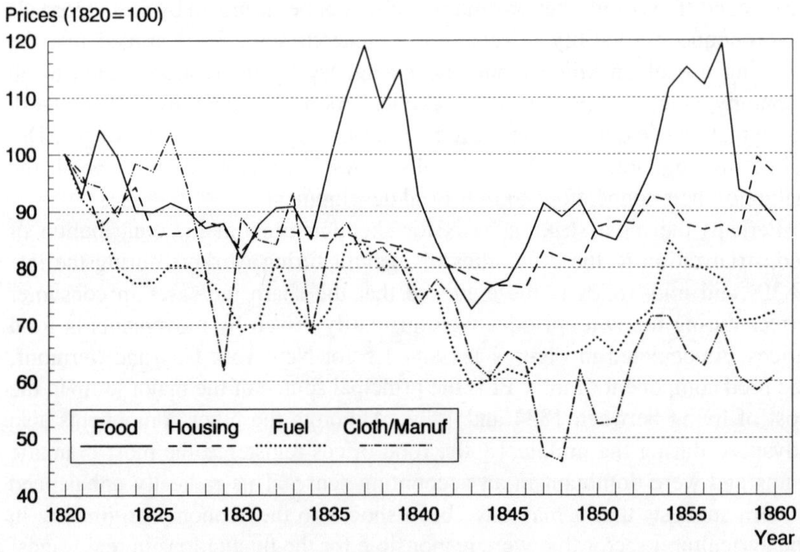

Fig. 1.4 Components of the New York City CPI
Source: See Appendix A.

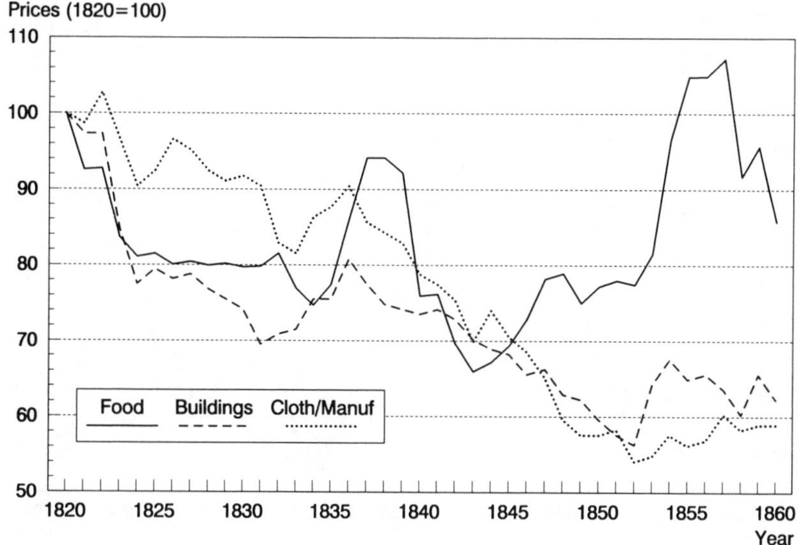

Fig. 1.5 Components of the Vermont CPI
Source: See Appendix A.

By decomposing food prices into subcomponents, one can document that spikes of several years' duration in the prices of grains, dairy, meat, and, to a lesser degree, fruit and vegetables explain much of the declines in real wages during the two episodes. Figures 1.6–1.9 present indexes for these components of food prices in New York City, Philadelphia, Boston, and rural Vermont. The plots reveal a strong correspondence across locations in price movements and indicate that the disturbances in food prices during the late 1830s and mid–1850s were extraordinary in magnitude and at least regional in scope. Although such events in food prices might in some contexts be related to features of industrial development, these seem instead to be more readily attributable to shocks exogenous to that process.

The major upturn in food prices beginning in 1835 seems rooted in exceptionally severe and widespread outbreaks of the wheat midge, the Hessian fly, and wheat rust in New York, Pennsylvania, and New England. These pests were common throughout the 1830s, but wheat output was especially hard hit in 1835 and 1836, when the crops were devastated in many areas and riots over food prices ultimately broke out in New York City.[34] The agricultural periodicals of the era are replete with accounts of the situation and support the hypothesis that an extreme shortfall in grains led to dramatic increases in

34. See the discussions in Percy W. Bidwell and John I. Falconer, *History of Agriculture in the Northern United States, 1620–1860* (New York, 1941); Paul W. Gates, *The Farmer's Age: Agriculture, 1815–1860* (New York, 1960); and Wilentz, *Chants Democratic*.

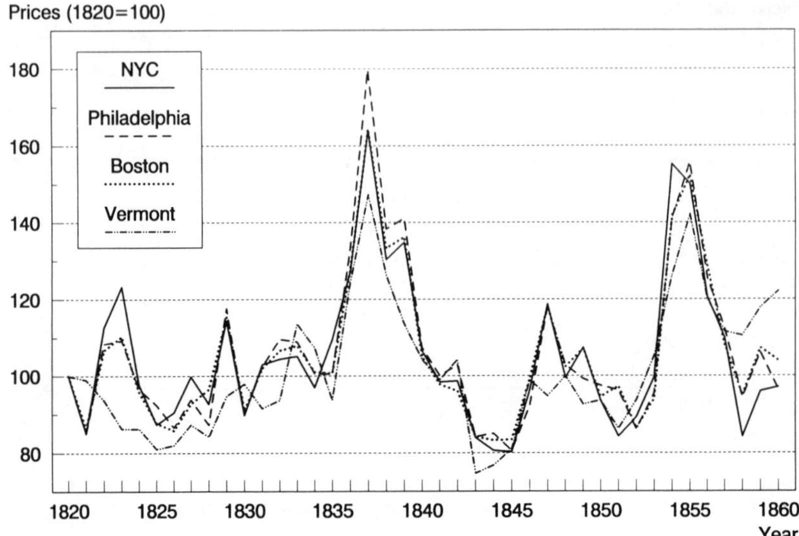

Fig. 1.6 Bread and Grain Prices in Selected Locations
Source: See Appendix A.

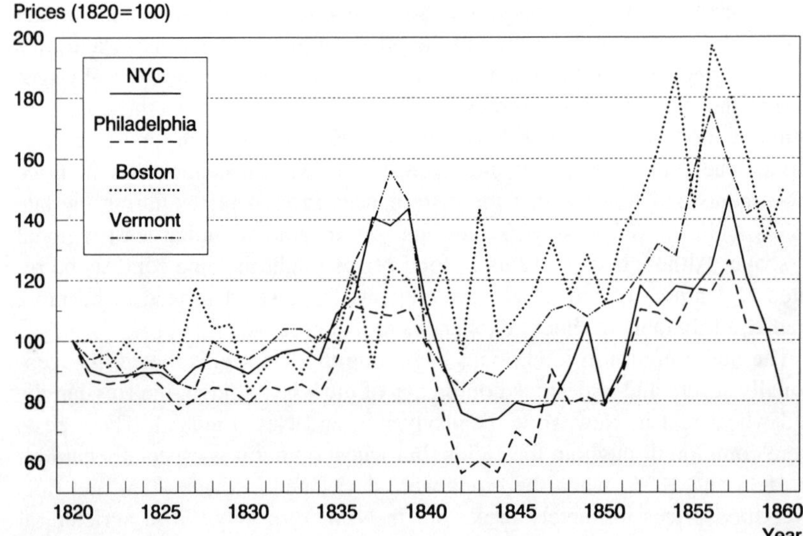

Fig. 1.7 Meat Prices in Selected Locations
Source: See Appendix A.

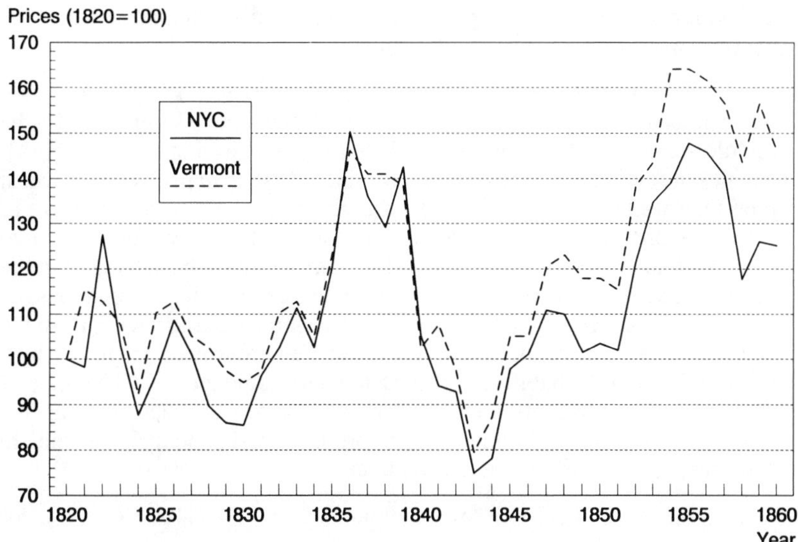

Fig. 1.8 Dairy Prices in New York City and Vermont
Source: See Appendix A.

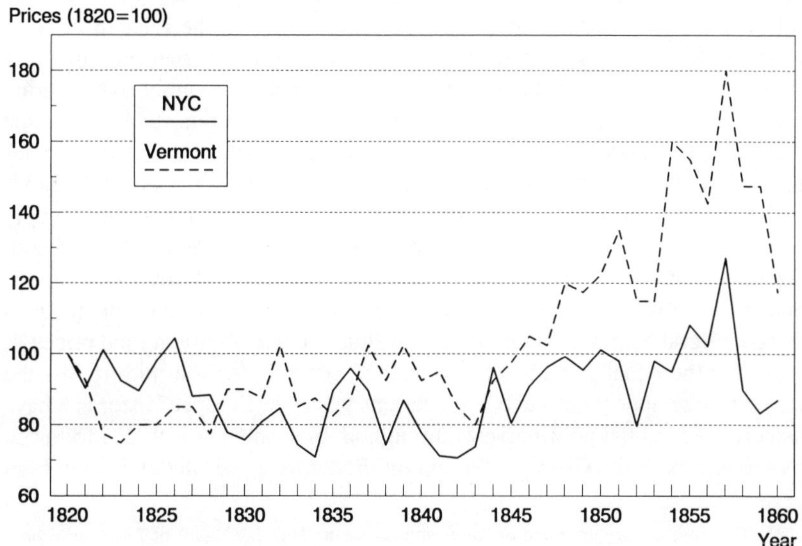

Fig. 1.9 Vegetable Prices in New York City and Vermont
Source: See Appendix A.

price, with corresponding and persistent effects on dairy and meat prices because of rising feed costs and smaller herds:

> The harvest prospect, so far as regards winter grain, is gloomy, as much so, we fear, as it was twelve months ago. Our accounts from Virginia, from the middle states, and from the wheat districts of our own state [New York], are all but favorable . . . we shall have little cause to expect a better wheat crop than we had in 1836. To show that the crop of 1836, fell far short of our consumption, it is only necessary to state, that there was imported into New-York alone, from Europe, in 1836, half a million-bushels, and in the current year, up to the 19th of April, eight hundred and fifty-seven thousand bushels . . . of wheat, besides rye and other grain—thus drawing from the country some millions of dollars for bread stuffs, our great staples, which we have been in the habit of exporting to a large amount. . . . The price of meats have been so high, and the scarcity of forage so great, that our live stock has been greatly diminished, and prudence and good management are necessary to replenish our herds and flocks.[35]

Indeed, grain prices began to fall precipitously in 1838, ahead of those for dairy and livestock products.

This evidence raises the possibility that the compensation of non-agricultural workers may simply have fallen with the short-term decrease in the value of their marginal product. Given the income-elastic demand for non-agricultural goods, the effect of the drop in national income would have reinforced the immediate impact of the supply shock on the relative price of food. In this view, agricultural labor should not have experienced much of a decline in real wages, and indeed Rothenberg's series is roughly stable during these years. Although the Margo-Villaflor series for laborers suggests that the recovery of real wages lagged the restoration of normal conditions in agriculture, the delay may be due to the contraction following the Panic of 1837, which could well have been related to the effects of the agricultural supply shock. Further study of this episode is certainly necessary, but the record seems to highlight a continued vulnerability of early industrial economies, and specifically real wages in the non-agricultural sector, to sharp fluctuations in agricultural output or other sources of short-run variability in food prices.[36]

As for the equally dramatic rise in food costs during the mid–1850s, the major source appears to have been circumstances in Europe. Historians have usually credited the poor harvests throughout the continent in 1853, followed by the effects of the Crimean War on the Baltic trade, for the extremely high

35. This commentary appeared on the front page of the May 1837 issue of *The Cultivator,* a popular monthly on agriculture published in Albany.

36. For a systematic examination of the responsiveness of wages to changes in the price level, see Claudia Goldin and Robert A. Margo, chap. 2 in this volume. See Peter Temin, *The Jacksonian Economy* (New York, 1969), for a monetary interpretation of the increase in the price level during the mid–1830s. An analogous specie-based story could also link the rising prices of the 1850s to gold strikes. Such theories do not easily account for the disproportionate adjustment of food prices.

world grain prices (and volume of U.S. exports) prevailing through 1856. The idea that the increased cost of living in the American Northeast had an international source is supported by parallel movements in consumer price indexes for Belgium, France, Germany, and Sweden during these years.[37] The link to dairy and livestock prices seems to have operated as it did earlier; grain prices began to fall in 1856 with the end of the war, but unambiguous decreases in dairy and livestock (as well as in vegetable) prices did not materialize until a year or two later. The situation may have been further exacerbated by the drought in New York, which was the primary dairy and an important gardening state, in 1854 and 1855. In the 1855 New York Census, for example, only 11 percent of the reporting dairies had attained their "normal yield" of butter and cheese in 1854, with 38 percent falling at least one-third short of this standard.[38]

In summary, neither of the two episodes of extreme short-term fluctuations in the cost of living between 1820 and 1860 appears attributable in any meaningful way to the process of industrialization. Exogenous shocks to the agricultural sector seem, instead, to bear chief responsibility. Although there may be questions about whether the cyclical effects of the supply-side disturbances may have persisted longer because industrial sectors adjust slowly to macroeconomic shocks, or about whether the influx of immigrants retarded the adjustment of labor markets in the 1850s case, steep but temporary drops in real wages for non-agricultural workers would have occurred regardless. Given this modest and indirect role of industrialization in accounting for the volatility, there is little reason to reject the implication of the real wage trends that these early stages of growth yielded substantial improvements in the material compensation of manufacturing workers.

1.5 Multivariate Analysis of Variation in Wages

The simple patterns of variation in wages seem to support the interpretation that workers and firms in the Northeast were quite flexible in responding to the structural and technological changes of early industrialization, and that the market for manufacturing labor generally operated well. At the same time that major shifts in the allocation of labor were taking place, virtually all segments of the work force appear to have shared in the improved compensation arising from increases in productivity. At our level of aggregation, there is no evidence that significant groups of manufacturing employees failed to make progress because of depreciated human capital or lack of mobility between industries or geographic districts. On the contrary, the greatest gains were

37. Lord Ernle, *English Farming Past and Present* (New York, 1922); Robert L. Jones, *History of Agriculture in Ontario, 1613–1880* (Toronto, 1946); J. D. Chambers and G. E. Mingay, *The Agricultural Revolution, 1775–1880* (London, 1966); Gates, *The Farmer's Age;* and B. R. Mitchell, *European Historical Statistics, 1750–1975* (New York, 1980).

38. State of New York, *Census of the State of New York for 1855* (Albany, 1857), p. liv.

realized by workers in once-outlying rural areas who were increasingly drawn into the growth process by the expansion of product markets. Instead of wider wage differentials, which one would expect if labor market participants adjusted slowly to altered circumstances, the gaps apparent in 1820 narrowed considerably.[39]

Even artisans appear to have adjusted well overall to the changing circumstances. Those who remained in small shops, for example, won wage increases equivalent in proportional terms to those of the typically less-skilled employees of medium- and large-sized establishments. Some might question whether this group was representative of artisans in general. If their employers were seeking to economize on labor costs, however, their wage rates should have reflected the opportunity cost for artisans working in other enterprises. Part of the improvement over time may have been compensation for the less amenable conditions of the work, including intensification and regimentation, implemented by manufacturers in the increasingly competitive environment. But given that such work practices are most commonly associated with the larger manufacturing establishments, this factor does not seem able to fully explain the pattern.

These findings could be sensitive to the limited controls for independent variables in the bivariate analysis. Accordingly, we have examined a variety of multivariate approaches, including the cross-sectional weighted regressions presented in Table 1.4 for each of the four years. They provide more comprehensive estimates of the patterns of variation by regressing the wage rate for adult males on dummy and interaction variables for firm characteristics. The qualitative results remain unchanged, however. Even after adjusting for industry, subregion, urbanization, and firm size, there is a marked convergence over time in wage rates between classes of workers. Employees in counties with major urban centers, for example, began in 1820 and 1832 with a statistically significant edge of approximately 15 to 20 percent (summing the coefficients on the urban and major urban dummies) over their rural counterparts, but the discrepancy fell to barely 10 percent in 1850 and was insignificant in 1860. Similarly, according to regressions (1), (3), (5), and (7) reported in the table, wage rates in small establishments rose from roughly 16 percent less than those in medium-sized firms (with an even greater deficit compared with large establishments) in 1820, to 9 percent less in 1832, to parity in 1850 and 1860. This pattern is robust to alternative specifications and suggests that labor markets were becoming so well integrated over time that influences on wages in one district would soon be reflected in other areas.

The one anomalous feature is that the gap between small and larger enterprises in the rural parts of the Middle Atlantic declined only modestly over the period, from about 30 percent in 1820 and 1832 to roughly 15 to 25 per-

39. In contrast, David R. Weir, "Labor Market Performance and Demographic Change in Nineteenth Century France," manuscript (New Haven, 1990), finds that the urban-rural wage gaps in England and France widen over much of the nineteenth century.

Table 1.4 **Cross-Sectional Wage Regressions for Adult Males in Northeastern Manufacturing: 1820, 1832, 1850, and 1860**

Dependent Variable: Log (Adult Male Wage)	Constant	Subregions: New England	Subregions: Northern New England	Subregions: Southern New England	Subregions: New York	Urbanization: Urban	Urbanization: Major Urban	Firm Size: Small	Firm Size: Large	Interactions: Small × New England	Interactions: Small × Urban New England	Interactions: Small × Urban Middle Atlantic	No. of Observations	R^2
1820														
(1)	5.519		−0.111	−0.072	−0.097	0.048	0.154	−0.162	0.062				623	0.26
	(117.62)		(−1.97)	(−1.89)	(−2.80)	(1.18)	(3.40)	(−3.82)	(1.88)					
(2)	5.544		−0.175	−0.125	−0.086	0.027	0.129	−0.298	0.069	0.343		0.224	623	0.28
	(118.23)		(−3.05)	(−3.15)	(−2.52)	(0.64)	(2.85)	(−5.76)	(2.11)	(4.331)		(2.35)		
1832														
(3)	5.654	0.036				0.109	0.110	−0.085	0.068				708	0.37
	(148.35)	(1.81)				(5.52)	(1.54)	(−1.93)	(2.33)					
(4)	5.676	0.016				0.104	0.101	−0.324	0.064	0.301	0.077		708	0.38
	(149.21)	(0.82)				(5.27)	(1.43)	(−4.50)	(2.22)	(3.78)	(0.83)			
1850														
(5)	5.570		0.082	0.066	0.015	0.043	0.074	−0.024	0.012				981	0.45
	(130.15)		(2.35)	(3.16)	(0.77)	(1.96)	(3.41)	(−0.82)	(0.48)					
(6)	5.618		0.017	0.043	0.009	−0.002	0.065	−0.160	0.025	0.225	0.019	0.156	981	0.46
	(127.82)		(0.43)	(1.98)	(0.45)	(−0.09)	(2.95)	(−3.72)	(0.99)	(3.43)	(0.24)	(3.30)		
1860														
(7)	5.595		0.040	0.087	−0.045	0.013	0.017	−0.053	0.057				858	0.20
	(99.22)		(0.88)	(3.13)	(−1.68)	(0.44)	(0.71)	(−1.33)	(1.84)					
(8)	5.657		−0.020	0.079	−0.046	−0.049	0.020	−0.253	0.060	0.312	0.010	0.248	858	0.22
	(97.73)		(−0.40)	(2.80)	(−1.74)	(−1.42)	(0.84)	(−4.17)	(1.94)	(2.69)	(0.07)	(3.88)		

Notes and Sources: See the notes to Tables 1.1 and 1.2. These regressions use the log of the nominal annualized wage as the dependent variable and were estimated with industry dummy variables which are excluded from the table. Each observation was weighted by the number of adult male employees. The selection of independent dummy variables was somewhat different for 1820 and 1832, because the sample from the former year included few small establishments in urban New England counties, and the sample from the latter consisted primarily of observations from Massachusetts and Pennsylvania. Coefficients are reported with t-statistics below in parentheses. The constant represents a medium-sized cotton textile firm operating in a rural county of Delaware, New Jersey, or Pennsylvania.

cent in the later years. This understates the extent of convergence, however. Wage levels were virtually uniform across small and medium-sized firms in New England and the urban counties of the Middle Atlantic throughout the period (evident in regressions [2], [4], [6], and [8]). Moreover, rural averages alone do not adequately convey the process of wage adjustment occurring as markets expanded into what had been remote districts. As falling transport costs brought them increasingly into competition with distant producers, rural firms were induced to raise their productivity and wage rates to competitive levels. These adjustments contributed to the relative advance of both wages and firm size in rural counties, and with the declining fraction of shops which were so insulated, the overall wage gap between small and medium enterprises fell to statistical insignificance by 1850 (see [5] and [7]). Small firms with lower wages did persist in isolated parts of the Middle Atlantic, as is apparent from (6) and (8), but their relative numbers dwindled over time.

The regressions confirm a relative increase over time in the wage rates offered by small establishments overall, but indicate that the pattern did not quite hold everywhere. An examination of the change over the cross sections in the coefficients on the dummy variables for firm size and on their interactions with region and urbanization reveals that these gains by workers in small shops were realized throughout New England, but only in the rural counties of the Middle Atlantic.[40] Even in the divergent Middle Atlantic cities, however, workers in small firms maintained their relative wages. In none of these areas, therefore, do artisans appear to have suffered in either absolute or relative terms.

The regressions in Table 1.5 differ in that they examine both the cross-sectional and temporal variation over a pooled sample, and accordingly subject the hypotheses about trends over time to more direct tests. The coefficients on the year dummies reflect substantial real wage growth over the period from 1820 to 1860, even after controlling for changes in industry, location, and firm size. Again, the pace of advance was most rapid during the 1820s and slowed to a virtual standstill during the 1850s. The results also provide further evidence of improved market integration. In particular, regression (2) indicates again that wages in small firms began in 1820 at a lower level but rose at a faster pace to overtake, or surpass in New England, those of larger enterprises as early as 1850. Although its statistical significance is reduced, the pattern continues to hold (regression [3]) when one allows for different relationships with firm size between New England and the Middle Atlantic.

Especially telling is regression (4), where the coefficients on the interaction variables between years and firm characteristics suggest that wages grew more rapidly in rural counties and in artisanal industries such as coaches and har-

40. Part of the average improvement is associated with the increasing proportion of the small firms located in urban counties.

Table 1.5 **Pooled Cross-Sectional Real Wage Regressions: 1820, 1832, 1850 and 1860**

	Dependent Variable: Log (Adult Male Wage)			
	(1)	(2)	(3)	(4)
Constant	6.053	6.041	6.055	6.081
	(218.00)	(215.84)	(215.63)	(180.97)
Sub-Regions:				
Northern New England	−9.020	−0.027	−0.034	−0.024
	(−0.62)	(−0.87)	(−1.09)	(−0.78)
Southern New England	0.007	0.006	0.005	0.018
	(0.25)	(0.21)	(0.17)	(0.67)
New York	−0.067	−0.068	−0.070	−0.064
	(−4.76)	(−4.82)	(−4.97)	(−4.54)
Urbanization:				
Urban	0.041	0.039	0.021	−0.048
	(3.24)	(3.04)	(1.56)	(−1.81)
Major urban	0.059	0.063	0.062	0.070
	(4.09)	(4.37)	(4.31)	(4.71)
Year:				
1820	−0.494	−0.474	−0.479	−0.517
	(−27.82)	(−24.81)	(−25.09)	(−16.27)
1832	−0.209	−0.194	−0.201	−0.250
	(−15.02)	(−13.47)	(−13.95)	(−9.88)
1850	−0.055	−0.055	−0.055	−0.083
	(−4.34)	(−4.00)	(−4.02)	(−2.52)
Firm Size:				
Middle-Atlantic × Small	−0.132	−0.080	−0.175	−0.198
	(−5.20)	(−2.41)	(−4.48)	(−4.94)
Middle-Atlantic × Large	0.020	0.022	0.024	0.030
	(0.95)	(1.07)	(1.18)	(1.46)
New England × Small	0.018	0.124	0.095	0.070
	(0.56)	(2.94)	(2.23)	(1.63)
New England × Large	0.017	0.021	0.024	0.028
	(0.83)	(0.99)	(1.17)	(1.33)
Other Interactions:				
Middle-Atlantic × Small × Urban			0.165	0.191
			(4.56)	(5.03)
Small × 1820		−0.126	−0.076	−0.042
		(−2.77)	(−1.64)	(−0.87)
Small × 1832		−0.199	−0.157	−0.188
		(−4.25)	(−3.31)	(−2.44)
Small × 1850		−0.021	−0.019	−0.004
		(−0.59)	(−0.53)	(−0.10)
Urban × 1820				0.126
				(3.37)
Urban × 1832				0.084
				(2.87)
Urban × 1850				0.037
				(1.09)

(*continued*)

Table 1.5 (continued)

	Dependent Variable: Log (Adult Male Wage)			
	(1)	(2)	(3)	(4)
Artisanal × 1820				−0.256 (−5.56)
Artisanal × 1832				−0.109 (−2.86)
Artisanal × 1850				−0.049 (−1.32)
No. of Observations	3,281	3,281	3,281	3,281
R^2	0.38	0.39	0.39	0.40

Notes and Sources: See the notes to Tables 1.1, 1.2, and 1.4. The industries classified as artisanal in the interactions are coaches and harnesses, clocks and jewelry, glass, and furniture and woodwork. Industry dummy variables were included in the regressions but are not reported here. The constant represents a medium-sized cotton textile firm operating in 1860 in a rural county of Pennsylvania, Delaware, or New Jersey. The wages were deflated by the New York City CPI.

nesses, clocks and jewelry, glass, and furniture and woodwork. This latter finding, which is robust to reasonable changes in classification, bolsters the case for our interpretation of the relative wage growth of artisans. All of the industries included in this artisanal group tended to rely on traditionally trained artisans, but shifted somewhat over time toward the use of greater numbers of less-skilled employees for carrying out the simpler tasks in the production process. That their workers on average realized more substantial increases in wages, after controlling for firm size, is important corroborating evidence.

In general, the results support the view that early industrialization boosted real wages for virtually all groups in manufacturing, but was of greatest benefit to employees in areas previously insulated from the broad markets. Decreases in transportation costs, as well as improvements in productivity stimulated by the extension of markets, led wages in such districts to rise to generally competitive levels. In those parts of the Northeast which were just beginning to engage in extensive commerce and develop substantial manufacturing activity, it is perhaps not surprising that skilled or artisanal labor became increasingly scarce and had its relative return bid up.

1.6 Labor Mobility

Much of our discussion of the market for manufacturing workers during early industrialization presumes that there was extensive trade and labor mobility within the Northeast. Even if manufacturing firms realized productivity growth, the fruits of this progress would not necessarily be shared with employees unless there were effective competing demands for the labor.[41] Similarly, the wages of artisans employed in small shops would not reflect those in other enterprises unless there was effective competition for jobs. One method of gauging the intensity of such competition would be to examine the frequency with which workers changed jobs and the associated changes in wage rates. Although the substantial sectoral shift of labor out of agriculture suggests that there must have been considerable occupational mobility, the current lack of job histories for individuals makes direct study of the question problematic. Another way of approaching the issue, however, is to examine the extent of geographic mobility.[42]

The samples of U.S. Army recruits drawn by Fogel and his colleagues contain information on places of birth and enlistment for each soldier and permit the estimation of migratory flows between locations as well as persistence rates.[43] Table 1.6 presents such a cross tabulation for northeastern-born recruits during the Civil War, showing their geographic mobility between cities or villages classified by size. The results indicate high rates of geographic mobility among the young men included in this randomly drawn and representative sample. Even with the use of such general categories for destination, the rates of persistence seem quite low. For example, only 54 percent of the recruits born in rural areas (cities or villages with populations less than 2,500 in 1860) enlisted in such districts, while the figures for recruits born in small and large cities were 63 percent and 80 percent, respectively. The actual persistence rates for enlisting in the city of birth were, of course, considerably lower (about 40 percent overall), but the rank ordering in which rural areas have the highest (and large cities the lowest) rates of outflow is preserved. Perhaps not surprisingly, there was net out-migration of native born from rural areas and net in-migration to small and large cities. The data for the four largest cities in 1860 (Boston, Brooklyn, New York, and Philadelphia) are also reported separately. Although they experienced a slight net outflow of native born, they also had higher persistence rates than either rural areas or small cities.

These estimates are consistent with our view that the Northeast was characterized by extensive geographic mobility during the early stages of industrialization and that employers of labor would have had to match wages for

41. This requirement could be satisfied by competing employers within the same district. Geographic mobility, however, would expand the scope of potential competitors, and thus increase the likelihood of a worker sharing in the returns to productivity growth.

42. For other evidence of mobility between jobs, see Alexander J. Field, "Sectoral Shift in Antebellum Massachusetts: A Reconsideration," *Explorations in Economic History,* (Apr. 1978), pp. 146–71; Prude, *Coming of Industrial Order;* and Stephan Thernstrom, *The Other Bostonians: Poverty and Progress in the American Metropolis* (Cambridge, 1973).

43. Fogel, "Nutrition and the Decline in Mortality;" and Georgia C. Villaflor and Kenneth L. Sokoloff, "Migration in Colonial America: Evidence from the Militia Muster Rolls," *Social Science History,* 6 (Fall 1982), pp. 539–70.

workers in other parts of the region. Indeed, with an extremely mobile population, a demonstrated ability on the part of workers to shift between industries, and expanding output markets, the basic requirements for a well-integrated labor market and wage convergence appear satisfied.

The estimates in Table 1.6 also provide information about the relative attractiveness of circumstances in cities as opposed to rural areas. It is especially interesting that the net movement of natives born in the Northeast is toward cities, even though the tendency of the immigrants to cluster there might be expected to have adversely affected housing costs, labor market conditions, and the disease environment.[44] The preference of these young men for cities also overrode the apparent increase between 1820 and 1860 in rural wages relative to urban. This flow of migrants undoubtedly contributed to the process of wage convergence and may have reflected an advantage for cities in the cost of living, in real incomes for natives, or in illiquid capital gains reaped by urban households during the years of exceptional city growth.

As David Galenson and Clayne Pope have argued, longstanding residents of an area might benefit disproportionately from rapid population growth through an increase in the relative value of the location-specific assets (human as well as physical) acquired earlier. Given that the tendency for native-born recruits to be disproportionately represented in the middle- and upper-class occupations was more pronounced in urban areas than rural, these data provide some support for the hypothesis.[45] If the theory is correct, our mean wages for various categories of manufacturing workers in 1860 would underestimate the average wage for the respective classes of only native-born employees and the extent of the bias would vary with the proportion of foreign born in the labor force. The presence of immigrants would have led to a bidding up of the returns to native labor in those districts where the immigrants concentrated, but would have obscured this effect in the gross wage data by occupying a larger fraction of the jobs and working at lower wage rates.

1.7 Conclusions

The early stages of industrialization no doubt posed a challenge to many workers. Through the same process that created new opportunities, old patterns of behavior were rendered less rewarding, if not totally lacking in viability. Not all people thrive under such conditions. It might seem remarkable, therefore, that the material benefits from the onset of growth in the American Northeast were widely shared and that all of the groups distinguishable in our

44. If one includes a variable for the percentage of the county population which was foreign born in cross-sectional wage regressions for 1850 or 1860, the estimated coefficient is not significantly different from zero. This finding is consistent with the view that the labor markets were well integrated throughout most of the Northeast.

45. David W. Galenson and Clayne L. Pope, chap. 7 in this volume; and Thernstrom, *The Other Bostonians*. The proportion of foreign-born recruits who were laborers relative to that for natives was higher in cities than in rural areas.

Table 1.6 **Geographic Mobility of Civil War Recruits Born in the Northeast**

	Place of Birth				
Place of Enlistment	Rural Areas	Small Cities	Large Cities	Four Largest Cities	Total
Rural areas	696	151	129	91	976
(a)	0.71	0.15	0.13	0.09	1.00
(b)	0.54	0.16	0.11	0.10	0.28
Small Cities	351	613	112	93	1,076
(a)	0.33	0.57	0.10	0.09	1.00
(b)	0.27	0.63	0.09	0.10	0.31
Large Cities	243	206	938	711	1,387
(a)	0.18	0.15	0.68	0.51	1.00
(b)	0.19	0.21	0.80	0.79	0.40
Four Largest Cities	43	71	635	579	749
(a)	0.06	0.09	0.85	0.77	1.00
(b)	0.03	0.07	0.54	0.65	0.22
Total	1,290	970	1,179	895	3,439
(a)	0.38	0.28	0.34	0.26	1.00
(b)	1.00	1.00	1.00	1.00	1.00

Notes and Sources: The table provides a cross tabulation of places of birth and enlistment for all of the individuals contained in the random sample of Civil War recruits for which they were reported. Proportions of row totals appear on lines (a), while proportions of column totals appear on (b). Rural areas consist of cities or villages with populations less than 2,500 in 1860; small cities include those with populations from 2,500 to 9,999; and large cities had populations of 10,000 or more. The next to last row and column of the table pertain to recruits born or enlisted in the cities of Boston, Brooklyn, New York, and Philadelphia. The figures for these "Four Largest Cities" are also counted in the "Large Cities" category.

data realized substantial increases in real wages over the period from 1820 to 1860. Indeed, those workers who were tested by having their insulation from the broad regional market eroded by improvements in transportation registered the greatest advances in compensation. This record of achievement under pressure tells us much about the people and the process of industrialization in the early Republic, and indicates that Americans were on the whole eager to pursue economic opportunities—whether this meant jobs with higher wages, goods at lower prices, or investments with better returns.

Many scholars have questioned how well traditional artisans coped with the challenges associated with early industrialization. This group had large investments in knowledge of general production skills, the value of which might have been depreciated by the direction and accelerated pace of technical change. Yet our estimates, though indirect, suggest that on average their wages grew more rapidly than those of other manufacturing workers. There were, obviously, individual artisans who did less well than this average, especially among the older workers who typically had more difficulty adjusting to new jobs or regimes. But one should not ignore the many opportunities that remained for the class as a whole and were evidently exploited. Their skills and knowledge continued to be valued in many industries because of the slow progress in standardizing the production of high-quality or customized goods and their usefulness to factories in the performance of specific tasks requiring general expertise.

Despite the substantial progress over time, the record of real wages in manufacturing between 1820 and 1860 was not one of continual improvement. Bad things do happen, and early industrial America was no exception to this law of nature. How much misfortune was due to industrialization is a question not easily answered. As for individual experiences, life can be punishing and there are always some who take losses. As for classes of manufacturing workers, however, none of the painful intervals that stand out in the record seem likely to be directly or primarily attributable to the path of industrial development. If the sharp fluctuations in real wages during the 1830s and 1850s were indeed driven by movements in food prices, the contributions of industrial organization, industrial labor markets, or technology to these bad spells seem reduced to issues of persistence. Similarly, the slowdown in real wage growth between 1850 and 1860, associated with a corresponding increase in the capital share of manufacturing income, is hard to link directly to industrialization. The most likely explanation is the immigration of the late 1840s and 1850s, but the unusually heavy flows of these years do not appear to have been endogenous with respect to domestic economic circumstances. On the contrary, they, like the other major shocks to the progress of manufacturing workers during early American industrialization, seem largely to have been imposed exogenously, rather than being naturally generated by the process. Whether the beginning of industrialization made the American Northeast more or less prone and sensitive to volatility in agricultural prices, labor supply, or other socioeconomic variables is an important question yet to be resolved. But the implication of the evidence examined here is that despite its material advantages and rapid secular advance, this small early industrial economy remained quite vulnerable to extreme fluctuations in agricultural conditions and other such disturbances.

Appendix

The Williamson and David-Solar price indexes are drawn respectively from Jeffrey G. Williamson, "American Prices and Urban Inequality," *Journal of Economic History,* 36 (June 1976), pp. 303–33, and Paul A. David and Peter Solar, "A Bicentenary Contribution." The former was meant to pertain to the urban poor in northeastern cities and the latter to the Northeast in general. The New York City and Vermont consumer price indexes, as well as those for

Boston and Philadelphia reported below, were constructed by adopting the rather conservative budget shares estimated for low-income urban households: 0.599 for food, 0.133 for housing, 0.061 for fuel and lighting, and 0.205 for clothing and other manufactured goods (Brady, "Price Deflators for Final Product Estimates" and "Consumption and the Style of Life"). This division of expenditures might be considered conservative, because it is at the high end of the estimates with respect to the share devoted to food, and food prices rose over the period relative to the prices of most other commodities. The budget shares for middle- and upper-income groups imply a somewhat greater decline in the cost of living over time. Since information on the prices of individual food products is relatively plentiful, separate indexes of food prices were prepared for each location by using budget shares for individual commodities derived from Hoover, "Retail Prices After 1850." This food component of consumer prices was divided between meat and fish (0.233), bread and baking goods (0.193), dairy products (0.163), fruits and vegetables (0.164), and other food products (0.247). Hoover's budget shares were estimated from late-nineteenth-century data and might also be considered conservative with respect to the extent of price decline before 1860, because she gave much less weight to expenditures on once-scarce commodities like tea and sugar, which loomed large in worker budgets of the early nineteenth century and yet fell substantially in price over the antebellum period (Larkin, *Reshaping of Everyday Life*, p. 175).

Where possible, the subcomponents of the food price indexes for Boston, New York City, and Philadelphia were estimated separately from city-specific wholesale (or retail, in the case of Boston) commodity series contained in Anne Bezanson, Robert D. Gray, and Miriam Hussey, *Wholesale Prices in Philadelphia, 1784–1861* (Philadelphia, 1937); Arthur H. Cole, *Wholesale Commodity Prices in the United States, 1700–1861*, 2 vols., (Cambridge, 1938); George G. Warren and Frank A. Pearson, *Prices* (New York, 1933); and Carroll Wright, *Sixteenth Annual Report of the Massachusetts Bureau of Statistics of Labor* (Boston, 1885). Among the individual commodities whose price series were employed are bread, flour, cornmeal, Indian meal, rye meal, and rice (bread and baking goods); bacon, beef, pork, fish, and halibut (meat and fish); and coffee, eggs, tea, molasses, sugar, gin, rum, and whiskey (other food products). For the dairy products and fruits and vegetables components, however, there were not sufficient data available to estimate separate indexes; hence, materials from all of these cities were pooled, with the price index for dairy products estimated from series for butter, cheese, and lard, as well as from the Bezanson average for dairy products. The price index for fruits and vegetables was estimated from series for potatoes, lemons, raisins, and apples, as well as from the Bezanson averages for beans, fruits, and condiments. The three cities also share the same price indexes for fuel and lighting, housing, and clothing and manufactured goods. The component for fuel and lighting was computed as an average of the Warren and Pearson, and Bezanson indexes; the Adams series for construction costs in Philadelphia is used as the housing component (Donald R. Adams, Jr., "Residential Construction in the Early Nineteenth Century," *Journal of Economic History,* 35 [Dec. 1975], pp. 794–816); and the clothing and manufactured goods component is a weighted average of commodity series for shoes, gloves, handkerchiefs, hose, calico, cambric, muslin, cotton yarn, and linen, as well as of interpolated series for the product prices in the coaches and harnesses, furniture, glass, and paper industries (Sokoloff, "Productivity Growth"). Further details on the construction of the indexes are available from the authors.

The Vermont index has been constructed anew from the information in Adams, *Prices Paid By Vermont Farmers*, on the retail prices paid by Vermont farmers and on the prices they received for their produce. Although Adams estimated an index of food prices directly from his data, we have modified his series because the pattern of expenditure on food of Vermont farmers seems unlikely to be representative of that of manufacturing workers. Specifically, we have used the Adams series on the prices farmers received for their livestock and vegetables as the components for meat and fish and fruits and vegetables, respectively. His series for the prices received for grains and dairy products are employed in Figures 1.7 and 1.9 above. Adams's food price series, which includes both local produce and agricultural goods obtained from afar, is used for the remaining parts of our overall Vermont food index. In addition, the Adams series on the cost of building materials and on the cost of clothing serve as the components for housing and clothing and other manufactured goods, respectively. The only set of non-Vermont prices employed is for the fuel and lighting component, where the average of the Warren and Pearson, and Bezanson indexes is again used.

Many of the choices about the weights for individual commodities, or between alternative price series, are to some degree arbitrary. In order to limit the significance of this potential problem, as well as to learn more about the patterns of price variation, extensive sensitivity analysis was carried out on many issues before settling on the particular specifications reported. In general, we were impressed with the robustness of the basic results. What stands out are the major declines in the prices of manufactures and imported food products, the modest declines in fuel and lighting costs, and the roughly stable or rising prices of meats, grains, and dairy products. This sharp change in relative prices, which was of course to the benefit of farmers, appears to have been especially pronounced in rural areas like Vermont, where improvements in transportation induced a convergence of local prices toward the levels prevailing in urban districts. As a consequence, the Vermont price index was the most sensitive to the weights used on the different components, and one should be cautious about accepting the implication of our estimates that the overall cost of living there for manufacturing workers fell relative to that in urban centers.

There are two potentially severe problems with the construction of our indexes, but they work in opposite directions. The first is the wholly inadequate series for housing costs, which likely understates the substantial run-up in large cities resulting from heavy immigration and domestic migration in the 1840s and 1850s. However, due to the limited share of housing in total consumption expenditures (13.3 percent), as well as caveats about the higher rentals reflecting the improved services arising from residence in a particular location, one should be careful before concluding that the qualitative results are an artifact of this deficiency. Moreover, the effects of the poor coverage of housing are to some degree offset by the failure to account for improvements in the quality of all kinds of products which are not reflected in price. Many scholars (e.g., see Brady, "Relative Prices," and Gordon, *Measurement of Durable Goods Prices*) have noted or demonstrated that the quantitative significance of this defect of conventional price indexes can be enormous, and one would expect this factor to have been important with the introduction of many new products and the competition over the ornament and design of even simple consumer items which characterized early and late American industrialization. Such improvements in quality were likely realized in agricultural products such as butter, cheese, and meat, as well as in housing and manufactures (Gates, *A Farmer's Age;* Brady, "Relative Prices"; and Larkin, *Reshaping of Everyday Life*). A related problem is that the price indexes fail to entirely capture the gains to consumers over the period arising from greater regularity in supply of products as well as easier access to retailers.

2 Wages, Prices, and Labor Markets before the Civil War

Claudia Goldin and Robert A. Margo

2.1 Economic Development, Nominal Wage Flexibility, and Antebellum Labor Markets

America experienced several expansions and contractions in economic activity between its founding and the Civil War. The Embargo of 1807 abruptly ended the export boom of the Napoleonic Wars, a recession followed the War of 1812, there was a panic in 1819, and a crisis in 1825. An expansion in the late 1820s and early 1830s gave way to several downturns; rapid recovery succeeded the first, a minor one in 1837, but the second, in 1839, was more prolonged. Minor contractions in the late 1840s and early 1850s were followed by another downturn in 1857. Associated with most of these expansions and contractions, especially the so-called Panic of 1837 and Panic of 1857, were sharp changes in the price level. While the existence of these fluctuations in economic activity is not in doubt, their severity has been questioned.

There are two opposing views of the antebellum economy. One is that the period was marked by at least one severe depression, from 1839 to 1843, and other lesser recessions. Aggregate economic activity, according to this view, was severely diminished during the downturns, and unemployment was both substantial and prolonged in cities and industrial towns. The other interpreta-

The wage data analyzed in this paper were collected by the Center for Population Economics, University of Chicago. The research assistance of Joseph Hunt and research support from Colgate University are gratefully acknowledged. The authors would like to thank Stanley Engerman, Kevin Hassett, Hugh Rockoff, and the participants at the 1990 NBER-DAE Summer Institute, the 1990 AEA-Cliometrics session, and the Cornell University economic history seminar for comments on an earlier draft.

tion is that antebellum fluctuations were more apparent than real; more often only prices, not quantities, changed. Furthermore, whatever unemployment may have been created did not endure for long; the unemployed, particularly laborers, teamsters, and other unskilled workers, migrated to the countryside and returned to industry when conditions turned more favorable.

According to the proponents of the first view, antebellum price changes are evidence of serious and sustained economic hardship.[1] Price fluctuations could have influenced real magnitudes if the antebellum wage lag was long. Real wages would then have decreased during periods of inflation, such as the mid–1830s, thereby sparking strikes and union activity. And real wages would have increased during periods of deflation, such as the early 1840s. Thus deflationary periods would have led to or been associated with unemployment. Labor market adjustment would have occurred largely through changes in employment, a real variable, rather than wages, a nominal variable.

Newspaper and other narrative accounts attest to considerable unemployment in cities following the Embargo of 1807, the Panic of 1837, and especially during the deflation of the early 1840s, and have led one historian to state that "more than half of New York's craft workers reportedly lost their jobs in the immediate wake of the panic" of 1837.[2] Many have claimed that artisans, in particular, were thrown out of employment during the well-known economic crises of 1837, 1839, and 1857, and that unemployment in general was high throughout the 1839 to 1842 period and during 1854 and 1855. But if deflation fostered unemployment, inflation must have caused strikes and other union activity, as many have documented for the mid–1830s and, to a lesser extent, in the 1850s.[3] The end result—inconstancy of work and distressed labor relations—were, according to many labor histories, the common ground around which working-class life, culture, and politics were shaped, and a dominant element in the emergence of working-class consciousness.[4]

But according to a revisionist view, even the most severe antebellum price fluctuations had little impact on aggregate real activity and employment. "The parallel between the 1840s and the 1930s," writes Peter Temin, "extends only to the monetary aspects of the economy. . . . Farmers, textile workers, and

1. See, for example, John R. Commons, et al., *History of Labor in the United States* (New York, 1916); William Sullivan, *The Industrial Worker in Pennsylvania, 1800–1840* (Harrisburg, 1955); Norman Ware, *The Industrial Worker, 1840–1860* (New York, 1924); Susan E. Hirsch, *Roots of the American Working Class: The Industrialization of Crafts in Newark, 1800–1860* (Philadelphia, 1978); Bruce Laurie, *Working People of Philadelphia, 1800–1850* (Philadelphia, 1980); Sean Wilentz, *Chants Democratic: New York City and the Rise of the American Working Class, 1788–1850* (New York, 1984); Steven J. Ross, *Workers on the Edge: Work, Leisure, and Politics in Industrializing Cincinnati, 1788–1890* (New York, 1985); and Robert W. Fogel, *Without Consent or Contract: The Rise and Fall of American Slavery* (New York, 1989).

2. Wilentz, *Chants Democratic*, p. 294.

3. Commons, et al., *History of Labor;* Stanley Lebergott, *Manpower in Economic Growth* (New York, 1964).

4. See especially Laurie, *Working People;* and Wilentz, *Chants Democratic*.

others found their money wages reduced. They were not unemployed, however, and their real incomes may not have fallen."[5]

The revisionist view is rooted in the belief that antebellum labor markets functioned like their textbook counterparts. Real wages, in the short and long runs, were the outcomes of real forces: the supply and demand for labor. A purely nominal shock—an unexpected increase in the money supply—would be swiftly followed by higher nominal wages, leaving no persistent deviation from the long-run growth path of real wages. The same would be true of real shocks. A permanent increase in labor productivity—caused, for example, by the introduction of the factory system—would result in a permanent increase in real wages but no permanent disequilibrium between wages and productivity.

We evaluate the revisionist view using an indirect method that measures the persistence of shocks to real wages. Short-run persistence is indicated by the degree to which the time-series properties of real wages deviate from those of a stochastic process following a deterministic trend, which measures the long-run path, plus a white-noise error. Long-run persistence is indicated by a "unit root" in real wages, which means that any shock today affects the expectation of the wage in the distant future. We test for a unit root using classical statistical procedures and measure its importance using a non-parametric technique.

Our results support a weak version of the revisionist model. In the long run, shocks to real wages eventually vanished, that is, the so-called random-walk component of real wages was small. But shocks had persistent effects on real wages in the short run, lasting as long as five years. The degree of persistence varied across occupations and regions. Persistence was less for agricultural and unskilled non-farm labor than for artisans and clerks, and less in the emerging Midwest than in the older Northeast or the South. Although our study concerns the antebellum period, we also report provisional evidence that shocks to real wages were more persistent in the late nineteenth century than before the Civil War, and post–World War II evidence suggests that the random-walk component of real wages is substantial today.

2.2 Antebellum Wages and Prices

Surprisingly little is known of the behavior of wages during the antebellum period. Standard nineteenth-century sources, like the *Weeks* and *Aldrich* reports, concentrate almost entirely on the Northeast, and even then the coverage is spotty.[6] Other sources, such as account books, firm records, and census

5. Peter Temin, *The Jacksonian Economy* (New York, 1969), p. 164.

6. The *Weeks* report is Joseph D. Weeks, *Reports on the Statistics of Wages in Manufacturing Industries with Supplementary Reports* (Washington, D.C., 1886). The *Aldrich* report is Nelson W. Aldrich, *Wholesale Prices, Wages, and Transportation,* 52nd Congress, 2nd Session, S.R.

manuscripts, provide valuable additional information on antebellum wages, but are limited to particular locations, occupations, or time periods.[7] We use a new source, the payroll records of civilian employees of the United States Army, which contain wages for various occupations and all parts of the country.[8] We assume here that the wage rates apply to the private sector and that the federal government paid workers the "going wage rate." The assumption is based on the fact that other wages series, derived from a variety of sources, track our series for the periods and regions of overlap.[9]

Previous work with the sample yielded annual dollar estimates and indices of nominal daily wages for artisans (blacksmiths, carpenters, machinists, masons, and painters), and laborers (common laborers and teamsters) from 1820 to 1856, for four census regions (Northeast, Midwest, South Atlantic, and South Central).[10] We have, in addition, constructed a new series—regional indices of nominal wages of clerks. This wage series is, we believe, the first for a white-collar occupation in the antebellum period. The nominal wage indices are graphed in Figures 2.1 and 2.2 and their numerical values are reported in Appendix A Tables 2A.1 (artisans), 2A.2 (laborers), and 2A.3 (clerks).[11]

1394 (Washington, D.C., 1893). Philip R. P. Coehlo and James F. Shepherd, "Regional Differences in Real Wages: The United States, 1851–1880," *Explorations in Economic History,* 13 (Jan. 1976), p. 205, point out that the *Weeks* data "exhibit a high degree of variability before 1860, probably due to a scarcity of data for . . . the 1850s."

7. See, for example, Robert G. Layer, *Earnings of Cotton Mill Operatives, 1825–1914* (Cambridge, Mass., 1955); Walter B. Smith, "Wage Rates on the Erie Canal," *Journal of Economic History,* 23 (Sept. 1963), pp. 298–311; Lebergott, *Manpower,* pp. 257–333; Donald R. Adams, Jr., "Wage Rates in the Early National Period: Philadelphia, 1785–1830," *Journal of Economic History,* 28 (Sept. 1968), pp. 404–26; Jeffrey Zabler, "Further Evidence on American Wage Differentials," *Explorations in Economic History,* 10 (Fall 1972), pp. 109–17; Donald R. Adams, Jr., "The Standard of Living During American Industrialization: Evidence from the Brandywine Region, 1800–1860," *Journal of Economic History,* 42 (Dec. 1982), pp. 903–17; "Prices and Wages in Maryland, 1750–1850," *Journal of Economic History,* 46 (Sept. 1986), pp. 625–45; and Kenneth Sokoloff, "The Puzzling Record of Real Wage Growth in Early Industrial America, 1820–1860" (manuscript, University of California, Los Angeles, 1986). See also Kenneth Sokoloff and Georgia Villaflor, chap. 1 in this volume.

8. The collection is known as the "Reports of Persons and Articles Hired, 1818–1905," Record Group 92, National Archives. For a detailed discussion of the characteristics of the "Reports," see Robert A. Margo and Georgia C. Villaflor, "The Growth of Wages in Antebellum America: New Evidence," *Journal of Economic History,* 47 (Dec. 1987), pp. 873–95.

9. See the discussion in Margo and Villaflor, "The Growth of Wages"; also see Robert A. Margo, "Wages and Prices before the Civil War: A Survey and New Evidence," in Robert E. Gallman and John Wallis, eds., *American Economic Growth and the Standard of Living Before the Civil War* (Chicago, 1992, forthcoming). Also, Wilentz, *Chants Democratic* (p. 419, figure 5) has data for masons and laborers in New York City over the 1835 to 1845 period that reasonably track those here for the Northeast.

10. The annual dollar estimates are in Margo and Villaflor, "The Growth of Wages," pp. 893–95. The annual indices are presented in Robert A. Margo, "Appendix: The Growth of Wages in Antebellum America," Colgate University, Department of Economics, Discussion Paper no. 88–06 (1988).

11. The construction of the annual dollar estimates involves the weighting of within-region wage estimates, while the construction of the indices does not; see Margo and Villaflor, "The

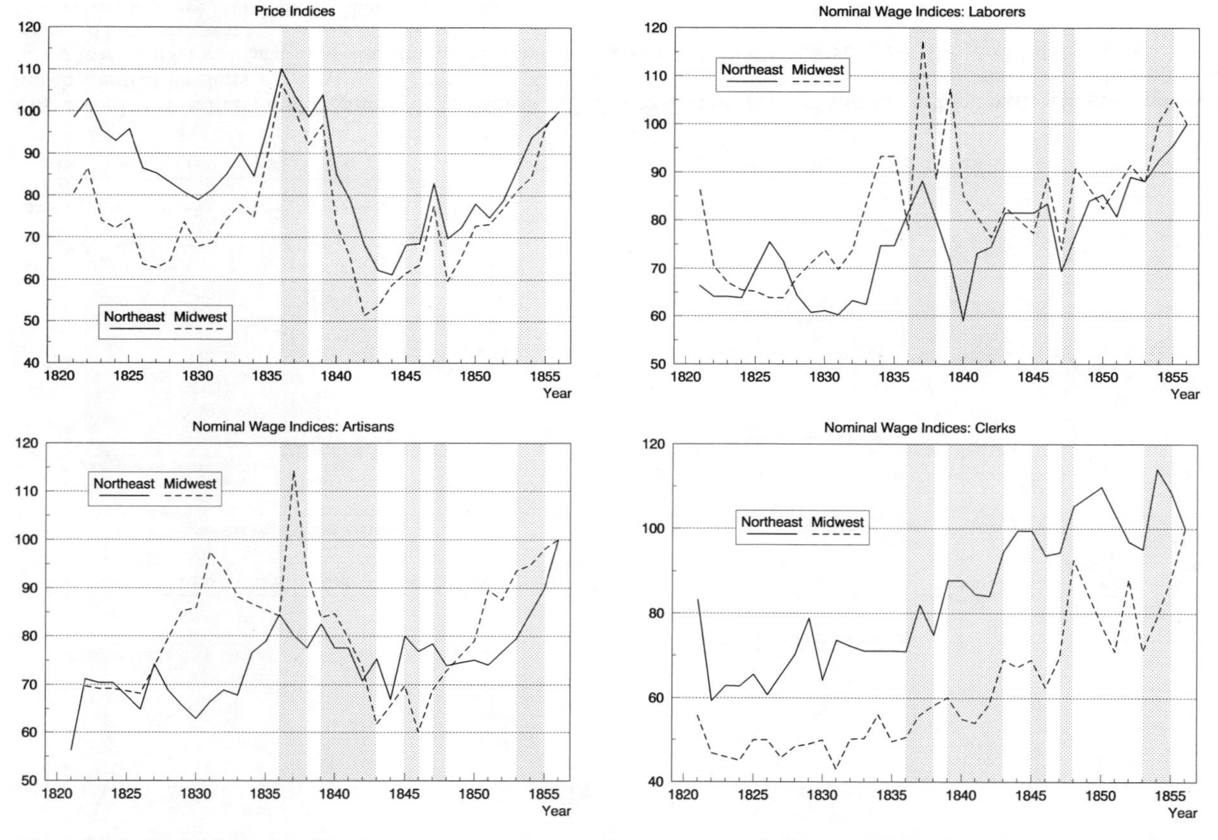

Fig. 2.1 Price Indices, and Nominal Wage Indices of Laborers, Artisans, and Clerks, in the Northeast and Midwest Regions

Notes: 1856 = 100 for all indices. Shaded areas are peak-to-trough periods of the NBER business cycle. The year 1834 begins the series and is a trough year.

Sources: See text. See also Appendix Tables 2A.1–2A.4.

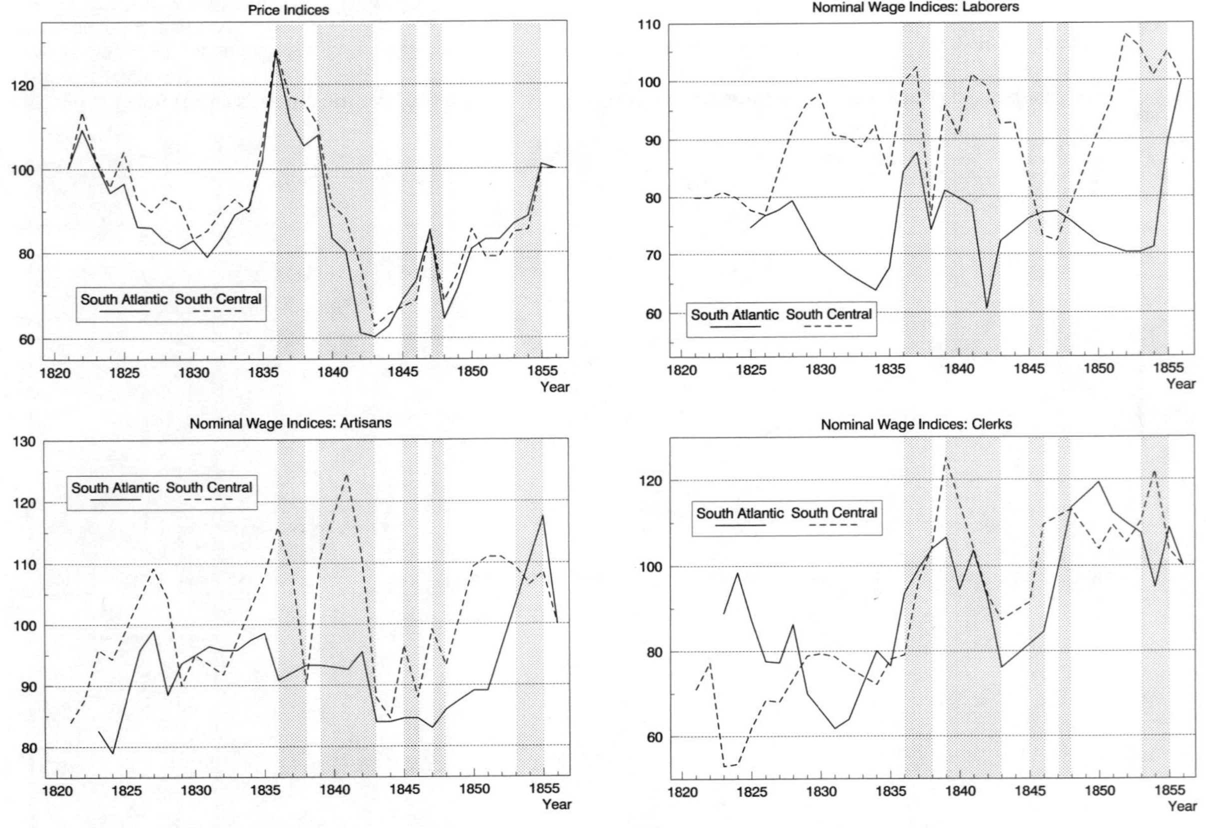

Fig. 2.2 Price Indices, and Nominal Wage Indices of Laborers, Artisans, and Clerks, in the South Atlantic and South Central Regions

Notes: 1856 = 100 for all indices. Shaded areas are peak-to-trough periods of the NBER business cycle. The year 1834 begins the series and is a trough year.

Sources: See text. See also Appendix Tables 2A.1–2A.4.

Because the series for clerks is new, Table 2.1 gives the distribution of clerk wage rates by decade and fort location. Approximately two-thirds of the wage observations are from forts in the Midwest and the South, and locations in the West North Central and West South Central states are also over-represented relative to the share of these regions in the general population. The total number of observations of clerk wages (6,673) exceeds 20 percent of the entire sample (32,709). Clerks were hired to maintain the forts' books, and to help quartermasters with purchasing and other commercial matters. They were, in effect, business managers, and thus the large number of clerks relative to other occupations should not be surprising. The vast majority of clerks were hired annually; many were employed at particular forts for lengthy periods of time, unlike artisans or common laborers who were often hired on a daily or monthly basis.

The construction of the indices of clerk wages follows the procedure previously used for the laborers and artisans. Hedonic regressions are estimated, for which the dependent variable is the log of the nominal monthly wage rate. The independent variables are dummy variables for the location of the fort (for example, St. Louis), characteristics of the worker associated with especially high or low wages (for example, chief clerk, apprentice clerk), whether the worker was paid daily, the number of army rations, the season of the year, and the time period (single years or groups of years, for example, 1834 to 1846).[12] Separate regressions were estimated for each census region.[13]

The coefficients of the time-period dummies are used to estimate annual indices of monthly wage rates. Because the dependent variable is measured in logs, the coefficients give the percentage difference in wages, controlling for other factors and relative to the base year, which is 1856. Let β_{ji} be the coefficient of the time dummy in the *j*th year (for example, 1844) for the *i*th census region (for example, the Northeast). Then the nominal wage index, I_{ji}, is

$$(1) \qquad I_{ji} = \exp(\beta_{ji}).$$

Antebellum price data, comparable in geographic scope to the wage data, are available for only certain commodities and only at the wholesale level. Retail price data, as well as data for various goods and services such as housing, are not presently available. We rely here on the extensive series of monthly wholesale prices collected by Arthur Cole and his associates.[14]

Growth of Wages," p. 879, and Margo, "Appendix: The Growth of Wages," p. 4. Essentially, the indices are constructed under the assumption that changes in wages within regions are the same regardless of location, while the dollar estimates adjust for within-region shifts in population. Because the dollar estimates are somewhat sensitive to the weighting scheme used, and because our focus in this paper is on changes in wages (not their dollar values), we rely instead on the wage indices.

12. Daily wages are converted to monthly wages using twenty-six days per month.

13. The regressions are in an appendix, available on request from Robert Margo.

14. Arthur Harrison Cole, *Wholesale Commodity Prices in the United States, 1700–1861* (Cambridge, Mass., 1938).

Table 2.1 Distribution of the Wage Rate Sample for Clerks, by Decade and Fort Location

	Number	Percent of Aggregated Total
Northeast		
1821–30	399	16.7
1831–40	596	24.9
1841–50	1,022	42.7
1851–56	376	15.7
Southern New England	265	11.1
Northern New England	68	2.8
New York City	462	19.3
Upstate New York	133	5.6
Philadelphia	871	36.4
Carlisle, Pennsylvania	111	4.6
Washington, D.C.	222	9.3
Baltimore	261	10.9
Total	2,393	35.9
Midwest		
1821–30	378	20.0
1831–40	758	40.1
1841–50	486	25.7
1851–56	267	14.1
Ohio, Western Pennsylvania	344	18.2
Illinois, Indiana	153	8.1
Michigan, Iowa, Wisconsin	357	18.9
Minnesota	99	5.2
Kansas	296	15.7
Missouri	967	51.2
Total	1,889	28.3
South Atlantic		
1821–30	198	18.2
1831–40	534	49.0
1841–50	245	22.5
1851–56	112	10.3
Virginia	261	24.0
South Carolina	279	25.6
Georgia	258	23.7
Florida	291	26.7
Total	1,089	16.3
South Central		
1821–30	167	12.8
1831–40	470	36.1
1841–50	376	28.9
1851–56	289	22.2
Kentucky, Tennessee	62	4.8
Mississippi	14	1.1
Arkansas	317	24.3

Table 2.1 (continued)

	Number	Percent of Aggregated Total
Baton Rouge, Louisiana	155	11.9
New Orleans, Louisiana	754	57.9
Total	1,302	19.5
Aggregated total	6,673	

Notes: The unit of observation is a person-month. Percentages may not add to 100 due to rounding.

Source: Margo-Villaflor sample of "Reports and Articles Hired," National Archives, Record Group 92.

The advantage of the Cole data is that price information is available for cities located in each of the census regions.[15] In using these data to construct regional price indices we chose commodities widely consumed by working-class households or proxies for finished goods: foods (for example, butter, pork), fuels (for example, coal), and clothing (proxied by wholesale prices of cotton and leather). We constructed annual commodity-specific price indices, with 1856 as the base year (that is, 1856 = 100 for each commodity index). The commodity-specific indices were then weighted into overall regional indices.[16]

The limitations of the price indices are many. Fluctuations in retail prices need not follow those in wholesale prices, although the fact that the series are annual, rather than monthly, should enhance the correspondence. The commodities included cover a large fraction of household expenditures, but one principal commodity—housing—cannot be included.[17] The indices presume that rural price changes were closely correlated with price changes in the urban areas represented in the Cole data. Although the assumption is reasonable for the Northeast, its validity cannot be assessed for the other regions.[18]

The price indices are presented in Figure 2.1a (also Figure 2.3a) for the Northeast and the Midwest regions and Figure 2.2a (also Figure 2.4a) for the South Atlantic and South Central regions. The actual data series are in Appendix Table 2A.4. Price series in all four regions have similar features, although that for the Midwest differs during the pre–1840 period. The Midwest was

15. The cities and associated census regions are New York and Philadelphia (Northeast), Cincinnati (Midwest), Charleston (South Atlantic), and New Orleans (South Central).

16. See Appendix B for a more detailed discussion of the construction of the price indices.

17. The exclusion of housing prices is important, because there is some evidence that the relative price of housing increased in northern cities in the 1850s; see Fogel, *Without Consent or Contract,* p. 356.

18. See Winifred B. Rothenberg, "The Market and Massachusetts Farmers," *Journal of Economic History,* 41 (June 1981), pp. 283–314, for a suggestive proof that rural and urban price changes were highly correlated during the period. Although see below for evidence that Rothenberg's price index does not have similar time-series properties to our Northeast price index.

growing rapidly from 1820 to 1840 but did not become integrated into the national market for goods until around mid-century.[19]

All four price series have numerous oscillations around a generally declining trend. There are two large deviations, one considerably larger than the other. The first is the well-known inflation of the post–1834 period with the subsequent collapse during 1837 and the rapid deflation from 1839 to 1842. Prices rose between 25 and 45 percentage points, depending on the region, during the 1834 to 1836/37 period and then plummeted by well over 40 percentage points during the deflation. Prices began a secular upward trend after 1842, with a spike in 1847 followed by a substantial decline and then continued increase during the years following the California gold rush. Except in the Midwest, where prices rose 19 percent from the 1820s to the 1850s, the long-term trend in prices was basically flat or slightly downward.

The nominal wage indices for the three occupational groups—laborers (including teamsters), artisans, and clerks—are shown in the remaining panels of Figure 2.1 for the Midwest and Northeast regions, and in Figure 2.2 for the South Atlantic and South Central regions. The series for laborers and artisans have been examined in detail elsewhere, and we summarize that discussion here.[20]

In the Northeast and Midwest, laborer (nominal) wages are level to around 1835. They spike, first up and then down, just after 1835, and then display an upward movement to 1856. In contrast, laborer wages in the South Atlantic first decline, then spike up and down in the 1830s, and end with a decade of virtual stability. Those of the South Central region have upward and downward movement throughout with no apparent tendency to mimic the price data.

The artisan wage series appears distinct from that for laborers in most of the regions. In the Midwest, for which the artisan and laborer series seem most similar, there are two spikes in the 1830s with secular growth before and after. But in the Northeast, while the general trend is similar to that for laborers, the large changes in the 1830s are absent. Oscillations in the South Central data are more numerous than in the laborer data, although the largest is during the period of greatest price fluctuation. The South Atlantic artisan data display no apparent relationship to the laborer data nor to the price series.

Indices of clerk wages are shown in Figure 2.1d for the Midwest and Northeast, and in Figure 2.2d for the South Atlantic and South Central regions (see also Appendix Table 2A.3). In the Northeast and Midwest, clerk wages grew more or less continuously during the entire period with no obvious relationship to the price series. In the two southern regions, however, wages increase and then decrease during the 1830s. But the two southern series deviate before the 1830s: South Central wages rise while those of the South Atlantic fall.

19. See, for example, Thomas Senior Berry, *Western Prices before 1861*, Harvard Economic Studies, vol. 74 (Cambridge, Mass., 1943).

20. See Margo and Villaflor, "The Growth of Wages in Antebellum America."

In general, nominal wages of clerks increase more rapidly in the 1840s than wages of artisans or laborers. As a result, the average annual growth rate of clerk wages (1820 to 1856) exceeds that for other occupations, and differences are especially large in the South. Previous work with the wage sample for artisans and laborers found no evidence of a surge in skill differentials—the ratio of artisan to unskilled wages—after 1820, as others have claimed.[21] That conclusion, however, must now be modified, because it appears that the wages of clerks, who were highly skilled, did grow more rapidly than wages of skilled or unskilled labor during the late antebellum period.[22]

Indices of real wages, based on the nominal wage and price indices, are presented in Figures 2.3 and 2.4 (also Appendix Tables 2A.5 to 2A.7). Real wages grew most among clerks, and they grew more rapidly in the North than the South. Real wages grew less in the newly settled Midwest than in the established Northeast, but the opposite holds when comparing the South Central and South Atlantic states. In every region real wages grew slowly during the 1830s, increased rapidly in the 1840s, and then decreased in the 1850s.

Real wages of artisans increased by 8 percent from the 1820s to the 1830s in the Northeast, compared with only 3 percent in the Midwest. Real wages continued to rise more rapidly in the Northeast than in the Midwest in the 1840s, before falling in both regions in the 1850s. Over the entire period, real wages of artisans rose at an average annual rate of 0.8 percent per year in the Northeast but at only 0.2 percent per year in the Midwest. Among common laborers and teamsters, real wage growth was similarly slow during the 1830s, but in both regions real wages rose rapidly in the 1840s before falling somewhat in the 1850s. Across the entire 35-year period, however, real wages of unskilled labor in the North grew more rapidly than did the real wages of artisans.[23]

21. The claim was originally made by Jeffrey Williamson and Peter Lindert, *American Inequality: A Macroeconomic History* (New York, 1980), pp. 67–75. Evidence against the surge hypothesis—that skilled wages grew more rapidly than unskilled wages—is presented in Margo and Villaflor, "The Growth of Wages," pp. 883–88.

22. This result is consistent with that in Richard Steckel, "Poverty and Prosperity: A Longitudinal Study of Wealth Accumulation, 1850–1860" (manuscript, Department of Economics, Ohio State University, 1988), p. 12. Steckel finds that, in terms of relative wealth, white-collar workers improved their economic position compared with blue-collar or unskilled workers during the 1850s.

23. When the price indices are applied to the annual dollar estimates of skilled and unskilled wages in Margo and Villaflor, "The Growth of Wages," pp. 893–94, the following annual growth rates (1821–30 to 1851–56) of real wages are obtained:

	Skilled	*Unskilled*
Northeast	0.9	1.2
Midwest	0.4	1.1
South Atlantic	0.5	0.3
South Central	0.7	1.0

These growth rates are similar to those in Appendix A, except for those in the Midwest which are higher. This difference is a consequence of the weighting procedure used in the construction of the dollar estimates; see Margo, "Appendix: The Growth of Wages," p. 24.

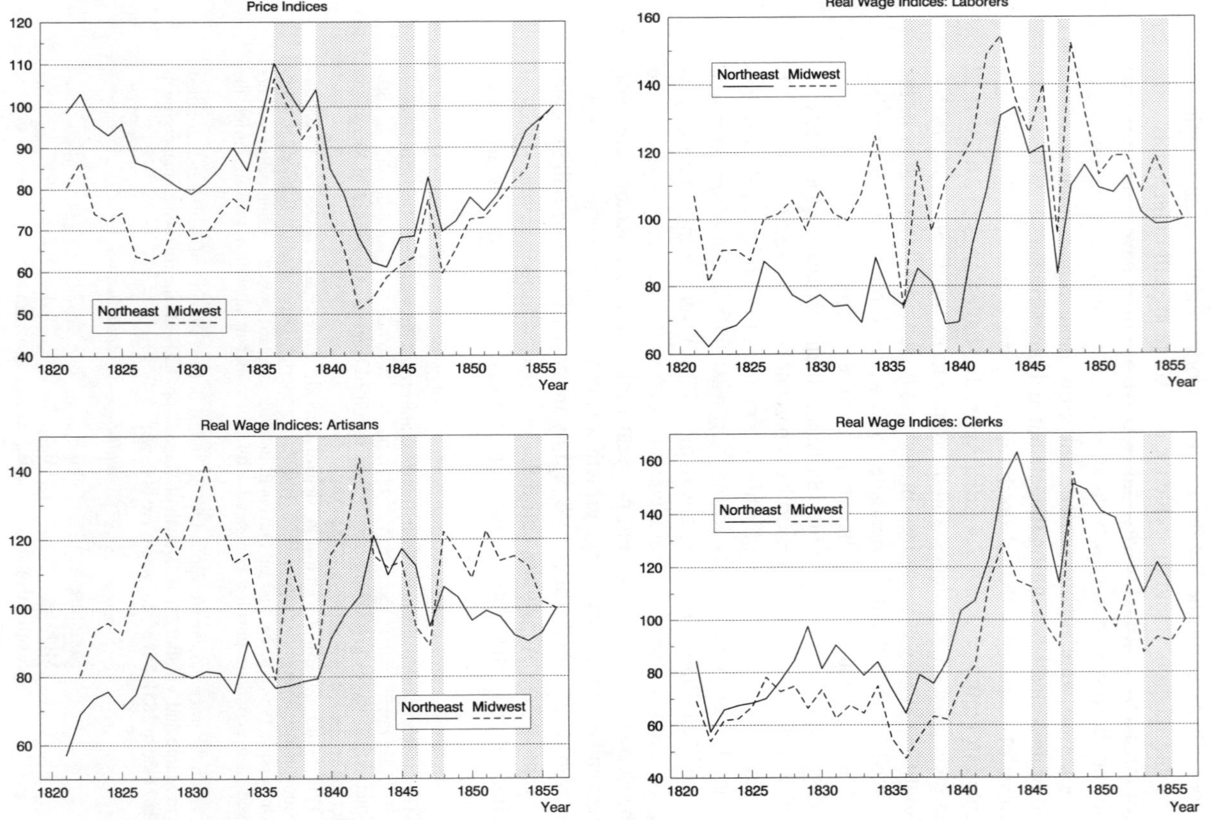

Fig. 2.3 Price Indices, and Real Wage Indices of Laborers, Artisans, and Clerks, in the Northeast and Midwest Regions

Notes: 1856 = 100 for all indices. Shaded areas are peak-to-trough periods of the NBER business cycle. The year 1834 begins the series and is a trough year.

Sources: See text. See also Appendix Tables 2A.4–2A.7.

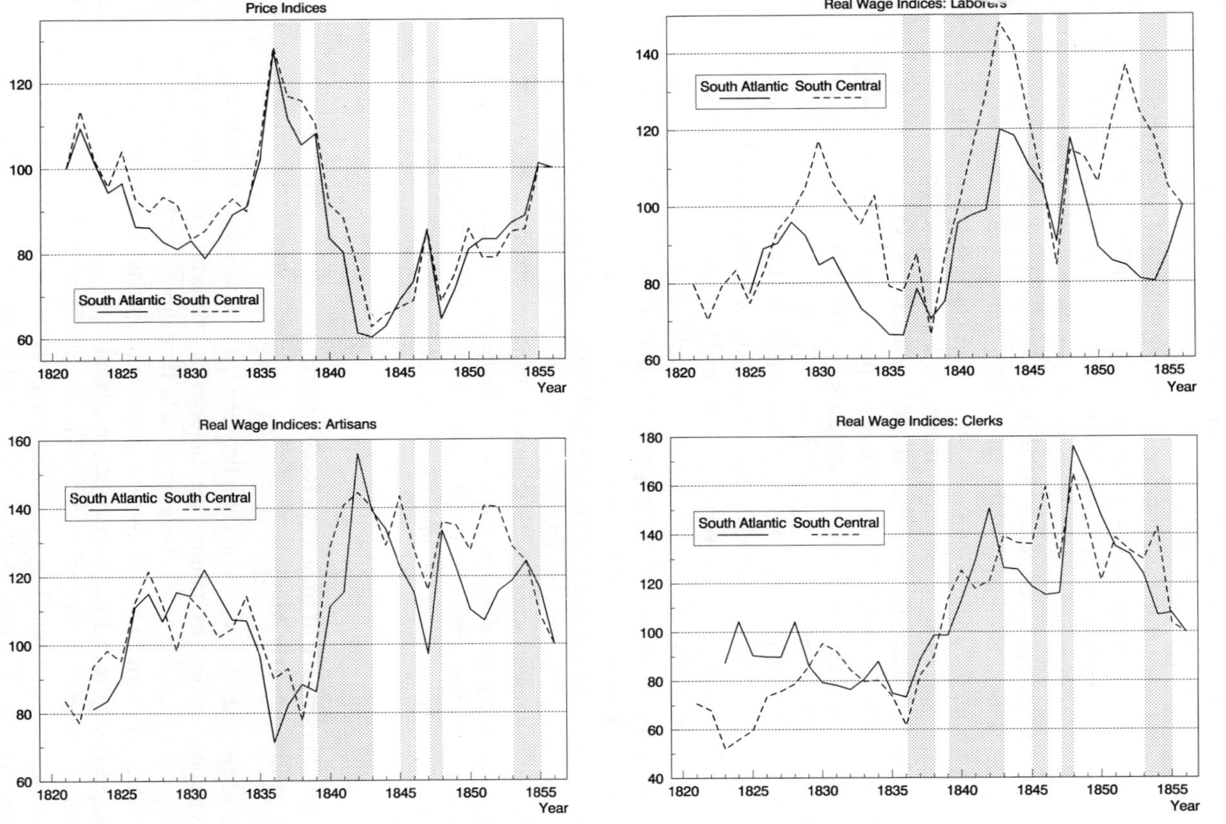

Fig. 2.4 Price Indices, and Real Wage Indices of Laborers, Artisans, and Clerks, in the South Atlantic and South Central Regions

Notes: 1856 = 100 for all indices. Shaded areas are peak-to-trough periods of the NBER business cycle. The year 1834 begins the series and is a trough year.

Sources: See text. See also Appendix Tables 2A.4–2A.7.

Real wages of artisans in the South Atlantic region increased in the late 1820s but fell sharply in the late 1830s, so that on average real wages were no higher in the 1830s than in the 1820s. As in the two northern regions, real wages rose in the 1840s before falling in the 1850s. Real wages of artisans in the South Central states did not increase on average from the 1820s to the 1830s, but they rose in the 1840s before falling in the 1850s. Overall, real wages grew more rapidly in the South Central states than the South Atlantic states, opposite to the pattern in the northern regions. Real wages of common laborers and teamsters in the South Atlantic states fell 14 percent from the 1820s to the 1830s, rose sharply in the early 1840s, before falling 18 percent in the 1850s from the 1840s average. In the South Central states, real wages of unskilled labor grew by 2 percent from the 1820s to the 1830s and rose by 33 percent in the 1840s, before falling slightly in the 1850s. Over the entire period, real wages of unskilled labor rose at 1.0 percent per year in the South Central states, but the growth rate was negative (−0.08 percent per year) in the South Atlantic states.

The real wages of clerks in the Northeast and South Central states were higher in the 1830s than in the 1820s, but the opposite was true in the Midwest and South Atlantic regions. In every region the real wages of clerks increased markedly in the 1840s, before falling again in the 1850s. On average, clerks experienced the greatest real wage growth among the three occupational groups across the entire 35-year period.

One feature of the six real-wage graphs in Figures 2.3 and 2.4 is the marked fluctuation in real wages, particularly during the 1840s. Such fluctuations could arise if nominal wages were relatively stable or responded with a lag while prices varied greatly. The question to which we now turn is how rigid nominal wages were across the four regions and among the three occupations. We approach this through an analysis of the persistence of shocks to real wages.

2.3 The Persistence of Shocks to Real Wages: An Econometric Analysis

The ideal method of distinguishing between the two views of the antebellum business cycle—examining the time-series properties of unemployment—is not available to us, because of data limitations for the nineteenth century. As an alternative procedure we examine the persistence of shocks to real wages using the real wage series just discussed.

Studies such as ours typically begin with an assumption that the time path of real wages is determined by a combination of real and nominal forces. The long-run, or "equilibrium," wage is determined by real forces—the supply and demand for labor given the price level. In the short run, however, the real wage can deviate from its long-run equilibrium value. For example, if nominal wages are slow to adjust to an increase in prices, real wages will fall below their equilibrium level (the opposite may occur for a reduction in prices). The shock to real wages may persist, possibly for several periods. Provided long-run neutrality holds, however, economic forces are set in motion to return the real wage to its equilibrium path.

We make use of two time-series techniques to examine the persistence of shocks to the real wage—parametric tests for a unit root and a related non-parametric technique. A time series x_t is termed $I(1)$, or *integrated of order 1* (has a unit root), if it can be written in the form

$$B(L)(1 - L)x_t = \mu + A(L)\varepsilon_t \tag{2}$$

where L is the lag operator; $B(L)$ and $A(L)$ are polynomials in the lag operator; μ is a constant, possibly zero ("drift"); and ε_t is a "white-noise" process (a mean zero, finite variance, serially uncorrelated error).[24] A random walk, $x_t = x_{t-1} + \varepsilon_t$, is the simplest example of an $I(1)$ series. Shocks to an $I(1)$ do not evaporate, but rather influence all future values; in the case of the random walk, note that $x_t = \varepsilon_t + \varepsilon_{t-1} + \ldots + \varepsilon_1$.

Suppose, instead, that the series x_t were *stationary* or *integrated of order 0*, $I(0)$. Then representation (2) would exist without the $(1-L)$ term on the left-hand side, that is, without first differencing. An example is a series with a constant mean. Alternatively, x_t could be *trend-stationary,* that is, have a mean which follows a deterministic time trend, as in

$$x_t = \beta + \mu t + A(L)\varepsilon_t. \tag{3}$$

In the case of (3), shocks eventually die out and the series returns to its long-run growth path given by the deterministic trend, $E(x_{t+k}) = \beta + \mu(t + k)$.

The antebellum trend in real wages was generally upward, as inspection of Figure 2.3 reveals, although there were often large fluctuations around trend. Testing representation (2) against (3) is a first step in determining whether annual fluctuations in antebellum real wages had permanent or merely transitory effects. Toward this end we estimate regressions of the form

$$(1 - L)(w/p)_t = \Delta(w/p)_t = \alpha + \beta t + \delta(w/p)_{t-1} + \varepsilon_t \tag{4}$$

where (w/p) is the log of the real wage. The null hypothesis is that (w/p) follows a random walk with drift, that is, it is $I(1)$ as in $x_t = x_{t-1} + \alpha + \varepsilon_t$. We can reject the null (and accept the hypothesis of trend-stationarity) if the F-statistic for the joint hypothesis $\beta = \delta = 0$ is sufficiently large. This procedure is known as the Dickey-Fuller (DF) test after its originators.[25]

24. The roots of the autoregressive polynomial $A(L)$ and the moving average polynomial $B(L)$ are assumed to lie outside the unit circle. Thus the first-differenced series, $(1 - L)x_t$, will be stationary—the roots of $A(L)$ lie outside the unit circle—and invertible—the roots of $B(L)$ lie outside the unit circle.

25. Lagged terms in $(1 - L)(w/p)$ are added to the regression until the residual term approximates white noise; see David A. Dickey and Wayne A. Fuller, "Distribution of the Estimators for Autoregressive Time Series with a Unit Root," *Journal of the American Statistical Association,* 74 (June 1979), pp. 427–31.

We estimate equation (4) for three occupations in four regions—twelve regressions in all. In every case we are unable to reject the null hypothesis that real wages possess a unit root.[26] The existence of a unit root indicates that shocks to antebellum real wages were, to some extent, permanent. But the test does not reveal the fraction of the variability in real wages that can be attributed to the permanent, or "random-walk," component.[27] If the random-walk component were small, shocks to real wages would still be primarily transitory in the long run. Further, the test reveals nothing about the short-run dynamics of wages and prices.

To investigate the size of the random-walk component and the short-run dynamics of real wages we make use of a non-parametric persistence estimator suggested by John Cochrane and given by

$$(5) \qquad \sigma_k^2 = (1/k) \times \mathrm{Var}\{(w/p)_t - (w/p)_{t-k}\} \times [T/(T-k+1)].$$

The statistic σ_k^2 is $(1/k)$ times the variance of the kth difference of real wages, adjusted for sample size (T = number of observations). Then σ_1^2 is the variance of the first difference of real wages. If real wages were a pure random walk, possibly with drift, the variance ratio (σ_k^2/σ_1^2) would equal one for all values of k. If real wages were the sum of a stationary series and a random walk, the variance ratio would approach a constant for large k. The closer the constant is to zero, the smaller is the random-walk component of real wages. As a short-run benchmark, we compare the actual variance ratios with the hypothetical ratio that would arise if real wages followed a deterministic trend plus a white-noise process.[28] The greater the deviation between the actual and the hypothetical ratio for small values of k, the greater is the short-run persistence of shocks to real wages.

The results of the Cochrane test, as we will term it, for the 1821 to 1856 period are graphed in Figure 2.5. Each panel is for one of the four regions, and in each there are four lines. Three of the lines are for the three occupational groups. The fourth is the hypothetical ratio and shows how the variance ratio changes with k, the number of years in the lag had there been a deterministic trend plus a white-noise process.[29]

The Cochrane tests reveal that the random-walk component (when k = 10 to 15 years) for all three occupations among the four regions was small.[30] But shocks to real wages persisted for many years. Even after five years, the vari-

26. A table containing the test statistics is available from Robert Margo on request.

27. A series with a unit root can be rewritten as the sum of a pure random walk, possibly with drift, and a stationary time series. See John H. Cochrane, "How Big is the Random Walk in GNP?", *Journal of Political Economy,* 96 (Oct. 1988), pp. 893–920.

28. If $(w/p)_t = \beta + \mu t + \varepsilon_t$, then $\sigma_k^2 = 1/k \times 2\sigma_1^2 \times [T/(T-k+1)]$ and the variance ratio is $[(1/k) \times T/(T-k+1)]$.

29. The hypothetical white-noise line depends on the number of observations which differs only slightly among the four regions and three occupations. We have drawn the line identical across the four panels, and it is thus an approximation for some.

30. A parametric way of measuring persistence is to estimate low-order ARMA (autoregressive, moving-average) models of the first difference of real wages, for example, equation (2). Rewrite equation (2) in its moving-average representation

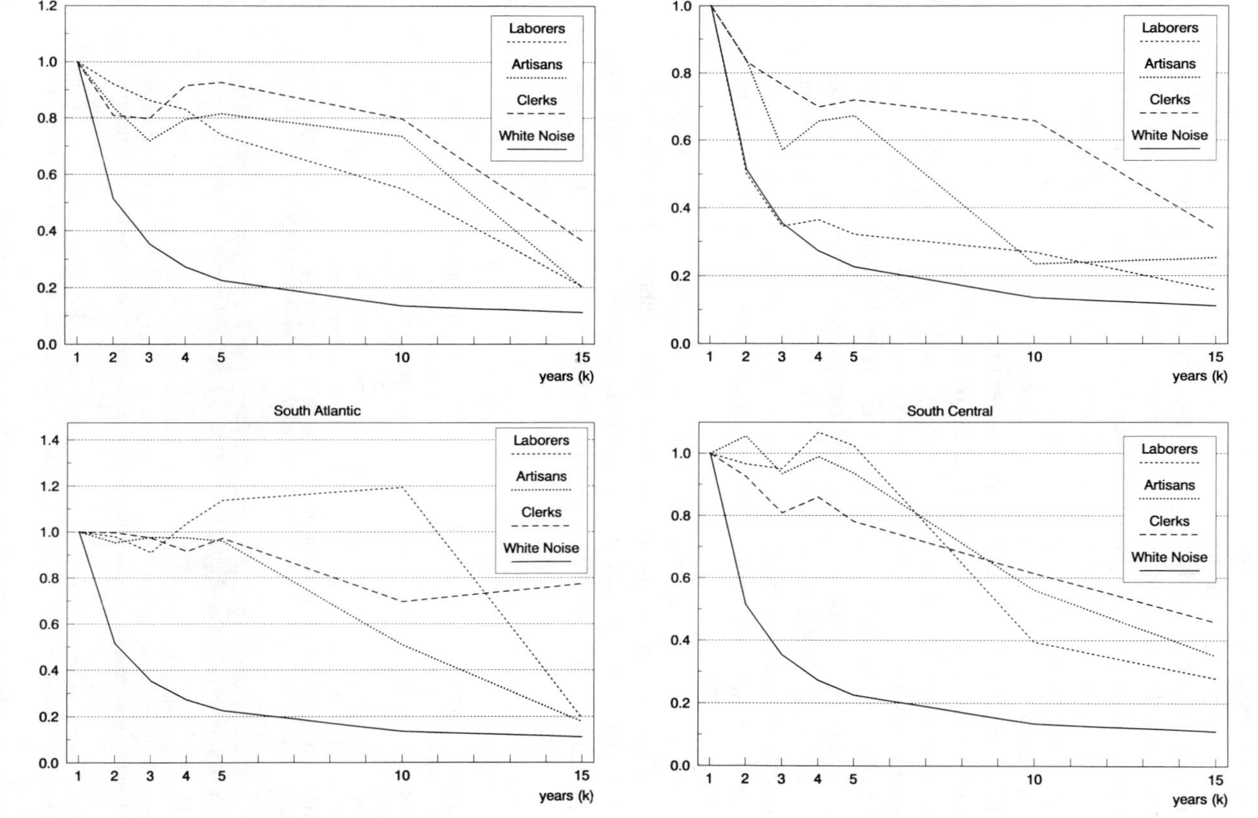

Fig. 2.5 σ_k^2/σ_1^2 for the Real Wage: Three Occupations across Four Regions, 1820–1856

Notes: $\sigma_k^2 = 1/k \times$ the variance of *k*-differences of the real wage, adjusted for degrees of freedom. White noise is σ_k^2/σ_1^2 for a deterministic trend plus a white-noise process, providing a base-line comparison for the other series. The greater the deviation from white noise, the larger the random-walk component.

Sources: See text.

ance ratio is only just below one, the value for the case of a pure random walk, in all but the Midwest region. After fifteen years the ratio is highest for clerks and generally lowest for laborers in all four regions.

On the basis of the Cochrane tests, we conclude that shocks to real wages were mostly transitory in the long run (the random-walk component was small), but that they were quite persistent in the short run. The Cochrane test also suggests the adjustment process was rapid in the Midwest for both laborers and artisans, was extremely protracted in the South Atlantic region, and was slowest for clerks everywhere.

Further evidence on the persistence of shocks can be found in the upper panel of Figure 2.6, which analyzes real wages of agricultural workers in the Northeast, 1821–55, using data collected by Winifred Rothenberg.[31] We have deflated Rothenberg's nominal wage series by our Northeast price index and by Rothenberg's agricultural price index.[32] Shocks to agricultural real wages appear to have been much less persistent than any of the series in Figure 2.5. Also in Figure 2.6, in the lower panel, are Cochrane tests on wages for cotton-mill operatives from Robert Layer's study, which we have deflated by our Northeast price index. Nominal wages for cotton-mill operatives are virtually flat over the period, and, not surprisingly, real wages demonstrate extreme persistence of shocks.

We have also estimated persistence measures for industrial workers in the late nineteenth century, during 1870 to 1908 and the subperiod 1870 to 1897, but we emphasize the provisional nature of these results.[33] We find that real wage data for the late nineteenth century demonstrate extreme persistence.

(2′) $$(1 - L)x_t = \mu' + A'(L)\varepsilon_t$$

where $A'(L) = A(L)/B(L)$ and $\mu' = \mu/B(L)$. Let $A'(1) = \Sigma a'_k$, the infinite sum of the moving average coefficients of $A'(L)$. If x_t is $I(1)$, then $A'(L)$ will converge to a finite and positive limit. This limit is the long-run "impulse-response" to a unit "innovation," or shock in ε_t. See J. Campbell and G. Mankiw, "Are Output Fluctuations Transitory?", *Quarterly Journal of Economics*, 102 (Nov. 1987), pp. 857–80. For example, if x_t were a random walk with drift ($x_t = \mu + x_{t-1} + \varepsilon_t$), then $A'(1) = 1$. Estimates of $\Sigma a'_k$ using the SAS PROC ARIMA procedure (available on request from Robert Margo) were less than one for all occupations in each region, which is consistent with the results of the Cochrane tests, which showed that the random-walk component of real wages was small.

31. See Winifred Rothenberg, "The Emergence of Farm Labor Markets and the Transformation of the Rural Economy: Massachusetts, 1750–1855," *Journal of Economic History*, 48 (Sept. 1988), pp. 537–66.

32. When we deflate by Rothenberg's agricultural price index (which she calls *PI* in "The Emergence of Farm Labor Markets"), the agricultural real wage (*WWI*/*PI*) is indistinguishable from a trend with white noise. Because our price index is heavily weighted toward agricultural commodities, the difference between the two indices seems curious. But Rothenberg apparently smoothed her price index with a three-year moving average (see Rothenberg, "The Market and Massachusetts Farmers," p. 311), and that procedure could explain the differences in using her agricultural index.

33. We use the index of average daily wages in all industries (D 574) spliced at 1891 to (average weekly hours × average hourly earnings) for workers in manufacturing (D 593–94). The price index is the Warren and Pearson wholesale price index for all commodities (E 1) spliced at 1890 to the Bureau of Labor Statistics wholesale price index (E 13). All series are from *Historical Statistics of the United States, Colonial Times to 1957* (Washington, D.C., 1960).

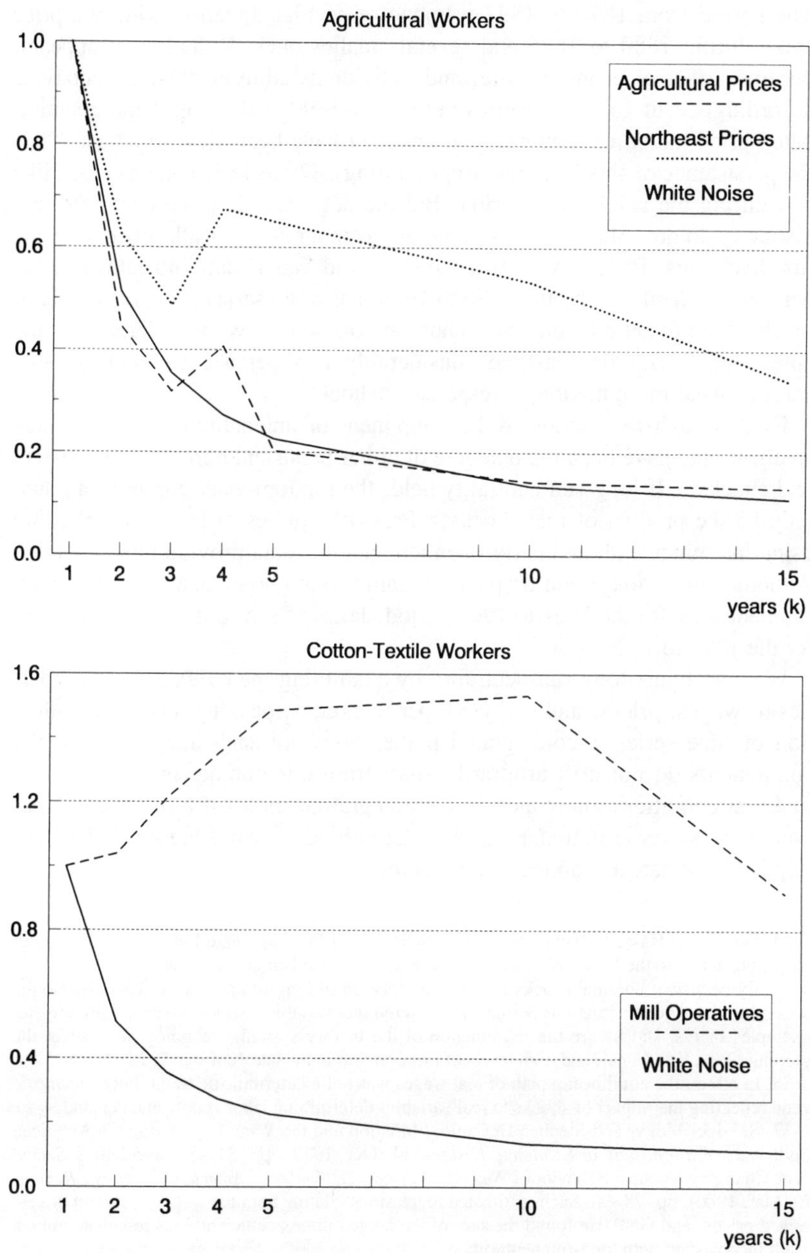

Fig. 2.6 σ_k^2/σ_1^2 for the Real Wage: Agricultural Workers in the Northeast, 1820–1855, and Cotton-Textile Operatives, 1825–1856

Notes: $\sigma_k^2 = 1/k \times$ the variance of k-differences of the real wage, adjusted for degrees of freedom. White noise is σ_k^2/σ_1^2 for a deterministic trend plus a white-noise process, providing a base-line comparison for the other series. The greater the deviation from white noise, the larger the random-walk component.

Sources: See text.

The period from 1870 to 1897 was one of secular deflation with one price spike during 1880 to 1885 and several smaller ones. Deflation, it appears, became a fact of economic life, and individuals adjusted their expectations accordingly. But gold discoveries in the mid–1890s led to rapid and unanticipated price increases, and expectations may have been slow to adjust. Thus the persistence of shocks to real wages during 1870 to 1897 appears much like that during the antebellum period. But the data including the post–1897 era distinctly do not. Shocks are as persistent as in a random-walk process for the first five years. Recent work using post–World War II data indicates that the persistence displayed by the 1870 to 1908 real wage series is characteristic of much of the twentieth century.[34] Thus, in comparison with the later data, the antebellum series demonstrate considerably less persistence, and nominal wages appear more flexible in response to shocks.

Even though the random-walk component of antebellum real wages was small, it may have been the outcome of either persistent nominal or persistent real shocks.[35] If long-run neutrality held, the random-walk component could only be the product of real shocks.[36] Previous studies of long-run neutrality using late nineteenth and early twentieth century data provide mixed results. Although Joel Mokyr and Stephen DeCanio found no evidence against long-run neutrality for the 1861 to 1900 period, Jeffrey Sachs did in his regressions for the 1897 to 1929 period.[37]

We investigate long-run neutrality by examining the *cointegration* properties of wages, prices, and real GNP per worker.[38] Speaking loosely, a collection of time series is cointegrated if the series are each integrated and the components do not drift arbitrarily apart from one another in the long run. The first condition, that concerning cointegration, holds if a linear combination of the series is stationary, even if the individual series are not.[39] The first step is to estimate a "cointegrating" regression

34. See Kevin Hassett, "Persistence and Cyclicality in the Aggregate Labor Market" (manuscript, presented to the Labor Workshop, University of Pennsylvania, Nov. 1988).

35. By persistent nominal shocks we mean a violation of long-run neutrality. There is also the possibility that price fluctuations permanently altered real variables, which we do not investigate. Examples of real shocks are the introduction of the factory system, technological change, the opening of the Erie Canal, and high levels of immigration in the late 1840s and early 1850s.

36. In effect, the equilibrium path of real wages was not a deterministic trend, but a *stochastic* trend reflecting the impact of shocks to real variables determining labor supply and demand.

37. See Joel Mokyr and Stephen DeCanio, "Inflation and the Wage Lag During the American Civil War," *Explorations in Economic History,* 14 (Oct. 1977), pp. 311–36; and Jeffrey Sachs, "The Changing Cyclical Behavior of Wages and Prices: 1890–1979," *American Economic Review,* 70 (Mar. 1980), pp. 78–90. Sachs estimated regressions relating nominal wages to current prices, lagged prices, and GNP. He found the sum of the lagged price coefficients was less than unity, a result inconsistent with long-run neutrality.

38. See Robert F. Engle and C. W. J. Granger, "Cointegration and Error-Correction: Representation, Estimation, and Testing," *Econometrica,* 55 (Mar. 1987), pp. 251–76, and *Econometric Modelling With Cointegrated Variables,* special issue of the *Oxford Bulletin of Economics and Statistics,* 48 (Aug. 1986), for discussions of cointegration.

39. Unit root tests of real wages show that wages and prices do not cointegrate. A test of the Gallman-Berry output series (see below) also could not reject the hypothesis that the series possesses a unit root.

$$w_t = \alpha_0 + \alpha_1 p_t + \alpha_2 gnp_t + \mu_t \quad (6)$$

for which all (lower-case) variables are in logs. The GNP variable is a combination of Robert Gallman's and Thomas Senior Berry's data for real gross national product in year t converted into a per-worker series. The Gallman-Berry index, as our spliced series will be called, is assumed to capture "real" factors determining the long-run equilibrium growth path of real wages.[40] The "cointegrating vector" $(1 - \alpha_1 - \alpha_2)$ gives the long-run coefficients of the stationary linear combination.[41]

Separate regressions are estimated for each of the three occupations in the four regions using the annual series reported in Appendix A. Two test statistics are calculated from the estimated regression residuals: the cointegrating regression Durbin-Watson test statistic (CRDW) and the augmented Dickey-Fuller test statistic (ADF). The test for cointegration is, in effect, a test whether the regression residuals are stationary.[42] As in the Dickey-Fuller test described earlier, the null hypothesis is that the three series are not cointegrated. The test results appear in Table 2.2. All of the CRDW statistics reject the null (accept cointegration) at the 5 percent level. The DF and ADF statistics are somewhat less conclusive, but still broadly support cointegration of wages, prices, and output per worker.

Interpreted literally, cointegration means that wages, prices, and per capita real output "moved together" in the long run. But the price coefficients in the cointegrating regressions (α_1 in Table 2.2) are substantially less than one, and those for clerks are negative in two cases, results that are inconsistent with long-run neutrality ($\alpha_1 = 1$). The price coefficients, however, are not robust to the estimating procedure. An equation regressing prices on wages, rather than the reverse, produces implied price coefficients that vary substantially and have ranges that include one.[43] Because the R^2's for the cointegrating regressions are low, the α_1's cannot be estimated with precision. We conclude that, while there is no evidence against long-run neutrality, there can be no definitive inference about the sources (nominal as opposed to real) of the random-walk component of real wages.

Having shown that wages, prices, and output per worker were cointegrated, our final step is to estimate "error-correction" regressions of nominal wages. Error correction refers to the notion that the coefficient δ, in equation (4), should be negative if the three series (wages, prices, and output per worker) were cointegrated. For example, if real wages were above their equilibrium value (a positive residual) in period $(t-1)$, then wages should fall in period t.

40. Thomas Senior Berry, *Production and Population since 1789: Revised GNP Series in Constant Dollars* (Richmond, 1988); and Robert E. Gallman, unpublished data (June 1965). Annual labor force estimates for intercensal years were linearly interpolated from census benchmarks. Census estimates of the labor force are from Thomas Weiss, "Appendix: Estimation of the Antebellum Labor Force Figures" (manuscript, University of Kansas, May 1990), table A–1.

41. The cointegrating vector, however, need not be unique; see Engle and Granger, "Cointegration and Error Correction."

42. Ibid., p. 266, describe the various test statistics for cointegration.

43. If β is the coefficient on wages in the reverse regression, then $\alpha_1 = 1/\beta$.

Table 2.2 **Price Coefficients and Cointegration Tests of Wages, Prices, and Real GNP Per Capita, 1821–1856**

	Northeast	Midwest	South Atlantic	South Central
Laborers				
α_1	0.060	0.350	0.239	0.140
CRDW	0.841*	1.555*	0.817*	0.943
DF	−2.872**	−4.654*	−2.237	−3.130*
ADF	−3.421*	−2.438	−2.388	−3.263*
R^2	0.434	0.465	0.141	0.258
Artisans				
α_1	0.247	0.486	0.164	0.221
CRDW	1.047*	0.974*	0.913*	0.902*
DF	−2.984**	−3.389*	−3.095**	−3.116**
ADF	−2.246	−3.188**	−2.825**	−3.863*
R^2	0.454	0.473	0.322	0.171
Clerks				
α_1	−0.367	−0.121	0.190	−0.078
CRDW	1.004*	0.843*	0.432*	0.601*
DF	−3.284**	−2.756	−1.861	−2.258
ADF	−2.145	−2.012	−2.133	−2.956**
R^2	0.679	0.703	0.221	0.478

Notes: α_1 is the coefficient on the log of prices from the cointegrating regression,

$$\ln W_t = \alpha_0 + \alpha_1 \cdot \ln P_t + \alpha_2 \cdot \ln GNP_t + \mu_t.$$

CRDW is the Durbin-Watson statistic from the above cointegrating regression. DF is the t-statistic on δ from the Dickey-Fuller regression

$$\Delta\mu = -\delta\mu_{-1} + \varepsilon.$$

ADF is the t-statistic on δ from the augmented Dickey-Fuller regression,

$$\Delta\mu = -\delta\mu_{-1} + \beta\Delta\mu_{-1} + \sigma\Delta\mu_{-2} + \varepsilon'.$$

The R_2's are those from the cointegrating regression. Critical values for CRDW, DF, and ADF statistics are from S. G. Hall, "An Application of the Granger and Engle Two-Step Estimation Procedure to United Kingdom Aggregate Wage Data," *Oxford Bulletin of Economics and Statistics*, 48 (Aug. 1986), p. 233.

*Indicates the test accepts cointegration at the 5% level.

**Indicates the test accepts cointegration at the 10% level.

The estimates of δ were, in fact, negative in all the regressions, and the majority were statistically significant. Because the sample sizes are small, the specification of the error-correction regressions is parsimonious:

$$(7) \qquad (1 - L)w = \alpha(1 - L)p + \beta(1 - L)gnp + \delta e_{-1} + \varepsilon$$

where e_{-1} is the lagged residual from the cointegrating regressions. The purpose of the regressions is to investigate the degree of contemporaneous responsiveness of wages to nominal Δp and real Δgnp shocks, that is, as revealed by the coefficients α and β.

Table 2.3 shows estimated values of α and β. Although few of the coefficients are statistically significant, the majority are positive in sign. For example, a positive productivity shock ($\Delta gnp > 0$) generally caused nominal

Table 2.3 Error-Correction Regressions: Coefficients on the Change in the Log of Price (Δp) and the Change in the Log of GNP (Δgnp)

	Northeast	Midwest	South Atlantic	South Central
Artisans				
p	0.310	0.127	−0.017	0.199
	(2.885)	(0.982)	(0.207)	(1.589)
gnp	−0.119	0.290	0.096	0.164
	(0.641)	(0.917)	(0.500)	(0.619)
Laborers				
p	−0.039	0.094	0.305	−0.017
	(0.231)	(0.613)	(2.213)	(0.128)
gnp	0.095	0.258	0.242	0.367
	(0.318)	(0.715)	(0.709)	(1.296)
Clerks				
p	−0.120	−0.140	0.238	0.039
	(0.736)	(0.922)	(1.508)	(0.224)
gnp	0.108	0.513	−0.034	−0.084
	(0.376)	(1.349)	(0.093)	(0.224)

Note: α and β are from regressions of the form given by equation (7):

$$(1-L)w = \alpha(1-L)p + \beta(1-L)gnp + \delta e_{-1} + \varepsilon$$

where e is the residual from the cointegrating regression; see Table 2.2. t-statistics are in parentheses.

wages to increase in the same period. Antebellum wages were "procyclical" in this sense. Similarly, a positive price shock ($\Delta p > 0$) resulted in higher nominal wages. The estimates of α, however, are all substantially less than one, implying that contemporaneous changes in prices and real wages were negatively related. Thus, the persistence of shocks to real wages in the short run is largely attributable to the slowness with which nominal wages adjusted to changes in the price level.

2.4 Implications for Antebellum Labor Markets

Our various findings, by region and occupation, reveal much about the functioning of antebellum labor markets and the effects of economic development. To reiterate, our main finding is that although shocks to real wages across all regions and (nonagricultural) occupations had little long-run persistence, there was a substantial short-run impact. Agricultural real wages, however, display considerably less persistence. At the two extremes, the Midwest and the South Atlantic were the most anomalous of the regions; the Midwest having the least persistent, and the South Atlantic having the most persistent, shocks to real wages. Agricultural workers and clerks (also cotton-mill operatives) were at the two extremes of the occupations.

Why did shocks to real wages persist in the short run? Price fluctuations in the antebellum period were generally monetary in origin. The United States was on a bimetallic standard but had no central bank to sterilize specie nor act as a "lender of the last resort" in times of banking crisis. Changes in specie, in the British discount rate, and in the cotton market led to sharp changes in the price level and often to banking panics.[44]

The precise mechanism underlying our results and causing monetary forces to have real effects may be related to Robert Lucas's "signal processing" theory.[45] A decrease in the money supply, for instance, is noticed by producers as a decrease in the price for their goods. But producers do not know whether the price change is general or relative, and they will attribute some of the change to each cause. Because they perceive that at least part of the decrease is specific to their industry or firm, they will decrease employment, investment, and other real variables by some amount. They perceive that they cannot lower nominal wages by the full amount, because, if part of the change is relative, the decrease in wages would lead to an exodus of labor. Because all producers lay off some workers, a downturn ensues, and nominal wages eventually do fall. The absence of information, thus the noisiness of the signal, causes a purely monetary phenomenon to have real effects.

Rather than attributing the relationship between the monetary and real phenomena simply to nominal wage rigidity, Lucas's signal processing theory is an equilibrium theory of adjustment in the face of imperfect information. Because the theory is more believable when information is limited, it seems particularly relevant to the nineteenth century when the public was less knowledgeable about the course of general economic variables. Agents may have had more difficulty discerning absolute from relative price changes in industrialized areas producing a heterogeneous mix of products, such as the Northeast, than in agricultural regions, such as the Midwest, where the product mix was more homogeneous. The lower persistence of shocks in the Midwest, especially among the unskilled, is also consistent with the view that a larger agricultural sector contributed to more flexible labor markets for free workers. The more persistent shocks in the Old South, however, appear to contradict claims that slavery enhanced the spatial efficiency of free labor markets, thereby inhibiting industrial development in the region.[46]

44. See, for example, Temin, *The Jacksonian Economy.* Recent work on financial crises suggests that antebellum banking panics could have had persistent effects on real wages. Disruptions in the credit mechanism resulting in credit rationing might have reduced the demand for labor, causing a reduction in real wages. On the real effects of financial crises, see Ben S. Bernanke, "Nonmonetary Effects of the Financial Crisis in the Propagation of the Great Depression," *American Economic Review,* 73 (June 1983), pp. 257–76.

45. See, for example, Robert Lucas, *Studies in Business-Cycle Theory* (Cambridge, Mass., 1981), in particular the reprinted article, "Expectations and the Neutrality of Money," and the essay "Understanding Business Cycles."

46. See Heywood Fleisig, "Slavery, the Supply of Agricultural Labor, and the Industrialization of the South," *Journal of Economic History,* 36 (Sept. 1976), pp. 572–97. Recent work by Gavin Wright suggests that inefficient labor markets may have inhibited southern economic growth after the Civil War; our results suggest that inefficiencies existed during the antebellum period as well; see Gavin Wright, *Old South, New South* (New York, 1986).

There is, however, a competing explanation for the behavior of midwestern wages. Land sales in the Midwest (and South Central regions) skyrocketed during the price inflation of the 1830s. In both regions land sales at the peak of the land boom, in 1836, were eight times their 1830 level.[47] The land boom, according to some, developed because land prices were fixed in nominal terms while output prices, especially cotton, were rapidly rising. Land, therefore, became an exceptional bargain.[48] Fluctuations in land sales appear strikingly similar to those of prices, although land sales are considerably more extreme. The demand for labor, particularly unskilled labor, may have increased with the land boom, thereby producing greater flexibility of wages in the Midwest.[49] The relationship between prices and nominal wages, therefore, may have been intermediated by a third factor—land. This explanation is appealing, but is not entirely consistent with the evidence. Real wages did not always increase during the land boom period; further, nominal wages in the South Central region, which also experienced a spectacular land boom, do not yield the same results.

We turn now to the implications of our findings for the functioning of labor markets. Most laborers in the antebellum period were paid by the day or the month and did not, it seems, have the explicit or implicit guarantees workers have today. Rigid nominal wages in the face of declining prices might then imply high levels of unemployment. If workers were relatively immobile, unemployment could have meant prolonged absence of work and wages. Given the signal processing model just sketched, price decreases, even if triggered by purely monetary phenomena, could have produced unemployment, economic depression, and, paradoxically, rising real wages for those who remained employed. Real wages did, in fact, rise during most episodes characterized by labor historians and others as ones of major unemployment, for example, 1839–42 and 1854–55.[50]

There is some evidence that workers laid off during periods of economic decline migrated to agricultural areas and later returned to their original employment when conditions improved.[51] Thus unemployment in the industrial

47. See the appendix in Stanley Lebergott, "The Demand for Land: The United States, 1820–1860," *Journal of Economic History,* 45 (June 1985), pp. 181–212.

48. See, for example, Temin, *The Jacksonian Economy.* It should also be noted that land became easier to purchase after 1832, when an act was passed which reduced the minimum acreage.

49. Because the price index does not include the cost of housing (which would have risen during the land boom), it is also possible that our real wage index overstates the flexibility of midwestern wages.

50. Layer, *Earnings of Cotton Mill Operatives,* notes employment was reduced during 1834, 1837, 1842, 1850, 1856. The episodes given are from Wilentz, *Chants Democratic.*

51. Alan Dawley, in *Class and Community: The Industrial Revolution in Lynn* (Cambridge, Mass., 1976), writes that "manufacturers . . . hired a large number of people to get the job done, and then laid off most of the employees when the orders were filled. . . . When the shoe industry expanded, new job opportunities attracted migrants to the city, and when it retrenched the inflow stopped. The boom of the 1830s came to an abrupt halt in 1837; for the next several years Lynn experienced an outright decline in population; then business revival in the mid–1840s brought renewed population growth" (p. 53).

sector may have been less severe than various historical accounts suggest. But migration from urban and industrial areas could have exacerbated the adjustment by preventing firms from observing the signal of general unemployment.

Price inflation, by similar reasoning, produced decreased real earnings and an increased demand for labor. Historically, labor unrest and strikes in the Northeast are easily linked to these episodes; important strikes occurred in virtually all the inflationary periods, for example, 1824–25, 1835–36, 1844–45, and 1853–54. According to the standard count of strikes between 1833 and 1837, when the price level rose sharply, the vast majority involved skilled workers in the Northeast; very few took place among the unskilled or in other regions.[52] Although striking for higher wages was not "the journeyman's sole or even major concern," there is no question that labor agitation was "clearly linked to the inflationary spiral."[53] Although persistence of shocks was somewhat diminished for northeastern artisans, compared with those in other regions, collective action did not greatly reduce it.

The persistence of shocks to clerks' wages is consistent with their relatively high degree of skill and the nature of white-collar work during the period. Often employed for long period of time at the same firm, there was less need for white-collar workers to resort to strikes and union activity, since real wage losses during inflationary periods would be balanced by gains during deflationary episodes.

Economic historians have long debated whether the existence of a wage lag helped finance the Union war effort during the Civil War.[54] An econometric study by Mokyr and DeCanio, using methods different from ours, concluded that a wage lag did exist during the Civil War, but they did not consider whether the lag was peculiar to the war period.[55] Our results suggest that the wage lag may have been a pervasive feature of American labor markets long before the Civil War and that it increased over time.

2.5 Summary

We have presented an econometric analysis of the persistence of shocks to real wages before the Civil War. The results suggest that the revisionist description of antebellum labor markets has merit. We found no evidence against the view that changes in prices were eventually reflected fully in nom-

52. Commons, et al., *History of Labor,* vol. 1, pp. 478–84 contains the list of strikes between 1833 and 1837.

53. Wilentz, *Chants Democratic,* p. 231. Wilentz also notes that a strike by journeyman cabinetmakers in 1835 was motivated by the fact that "the price book [for standard journeyman wages] used by their masters was more than a quarter of a century old. . . . The old book failed to keep up with the cost of living" (p. 232).

54. The wage-lag hypothesis was first articulated by Wesley Clair Mitchell, *A History of the Greenbacks* (Chicago, 1903). Mitchell's hypothesis was criticized by, among others, R. A. Kessel and A. A. Alchian, "Real Wages in the North During the Civil War: Mitchell's Data Reinterpreted," *Journal of Law and Economics,* 2 (Oct. 1959), pp. 95–113.

55. Mokyr and DeCanio, "Inflation and the Wage Lag During the American Civil War."

inal wages, controlling for real factors. In the short run, however, shocks to real wages had persistent effects. Real wages generally fell during periods of inflation and rose during periods of deflation. Antebellum deflations went hand in hand with recession or depression, and almost all involved episodes of reduced employment in industry and urban areas. Only fully employed workers, therefore, benefited from real wage growth during deflations. Others, it seems, were either out of work or migrated to agriculture. The emphasis labor historians have given to the wage lag in explaining labor strife, and in accounting for the importance of inconstant employment in working class culture and politics, seems deserved. But the flexibility of the antebellum labor force and the role of the agricultural hinterland in shielding labor from unemployment requires further investigation.

Appendix A

Table 2A.1 Indices of Nominal Wages of Artisans, 1820–1856

Year	Northeast	Midwest	South Atlantic	South Central
1820	79.4	n.a.	n.a.	80.2
1821	56.3	n.a.	n.a.	84.0
1822	71.2	69.7	n.a.	87.7
1823	70.4	69.2	82.6	95.9
1824	70.4	69.2	79.0	94.3
1825	67.7	68.7	87.4	99.2
1826	64.9	68.2	95.8	104.2
1827	74.3	73.9	99.0	109.2
1828	68.9	79.6	88.5	104.4
1829	65.7	85.3	93.6	90.0
1830	62.9	85.9	95.0	95.0
1831	66.4	97.5	96.4	93.4
1832	68.9	93.8	95.8	91.8
1833	67.8	88.2	95.8	97.3
1834	76.6	86.8	97.5	102.8
1835	78.9	85.5	98.6	108.0
1836	84.5	84.2	90.9	115.8
1837	80.3	114.3	92.1	108.8
1838	77.6	92.8	93.3	90.2
1839	82.5	83.9	93.3	110.6
1840	77.6	84.7	93.0	117.6
1841	77.6	79.5	92.6	124.5
1842	70.8	73.6	95.5	111.2
1843	75.4	61.8	84.0	87.9
1844	67.0	65.7	84.0	84.6
1845	80.0	69.8	84.6	96.5
1846	76.9	60.1	84.6	88.0
1847	78.4	68.9	83.0	99.2
1848	74.0	72.9	86.0	93.3
1849	74.6	76.0	87.6	101.4
1850	75.1	79.0	89.1	109.4
1851	74.1	89.6	89.1	110.0
1852	76.8	87.5	96.2	110.0
1853	79.5	93.6	103.3	109.4
1854	84.7	94.8	110.4	106.5
1855	89.9	98.1	117.5	108.5
1856	100.0	100.0	100.0	100.0
Decadal averages (1821–30 = 100):				
1821–30	100.0	100.0	100.0	100.0
1831–40	113.1	122.6	105.1	107.5
1841–40	111.5	95.0	96.7	103.3
1851–56	125.2	126.2	114.1	111.4
Rate of growth[a]	0.8	0.8	0.5	0.4

Notes: See also Appendix B for a procedure to convert the wage indices to wage levels.

Source: Margo-Villaflor sample of "Reports and Articles Hired," National Archives, Record Group 92.

n.a. = not available.

[a]Rate of growth is the average annual rate of growth, 1821–30 to 1851–56.

Table 2A.2 Indices of Nominal Wages of Laborers, 1820–1856

Year	Northeast	Midwest	South Atlantic	South Central
1820	n.a.	84.5	n.a.	73.9
1821	66.4	86.3	n.a.	79.9
1822	64.1	70.5	n.a.	79.9
1823	64.1	67.1	n.a.	80.9
1824	63.8	65.5	n.a.	79.9
1825	69.7	65.2	74.8	77.8
1826	75.5	63.8	76.8	77.0
1827	71.5	63.8	77.8	84.3
1828	64.3	68.2	79.4	91.6
1829	60.7	71.1	74.9	96.0
1830	61.1	73.8	70.4	97.7
1831	60.2	69.8	68.5	90.8
1832	63.2	73.8	66.6	90.3
1833	62.4	83.6	65.2	88.6
1834	74.7	93.3	63.8	92.4
1835	74.7	93.3	67.6	83.8
1836	81.8	78.0	84.3	99.8
1837	88.2	117.4	87.6	102.3
1838	80.1	88.6	74.3	76.7
1839	71.5	107.4	81.1	95.7
1840	59.0	85.1	79.8	90.8
1841	73.1	80.8	78.4	101.1
1842	74.4	76.4	60.6	99.1
1843	81.5	82.7	72.3	92.7
1844	81.5	80.0	74.3	92.9
1845	81.5	77.3	76.3	83.1
1846	83.4	88.9	77.3	73.3
1847	69.4	73.9	77.5	72.4
1848	76.7	90.8	75.9	78.6
1849	84.0	86.6	74.0	84.9
1850	85.3	82.4	72.1	91.1
1851	80.7	87.0	71.2	96.8
1852	89.0	91.5	70.3	108.0
1853	88.1	87.8	70.3	105.7
1854	92.4	100.5	71.2	100.9
1855	95.5	105.2	89.4	105.0
1856	100.0	100.0	100.0	100.0
Decadal averages (1821–30 = 100):				
1821–30	100.0	100.0	100.0	100.0
1831–40	108.3	128.5	97.6	107.8
1841–40	119.5	118.0	97.6	103.4
1851–56	137.6	137.1	104.0	121.5
Rate of growth[a]	1.1	1.1	0.1	0.7

Notes: See also Appendix B for a procedure to convert the wage indices to wage levels.

Source: Margo-Villaflor sample of "Reports and Articles Hired," National Archives, Record Group 92.

n.a. = not available.

[a]Rate of growth is the average annual rate of growth, 1821–30 to 1851–56.

Table 2A.3 Indices of Nominal Wages of Clerks, 1820–1856

Year	Northeast	Midwest	South Atlantic	South Central
1820	89.9	49.7	n.a.	n.a.
1821	83.2	55.8	n.a.	71.0
1822	59.3	46.8	n.a.	77.3
1823	62.9	45.9	88.9	53.0
1824	62.8	45.1	98.5	55.5
1825	65.6	49.9	87.3	62.0
1826	60.7	49.9	77.6	68.4
1827	65.6	45.7	77.3	68.1
1828	70.3	48.3	86.3	73.5
1829	78.8	48.9	69.9	78.9
1830	64.2	49.9	65.9	79.4
1831	73.6	43.0	61.8	78.7
1832	72.2	50.1	63.9	76.0
1833	71.1	50.2	72.0	74.1
1834	71.1	56.0	80.1	72.1
1835	71.1	49.5	76.5	78.1
1836	71.0	50.5	93.5	79.1
1837	82.0	55.9	99.2	96.2
1838	74.8	58.2	104.0	104.3
1839	87.8	60.1	106.6	125.1
1840	87.8	55.0	94.4	114.6
1841	84.5	54.0	103.6	104.1
1842	84.1	58.6	92.3	93.2
1843	94.7	69.1	76.1	87.3
1844	99.5	67.3	78.9	89.4
1845	99.5	69.1	81.7	91.5
1846	93.7	62.5	84.5	109.6
1847	94.4	69.6	99.0	111.4
1848	105.3	92.7	113.5	113.1
1849	107.6	85.0	116.5	108.5
1850	109.9	77.3	119.4	103.9
1851	103.3	71.0	112.4	109.5
1852	96.9	88.1	109.9	105.5
1853	95.1	71.1	107.6	110.3
1854	114.1	78.9	95.0	122.1
1855	108.6	88.3	108.9	103.7
1856	100.0	100.0	100.0	100.0
Decadal averages (1821–30 = 100):				
1821–30	100.0	100.0	100.0	100.0
1831–40	113.4	108.8	104.5	130.7
1841–40	144.6	145.1	118.5	147.3
1851–56	153.0	170.5	129.6	157.9
Rate of growth[a]	1.5	1.9	0.9	1.6

Notes: See also Appendix B for a procedure to convert the wage indices to wage levels.

Source: Margo-Villaflor sample of "Reports and Articles Hired," National Archives, Record Group 92.

n.a. = not available.

[a]Rate of growth is the average annual rate of growth, 1821–30 to 1851–56.

Table 2A.4 Price Indices, 1821–1856

Year	Northeast	Midwest	South Atlantic	South Central
1821	98.6	80.6	100.1	100.3
1822	103.0	86.6	109.5	113.6
1823	95.5	74.1	101.6	102.2
1824	93.0	72.2	94.4	95.8
1825	95.8	74.4	96.6	104.1
1826	86.5	63.7	86.3	92.8
1827	85.3	62.8	86.1	89.9
1828	83.1	64.5	82.8	93.3
1829	80.8	73.7	81.1	91.6
1830	78.9	67.9	83.1	83.4
1831	81.4	68.7	79.0	85.4
1832	85.0	74.2	83.5	89.8
1833	90.1	77.8	89.2	92.9
1834	84.6	74.8	91.0	89.9
1835	96.4	90.0	102.1	106.0
1836	110.2	106.5	127.5	128.5
1837	103.7	100.2	111.7	116.9
1838	98.7	92.0	105.5	115.9
1839	103.9	96.8	108.1	110.4
1840	85.0	73.1	83.6	91.5
1841	78.8	65.3	80.3	88.4
1842	68.3	51.3	61.3	77.0
1843	62.2	53.6	60.3	62.7
1844	61.1	58.7	62.8	65.6
1845	68.2	61.5	68.9	67.3
1846	68.5	63.5	73.4	68.8
1847	82.9	77.4	85.4	85.6
1848	69.7	59.6	64.5	68.7
1849	72.3	65.4	71.6	75.2
1850	78.0	72.7	80.9	85.8
1851	74.7	73.1	83.3	79.0
1852	78.8	76.9	83.3	79.1
1853	86.4	81.3	87.0	85.1
1854	93.8	84.5	88.8	85.6
1855	96.8	96.3	101.1	100.1
1856	100.0	100.0	100.0	100.0
Decadal averages (1821–30 = 100):				
1821–30	100.0	100.0	100.0	100.0
1831–40	104.2	118.6	106.5	106.2
1841–40	78.8	87.4	77.0	77.0
1851–56	98.0	118.6	98.4	91.2
Rate of growth[a]	−0.07	0.6	−0.06	−0.3

Source: See Appendix B and text.

[a]Rate of growth is the average annual rate of growth, 1821–30 to 1851–56.

Table 2A.5 **Indices of Real Wages of Artisans, 1821–1856**

Year	Northeast	Midwest	South Atlantic	South Central
1821	57.1	n.a.	n.a.	83.7
1822	69.1	80.5	n.a.	77.2
1823	73.7	93.4	81.3	93.8
1824	75.7	95.8	83.6	98.4
1825	70.7	92.3	90.5	95.3
1826	75.0	107.1	110.0	112.3
1827	87.1	117.1	115.0	121.5
1828	82.9	123.4	106.8	111.9
1829	81.3	115.7	115.4	98.3
1830	79.7	126.5	114.3	113.9
1831	81.6	141.9	122.0	109.4
1832	81.1	126.4	114.7	102.2
1833	75.2	113.3	107.3	104.7
1834	90.5	116.0	107.1	114.3
1835	81.8	95.0	96.6	101.9
1836	76.7	79.1	71.3	90.1
1837	77.4	114.1	82.5	93.1
1838	78.6	100.9	88.4	77.8
1839	79.4	86.7	86.3	100.2
1840	91.3	115.9	111.2	128.5
1841	98.5	121.7	115.3	140.8
1842	103.7	143.5	155.8	144.4
1843	121.2	115.3	139.3	140.2
1844	109.7	111.9	133.8	129.0
1845	117.3	113.5	122.8	143.4
1846	112.3	94.6	115.3	127.9
1847	94.6	89.0	97.2	115.9
1848	106.2	122.3	133.3	135.8
1849	103.2	116.2	122.3	134.8
1850	96.3	108.7	110.1	127.5
1851	99.2	122.6	106.9	139.2
1852	97.5	113.8	115.5	139.1
1853	92.0	115.1	118.7	128.6
1854	90.3	112.2	124.3	124.4
1855	92.9	101.9	116.2	108.4
1856	100.0	100.0	100.0	100.0
Decadal averages (1821–30 = 100):				
1821–30	100.0	100.0	100.0	100.0
1831–40	108.2	102.9	96.7	101.5
1841–40	141.2	107.5	121.9	133.2
1851–56	126.7	104.8	111.3	122.6
Rate of growth[a]	0.8	0.2	0.4	0.7

Sources: Tables 2A.1 and 2A.4.

n.a. = not available.

[a]Rate of growth is the average annual rate of growth, 1821–30 to 1851–56.

Table 2A.6 Indices of Real Wages of Laborers, 1821–1856

Year	Northeast	Midwest	South Atlantic	South Central
1821	67.3	107.1	n.a.	79.7
1822	62.2	81.4	n.a.	70.3
1823	67.1	90.6	n.a.	79.2
1824	68.6	90.7	n.a.	83.4
1825	72.8	87.6	77.4	74.7
1826	87.3	100.2	89.9	82.9
1827	83.8	101.6	90.4	93.8
1828	77.4	105.7	95.9	98.2
1829	75.1	96.4	92.4	104.8
1830	77.4	108.7	84.7	117.1
1831	74.0	101.6	86.7	106.3
1832	74.4	99.5	79.8	100.6
1833	69.3	107.5	73.1	95.4
1834	88.3	124.7	70.1	102.8
1835	77.5	103.7	66.2	79.1
1836	74.2	73.2	66.1	77.7
1837	85.1	117.2	78.4	87.5
1838	81.2	96.3	70.4	66.2
1839	68.8	111.0	75.0	86.7
1840	69.4	116.4	95.5	99.2
1841	92.8	123.7	97.6	114.4
1842	108.9	148.9	98.9	128.7
1843	131.0	154.3	119.9	147.8
1844	133.4	136.2	118.3	141.6
1845	119.5	125.7	110.7	123.5
1846	121.8	140.0	105.3	106.5
1847	83.7	95.5	90.7	84.6
1848	110.0	152.3	117.7	114.4
1849	116.2	132.4	103.4	112.9
1850	109.4	113.3	89.4	106.2
1851	108.0	119.0	85.5	122.5
1852	112.9	119.0	84.4	136.5
1853	102.0	108.0	80.8	124.2
1854	98.5	118.9	80.2	117.9
1855	98.7	109.2	88.4	104.9
1856	100.0	100.0	100.0	100.0
Decadal averages (1821–30 = 100):				
1821–30	100.0	100.0	100.0	100.0
1831–40	103.1	108.4	86.0	102.0
1841–40	152.5	136.3	118.9	133.6
1851–56	139.9	115.9	97.9	133.1
Rate of growth[a]	1.2	0.5	−0.08	1.0

Sources: Tables 2A.2 and 2A.4.

n.a. = not available.

[a]Rate of growth is the average annual rate of growth, 1821–30 to 1851–56.

Table 2A.7 Indices of Real Wages of Clerks, 1821–1856

Year	Northeast	Midwest	South Atlantic	South Central
1821	84.4	69.2	n.a.	70.8
1822	57.5	54.0	n.a.	68.0
1823	65.9	61.9	87.0	51.9
1824	67.5	62.5	102.8	57.9
1825	68.5	67.1	94.1	59.6
1826	70.1	78.3	83.6	73.7
1827	76.9	72.8	86.0	75.8
1828	84.6	74.9	92.5	78.8
1829	97.5	66.4	76.3	86.1
1830	81.3	73.5	79.0	95.2
1831	90.4	62.6	72.4	92.2
1832	84.9	67.5	71.2	84.6
1833	78.9	64.5	77.5	79.8
1834	84.0	74.9	89.1	80.2
1835	73.7	55.0	72.2	73.7
1836	64.5	47.4	72.8	61.6
1837	79.1	55.8	84.9	82.3
1838	75.7	63.2	89.7	90.0
1839	84.5	62.1	96.6	113.3
1840	103.3	75.2	103.7	125.2
1841	107.3	82.7	117.2	117.8
1842	123.1	114.2	119.9	121.0
1843	152.3	128.9	121.4	139.2
1844	162.8	114.7	120.3	132.8
1845	145.9	112.4	121.4	136.0
1846	136.8	98.4	122.8	159.3
1847	113.9	89.9	115.7	130.1
1848	151.1	155.5	165.2	164.6
1849	148.9	129.9	154.9	144.3
1850	140.9	106.3	139.2	121.1
1851	138.4	97.1	141.9	138.6
1852	122.9	114.6	138.9	133.4
1853	110.1	87.5	126.4	129.6
1854	121.6	93.3	111.0	142.6
1855	112.2	91.7	108.8	103.6
1856	100.0	100.0	100.0	100.0
Decadal averages (1821–30 = 100):				
1821–30	100.0	100.0	100.0	100.0
1831–40	108.6	92.2	93.5	123.0
1841–40	183.4	166.3	148.0	190.3
1851–56	155.8	143.0	138.2	173.5
Rate of growth[a]	1.6	1.3	1.2	2.0

Sources: Tables 2A.3 and 2A.4.

[a]Rate of growth is the average annual rate of growth, 1821–30 to 1851–56.

Appendix B
Construction of the Wage and Regional Price Indices

Wage Indices

The nominal wage indices in Tables 2A.1–2A.3 are constructed so that 1856 = 100, and therefore cannot be used to compute skill differentials or ratios. The following are a set of nominal wages for 1856 that can be used to produce nominal wages for all years.

	Northeast	Midwest	South Atlantic	South Central
Artisans	1.91	2.21	1.74	1.91
Laborers	1.26	1.36	1.02	1.22
Clerks	2.14	2.21	2.35	2.52

Notes: Artisans includes carpenters, painters and plasterers, blacksmiths and machinists. Laborers includes common laborers and teamsters. Clerks includes inspectors and foragers.

Because the wages analyzed here have been computed using a hedonic regression, those given above for 1856 depend on the weights placed on the coefficients. The procedure used is as follows. The coefficients from the hedonic wage regression for the fort and occupation dummies were weighted by the sample shares (e.g., the coefficient of the fort dummy for Detroit in the Midwest laborer regression was weighted by the share of observations from Detroit). Coefficients of the seasonal dummies were each weighted by ¼, and all other variables were set equal to zero. The estimates, therefore, can be interpreted as the daily wage (without rations) in the particular occupational group in 1856 averaged across forts in the region and across seasons.

To produce similar estimates for other years, multiply the wage estimate for 1856 by the index numbers reported in the appendix tables and divide by 100. For example, the index number for clerks in the Northeast in 1840 is 87.8. Thus the estimated clerks' wage at Northeast forts in 1840 is $1.88 (= $2.14 × 0.878). We emphasize, however, that wage estimates for artisans and laborers produced in this manner are not comparable to those in Robert A. Margo and Georgia C. Villaflor, "The Growth of Wages in Antebellum America: New Evidence," *Journal of Economic History,* 47 (Dec. 1987), pp. 873–95, because they were produced using a different weighting procedure than that just described.

Price Indices

For each census region a set of commodities was selected from Arthur H. Cole's compendium of price data. Average annual prices were calculated, and commodity-specific indices were formed (base year is 1856) in the usual manner. The regional price indices are geometric weighted averages of the commodity-specific indices:[56]

56. See Cole, *Wholesale Prices*. Although geometric weighted-average price indices are theoretically inferior to other functional forms, the information required to calculate more complicated

$$P = \Pi_i p_{it}^{s(i)}$$

where p_{it} is the value of the commodity-specific index in year t, and the $s(i)$'s are weights. The weights are analogous to budget shares and are derived from Ethel Hoover's study of consumer prices.[57] Using the Carroll Wright sample of Massachusetts families, Hoover divided household expenditures into nine categories. For six of these categories (cereal and bakery products, meat and fish, dairy, other foods, clothing, and fuel), prices could be found in the Cole collection for commodities within each category. The Cole collection also contains price quotations for a tenth group, liquor, which Hoover did not include in her consumer price index.[58] Commodity-specific indices were then calculated and weights assigned to each index depending on the relative budget shares within categories.

To take a specific example, consider the category "cereal and bakery products" for the Northeast. The Cole collection contains prices for three commodities within this group—flour, cornmeal, and rice—for New York and Philadelphia. According to Hoover's calculations, flour accounted for 88 percent of all cereal and bakery expenditures on flour, cornmeal, and rice; the other relative shares are: cornmeal (0.10), rice (0.02). Cereal and bakery products, according to Hoover, made up 10.8 percent of all household expenditures, and expenditures on the seven groups represented were 70.7 percent of all household expenditures. Thus the Northeast weight for flour (see below) is 0.134 ($0.88 \times 0.108/0.707$). The remaining weights, listed below, were derived in a similar manner.

It is important to note that the South Atlantic index is the least satisfactory. The Cole collection contains no usable data for fuel prices for Charleston (either coal or wood) covering the entire period. Furthermore, the "meats and fish" and "clothing" categories cover only a single commodity each (bacon and cotton, respectively). If prices for these commodities evolved in a different way than for the other commodities in the category, the regional index may be biased. Investigating such biases would require the collection of additional price data, which is beyond our scope here.

indices is not available. Furthermore, a geometric index would appear to be more consonant with consumer theory than, for example, an algebraic weighted-average. Specifically, the geometric average is consistent with a Cobb-Douglas utility function, while an algebraic index is inconsistent with utility maximization. On price indices in general see W. E. Diewert, "Index Numbers," in J. Eatwell, M. Milgate, and P. Newman, eds., *The New Palgrave: A Dictionary of Economics,* vol. 2 (New York, 1987), pp. 767–80.

57. Ethel D. Hoover, "Retail Prices After 1850," in Conference on Research in Income and Wealth, vol. 24, *Trends in the American Economy in the Nineteenth Century* (Princeton, 1960), pp. 177–78.

58. The budget share for liquor (0.02 of total consumer expenditures) is assumed to be the same for all regions and is derived from regressions in Michael Haines, "Consumer Behavior and Immigrant Assimilation: A Comparison of the United States, Britain, and Germany, 1889/1890" (manuscript, Department of Economics, Wayne State University, Jan. 1988).

1. Northeast, commodities and weights:
    1.1 Cereal and bakery products: flour (0.134), cornmeal (0.015), rice (0.003)
    1.2 Meats and fish: beef (0.113), pork (0.024), bacon (0.026), fish (0.024)
    1.3 Dairy: butter (0.130)
    1.4 Other foods: molasses (0.003), coffee (0.067), tea (0.022), lard (0.025), sugar (0.075)
    1.5 Clothing: cotton (0.156), leather (0.054)
    1.6 Fuel: coal (0.098)
    1.7 Liquor: whiskey (0.028)

    Percent of household expenditure accounted for by above commodities = 70.7%[59]

2. *Midwest, commodities and weights:*
    2.1 Cereal and bakery products: flour (0.150), rice (0.003).
    2.2 Meats and fish: pork (0.087), bacon (0.102)
    2.3 Dairy: butter (0.130)
    2.4 Other foods: coffee (0.075), sugar (0.085), lard (0.029), molasses (0.004)
    2.5 Clothing: cotton (0.156), leather (0.054)
    2.6 Fuel: coal (0.098)
    2.7 Liquor: whiskey (0.028)

    Percent of household expenditure accounted for by above commodities = 70.7%

3. *South Atlantic, commodities and weights:*
    3.1 Cereal and bakery products: flour (0.167), rice (0.003)
    3.2 Meats and fish: bacon (0.209)
    3.3 Dairy: butter (0.144)
    3.4 Other foods: coffee (0.083), lard (0.032), sugar (0.094), molasses (0.004)
    3.5 Clothing: cotton (0.233)
    3.6 Liquor: (0.031)

    Percent of household expenditure accounted for by above commodities = 65.1%

59. Of the expenditures of a typical antebellum household, 70.7 percent were on the listed commodities, in all but the South Atlantic region. The major excluded commodity is housing, for which there is no information in Cole's collection. For the South Atlantic, the commodities included account for slightly less of total expenditure.

4. South Central, commodities and weights:

4.1 Cereal and bakery products: flour (0.150), rice (0.003)

4.2 Meats and fish: beef (0.113), pork (0.024), bacon (0.026), fish (0.024)

4.3 Dairy: butter (0.130)

4.4 Other foods: coffee (0.067), tea (0.022), sugar (0.075), lard (0.025), molasses (0.003)

4.5 Clothing: cotton (0.211)

4.6 Fuel: wood (0.098)

4.7 Liquor: whiskey (0.028)

Percent of household expenditure accounted for by above commodities = 70.7%

3 Structural Change in the Farm Labor Force

Contract Labor in Massachusetts Agriculture, 1750–1865

Winifred B. Rothenberg

America's genuinely "peculiar institution" may not have been plantation slavery at all, but free labor on the farms of New England. Varieties of bondage—slavery, serfdom, truck, peonage, the *encomienda,* indentured servitude, the interlinking of forced labor to ill-functioning markets for land and credit, the buying and selling of foreign workers by *padrones, partidaros,* and labor bosses, and the more subtle but no less coercive tyranny of familial production—have characterized agrarian labor systems throughout the world since time immemorial.[1] There is nothing "peculiar" about them. But an agricul-

Even after many years of doing so, it is still a pleasure to acknowledge the assistance of the staffs of the Pocumtuck Valley Memorial Association Library at Historic Deerfield, Old Sturbridge Village Library, and the Manuscripts and Archives Collection of Baker Library at the Harvard Business School. This study owes most to Ellen Rothenberg, Stanley Engerman, and Kenneth Sokoloff; to Jack Larkin, Chief Historian of the Research Department at Old Sturbridge Village, whose generous willingness to share the data base for his study of farm laborers on the Ward family farm is deeply appreciated; to David Garman and Oliver Hart whose insights have proved most helpful; and to Claudia Goldin who, in honoring Robert Fogel, has—repeatedly—stretched my grasp beyond my reach.

1. On the tyranny of familial production in traditional societies, see J. C. Caldwell, "The Mechanisms of Demographic Change in Historical Perspective," *Population Studies,* 35 (March 1981), pp. 5–27. On the tyranny of familial production in the United States, see William N. Parker, "Agriculture," in Lance E. Davis, Richard A. Easterlin, and William N. Parker, eds., *American Economic Growth: An Economist's History of the United States* (New York, 1972), especially p. 395. On bound labor on the American frontier, see Howard Lamar, "From Bondage to Contract: Ethnic Labor in the American West, 1600–1890," in Steven Hahn and Jonathan Prude, eds., *The Countryside in the Age of Capitalist Transformation: Essays in the Social History of Rural America* (Chapel Hill, 1985), pp. 293–324; and William S. Hallagan, "Labor Contracting in Turn-of-the-Century California Agriculture," *Journal of Economic History,* 40 (Dec. 1980), pp. 757–76. On forms of interlinked labor, credit, and tenurial contracts in developing economies, see Hans P. Binswanger and Mark R. Rosenzweig, eds., *Contractual Arrangements, Employment, and Wages in Rural Labor Markets in Asia* (New Haven, 1984). On truck, see Rosemary E. Ommer, ed., *Merchant Credit and Labour Strategies in Historical Perspective* (Fredericton, New Brunswick, 1990).

tural labor force, unconstrained and free to move, may well be a New England innovation.[2]

In an earlier paper I attempted to understand the developmental role played by the emergence of a market for free labor working by the day on Massachusetts farms between 1750 and 1850.[3] Here I explore the complementary role played by live-in laborers hired on monthly contracts "to work with" (or "to work for") Massachusetts farmers.

The distinction between day labor and contract labor in New England agriculture can be traced to the distinction made in English feudal law between free and unfree tenants, a difference that apparently had less to do with the tenure on which the land was held and more to do with what was called the certainty of the work. If the tenants must work at the will of the lord—if "when they go to bed on Sunday night they do not know what Monday's work will be: it may be threshing, ditching, carrying; they can not tell"—then they are unfree. "The tenure is unfree, not because the tenant 'holds at the will of the lord,' in the sense of being removable at a moment's notice, but because his services, though in many respects minutely defined by custom, can not be altogether defined without frequent reference to the lord's will."[4]

From the sixteenth to the mid-nineteenth centuries, much of the labor on English farms was done by "servants-in-husbandry" on annual contracts, an important institution which evolved in response, on the one hand, to desperate labor shortages after each visitation of the plague and, on the other, to the increasingly urgent demand for labor on the larger, enclosed, pastoral farms. Servants-in-husbandry were unmarried young people usually between the ages of 15 and 24, the sons and daughters of farmers who had, for a variety of reasons, shed their adolescent children and taken on someone else's. Servants were hired every Michaelmas at job fairs to live with and in the family (that is, as a member of the household) of the master and to do all manner of farm work for twelve months from harvest to harvest. Until the eighteenth century, the wage was set by fiat; thereafter it was set in the open market. The annual contracts, while not always written, were made public, were constrained by custom and law, and were enforceable in the courts.[5]

2. Free, even, to quit in breach of contract without penalty. It is a matter of some significance, I think, that none of the farmers in my sample withheld the wages earned by workers who quit early in breach of contract, although the courts had held that labor service contracts bar recovery in *quantum meruit*. With the solitary exception of *Britton* v. *Turner*, (N.H., 1834), state courts had consistently held that employers had a right at law to withhold wages from laborers who failed to fulfill an express contract, "whether the wages are estimated at a gross sum, or are to be calculated according to a certain rate per week or month, or are payable at certain stipulated times, provided the servant agree for a definite and whole term." The curious thing, then, is why the farmers in my sample did not withhold wages in fact. See Morton J. Horwitz, *The Transformation of American Law, 1780–1860* (Cambridge, Mass., 1977), pp. 332, n. 148, and 186–87.

3. See my "The Emergence of Farm Labor Markets and the Transformation of the Rural Economy: Massachusetts, 1750–1855," *Journal of Economic History*, 48 (Sept. 1988), pp. 537–66.

4. Frederick Pollock and Frederick W. Maitland, *The History of English Law before the Time of Edward I* (1st edn., 1895; 2d edn., 1898; reprinted Cambridge, 1978), vol. 1, p. 371.

5. The 52-week residency in the parish required for a settlement under the English Poor Law deterred servants from running away in breach of contract, but employing farmers were all too

It is likely that most of the early settlers of Massachusetts had had servants-in-husbandry in England and expected to transport the institution to New England, for it has been estimated that nearly three-quarters of the yeomen, nearly one-half of the husbandmen, and nearly a quarter of the tradesmen in early modern England had a live-in laborer.[6] But farm laborers as a class quickly disappeared in Massachusetts. Estimates put the proportion of servants in seventeenth century Essex County at no more than 4 percent, and in Dedham at less than 5 percent, of the farm population.[7] That first generation of settlers faced not only a dearth of live-in help but a "withering" of day labor as well.[8] Farmers breaking a wilderness to grain agriculture could count only on the field labor of their sons or, if sufficiently prosperous, of their tenants.

While Massachusetts farmers may have had little, if any, live-in help in the seventeenth century, farm account books document the appearance of labor contracts by the mid-eighteenth century. Although contract labor was used with increased frequency after 1800, so was day labor. Both forms of labor were used throughout the sample period and, averaged over quinquennia, there is no change in the composition of man-days of labor. Yet there was an increase in the use of contract labor in terms of the number of contract-months hired per farmer. Measuring the magnitude of that increase, which occupies much of the remainder of this study, will prove problematical, but what increase there was directs our attention to the advantages of labor contracts, advantages that to this day continue to make contractual arrangements the dominant mode of organizing agricultural labor throughout the developing world.

The prevalence of labor contracts (in unionized industries, of course, more conspicuously than in agriculture) poses a challenge to conventional labor market theory. Where conventional theory puts current wages at the center of the process, contract markets "tend to insulate contracting parties from short-run external shocks which take current wage rates 'out of competition' in allocating labor resources." Where in conventional theory labor inputs adjust to the market wage in a perpetual and timeless equilibrium process, in contract theory all options that existed ex ante are closed ex post. In sum, where competitive markets are governed by the invisible hand, contract markets are governed by "the invisible handshake."[9]

Several motivations for labor contracts have been identified in the theoretical literature. There is, first, the insurance motive. The theory of contracts

---

often able to impose the infamous 51-week contracts that left servants disqualified for a settlement. See Ann Kussmaul, *Servants in Husbandry in Early Modern England* (New York, 1981).

6. Daniel Vickers, "Working the Fields in a Developing Economy: Essex County, Massachusetts, 1630–1675," in Stephen Innes, ed., *Work and Labor in Early America* (Chapel Hill, 1988), p. 55.

7. Ibid., p. 55, n. 13.

8. Ibid., p. 60.

9. See Sherwin Rosen, "Implicit Contracts: A Survey," *Journal of Economic Literature*, 23 (Sept. 1985), pp. 1144–75. The passages quoted appear on pp. 1145 and 1149.

suggests that the primary beneficiary of a labor contract is the worker who is assumed to be more risk-averse than the employer. In adjusting output to falling seasonal demand, the employer may be indifferent as to lowering wage rates and keeping employment constant or keeping wage rates constant and laying off workers, but the worker is not. Where both contract and day labor are used, the brunt of periodic layoffs is borne by the day workers, while the contract workers accept a wage below their marginal revenue product and considerably below the spot wage of the day worker in return for employment security for the duration of the contract. Sherwin Rosen calls this bargain struck by the contracting parties, "implicit payments of insurance premiums by workers in favorable states of nature and receipt of indemnities in unfavorable states."[10]

Another motivation concerns the hoarding of labor. If the local supply of labor cannot be counted upon to satisfy peak seasonal demands, the employer may have an incentive to secure "downstream" labor in the off-season, at off-season wages, even if it means hoarding wage labor for many months. As a corollary, the employer-farmer will have an incentive to restructure the farm enterprise so that the labor he is "storing" at considerable expense can be gainfully employed in the off-season. Diversifying the crop mix, home manufacturing, hiring out "my hand" to neighboring farmers, shifting to dairying and animal husbandry which use labor throughout the year, can all be understood as responses to the need to provide year-round employment for workers on long-term contracts.[11]

It is difficult to understand the ubiquity of long-term wage and tenancy contracts in labor-surplus economies where the marginal productivity of family labor approaches zero and the probability of recruiting harvest workers on the spot is very high. Yet the major incidence of agricultural labor contracts today is in just such economies.[12] It would appear that contracts under these conditions disguise as labor recruitment strategies what are primarily arrangements for workers to obtain access to credit and land in the absence of well-functioning credit and land markets. The interlinking of labor, land, and credit transactions is facilitated by the sunk investment the parties have made in the relationship, that is, by what Oliver Hart and Bengt Holmstrom have called a

10. Ibid., p. 1145.

11. See, for example, Ralph V. Anderson and Robert E. Gallman, "Slaves as Fixed Capital: Slave Labor and Southern Economic Development," *Journal of American History,* 64 (June 1977), pp. 24–46.

Of course, not all farmers will be willing to absorb the costs of hoarding labor, together with the related costs of restructuring the farm calendar. They would be particularly reluctant if "worker opportunism," that is, quitting in breach of contract, is not heavily penalized by custom as well as by law. "Contracts break down if workers accept insurance payments opportunistically in bad times and renege on premium payments by skipping out in good times" (Rosen, "Implicit Contracts," p. 1170). It is for this reason that I attach considerable importance to the finding in farm account books that wages in *quantum meruit* were in fact paid on incomplete contracts.

12. See Binswanger and Rosenzweig, *Contractual Arrangements.*

"lock-in effect."[13] The long-term contract acts in lieu of collateral for the debtor borrowing against his wages and acts as a screening device for the creditor.[14]

Finally, long-term contracts are, above all else, a means by which both sides seek to save on the costs of time spent in negotiation, in matching, in monitoring and enforcement, and in search.[15] While it is well known that a wage contract provides less incentive than a land-tenure contract for a worker to perform at maximum effort, the notion of "lock-in" as Hart and Holmstrom use the term—that is, of a relation-specific investment which has a higher value to both parties inside the relationship than outside it—provides what incentives there were.

Presumably all these factors played a role in motivating the use of monthly contracts on Massachusetts farms between 1750 and 1865. In my attempt to measure the incidence of farm labor contracts, to assess their relationship to seasonality, to analyze the pattern of seasonal and structural wage differentials, and to raise questions about the segmentation of the farm labor force,

13. Oliver Hart and Bengt Holmstrom, "The Theory of Contracts," in Truman F. Bewley, ed., *Advances in Economic Theory* (New York, 1987). The term "lock-in" as used by Hart and Holmstrom refers to "situations where a small number of parties make investments which are to some extent relationship-specific; that is, once made, they have a much higher value inside the relationship than outside. Given this 'lock-in' effect, each party will have some monopoly power ex post, although there may be plenty of competition ex ante before investments are sunk," p. 72.

Although Hart and Holmstrom did not have farm labor contracts in mind, Hart has suggested in private conversation with the author that among the "investments which are to some extent relationship-specific" (that is, among lock-in situations) may indeed be the commitment a farmer made to a worker who had foregone alternatives, left home and family, and traveled perhaps a considerable distance to move into a quid pro quo relationship where "a considerable amount of time may elapse between the quid and the quo," p. 71.

Clearly, the term lock-in is being used in the theory-of-contract literature in quite a different sense from the way the term has been used by economic historians of the postbellum South where it refers to the intricate web of cause and effect that produced "debt peonage and the power of the merchant to force farmers into overproduction of cotton" (Roger L. Ransom and Richard Sutch, *One Kind of Freedom: The Economic Consequences of Emancipation* [New York, 1977], p. 164).

14. It is in this connection that changes in the quality of the farm labor force after 1830, discussed below, may have been most telling. Monthly workers hired "off the road" had not been screened.

15. "As I have now little or no Hope of recovering Enoch, I mounted for Hopkinton p.m. to hire a man," wrote Ebenezer Parkman on 14 July 1768, after his hired hand quit. He scoured the countryside again the following March and April, riding from Westborough to Hopkinton, Grafton, Mansfield, Brookfield, Paxton, Needham, and Upton in search of a young man to live in and work for the season (Francis B. Walett, ed., *The Diary of Ebenezer Parkman, 1703–1782*, American Antiquarian Society [Worcester, 1974], part 2).

On the other side of the search process is Abner Sanger, a farm laborer from Keene, New Hampshire, who wrote in his journal on Saturday, 1 July 1775, "I go over to Captain Wyman's to see if they want me to work for them and let me take the pay in grain. Mrs. Wyman don't know, so I come home." He returned on Monday "to see if they will take work and let me have some grain. I have to wait until night." When he went back that night he learned that young Isaac Wyman, with whom he often worked, had come down with smallpox. On this occasion Sanger lost two days looking for work; and because he seldom if ever worked by the month, this desperate pattern recurred throughout his life. Abner Sanger's extraordinary journal is now annotated, edited, and published in full by Lois K. Stabler, ed., *Very Poor and of a Lo Make: The Journal of Abner Sanger* (Portsmouth, N.H., 1986).

this study is intended as a contribution to the unfinished task of understanding free labor, America's "peculiar institution."

3.1 The Quantitative Importance of Labor Contracts

The data base for this study is a sample of 692 monthly contracts I have drawn from 36 account books of farmers who used contract labor during the period, giving name of farmer, town of farmer, name of hired "hand," year and month of starting work, duration of contract, wage in dollars per month, and any additional information available including age and town of laborer, sudden quits or terminations, special characteristics of the arrangement, and so on. The sample of workers employed by these 36 farmers is augmented on occasion by a data base of 227 contract workers and 181 day workers hired to work on the Ward farm in Shrewsbury, Massachusetts, between 1787 and 1865.[16]

The first set of questions to address with the data is what they tell us about the quantitative importance of contract labor on Massachusetts farms in the period 1750 to 1865. Was there an increase in the number of farmers hiring contract workers? Did individual farmers increase the number of contract workers they hired per year? Did they attempt to increase the length of the contract term? Is there evidence of a shift, a substitution, away from day labor to monthly live-in labor?

Table 3.1 presents several alternative ways of calculating the incidence of contract labor on Massachusetts farms. Column 1 indicates the number of farm account books that appear in the sample for each five-year period. Column 2 counts the number of individual farmers with one or more contracts in each period. (For example, in the first period, two farmers accounted for the eighteen contracts, totalling 96 man-months; the other four books whose coverage spanned this period used no monthly labor in this quinquennium.) The number of contracts in each quinquennium is given in column 3. But number of contracts is an unreliable indicator of changes in the importance of contract labor for two reasons. First, column 3 is drawn from a sample—see column 1—whose size is itself changing as account books varying in time-span enter and leave the sample. Second, the number of contracts, because it does not acknowledge variations in length of contracts, misrepresents their importance. Twelve one-month contracts will loom large but may have less signifi-

16. The Ward Family Farm Laborers' File, compiled by Holly Izard under the supervision of Jack Larkin, Chief Historian, Research Department, Old Sturbridge Village, was generously made available to me by Mr. Larkin. See his discussion based on these data in "'Labor is the Great Thing in Farming': The Farm Laborers of the Ward Family of Shrewsbury, Massachusetts, 1787–1860," *Proceedings of the American Antiquarian Society,* 99 (1989), pp. 189–226. This same volume of the *Proceedings* contains two additional studies of farm laborers: Ross W. Beales, Jr., "The Reverend Ebenezer Parkman's Farm Workers, Westborough, Massachusetts, 1726–82," pp. 121–49; and Richard B. Lyman, Jr., "'What is Done in My Absence?': Levi Lincoln's Oakham, Massachusetts, Farm Workers, 1807–20," pp. 151–87.

Table 3.1 **The Incidence of Monthly Farm Labor Contracts, 1763 to 1865**

	(1)	(2)	(3)	(4)	(5)	(6)	(7)
					Average Man-Months of Contract Labor:		
Period	Number of Books	Number of Farmers with Contracts	Number of Contracts Specifying Length	Total Man-Months of Contract Labor	Per Contract (4)/(3)	Per Farmer (4)/(1)	Per Farmer with Contracts (4)/(2)
1763–69	6	2	18	96.0	5.3	16.0	48.0
1770–74	6	5	7	38.2	5.5	6.4	7.6
1775–79	6	3	7	22.2	3.2	3.7	7.4
1780–84	9	5	6	34.5	5.8	3.8	6.9
1785–89	11	4	14	80.2	5.7	7.3	20.1
1790–94	12	8	22	110.0	5.0	9.2	13.8
1795–99	12	6	23	114.5	5.0	9.5	19.1
1800–1804	15	7	34	179.2	5.3	11.9	25.6
1805–09	15	9	53	326.1	6.2	21.7	36.2
1810–14	14	10	69	374.7	5.4	26.8	37.5
1815–19	15	10	36	168.8	4.7	11.3	16.9
1820–24	14	12	63	283.3	4.5	20.2	23.6
1825–29	12	8	36	185.8	5.2	15.5	23.2
1830–34	13	9	38	188.6	5.0	14.5	20.9
1835–39	13	8	29	160.4	5.5	12.3	20.1
1840–44	15	11	47	277.3	5.9	18.5	25.2
1845–49	16	15	58	354.4	6.1	22.2	23.6
1850–54	13	7	34	168.2	4.9	12.9	24.0
1855–59	11	3	8	44.8	5.6	4.1	14.9
1860–65	5	2	15	68.8	4.6	13.8	34.4

Notes: Contracts that extended beyond a calendar year are assigned to the year in which they began. The contracts are drawn from a sample of thirty-six account books for thirty-six farmers, all of whom hired contract labor, but not necessarily in every year covered by their books. Of all the contracts in the sample, six hundred and twenty specified length. Three, dated 1713, 1752, and 1753, are omitted from the table.

Source: Rothenberg sample of farm account books.

cance than one twelve-month contract in terms of the insurance, hoarding, interlinking, screening, and cost-saving motives for hiring labor by the month.

Once the number of man-months under contract in each period is known (column 4), then we can compensate for shifting sample size by calculating man-months per contract (column 5), man-months per account book or per sample farmer (column 6), and man-months per contracting farmer (column 7).

As noted above, not all sample farmers hired contract labor in every five-year period. It is the presence of zero entries in column 6 that accounts for the difference between it and column 7. Both measures are given because Table 3.1 is measuring, in effect, the diffusion of an innovation and, in a diffusion measure, zero entries are relevant.

The finding in column 5 that for one hundred years farm labor contracts, on average, did not lengthen much beyond five months is supported by Table 3.2, a frequency distribution of contracts by length. There is no discernible shift to more frequent use of nine- to twelve-month contracts, no marked increase in the proportion of annual as opposed to seasonal commitments. Between 60 and 75 percent of contracts, depending on decade, ran six months or less.[17] This finding suggests that the motives for long commitments discussed above—particularly the insurance motive, which is closely related in the theoretical literature to the Hart-Holmstrom notion of lock-in—were overwhelmed by other factors, principally by the inexorable seasonality of New England agriculture.[18]

3.2 Contract Labor and the Seasonality of Agricultural Employment

A decade ago, Carville Earle and Ronald Hoffman published a study in which America's early and successful industrialization was attributed to a surplus, not a scarcity, of unskilled labor made cheap by long periods of seasonal layoffs in agriculture.[19] While recent research indicates that there is much to fault in their analysis, it is to be acknowledged for having put the seasonality of agriculture at the very center of a model of American industrial development.[20]

17. Man-months per contract averaged 5.2 across quinquennia, 4.9 when averaged annually.

18. What I am suggesting here is that there is a difference between one long contract and two sequential short contracts. It will be recalled that the theory of labor contracts "is based on the idea that a firm offers its risk-averse workers wage and employment insurance via a long-term contract. . . . If the lock-in effect that is responsible for the long-term relationship in the first place is small, . . . the insurance element of the contract will be put under severe pressure" (Hart and Holmstrom, "Theory of Contracts," pp. 106, 110).

19. Carville Earle and Ronald Hoffman, "The Foundation of the Modern Economy: Agriculture and the Costs of Labor in the United States and England, 1800–60," *American Historical Review,* 85 (Dec. 1980), pp. 1055–94.

20. First, recent research based on harvest wage premia finds considerably less seasonality, not more, in American grain agriculture than in British, a result which undermines the Earle-Hoffman

Table 3.2 Frequency Distribution of Monthly Contracts by Length in Months, by Decade, 1763 to 1865

		Percentage Distribution			
Years	Total Number	0 to 3 months	Over 3 to 6 months	Over 6 to 9 months	Over 9 to 12 months
1763–69	18	39%	22%	22%	17%
1770–79	14	43	43	7	7
1780–89	20	40	20	10	30
1790–99	45	36	36	18	11
1800–1809	87	31	30	21	17
1810–19	105	34	36	22	7
1820–29	99	36	34	23	6
1830–39	67	22	43	28	6
1840–49	105	20	46	23	12
1850–65	57	42	33	12	12

Note: Of all the contracts in the sample, 620 specified length. Three, dated 1713, 1752, and 1753, are omitted from the table.
Source: Rothenberg sample of farm account books.

In their recent study, Stanley Engerman and Claudia Goldin estimate the loss of national income due to seasonal unemployment in both agriculture and manufacturing, and therefore the "fillip" added to economic growth late in the nineteenth century as a consequence of "surmounting" seasonality, a process they confirm from the decline of the seasonal wage premium between 1880 and 1900.[21] While the credit for reducing seasonality goes principally to the shift out of agriculture, to structural changes within agriculture (mechanization and changes in crop mix), and to the seasonal migration of workers between sectors whose seasonal demands for labor "meshed," Engerman and

explanation for the relative capital-deepening of American and British industrial technology (David Dollar and Kenneth Sokoloff, "Agricultural Seasonality and the Organization of Manufacturing in Early Industrial Economies: The Contrast Between Britain and the U.S.," Working Paper, University of California at Los Angeles, 1991). Second, seasonally unemployed farm hands in the Midwest, in the very grain-growing regions Earle and Hoffman target, sought jobs not in manufacturing but in logging, teamstering, droving, or moved down-river looking for work as itinerant farm workers. If they could not land one of those jobs, they wintered in town, dissipating all their savings on room and board, or stayed on a farm all winter, even for no pay, but with free room and board. See David E. Schob, *Hired Hands and Plowboys: Farm Labor in the Midwest, 1815–60* (Urbana, 1975), pp. 255–56. Lastly, the Earle-Hoffman story depends on the degree to which there was sufficient "meshing" between the seasonal patterns of agriculture and those of manufacturing in the early stages of industrial development. A recent study of seasonality in the late nineteenth century concludes, "After weighing all the evidence, we believe [seasonal unemployment] was not reduced by a movement of laborers across sectors having seasons that meshed" (Stanley Engerman and Claudia Goldin, "Seasonality in Nineteenth Century Labor Markets," NBER Historical Factors in Long-Run Growth Working Paper no. 20 [Jan. 1991], p. 21). There is likely to have been even less meshing in the early years of the century.

21. Engerman and Goldin, "Seasonality in Nineteenth Century Labor Markets," p. 3.

Goldin acknowledge that annual labor contracts may have played a role in diminishing seasonal layoffs within agriculture by 1900.[22]

To posit some relationship between the diffusion of long-term labor contracts and reduced seasonality in agricultural employment is not to posit a direction of causation. Long-term (and off-season) contracts may have been a response to output shifts which lengthened the crop year. Or strategies to lengthen the crop year may have been a response to conditions in the labor market (heightened risk-aversion, for example) which favored long-term and off-season contracts. Or, both the extended use of contracts and the shift in output mix may have been the result of some third factor, say, the growth and spread of markets. While the choice among these causal scenarios is beyond the scope of this paper, it raises three empirical questions that can be addressed with the data presented here. Did the length of labor contracts increase over time to provide more off-season employment? Did the frequency of off-season (winter) contracts, regardless of their length, increase over time? Did farmers alter their crop mix to produce outputs that lengthened the crop year?

It has already been remarked that man-months per contract did not lengthen over time (Table 3.1, col. 5) nor did the frequency of annual contracts increase over time (Table 3.2). There are 77 nine- to twelve-month contracts in my sample—over 12 percent of the 620 contracts in which length was specified—but that number failed to increase over a period in which, as will be discussed below, contract workers accounted for a far larger proportion of man-days of hired farm labor than did day workers.

But even short-term monthly contracts can have worked to smooth seasonal discontinuities in agricultural employment if it can be shown that an increasing proportion of them began in or extended into the winter months. Overall, more than 24 percent of the man-months under contract were for winter work.[23] The number of man-months of off-season (winter) work increased markedly from 21 in the 1760s to 151 in the 1840s, but as a percentage of total man-months there is no evidence of a rising time-trend (see Table 3.3).

Table 3.4, a calendar of farm activities drawn from several unusually detailed farm diaries, daybooks, and account books serves to identify those tasks reserved for the winter months of November through March. The hewing, drawing, and scoring of timber, and the chopping, cutting, and carting of wood took up so much of every winter day that these tasks alone might have

22. "About 25 percent of all nonfamily farm workers in 1900 were unemployed sometime during the year and . . . most of these workers experienced 3 to 4 months of unemployment. Whether or not many of the 75 percent who did not report unemployment during the year were involved in a meshing of the sectors through migration, depends on the proportion of farm laborers who found yearly employment in agriculture. Reliable sources indicate that about 25 to 35 percent of all farm laborers were hired on annual contract, although some additional fraction may have found yearly employment in the agricultural sector on monthly, seasonal, and daily bases" (Engerman and Goldin, "Seasonality in Nineteenth Century Labor Markets," pp. 20–21).

23. "Winter" is defined here as the five months from November through March, so 24 percent of the man-months under contract were for 42 percent of the months.

Table 3.3 **Winter Work on Monthly Contract, 1763 to 1865**

Date	(1) Number of Man-Months of Winter Work	(2) Total Man-Months Worked	(1)/(2) Winter Months Worked as a percentage of Total Man-Months Worked
1763–69	21 months	96 months	22%
1770–79	11	60	18
1780–89	37	115	33
1790–99	64	147	44
1800–1809	143	500	29
1810–19	104	544	19
1820–29	82	477	17
1830–39	66	349	19
1840–49	151	636	24
1850–59	72	213	34
1860–65	22	69	31
Total	777	3,210	24

Note: Winter is defined as November through March.
Source: Rothenberg sample of farm account books.

kept a hired hand fully occupied. Market trips were sometimes left until winter because sledding loads of produce or livestock on snow and ice was much faster than hauling it in wagons over rutted or muddy roads. Threshing was typically done in the winter: 100 bushels of small grains (wheat, rye, oats, and barley), flailed at the rate of 5 bushels a day, would have occupied one man full time for nearly a month, and several of the farmers sampled produced considerably more than 100 bushels of small grains.[24] Corn did not suffer, as did the small grains and hays, from being left late in the field and could be harvested, cut, stacked, and husked in winter. The first snow each winter was believed to impart special nutrients to the soil and that, presumably, accounts for the many instances of plowing in December. And there were always hogs to butcher, sugar maples to tap, brooms to make, fields to manure, cider to press, and winter rye and wheat to sow.

While the incidence of long-term and off-season contracts did not increase, there was a marked shift in the composition of output which worked to extend the crop year. Plant species cannot, of course, be "deseasonalized." They

24. "New England farmers hailed mainly from England and Scotland and brought with them the strong preference for flailing that dominated pre-mechanical threshing systems throughout the British Isles. . . . The slower and more individualistic flailing technique suited regional needs and became a common task carried out during the long New England winters" (J. Sanford Rikoon, *Threshing in the Midwest, 1820–1940* [Bloomington, Ind., 1988], p. 2). The estimate of 5 bushels a day appears on p. 7. Outputs of up to 400 bushels of small grains are reported for some of my sample farmers in U.S. Census Office, Seventh Census (Manuscript), Massachusetts, 1850, Productions of Agriculture.

Table 3.4 **A Calendar of Farm Work**

Farm Chore	January	February	March	April	May	June	July	August	September	October	November	December
Altering animals				x	x							
Berrying								x				
Birthing calves, lambs, piglets	x	x	x	x								
Breaking up soil					x							
Bringing in cattle for winter									x	x		
Burning over/clearing new land						x		x				
Butchering	x	x	x	x			x		x	x	x	x
Carding wool	x											
Carting hay to markets		x	x	x			x		x	x	x	x
Carting wheat to markets								x				
Carting/spreading dung				x	x	x	x			x	x	x
Chopping wood	x	x	x	x		x					x	x
Cutting ice	x										x	x
Cutting & hanging tobacco								x	x			
Destroy caterpillars					x							
Digging carrots, turnips, etc.											x	
Digging potatoes		x							x	x	x	
Digging stones				x							x	x
Drawing logs to sawmill	x	x	x								x	x
Dressing flax	x											
Gathering poultry & turkey eggs			x									
Getting in stalks and rowen				x					x	x		
Grafting fruit trees				x	x				x			

Harrowing tillage ground				x	x	x			x	x		x
Harvesting corn, beans							x		x	x	x	x
Haying					x		x	x	x	x		
Hewing timber/drawing logs	x		x	x	x					x	x	x
Highway/road work		x	x	x	x	x				x	x	
Hilling/half-hilling corn			x	x		x	x					
Hoeing corn, potatoes, beans				x	x	x	x					
Husking, shelling corn	x								x	x	x	
Make brooms from broomcorn	x											
Making cider	x							x	x	x	x	
Mending dams, walls, fences				x	x			x	x	x	x	
Milling wheat												x
Mowing bushes				x		x		x	x			
Mowing hay meadow						x	x	x	x	x		
Picking hops									x			
Plant broomcorn, cranberries					x							
Plant cabbages, sweet corn, squash				x								
Plant peas, beets, carrots, parsnips				x								
Plant watermelon, cucumbers					x							
Planting corn				x	x							
Planting potatoes, beans, etc.					x							
Planting tobacco						x						
Plowing tillage, meadow, garden				x	x	x	x	x	x	x	x	x
Pruning, trimming fruit trees				x								
Pulling bark for tanning						x						

(*continued*)

Table 3.4 (continued)

Farm Chore	January	February	March	April	May	June	July	August	September	October	November	December
Reaping/cradling oats, rye, wheat			x		x		x	x	x			
Shaking/picking apple trees									x	x		
Shearing sheep					x	x						
Shoemaking		x										
Shoot wild geese											x	
Shoot wild pigeons			x									
Sledding wood	x	x	x								x	x
Sowing clover seed			x	x		x		x				
Sowing flaxseed				x								
Sowing oats				x	x							
Sowing rye (winter & summer)					x	x		x	x	x		
Sowing wheat (winter & summer)				x				x	x			x
Stable and fatten cattle												x
Stripping tobacco	x									x		
Take calves from cows			x									
Taking cattle to outpastures				x	x	x						
Tapping maple trees		x	x									
Threshing barley, oats, rye	x	x	x					x	x	x	x	x
Washing sheep				x		x						
Winnowing grains									x			

Sources: Account and Day Books of William Hosmer of Westfield, Julian Robbins of Deerfield, David Hoyt of Deerfield, and Harrison Howard of North Bridgewater.

carry their seasonality in their genetic codes: corn matures in 2,000 growing-degree-days, and no reorganization of labor on the farm will alter that.[25] But in the interest of distributing labor inputs and farm income more evenly across the year, the plant mix can be diversified. An important example was the cultivation of broomcorn in the Connecticut River Valley. The home manufacture of brooms for urban markets not only linked farmers to industrial out-work (as palm-leaf braiding linked their wives), but provided remunerative (and very labor-intensive) winter work for males.[26]

When the broomcorn bonanza faded, tobacco took its place in the valley. As early as September 1738, and hardly aware that it was a harbinger of momentous things to come, Ebenezer Parkman noted in his diary a shipment of 500 hogsheads of tobacco being sent down river en route to the West Indies. In 1850 Massachusetts farmers were growing 138,000 pounds of the stuff and, by 1860, 3.2 million pounds. Shade-grown tobacco (for cigar wrappers) had become the region's major agricultural staple, cultivated specifically for the New York market, and remained so for a hundred years. What makes tobacco singularly important for a study of farm labor is that its cultivation, picking, smoke-drying, leaf selection, and packing are highly labor- intensive. Given the heavy labor requirements of the crop, the case has been made that its success is inextricably linked to the creation of a "permanent agricultural proletariat" in Massachusetts by the mid-nineteenth century.[27]

The making of brooms and the packing of tobacco provided off-season employment, but their growing seasons competed for labor with all other crops grown in the regular season. On the other hand, the double-cropping of rye and (to a lesser extent) of wheat allowed cultivation to be spread across the year: the winter crop was sown in August and September (one farmer even sowed Black Sea wheat in December) and was brought in in March and April; the spring crop was sown in May and was brought in in July. Grass seed, usually sown in the spring, could just as well be sown in August, as one farmer noted, just after haying.

In addition, with the expansion and integration of markets, New England farm families were expanding their traditional diet of baked beans, cheese, rye-'n-injun bread, Indian pudding, potatoes, salt pork, salt beef, and cider,

25. Growing-degree-days are the cumulative number of degrees Fahrenheit above the "base temperature" (which is the temperature at which a crop begins to grow). Corn begins to grow at 50 degrees F. To calculate the number of summer days it takes for corn to mature, divide 2,000 by the difference between the actual summer temperature and 50 degrees. The enormous effort devoted to corn hybridization has increased yields (over 400 percent between 1930 and 1980!) and pest resistance, but has not affected corn's "seasonality." See Jack Ralph Kloppenburg, Jr., *First the Seed: The Political Economy of Plant Biotechnology, 1492–2000* (New York, 1988), pp. 5, 120, 168.

26. Broomcorn cultivation apparently required two to three times as much labor as corn (Percy W. Bidwell and John I. Falconer, *History of Agriculture in the Northern United States, 1620–1860* [New York, 1941, reprint], p. 245).

27. On tobacco cultivation in the Connecticut River Valley, see Christopher Clark, *The Roots of Rural Capitalism: Western Massachusetts, 1780–1860* (Ithaca, 1990), pp. 295–304.

by growing and eating and marketing poultry, winter wheat, winter rye, fluid milk, fresh butter, green herbs, celery, rutabagas, beets, winter squashes, pumpkins, mangel wurtzels, carrots, parsnips, turnips, cabbages, onions, tomatoes, asparagus, string beans, green peas; peaches, pears, rhubarb, strawberries, cherries, damson plums, quinces, cranberries, wine grapes; salmon, smelts, alewives, clams, haddock, shad, and mackerel. The cultivation of some of these crops did expand the growing season: turnips could be planted in August and pulled in November, asparagus was picked in May, cranberries in September, apples in October.[28]

The increased emphasis on dairy products alone—on fluid milk and butter for nearby urban markets, and on cheese for local cheese factories—meant that more cows were wintered, fattened, kept in milk for most of the year, and stall-fed, a year-round commitment of labor time. So commonplace that it was rarely mentioned in farm account books, milking was nonetheless "the most time-consuming chore."[29] It is still not clear to me who did the milking on Massachusetts farms—wives and daughters, or sons and hired hands—but the heaviest demands dairying made upon hired labor must have been in activities other than milking. These non-milking jobs included cleaning stalls and barns, washing milk cans, delivering milk, and, most of all, in restructuring farm space—mending fences, year-round stabling and stall-feeding of cattle, plowing and seeding and cultivating meadow, upgrading pasture, growing and preparing better feeds, collecting and spreading dung, and so on.[30]

Despite a variety of techniques for mitigating seasonality, its persistence can be read in the persistence of seasonal wage differentials written, on occasion, into annual contracts. In 1771, Joseph Barnard of Deerfield agreed to pay Daniel Rider 24s a month ($4) from January to mid-March, 36s a month ($6) from April to October, and 24s ($4) a month from December to March. In 1788, John Hill's contract with David Hoyt of Deerfield fixed his monthly

28. See Sarah McMahon, "A Comfortable Subsistence: The Changing Composition of Diet in Rural New England, 1620–1840," *William & Mary Quarterly,* 3rd series, 42 (Jan. 1985), pp. 28–65; "Laying Foods By: Gender, Dietary Decisions, and the Technology of Food Preservation in New England Households, 1750–1850" (manuscript, Bowdoin College, 1989); and "'All Things in Their Proper Season': Seasonal Rhythms of Diet in Nineteenth Century New England," *Agricultural History,* 63 (Spring 1989), pp. 130–51.

29. Jeremy Atack and Fred Bateman, *To Their Own Soil: Agriculture in the Antebellum North* (Ames, Iowa, 1987), p. 153.

30. See Fred Bateman, "Labor Inputs and Productivity in American Dairy Agriculture, 1850–1910," *Journal of Economic History,* 29 (June 1969), pp. 206–29. There is some question about gender roles in dairy farming. Bidwell and Falconer quote the following passage from a tract published by the Western Reserve Historical Society: "Except in a Yankee family, no man or boy could be induced to milk the cows, it being regarded as woman's work. But wherever a New Englander was found he and the boys did the 'pailing' of the cows" (*History of Agriculture,* p. 163). On the other hand, I have found only two references in Massachusetts farm account books to men milking, but it may be the case that "chores," of which milking was one, were sufficiently taken for granted not to be entered in account books. Schob quotes *The Prairie Farmer,* "If the hands had worked hard and well [at harvesting] they were not expected to milk the cows prior to dinner" (*Hired Hands and Plowboys,* p. 93). But this suggests that men in the Midwest *did* do the milking.

wages at $11.67 in spring and summer, $6.67 in fall, and $5 in winter. James Bean, Jr., worked for Samuel Plumer of Epping, New Hampshire, for $10 a month from April to December of 1805 and for $6 a month from December to the following April. William Till worked for Charles Phelps, Jr., of Hadley for $6 a month between January and April of 1811, and $11.50 a month from May to November. William Rice worked a year for Phelps in 1814 for $14 a month from April to November, $10 a month from November to January, $12 a month from January to March. In Plymouth, Michael Jacobs in 1847 agreed to pay Henry Barns $8 for the month of October and $6 for each of the following five winter months. William Dowd, who worked faithfully for William Odiorne of Billerica twelve months a year from 1848 to 1853, was paid $14 a month from April to November and $8 a month from December to March.

Long-term contracts like these, in which seasonal wage differentials were written in, appear to have been rare: 90 percent of the 77 nine- to twelve-month contracts in my sample stipulated a flat monthly rate.[31] But it is clear that some of the most interesting issues raised by monthly contracts are to be found in the structure of wage differentials.

3.3 Wage Differentials Between Contract and Day Labor

The structure of day wages in antebellum Massachusetts agriculture was complex and rested, I have argued elsewhere, upon stratification by task.[32] The connection between task and season in farming is so intimate that it may be difficult to disentangle them, but that there is a distinction worth making between them is seen by comparing July/August day wages for non-harvest work with July/August day wages for harvest work (that is, mowing, haying, and reaping). Holding season constant in this way, wages for harvest work were on average 30 percent higher.[33] Overlaying the season- and task-specific structure of farm wages was yet a third pattern: the differentials between day

31. But the seasonal differential is implicit in the flat monthly rate. Workers earned a wage below their marginal revenue product (the cost of employment insurance) in season and above it (the indemnity) off-season.

Engerman and Goldin assume that the flat monthly wage is a weighted average of the seasonal wage and the off-season wage. Assuming the season to be six months, then "$M_a = .5M_s + .5M_{ns}$, where M_a is the average monthly wage on an annual contract, M_s is the average monthly wage for seasonal labor, and M_{ns} is the implicit average monthly wage during the off season" ("Seasonality in Nineteenth Century Labor Markets," p. 7 and table 2, part B).

From the seasonal premia expressly written into annual contracts, it is clear that farmers often thought in terms of three seasons, not two, the length of which varied from season to season and from farmer to farmer.

32. "The Emergence of Farm Labor Markets."

33. A further illustration of the need to distinguish between season and task concerns wages for the month of June. June is of course a summer month, but the dominant tasks done in June were all low-paying tasks—hoeing, half-hilling, weeding, and picking corn. For the purpose of calculating the harvest premium, to include June with July and August would bias the differential downward.

wages and monthly per diem wages. It is to this that we now turn our attention.

That the per diem wage of workers on monthly contracts was considerably below the daily wage of day workers is well known and much—though not all—of the gap is easily explained. Since as a rule contract workers lived with the farm family, it was understood that they received part of their wages in room, board, washing, mending (and, on occasion, clothing, boots, militia training days and election days off, and the use of a horse for a visit home), while day workers "found" for themselves.[34] To make day wages and live-in wages comparable, researchers have valued the income in kind of contract workers at approximately 50 percent of their money wages.[35]

But multiplying monthly wages by a factor of 1.5, as did Larkin, hardly closes the gap between contract and day wages. The actual differential between (non-harvest) day wages and monthly per diems was far larger—on average 80 percent (see Table 3.6, col. 4, below)—suggesting that more than the imputed cost of room and board separated the per day wages of day labor and contract labor. Tables 3.5 and 3.6 will suggest that part of the unexplained differential is a seasonal premium, part a harvest premium—neither of which is fully captured by monthly wages—and part reflects the working of a dual labor market in Massachusetts agriculture.

Table 3.5 aggregates to the level of decadal averages two sets of wage data I have collected from farm account books: monthly per diems (that is, monthly wages divided by twenty-six working days per month) from the sample of labor contracts, and nearly 3,200 day wages from my previous study of day labor. Of the monthly contracts there were 553, over the period 1764 to 1860, that were fully specified, that is, that gave the monthly wage,

34. Schob gives this staggering description of a day's food consumed by hired hands on a midwestern farm: "For Breakfast—Coffee or tea, with cream and sugar, just as much as is desired. Fried bacon, and in the season, eggs always. Cold beef or hash, or perhaps fish, and often fresh meat. Irish or sweet potatoes, good butter and plenty of it; cheese, ditto; pickles, stewed dried fruit, light and white flour bread, cornbread, or hot cakes, hot biscuit, often pies or cakes. For Dinner—Coffee, sweet milk, or sour, or buttermilk, as may be preferred. Boiled pork, beef, potatoes, turnips, cabbages, beets, &c. White loaf bread and butter, cheese, pickles, stewed fruit, and almost always pie or pastry. Supper—The cold meats and vegetables from dinner, or perhaps a hot dish of meats or fish, or some broiled chickens, and coffee or tea, of course, with bread, as before, to which add a little 'tea cake'. At each meal, all the condiments and provocatives of appetite, such as mustard, catchup vinegar, pepper, salt, pickles, &c, are usually on the table. During harvest time, a lunch in the forenoon and afternoon, of cold meats or fowls, with fresh wheaten loaves or biscuits, cakes or pies, and often accompanied by hot coffee, with cream and sugar, always as a matter of course." Quoted from the *American Agriculturist,* 1849, in Schob, *Hired Hands and Plowboys,* p. 97.

35. In the database for his study of laborers on the Ward Farm, Larkin multiplies monthly wages by a factor of 1.5 to account for the imputed value of room and board. Earle and Hoffman adjusted monthly live-in wages by a factor of 1.33 to 1.45 ("Foundation of the Modern Economy," p. 1069). The Department of Agriculture series on farm wages per month, 1866–1927, showed a slight but steady decline in the differential between with and without board, from 54 percent to 41 percent and averaging 44 percent over the period. U.S. Department of Labor, *History of Wages in the United States From Colonial Times to 1928,* Bureau of Labor Statistics Bulletin No. 499 (Washington, D. C., Oct. 1929), Table D–2, p. 227.

year, starting month, and duration of the contract.[36] The monthly per diems were entered for each month for the duration of each contract.[37] Day wages for mowing, reaping, and haying were averaged and entered as harvest wages in July and August of the year in which they were observed. Non-harvest day wages are the day wages for all other tasks and were entered in the month and year in which they were observed.

In Table 3.6 the monthly data in Table 3.5 are aggregated, and the ratios are calculated that define the overlying pattern of wage differentials. The ratio of (non-harvest) day wages to monthly per diems (which might be called the day-labor premium) averaged 1.8; the ratio of harvest day wages to non-harvest day wages (the harvest premium) averaged 1.3; the ratio of harvest day wages to monthly per diems (which might be called the spot-market premium) averaged 2.3. And the seasonal premium, the ratio of peak-month wages to trough-month wages, averaged 1.3 for contract workers and 1.6 for (non-harvest) day labor. Of all these, the only differential that narrowed during the antebellum period was the seasonal differential for contract workers, from 1.5 in the 1770s to 1.1 in the 1840s.

If decomposing the differential into its several components explains its magnitude, it does not explain its persistence. Why did wage differentials so lavishly favoring day workers persist for ten decades? Was it more difficult to recruit day workers than contract workers? Did day workers, residing off the farm, have to be compensated for travel costs? For the costs of job search? For leaving their own farms? For bearing the brunt of seasonal unemployment? Or does the persistence of the wage differential owe something to group characteristics distinguishing the populations of day and monthly workers and relevant to their relative productivities? In the next section, a case study will cast light on the proposition that the persistence of wage differentials between day and monthly workers not otherwise explained testifies to a considerable degree of segmentation in the farm labor market.

3.4 The Comparative Demographics of Farm Laborers: The Case of the Ward Farm

Each of the laborers on the Ward farm in Shrewsbury, Massachusetts, a farm that used a great deal of both day and contract labor from 1787 to 1890, has been identified at Old Sturbridge Village by linkage to genealogical records. Comparison of the two groups with respect to age, marital status, and place of birth strongly supports the conclusion that these two segments of the farm labor force were being drawn from two quite different populations, in

36. In the few cases where wage and starting month were given but duration was not, the wage was applied to the starting month only.

37. The per diems were entered each month for the duration of the contract even in the case of quits, since it is the intentions of the parties to the wage-setting process that interests us here.

Table 3.5 **The Seasonality of Farm Wages, Massachusetts, 1760s through 1850s: Day Wages of Contract Workers, Day Workers, and Harvest Workers (decadal averages, in dollars)**

Years	Category	January	February	March	April	May	June	July	August	September	October	November	December
1764–69	Monthly Per Diem	.199	.199	.207	.208	.209	.205	.205	.205	.205	.203	.195	.188
	Day Work	.360	.338	.330	.385	.412	.418	.415	.424	.367	.380	.434	.468
	Harvest							.455	.455				
	N = 17												
1770–79	Monthly Per Diem	.158	.161	.161	.224	.241	.238	.238	.238	.234	.217	.187	.187
	Day Work	.330	.365	.368	.398	.393	.396	.436	.388	.411	.384	n.a.	.388
	Harvest							.484	.484				
	N = 10												
1780–89	Monthly Per Diem	.187	.197	.251	.245	.246	.249	.255	.262	.238	.231	.205	.188
	Day Work	.330	.290	.383	.499	.437	.404	.423	.417	.330	.260	.520	.415
	Harvest							.493	.493				
	N = 16												
1790–99	Monthly Per Diem	.208	.208	.243	.241	.250	.246	.272	.263	.258	.241	.200	.216
	Day Work	.323	.375	.427	.439	.437	.460	.504	.538	.531	.386	.476	.382
	Harvest							.589	.589				
	N = 36												
1800–1809	Monthly Per Diem	.273	.270	.302	.351	.351	.369	.365	.357	.351	.342	.318	.295
	Day Work	.432	.531	.532	.569	.531	.571	.653	.572	.611	.490	.464	.528
	Harvest							.700	.700				
	N = 77												

1810–19	Monthly Per Diem	.332	.341	.328	.366	.391	.395	.403	.401	.397	.371	.383	.360
	Day Work	.606	.594	.658	.633	.678	.731	.796	.828	.711	.687	.645	.621
	Harvest							.919	.919				
	N = 95												
1820–29	Monthly Per Diem	.303	.319	.331	.362	.370	.361	.356	.359	.355	.344	.317	.328
	Day Work	.700	.563	.655	.684	.667	.625	.718	.698	.593	.610	.624	.666
	Harvest							.867	.867				
	N = 89												
1830–39	Monthly Per Diem	.354	.382	.379	.407	.429	.443	.445	.455	.436	.453	.383	.368
	Day Work	.681	.635	.563	.704	.716	.762	.880	.695	.701	.678	.746	.730
	Harvest							.991	.991				
	N = 63												
1840–49	Monthly Per Diem	.457	.463	.462	.483	.491	.501	.507	.498	.493	.503	.505	.453
	Day Work	.604	.612	.767	.750	.762	.802	.901	1.00	.859	.778	.760	.695
	Harvest							1.03	1.03				
	N = 102												
1850–59	Monthly Per Diem	.360	.348	.383	.490	.502	.502	.501	.502	.487	.478	.424	.375
	Day Work	.645	.700	.855	1.25	.855	.830	.950	1.06	1.08	.821	.500	.835
	Harvest							1.15	1.15				
	N = 48												

Notes: Monthly Per Diem is a decadal average of contract wages per month, divided by 26, which have been entered for every month of each contract. Day Work is a decadal average of the wages paid to day workers for all tasks other than haying, reaping, and mowing, for the month in which it appears in the table. Harvest is a decadal average of the wages for the tasks of mowing, haying, and reaping only, and performed by day workers in July and August. N is the number of fully specified contracts stipulating year, starting month, duration, and wage. The total number of such contracts was 553. n.a. = not available.

Sources: Day wages and monthly contract wages are from Rothenberg sample of farm account books. For sources of day wages, see my "The Emergence of Farm Labor Markets and the Transformation of the Rural Economy: Massachusetts, 1750–1855," *Journal of Economic History,* 48 (Sept. 1988), pp. 562–63.

Table 3.6 **Harvest, Seasonal, and Day Wage Differentials, 1760s through 1850s, by Decade (wages in dollars per day)**

	(1)	(2)	(3)	(4)	(5)	(6)	(7)	(8)
					Harvest Premium		Seasonal Premium	
Years	Average Monthly Per Diem	Average Non-harvest Day Wage	Average Harvest Day Wage	Day Wage Premium/Monthly Per Diem (2)/(1)	Harvest Wage/ Non-harvest Day Wage (3)/(2)	Harvest Wage Monthly Per Diem (3)/(1)	High Month/Low Month for Non-harvest Day Wages	High Month/Low Month for Monthly Per Diems
1764–69	0.202	0.394	0.455	1.95	1.15	2.25	1.42	1.11
1770–79	0.207	0.387	0.484	1.87	1.25	2.34	1.32	1.53
1780–89	0.230	0.392	0.493	1.70	1.26	2.14	1.92	1.40
1790–99	0.237	0.440	0.589	1.86	1.34	2.49	1.67	1.36
1800–1809	0.329	0.540	0.700	1.64	1.30	2.13	1.51	1.37
1810–19	0.372	0.682	0.919	1.83	1.35	2.47	1.39	1.23
1820–29	0.342	0.650	0.867	1.90	1.33	2.54	1.28	1.22
1830–39	0.411	0.708	0.991	1.72	1.40	2.41	1.56	1.29
1840–49	0.485	0.774	1.03	1.60	1.33	2.12	1.63	1.12
1850–59	0.446	0.866	1.15	1.94	1.32	2.57	2.50	1.44
Means				1.80	1.30	2.35	1.62	1.31

Notes: Column 1 is based on per month wages for contract labor divided by 26. Monthly per diems were entered for every month for the anticipated duration of each contract, even in the case of sudden quits. Column 2 is based on day wages for all tasks except haying, mowing, and reaping. Column 3 is based on day wages for haying, mowing, and reaping.

Source: Table 3.5.

which case some of the pay differential, or at any rate its persistence, may be explained as the working of a dual labor market.[38]

Table 3.7 summarizes personal characteristics in the Ward Farm Laborers' Biographical File by decade, from 1787 to 1866.[39] Taking the period as a whole, half of the day laborers, but only one-quarter of the contract laborers, were born in Shrewsbury. The proportion of foreign- born contract workers was twice that of day workers. The average age of day workers was 41.6 years and several men were in their seventies, but the average age of contract workers was only 26.5 years.[40] Over 80 percent of the day workers were married, while over 86 percent of the contract workers were unmarried.

But the period should not be taken as a whole, for 1830 was a turning point. Before 1830, nearly 70 percent of contract workers came from within twenty miles of Shrewsbury; after 1830 it was less than 10 percent. After 1830, the foreign-born came not from England and Scotland but from Ireland and French Canada. The rate of sudden quits rose from 16 percent to 33 percent.

38. I do not intend, by the use of the term "dual labor market," to engage in a political controversy over whether the market for rural labor "worked," in the neoclassical sense. After all, unlike race, ethnicity, gender, and educational deficits, the contract workers who were too young, too single, too uprooted, and too Irish or Acadian, would in time become as old, as married, and as "American" as more respected workers. Nevertheless, in the short run they were identifiable as having more limited options.

39. Property holdings may be as important as place of birth, marital status, and age in describing these two populations. In fact, the Wards' day laborers were poor: one-third were without property in the 1790s, over half in the 1800s, over two-thirds in the 1810s, and all were propertyless in the 1820s and again in the 1850s (Larkin, "'Labor is the Great Thing in Farming,'" p. 205).

In this respect, too, the day laborers' status was as ambiguous in nineteenth-century Shrewsbury as in early modern England, where day laborers were at the very bottom of the agricultural ladder, yet were looked to for special skills. According to Kussmaul, in *Servants in Husbandry,* "The hierarchy of farmworkers ran from the farmer's sons down to servants [-in-husbandry] and finally to [day] labourers. . . . To be a servant was to be a potential farmer, but to be a labourer was to be a realized failure" (p. 80). On the other hand, she notes elsewhere that "skilled . . . work continued to be done by day-labourers" (p. 101).

40. Seven contract workers and eight day workers were boys under 16 years of age; the youngest, a day worker, was 11. The reasons in 1836 for "putting out" young George Homer, age 12, to work for the Wards for thirty-five months may have been the same as those in Plymouth two centuries earlier: to teach him to read and write and an artisan skill, "to bring him up in his imploymt of husbandry," to remove him from an impoverished home, or to be his guardian if he had been orphaned. See John Demos, *A Little Commonwealth: Family Life in Plymouth Colony* (New York, 1970). The quote is from p. 71.

While I do not know how George Homer fared in the Ward household, there are some hints about the effectiveness of such apprenticeships to be gleaned from the account book of Jabez B. Low, a farmer and comb maker of Leominster, Massachusetts:

1813 November the 19: Phineas Prowty come to live with me and will be 15 years in february Next the 15 day. 1815, Febr 4: the above Phineas went from School. and I know not whare.

1815 June 21: Elize Chandler Come to live with me and was 8 years old th 12 of April Last. 1818 Decr 16: Elize Chandler Left my house & hath not Returned.

1820 June 19: Persis Warner come to live with me & was 13 years old the 24 of Febr Last. November 18: Carried Persis to hir Fathers & Left hir.

1830 Septr 7th: Andrew Low Left my house when I was gone to Albany and without a justifiable cause.

Table 3.7 **Comparative Demographics of Contract and Day Workers on the Ward Farm, 1787–1866**

					Place of Birth				
Decade	Number of Observations	Age	Married	Single	Shrewsbury	Within 15 miles of Shrewsbury	Massachusetts	Native born, Out of Massachusetts	Foreign born
					Contract Workers				
1787–96	18	23.0	0	13	9	3	3	0	0
1797–1806	14	27.5	2	6	1	7	3	0	1
1807–16	36	25.9	4	16	14	9	4	0	0
1817–26	66	21.4	2	38	23	18	8	2	4
1827–36	49	23.4	4	25	3	5	16	3	14
1837–46	20	28.7	2	5	0	1	12	0	4
1847–56	26	31.1	3	15	0	2	6	6	5
1857–66	29	30.6	5	13	1	3	2	5	13
					Day Workers				
1787–96	59	37.5	47	6	34	2	7	1	6
1797–1806	71	38.5	66	3	27	12	10	1	18
1807–16	67	36.6	42	22	37	14	13	0	1
1817–26	138	42.4	54	43	76	17	29	2	3
1827–36	144	40.0	109	30	69	16	35	4	5
1837–46	74	42.4	62	6	19	9	30	3	6
1847–56	56	45.2	44	6	17	5	17	7	7
1857–66	59	50.5	40	6	12	2	3	20	11

Notes: Summing across marital status or across place of birth often does not equal the number of observations because of missing information.

Source: Ward Farm Laborers' File (Old Sturbridge Village, courtesy of Jack Larkin).

After 1830, the rural labor force was becoming not only segmented but perversely segmented, by which I mean that irregular day work was being done by stable, older, married men, born and rooted in the community, while steady, live-in work was being done, increasingly over time, by "travel-weathered men from much further away, most of them culturally alien, more migratory but less hopeful," transients, migrants, passersby who "come here to work," hired in the case of the Wards, quite literally, off the road.[41]

Arrangements with such men frequently began cautiously, conditionally, "as long as I want him," "no stated time agreed upon to stay," with the first month a probationary period at a lower wage, to be regularized "if he live with me a year," "if I want so long," "if we like," "if he is faithful and learns to work well."[42] Many of them did not. In my sample there are sixty-eight instances of sudden quits, just about 10 percent of total contracts. In August 1820, Samuel Plumer of Epping, New Hampshire hired one worker on contract who quit after eight days, another in September who quit after two weeks, another in November who quit after four days, and another the following January to work through the winter who left before the month was out.

From a broad perspective one might well ask, "How much of observed, voluntary turnover [that is, quitting] reflects opportunism and how much of it is the rational outcome of moving workers from lower to higher valued uses?"[43] Merely to raise the question, even if it cannot be answered, suggests that with "higher valued" opportunities opening up outside of farming, there was a pronounced change in the quality of those who remained.[44] The deterioration would be particularly pronounced in the pool of full-time farm workers.

If day workers and monthly farm laborers were indeed drawn from two

41. Larkin, "'Labor is the Great Thing in Farming,'" p. 218.

Dual-labor-market theory distinguishes between primary and secondary labor markets, the primary composed of better jobs, the secondary composed of low-paying jobs "held by workers who have unstable working patterns" (Glen G. Cain, "The Challenge of Segmented Labor Market Theories to Orthodox Theory: A Survey," *Journal of Economic Literature,* 14 (Dec. 1976), p. 1222). "There are distinctions between workers in the two sectors which *parallel* those between jobs" (Peter B. Doeringer and Michael J. Piore, *Internal Labor Markets and Manpower Analysis* [Lexington, Mass., 1971], p. 65, emphasis mine). In calling the market for rural labor after 1830 "perversely segmented," I wish to make the point that the distinctions between workers' characteristics in the two sectors (that is, between daily and monthly laborers) after 1830 did *not* parallel those between jobs.

42. Back-end loading—"the worker gets less than his marginal product at date 0 and at least his marginal product at date 1"—was clearly a defense against worker quits. "One may ask why the contract cannot specify either that a worker cannot quit at all, or (less extremely) that a quitting worker must compensate the firm by paying an 'exit fee'" (Hart and Holmstrom, "Theory of Contracts," p. 111). Instead, and in fact, as has been said repeatedly in this paper, quitting workers were paid in *quantum meruit.*

43. Rosen, "Implicit Contracts," p. 1170.

44. It will be recalled that whaling, too, suffered after 1820 from the deterioration in the quality of crews when alternative occupations ashore became more attractive. It is estimated that productivity in whaling fell 0.3 points between 1820 and 1860 as a consequence of a 52-point increase in wages ashore. See Lance E. Davis, Robert E. Gallman, and Teresa D. Hutchins, "Productivity in American Whaling: The New Bedford Fleet in the Nineteenth Century," in David W. Galenson, ed., *Markets in History: Economic Studies of the Past* (New York, 1989), p. 136.

increasingly different populations, it might be possible, even in the socially fluid society of antebellum America, to confirm that fact in their subsequent careers. What follows is an admittedly preliminary attempt to discover what became of them by linking some of the contract workers in my sample and in the Ward file to the 1850 federal manuscript census.[45]

Table 3.8 traces some of the monthly laborers of several major employers of contract labor: the Wards of Shrewsbury, a group of several farmers in Deerfield, Charles Phelps of Hadley, David Goodale of Marlborough, and an anonymous "market gardener" in West Cambridge (now Arlington). By 1850, 92 percent of the contract workers who had worked on the Ward farm in the four or five preceding decades had left Shrewsbury; 88 percent of Phelps's monthly workers had left Hadley; 96 percent of the men who worked on contract for the Deerfield farmers had left Deerfield; 68 percent of David Goodale's monthly workers had left Marlborough. Perhaps because of its access to major urban areas, only 43 percent of the men who worked on contract for the market gardener in West Cambridge had left town by 1850, and some of these were found nearby in Cambridge, Brookline, and Boston. Nearly half the men who had worked on contract in Deerfield and Shrewsbury had not only left town and county but could not be found in Massachusetts by 1850. Segmentation in the farm labor force, then, may have played a role in explaining the persistence of pay differentials between day and monthly workers.

3.5 Conclusion: Evidence of Structural Change in the Farm Labor Force

Is there evidence of a shift to contract labor, what I term here "structural change," in the proportions of day and monthly labor used on Massachusetts farms? To argue from a small group of account books to the farm population as a whole raises sampling issues, but the experiences of individual farmers may be instructive. Charles Phelps, Jr., of Hadley, David Goodale of Marlborough, and the Ward family of Shrewsbury all used large numbers of hired labor. In the case of Phelps and Goodale, it is possible to count man-days of monthly labor (number of contract months multiplied by twenty-six working days per month) and man-days of day labor recorded in their books. In the case of the Ward farm the number of day and contract laborers is in the data

45. The effort to link names in Massachusetts records is always subject to error because the long tradition of necronyms, patronyms, and Bible-naming patterns seriously limited the pool of first names; and two hundred years of very little immigration or in-migration seriously limited the pool of last names. There are not only a large number of John Hunts and William Johnsons, but several Ithamar Wards. See Daniel Scott Smith, "Child-Naming Patterns and Family Structure Change: Hingham, Massachusetts, 1640–1880," *Newberry Papers in Family and Community History,* paper 76-5 (Jan., 1977). Also, tracing individuals to the 1850 manuscript census requires truncating the sample on both ends. Farm workers who appeared in the sample much before 1800 are unlikely to be alive in 1850, and those who first appear in the sample near or after 1850 are beside the point.

Table 3.8 Tracing Monthly Contract Workers to 1850 (by source, town, and county)

	Ward File Shrewsbury Worcester County	Deerfield Farmers Deerfield Hampshire/Franklin County	Charles Phelps Hadley Hampshire County	David Goodale Marlborough Middlesex County	Anonymous Market Gardener West Cambridge Middlesex County
Number of names searched	50	80	34	31	21
Period of their contracts	1825–50	1800–1849	1805–30	1820–47	1836–43
Number (%) who left Massachusetts	22 (44%)	39 (49%)	9 (26%)	5 (16%)	2 (9.5%)
Number in Massachusetts but left county	9	16	14	13	3
Number in county but left town	15	22	7	3	4
% Who left town	92%	96%	88%	68%	43%
Number remaining in town	4	3	4	10	12
Number in town with no real estate	3	2	0	3	3

Sources: Ward Family Farm Laborers' File (Old Sturbridge Village, courtesy of Jack Larkin), Rothenberg sample of farm account books, and the 1850 manuscript census.

base, as is the number of man-months of contract labor, but unfortunately the number of days worked by day labor is not. However, with the Ward data it is possible to infer the magnitudes of day and monthly labor from the share of each in their total wage bill (Table 3.9).

For all three farmers, although the number of day laborers hired exceeded the number of contract laborers, man-days hired on contract swamped man-days of day labor. In most of the years between 1787 and 1890, the Ward farm expended more than 75 percent of its total wage bill on monthly labor. In most of the 21 years for which I have Phelps's records, he employed at least four times—and in 1815 eighteen times—as many man-days of contract labor as of day labor. Goodale relied even more heavily on contracts, using over ten times as many man-days of monthly as of daily labor in ten of the 28 years covered by his accounts, climaxing in 1835 when he hired 143 man-days of monthly labor, and only one day of day labor.Persuasive as these numbers may be, day labor, though relatively expensive, never disappeared. Every farm account book bears witness to the use of labor hired by the day either to "work" or to do specified farm tasks. And every farmer relied on gangs of day laborers to bring in his hay. William Odiorne of Billerica, for example, had two workers on annual contract, but in 1848 hired 90 man-days of day labor for the haying. Although the mix on individual farms was erratic, day labor remained important even as late as 1890.

The introduction of contract labor roughly coincided with the upturn in agricultural labor productivity that I have dated, in previous work, to the late 1780s. That there may have been a relation between productivity growth and the introduction of contract labor cannot be established with certainty, but contract labor may at least be understood as a way of restructuring the farm enterprise in time, analogous to restructuring the farm in space that became central to the agricultural reform movement of the antebellum years.[46] Contract workers do to time what connected farm buildings do to space: they bridge the diverse activities of mixed farming, dairying, home manufactures, and artisanal by-employments; and shelter the coming and going between them from inclemencies of market as from inclemencies of weather. "Connected farm buildings were the manifestation of a powerful will to succeed by farming," and the commitment a farmer makes when he hires a young man to live and work with him for five or six months is also a "manifestation of a powerful will to succeed by farming."[47] The live-in worker is likewise a

46. For new research on the relation between the reform impulse and changes in farm space, see Alan Synenki, ed., *Archeological Investigations of Minute Man National Historical Park*. Vol. 1: *Farmers and Artisans of the Historical Period,* Cultural Resources Management Study No. 22, National Park Service, United States Department of the Interior (Boston, 1990); and Jack Larkin, "From 'Country Mediocrity' to 'Rural Improvement': Transforming the Slovenly Countryside in Central Massachusetts, 1771–1840" (Old Sturbridge Village, 1991).

47. Thomas C. Hubka, *Big House, Little House, Back House, Barn: The Connected Farm Buildings of New England* (Hanover, N.H., 1984), p. 180.

Table 3.9 **Monthly Labor as a Share of Total Labor on Three Massachusetts Farms**

Years	Ward Farm, Shrewsbury Share of Total Wage Bill Expended Annually for Contract Labor	Years	Phelps Farm, Hadley Man-days of Contract Labor Hired Annually, as Share of Total Man-days Hired	Years	Goodale Farm, Marlborough Man-days of Contract Labor Hired Annually, as Share of Total Man-days Hired
1790–94	0.82	1805	416/463 = 0.90	1819	0/2 = 0.00
1795–99	0.74	1806	728/781 = 0.93	1821	0/1 = 0.00
1800–1804	0.47	1807	364/431 = 0.84	1822	0/9 = 0.00
1805–09	0.92	1808	572/609 = 0.94	1823	0/24 = 0.00
1810–14	0.88	1809	728/789 = 0.92	1824	52/107 = 0.49
1815–19	0.76	1810	676/780 = 0.87	1825	104/127 = 0.82
1820–24	0.71	1811	832/916 = 0.91	1826	227/246 = 0.92
1825–29	0.68	1812	936/1,023 = 0.91	1827	234/244 = 0.96
1830–34	0.78	1813	572/678 = 0.84	1828	117/136 = 0.86
1835–39	0.88	1814	286/457 = 0.63	1829	156/165 = 0.95
1840–44	0.45	1815	468/494 = 0.95	1830	299/312 = 0.96
1845–49	0.79	1829	0/96 = 0.00	1831	390/405 = 0.96
1850–54	0.81	1830	307/372 = 0.83	1832	370/386 = 0.96
1855–60	0.54	1831	226/285 = 0.79	1833	208/219 = 0.95
		1836	0/90 = 0.00	1834	357/368 = 0.97
		1837	130/498 = 0.26	1835	143/144 = 0.99
		1838	224/284 = 0.79	1836	188/191 = 0.98
		1851	130/344 = 0.38	1837	0/10 = 0.00
		1852	260/448 = 0.58	1838	139/160 = 0.87
		1853	442/668 = 0.66	1839	130/244 = 0.53
		1854	234/352 = 0.66	1840	182/341 = 0.53
				1841	182/298 = 0.61

Notes: The share of the wage bill was used for the Ward farm because man-days of day labor are not available. The wage bill for monthly contract labor was adjusted (by Jack Larkin, see below) by multiplying by 1.5 to include the imputed cost of room and board.

Sources: Ward Farm Laborers' File (Old Sturbridge Village, courtesy of Jack Larkin), and the account books of Phelps and Goodale.

bridge, available "at the will of the lord," "to take and do one sort of Business as well as another, whether Husbandry or Carpenters, or whatever I have to be done, that he is able to do; and to be as handy and helpfull as he can in the Family also."[48]

48. Walett, *Diary of Ebenezer Parkman,* 26 March 1736.

4 Farm Tenancy in the Antebellum North

Donghyu Yang

Economic historians and theorists have made contributions to the literature on agricultural tenancy, including theoretical models of the causes and consequences of farm tenancy and empirical tests using historical data.[1] Sharecropping in the postbellum South has received special attention as part of the general reinterpretation of the economic history of that region. The most widely accepted view of sharecropping now favorably interprets the relationship between landlord and tenant as an "understandable market response," using Joseph Reid's phrase. According to this view, sharecropping minimized risk and transactions costs but did not necessarily depress productivity or cause soil depletion.[2] But the notion that sharecropping was the source of numerous long-term problems in the South still has many supporters.

The author acknowledges helpful comments on an earlier draft by D. Gale Johnson, David W. Galenson, Lee J. Alston, and Jeremy Atack. Portions of this paper were presented at the Economic History Association meetings in Montreal, Canada, September 1990.

1. Some of the important works in the earlier literature are D. Gale Johnson, "Resource Allocation under Share Contracts," *Journal of Political Economy,* 58 (Apr. 1950), pp. 111–23; Steven N. S. Cheung, *The Theory of Share Tenancy: With Special Application to Asian Agriculture and the First Phase of Taiwan Land Reform* (Chicago, 1969); Joseph D. Reid, Jr., "Sharecropping as an Understandable Market Response: The Postbellum South," *Journal of Economic History,* 33 (Mar. 1973), pp. 106–30.

2. See, among others, Robert Higgs, "Race, Tenure, and Resource Allocation in Southern Agriculture, 1910," *Journal of Economic History,* 33 (Mar. 1973), pp. 149–69; "Patterns of Farm Rental in the Georgia Cotton Belt, 1880–1900," *Journal of Economic History,* 34 (June 1974), pp. 468–82; *Competition and Coercion: Blacks in the American Economy,* 1865–1914 (Cambridge, Mass., 1977); "Sharecropping as an Understandable Market Response"; "White Land, Black Labor, and Agricultural Stagnation: The Causes and Effects of Sharecropping in the Postbellum South," *Explorations in Economic History,* 16 (Jan. 1979), pp. 31–55; Roger L. Ransom and Richard Sutch, *One Kind of Freedom: The Economic Consequences of Emancipation* (Cambridge, Mass., 1977); Lee J. Alston, "Tenure Choice in Southern Agriculture, 1930–1960," *Explorations in Economic History,* 18 (July 1981), pp. 211–32; Alston and Higgs, "Contractual Mix in Southern Agriculture since the Civil War: Facts, Hypotheses, and Tests," *Journal of Economic History,* 42 (June 1982), pp. 327–53; Gavin Wright, "Cheap Labor and Southern Textiles before 1880," *Journal of Economic History,* 39 (Sept. 1979), pp. 655–68.

The modern debate is a reformulation of an older one between those who supported "the speculator thesis" and those who supported the "agricultural ladder thesis." The speculator thesis held that speculators and large estateholders took advantage of federal land policies to concentrate landholdings and exploit tenants. The agricultural ladder thesis viewed tenancy as a viable and efficient economic institution, a rationally chosen rung on the ladder from farm laborer to farm owner. The ladder thesis dates back to the nineteenth century and was subsequently espoused in studies by the U.S. Department of Agriculture in the 1910s and the 1920s.[3] During the Great Depression, however, the speculator thesis gained adherents whose opinions filled the pages of the report of the Special Committee on Farm Tenancy in 1937.[4] The speculator view also dominates works by noted agricultural historians, such as Paul Gates and Fred Shannon. The ladder thesis, however, was rejuvenated by two other well-respected historians of America's farmlands, Allan Bogue and Clarence Danhof.[5] Traditional studies relating to either thesis focused on the resource endowments of landlords and tenants. Recent research on postbellum southern sharecropping enrich the analysis by affording greater attention to other variables such as risk and transactions costs.

A second debate concerning the efficiency of production under different types of landholding has also received considerable attention. According to one economic theory, a share renter will not supply the efficient amount of inputs (except when the contract stipulates the exact amount to be supplied) since the share renter chooses an outlay on inputs at which the share of marginal revenue equals marginal cost. This is the famous doctrine of inefficiency of sharecropping espoused by economists from Adam Smith to Alfred Marshall.[6] A farmer on a short-term lease, moreover, will have no interest in the long-term condition of the property (unless given a compensatory payment) and will concentrate on activities that yield immediate benefits. Economists more recently have endeavored to formalize the conditions under which share renters behave as efficiently as owner-operators. Beginning with D. Gale Johnson's influential work, Steven Cheung, Joseph Reid, and others have ar-

3. For an early statement of the speculator thesis, see William Kent, "Land Tenure and Public Policy," *American Economic Review,* 9 suppl. (Mar. 1919), pp. 213–25; however, see also papers by W. J. Spillman, and by Richard T. Ely and Charles J. Galpin, and the discussions of them that appeared in the same issue, pp. 170–212, 226–32.

4. U.S. Special Committee on Farm Tenancy, *Farm Tenancy: Report to the President's Committee,* prepared under the auspices of the National Resources Committee (Washington, D.C., 1937).

5. Paul W. Gates, *Frontier Landlords and Pioneer Tenants* (Ithaca, 1945); and essays contained in Gates, *Landlords and Tenants on the Prairie Frontier: Studies in American Land Policy* (Ithaca, 1973); Fred A. Shannon, *The Farmer's Last Frontier: Agriculture, 1860–1897* (New York, 1945); Allan G. Bogue, *From Prairie to Corn Belt: Farming on the Illinois and Iowa Prairie in the Nineteenth Century* (Chicago, 1963); Clarence H. Danhof, *Change in Agriculture: The Northern United States, 1820–1870* (Cambridge, Mass., 1969).

6. For a good summary of the history of thought on farm tenancy, see William B. Bizzell, *Farm Tenancy in the United States,* Texas Agricultural Experiment Station, Bulletin No. 278 (College Station, 1921), chaps. 3–6; or Johnson, "Resource Allocation under Share Contracts."

gued that if landlords set their tenants' intensity of effort, then the productive efficiency of share tenants need not be below that of owner-operators. Reid, moreover, provided impressive evidence that a variety of devices were used in the postbellum South to specify the tenants' labor inputs, crop outputs, and other details of the production process.[7]

Most of the discussion regarding tenancy in American economic history has focused on the South, and until recently tenant farming in the North was relatively neglected. In separate studies, Seddie Cogswell and Donald Winters tried to support the agricultural ladder thesis by analyzing a carefully collected micro-data set for northern farms, but their work lacks the theoretical rigor of the studies on southern tenancy.[8] Further, both Cogswell and Winters concentrated on only one state, Iowa, and gave far less attention to the antebellum era. Studies by Jeremy Atack and Fred Bateman, published after most of my work was completed, also investigated northern tenancy. While we use the same data set, I use a simultaneous model to explain tenure choice, and I examine the relationship between productivity and tenure.[9]

This essay explores the determinants of tenancy, and thus the speculator and ladder hypotheses, and the determinants of productivity, and thus the possibility of Marshallian inefficiencies.

4.1 The Data

My data come from a sample of 21,118 rural households taken from the manuscript census of 1860 under the direction of Fred Bateman and James D. Foust.[10] The sample includes all households in a single township from each of 102 randomly selected counties, scattered across 16 northern states, and contains agricultural production data linked to demographic and economic information about the farm operators.

As I have discussed elsewhere, one can distinguish tenant farmers from owner-operators in this sample, even though census takers were not required until 1880 to ask farmers if they owned or rented their farms. Farmers enu-

7. Johnson, "Resource Allocation under Share Contracts"; Cheung, *The Theory of Share Tenancy;* Reid, "Sharecropping as an Understandable Market Response."

8. Seddie Cogswell Jr., *Tenure, Nativity and Age as Factors in Iowa Agriculture, 1850–1880* (Ames, Iowa, 1975); Donald L. Winters, *Farmers Without Farms: Agricultural Tenancy in Nineteenth Century Iowa* (Westport, 1978). For an historiographical survey see Winters, "Agricultural Tenancy in the Nineteenth Century Middle West: The Historiographical Debate," *Indiana Magazine of History,* 78 (June 1982), pp. 128–53.

9. See Jeremy Atack and Fred Bateman, *To Their Own Soil: Agriculture in the Antebellum North* (Ames, 1987); Atack, "Tenants and Yeoman in the Nineteenth Century," *Agricultural History,* 62 (Summer 1988), pp. 6–32; "The Agricultural Ladder Revisited: A New Look at an Old Question with Some Data for 1860," *Agricultural History,* 63 (Winter 1989), pp. 1–25.

10. Fred Bateman and James D. Foust, "A Sample of Rural Households Selected from the 1860 Manuscript Censuses," *Agricultural History,* 48 (Winter 1974) pp. 75–93; Yang, "Notes on the Wealth Distribution of Farm Households in the United States, 1860: A New Look at Two Manuscript Census Samples," *Explorations in Economic History,* 21 (Jan. 1984), pp. 88–102.

merated together with full production data in the agricultural schedules and no real property in the population schedules were considered tenants.[11]

Out of 11,940 households with agricultural production information in the sample, 3,382 were excluded from the analysis for one or more of the following reasons: (1) the household was in a slave state, Missouri or Maryland; (2) the head of the household had a nonfarm occupation;[12] (3) the information needed to estimate the farm's labor input was missing, owing to an inability to match the household in the population schedule with the household in the agricultural schedule, or for some other reason; (4) the size of the household given in the population schedule differed by more than one person from the size of the household coded as a separate variable in the sample; (5) improved acreage or the value of the farm was not reported; (6) the value of farm implements was not reported; (7) there was no farm output; and (8) there were obvious recording errors for key variables. After removing these observations, 7,740 owner-operated farms and 818 tenant farms remained.

Tenant farms might be further classified, for instance as sharecropping, share renting, and cash renting.[13] Because these lease arrangements cannot be identified from the census data of 1860, I treat tenants as a single group. Neglecting the composition of the tenantry could impart a bias if the type of contract varied with the principal crop in an area. Typically, however, the terms of share contracts do not appear to have differed very much across regions.[14]

Characteristic features of tenants and tenant farms in comparison with owner-operated farms are summarized in Tables 4.1–4.3. Table 4.1 reaffirms

11. These are the type A and type B farmers, respectively, as defined in Yang, "Notes on the Wealth Distribution," table 1. For geographic variations in the tenancy rate see ibid., table 2; and Atack and Bateman, *To Their Own Soil,* chap. 7.

12. This criterion was absent in my previous work, see Yang, "Agricultural Productivity in the Northern United States, 1860," in Robert W. Fogel and Stanley L. Engerman, eds., *Without Consent or Contract: Technical Papers on Slavery* (New York, 1991). There the objective was to explain total agricultural production, whether the farm operator was an owner-operator, tenant, or non-farmer by occupation. Here eliminating the non-farmer–headed farms will help distinguish tenant farmers from owner-operator farmers.

13. Studies by the Department of Agriculture during the 1910s and 1920s reported a variety of terms under which farms were leased. In the northwestern wheat belt at least six major classes of renting were identified; for the dairy farms in Wisconsin and Illinois, two important types of tenure were described.These and other studies are summarized in E. A. Goldenweiser and Leon E. Truesdell, *Farm Tenancy in the United States,* U.S. Bureau of the Census, Census Monograph No. 4 (Washington, D.C., 1924). Generally, cash renters were responsible for supply of labor and all working capital. The contribution of productive factors by landowner increased with the share of the crop he received.

14. A Department of Agriculture bulletin in 1918, based on the study of 258 lease contracts and the survey records of 2,907 tenant farms, reported the pattern of renting farms according to crops. Although there was considerable variation, the most frequent share of the landlord (when the work stock, machinery, and labor were furnished by tenants) was one half for corn, hay, and potatoes and one third for wheat, peas, and beans. The products of breeding and milking dairy cattle and of raising beef cattle and hogs were divided half and half when the expenses for working capital were shared equally (E. V. Wilcox, *Lease Contracts used in Renting Farms on Shares,* U.S. Department of Agriculture, Bulletin No. 650 [Washington, D.C., 1918]). This description, however, may not apply to 1860.

Table 4.1 **Percentage Tenant by Age and Region, 1860**

	Percentage Tenant		
Age	North	Northeast	North Central
29 and under	20.3%	18.2%	21.1%
30–39	12.0	8.4	13.5
40–49	8.0	7.2	8.4
50–59	5.3	3.8	6.4
60–69	4.5	2.6	6.3
70 and over	0.3	0.0	1.3
Number of farms (tenant and non-tenant):			
	8,558	3,175	5,383

Source: Computed from the Bateman-Foust sample.

Table 4.2 **Tenancy Rates by Place of Birth in the Rural North, 1860**

	North			Northeast			North Central		
Birthplace	Owner	Tenant	Tenancy Rate	Owner	Tenant	Tenancy Rate	Owner	Tenant	Tenancy Rate
Total	7,740	818	9.56%	2,959	216	6.80%	4,781	602	11.18%
Born in state	3,075	290	8.62	2,364	185	7.26	711	105	12.87
Born out of state	3,393	402	10.59	437	11	2.46	2,959	391	11.68
Foreign-born	1,267	124	8.91	158	20	11.24	1,109	104	8.57
English-speaking	599	48	7.42	109	14	11.38	490	34	6.49
British Isles	289	18	5.86	63	2	3.08	226	16	6.61
Ireland	274	24	8.05	40	9	18.37	234	15	6.02
Canada	35	6	14.63	6	3	33.33	29	3	9.38
Others	1	0	0.00	0	0	—	1	0	0.00
Low countries	122	2	1.61	0	0	—	122	2	1.61
France	30	3	9.09	4	0	0.00	26	3	10.34
Germany	403	39	8.82	30	4	11.76	373	35	9.38
Switzerland	31	4	11.43	14	2	12.50	17	2	10.53
Northern Europe	75	27	26.47	0	0	—	75	27	26.47
Others	7	1	12.50	1	1	50.00	6	0	0.00
At sea	1	0		0	0		1	0	
Unknown	4	2		0	0		4	2	

Source: Computed from the Bateman-Foust sample.

an observation found in numerous sources that tenant farmers were younger than owner-operators. This finding was frequently used to support the agricultural ladder thesis, because it was presumed that young renters eventually became older owner-operators.[15] The phenomenon is more conspicuous in the

15. For recent examples, see Winters, *Farmers Without Farms;* and Reid, "White Land, Black Labor."

Table 4.3 **Average Measures by Land-Tenure Status in the Rural North, 1860**

	North		Northeast		North Central	
	Owner	Tenant	Owner	Tenant	Owner	Tenant
Number of farms	7,740	818	2,959	216	4,781	602
Age (years)	44.7	37.6	47.4	38.4	43.1	37.3
Percentage born:						
In state	39.7	35.5	79.9	85.6	14.9	17.4
Out of state	43.9	49.3	14.8	5.1	61.9	65.3
Foreign	16.4	15.2	5.3	9.3	23.2	17.3
Length of residency (years)	29.7	22.5	42.3	35.5	22.0	17.9
Real property	\$3,315	0	4,052	0	2,859	0
Personal wealth	\$941	497	1,260	864	744	365
Acreage:						
Improved (*I*)	74.4	58.8	84.8	80.5	67.9	51.0
Unimproved (*U*)	55.5	53.0	33.9	41.4	68.9	57.2
Value (\$) of:						
Farm (*F*)	\$3,126	2,342	3,897	4,199	2,649	1,676
Farm adjusted for location (*T*)	2,746	2,039	3,277	3,562	2,418	1,493
Machinery (*K*)	117	85	142	141	102	64
Livestock (*V*)	481	344	555	514	434	283
Labor (*L*): equivalent hands	1.58	1.44	1.54	1.48	1.60	1.43
Output (*Q*)	\$588.3	527.2	582.3	561.3	592.0	515.0
Q/*I*	7,907	8,966	6,867	6,973	8,719	10,098
Q/*T*	.2141	.2585	.1776	.1575	.2448	.3449
Q/*K*	5.025	6.226	4.099	3,975	5.827	7.997
Q/*L*	372.3	366.1	378.1	379.3	370.0	360.1
Total factor productivity index (owner = 100)	100.0	106.2	94.1	90.6	104.7	116.8
Value (\$) of:						
Beef	\$ 75.4	49.3	83.2	71.5	70.7	41.4
Dairy	117.2	78.8	200.6	183.4	65.5	41.3
Pork	114.5	98.7	53.6	81.6	152.2	104.9
Corn	161.4	231.2	53.0	73.7	228.6	287.7
Wheat	84.2	68.7	35.2	58.5	114.5	72.3
Corn/*Q*	.274	.439	.091	.131	.386	.559
Wheat/*Q*	.143	.130	.060	.104	.193	.140
Animal products/*Q*	.536	.436	.602	.612	.496	.368
Pork/animal products	.373	.435	.159	.242	.528	.559

Note: Total factor productivity was computed by taking the geometric average of *Q*/*L*, *Q*/*K*, and *Q*/*T* with the weights of .63, .05, and .32, derived from the factor shares in total cost. See Yang, "Aspects of United States Agriculture circa 1860" (Ph.D. diss., Harvard, 1984), chap. 2; and "Agricultural Productivity in the Northern United States, 1860," in Robert W. Fogel and Stanley L. Engerman, eds., *Without Consent or Contract: Technical Papers on Slavery* (New York, 1991), for more detail.

Source: Computed from the Bateman-Foust sample.

long-settled Northeast. But, as I will show, age was actually more significant in the North Central region, where tenancy was, in fact, a more effective route to ownership because settlement was still in progress.

As Table 4.2 shows, foreign-born farmers were more likely to be tenants in the Northeast than in the North Central region, in part because in the North Central region foreign-born farmers tended to be older than native farmers. Immigrants from English-speaking countries had lower tenancy rates than other foreign-born farmers.[16]

Table 4.3 reports the length of in-state residence, another measure relevant to the agricultural ladder thesis. The census schedules did not include a question on the years of residency, but one can generate a range for the length of time a farm operator could have resided in-state from the age and birthplace of his children. In most cases, one can use the age of a farmer born in a state as his length of residence. If the head of the household was not born in the state, then the age of the oldest child born in-state generally sets a lower bound on his years of residency, and the age of the youngest child born out of the state sets an upper bound.[17] If no children were born in-state, then the minimum residency is zero. Averaging the maximum and minimum gives the probable period of residency. Since the range is fairly wide (averaging about fourteen years) and family relationships had to be reconstructed (the census did not collect information on relationships among members of a household before 1880), the measure is subject to a substantial error.[18] Even so, it is clear that length of residency was shorter for tenants than owners, a finding consistent with the idea that tenants eventually worked their way up to become owners.

Output, input, and productivity (measured according to the procedures described in my study of northern agricultural productivity) are also reported in Table 4.3.[19] A brief description, however, may clarify the meaning of the productivity measures. Physical units of crop outputs reported in the agricultural schedules were converted into dollar amounts (after adjusting for seed and feed allowances) by using 1860 national prices. Meat output was computed

16. Female-headed households were minimal, about 4 percent, and there were almost no black farmers, so we cannot shed any light directly on the racial issues that are the focus of attention in the study of postbellum southern tenancy.

17. There are very few odd cases in the Bateman-Foust sample, such as intermediate children born in-state but first and last born out of state.

18. A similar measure was employed by Cogswell, *Tenure, Nativity and Age,* chap. 6. The family relation was reconstructed by following the methods (with some minor variations) of Richard A. Easterlin, George Alter, and Gretchen A. Condran, "Farms and Farm Families in Old and New Areas: The Northern States in 1860," in Tamara K. Hareven and Maris A. Vinovskis, eds., *Family and Population in Nineteenth-Century America* (Princeton, 1978). Households were classified into three headships: husband-wife headed, other male headed, and female headed. The recognition that all the property-holding members of a household were listed before the non-property holders saved many unnecessary steps, such as identifying grandparents and stepchildren. Restrictions on the age differentials between spouses and between mother and children were slightly loosened.

19. Yang, "Agricultural Productivity."

by multiplying the number of head of each type of animal by their slaughter-to-live-weight ratio, their average live weight, and their price per pound of live weight. Capital was measured by the value of implements and machinery; land was measured by the value of the farm. Capital and land values were taken directly from the agricultural schedules. The locational component of the land value was estimated as the difference between the coefficients from a linear regression of the value of the land on improved acreage and unimproved acreage. The locational component was removed from the value of the farm (*F*) to create an adjusted land input (*T*). The labor input was estimated in equivalent full hands using the information in the population schedules. To convert the farm population into full hands, I used the same age-sex weights employed in related work for southern labor. These weights were obtained from slave hire-rate profiles, and in turn multiplied by the assumed labor force participation rates of 1.0 for males and 0.25 for females. Labor input estimates are likely to be downwardly biased (as much as 25 percent) because hired hands were not counted, but the bias may not be very serious when comparing owner-operated with tenant farms.[20]

Looking at the input mix and output mix by tenure in Table 4.3, one may be surprised by the differences between the two regions. The scale of farming (improved acreage) was smaller for tenants than owners in the North Central region, as might be expected from the agricultural ladder thesis, but it was higher in the Northeast. Indeed, the average value of tenant farms was actually greater than that of owner-operated farms in the Northeast. Similarly, the investment in machinery and livestock on tenant farms was far less than on owner-operated farms in the North Central region but was about equal in the Northeast. As a consequence, North Central tenants had higher capital and land productivity and lower labor productivity than owners, while just the reverse held in the Northeast. Tenants had 11 percent higher total factor productivity than owners in the North Central region, but 4 percent lower total factor productivity than owners in the Northeast. Crop mix was also different. Tenants grew a greater proportion of corn, a smaller proportion of wheat, and produced a smaller share of animal products than owners in the North Central region, but again these comparisons are reversed in the Northeast.[21] These figures suggest that the institution of tenancy operated very differently in the two regions.

20. If we allocate hired hands available outside farms proportionally to the improved acreage of each farm, the downward bias of the labor input appears to be about 20 percent for owner-operated farms and 18 percent for tenant farms. The influence of the differential bias on the productivity comparison between owner and tenant turns out to be negligible.

21. It is noteworthy that the Bateman-Foust sample does not cover urban townships, where the growth of labor-intensive market gardening led to an increase in tenancy, especially in the Northeast. "High land values in connection with ready markets produced tenancy near the large cities, a condition of land tenure almost unknown elsewhere in the North. Many of the truck farms were leased by immigrants, who had learned gardening in Europe" (Percy W. Bidwell and John I. Falconer, *History of Agriculture in the Northern United States, 1620–1860* [Washington, D.C., 1925], p. 242).

Differences in crop mix and input composition by tenure status have been observed in other contexts, and explanations have been offered for them. Lower livestock investment, emphasis on swine within the livestock category, and a higher share of corn in the total output of tenants have all been interpreted as rational utility maximizing behavior. The following interpretation is typical of the literature: "Since tenants were generally in a poorer capital position, they were unable to invest in livestock to the same extent as owner-operators. Moreover, meat production provided a slower turnover on investment than did grain production. It took two to three years to fatten a steer for a market and about half the time for a pig. . . . Renters were likewise reluctant to make investments in dairy cattle or sheep that would be difficult to liquidate if their leases were not renewed."[22] This statement is based on implicit assumptions about the state of the capital market, terms of the lease contract, and attitudes toward risk. This is especially clear in our case since the Northeast showed a pattern almost contrary to what the quotation would predict. Accounting for the behavior of farmers in the Northeast requires a more elaborate theoretical model and a reevaluation of the farm-level data.

4.2 A Model of the Farm-Rental Market

The economic theory of farm tenancy was developed from various perspectives. Some writers have emphasized relative resource endowments, while others have given more weight to risk and transactions costs. All have assumed that the contractual form is determined by a market process of interacting demand and supply, not merely by custom or unilateral pressures from landowners. Thus, they provide not competing, but complementary explanations of tenure choice. Most previous empirical tests, however, have focused on a particular aspect of the market within the confines of a specific theory.[23] I develop and test a market-equilibrium model that simultaneously incorporates many of the explanatory variables identified in previous research.

Transactions in the rental market involve bilateral contracts whereby the landowner transfers to a tenant the right to use a unit of land in return for an agreed rental payment. We may assume that each owner has some "reservation rent," defined as the minimum rent he is prepared to accept for leasing his unit, and that each prospective tenant farmer has some "limit rent," defined as

22. Winters, *Farmers Without Farms*, p. 40.

23. For a survey of the literature, see Alston and Higgs, "Contractual Mix in Southern Agriculture." The recent empirical tests emphasizing the tenure ladder are Reid, "White Land, Black Labor"; Wright, "Cheap Labor and Southern Texiles"; and Winters, *Farmers Without Farms*. Risk sharing is emphasized in Higgs, "Race, Tenure, and Resource Allocation; "Patterns of Farm Rentals"; and *Competition and Coercion*. Enforcement and supervision costs are emphasized in Alston, "Tenure Choice in Southern Agriculture"; and Alston and Higgs, "Contractual Mix in Southern Agriculture." The balance between transaction costs and risk is emphasized in Phillip T. Hoffman, "The Economic Theory of Sharecropping in Early Modern France," *Journal of Economic History*, 44 (June 1984), pp. 309–19.

the maximum rent he would be prepared to pay for a unit of land.[24] The lower the reservation rent of the owner and the higher the limit rent of the prospective tenant, the greater the number of transactions that will take place in the rental market. The precise contract rent will be set at market-clearing level. In other words, the two-equation system,

$$(1) \qquad T^d = T^d(R - R_r),\ T^{d\prime} > 0$$

$$(2) \qquad T^S = T^S(R_l - R),\ T^{S\prime} > 0$$

can be solved for a reduced form,

$$(3) \qquad T = T(R_r, R_l)$$

where T denotes the extent of tenancy (expressed as a probability at the individual level), R_r the reservation rent, R_l the limit rent, R the actual contract rent, and the superscripts d and s denote the demand for and supply of tenant farmers respectively, with $\partial T/\partial R_r < 0$ and $\partial T/\partial R_l > 0$.

The problem now reduces to identifying the determinants of the reservation and limit rents. The landowner's reservation rent reflects his choice between leasing the land and hiring farm laborers. It will depend on his resource endowments and on the specific nature of the farming unit. The amount of agriculture-specific human capital the owner has, holding other variables constant, determines how likely the owner is to operate the farm or to rent it. The reservation rent must be higher to compensate for the lower earnings of the owner's human capital in alternative employment. The accumulation of managerial expertise, work stock, and tools were the most frequently cited forces enabling a farmer to move up the tenure ladder from wage hand to cropper, to share tenant, to fixed-payment renter, to owner-operator. The proxies for human capital chosen from the manuscript census data are age, literacy, nativity, and length of residency. Physical capital was measured by the personal property variable, since it consisted mainly of livestock and implements.

The nature of the farming unit influenced the landlord's demand for tenant farmers through two major channels: risk and transactions costs. Assuming risk-aversion, the higher the risk attached to the operation of the farm, the lower the reservation rent. When the owner works his own farm, he bears all the risk. But he bears only a part of the risk when he rents out the farm. Variance of yields and prices provide a good measure of the risk, but the cross-sectional variance of farm income is not readily available. Crop mix may serve as a proxy. Corn was long regarded as less risky than wheat, its major alternative. Wheat was vulnerable to disease, insects, and harsh weather, and had a shorter harvest period. As early as 1843, an English pamphlet to emigrants noted that corn "is not like other grain easily injured; but once ripe, there it stands, setting at defiance rain, frost, snow, and avery [sic] vicissitude of cli-

24. The model below follows the spirit of J. M. Currie, *The Economic Theory of Agricultural Land Tenure* (Cambridge, 1981).

mate, often through great part of winter."[25] While the price of corn fluctuated widely (usually along with the price of hogs), it fluctuated no more than the price of wheat. Major declines in the price of corn did not occur until 1861. Thus, the proportion of corn acreage in total cropland can be taken as an index of risk. The estimated value of corn divided by the value of total farm output was used, however, because the 1860 census did not collect crop acreage.[26]

The costs of hiring, enforcing, and supervising wage labor probably increased disproportionately with the size of the work force, because the supply of enforcement and supervision was probably inelastic. "Tenant farming tends to increase where the average acreage per farm is large, and methods of cultivation relatively simple."[27] The size of a farm (improved acreage) provides a measure of the cost of using hired labor.

Thus, the reservation rent should be positively related to age, literacy, length of residency, personal property, and share of corn in output, and inversely related to improved acreage per farm. The effect of nativity is uncertain.

The limit rent of a prospective tenant is more difficult to analyze, because the tenant's alternatives to renting a farm include being hired as a farm worker, working outside agriculture, and buying a farm. I will confine my attention to the choice between renting and buying a farm, because I can only compare owners with tenants. This limitation does not create problems if the labor market is similar across geographic regions, but may when explaining spatial variation in the tenancy rate (see the discussion below of Table 4.5).

Relative resource endowments and the nature of a farm also play a role in determining the limit rent. Potential farmers who were well endowed with managerial expertise, work stock, and implements would have a lower limit rent, while those with less human capital would desire advice and supervision from the landlord. The willingness of potential tenants to pay for these services would increase their limit rent. Assuming risk-aversion, the limit rent will be lower for the farm that involves riskier operations. Therefore, all the variables representing resource endowments and risk enter as arguments influencing the limit rent.

25. William Oliver, *Eight Months in Illinois: With Information to Emigrants* (New Castle Upon Tyne, 1834), p.85, cited in Bogue, *From Prairie to Corn Belt*, p. 129.

26. Corn production includes raising of feed for animals. However, since the share of animal products in the total output will enter the regression equation, the estimated coefficient of the corn share variable will reflect the marketed corn crop only. Table 4.3 above shows that the proportion of marketable corn in gross corn output was higher for tenant farms than for owner-operated farms. Alternatively, the corn product net of animal feed can be used in the regression instead of the gross value of the corn output but the results would not be very different.

27. Bizzell, *Farm Tenancy in the United States*, p. 175. This relation is discussed at some length in ibid., chap. 14. Lee Alston, Samar K. Datta, and Jeffrey B. Nugent, "Tenancy Choice in a Competitive Framework with Transactions Costs," *Journal of Political Economy*, 92 (Dec. 1984), pp. 1121–33, suggest, however, that there may be economies of scale in supervision up to a point. Lee Alston pointed out to me in a letter that the Midwest was characterized by higher percentage of kin-tenants. This would surely affect supervision costs but it is not clear how or if it influenced contractual mix. It is hoped that regressions for separate regions may circumvent this problem.

Because leases had limited terms, the limit rent of a prospective tenant will be lower for the farm where the principal operation needed long-term investment, for example building and maintaining the barns, silos, cribs, and fences necessary for stock farming. I chose two variables to measure the impact of long-term investment requirements, namely, the share of beef in the total value of output and the share of total animal products (beef, pork, and dairy) in total production. The share of beef captures the longer time it takes to raise cattle than swine, and the share of total animal products captures the longer time involved in raising livestock compared with other food crops.[28]

To sum up, the limit rent is expected to be negatively related to age, literacy, length of residence, value of personal property, and share of beef and animal products in output, and positively related to the share of corn. Nativity is again of uncertain significance.

Other forces affected the rental market that did not work directly through the demand or supply of tenant farmers. Among those discussed in the literature are the price of land per acre and the availability of public lands. The relation between land prices and tenancy is somewhat complicated to analyze, although the positive correlation between the two has been observed and discussed for some time.[29] To the extent that farm value capitalizes the productivity of land and its proximity to market, and that prospective tenants perceive these facts, the limit rent will be higher. However, the reservation rent of the owner will also be higher. Thus, farm value per acre should enter both the limit rent and the reservation rent equations. These two impacts will offset each other if the subjective evaluation of land productivity and proximity to market are the same for owner and tenant.

If, for speculative or other reasons, the price of a farm stays above its equilibrium level, the farm will not be purchased or maintained by a bona fide owner-operator who will compare the land price to the prospective income stream. This implies that the speculator may have a lower reservation rent than an owner-operator. Because the rental market is not likely to be motivated by concerns about capital gains or the prestige of landownership, one would expect higher tenancy rates on overvalued farms. I used farm value per acre to capture this effect.

28. When interpreting the estimated coefficients, these two variables should be considered together, since they are closely related to each other.

29. Early writers correctly identified the relationship, but their discussion frequently was limited to a single aspect. For example, W. J. Spillman and E. A. Goldenweiser, "Farm Tenantry in the United States," in U.S. Department of Agriculture, *Yearbook of Agriculture,1916* (Washington, D.C., 1917), p. 335, tried to explain it with a version of the agricultural ladder hypothesis, stating that "where the value of farm land is high a longer time is required for the tenant to accumulate the capital necessary for making a first payment on a farm than where it is low." See also Goldenweiser and Truesdell, *Farm Tenancy in the United States,* chap. 6. Recently, Alston and Higgs, "Contractual Mix in Southern Agriculture," contended that the more valuable the land, the more numerous would be wage workers relative to tenants. This is because, they argue, more valuable lands were given more supervision, and because the marginal cost of supervising wage labor is decreasing. However, this influence, if it existed, would have been dominated by other forces that are discussed below.

Availability of public lands is another factor claimed to influence tenancy. Where the settlement of desirable new land was in rapid progress, it has been argued, the opportunity for acquiring land was so great that there was little reason for the rental market to develop. On the other hand, speculators and landlords who took advantage of the federal land policy leased out their lands to tenants.[30] The direction of influence of the settlement level, thus, cannot be determined a priori, but the sign of the estimated coefficient may discriminate between the two opposing views. I took the proportion of farm land improved by 1860 to the ever-improved agricultural land in the county as the measure of farm settlement.[31]

Solving the demand and supply equations and adding the two variables considered separately yields a reduced-form equation which predicts that the rate (or probability) of tenancy varies negatively with the age, literacy, length of residency, and personal property of the farm operator, negatively with the share of beef and animal products in output, and positively with improved acreage. The effects of nativity, share of corn, value of farm per acre, and settlement level are more difficult to determine. The expected sign of the share of corn is ambiguous because risk decreases both the limit rent and the reservation rent. If tenants were more risk averse than owners because they were less wealthy and had less access to credit, then the limit effect would dominate and a positive sign would be expected.[32] The value of the farm also affects both the limit rent and reservation rent in the same direction. If speculators were the key players, the sign of value per acre would be positive and the sign of settlement negative.

4.3 Northern Tenancy Decisions in 1860

Farm-level regressions are shown in Table 4.4. The equations were estimated using the binary logit technique, with the dependent variable equal to zero if the farm was owner-operated and one if tenanted. Human capital variables were specified in logarithms to allow for diminishing returns and, for the same reason, the settlement variable was entered as a quadratic.[33] The interaction terms of age and residency with settlement were added to capture any differential in the effect of human capital over the settlement stage.

In the regression for the North as a whole, every variable, except stock farming (beef share and the share of animal products) and nativity, is significant at the .05 level and has the expected sign. The sign of the interaction terms shows that age gained importance over the settlement stage, but length

30. See the introductory part of the text for a related discussion.

31. This measure is based on the procedure used by Easterlin et al., "Farms and Farm Families." The index was constructed from decennial census data by dividing the improved acreage in 1860 by the improved acreage of 1870, 1880, 1890, 1900, 1910, whichever was largest.

32. For a similar argument, see Higgs, "Patterns of Farm Rental."

33. It was not entered in logarithms because it is already a ratio variable constrained to fall between zero and one.

Table 4.4 Logit Regression of Farm-Level Tenancy

	North	Northeast	North Central
Intercept	2.0390*	−0.8748	2.1903*
	(1.2230)	(6.1490)	(1.2602)
Log (age)	−0.8752***	−2.9276	−0.8574**
	(0.3101)	(2.0814)	(0.3481)
Dummy for literacy	−0.6198***	−1.0544***	−0.5290***
	(0.1347)	(0.4053)	(0.1472)
Dummy for born in state	0.0594	0.4766	−0.1642
	(0.1178)	(0.3777)	(0.1468)
Dummy for foreign-born	−0.0066	1.2186**	−0.1769
	(0.1413)	(0.5583)	(0.1506)
Dummy for born in English-speaking countries	−0.3423*	−0.3372	−0.5087**
	(0.2000)	(0.5526)	(0.2272)
Log of length of residency	−0.4985***	0.6339	−0.4087***
	(0.0984)	(1.4825)	(0.1077)
Personal property	−0.001006***	−0.000345***	−0.002300***
	(0.000106)	(0.000109)	(0.000189)
Log (age) × settlement	−1.2415**	0.8589	−0.9284
	(0.5046)	(2.3272)	(0.6836)
Log (residency) × settlement	0.6158***	−0.6845	0.3860
	(0.2047)	(1.5821)	(0.2402)
Settlement	4.1890**	15.1011*	3.6939
	(1.8314)	(8.5417)	(2.5277)
$Settlement^2$	−1.3907**	−10.3441***	−1.7689**
	(0.5930)	(3.5747)	(0.7221)
Corn share	1.2030***	2.4151***	1.4535***
	(0.1514)	(0.5516)	(0.1773)
Improved acreage	0.001633**	0.003799***	0.001888**
	(0.000718)	(0.001435)	(0.000915)
Beef share	−0.6018	−3.7532***	−0.1545
	(0.4438)	(1.1703)	(0.4470)
Animal-product share	0.1982	1.2067***	0.0493
	(0.1373)	(0.3329)	(0.1513)
Value per acre	0.004794***	0.003047*	0.012119***
	(0.001283)	(0.001663)	(0.003659)
N	8,558	3,175	5,381
Log likelihood	−2,406.76	−702.39	−1,623.09

Notes: Standard errors are in parentheses. Dependent variable = 0 if owner, = 1 if tenant.
Source: Computed from the Bateman-Foust sample.
*Significant at the .10 level.
**Significant at the .05 level.
***Significant at the .01 level.

of residency did not. The North Central region follows the same pattern as the North as a whole, except that the interaction terms between human capital and settlement lose their significance. For the Northeast, however, the results are generally poor. All the human capital variables except literacy are insignificant, and the size of the coefficient for the physical capital variable (personal property) is very small compared with that of the North Central region. The share of animal products has a positive sign, indicating that raising livestock other than beef cattle (probably swine) attracted tenants.

The lack of significance for the stock farming variables indicates that the limited length of lease contracts may not have greatly influenced the demand by tenants for rental farms. A Department of Agriculture bulletin published in 1918 observed: "The landlord almost universally furnishes all materials needed in repairing buildings and fences, and in making other permanent improvements as required, while the tenants furnishes all labor except skilled labor necessary for making the required repairs and improvements. The tenant, however, is commonly paid wages for work on extensive improvements, such as ditching, tile draining, building silos, etc. . . . In the case of extensive improvements the landlord may supply all labor while the tenant is required to board the laborers."[34] The same source reported that annual lease contracts were generally renewed repeatedly.

Except for the apparent differences in the age distribution and length of residency, there does not seem to be much evidence for an agricultural ladder in the Northeast. Once farm characteristics are controlled, the relative resource endowment variables lose their explanatory power. One may infer that the tenure ladder was meaningful only in the North Central region, where settlement was still in progress, and that in the Northeast, where agriculture was already declining, farmers on the lower rung of the ladder were constantly drawn off by the increasingly attractive industrial labor market and by the lure of westward migration.[35] The average age of farm operators, given in Table 4.3, shows that there were fewer young farmers in the Northeast than in the North Central region.

The value of farm per acre has a larger and more significant coefficient in the North Central region than in the Northeast. This variable may have captured the prevalence of land speculation in the newly settled area of the North Central region. The squared settlement variable has a significant positive sign in the equation for the North Central region. This result, together with the significant positive sign of the land price variable, indicates that the speculator

34. Wilcox, *Lease Contracts used in Renting Farms on Shares,* p. 21. See also Bizzell, *Farm Tenancy in the United States,* pp. 195–96; and Spillman and Goldenweiser, "Farm Tenantry in the United States," pp. 343–46. This may not apply to the period around 1860.

35. For related discussions, see Alexander Field, "Sectoral Shifts in Antebellum Massachusetts: A Reconsideration," *Explorations in Economic History,* 15 (Apr. 1978), pp. 146–71; and Wright, "Cheap Labor and Southern Textiles."

thesis cannot be easily rejected.[36] In the North Central region, tenancy, it appears, is hard to explain with a monocausal theory.

I now use the model of the farm-rental market to explain geographic variation of the tenancy rate across townships. Excluding townships with fewer than five farms, the rate of tenancy varied from zero to a high of 74 percent. Table 4.5 shows the results of the township-level regressions.[37] Coefficients of practically all variables have the expected signs, and together they explain more than a half of the spatial variation in the tenancy rate. As noted previously, this specification assumes a uniform state of the labor market across geographic areas.

The second equation of Table 4.5 takes into account variation in the labor market by including the wage rate.[38] The higher the wage rate, the lower the limit rent of a prospective tenant will be, because the value of his labor in the alternative employment is higher. Likewise, the reservation rent of a landlord will be lower, because the costs of hiring and keeping wage laborers will be higher. Thus, the direction of influence on the tenancy rate is ambiguous and will be determined by the relative sensitivities of demand and supply in the rental market.[39]

The inclusion of wages decreases the residual variance by about 6 percentage points. The highly significant negative coefficient of the wage variable indicates that the tenant's response was more sensitive to labor market conditions than the owner's.

4.4 The Productivity of Tenants and Owner-Operators

The empirical literature has not yet produced a consensus concerning the economic performance of tenant farming. Among others, Winters reported that grain yields were not less for tenants than owners in postbellum Iowa. Lewis Gray, echoing others, noted that "the question whether tenants or owner

36. The role of speculators can also be viewed in a more sanguine light. "We can rightly regard the operations of the speculator as a means of sending capital to regions that were desperately in need of it" (Bogue, *From Prairie to Corn Belt,* p. 45).

37. Since the dependent variable is a proportion bounded by zero and one, I transformed it into the log of the odds ratio, log [tenancy rate/(1 − tenancy rate)], and ran weighted regressions to correct for heteroscedasticity. The weight was (tenancy rate) × (1 − tenancy rate) × (number of farms in the township).

38. Agricultural wage rates for 1860 by state were taken from Stanley Lebergott, *Manpower in Economic Growth: The American Record Since 1800* (New York, 1964), p. 539.

39. The model of P. K. Bardhan and T. N. Srinivasan, "Cropsharing Tenancy in Agriculture: A Theoretical and Empirical Analysis," *American Economic Review,* 61 (Mar. 1971), pp. 48–64, derives a positive relation between wage and tenancy rate. This came from an unusual property of their equilibrium solution: zero marginal product of land is retained with the concave production function of share tenants. David Newberry pointed out that their equilibrium is not only noncompetitive but also unstable. Modified to meet the existence problem, "the final outcome will depend on the relative strength of the two effects and cannot be predicted a priori" (David M. G. Newberry, "The Choice of Rental Contract in Peasant Agriculture," in Lloyd G. Reynolds, ed., *Agriculture in Development Theory* [New Haven, 1975], p. 126).

Table 4.5 Township-Level Regression of Tenancy Rate

	Equation 1	Equation 2
Intercept	37.9359**	71.9157***
	(18.6784)	(21.6249)
Log (age)	−9.7646*	−14.1596***
	(5.1927)	(5.1489)
Literacy	−0.9632	−0.0379
	(1.8728)	(1.7991)
Born in state	1.0655	−0.8163
	(1.3727)	(1.4605)
Foreign-born	2.2637**	1.7901**
	(0.9018)	(0.8681)
Born in English-speaking countries	−4.2391**	−3.3816**
	(1.6994)	(1.6336)
Log of length of residency	−1.8084**	−1.2696
	(0.7902)	(0.7706)
Personal property	−0.000240	−0.000249
	(0.000371)	(0.000350)
Log (age) × settlement	2.7364	7.5842
	(8.3375)	(8.0610)
Log (residency) × settlement	4.2526	5.3079**
	(2.2696)	(2.1760)
Settlement	−15.4744	−39.0416
	(28.5745)	(28.2669)
Settlement^2	−7.6150***	−6.0746**
	(2.6685)	(2.5791)
Corn share	1.7729*	2.1689**
	(0.9048)	(0.8659)
Improved acreage	0.001596	0.002492
	(0.007087)	(0.006699)
Beef share	0.1890	2.2931
	(4.8503)	(4.6411)
Animal-product share	−1.5284	−1.3905
	(1.5061)	(1.4229)
Value per acre	0.01297*	0.00807
	(0.00727)	(0.00709)
Log (wage)		−7.4822***
		(2.6767)
Degrees of freedom	56	55
R^2	.503	.564
F-ratio	3.53	4.19

Notes: Standard errors are in parentheses. Dependent variable = log of the odds ratio of the tenancy rate. Weight = tenancy × (1 − tenancy) × number of farms.

Source: Computed from the Bateman-Foust sample.

*Significant at the .10 level.

**Significant at the .05 level.

***Significant at the .01 level.

farmers are the more efficient as measured by crop production per acre can not be conclusively answered except with reference to the particular locality under consideration." Roger Ransom and Richard Sutch claimed lower labor productivity, while Jon Moen calculated that the total productivity measure of tenants was greater than that of owners in 1880 in the cotton South.[40]

As Table 4.3 above shows, tenants had lower labor productivity and higher land, capital, and total factor productivity in the North as a whole and in the North Central region in 1860, while the opposite was true in the Northeast. In the North, total factor productivity of tenants was 6 percent higher than total factor productivity of owner-operators. In the North Central region tenants were 11 percent more productive, but in the Northeast tenants were 4 percent less productive. Was it because northeastern tenants were subject to static Marshallian inefficiencies, while the North Central tenants enjoyed productive efficiency in the sense of Cheung and Reid? Paradoxically, the similar pattern of input mix and output mix of owners and tenants in the Northeast suggests direct supervision by landlords, yet it is here that tenants are less efficient.

Agricultural productivity calculations have been widely employed to trace technological change over time or to compare the performance of different agricultural regions. Whether in temporal or spatial comparison, differences in total factor productivity call for an explanation, which usually turns on the existence of unmeasured inputs, changes in resource allocation, economies of scale, and so on. One way to approach the issue is to specify a production function containing more inputs. For example, Zvi Griliches introduced an education variable to represent labor-quality differentials and variables reflecting the output mix of different regions.[41]

Table 4.6 reports the results of production-function estimates. In addition to the conventional inputs of labor, land, and capital, the personal characteristics of farm operators were added to capture labor quality and managerial experience. The nature of the farm was represented by output-mix variables (shares of corn, beef, and animal products), scale of operation (improved acreage), and the settlement stage.

The effect of length of residency is not significantly different from zero in all three equations, probably because of measurement errors. Personal characteristics generally have significant coefficients of expected sign in the regressions for the North as a whole and for the North Central region. Again, this is not true of the Northeast. The most important human capital variables,

40. Winters, *Farmers Without Farms,* chap. 5; Lewis C. Gray et al., "Farm Ownership and Tenancy," in U.S. Department of Agriculture, *Yearbook of Agriculture, 1923* (Washington, D.C, 1924), pp. 574–75; Ransom and Sutch, *One Kind of Freedom;* Jon R. Moen, "Changes in the Productivity of Southern Agriculture, 1860–1880," in Robert W. Fogel and Stanley Engerman, eds., *Without Consent or Contract: Technical Papers on Slavery* (New York, 1991). I have reservations concerning the latter two citations, because the samples do not have adequate information to measure productivity by tenure.

41. Zvi Griliches, "Estimates of the Agricultural Production Function from Cross-Sectional Data," *Journal of Farm Economics,* 45 (May 1963), pp. 419–28.

Table 4.6 Production-Function Estimates with Tenure Dummy

	North	Northeast	North Central
Intercept	3.5487***	2.8343***	3.2952***
	(0.1026)	(0.2400)	(0.1212)
Log (labor)	0.1874***	0.1814***	0.1771***
	(0.0122)	(0.0167)	(0.0174)
Log (capital)	0.2522***	0.3354***	0.1814***
	(0.0084)	(0.0143)	(0.0104)
Log (land)	0.1925***	0.1809***	0.2391***
	(0.0075)	(0.0106)	(0.0107)
Log (age)	0.0703***	0.0274	0.1226***
	(0.0234)	(0.0503)	(0.0294)
Dummy for literacy	−0.0754***	−0.1029	−0.0768***
	(0.0273)	(0.0695)	(0.0295)
Dummy for born in state	−0.0416**	−0.1014***	0.0309
	(0.0190)	(0.0359)	(0.0246)
Dummy for foreign-born	−0.0834***	−0.1357*	−0.0382**
	(0.0235)	(0.0769)	(0.0250)
Dummy for born in English-speaking countries	0.1067***	0.0898	0.0626*
	(0.0306)	(0.0864)	(0.0330)
Log length of residency	0.0053	0.0200	0.0079
	(0.0103)	(0.0370)	(0.0108)
Personal property	5.858×10^{-5}***	3.617×10^{-5}***	7.907×10^{-5}**
	(0.504×10^{-5})	(0.610×10^{-5})	(0.845×10^{-5})
Settlement	0.1780*	2.7224***	−0.1082
	(0.1011)	(0.4619)	(0.1167)
Settlement^2	−0.5015***	−2.0982***	−0.2294**
	(0.0850)	(0.3032)	(0.1069)
Corn share	0.1341***	−1.6376***	0.3434***
	(0.0488)	(0.1761)	(0.0527)
Improved acreage	0.00161***	-4.024×10^{-5}	0.00116***
	(0.00029)	(46.498×10^{-5})	(0.00038)
Beef share	−1.0717***	−3.3514***	−0.3198**
	(0.1114)	(0.3343)	(0.1248)
Animal-product share	−0.2822***	0.1863	−0.7022***
	(0.0630)	(0.1348)	(0.0781)
Dummy for tenant	−0.0397*	−0.0207	−0.0672***
	(0.0210)	(0.0379)	(0.0248)
Dummy for Northeast	−0.1106***		
	(0.0560)		
Number of farms	8,556	3,175	5,381
R^2	.450	.509	.456
F-ratio	388.69	192.47	264.84

Notes: Standard errors are in parentheses. Dependent variable = log of value of farm output.

Source: Computed from the Bateman-Foust sample.

*Significant at the .10 level.

**Significant at the .05 level.

***Significant at the .01 level.

age and residency, lack significance in the regression for Northeast. It may be that younger farmers in the region shifted to the industrial sector or migrated westward and did not stay on the farm during the costly process of learning by doing.

The size and sign of the coefficients of the settlement variables indicate that the productivity of a farm increased in the initial stage of settlement but slowly declined thereafter. This may have reflected changing external economies. The sign of the size of a farm (improved acreage) is positive and significant for the North Central region and negative but insignificant for the Northeast. The sign on corn share is negative in the Northeast and positive in the North Central region, but the sign on animal-product share is positive in the Northeast and negative in the North Central region. These results reflect the pattern of the comparative advantage by region (corn for the North Central, dairy for Northeast); specialization raises efficiency.

It appears that the paradox of relatively low tenant productivity in the Northeast and high tenant productivity in the North Central region can now be resolved. The coefficients on the tenant dummy all have negative signs, which are statistically significant for the North Central region and for the North as a whole. In the North Central region, where the crude total productivity measures gave tenants 11 percent higher productivity than owner-operators, tenants seem to have been, other things equal, less productive than owners by about 7 percent. Tenants in the North Central region appeared more productive because they operated farms which produced a higher proportion of corn. This finding is hard to dismiss as a mere statistical artifact because the characteristics of the tenant farmer, such as age, length of residency, and the value of personal property, all imply lower agricultural productivity, unless fully supplemented by the landlord's supervision. According to Allan G. Bogue, "In general, tenants were most common where the soils were highly productive," and from a census monograph by Goldenweiser and Truesdell, published in 1924, "tenants are likely to lease farms situated on better land, while the farms on poor soil are most likely to be operated by their owners."[42] Likewise, tenants in the Northeast appeared less productive because they operated farms that produced a higher proportion of corn and a lower proportion of dairy product which went against the comparative advantage of the region.

If we rely on the results of the production-function estimates, then, other things being equal, the tenants in the Northeast were as productive as owners, and those in the North Central region were approximately 7 percent less productive than owners. My conclusion is that the substantial difference in the input mix in the North Central region suggests the possibility of a Marshallian misallocation, while the almost identical input and output mix of owner-operators and tenants in the Northeast suggests that in this region, supervision by landlords might have overcome any tendency toward inefficiency.

42. Bogue, *From Prairie to Corn Belt*, p. 66; Goldenweiser and Truesdell, *Farm Tenancy in the United States*, p. 65.

4.5 Conclusions

Generalizations about northern farming that do not take interregional differences into account are bound to be misleading. The characteristics of tenants compared with owners, and of tenant farms compared with owner-operated farms, were distinctly different in the North Central and Northeastern regions. In the North Central region tenants were generally younger than owner-operators and a higher proportion were migrants from out of state. Among those who were foreign-born, English-speaking countries were less represented among the tenantry. Tenant farms were smaller, more labor intensive, and produced relatively more corn than wheat or animal products. Within livestock husbandry, hog farming was more common among tenants than cattle raising or dairy farming. In the Northeast, on the other hand, almost none of these generalizations held.

The decision to lease a farm was largely determined by economic factors such as relative resource endowments, risk, and transactions costs, although in the Northeast the effect of resource endowments assumed less importance. A good part of the geographic variation in the tenancy rate can be explained by these forces. But, at the same time, some effect from speculation in the North Central region cannot be dismissed easily.

Ownership was a stage that could be reached only after accumulating a stock of human and physical capital. In the North Central region, where the capital market and the communication network of farm-management knowledge might not have operated well, tenancy served as a stepping stone to farm ownership. On the other hand, in the Northeast, where younger farmers were constantly drawn from the farm, the agricultural ladder hypothesis performs less well. Even six decades later, the pattern seems to have been intact. "In the United States as a whole [in 1920], 42 percent of the owner farmers reported no previous farm experience as wage hands or tenants. . . . The percentage is high in New England [59 percent], where tenancy is an unimportant step in the tenure ladder."[43] Thus, the institution of tenancy depended on the market environment where it operated.

Throughout the North, farm characteristics reflecting risk, transactions costs, and the condition of the market for land were important determinants of tenancy. The emergence and dispersion of tenancy can be explained fairly well by the market-equilibrium model. The model, moreover, can be extended to incorporate the influence of the labor market.

Tenants had lower labor productivity but approximately 6 percent higher total factor productivity than owner-operators. However, after adjusting for characteristics of farm and farm operators, the superiority of tenant farming disappears. In other words, tenants appeared more productive because they rented more productive farms. The finding is more apparent in the North Central region, where the apparent 11 percent superiority in total factor productiv-

43. Gray et al., "Farm Ownership and Tenancy," p. 554.

ity of tenants can be more than explained away by the characteristics of the farms. Tenants in this region may have been about 7 percent less productive than owner-operators, suggesting the possibility of Marshallian inefficiency. In the Northeast, on the other hand, the almost identical input and output mixes of tenants and owner-operators suggest that supervision by landlords may have been more effective. On the whole, the findings imply that, although the institution of farm leasing functioned reasonably well, the higher productivity exhibited by tenants in the crude comparisons originated in farm characteristics.

II Markets in Capital and Credit

5 Regional Interest Rates in Antebellum America

Howard Bodenhorn and Hugh Rockoff

5.1 The Debate Over the Short-term Capital Market

In one of the most famous papers in the literature of economic history, Lance Davis showed that short-term regional interest rates in the United States varied widely in the immediate postbellum years and converged slowly.[1] This paper stirred enormous interest among economic historians because it challenged the conventional wisdom that financial markets quickly and completely eliminate price differentials among assets bearing the same risk. A number of explanations of the pace and degree of convergence have been offered. Davis stressed the extension of the commercial-paper market; Richard Sylla, increased competition in banking and especially the provision for smaller national banks in the Gold Standard Act of 1900; Gene Smiley, risk and uncertainty as well as developments in the commercial-paper market; John James, the revival of free banking; Jeffrey Williamson, changing demands for capital; and Marie Elizabeth Sushka and Brian W. Barrett, the development of the stock market; and one of the authors of this paper, a number of years ago, argued that the risk of bank failure was a crucial determinant of the differences in the rate of return to bank capital.[2] Various attempts have also

The authors wish to thank Michael Bordo, Stanley Engerman, John James, Richard Keehn, Gene Smiley, Richard Sylla, and Eugene White for numerous helpful comments on previous drafts. As usual, any remaining errors are our responsibility.

1. Lance Davis, "The Investment Market, 1870–1914: Evolution of a National Market," *Journal of Economic History,* 25 (Sept. 1965), pp. 355–99.

2. Richard Sylla, "Federal Policy, Banking Market Structure, and Capital Mobilization in the United States, 1863–1913," *Journal of Economic History,* 29 (Dec. 1969), pp. 657–86; Gene Smiley, "Interest Rate Movements in the United States, 1888–1913," *Journal of Economic History,* 35 (Sept. 1975), pp. 591–620; John James, "The Development of the National Money Market," *Journal of Economic History,* 36 (Dec. 1976), pp. 878–97; Jeffrey G. Williamson, *Late Nineteenth Century American Development: A General Equilibrium History* (New York, 1974), chap. 6, pp. 119–45; Marie Elizabeth Sushka and Brian W. Barrett, "Banking Structure and the National Capital Market 1869–1914," *Journal of Economic History,* 44 (June 1984), pp. 463–77;

been made to refine Davis's estimates, as well as to see whether a similar phenomenon can be observed within a given state or in other countries.[3] Barry Eichengreen has examined the degree of integration in the mortgage market in 1890.[4]

But so far no attempt has been made to ask whether a related pattern held in the United States before the Civil War. Such an effort is important for several reasons. For one thing, the standard interpretation of the postbellum years may be misleading. The divergent character of rates in the aftermath of the Civil War may be a product of the disruption of the capital market during the war. This is most likely to be the case for the South, a major contributor to the impression that rates were divergent until late in the nineteenth century, and for the Pacific Coast which was left with a different monetary standard until specie payments were resumed in 1879.

If this conjecture were true, it would shed new light on the controversy over the convergence of the postwar rates. If interest rate differentials were the result of irrational prejudices against investing in capital-poor regions, we would expect the late antebellum period to exhibit the same interest rate profile as the early postbellum period. But if, for example, the postbellum pattern was the result of the disruptions caused by the war, including the local bank monopolies fostered by the National Banking Act (Sylla's thesis), then we would expect to see prewar rates close together, or at least exhibiting a different pattern of divergence. In any case, the war caused major disturbances to the normal functioning of the capital market. By looking at the antebellum rates we can establish a better benchmark for our examination of postbellum trends.

Antebellum rates would also be relevant to an issue that has been of special interest to Robert Fogel. One of the questions explored in *Time on the Cross* is whether slavery was profitable in the conventional business sense of the term. After the profitability of slavery is measured, the question becomes, With what alternative investment should we compare slavery? In *Time on the Cross,* Fogel and Stanley Engerman compare the rates of return to slavery

---

Hugh Rockoff, "Regional Interest Rates and Bank Failures," *Explorations in Economic History,* 14 (Winter 1977), pp. 90–95. This list is not intended to be complete. The point is simply to illustrate the wide range of work stimulated by Davis's paper.

3. For the former, see Gene Smiley, "Interest Rate Movements"; and John James, "Banking Market Structure, Risk, and the Pattern of Local Interest Rates in the United States, 1893–1911," *Review of Economics and Statistics,* 58 (Nov. 1976), pp. 453–62. For studies on the latter, see Richard Keehn, "Market Power and Bank Lending: Some Evidence from Wisconsin, 1870–1900," *Journal of Economic History,* 35 (Sept. 1975), pp. 591–620; Kenneth A. Lewis and Kozo Yamamura, "Industrialization and Interregional Interest Rate Structure: The Japanese Case, 1889–1925," *Explorations in Economic History,* 8 (Summer 1971), pp. 473–99; and David F. Good, "Financial Integration in Late Nineteenth-Century Austria," *Journal of Economic History,* 37 (Dec. 1977), pp. 890–910.

4. Barry Eichengreen, "Mortgage Interest Rates in the Populist Era," *American Economic Review,* 74 (Dec. 1984), pp. 995–1015.

with those to northern textile mills and southern railroads. Robert Evans presented data on short-term financial instruments and northern and southern railroads. Alfred H. Conrad and John R. Meyer relied on the rate of return on government bonds in their pioneering research.[5] Banking was an institution with which southern planters were familiar, and it provided a reasonable alternative for a planter seeking to shift some of his wealth into financial assets. So antebellum rates of return constructed from the type of data explored in the literature on postbellum regional rates could help clarify where slavery fell in the spectrum of available returns.

For these reasons we have combined information from a variety of sources to create a portrait of regional interest rates in the United States in the four decades before the Civil War. We discuss possible measures of interest rates from a theoretical point of view in section 5.2. The data and methods we use to derive our estimates follow in section 5.3. We present our basic interest rate series in section 5.4. These series, we believe, provide strong evidence that the interregional short-term capital market was integrated well before the Civil War. In section 5.5 we take a closer look at a cross section of states in the early 1850s, when additional data are available, which reinforces the conclusions drawn from the longer time series. In section 5.6 we tentatively reject an alternative explanation of the finding that regional interest rates were close together before the Civil War, that rates were held to the same level by usury laws. We examine evidence on the rate of return to bank capital, a long-term rate relevant to the debate over the profitability of slavery, in section 5.7. In section 5.8 we examine the impact of the Civil War on the regional dispersion of rates. Lastly, in section 5.9 we summarize our major findings and conclusions.

5.2 Measures of Interest Rates Derived from Bank Data

In the postbellum period the reports required by the National Banking Act provided data on bank earnings and earning assets. So it is relatively simple to derive a measure of short-term interest rates by taking a ratio of the two. It is true that this variable is not identical to an average of the rates specified in loan agreements. It is only a proxy for this purpose. But the net earnings ratio is more relevant than the average interest rate on loan agreements to decisions to allocate capital within the banking system. The net earnings ratio, in other words, is the right variable to use in a test for capital market integration.

Only limited sorts of data are available for the antebellum period, so it is necessary to consider in some detail how the surviving records can be used to

5. Robert W. Fogel and Stanley L. Engerman, *Time on the Cross: The Economics of American Negro Slavery* (Boston, 1974), vol. 1, p. 70; Robert Evans, Jr., "The Economics of American Negro Slavery," in *Aspects of Labor Economics: A Conference of the Universities–National Bureau Committee for Economic Research* (Princeton, 1962), pp. 203–08; Alfred H. Conrad and John R. Meyer, "The Economics of Slavery in the Ante Bellum South," *Journal of Political Economy,* 66 (Apr. 1958), pp. 43–92.

compute net earnings measures analogous to those computed for the postbellum period. Typically, we can find balance sheets for banks or groups of banks, usually on an annual basis, and, more rarely, dividend rates. From these bits of information several rates of return can be calculated. A typical antebellum balance sheet is given below.

Assets	Liabilities
Specie	Circulation
Notes of Other Banks	Deposits
Due from Other Banks	Other Liabilities
Loans and Discounts	Contingent Fund
Bonds	Surplus
Real Estate and Other Assets	Capital

The specie of the bank is the bank's gold and silver reserve and, of course, earns no interest. "Notes of Other Banks" and "Due from Other Banks" stand next to specie in terms of liquidity, and we have treated them as if they typically bear no interest. Some bankers' balances paid interest, but we do not know of any evidence on actual rates paid. In any case, bankers' balances would have paid a relatively low rate and were typically a small proportion of assets. "Loans and Discounts" are the main earning assets of the banks. The term "discount" was used frequently because a typical method of lending was the discounting of promissory notes. A bank might also own municipal, state, federal, railroad, or canal bonds. These could be sold on a national market and bore a lower rate of interest than loans to individuals. The last item, "Real Estate and Other Assets" includes the building, the flagpole, and any earning properties the bank owned. We have treated this item, normally rather small due to legal restrictions, as a non-earning asset.

On the liability side of the balance sheet we find the bank's "Circulation." This is the currency the bank issues which then "circulates" from hand to hand as money. Bank notes bore no interest. Deposits may be either interest bearing or non-interest bearing, although our limited information for New England suggests that the proportion of interest bearing deposits was normally rather small.

The final entries consist of the equity accounts. Paid-in capital is the amount of capital stock of the corporation outstanding. It is the "Contingent Fund" and "Surplus" accounts that are of importance in this study. In modern vernacular, these funds are equivalent to loan-loss and retained earnings accounts, respectively. In some states the legislative charters required the banks to retain a contingent fund to be used against future bad debts, or uncollectible loans or discounts. In other cases, banks adopted the practice as part of a sound banking policy.[6] The surplus or profit-and-loss account is equivalent to

6. After the collapse of the Bank of the Commonwealth in 1834–35, the legislature required that the banks could not pay dividends unless a contingent fund equal to 2 percent of the capital

a modern retained earnings fund. Any current net earnings not paid out as current dividends were transferred to this account to be paid out at a later date.

From these balance sheet items, and from the dividends paid to shareholders, we can construct several rates of return. Below we concentrate on two measures. First, we view the matter from the point of view of a bank manager and compute the ratio of dividends plus change in surplus less interest on bonds divided by loans. These measures address the issue of whether local net-lending rates were equalized by competition among banks and other intermediaries. Second, we view the matter from the point of view of a bank investor and measure the ratio of dividends plus retained earnings to capital plus surplus.

Equalization of one of these rates across regions, of course, is neither necessary nor sufficient to prove that the capital market was efficient. Risk, uncertainty, the costs of acquiring information about borrowers, and other costs of banking might differ from region to region. This is the burden of George Stigler's criticism of Davis's work.[7] Our basic response is to take a comparative approach, to see whether the differences we observe in the antebellum period are large or small when compared with differences observed in markets (generally at a later date or within a region) that qualitative evidence suggests we should regard as unified.

But how should differences between interest rates be measured? Should we look at the relative difference in rates or the absolute difference? For example, assume that initially the rate in region A was 8 percent and in region B, 10 percent. Later the rate fell to 2 percent in A and 3 percent in B. In absolute terms the gap has narrowed from 2 percent to 1 percent. But in relative terms it has widened from 22 percent in the initial period (2/9) to 40 percent (1/2.5) in the later period.

The consensus in the literature is that absolute differences are what count. Smiley's use of the coefficient of variation to measure dispersion, for example, was criticized by both Sylla and James whose argument is simply that a dollar is a dollar.[8] If arbitrageurs can make additional profits by moving money from region A to region B, they will do so, and the supply response will depend on the size of the gain. We must confess to some uneasiness about this argument. It seems to neglect the declining marginal utility of further gains when interest

stock was maintained ("Statement of the Bank of Kentucky and Branches," *Journal of the House of Representatives of Kentucky* [1859–60], pp. 296–97).

Although no law was found stating that banks were required to hold a contingent fund, most of the Virginia banks reported such a fund separately, as did several of the Philadelphia banks.

7. George Stigler, "Imperfections in the Capital Market," *Journal of Political Economy,* 75 (June 1967), pp. 113–22, reprinted in *The Organization of Industry* (Homewood, 1968), p. 116.

8. Richard Sylla, "Financial Intermediaries in Economic History: Quantitative Research on the Seminal Hypotheses of Lance Davis and Alexander Gerschenkron," in *Recent Developments in the Study of Business History: Essays in Memory of Herman E. Krooss,* Robert E. Gallman, ed., *Research in Economic History,* supplement 1 (1977), p. 68; John James, "The Development of the National Money Market," pp. 879–80.

rates are already high. Will an investor in region A be as likely to move capital to region B in response to a small absolute gain when the rate in region A is 8 percent as when it is only 2 percent? But, in the analysis below, we will concentrate on absolute differentials to maintain comparability with postbellum studies.

5.3 The Sources of the Data and the Computation of the Rates

As all students of American banking history are aware, bank data for the antebellum period are scarce and scattered. One advantage of the National Banking Act is that uniform bank reports were collected and published by the Comptroller of the Currency. During the antebellum period, states were the regulators of the banks within their jurisdictions. Most states required that banks return quarterly or annual reports of condition to the legislature. These reports were typically then printed in the state's legislative documents or journals and often found their way into contemporary journals, such as *The Bankers' Magazine,* Hunt's *Merchants' Magazine and Commercial Review,* and local newspapers. Most of the data used here, however, are from the original sources—state legislative reports and documents. In some cases it was necessary to use the Reports of the Secretary of the Treasury of the United States as reported in the *House Executive Documents*.[9] The results reported here are calculated from data for eight states for the period 1815 to 1860.[10] No claim is made that the data assembled are exhaustive, but they should reasonably reflect the regional pattern of interest rates from 1815 through 1860. Further research could add more series to the present study, but it is unlikely that they would contradict the findings reported here.

We included at least one state from each of the four regions east of the Mississippi defined by Davis: New England, Middle Atlantic, South, and the Old Northwest. Our data come primarily from Massachusetts, Rhode Island, New York City, Pennsylvania, Virginia, South Carolina, Tennessee, Kentucky, and Indiana. The Indiana figures are those of the State Bank of Indiana, which was a state-owned, statewide banking monopoly until 1856. The South Carolina figures are those of the state-owned Bank of the State of South Carolina. Although the South Carolina bank was not a monopoly, it had three branches and was the largest institution in the state. Kentucky, too, had a state-owned, state-branched bank—The Bank of the Commonwealth—until its liquidation began in 1835.

9. The Secretary of the Treasury of the United States collected the data for several years, from 1834 to 1862, but the reporting is sketchy in the early years, and no reports were collected or published during the Polk administration (i.e., the 27th and 28th congresses).

10. Reporting dates varied widely across states and even within states from year to year. The reports used here were those closest to year-end when a choice of dates was possible. In a few cases, linear interpolation was used to develop statements not available, but this was kept to an absolute minimum.

The annual net profit of the individual bank is calculated as dividends paid out in the past year plus changes in the surplus and contingent fund accounts since the last annual statement. This figure is then corrected in two respects. Bank portfolios included government securities, railroad and canal securities, and in some cases, direct loans to the state.[11] To obtain an accurate proxy for bank lending rates, income from these sources is subtracted. The simplest method is employed here, by subtracting 5 percent of each bank's reported holdings of public and private securities. Most federal, state, and city bonds as well as private bonds were issued with a nominal interest rate of 4 to 6 percent throughout the antebellum period.[12] Actual yields varied depending on the price paid for the security, but bank statements rarely revealed the type of security nor the price paid for them so more sophisticated adjustments are not possible.

The second adjustment made was the addition of taxes paid by the banks. Tax rates and taxing systems varied widely across states, but some general statements can be made. States adopted one of two schemes or some combination thereof. The New England states placed an annual tax on the paid-in capital of the bank, while states in the Middle Atlantic region and the South imposed taxes on dividend payments. For a statement of tax schemes and rates in various states, see Table 5.1.

The calculation of the interest rate proxies is then:

$$\text{Rate of Return on Earning Assets} = \text{Net Earnings}_{(t)}/\text{Earning Assets}_{(t-1)}$$

where Net $\text{Earnings}_{(t)}$ = [$\text{Dividends}_{(t)}$ + $\text{Surplus}_{(t)}$ − $\text{Surplus}_{(t-1)}$ − Securities $\text{Earnings}_{(t)}$ + $\text{Taxes}_{(t)}$]; Earning Assets = Discounts + Bills of Exchange.[13]

A number of potential refinements are possible in this measure. But experiments with data from the 1850s suggest that such refinements do not significantly alter the results. It could be argued, as we noted above, that interest paid on deposits should be added to the numerator since it is part of the gross earnings of a bank. We were able to make such an adjustment for Massachu-

11. In most Pennsylvania bank charters, a clause was inserted requiring the bank to loan to the state at short notice during fiscal emergencies at 5 percent annual interest. See Anna J. Schwartz, "The Beginning of Competitive Banking in Philadelphia, 1782–1809," *Journal of Political Economy,* 55 (Oct. 1947), pp. 417–31.

12. Sidney Homer, *A History of Interest Rates* (New Brunswick, 1963), chap. 16, pp. 274–326.

13. For the calculation of Net Earnings, New York City was one exception. We have been unable to determine the tax rate, if any, on New York banks. Therefore, we have not added in the tax component; neither have we subtracted out the security earnings term. This may introduce some bias, but our experience with the other states indicates that the two terms are about equal.

For Earning Assets, we followed the example of John James, "Banking Market Structure," p. 461, so that the divisor is the value of Earning Assets lagged one period. James argues that using a contemporaneous value of the divisor biases the calculation during periods of either rapid expansion or contraction. Alternative specifications using contemporaneous values and averages of (t) and $(t - 1)$ values altered the results very little.

Table 5.1 Bank Tax Schemes and Rates by State

State	Years	Rate	Base
Massachusetts	1820–60	1%	Paid-in capital
Rhode Island	1820–47	0.125	Paid-in capital
	1848–60	0.667	Paid-in capital
Pennsylvania	1815–34	8	Annual dividend
	1835–60	8–50	Annual dividend
Virginia	1820–60	0.5	Paid-in capital
Kentucky	1835–60	1	Paid-in capital

Note: The Pennsylvania tax rate from 1835 to 1860 was a graduated scale depending on the dividend percentage. Dividends of 6 percent of capital were taxed at 8 percent, with rates increasing to 50 percent with dividends of 12 percent or more.

Sources: N. S. B. Gras, *Massachusetts First National Bank of Boston* (Cambridge, Mass., 1937); Rhode Island *Acts and Resolves,* 1820–1860; J. Van Fenstermaker, *The Development of American Commercial Banking, 1782–1837* (Kent, Ohio, 1965); *Virginia House Documents,* 1820–1860; and *Kentucky Legislative Documents,* 1841–1860.

setts and Rhode Island, and this adjustment made almost no difference in the results; the proportion of deposits bearing interest was small and declining. In some cases the month in which balance sheets are reported differ from year to year. But again, experiments for the 1850s showed that interpolating all balance sheet data to June dates did not significantly alter the results. All bonds were assumed to pay interest at 5 percent. This rate is appropriate for government bonds, but it is conceivable that some securities held by banks—canal bonds, railroad bonds, some state bonds, and so on—paid somewhat higher rates. This would more likely be the case in the western and southern states, so our assumption biases the computations against finding interregional integration. But in any case, the ratio of bond holdings to loans was too small in all of the states we looked at for such adjustments to materially affect the rates of return.

5.4 The Results

The results of our computations are reported in Table 5.2 and Figures 5.1–5.4. The figures (which show three-year moving averages) reveal a remarkable degree of interregional financial integration before the Civil War.[14] Interest rates in most of the states shown were close to, and varied around, the rate in New York City, the nation's emerging financial center. The pattern holds, moreover, from the mid–1830s when most of our time-series begin. Indeed, in a few cases where we have the data, the pattern seems to have held even in the 1820s. We take these results to mean that the business of banking was

14. New England includes Rhode Island and Massachusetts. The Middle Atlantic includes New York and Pennsylvania. The South includes South Carolina and Virginia. The West includes Indiana, Kentucky, and Tennessee.

Table 5.2 Net Rates of Return on Earnings Assets

Year	Boston	Massachusetts (except Boston)	Rhode Island	New York City	Philadelphia	Pennsylvania (except Philadelphia)
1815					4.62%	
1816					5.70	
1817					3.69	
1818					5.55	
1819	5.48%	4.99%			3.84	
1820	6.12	5.34			5.60	4.24%
1821	5.61	4.76			4.78	4.16
1822	4.28	4.61			5.65	4.52
1823	4.70	4.65			3.42	4.35
1824	n.a.	n.a.			5.21	3.92
1825	n.a.	n.a.			4.24	4.48
1826	n.a.	n.a.			5.86	4.32
1827	4.05	5.50			4.95	4.28
1828	4.64	5.08			5.82	4.62
1829	4.93	5.07			4.58	4.37
1830	4.88	n.a.			4.97	5.89
1831	5.42	n.a.			5.15	5.19
1832	4.05	n.a.			4.48	5.61
1833	4.94	5.21		5.03%	6.54	5.95
1834	4.31	5.07		5.69	3.41	4.04
1835	4.52	5.19	6.24%	5.11	6.12	5.69
1836	4.56	5.28	5.78	6.82	5.74	6.35
1837	5.09	5.53	4.88	5.91	4.75	4.96
1838	5.21	5.30	5.27	5.33	5.47	4.05
1839	6.09	4.94	5.46	4.24	3.44	4.78
1840	5.45	4.83	4.39	5.57	5.73	4.34
1841	5.46	n.a.	5.80	5.27	4.41	4.81
1842	5.51	n.a.	5.34	3.95	2.50	n.a.
1843	4.89	n.a.	4.86	5.37	3.72	3.40
1844	4.28	n.a.	3.94	5.80	5.18	5.13
1845	4.31	4.34	5.40	5.21	4.20	4.82
1846	5.25	5.00	6.03	4.69	6.39	4.13
1847	4.51	4.92	5.57	5.04	5.21	4.08
1848	5.87	5.10	4.58	5.32	4.83	4.97
1849	6.02	5.49	6.18	7.17	6.35	4.48
1850	5.15	5.16	5.31	5.62	6.47	4.79
1851	5.14	5.23	5.58	6.32	4.69	5.07
1852	5.13	5.42	5.24	7.23	5.56	4.07
1853	5.73	5.92	5.94	4.99	5.10	5.50
1854	5.57	5.47	5.82	4.98	5.31	5.84
1855	5.87	5.75	5.20	5.87	5.70	5.96
1856	6.11	5.90	5.18	6.09	4.45	6.19
1857	6.01	5.59	5.81	5.45	3.16	5.28
1858	4.75	5.58	5.53	4.95	6.46	5.32
1859	4.67	5.18	5.49	4.62	4.32	6.04

(*continued*)

Table 5.2 (continued)

Year	Virginia	South Carolina	New Orleans	Kentucky	Tennessee	Indiana
1815		8.55%				
1816		5.55				
1817		5.45				
1818		8.35				
1819		4.23				
1820		4.36				
1821		4.34				
1822	4.08%	5.77		6.33%		
1823	3.81	4.86		4.42		
1824	4.14	4.62		4.01		
1825	4.61	4.15		3.93		
1826	3.97	2.53		3.00		
1827	4.97	7.81		3.12		
1828	3.97	4.50		3.83		
1829	4.23	4.09		3.51		
1830	4.45	4.14		5.02		
1831	4.84	4.49		3.48		
1832	6.28	4.24		3.35		
1833	8.02	4.37		2.85		
1834	3.75	3.54	6.82%	n.a.		
1835	4.43	4.12	7.54	5.89		7.97%
1836	7.22	4.37	7.16	7.97		7.60
1837	5.70	6.11	11.28	6.03		8.50
1838	4.41	6.00	7.68	5.93		8.35
1839	6.78	5.11	10.15	4.38		n.a.
1840	5.43	3.10	9.01	3.30	6.85%	n.a.
1841	4.21	5.75	8.86	4.91	5.48	7.65
1842	4.20	5.97	8.85	6.88	7.41	5.05
1843	4.12	6.20	n.a.	6.02	4.85	2.85
1844	4.15	6.03	n.a.	6.41	6.99	5.74
1845	5.10	5.76	n.a.	6.29	4.24	7.86
1846	3.95	5.42	n.a.	5.72	5.66	n.a.
1847	4.99	7.11	n.a.	5.44	4.92	6.32
1848	4.43	5.07	7.73	7.57	5.62	8.36
1849	4.19	6.03	4.84	5.02	5.50	7.77
1850	4.53	9.28	7.42	6.22	4.01	9.45
1851	4.72	7.67	7.79	7.00	6.08	5.95
1852	5.53	6.38	7.91	7.01	4.77	6.81
1853	4.46	6.71	7.38	5.80	4.38	6.37
1854	5.04	5.57	8.50	5.00	5.19	7.70
1855	5.18	6.03	12.81	8.42	4.65	10.89
1856	4.29	6.30		4.80	7.35	9.25
1857	3.88	5.93		4.96	7.46	
1858	2.92	5.98		5.78	6.79	
1859	5.96	6.76		6.25	4.48	

Notes: All values are simple averages for all reporting banks in each year for which sufficient information existed to make the rate of return calculations. For a complete list of all banks used in the sample, see Howard Bodenhorn, "Banking and the Integration of Antebellum American Capital Markets, 1815–1859" (Ph.D. dissertation, Rutgers University, 1990), appendix C. n.a. = not available.

Table 5.2 (continued)

Sources: **United States Documents**: U.S. House of Representatives, *Executive Document,* No. 105, 22d Cong.; Nos. 498 and 190, 23d Cong.; No. 65, 24th Cong.; Nos. 79, 471, and 227, 25th Cong.; No. 172 and 111, 26th Cong.; Nos. 226 and 120, 29th Cong.; No. 77, 30th Cong.; No. 68, 31st Cong.; Nos. 122 and 66, 32d Cong.; Nos. 102 and 82, 33d Cong.; Nos. 102 and 87, 34th Cong.; Nos. 107 and 112, 35th Cong.; Nos. 49 and 77, 36th Cong. **Massachusetts**: "A True Abstract of the Statements of Several Bank Corporations in the Commonwealth of Massachusetts," broadsides printed by order of the Senate, 1819, 1820, 1822–23, 1827–29. **Rhode Island**: "Returns of the Several Banks made to the General Assembly," *Acts and Resolves,* 1834, 1837–45, 1848. **New York State Documents**: *Assembly Documents,* 1832–33, 1835–37, 1839–48, 1856, 1858–59; "Report of the State Banking Department," 1860. **Pennsylvania**: "Report of the Auditor General, Accompanied with a Statement of Certain Banks," *Senate Journal,* 1814–17, 1819–31, 1833–38, 1841–52; *House Journal,* 1818, 1832, 1840; *Legislative Documents,* 1853–60. **Virginia**: *House Journal,* 1822–24, 1827–31; *House Documents,* 1825, 1826, 1832–60. **South Carolina**: *Reports and Resolutions of the General Assembly of South Carolina,* 1844, 1852–54, 1860; *Compilation of all the Acts, Resolutions, Reports and Other Documents in Relation to the Bank of the State of South Carolina, Affording Full Information Concerning that Institution* (Columbia, 1848). **Kentucky**: *House Journal,* 1822, 1825, 1832–33, 1860; *Senate Journal,* 1823–24, 1826–32, 1834–38, 1840; *Legislative Documents,* 1841–51, 1856, 1858. **Tennessee**: *House Journal,* 1845, 1848–49, 1851, 1853–55, 1859; *Senate Journal,* 1842–43, 1849. **Other Sources**: Norman Scott B. Gras, *The Massachusetts First National Bank of Boston, 1784–1934* (Cambridge, Mass., 1937), pp. 711–40; J. Mauldin Lesesne, *The Bank of the State of South Carolina: A General and Political History* (Columbia, South Carolina, 1970), pp. 185–86; Joseph G. Martin, *Twenty-One Years in the Boston Stock Market* (Boston, 1927); Nicholas B. Wainwright, *History of the Philadelphia National Bank* (Philadelphia, 1953), pp. 244–45; Lawrence Lewis, Jr., *A History of the Bank of North America* (Philadelphia, 1882), pp. 152–53; William F. Harding, "The State Bank of Indiana," *Journal of Political Economy,* 4 (Dec. 1895), pp. 1–36 and appendix; *Albany Daily Argus* (Albany), various issues, 1849–52; *Bicknell's Counterfeit Detector, Banknote Reporter and General Prices Current,* various issues, 1830–57; *Philadelphia Price Current,* various issues, 1827–30; *Commercial and Shipping List and Philadelphia Price Current,* various issues, 1830–59; *New Orleans Price Current,* various issues, 1835–59; *Daily Picayune,* various issues, 1834–60; *New York Herald Tribune,* various issues, 1842–60; *Banker's Magazine and Statistical Register,* various issus, 1848–60.

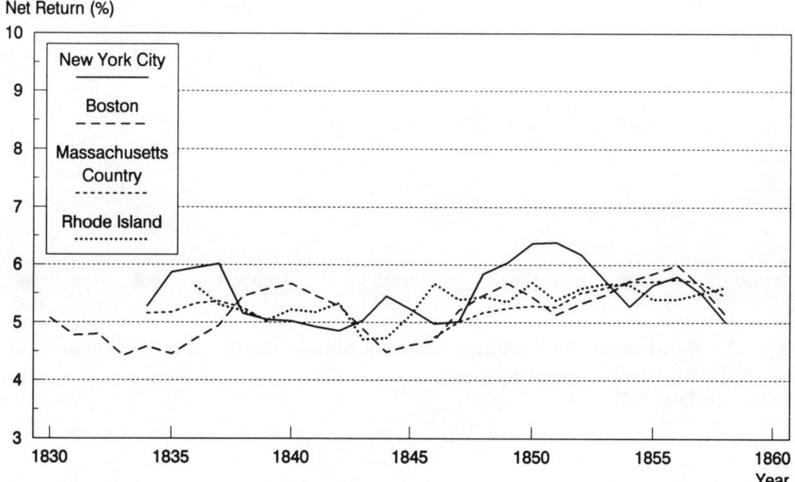

Fig. 5.1 Returns on the Earnings Assets of Banks: New England Region
Note: Returns are three-year moving averages.
Source: See Table 5.2.

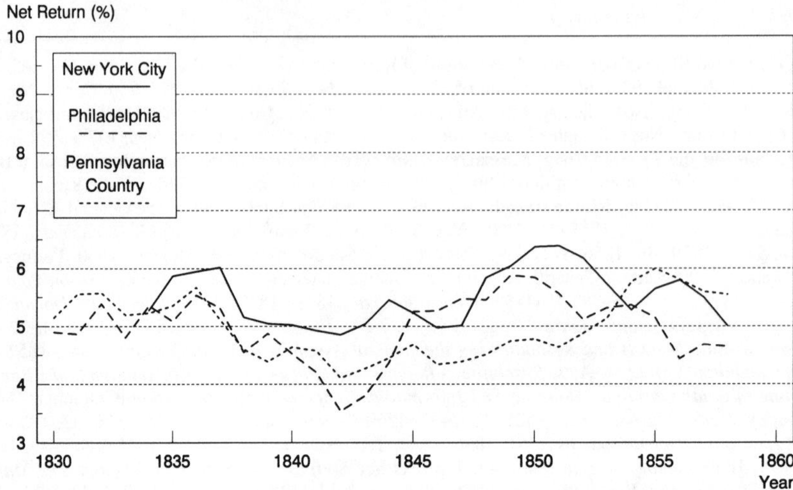

Fig. 5.2 Returns on the Earnings Assets of Banks: Middle Atlantic Region
Note: Returns are three-year moving averages.
Source: See Table 5.2.

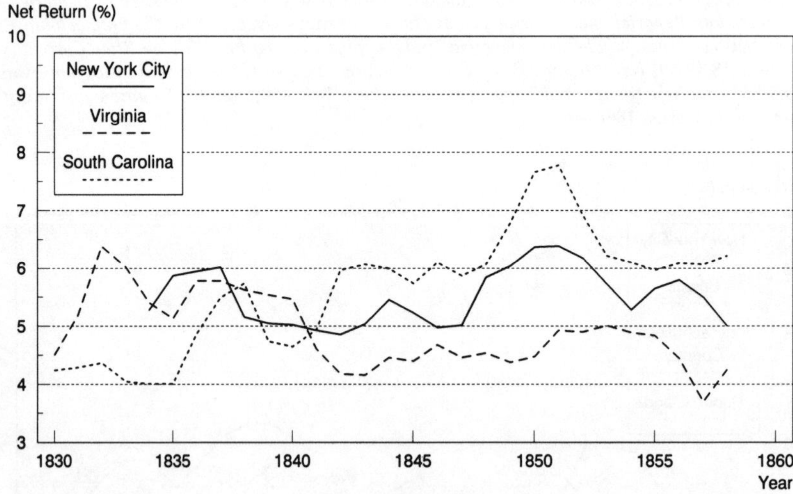

Fig. 5.3 Returns on the Earnings Assets of Banks: South Atlantic Region
Note: Returns are three-year moving averages.
Source: See Table 5.2.

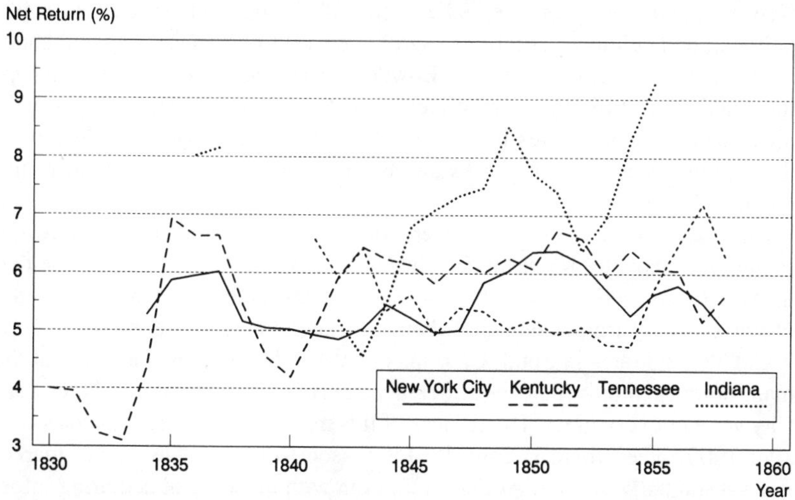

Fig. 5.4 Returns on the Earnings Assets of Banks: Western and Southwestern Regions

Note: Returns are three-year moving averages.
Source: See Table 5.2.

similar in developed regions of the country (risks and administrative costs were similar) and that short-term capital was reallocated until returns were roughly equalized.

Some of the results are, perhaps, to be expected. Boston, Philadelphia, and New York City were all thriving financial centers. Merchants and bankers in these cities would have been informed of market conditions and could have readily moved funds from one city to another. Nor is it surprising that rates within New England were fairly close together and consistent with New York City (Figure 5.1). A strong case can be made that if any region of the country constituted a unified capital market before the Civil War, it was New England. Even by the 1850s, banking had a long history in the region, and its banks, moreover, were subject to the Suffolk system of note redemption.[15] Banking regulations (including usury laws) were similar from state to state. There was very little in the way of free banking in New England, but it has been argued that legislatures in this region were relatively free in granting charters.[16] Even the accounting frameworks within New England seem to have been similar. But such considerations are only part of the story. More important was that

15. The Suffolk was a bank in Boston. By agreement of the Boston banks, all out of city notes were turned over to the Suffolk for redemption. This arrangement had the effect of keeping New England notes at par.

16. See Richard Sylla, "Early American Banking: The Significance of the Corporate Form," *Business and Economic History,* 14 (Mar. 1985), pp. 105–23. Schwartz, "The Beginning of Competitive Banking," demonstrates that competition can take hold quickly, even in a system that requires a legislative charter for each new bank.

New England was a long-settled region with limited variation in its legal, political, and cultural institutions. Surely networks of businessmen and bankers existed—former classmates at Bowdoin or Harvard —through which capital could move from one part of New England to another. The differences in interest rates among states in New England, in other words, were as low as the technology and varying risks and business conditions of the time would allow.

The results for the South, however, are somewhat unexpected. As shown in Figure 5.3, short-term rates in South Carolina and Virginia seemed to be tied in with those in New York City throughout the antebellum period. In the 1850s, rates in Virginia averaged about 100 basis points less than rates in New York City, and rates in South Carolina about 100 basis points more.[17] But the main point is simply that the differences between the South and New York City were not very great. Differences of this magnitude appear in Davis's data after 1900, when there is considerable reason to believe the capital market was substantially unified. At that time, even with the costs of acquiring information much reduced by improved communication and National Banks operating within a common regulatory framework, rate differentials of 75 to 100 basis points were still common between regions. Over the period 1908 to 1914, for example, net rates of return for non-reserve-city banks in the region containing South Carolina and Virginia averaged almost 70 basis points more than those in New York City.[18]

It would be useful to have a long series for bank rates in New Orleans, but we have not been able to locate many dividend rates. Table 5.2 shows the rate for the Canal Bank. The rate earned by this bank appears to have been somewhat higher than the others we have been examining. But the Canal Bank also received income from its Canal Company, and the computations may not adjust fully for the income from this source. We also found dividend rates for all banks in New Orleans in 1858.[19] In that year, the dividend to earnings asset ratio was 6.16 percent, a rate that might be expected in the West. It is possible that net earnings were lower than dividends. The gap between assets and liabilities in the balance sheets in *De Bow's Review* declined from + $1,636 in September 1857 to − $664,993 in August 1858.[20] Adjusting for this decline would make the net return on earnings assets 3.57 percent. But the absence of complete balance sheets and a longer time-series make it hard to draw firm

17. To some extent this might be accounted for by regulatory differences. The South Carolina rates were produced by a state-owned banking system, while the Virginia rates were produced by a system that was highly competitive owing to the presence of branch banking.

18. Davis, "The Investment Market," p. 365.

19. *De Bow's Review,* 18 (1858), p. 562.

20. George D. Green, *Finance and Economic Development in the Old South: Louisiana Banking, 1804–1861* (Stanford, 1972), p. 204, shows a total for all of Louisiana, "other liabilities," that includes capital accounts. This item declines from $2.21 million in December 1857 to $0.46 million in January 1859.

conclusions about New Orleans. On the whole we are inclined to believe that rates there may have been somewhat higher than the eastern norm.

The finding that the older states of the South were integrated financially with the North, we should add, is only surprising if it is assumed that capital markets were fragmented before the Civil War and that the South was a separate region, poor in capital and lacking in entrepreneurial skills. The results are not so surprising when we start from the more recent view that the antebellum South had a rational, albeit morally abhorrent, economy.[21]

When we turn to the West (Figure 5.4), the results are similar although less clear-cut. In Kentucky (perhaps as much a southern as a western state) the rates are similar to those in the East. The Kentucky rate conforms to the New York City rate from the time our New York City rate becomes available in the 1830s. In the 1850s the Kentucky rate averaged only about 50 basis points more than the New York City rate. The Kentucky rates for the 1820s seem unusually low, and there is an interesting story behind them. The Panic of 1819 was particularly devastating for the farmers of Illinois, Tennessee, and Kentucky. In response, the three legislatures formed banks with the express purpose of relieving the "distresses of the community."[22] For example, the Bank of the Commonwealth of Kentucky was required by charter to extend low-interest loans to farmers and planters throughout the state. That the legislature was successful is evidenced by the relatively low rates during the period.

In Indiana, by way of contrast, rates appear to have been significantly above those in the East during the 1830s and 1840s. To some extent this may have been due to the monopoly position of the State Bank of Indiana. Note that in the mid–1850s, when the State Bank was challenged by banks established under a free-banking law, the rate appears to have fallen substantially. The high rates for 1855 and 1856, moreover, may be misleading since we are unable to separate current earnings from the realization of capital gains produced by the winding up of the affairs of the State Bank.[23] In short, we cannot rule out the possibility that there was a frontier premium in Indiana during part of our period. But in any case, rates in Indiana were approaching the eastern norm by the early 1850s.

21. Charles W. Calomiris and Larry Schweikart have reached a view of southern banking similar to ours based on balance sheet data and the performance of the southern systems in financial crises. See "Was the South Backward? North-South Differences in Antebellum Bank Performance during Normalcy and Crises" (manuscript, Northwestern University, 1988).

22. This section follows J. Van Fenstermaker, *The Development of American Commercial Banking, 1782–1837* (Kent, 1965), pp. 25–26. The quote is from p. 26.

23. Some of the earlier rates may also be overstated. There were several items on the balance sheet that we could not positively identify. These may have been short-term loans to the state. Deducting an interest allowance for these assets would further reduce the measured return on loans and discounts. The 5 percent rate we use for the return on stocks and bonds in the bank's portfolio may also be an understatement.

The question that naturally follows is how well the rates we have calculated reflect actual commercial bank lending rates. It is not necessary, to reiterate a point made above, that net returns mimic lending rates for net returns to provide us with useful information about the integration of the financial markets. But for many purposes, rates paid by borrowers are at issue. A few bits of data are available. Donald Adams has investigated Stephen Girard's private bank that operated in Philadelphia between 1812 and 1831. He calculated the average monthly discount rate charged by Girard's bank from January 1812 through October 1831, and Table 5.3 reproduces his results. Comparisons with our rates for Philadelphia reveal a near equality in most years. Results this close are somewhat unexpected, because the Girard Bank figures are gross while the Philadelphia numbers are net. But Stephen Girard was generally very conservative, investing heavily in government securities and "prime double-name paper."[24] The chartered Philadelphia banks, however, could not be as selective. Charter clauses mandated that the Philadelphia banks (and all Pennsylvania banks generally) make loans equaling at least 20 percent of their paid-in capital to farmers and mechanics in the state.[25] Since agriculture is traditionally risky and real estate security would have to be taken, these loan rates were probably higher than those for prime commercial paper.[26] Provided that default rates were low, both the gross and net returns would be higher if a substantial portion of a bank's portfolio was held in higher return assets.

We also examined the discount rates in New York City, Philadelphia, Boston, and New Orleans on various commercial instruments as reported in *Bankers' Magazine* and in local newspapers. These figures provide further evidence that the bank rates we calculate represent fairly accurately the pattern of financial integration in early America from the borrower's point of view. Table 5.4 shows the quotes on prime or first-class paper in all four cities. The discount rate on "prime paper" in New York City is closely followed by changes in the rates on similar instruments in the other cities. The only real exception is in 1858, when New York City rates were 3 percent while New Orleans reported an 8 percent rate.[27]

24. See Donald R. Adams, Jr., *Finance and Enterprise in Early America: A Study of Stephen Girard's Bank, 1812–1831* (Philadelphia, 1978). In 1815 almost 75 percent of the Girard Bank's earnings assets was in government debt. In 1816 and 1817 the figures were 45 and 46 percent, respectively (table 2, p. 33).

25. Van Fenstermaker, *The Development of American Commercial Banking*, p. 18.

26. The Philadelphia Bank operated an agent in Wilkes-Barre, probably for the purpose of extending loans primarily to farmers, to comply with the condition of its charter. The Pennsylvania Bank operated a branch at Easton for several years, as well. The debts outstanding at these branches were generally secured by bonds and mortgages ("Auditor General's Report on Banks," *Pennsylvania House Journals*, 1825–1829).

27. Borrowing rates might also differ from the net rates we examine because of cost differences among regions. But we have not found sufficient data to address this issue.

Table 5.3 **Average Discount Rates at Girard's Bank, Philadelphia: 1815–1831**

Year	Quarter I	Quarter II	Quarter III	Quarter IV
1815	6.07%	6.15%	5.39%	5.50%
1816	5.69	5.84	5.78	5.75
1817	5.79	5.36	5.62	5.85
1818	5.42	5.48	5.52	5.33
1819	5.45	5.35	5.81	5.63
1820	5.43	5.54	5.41	5.24
1821	5.07	5.43	5.53	5.43
1822	5.55	5.60	5.47	5.59
1823	5.40	5.64	5.54	5.63
1824	5.37	5.84	5.14	5.97
1825	5.32	5.88	5.57	5.62
1826	5.19	5.46	5.51	5.67
1827	5.88	5.47	5.80	5.43
1828	5.34	5.23	5.15	5.00
1829	4.92	5.47	5.03	5.90
1830	5.91	6.06	6.14	6.02
1831	5.12	5.95	5.45	n.a.

Source: Donald R. Adams, Jr., *Finance and Enterprise in Early America: A Study of Stephen Girard's Bank* (Philadelphia, 1978), p. 107. Used by permission of the author.
n.a. = not available.

5.5 A Cross Section for the First Half of the 1850s

Table 5.5 shows the rates earned for a list of states, including both those examined above and some additional states for which we have data for only a few years or data that are not strictly comparable. In New England we have added rates for Maine. These appear to be in line with the other rates and strengthen the picture of a unified capital market along the east coast. For the period 1850 to 1854, the rate in Maine averaged 4.73 compared with 5.83 in New York City. In the South we have added a few observations for the banks of Baltimore where the rates seem to have been low.

In the West we have added data for Ohio from Charles Clifford Huntington's classic history which contains earnings of Ohio banks in 1850, 1851, and 1853.[28] Table 5.5 presents rates based on these data for the years 1850 to 1853 by class of bank. The banking situation in Ohio was confused by the presence of four regulatory systems: the State Bank, the chartered banks, the independent banks, and free banks. The State Bank (a federation on the Indiana model) and the older chartered banks were relatively unconstrained in their selection of assets. The independent banks and the free banks, on the other hand, had bond-secured note issues. Our calculations for the latter two

28. Charles C. Huntington, *A History of Banking and Currency in Ohio Before the Civil War, Ohio Archaeological and Historical Publications,* vol. 24 (Columbus, 1915), pp. 440–41.

Table 5.4 Commercial-Paper Rates at Selected Cities, 1841–1859

Year	New York City	Philadelphia	Boston	New Orleans
1841	7%	8%	6%	
1842	7	9	8	
1843	3	5	4	
1844	4	5	5	
1845	5	6	6	
1846	7	7	9	
1847	5	6	6	
1848	8	7	18	
1849	5	6	9	
1850	5	7	7.5	
1851	6	7	7	
1852	4	6	5.5	
1853	5	7	8	8.5%
1854	8	12	11	10
1855	5	6	6	6
1856	6	7	8	6
1857	8	9	8	12
1858	4		4.5	6
1859	6		7	6

Note: Rates on high-grade paper. All observations are closest to the end of June of each year. When a spread was given in the source, the lower quote is reported in the table.

Sources: New York Herald Tribune, various issues, 1841–60; *New York Journal of Commerce,* various issues, 1841–60; *Bicknell's Counterfeit Detector, Banknote Reporter, and General Prices Current,* various issues, 1831–57; New Orleans *Daily Picayune,* various issues, 1853–59; and Frederick R. Macaulay, *The Movements of Interest Rates, Bond Yields and Stock Prices in the United States since 1856* (New York, 1938), pp. A248–A250.

classes are unusually sensitive to the assumption made about the interest paid on the bonds. According to Huntington, the bonds deposited normally bore 5 to 6 percent interest, but the banks often borrowed the securities, paying the owner 1 or 2 percent for their use.[29] In our calculations we have assumed a net return of zero, assuming, in other words, that income earned on bonds was offset in the aggregate by interest paid to lenders of the securities. Altogether, the Ohio rates during the period appear similar to, perhaps a bit below, the rates in Indiana and Kentucky, and are not substantially higher than rates in the eastern financial centers.

Finally, we have added some rates for California. Because these are not bank rates, they are not strictly comparable with the others we have computed. It seems likely that rates on the assets normally acquired by banks would have been lower. Nevertheless, the sketchy evidence we have found suggests that rates in California were extraordinarily high in the early 1850s. According to Hubert H. Bancroft, the interest rate "ruled at ten percent per month even after

29. Ibid., p. 441.

Table 5.5 **A Cross-Section of Rates, 1850–1854**

	1850	1851	1852	1853	1854	Average
New York City	5.62%	6.32%	7.23%	4.99%	4.98%	5.83%
Prime paper	6.00	6.00	4.50	7.00	8.00	6.30
Boston	5.15	5.14	5.13	5.73	5.57	5.34
Prime paper	7.00	6.25	5.00	6.00	n.a.	6.06
Massachusetts (except Boston)	5.16	5.23	5.42	5.92	5.47	5.44
Rhode Island	5.31	5.58	5.24	5.94	5.82	5.58
Maine	4.29	4.94	3.97	5.20	5.24	4.73
Philadelphia	6.47	4.69	5.56	5.10	5.31	5.43
Prime paper	7.00	7.00	6.00	8.00	12.00	8.00
Pennsylvania (except Philadelphia)	4.79	5.07	4.07	5.50	5.84	5.05
Baltimore	3.86	3.47	n.a.	n.a.	n.a.	3.67
Virginia	4.53	4.72	5.53	4.46	5.04	4.86
South Carolina	9.28	7.65	6.38	6.71	5.57	7.12
Tennessee	4.01	6.08	4.77	4.38	5.19	4.89
New Orleans[a]	7.42	7.79	7.91	7.38	8.50	7.80
Prime paper	n.a.	n.a.	n.a.	8.50	10.00	9.25
Indiana	9.45	5.95	6.81	6.37	7.70	7.26
Ohio						
State	5.46	5.91	6.07	6.23	n.a.	5.87
Chartered	7.00	5.00	n.a.	n.a.	n.a.	6.00
Independent	2.30	5.16	4.96	4.76	n.a.	4.07
Free	n.a.	n.a.	n.a.	6.52	n.a.	6.52
Kentucky	6.22	7.00	7.01	5.80	5.00	6.21
California	213.84	213.84	55.80	34.49	n.a.	129.49

Sources: **Maine**: *Annual Reports* of the Secretary of the Treasury on the Banks (see the House documents listed in Table 5.2). **Baltimore**: Dividends 1849–51—*Banker's Magazine,* vol. 6, p. 749; dividends 1852—vol. 7, p. 166; balance sheets: *Annual Reports* of the Secretary of the Treasury on the Banks. **Ohio**: Charles C. Huntington, *A History of Banking and Currency in Ohio Before the Civil War, Ohio Archaeological and Historical Publications,* vol. 24 (Columbus, 1915), pp. 440–41. **California**: Hubert Howe Bancroft, *History of California,* vol. 7 (San Francisco, 1890), pp. 161–62. The remaining rates are from Tables 5.2 and 5.4.

[a]Canal Bank.

n.a. = not available.

1849, or even double that for short loans. In 1852 it declined to three and soon after to two and a half percent per month, at which it stood for some time, while operations adjusted themselves more and more to eastern forms."[30] Sidney Homer records a number of private transactions in California at rates of 60 percent and more per year, and a loan on which the city of San Francisco paid 24 percent per year.[31] To some extent this state of affairs may have been

30. Hubert Howe Bancroft, *History of California,* vol. 7 (San Francisco, 1890), pp. 161–62.
31. Homer, *A History of Interest Rates,* p. 323.

due to legal restrictions. California's constitution prohibited the state from chartering note-issuing banks, and subsequent legislation made clear that the prohibition on note issue applied to private banks as well. Although this restriction may have been violated at times, it may have served to restrict the supply of loanable funds. But Bancroft's emphasis on "the enterprise stirred by the fast-developing resources of a new country" may well be the right one. The demand for capital was high and firms, and sometimes whole industries, lacked the track record that made fine calculations of risk possible.[32]

5.6 Usury Laws and the Antebellum Pattern of Interest Rates

A potential alternative explanation for the observed pattern of interest rates is that usury laws placed a binding ceiling on the rates banks could charge. The pattern of rates seen in Figures 5.1–5.4, in other words, might be the result of usury ceilings and the cost functions of banks, rather than market integration. A cursory glance at Table 5.6, which shows legal interest rates in 1841, would seem to confirm the contention that usury laws explain the pattern of antebellum interest rates. Most of the states had rates of 6 or 7 percent. The effectiveness of these laws, it might then be argued, is reflected in the net rates reported in Table 5.2, which are concentrated around 5½ to 6 percent.[33]

But before we can attribute a causal role to usury laws in producing the pattern of antebellum interest rates, we need to consider how effective they were. Legal rates were often ignored when economic conditions warranted higher rates. On 19 August 1851, the "Money Market" column in *Bicknells' Counterfeit Detector, Banknote Reporter, and General Prices Current* quoted the going rate on first-class paper at 1 percent per month and noted that it was twice the legal rate. Banks, moreover, were among those lending at these extraordinary rates. In New York City, to take another example, the legal rate was 7 percent, but in June 1848 the going rate for prime paper was 12 to 18 percent. If debtors were litigious, such lending would be a courageous act since the penalty for a usurious contract was forfeiture of both principal and interest. It is also apparent that money was lent at higher than legal rates from the rate of return figure for New York City in 1849. The average net rate of return was 7.17 percent. In 1852, it was 7.23 percent.

There were, as well, legal methods of collecting interest in excess of rates

32. Adam Smith would not have been surprised that interest rates were higher in the regions of new settlement (*An Inquiry into the Nature and Causes of the Wealth of Nations* [New York, 1937; orig. pub. 1776], pp. 92–93).

33. A number of the usury laws in the frontier states, however, contained an important escape clause, perhaps reflecting higher rates in this region. Here the laws allowed for higher rates of interest if specified in the contract. In Wisconsin, for example, if no mention were made on the promissory note of the rate to be paid, the maximum legal discount rate was 7 percent. If a special clause were inserted specifying the rate to be charged, the maximum allowable rate was 12 percent. Similar laws prevailed in Indiana (the State Bank of Indiana, however, appears to have been restricted to 6 percent), Illinois, Missouri, Mississippi, Arkansas, and Iowa.

Table 5.6 Legal Interest Rates and Usury Penalties, 1841

State	Legal Rate	Usury Penalty
Maine	6%	Forfeiture of debt
New Hampshire	6	Three times the usury
Vermont	6	Recovery of usury, with costs
Massachusetts	6	Three times the usury
Rhode Island	6	Forfeiture of interest
Connecticut	6	Forfeit interest and principal
New York	7	Contract unenforceable
New Jersey	6	Forfeit interest and principal
Pennsylvania	6	Forfeit interest and principal
Delaware	6	Forfeit interest and principal
Maryland	6	Contract void
Virginia	6	Two times the usury
North Carolina	6	Two times the usury
South Carolina	7	Forfeit interest, with costs
Georgia	8	Three times the usury
Alabama	8	Forfeit interest and usury
Mississippi	8	Forfeit the usury, 10% legal
Louisiana	5	Contract void. Bank rate, 6%
Tennessee	6	Contract void
Kentucky	6	Forfeit usury, with costs
Ohio	6	Contract void
Indiana	6	Two times the usury, 10% legal
Illinois	6	Three times the interest
Missouri	6	Forfeit interest
Michigan	7	Forfeit usury and one-fourth principal
Arkansas	6	Forfeit usury, 10% legal
Florida	8	Forfeit interest and usury
Wisconsin	7	Three times usury, 12% legal
Iowa	7	Three times usury, 12% legal

Note: A percentage listed in the penalty column means that if both parties agreed to the interest rate in writing, it could be as high as the percentage indicated.
Source: Hunt's *Merchants' Magazine and Commercial Review,* vol. 4 (1841), p. 268.

allowed under the usury laws. One method was by overcharging for the so-called sight exchange. One common way of borrowing was through the bill of exchange. Consider, to make the argument concrete, a bill of exchange drawn by a tobacco factor in Philadelphia on the Bank of Kentucky, payable in sixty days to a Philadelphia commission merchant. As the Philadelphia merchant was unlikely to travel to Louisville in sixty days to collect on the bill, he would rediscount it at a bank or exchange broker in Philadelphia. The discount charged by the bank or exchange broker would include an amount beyond the opportunity cost of the money that reflected the cost of collection—the "sight exchange." The going rate for sight exchange (it might range from ¼ percent to 3 percent or more, depending on the time and date) was widely reported in the commercial press. With a 1½ percent sight exchange (a typical charge for exchange between Louisville and Philadelphia), the banker or exchange broker would value the $100 bill at $98.50 and then charge an additional discount to reflect the interest on the sixty-day loan.

The effective discount, therefore, on bills of exchange can be broken down into two parts—the interest rate and the sight exchange, or the cost to bring the money home.[34] It was through the use of sight exchange that usury laws could be effectively circumvented. If usury were alleged by a borrower, the creditor could claim that only the legal interest rate was charged and any excess represented the cost of collection.[35] According to one authority, "it was widely possible by the time of the Civil War to arrange usurious transactions in such a way as to entirely avoid running afoul of the usury laws."[36]

Further evidence against the usury explanation is provided in Table 5.7 which reports Spearman rank-correlation tests for various periods for rates between New York City or Philadelphia and Virginia, South Carolina, Kentucky, and Rhode Island.[37] If usury laws were the source of the apparent conformity of rates and the markets were not integrated, then regional rates should move independently. The correlations, however, show that the direction of influence was from the eastern financial centers—New York City and Philadelphia—to other regions.

While this evidence does not rule out some effect from usury laws, we doubt that they can explain much of the congruence in the regional interest rate series.

5.7 The Rate of Return to Equity

The rate of return to bank equity has received less attention in the literature on postbellum rates than the short-term rate. But the return to equity is presumably the determinant of the allocation of bank capital. Investors could have figured out where returns were highest, in part by relying on the same data that we have, and tried to earn the high returns by investing in bank stock (although higher stock prices would have capitalized high returns if widely anticipated) or by actually organizing a bank. The net rates of return to equity by quinquennia are displayed in Table 5.8. While outliers exist (the Pennsylvania and Kentucky rates in the 1850s, and the Tennessee rates in the late 1850s), the overall impression is that most rates were in the 7 to 8 percent range. There is little evidence here of a regional gradient.

This table, we should point out, provides evidence relevant to the contro-

34. This section is developed largely from Hugh Rockoff, "Origins of the Usury Provision of the National Banking Act," (manuscript, Rutgers University, 1988), pp. 17–18.

35. This method of applying the usury law was accepted in Maine. See ibid., p. 18.

36. Morton J. Horwitz, *The Transformation of American Law* (Cambridge, Mass., 1977), p. 244, quoted in ibid., p. 18.

37. Conventional parametric correlations, however, were not statistically significant, possibly because of the distorting effects of the very high rates in certain cities during financial crises.

Table 5.7 **Spearman Rank-Correlation Coefficient Tests**

	Virginia	South Carolina	Kentucky	Rhode Island
1825–59				
Philadelphia (−1)	0.38**	0.28*	0.14	
1830–59				
Philadelphia (−1)	0.37**	0.28*	0.22	
1835–59				
Philadelphia (−1)	0.58***	0.39**	0.19	0.11
New York (−1)	−0.09	0.28	0.00	0.13
1840–59				
Philadelphia (−1)	0.50**	0.53**	0.11	0.27
New York	−0.13	0.30	0.04	0.55**

Notes: (−1) denotes a one-period lag.
Source: Table 5.2

*Denotes significance at the 90% level.
**Denotes significance at the 95% level.
***Denotes significance at the 99% level.

Table 5.8 **Antebellum Rates of Return to Bank Equity**

	1830–34	1835–39	1840–44	1845–49	1850–54	1855–59
New York City	8.85%	8.36%	5.17%	8.54%	8.28%	7.20%
Boston	7.03	7.06	7.29	9.10	9.29	8.29
Massachusetts (except Boston)	7.60	7.32	n.a.	8.00	8.58	8.64
Providence	n.a.	6.71	5.95	6.77	7.30	7.05
Philadelphia	8.46	7.31	5.39	7.03	9.94	8.08
Pennsylvania (except Philadelphia)	8.21	7.72	6.83	7.85	9.17	9.58
Virginia	7.93	9.11	5.43	7.01	8.40	8.36
South Carolina	7.24	6.64	4.52	6.67	7.64	6.58
New Orleans	n.a.	7.13	6.17	n.a.	5.98	n.a.
Kentucky	n.a.	6.66	4.00	8.19	9.43	9.08
Tennessee	n.a.	n.a.	6.88	5.94	7.22	10.10
Indiana	8.85	8.36	5.17	8.54	8.28	7.20

Sources: See Table 5.2.
n.a. = not available.

versy about the profitability of slavery. Fogel and Engerman estimated that slave owners earned about 10 percent on their investment.[38] Slave owners could have moved their capital into banking, but as the rates for South Carolina, Virginia, Kentucky, and Tennessee show, it would not have been profitable to do so. A definitive comparison would have to make risk adjustments to both the returns to slaveholding and banking. But the unadjusted figures confirm Fogel and Engerman's claim that the rates of return earned by slave-

38. Fogel and Engerman, *Time on the Cross,* p. 70.

holders were equal to or higher than the rates that could have been earned with alternatives.

Antebellum rates of return to bank equity appear to have been no more dispersed than similar postbellum rates; indeed the antebellum rates may have fallen within a narrower band. Some long-term averages for the postbellum period are shown in Table 5.9, which is based on data published by Keith Powlison in 1931. Evidently there were substantial interregional differences even in the period 1904 to 1914. Whatever the explanation for the persistence of differences in the returns to equity, the main point for our purposes is that a wide dispersion in this measure existed even after the turn of the century, when the consensus is that the short-term market was effectively integrated.[39] So the small number of outliers in the prewar period cannot be a basis for doubting that the short-term antebellum market was integrated.

5.8 The Impact of the Civil War

There are two regions that are outliers in the picture of postbellum interest rates: the South and the Pacific Coast. In both cases the explanation for the high rates prevailing in these regions in the immediate postbellum years can be traced, at least in part, to disruptions caused by the Civil War. The case of the South is obvious, for it suffered enormous losses of human, physical, and financial capital. Many southern banks, heavily invested in Confederate government securities fell with the Confederacy.[40] The Bank of the State of South Carolina, for instance, held over $6,813,000 in Confederate securities and notes in October 1865, which accounted for 41 percent of its total assets, and much of the remainder was held in South Carolina securities. Only 12 percent of assets were in discounted notes and bills of exchange.[41] William Royal cites the same reason for the failure of the Virginia banks.[42] In South Carolina, only the Bank of Charleston survived the Civil War and Reconstruction.[43] None of Virginia's twenty-two banks survived. Only Missouri appears to have escaped relatively unscathed, and this was due, in large part, to the survival of the Bank of the State of Missouri. Virginia recovered rather quickly in terms of the number of banks, but in terms of paid-in capital it, too, was far worse off than it was in 1860. Louisiana, North Carolina, and South Carolina were the hardest hit. In 1867 South Carolina had recovered only 4 percent of its prewar

39. See Rockoff, "Regional Interest Rates," for one explanation of the persistence of these differentials based on regional differences in the rates of bank failure.

40. William Royal, *A History of Virginia Banks and Banking Prior to the Civil War* (New York, 1907), p. 39.

41. "Report of the President and Directors of the Bank of the State of South Carolina," *Reports and Resolutions of the General Assembly of the State of South Carolina* (1865), pp. 55–65.

42. Royal, *A History of Virginia Banks*, p. 39.

43. James G. Lindley, *South Carolina National: The First 150 Years* (New York, 1985) p. 7. The bank continues to this day to operate as the South Carolina National Bank.

Table 5.9 Postbellum Rates of Return to Bank Capital

Region	1870–91	1891–1904	1904–14
New England	6.99%	5.32%	7.26%
Middle Atlantic	8.09	8.25	8.88
South	9.90	8.48	10.50
Middle West	9.94	7.76	9.21
West	13.63	8.12	13.55
Pacific Coast	13.78	8.64	11.64

Notes: *New England*: Maine, Vermont, New Hampshire, Massachusetts, Connecticut, and Rhode Island. *Middle Atlantic*: New York, New Jersey, Pennsylvania, Delaware, and the District of Columbia. *South*: Virginia, West Virginia, North Carolina, South Carolina, Georgia, Florida, Alabama, Mississippi, Louisiana, Texas, Arkansas, Kentucky, and Tennessee. *Middle West*: Ohio, Indiana, Illinois, Michigan, Wisconsin, Minnesota, Iowa, and Missouri. *West*: North Dakota, South Dakota, Nebraska, Kansas, Wyoming, Colorado, New Mexico, Oklahoma, and the Indian Territory. *Pacific*: Washington, Oregon, California, Idaho, Utah, Nevada, and Arizona.

Source: Hugh Rockoff, "Regional Interest Rates and Bank Failures, 1870–1914," *Explorations in Economic History*, 14 (Winter, 1977), p. 92; based on Keith Powlison, *Profits of the National Banks* (Boston, 1931), pp. 105–6.

banking capital in nominal terms (prices were multiplied by a factor of about 1.75); Louisiana, only 7 percent; and North Carolina, 9 percent.[44]

So it is not surprising that rates were higher in the South than in the North during the immediate postbellum years. The relatively long time it took the South to fall in line, however, is more surprising. The difficulties in reestablishing an effective banking system within the constraints imposed by the National Banking Act appear to be the answer, as has been documented by Sylla and James.

The less obvious case is the Pacific Coast. During the Civil War the United States left the gold standard. In the East the greenback dollar became the unit of account and gold, now useful mostly as foreign exchange or to pay customs duties, went at a premium which varied over time with market conditions. On the Pacific Coast, however, the reverse occurred. The gold dollar remained the unit of account and the greenback went at a discount. The United States consisted of two currency areas linked by a fluctuating exchange rate. This situation prevailed until 1879 when specie payments were resumed. For an eastern investor contemplating investment on the Pacific Coast, the expected change in the exchange rate and the risk of fluctuations in that rate became important factors to be taken into account. Since the greenback was appreciating over most of this period (the gold price of greenbacks was rising), an eastern investor considering an investment on the Pacific Coast would have regarded the

44. Paid-in bank capital for 1860 are from U.S. Census Office, Eighth Census, 1860, *Population of the United States in 1860* (Washington, D.C., 1864), p. 292; for 1867, *Report of the Comptroller of the Currency* (Washington, D.C., 1867), p. 1. The numbers for 1867 may be slight underestimates because the Comptroller's Report included only national banks.

potential change in the exchange rate as a loss to be deducted from any gain from moving funds. In equilibrium, in other words, interest rates on the Pacific Coast from 1862 to 1879 would have exceeded interest rates in the East by the expected appreciation of the greenback. This is, of course, an oversimplification that does not allow for the risk associated with fluctuations in the exchange rate. In fact, the gold price of greenbacks rose fairly steadily after the Civil War, but it might have risen or fallen in any given year.

Table 5.10 contains the data needed to assess the role of greenback appreciation. It shows the interest rates in New York City and the Pacific Coast, the differential, the appreciation of the greenback in terms of gold, and the net differential. The appreciation of the greenback on average explains almost half the differential during the period prior to resumption (compare the gross with the net differential), and the negative net differentials in some years suggest that exchange risk was also a factor capable of deterring interregional capital movements in this period.

In both the South and the Pacific Coast, to sum up, regional differentials in the immediate postwar period were distorted by the Civil War. To that extent, an analysis that begins in 1870 gives an exaggerated picture of the extent to which the market was naturally fragmented.

5.9 Summary and Conclusions

Our most important findings are illustrated in Table 5.11 which shows the difference between the rate in each of four regions and New York City at five-year intervals from 1835 to 1914. It is clear at once that three of the regions—New England, the Middle Atlantic, and the South—were (by the usual standard of a narrow differential) integrated with New York City before the Civil War. The differentials in 1850, 1855, 1859, or even earlier are similar to those realized in 1900, 1905, or 1914. The South, for example was 39 basis points higher than New York City in 1850, 20 basis points higher in 1855, and 124 basis points higher in 1859; but it was 134 basis points higher in 1900, 241 basis points higher in 1905, and 24 basis points higher in 1914. Yet most financial historians would probably agree that the capital market was integrated after the turn of the century. Indeed, one would expect smaller differentials at the later dates due to the impovements in communication and transportation. The conventional portrait of increasing integration in the postbellum era is sharply colored by the large differentials realized in the years immediately following the Civil War. A few of our series, moreover, cover the 1820s; the Philadelphia and South Carolina series, the longest, begin in 1815. Even at these early dates the simplest interpretation of the data is that the market was integrated.

The same cannot be said for our midwestern rate because it is consistently higher than the New York City rate during the antebellum period. For this region, however, we have had to rely primarily on the returns of the State

Table 5.10 Rates on the Pacific Coast and Appreciation of the Greenback

Year	New York City	Pacific Coast	Gross Differential	Appreciation of Greenback	Net Differential
1869	6.32%	12.52%	6.20%	1.80%	4.40%
1870	5.78	8.81	3.03	10.90	−7.87
1871	5.36	18.62	13.26	8.99	4.27
1872	5.33	15.24	9.91	0.62	9.29
1873	5.50	7.40	1.90	−2.83	4.28
1874	5.41	9.17	3.76	2.38	1.38
1875	4.91	10.25	5.34	−0.62	5.96
1876	3.87	8.36	4.49	−1.15	5.64
1877	3.29	8.55	5.26	5.50	−0.24
1878	3.03	5.92	2.89	5.13	−2.24
1879	2.84	7.48	4.64	2.47	2.17
1880	3.51	6.90	3.39	.00	3.39
1881	3.70	8.53	4.83	.00	4.83
1882	3.37	6.84	3.47	.00	3.47

Sources: Interest rates: Lance Davis, "The Investment Market, 1870–1914: Evolution of a National Market," *Journal of Economic History*, 25 (Sept. 1965), p. 365, col. I (1), VI (1). Gold price of the greenback: James K. Kindahl, "Economic Factors in Specie Resumption," in *The Reinterpretation of American Economic History*, Robert W. Fogel and Stanley L. Engerman, eds. (New York, 1971), p. 472, col. (4).

Table 5.11 Interest Rate Differentials with New York City

Year	New England	Middle Atlantic	South	Midwest
1835	0.21%	0.80%	−0.30%	2.86%
1840	−0.68	−0.54	−0.90	2.03
1845	−0.53	−0.70	0.14	2.44
1850	−0.41	0.01	0.39	3.83
1855	−0.26	−0.04	0.20	5.02
1859	0.49	0.56	1.24	n.a.
1870	2.29	1.13	3.93	1.67
1875	1.59	1.14	1.33	1.99
1880	−0.20	−0.44	0.00	0.29
1885	0.37	0.92	1.59	1.77
1890	0.18	0.51	1.65	0.78
1895	0.57	1.23	1.09	0.79
1900	0.57	1.00	1.34	0.40
1905	0.48	0.44	2.41	0.82
1910	−0.31	−0.54	0.24	−0.70
1914	−0.05	−0.16	0.80	0.09

Sources: 1835–59: See Table 5.2. For this period we used an average for all states and cities on which we had data. 1870–1914: Lance Davis, "The Investment Market, 1870–1914: The Evolution of a National Market," *Journal of Economic History,* 25 (Sept. 1965), pp. 362–65. For this period we used average of the rates for reserve-city and non-reserve-city banks. Definitions of the regions are given in Table 9.5.

Bank of Indiana. It may be that this bank enjoyed some monopoly power. Its rates were somewhat lower in the mid–1850s when there was competition from free banks. And the rates in Ohio in the early 1850s and Kentucky over a long run of years were somewhat lower than at the State Bank of Indiana and not much higher than in New York City.[45] But we cannot rule out the possibility that rates in this region were somewhat higher than in the eastern financial centers due to a frontier effect.

By integrated we do not mean that rates were everywhere the same. Differentials could and did exist for a variety of reasons—the monopoly power of certain banks, differences in risk, or bad times that led to differences in the realized yields measured here. Nor do we want to claim that developments after the Civil War had no impact on the market. The view we reject is one in which interregional differences were large, persistent, and hard to explain except on the basis of irrational fears and prejudices.

We have not explored here the institutional structure that permitted antebellum financial markets to achieve such unity. But it is evident that beneath the tables and figures we present there lay a structure of banks, private bankers, and bill brokers, who were in constant communication. Assets of similar risk would not trade for long at large premiums or discounts. The story of how these institutions functioned—how individuals communicated, valued risks, and so on—is an important and potentially fascinating part of the story, but must be left for another paper.

The finding that antebellum American financial markets were well integrated should come as no surprise to students of the history of international capital and financial markets. Studies by Larry Neal have shown that the London and Amsterdam stock markets were integrated as early as 1723.[46] Only wars and severe financial panics pulled them apart. The markets examined by Neal reintegrated quickly after a war which Neal attributes to their being unfettered by government restrictions.[47] American markets, in contrast, were forced to reintegrate after the Civil War under the strain of a monetary policy aimed toward gradual resumption and fettered by the National Banking Act. As desirable as these policies may have been on other grounds, it is clear that they hampered the smooth return of the capital market to its prewar pattern of regional integration.

45. The rates for Ohio presented here suggests the need to revise the conclusion drawn by one of us, Hugh Rockoff, "The Free Banking Era: A Reexamination," *Journal of Money, Credit, and Banking*, 6 (May 1974), pp. 159–60, that the introduction of free banking in Ohio had a substantial impact.

46. Larry Neal, "Integration of International Capital Markets: Quantitative Evidence from the Eighteenth to Twentieth Centuries," *Journal of Economic History*, 45 (June 1985), pp. 219–26; "The Integration and Efficiency of the London and Amsterdam Stock Markets in the Eighteenth Century," *Journal of Economic History*, 47 (Mar. 1987), pp. 97–116; and *The Rise of Financial Capitalism: International Capitalism in the Age of Reason* (New York, 1990).

47. Neal, "The Integration and Efficiency of the London and Amsterdam Stock Markets," p. 115.

Most of the rates examined here, we should also note, come from states within the frontier. Capital markets on the Pacific Coast may truly have been different. Scattered evidence for California, we noted previously, suggests that rates there may have been fabulously high. Beyond the frontier the costs of acquiring information about potential investments, and the costs of supervising them, may have effectively prevented rate-equalizing capital flows.

Historians have long believed that changes in financial markets that took place during the Civil War, in particular the National Banking Act, were crucial to postwar economic development. Action by the federal government, in other words, was needed to create a unified currency to permit rapid economic expansion. The evidence assembled here disputes that view. The National Banking Act, whatever its plusses and minuses, was not needed to knit together regional capital markets. Capital would have found its way to profitable ventures even in the absence of a partial centralization of the bank regulatory environment.

Instead, it appears that the Civil War, and to some extent the National Banking Act, were disruptive elements that separated the South (because of the destruction of its banking system) and the Pacific Coast (because of the separation of the currency) from the eastern capital market. The slow reintegration of the short-term capital market after the Civil War noted by a number of scholars was a return to the status quo ante bellum.

This summary leads us to a final question. At what date did the capital market first became integrated? While more work is needed to push our measures of interest rates back in time and across a wider range of locations, it may make sense to assume, at least tentatively, that capital markets in the United States have always been integrated. The idea of separate centers of savings and investment emerging on a wide plain of settlement and then being knit together is probably the wrong way to view the evolution of the capital market in the United States. Instead, settlement proceeded because capitalists made decisions to invest funds in new regions. The frontier separated those regions in which investment decisions could be based on a long experience with similar investments from regions where rates of return, although potentially very high, were a matter of conjecture. The frontier, to use Frank Knight's terminology, was the line that separated risk from uncertainty.[48]

48. A model of separate markets being gradually knit together, however, may make more sense for other countries. See, for example, Good, "Financial Integration in Late Nineteenth-Century Austria."

6 Money versus Credit Rationing
Evidence for the National Banking Era, 1880–1914

Michael D. Bordo, Peter Rappoport, and Anna J. Schwartz

6.1 Introduction

The provisions of the Acts of 1863 and 1865 that established the national banking system were designed to remedy two perceived defects of the antebellum state banking systems. One was the circulation of a wide variety of state bank notes, often at a discount, which made for an inefficient payments system. The second defect was instability of the note issue, marked by overissue, bank runs and failures, and periodic suspensions of convertibility into specie. To remedy the first defect, state bank notes were replaced by national bank issues of U.S. bond-secured currency. To remedy the second defect, stringent reserve and capital requirements, oversight, and regulation by the Comptroller of the Currency were conditions for national bank charters. Unfortunately, the remedies did not work as intended by the architects of the national banking system. Instead, the system was characterized by monetary and cyclical instability, four banking panics, frequent stock market crashes, and other financial disturbances.

In this paper we examine the evidence for two competing views—monetarist and credit-rationing—on how monetary and financial disturbances influenced the real economy during the national banking era. These views stress either the asset or the liability side of the banking system's balance sheet as the way in which monetary shocks are transmitted.

According to the monetarist view, the way in which monetary disturbances—such as gold flows and banking panics in the national banking era—affected the real economy was through changes on the liability side of the banking system's balance sheet.[1] Changes in bank deposits impinge directly

The authors thank Bernhard Eschweiler for valuable research assistance and Charles Calomiris, Bill Lang, Donald McCloskey, and Hugh Rockoff for helpful comments.

1. Milton Friedman and Anna J. Schwartz, *A Monetary History of the United States, 1867 to 1960* (Princeton, 1963).

and indirectly (through changing interest rates) on spending, while the composition of bank portfolios (reflected on the asset side of the balance sheet) is not important in explaining transmission.

According to the alternative, credit-rationing view, the composition of the asset side is important: changes in bank loans and other credit variables, independent of changes in the quantity of money, are the determinants of real fluctuations in the national banking period.[2] Banks engage in credit rationing rather than raise interest rates because in a world of asymmetric information, a rise in interest rates may encourage adverse selection, that is, borrowing by individuals and firms more likely to default. This approach follows an older tradition stressing the asset side of the balance sheet.[3]

Theoretically, credit rationing has been cast as an equilibrium concept. Several authors have suggested that changes in the equilibrium quantity of credit rationing can explain short-run fluctuations in real output.[4] The idea is that changes in the "level of uncertainty" in the economy induce changes in the equilibrium quantity of loans, and thereby affect real activity.

Recently Charles Calomiris and Glenn Hubbard provided support for the credit-rationing view for the national banking period.[5] We have followed their approach but expand their simultaneous equations model by considering additional factors that could explain the link they find between credit and the real economy. Our evidence suggests that it is difficult to distinguish between the two views. When monetary variables are introduced into the credit model, money is significant and credit declines in importance though its contribution is not eliminated. When credit variables are introduced into the monetarist model, money is robust but credit effects are also significant.

The inconclusive simultaneous equations results have led us to examine institutional data for the national banking period for evidence that helps distinguish between the two views. The key feature is the intimate connection between the stock market and the national banking system. A substantial fraction of the reserves of all national banks ended up being invested in the New York City call loan market. We show that loans secured by stock in New York City were volatile, but other loans were not. A similar but more muted pattern is found for the United States as a whole. Yet other loans comprise direct loans

2. Charles W. Calomiris and R. Glenn Hubbard, "Price Flexibility, Credit Availability, and Economic Fluctuations: Evidence from the United States, 1894–1909," *Quarterly Journal of Economics* 104 (Aug. 1989), pp. 429–52.

3. Joseph Stiglitz and Andrew Weiss, "Credit Rationing in Markets with Imperfect Information," *American Economic Review* 71 (June 1981), pp. 393–410; "Credit Rationing with Many Borrowers," *American Economic Review* 77 (Mar. 1987), pp. 228–31; Mark Gertler and R. Glenn Hubbard, "Financial Factors in Business Fluctuations," in *Financial Market Volatility* (Federal Reserve Bank of Kansas City, 1988), pp. 33–71.

4. Ben Bernanke, "Alternative Explanations of the Money-Income Correlation," *Carnegie-Rochester Conference Series on Public Policy* 25 (Autumn 1986), pp. 49–99; Calomiris and Hubbard, "Price Flexibility," pp. 429–52.

5. Calomiris and Hubbard, "Price Flexibility," pp. 429–52.

to businesses and so are the principal candidates for credit effects, if such effects were present.

This pattern suggests that disturbances in the stock market were mirrored in the call loan market, which in turn dominated total New York City bank loans and, to a lesser extent, total U.S. loans. Thus the significant influence of bank loans found in credit models may simply be reflecting volatility in the stock market. To test this possibility, we introduce a stock price index and the call loan rate into a simultaneous equations model incorporating both loans and money. The effect is to reduce greatly the influence of bank loans on real activity. The influence of money, however, remains robust.

The rest of the paper is organized as follows. Section 6.2 explains the money and credit-rationing views. We first set out the credit-rationing story and contrast it with the money story. We then trace the effects to be expected from various shocks according to the two views, beginning with the more familiar modern setting in which a central bank engages in open market sales that reduce bank reserves and money supply, with contractionary effects on national income. Then we turn to a gold standard setting, subject to gold outflows, in which banking panics occur. Section 6.3 reviews past attempts to assess the roles of money and credit in the transmission mechanism, and then turns to the empirical results of four simultaneous equations models of quarterly data that we present to test the two views.

In section 6.4 we examine the role of the stock and call loan markets. We describe the relation between the inverted pyramid of credit and the call loan market. Data from the Comptroller of the Currency's annual reports reveal the diverse pattern of loans secured by stock and of other bank loans. We present a simultaneous equations model incorporating stock market variables, money, and U.S. loans. Section 6.5 summarizes the paper, drawing lessons for research strategy.

6.2 Money versus Credit-Rationing: Theory

A considerable theoretical and empirical literature exists on whether the monetary system affects the real economy through the liability or the asset side of the banking system.[6]

Emphasis on bank credit as an alternative or additional channel to money goes back to Adam Smith and the classical economists. The real bills doctrine that dominated both nineteenth and early twentieth century thinking stressed that bank lending based strictly on self-liquidating commercial bills would always be sufficient to finance economic activity. John Maynard Keynes in *The General Theory* suggested the possibility of credit rationing. That sugges-

6. For a useful survey, see Mark Gertler, "Financial Structure and Aggregate Economic Activity: An Overview," *Journal of Money, Credit and Banking* 20 (Aug. 1988, pt. 2), pp. 559–88.

tion led to the availability doctrine, whereby the Federal Reserve would influence the availability of bank loans through its open market operations.[7] It was assumed that changes in bank deposits would be offset by substitution into nonmonetary assets. Hence the only way the monetary authorities could affect spending was by influencing total credit.[8] A modern proponent of these views bases them on extensive empirical evidence showing a close connection between various credit aggregates and economic activity.[9]

In the past decade, various authors have given a new impetus to the credit approach. Based on the theory of incomplete information and the seminal "lemons" article, they have argued for a theory of "equilibrium credit rationing."[10] In their view, the market for loans is a customer market where factors other than price are important, unlike the auction markets which characterize many other commodities. Specifically, because of asymmetric information available to lenders and borrowers, a rise in the loan rate, by encouraging adverse selection (a predominance of loan applicants with risky projects) and moral hazard (engaging in risky behavior after receiving a loan) on the part of borrowers, can increase the incidence of defaults and reduce the real return earned by the lenders. Under these circumstances, banks will charge a "lemons premium" to highly qualified borrowers, causing them to reduce their borrowing, and will restrict loans to marginal borrowers. With equilibrium credit rationing, loan rates will not rise to clear the loan market. The supply curve is backward bending. In a macro setting, this theory predicts that restrictive monetary policy will lead to a reduction in bank lending with little influence on interest rates. Extensions of this approach view commercial banks as important because they use their expertise to screen borrowers, and hence reduce the information asymmetry. One device used is the posting of collateral. In this context, restrictive monetary policy, if it produces bankruptcy and declines in net worth because of debt deflation, will disrupt the valuable credit-intermediation network created by the banking system, further reducing bank lending and economic activity.[11]

With these views in mind, we trace the transmission of both monetary and

7. Robert Roosa, "Interest Rates and the Central Bank," in *Money, Trade and Economic Growth: Essays in Honor of John H. Williams* (New York, 1951), pp. 270–95.

8. Committee on the Working of the Monetary System (Radcliffe), *Report,* Cmnd. 827 (H.M.S.O., 1959); Commission on Money and Credit, *Money and Credit: Their Influence on Jobs, Prices, and Growth* (New York, 1961); John Gurley and Edward Shaw, *Money in a Theory of Finance* (Washington, D.C., 1960).

9. Benjamin Friedman, "Debt and Economic Activity in the United States," in B. Friedman, ed., *The Changing Role of Debt and Equity in Financing U.S. Capital Formation* (Chicago, 1982).

10. Stiglitz and Weiss, "Credit Rationing in Markets with Imperfect Information," pp. 393–410; "Credit Rationing with Many Borrowers," pp. 228–31; Joseph Stiglitz, "Money, Credit and Business Fluctuations," *The Economic Record* 64 (Dec. 1988), pp. 307–22; George Akerlof, "The Market for Lemons: Qualitative Uncertainty and the Market Mechanism," *Quarterly Journal of Economics* 84 (Aug. 1970), pp. 488–500.

11. Ben Bernanke, "Nonmonetary Effects of the Financial Collapse in the Propagation of the Great Depression," *American Economic Review* 73 (June 1983), pp. 257–76.

real shocks according to the money and credit-rationing views. We initially focus on a modern setting, and then on the pre–Federal Reserve System and the classical gold standard.

6.2.1 The Modern Setting

We compare the two views of transmission, first, following an open market sale of government securities and second, following an unexpected decline in exports.

An Open Market Sale of Government Securities

In the simplest version of the money view, an open market sale reduces the reserves of the commercial banks (we neglect the distinction between borrowed and nonborrowed reserves). In the face of declining reserves (assuming no excess reserves), the banks sell investments and call in (do not renew) their loans. As a result deposits decline. The decline in deposits leads to a fall in expenditures, which in turn reduces output and the price level. Rising market interest rates as well as implicit rates connecting assets to service flows will be a key conduit connecting money supply to spending. This approach assumes that deposits and other financial assets are not close substitutes, whereas loans and other earning assets are.[12]

In the credit view, the open market sale reduces reserves and leads to a decline in bank loans (presumably, because loans and investments are not close substitutes, the former decline more). As in the money view, deposits are reduced, but because of a high degree of substitution between transaction balances and near-monies, there is little effect from this source on spending. In the approach put forward by Joseph Stiglitz and Andrew Weiss, as the decline in lending threatens to raise interest rates, the danger of adverse selection and moral hazard increases for lenders, so banks reduce their lending further (they engage in credit rationing). If the contractionary policy leads to bankruptcies, a stock market crash, or deflation, then the decline in the net worth of firms subjects lenders to greater moral hazard and increases adverse selection. The reduction in the value of collateral can lead to further declines in bank loans.

12. The story can be complicated by distinguishing between certificates of deposit and other deposits, with the former being close substitutes for marketable securities. In this case, as Eugene F. Fama, "What's Different About Banks?" *Journal of Monetary Economics* 15 (Jan. 1985), pp. 24–39, and Christina Romer and David Romer, "New Evidence on the Monetary Transmission Mechanism," *Brookings Papers on Economic Activity* 1 (1990), pp. 149–213, have demonstrated, if the reserve requirements on certificates of deposit were the same as on demand deposits, the reduction in bank liabilities would have no effect on interest rates and bank loans would dominate in the transmission mechanism. Since reserve requirements on certificates of deposit are considerably lower than on demand deposits, this is unlikely.

According to Karl Brunner and Allan H. Meltzer, loans and other assets (bonds) are not perfect substitutes (see Brunner and Meltzer, "Friedman's Monetary Theory," in Robert J. Gordon, ed., *Milton Friedman's Monetary Framework: A Debate with His Critics* (Chicago, 1976), pp. 63–76. They construct a monetarist model including a credit market, in which the effects of money dominate those of credit.

Both views assume that the central bank will act as a lender of last resort to prevent the onset of a banking panic. The two views differ, however, with respect to the empirical behavior of interest rates and loan aggregates at the business cycle peak. According to the money view, money growth decelerates during mid-expansion and is accompanied by a rise in interest rates that persists beyond the business cycle peak and well into the recession phase. According to the credit-rationing view, interest rates do not exhibit this pattern because of the adverse selection problems banks are assumed to confront should interest rates rise. According to the money view, the allocation of credit between loans and investments in bank portfolios has no effect on the aggregate of deposits. Banks expand their portfolios and deposits with the availability of reserves. According to the credit-rationing view, banks withdraw from loan expansion when their attitude toward loan applicants hardens. It is precisely that behavior which proponents of this theory claim causes a contraction of the economy.

A Decline in Exports

The outcome of a transitory real shock, such as a decline in exports, according to the money view, depends on the actions of the central bank. In the absence of a shock to bank reserves, banks will hold excess reserves and will lower interest rates. If demand for loans does not increase in response to the interest rate decline, banks will expand their portfolio of investments. A stable money supply and lower interest rates will eventually provide a stimulus to the economy.

In the credit view, a transitory real shock that lowers the demand for loans may be exacerbated if the degree of uncertainty is affected.[13] If uncertainty is increased, this will cause banks to reduce their lending further, because of the adverse selection and moral hazard problems mentioned above. Unlike the money view, the credit-rationing view, as represented by Stiglitz, provides no role for accommodating monetary policy to mitigate the effects of a real shock.[14]

6.2.2 The National Banking Era

In the pre–Federal Reserve setting, two key institutional differences affected the transmission mechanism: the absence of a central bank and the classical gold standard. The first factor was important because an effective lender of last resort did not exist.[15] The importance of the second factor was that a

13. William W. Lang and Leonard I. Nakamura, "The Dynamics of Credit Markets in a Model with Learning," *Journal of Monetary Economics* 26 (Jan. 1990), pp. 305–18; and Stiglitz, "Money, Credit and Business Fluctuations."

14. Stiglitz, "Money, Credit and Business Fluctuations."

15. On a number of occasions, the clearing houses, a consortium of large New York City commercial banks, and the U.S. Treasury performed this role.

gold outflow, induced typically either by a rise in Bank Rate by the Bank of England or by a severe harvest failure—a real shock that led to a deficit in the current account—reduced monetary gold reserves.

A Gold Outflow

If the Bank of England raised its discount rate, a short-term capital outflow from the United States ensued, as did a gold outflow that reduced the reserves of the commercial banks.[16] According to the money view, both loans and investments declined, *pari passu* with deposits, interest rates rose, and spending declined along with output and prices. A key difference from the modern setting could, however, arise. There was no ready source of high-powered money to replace the loss of monetary reserves. In addition, if the external drain was also accompanied by an internal drain, such as a seasonally induced demand for reserves by country national banks, the possibility arose of a banking panic generated by a decline in the public's deposit-currency ratio as well as the banking system's deposit-reserve ratio.[17] This could produce a further decline in the money supply. Resultant bank failures could lead to bankruptcies, reductions in firms' net worth, and further bank failures, as the value of bank assets declined. This process could continue unless some authority intervened as a lender of last resort or the convertibility of deposits into currency was suspended.

In the credit view, the decline in bank reserves reduced loans (more than investments and more than deposits), as it would today, but the incipient rise in interest rates could lead to credit rationing because of adverse selection and moral hazard. The fall in activity and the price level would reduce the value of bank collateral, causing a further reduction in bank loans. If a banking panic ensued, this exacerbated the process, leading to a rise in the cost of intermediation. A stock market crash also would reduce the net worth and collateral of firms, in turn reducing bank lending.

A Harvest Failure

In the money view, a transitory real shock such as a harvest failure reduced output. If country banks withdrew reserve balances from their city correspondents and reduced loans and deposits, the national banking system contracted. A fortuitous short-term capital inflow from abroad could, however, cut short this process of decline. If the inflow did not occur, interest rates fell, leading

16. Friedman and Schwartz, *A Monetary History*, chap. 3. See section 6.4 below for an elaboration of the institutional framework of the U.S. banking system in this period.

17. For alternative explanations of banking panics in this period, see Michael D. Bordo, "The Contribution of *A Monetary History of the United States, 1867–1960* to Monetary History," in Michael D. Bordo, ed., *Money, History, and International Finance: Essays in Honor of Anna J. Schwartz* (Chicago, 1989), pp. 15–70; and Charles W. Calomiris and Gary Gorton, "The Origins of Banking Panics: Models, Facts, and Bank Regulation," in R. Glenn Hubbard, ed., *Financial Crises and Financial Markets* (Chicago, 1991).

to a gold outflow. The gold outflow reduced the money supply, output, and the price level until equilibrium was restored. If a banking panic ensued, further declines in the money supply occurred.

In the credit-rationing view, the story is the same for the modern period and the national banking era. The real shock reduced the demand for loans and the level of interest rates. If uncertainty increased, bank lending would be reduced, reflecting adverse selection and moral hazard. If bankruptcies, declines in net worth, and debt deflation ensued, then further declines in bank lending occurred. Finally, if the real shock caused a stock market crash, then equity rationing might follow, as declines in the net worths of firms made it harder for them to obtain external finance.[18]

6.3 Money versus Credit: Some Empirical Results

An early approach to these issues compared correlations between bank loans (and other credit aggregates) and economic activity, and those between various monetary aggregates and activity in the post–World War II United States, with the result that credit usually dominated.[19] Two later studies based on Granger-causality tests and standard vector autoregressions (VARs) led to the conclusion that both money and credit together explain variations in real output.[20]

The Granger-causality tests examine the reduced-form predictive power of money and credit variables, which is not necessarily the same as their causal role. In particular, it is necessary to abstract from contemporaneous effects of output on financial variables. One approach was to run a race between money and credit by identifying episodes in the post–World War II period when a contractionary monetary policy was adopted independent of the state of the real economy.[21] In this approach, univariate forecasting regressions lead to the conclusion that money is an active force in transmission, with bank lending a reflecting force.

Another approach, using structural VARs, makes explicit allowance for contemporaneous interactions between output and credit and money, and finds that bank loans account for at least as much of the variance of output as

18. Dwight Jaffee and Joseph Stiglitz, "Credit Rationing," in Benjamin M. Friedman and Frank H. Hahn, eds., *Handbook of Monetary Economics,* vol. 2 (Amsterdam, 1990), chap. 16, pp. 838–98.

19. Friedman, "Debt and Economic Activity."

20. Benjamin Friedman, "Monetary Policy with a Credit Aggregate Target," *Carnegie Rochester Conference Series on Public Policy* 18 (1983), pp. 117–18, and "The Roles of Money and Credit in Macroeconomic Analysis," in *Macroeconomics, Prices and Quantities,* James Tobin, ed. (Washington, D.C.: Brookings Institution), pp. 161–99. Stephen King, "Monetary Transmission: Through Bank Loans or Bank Liabilities?" *Journal of Money, Credit and Banking* 18 (Aug. 1986), pp. 290–303, in his VAR found that money dominated credit. The relationship of VARs to other methods of estimating simultaneous equations systems is discussed below.

21. Romer and Romer, "Monetary Transmission Mechanism," pp. 149–213.

money. Subsequently the approach was applied to the pre–1914 national banking era.[22]

Assessing the relative merits of the money and credit-rationing explanations requires that one disentangle a complex set of interactions among economic variables. This task is complicated by different views about the structure of these interactions held by the two schools of thought. In this section of the paper, we use a structural VAR approach to analyze a number of different models of the relationships among the variables of central concern to the money and credit views.

Structural VARs involve a strategy for identifying parameters in a simultaneous equations model that preserves some of the intent of the original Cowles Commission approach, while remaining sensitive to Christopher Sims's criticism of the "incredible" identification assumptions it necessitated.[23] The cost of this compromise is that the structural VAR approach requires the investigator to have great faith in the validity of all apects of the model.

The structural and reduced forms of a linear simultaneous system can be expressed as

$$Y_t\Gamma + X_t B = V_t \quad E(V_t{}'V_t) = \Sigma \tag{1}$$

$$Y_t = X_t\Pi + U_t \tag{2}$$

$$\Pi = -B\Gamma^{-1} \tag{3}$$

$$U_t\Gamma = V_t \tag{4}$$

$$E(U'_tU_t) = \Gamma^{-1\prime}\,\Sigma\Gamma^{-1} = \Omega \tag{5}$$

Here, Y_t and X_t are row vectors, respectively, of observations on the K endogenous and M exogenous or predetermined variables. U_t and V_t are K-element row vectors of reduced form and structural errors, respectively. The structural parameters are contained in the matrices Γ, B, and Σ, whose respective dimensions are $K \times K$, $M \times K$, and $K \times K$, while Π and Ω are $M \times K$ and $K \times K$ matrices of reduced-form coefficients that can be estimated consistently from ordinary least squares regression of Y on X.

Identification is accomplished by placing sufficient restrictions on the structural coefficient matrices—that a unique solution for Γ, B, and Σ is possible

22. This approach was first applied in this context by Bernanke, "Money-Income Correlation," pp. 49–99. The Bernanke method was applied to the pre–national banking era by Calomiris and Hubbard, "Price Flexibility," pp. 429–52.

23. Structural VARs were conceived by Bernanke, "Money-Income Correlation," and Christopher Sims, "Are Forecasting Models Usable for Policy Analysis?" *Federal Reserve Bank of Minneapolis Quarterly Review* (Winter 1986), pp. 2–16. For a discussion of the Cowles Commission approach, see Thomas Cooley and Stephen LeRoy, "Atheoretical Macroeconomics: A Critique," *Journal of Monetary Economics* 16 (Nov. 1985), pp. 283–308. For his criticism, see Christopher Sims, "Macroeconomics and Reality," *Econometrica* 48 (Jan. 1980), pp. 1–48.

from equations (3) and (5), given Π and Ω.[24] The three prominent approaches to identification can be summarized as:

(a) Restrict Γ and B, and leave Σ unrestricted (Cowles).
(b) After ordering the endogenous variables in a suitable manner, make Γ triangular, Σ diagonal, and leave B unrestricted (standard VAR).
(c) Impose $K(K - 1)$ restrictions on Γ and Σ, and leave B unrestricted (structural VAR).

The rationale for the Cowles approach was that the structural errors contained the effects of variables not captured by the model, and since there could be no presumption that the same variables had not been omitted from more than one equation, one would expect the elements of V_t to be correlated contemporaneously. This implied that a total of $K(K - 1)$ zero restrictions needed to be placed on the Γ and B matrices.

Sims criticized this approach, arguing that it was difficult to believe the exclusion restrictions typically used, especially in the light of rational expectations models that conditioned people's behavior, and therefore observable variables, on all available past data.[25] He advanced the standard VAR approach, without claiming it represented structural relationships. However, several authors argued that little meaningful could be said unless a structural interpretation were placed on the triangular form of Γ used in Sims's approach, which, in turn, did not seem plausible.[26]

The structural VAR approach adopts Sims's skepticism concerning restrictions on B, but sides with the Cowles approach in maintaining that restrictions on Γ are sensible. There are $K(K - 1)$ free elements in Γ, which is the number of restrictions required for identification. The fewer restrictions placed on Γ, the more must be imposed on Σ. Typically, the maximum of $K(K - 1)/2$ restrictions are placed on Σ, making it diagonal.[27] This strains credibility from the Cowles viewpoint, since it does not allow for correlation among variables omitted from equations: it is tantamount to an extreme expression of faith in the specification of the model.

In identifying the models that follow, we use the diagonal-Σ structural VAR strategy. This, in turn, necessitates that $K(K - 1)/2$ of the elements of Γ be zero. Since we are very far from believing any of these models to be the last word, we shall attempt to trace patterns that are consistent with the results of all the models.

24. Aside from K restrictions on Γ that normalize to unity the coefficient of one endogenous variable per equation.

25. Sims, "Macroeconomics and Reality," pp. 1–48.

26. The authors include Cooley and Leroy, "Atheoretical Macroeconomics," pp. 283–308; Rodney L. Jacobs, Edward Leamer, and Michael P. Ward, "Difficulties with Testing for Causation," *Economic Inquiry* 17 (July 1979), pp. 401–13; and Bernanke, "Money-Income Correlation," pp. 49–99.

27. An exception is Bernanke, "Money-Income Correlation," who, in a six-variable system, permits one off-diagonal element of Σ to be non-zero.

In all, we present four models in this section. The first two specifications we estimate include only the variables considered relevant to the determination of real output by proponents of the money and credit views, respectively. The drawback with these models is that neither allows for the effects of variables considered important by the other story: neither is sufficiently rich to distinguish the roles of the asset and liability sides of the banks' balance sheets. In order to compare the merits of the two stories, we need to nest the two models in a larger model. Unfortunately, such a system would be computationally intractable, and so we present a separate generalization for each model.

All models are estimated using quarterly data spanning the period 1880.I to 1914.IV. All variables except those involving interest rates enter the estimated models as quarterly rates of change, but, for the sake of brevity, we refer to these changes as M2, real GNP, etc. The sources of the data series used are described in the Appendix. The same estimation procedure is used for all the structural VAR specifications that we examine, and it will prove useful to describe it in detail in the context of the first model we discuss.

6.3.1 Monetarist Model

Our basic monetarist model involves five variables, the monetary base, M2, real GNP, the commercial paper rate, and the GNP deflator. Thus the vector Y_t in equation (1) is a row vector with five elements, the observations at time t on these five variables. The first step in implementing the structural VAR approach is to run a vector autoregression of the system, which is equivalent to estimating the reduced-form (2). The variables in X_t are four lagged values of each of the five variables, a constant term, time trend, and three seasonal dummies. These reduced-form regressions produce estimates of the reduced form errors, U_t, which are related to the structural errors, V_t, by the linear transformation Γ, as shown in equation (4). The object of the second stage of the estimation procedure is to extract estimates of Γ and Σ from the estimated reduced-form errors, essentially by using equation (5), which shows how the covariance matrix of U_t is related to these two parameter matrices.[28] Equation (5) contains $[K + K(K - 1)/2]$ (that is, 15) distinct relationships. Before the imposition of identification restrictions, Σ has $[K + K(K - 1)/2]$ (15) distinct parameters, and Γ has K^2 (25). For a unique solution to equation (5), K^2 (25) restrictions on the parameters are required (to produce as many equations as

28. The actual estimation procedure used is full information maximum likelihood (FIML) which converges in probability to the same values as the "method of moments" solution of equation (5) mentioned in the text. FIML minimizes the concentrated likelihood function:

$$-2\ln|\Gamma| + \sum_{i=1}^{K} \ln(\Gamma'\Omega\,\Gamma)_{ii}$$

over the unrestricted elements in Γ. The sample covariance matrix of U_t, Ω, is used in place of Ω, for which it is a consistent estimator. The covariance matrix of the structural errors, Σ, is then estimated as $\hat{\Gamma}'\,\hat{\Omega}\,\hat{\Gamma}$.

unknowns). As discussed above, K (5) of these come from normalizing diagonal elements of Γ to unity, $[K(K - 1)/2]$ (10) come from restricting Σ to be diagonal, and the remaining $[K(K - 1)/2]$ (10) come from setting elements of Γ to zero. The last type of restriction is a limitation on the contemporaneous interactions among variables.[29] Equivalently, in view of equation (4), it involves restrictions on the way the observable reduced-form errors, U_t, are composed of the unobserved structural errors, V_t.

Using the letters b, m, y, i, and p to refer to the base, M2, real GNP, commercial paper rate, and GNP deflator, respectively, and $g_{ij} = -\Gamma_{ij}$, the contemporaneous interactions we identify in the monetarist model are[30]

$$\begin{aligned} u_b &= g_{41}^{(+)}u_i + g_{51}^{(-)}u_p + v_b \\ u_m &= g_{12}^{(+)}u_b + g_{42}^{(-)}u_i + v_m \\ u_y &= g_{23}^{(+)}u_m + g_{43}^{(-)}u_i + g_{53}^{(+)}u_p + v_y \\ u_i &= g_{24}^{(-)}u_m + g_{34}^{(-)}u_y + v_i \\ u_p &= g_{25}^{(+)}u_m + v_p \end{aligned}$$

The monetarist model allows the base to be affected contemporaneously only by interest rate and price shocks, reflecting the operation of the gold standard.[31] Increases in the interest rate and decreases in the inflation rate are postulated to increase the base, via capital inflows. Some authors have argued that, during this period, interest rate and price shocks from abroad were reflected fully and quickly in domestic interest rate and price movements.[32] These effects are allowed for by the interest rate and price channels included in the base equation. This explains why it is unnecessary to include explicit open economy variables. The money multiplier drives the dependence of the money supply on the base, while liquidity preference accounts for the presence of the interest rate. The presence of M2 in the output equation reflects demand shocks, and the interest rate and inflation rate are inserted to allow for the possibility of supply side, or real interest rate shocks. The interest rate is influenced by M2 and real output as a result of the demand for money. Finally, inflation is driven by shocks to the quantity of money. Notice that, since Σ is assumed to be diagonal, the shocks to each variable (v_b, v_m, etc.) are assumed independent of each other.

The estimates of the contemporaneous interactions are shown in the top

29. The ith column of Γ contains the contemporaneous coefficients in the structural equation for the ith variable. Thus, in the monetarist model for example, one would impose the restriction that M2 does not contemporaneously affect the base by restricting Γ_{21} to be zero.

30. The signs are those of the g_{ij} terms. Since K equals 5 in the monetarist model, ten of the off-diagonal elements of Γ are restricted to be zero.

31. We also ran the model with gold flows in place of the monetary base. The results are similar to those with the base, though less pronounced.

32. See Donald N. McCloskey and J. Richard Zecher, "How the Gold Standard Worked," in Jacob A. Frenkel and Harry G. Johnson, eds., *The Monetary Approach to the Balance of Payments* (Toronto, 1976), pp. 357–85.

panel of Table 6.1. As the table shows, three of the ten coefficients do not have the anticipated signs. Several factors may be involved here, besides the obvious possibility that the model is misspecified. First, the theory we are using to predict the signs of these interactions is comparative static in nature and does not necessarily require that the predicted effects be contemporaneous. Second, even if the theory were to apply to contemporaneous relationships, the synchronization of the available data leaves much to be desired.[33] For both of these reasons, we believe it to be more appropriate to examine jointly the contemporaneous and lagged influence of one variable on another, by using impulse response functions and decompositions of the variance of forecast errors.

Figure 6.1 shows the response of real output to innovations in the base, M2, and the interest rate. Shocks to the *levels* of M2 and the base have positive but permanent effects on output. Innovations in the interest rate have approximately a zero output effect on net, although the response is initially positive for four quarters.

The relative importance of shocks assigned to each variable can be assessed from the decomposition of the variance of the forecast errors, which is shown in the lower panel of Table 6.1. Here the columns correspond to the sources of the shocks (i.e., which element of V is responsible), and the row names are those of the variable being predicted. The horizon of the forecasts is twelve quarters in all cases. The salient feature of these results is that 26.8 percent of the variance of output forecast errors is assigned to base and M2 innovations. It is also worth noting that two-thirds of the variability of the interest rate comes from the innovations to the base and the money supply, while innovations to the interest rate have a considerably smaller effect.

In summary, there is little in these results that would lead a monetarist to revise his or her views on the nature of the transmission mechanism.

6.3.2 Credit Model

Table 6.2 describes the results of estimating a model designed to capture the effects of variables important to the credit view. This model was developed by Calomiris and Hubbard and is described in detail in their paper.[34] In their structural VAR, in addition to prices, output, and interest rates, they introduce three variables to capture the role of credit: real bank loans, a spread between risky and riskless assets of similar maturity, and the liabilities of business failures. These variables capture both traditional credit interpretations and the determinants of equilibrium credit rationing. The spread and business failures variables are intended to capture the increased "agency costs" faced by lower

33. For example, output and prices are quarterly averages, while the financial variables are measured at the end of each quarter.

34. Calomiris and Hubbard, "Price Flexibility," pp. 429–52.

Table 6.1 Monetarist Model

Interactions Among Contemporaneous Variables

Equation	Base	M2	Real GNP	Commercial Paper	Deflator
Base				1.077^{+}	0.118^{-}
				(0.498)	(0.021)
M2	0.43^{+}			0.886^{-}	
	(0.264)			(0.469)	
Real GNP		0.876^{+}		0.531^{-}	0.017^{+}
		(2.51)		(3.49)	(0.02)
Commercial paper		-0.818^{-}	-0.192^{-}		
		(0.633)	(0.833)		
GNP deflator		0.246^{+}			
		(0.038)			

Variance Decomposition (percent)

	Source of Innovation				
Equation	Base	M2	Real GNP	Commercial Paper	Inflation
Base	64.5	12.1	2.9	16.5	3.9
M2	30.1	30.7	6.9	24.5	7.8
Real GNP	8.5	18.3	52.2	12.1	8.9
Commercial paper	35.8	32.0	4.8	18.8	8.8
Inflation	11.0	2.9	2.2	4.0	80.0

Notes: The entries in the table are the negative of the respective elements of the transpose of Γ. For example, the entry 0.43 means that the coefficient of the contemporaneous effect of Base growth on M2 growth is 0.43. The plus sign to the right of a coefficient signifies that its expected sign is positive; the minus sign, negative. All variables except those involving interest rates are percentage rates of change. Standard errors are in parentheses.

quality firms in their efforts to raise funds in a downturn.[35] They do not include money in their model on the assumption that the money supply was endogenous under the classical gold standard.[36]

The model focuses on the effects of the loan market on economic activity, and so relates the *real* volume of loans to the spread between interest rates on low- and high-grade loans, and the rate of business failures.[37] Calomiris and Hubbard used a monthly series on loans extended at national banks in New York, Boston, and Philadelphia, while we use total national bank loans for the

35. See Frederic S. Mishkin, "Asymmetric Information and Financial Crises: A Historical Perspective," in R. Glenn Hubbard, ed., *Financial Crises and Financial Markets* (Chicago, 1991).

36. As evidence for this position, they cite studies showing interest rate and price arbitrage between the United States and Britain, and unpublished evidence that gold shocks reversed themselves within a short period of time.

37. The spread variable was constructed from rates on different grades of commercial paper, which are only available for Calomiris and Hubbard's 1894 to 1909 sample period. We used the spread between rates on low- and high-grade railroad bonds, constructed by Mishkin (see Appendix).

a) Response of real GNP to a one-standard-deviation shock in base and money

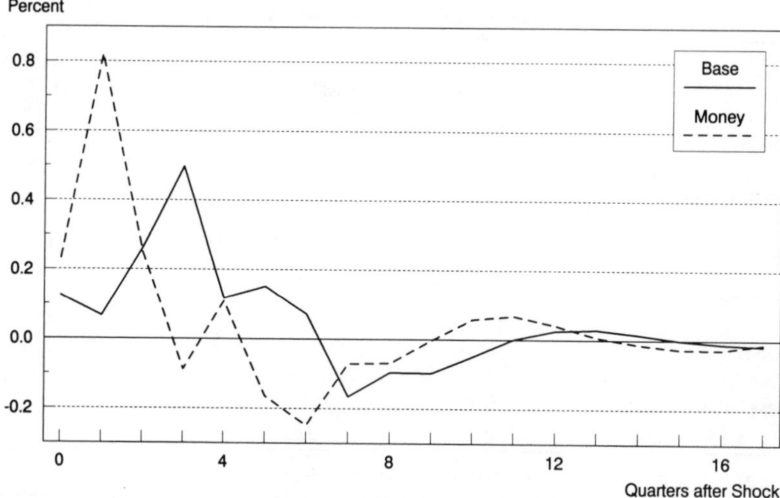

b) Response of real GNP to a one-standard-deviation shock in the commercial paper rate

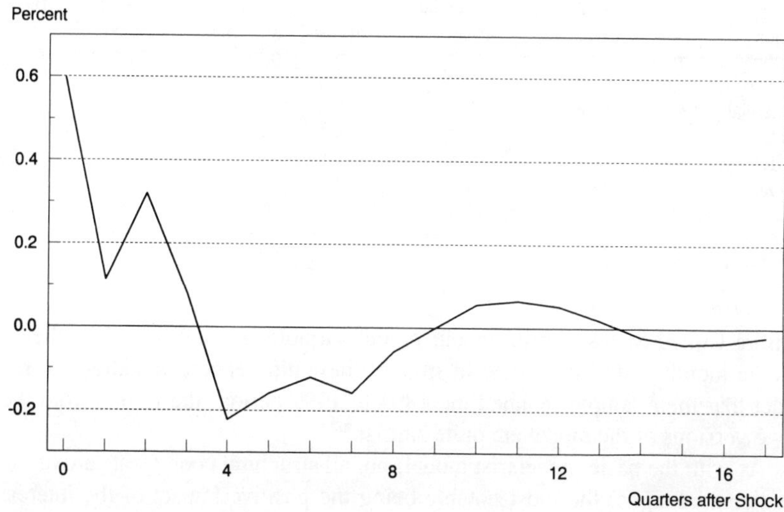

Fig. 6.1 Impulse Response Functions: Monetarist Model
Source: See text.

Table 6.2 **Credit Model**

Interactions among Contemporaneous Variables

Equation	Real Loans	Commercial Paper	Spread	Deflator	Real GNP	Business Failures
Real loans			1.55^{-}			0.364^{-}
			(4.64)			(0.90)
Commercial paper	-0.187^{-}					
	(0.037)					
Spread		0.031^{+}		-0.001^{-}		0.032^{+}
		(0.006)		(0.003)		(0.016)
GNP deflator		-0.071^{+}				0.871^{-}
		(0.19)				(0.544)
Real GNP	0.453^{+}	0.37^{-}	-2.13^{-}	0.38^{+}		-0.246^{-}
	(0.083)	(0.23)	(2.76)	(0.100)		(0.541)
Business failures		0.165^{+}				
		(0.031)				

Variance Decomposition (percent)

	Source of Innovation					
Equation	Real Loans	Commercial Paper	Spread	Deflator	Real GNP	Business Failures
Real loans	82.2	7.9	5.8	2.1	0.7	1.2
Commercial paper	35.8	35.5	5.5	18.0	1.7	3.6
Spread	12.2	13.0	69.1	2.2	1.4	2.2
GNP deflator	10.7	4.5	1.9	76.2	2.7	3.9
Real GNP	35.9	3.4	3.3	16.8	37.2	3.2
Business failures	8.5	12.3	0.7	6.1	0.4	71.9

Notes: See Table 6.1.

entire United States. Similarly, our output variable is real GNP, while their's is the monthly pig-iron series. In spite of these differences, in addition to the fact that their sample spanned the 1894 to 1909 period, the results from the two versions of the model are quite similar.[38]

As with the basic monetarist model, not all structural coefficients are of the anticipated signs, the most notable being the positive impact of the interest rate on output. The impulse response functions show a healthy impact of loan innovations on output, and also exhibit the initial positive response to interest rate shocks found in the monetarist model (Fig. 6.2). The most striking feature of the results is the 35.9 percent of output forecast-error variance explained by loan innovations. Calomiris and Hubbard found that only 10.6

38. A minor difference between the two specifications is that we do not include the spread variable in the inflation equation, which aids the convergence of our estimation procedure. This interaction was not statistically significant in Calomiris and Hubbard's work.

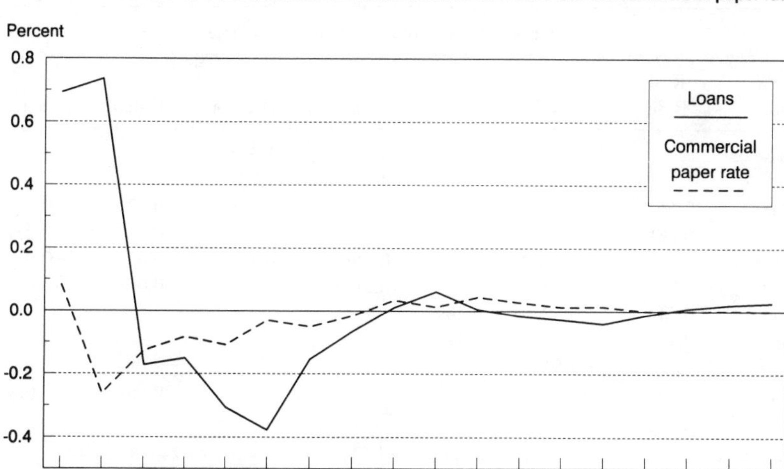

Fig. 6.2 Impulse Response Functions: Credit Model
Source: See text.

percent of this variance could be explained by real loan shocks in their monthly data. We will have occasion to return to this difference in section 6.4 below. In summary, the basic credit model, applied to the national banking era, does not turn up any evidence that would lead one to doubt it.

6.3.3 Hybrid Monetarist Model

Table 6.3 describes the results of estimating a hybrid monetarist model, expanded by adding credit variables. Thus, we add business failures and the spread variable to the five variables of the basic monetarist specification. In addition, we use the *real* money supply and base, since, from the credit viewpoint, it is real balance sheet variables that are important. Unfortunately, we are not able to add the loans variable to the basic monetarist model, because of the close relationship between movements in the quantity of loans on the one hand, and the base and money supply on the other. Of course, this difficulty dogs all tests of the relative merits of the two views.[39] This omission is remedied in the fourth model, discussed below.

The identification restrictions in the top part of Table 6.3 are driven by those in the two basic models. Thus, increases in business failures and the spread are anticipated by the credit view to have a depressing effect on M2, real GNP,

39. See Alan Blinder and Joseph Stiglitz, "Money, Credit Constraints, and Economic Activity," *American Economic Review* 73 (May 1983), pp. 297–302; and Karl Brunner and Allan H. Meltzer, "Money and Credit in the Monetary Transmission Process," *American Economic Review* 78 (June 1988), pp. 446–51.

Table 6.3 **Hybrid Monetarist Model**

Interactions among Contemporaneous Variables

Equation	Real Base	Real M2	Real GNP	Commercial Paper	Deflator	Business Failures	Spread
Real base				−3.24	−1.25^{-}		
				(2.81)	(1.03)		
Real M2	−2.66^{+}			2.33^{-}		0.271^{-}	0.100^{-}
	(6.88)			(8.0)		(0.7)	(0.27)
Real GNP		−0.012^{+}		−0.358^{-}	−0.150^{+}	−0.071^{-}	−0.01^{-}
		(0.24)		(0.28)	(0.18)	(0.06)	(0.03)
Commercial paper	0.514^{-} (0.13)	−0.827^{-} (0.29)	0.149^{-} (0.11)				
GNP deflator		−0.848^{-} (0.08)				−0.054^{-} (0.03)	−0.023^{-} (0.02)
Business failures				1.29^{+} (0.34)			
Spread				2.733^{+}	−0.017^{-}	−0.429^{+}	
				(0.67)	(0.54)	(0.17)	

Variance Decomposition (percent)

Equation	Source of Innovation						
	Real Base	Real M2	Real GNP	Commercial Paper	Deflator	Business Failures	Spread
Real base	13.6	73.1	1.5	2.3	4.3	3.2	1.9
Real M2	4.4	48.2	5.8	17.9	10.4	1.9	11.3
Real GNP	12.3	12.7	52.2	4.2	8.9	4.1	5.5
Commercial paper	32.4	24.6	5.4	8.7	10.9	5.4	12.5
GNP deflator	2.3	48.7	3.0	21.0	18.2	3.3	3.5
Business failures	8.9	12.6	0.8	5.3	4.4	66.8	1.1
Spread	10.4	4.2	0.5	3.0	4.8	3.4	73.7

Notes: See Table 6.1.

and the deflator, after the monetarist effects of the first model have been accounted for, while an increase in business failures is expected to increase the spread between rates on low- and high-quality bonds. The dependence of business failure and spread innovations on interest rate and price innovations is as specified in the basic credit model. A substantially higher proportion of the contemporaneous interactions have the wrong sign than in the basic monetarist model, the most egregious being the response of M2 to the base, and of real output to money. However, there is a strong positive response of output to M2 innovations after two quarters have elapsed (Fig. 6.3). Money innova-

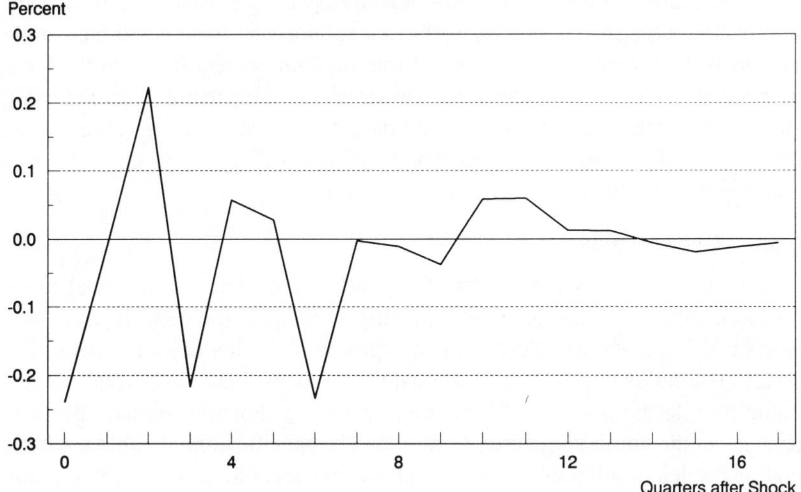

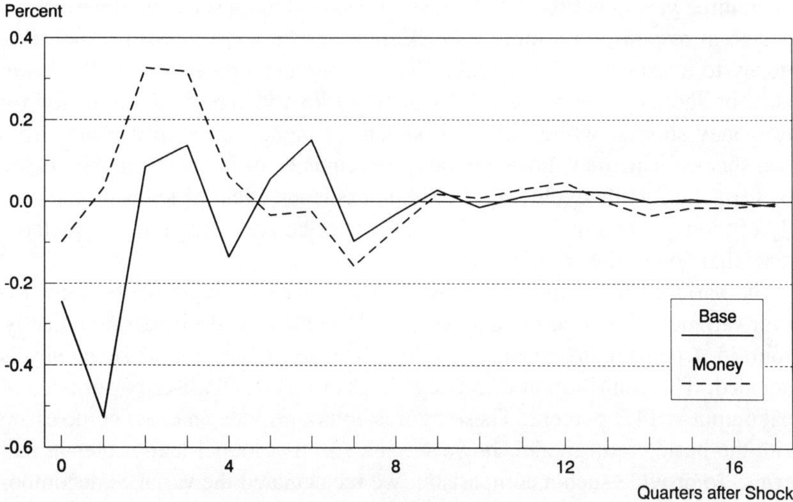

Fig. 6.3 Impulse Response Functions: Hybrid Monetarist Model
Source: See text.

tions appear to have a smaller permanent effect on the level of output, and the permanent effect of base innovations has disappeared.[40] Similarly, the proportion of the output forecast-error variance explained by money and base innovations is 25 percent, little changed from the 26.8 percent found in the basic monetarist model. We also note that the variables added to represent the credit story—the interest rate spread and the rate of business failures—together explain only 9.6 percent of the variability of real GNP, which approximately matches their performance in the basic credit model.

6.3.4 Hybrid Credit Model

Table 6.4 describes the results of expanding the basic credit model to include the effects of changes in the quantity of money. The delicate issue here is whether loans and money should be expressed in real or nominal terms. The credit view holds that it is the real quantity of loans that is important for real output, while the monetarist view focuses on the short-run output effects of changes in the nominal quantity of money. The specification of Table 6.4 casts both variables in nominal terms, but allows for real effects to be consistently estimated by including the inflation rate in the output and loans equations.[41]

The responses of real GNP to nominal loans and money both die out after about three years, as Figure 6.4 shows. Loans exhibit a substantial permanent change in response to a money shock, but there is not a marked response of money to a loan shock. Similarly, the variance decompositions in the lower panel of Table 6.4 show that 14.4 percent of loan variability is accounted for by money shocks, while only 5.9 percent of money variability comes from loan shocks. This may, however, be a consequence of including money in the loan equation while excluding a contemporaneous effect of loans on the supply of money. For this reason, the model is to be understood as a monetarist generalization of the credit model.

The variance decomposition also shows that the fraction of the forecast-error variance of real output attributable to loan shocks declines dramatically, from 35.9 percent in the basic credit model to 16 percent when money is included. The contribution of money shocks to the forecast-error variance of real output is 14.3 percent. These figures do not provide an exact comparison with the basic credit model, however, since in that model loans enter in real terms. To provide such a comparison, we recalculated the variance decomposition to assess the effect of real loan shocks on real output, leaving money in nominal terms. The results, which are shown in the addendum to Table 6.4, are little changed, although the influence of money shocks declines slightly

40. The permanent or long-run effect on the *level* of real GNP is the sum of the impulse responses over the time horizon.

41. We also ran the model using real loans, nominal money, and the deflator, and found that the deflator coefficient in the real loans equation was -0.94. This suggests that deflation of the loans series was inappropriate in this model.

Table 6.4 **Hybrid Credit Model**

Interactions among Contemporaneous Variables

Equation	Loans	Commercial Paper	Spread	Deflator	Real GNP	Business Failures	M2
Loans			-1.35^{-}	0.302^{+}		0.053^{-}	0.58^{+}
			(2.95)	(0.09)		(0.06)	(0.16)
Commercial paper	-0.184^{-}						
	(0.04)						
Spread		0.0328^{+}		-0.0124^{-}		0.0024^{+}	
		(0.01)		(0.01)		(0.002)	
GNP deflator		0.0169^{+}	11.11^{+}			-0.089^{-}	0.433^{+}
		(0.54)	(16.6)			(0.07)	(0.18)
Real GNP	0.437	0.402^{-}	-3.04^{-}	-0.0717^{+}		-0.0209^{-}	-0.038^{+}
	(0.09)	(0.22)	(2.72)	(0.08)		(0.05)	(0.16)
Business failures		0.136^{+}					
		(0.03)					
M2		-0.236^{-}				-0.0749^{+}	
		(0.11)				(0.03)	

Variance Decomposition (percent)

Equation	Loans	Commercial Paper	Spread	Deflator	Real GNP	Business Failures	M2
Loans	49.6	5.4	6.4	10.3	1.5	0.5	14.4
Commercial paper	16.2	41.7	9.3	7.7	2.9	3.0	19.1
Spread	9.6	9.9	57.1	10.8	1.2	2.9	8.5
Inflation	0.9	4.1	9.5	70.4	2.7	3.8	8.6
Real GNP	16.0	5.2	7.0	7.5	47.1	2.8	14.3
Business failures	3.6	8.2	0.8	5.0	0.5	76.0	5.8
M2	5.9	6.9	18.3	6.5	2.1	3.2	57.3
Addendum: Model Using Real Loans							
Real output	18.5	3.1	9.4	6.0	47.1	2.9	13.0

Notes: See Table 6.1.

while that of real loan shocks is 2.5 percentage points larger than that of nominal loan shocks.

The central message of this "hybrid credit model" is that the channel of influence on output that operates through the money supply cannot be ignored. Of course, loan shocks still account for a respectable fraction of the variance of output forecast errors, even after money shocks have been allowed for, and this is perhaps a greater surprise to the monetarist camp than to those

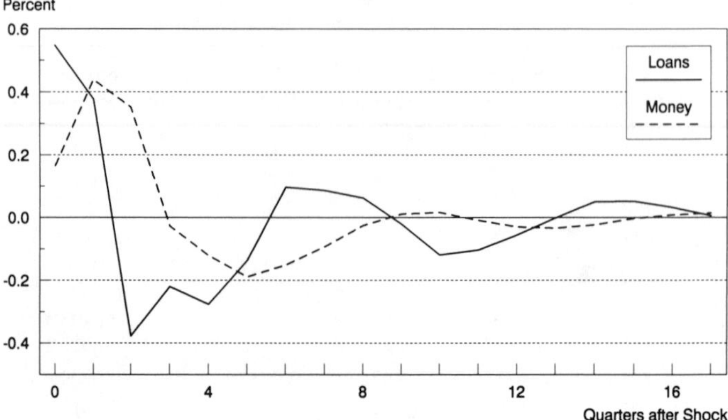

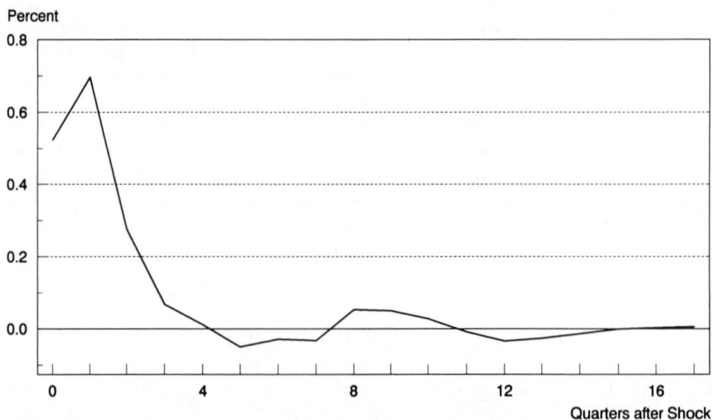

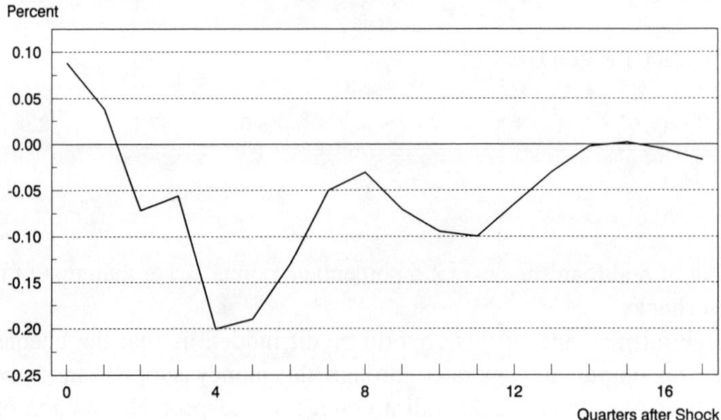

Fig. 6.4 Impulse Response Functions: Hybrid Credit Model
Source: See text.

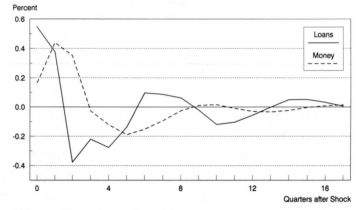

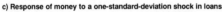

holding the credit view. However, it is always possible that the loan variable is picking up shocks to the base, which is not included in this model.

The message of this section thus turns out to be generally negative as to the possibility of a clear choice between the two schools of thought, using such aggregate data. The basic models both appear reasonably soothing to members of the associated school. The hybrid monetarist model leaves the money story intact when the interest rate spread and business failures are added, but credit proponents could argue that the base variable is accounting for the effects of loans. The hybrid credit model suggests that money effects are important in addition to those said to operate through the asset side of the banks' balance sheets, but it is not a plank of the credit platform to say that money does not matter at all. The close comovement between loans, money, and the base also clouds the interpretation here: monetarists could argue that the incremental explanatory power of the loans variable arises because its inclusion helps to separate base shocks from money demand shocks.

It therefore appears that other data must be consulted, if we are ultimately to be able to assess the relative merits of the two views. We offer a first step in this direction in the next section, by examining the composition of loans.

6.4 The Role of the Stock Market and Call Loan Market in the Institutional Framework, 1880 to 1914

The results of the VARs in the preceding section, if taken at face value, suggest that both bank loans and money are important in the transmission mechanism. However, the institutional structure of the national banking era directs attention to the fundamental reason for the importance of bank loans in this period—the intimate connection between the stock market and the national banking system established by the inverted pyramid of credit and the New York City call loan market. Disturbances to the stock market were transmitted to the call loan market, which in turn had a dramatic impact on total bank loans in New York City and in the rest of the country.

A key feature of the regulations that defined the national banking system was the imposition of different reserve requirements on three separate classes of national banks. Specifically, the Act of 1874 required country banks to hold 15 percent against their deposits, three-fifths of which, or 9 percent, could be held as bankers' balances with correspondent national banks in reserve cities (with populations greater than 50,000) or in central-reserve cities (New York City and, after 1887, also Chicago and St. Louis). These balances earned interest up to 2 percent. The remaining two-fifths of required reserves were to be held in lawful money (U.S. notes, specie, gold, and clearing-house certificates). Reserve-city national banks were required to hold 25 percent of their deposits in reserves, half of which had to be held in lawful money, the other half available to be held as bankers' balances in central-reserve-city national banks. Central-reserve-city national banks were required to hold 25 percent of their deposits in lawful money.[42] Country and reserve-city banks kept excess reserves far above the required levels in the form of bankers' balances in central-reserve cities. These funds were a form of secondary reserves. The reserve structure of the national banking system has been described as an inverted pyramid, whereby most of the nation's reserves ended up as bankers' balances in the central-reserve cities, but especially in New York City.[43]

Most of the reserves held as bankers' balances in New York City national banks were invested in the call loan market. Call loans were demand loans secured by stock traded on the New York Stock Exchange and also by U.S. and other bonds. Most of the loans were made to brokers who would then consign the stock serving as collateral to the banks. The commercial banks considered call loans the most liquid form of investment, since they could be called at any time. The New York national banks dominated the call loan market, with between a third and a half of their loan portfolios in call loans during the period we cover.[44] Close to 75 percent of bankers' balances in New York were held in call loans between 1880 and 1904, the amount to be expected if the New York banks held the required 25 percent reserve requirement against those balances. In addition, country and reserve-city national banks and state commercial, savings, and trust companies invested directly in the call loan market (using their central-reserve-city correspondents as intermediaries) whenever the call loan rate rose significantly above the 2 percent earned on bankers' balances. Thus an inverse relationship existed between the call loan rate and bankers' balances in New York City, and a direct one between the call loan rate and country bank excess reserves invested directly in the call loan market.[45]

The inverted pyramid as well as the correspondent balance arrangement and its intimate connection to the call loan market are widely regarded as key elements in financial crises that punctuated the era.[46] All the major banking

42. Although Chicago and St. Louis were important regional centers, New York held the lion's share of bankers' balances. National banks in central-reserve cities also held substantial correspondent balances of state banks, private banks, and trust companies.

43. The inverted pyramid was a natural outgrowth of the extensive correspondent network developed before the Civil War. See John James, *Money and Capital Markets* (Princeton, 1978), chap. 4; and Margaret Myers, *The New York Money Market* (New York, 1935), chap. 12. In the unit-banking system that arose earlier in the century, holding balances with city correspondents represented a valuable way in which a country bank could gain access to an interregional clearing mechanism (obtain domestic exchange and clear out-of-town checks), obtain additional sources of credit (by interbank loans and rediscounts, although rarely extended in this period), and earn interest on excess reserves. The city banks on their part had access to the interior and secured compensation for their services to the country banks. The national banks thus extended an existing framework.

44. Myers, *The New York Money Market,* p. 290.

45. Myers, *The New York Money Market,* p. 290; James, *Money and Capital Markets,* p. 304.

46. Oliver M. W. Sprague, *History of Crises Under the National Banking System.* National Monetary Commission, 61st Cong., 2d sess., S. Doc. 538 (Washington, D.C., 1910); Myers, *The New York Money Market.*

panics of the period (1873, 1884, 1893, 1907) were marked by withdrawals of bankers' balances (especially those representing excess reserves) by the country and reserve-city banks from the New York banks. The decline in bankers' balances in turn put pressure on the call loan market, causing call loan rates to rise and stock prices to fall—possibly inducing a stock market crash. The decline in New York bank reserves could on occasion be so severe as to precipitate a panic, which could only be stopped by the restriction of convertibility of deposits into currency.

The evidence is mixed on whether the combined incidence of stock market crashes and banking panics during the national banking era reflects causation from the banking system or vice versa.[47] Although there were twice as many crashes as there were panics, all of the major banking panics also occurred close to stock market crashes. On two occasions (1899 and 1901), syndicates of prominent financial institutions were able to reverse the pressure on the New York call loan market.[48] On other occasions, panic was averted by the issue of clearing-house certificates by the New York Clearing House and/or by Treasury intervention (1884, 1890). However, on three occasions (1873, 1893, 1907), this intervention was insufficient to prevent panic. Only a restriction of convertibility of deposits into currency sufficed.

This experience suggests that a potential source of volatility in bank loans may lie in call loans. If that is the case, this makes questionable the importance of credit rationing. To consider this possibility we examine more closely the composition of loans in New York City national banks and in national banks in the rest of the country.

Bank loans were either demand or time loans, some secured by different types of collateral: stocks and bonds, merchandise, and receivables. The latter two categories of secured loans were typically issued on the real bills principle that they would be self-liquidating.[49] The balance sheets of the New York City national banks had similar categories to those of the country national banks, but the composition was quite different, reflecting the absence of excess reserves in New York City.

Of the categories of assets just noted, credit rationing would refer to loans

47. Jack W. Wilson, Richard E. Sylla, and Charles P. Jones, "Financial Market Panics and Volatility in the Long Run, 1830–1988," in Eugene N. White, ed., *Crashes and Panics: The Lessons from History* (New York, 1990). According to Calomiris and Gorton, "The Origins of Banking Panics," however, banking panics happened only if there had been prior bad news in the stock market combined with increased commercial failures.

48. Myers, *The New York Money Market*, p. 286.

49. Other earning assets of the national banks were discounts and investments. Discounts were usually not secured by collateral, and differed from loans in that the interest charge was collected in advance. Discounts consisted primarily of commercial paper, either in the form of trade acceptances or lenders' acceptances. Commercial paper bore either two names or one name, with the latter eclipsing the former by the end of the period. These instruments usually traded in an active national market, and the commercial paper rate fluctuated widely, reflecting changing conditions in the money market. Investments consisted of eligible U.S. securities required to back the note issue and other U.S. securities held as a form of secondary reserves.

secured primarily by merchandise, since discounts and call loan rates were determined in active national markets. We show in Figures 6.5 and 6.6 data for one call date annually (usually in September), 1880 to 1914, two categories of national bank loans, as well as total national bank loans for New York City and for all national banks.[50] The two categories are loans secured by stocks and other loans.[51]

The pattern that emerges from these figures is quite striking. New York City loans secured by stock are highly volatile, exhibiting sharp declines in the panic years 1884, 1893, and 1907, and slight declines in two years with stock market crashes and no banking panics (1895 and 1899). Other New York City loans by contrast are distinctly stable, with a mild upward trend, and the movement of total New York City loans reflects that of loans secured by stock.[52]

For the United States as a whole, the pattern of loans secured by stock is much less volatile than for New York City, but declines in the panic years can be discerned. Other loans have a stable upward trend. While total U.S. loans pick up some of the volatility of New York City loans, they are considerably more stable.[53]

The stable pattern of other loans compared to loans secured by stock in New York City and, to a lesser extent, a similar difference in the composition of loans in the United States as a whole, in country banks, and in the United States minus New York City, suggest that whatever procyclical influence is exhibited by loans in New York City and for the United States as a whole can be explained by the behavior of the call loan market. On the face of it, this

50. The source is U.S. Comptroller of the Currency, *Annual Report,* 1880 to 1914.

51. For 1880–88, the Comptroller showed four categories of loans: (1) loans on U.S. bonds on demand; (2) loans on other stocks, bonds, etc., on demand; (3) loans on single-name paper without other security; and (4) all other loans. From 1891 to 1914, the Comptroller showed five categories: (1) loans on demand paper with one or more individual or firm names; (2) loans on demand, secured by stocks, bonds, and other securities; (3) loans on time, paper with two or more individual or firm names; (4) loans on time, single-name paper (person or firm) without other security; and (5) loans on time, secured by stocks, bonds, and other personal securities, or on mortgages or other real estate securities. For 1889 and 1890, the Comptroller showed different categories, not readily comparable to those of the preceding and subsequent periods, and they are consequently omitted from the figures.

The first category of loans that we show in Figure 6.5—loans secured by stocks—consists for 1880 to 1888 of categories (1) and (2), and for 1891 to 1914 of categories (2) and (5). The second category in Figure 6.5—other loans—consists for 1880 to 1888 of categories (3) and (4), for 1891 to 1914 of categories (1), (3), and (4).

We compared demand loans secured by stock (i.e., call loans)—category (2)—with the rest. The pictures are similar to those presented here. We also drew similar figures for country banks and total United States minus New York City. However, to save space we discuss but do not present the former, and the pattern of the latter, which includes country banks, reserve-city banks, and central-reserve cities other than New York, can be inferred from the figures we present.

52. Within the category of other loans, one of the subcategories exhibited more volatility than the total.

53. For country banks, loans secured by stock were also more volatile than other loans, but the difference between the two categories was not as marked as for New York City. Results are similar for the U.S. minus New York City.

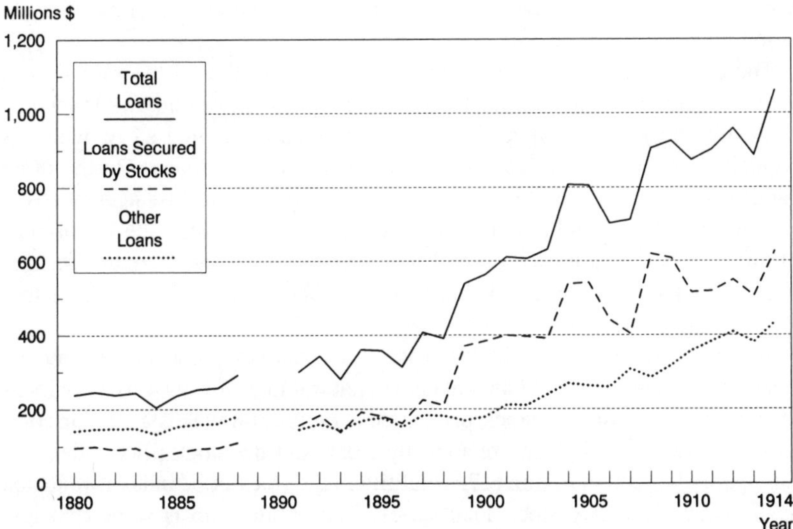

Fig. 6.5 Composition of New York City National Bank Loans, 1880–1914
Source: See Appendix.

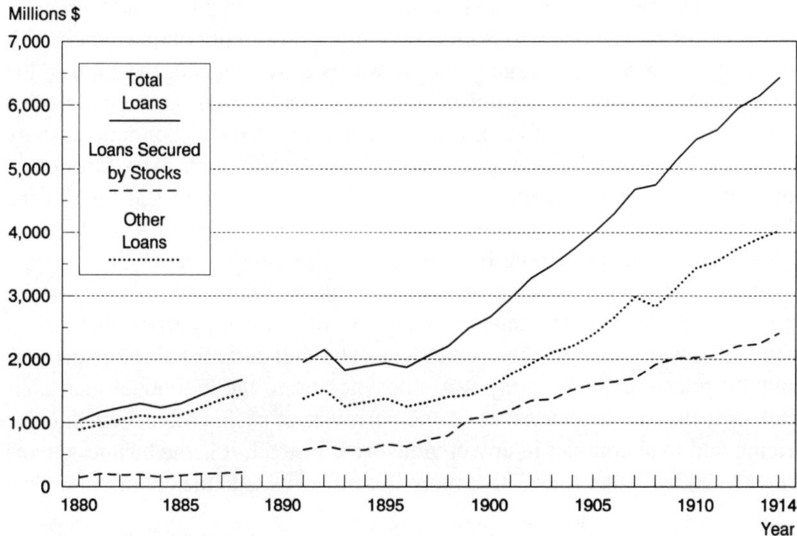

Fig 6.6 Composition of U.S. National Bank Loans, 1880–1914
Source: See Appendix.

leaves little room for an independent influence on output variability of credit rationing.

There remains, however, the link between the decline in the valuation of firms reflected in a fall in stock prices and declines in real output. On the one hand, this does not impinge directly on the credit-rationing story, which is typically limited to borrowers who must resort to bank loans. On the other hand, some have argued that a stock market crash can increase agency costs, causing investment and real activity to decline.[54] To measure the importance of this channel of influence on real output, it is necessary to control for that part of stock price movements that is due to changes in fundamentals, a subject for possible future research.

To demonstrate the link between the stock market and loans secured by stock, we plot in Figure 6.7 annual data in natural logs of New York City loans secured by stock and the stock price index. Figure 6.8 makes a similar comparison between U.S. loans secured by stock and the stock price index. As can readily be seen in Figure 6.7, volatility in the stock price index is reflected in the New York City stock loan series. The relationship is somewhat less transparent in Figure 6.8 for U.S. loans secured by stock.

One inference that can be drawn from Figures 6.7 and 6.8 is that the significant results obtained for bank loans and other credit variables in the VARs reported in section 6.3 reflect stock market disturbances, where the principal stocks traded were railway stocks. These disturbances in turn could be reflecting earlier or contemporaneous monetary shocks, or future output shocks.[55] It is a mistake, however, to argue that the waves of railroad construction in the late nineteenth century were independent of financial markets, on the ground that "there was no central bank to mistakenly squeeze off economic activity by letting the money supply grow too slowly."[56] The stock market reflected banking panics and concerns about the stability of the gold standard in the United States from 1890 to 1897. External finance that the stock market provided either advanced or retarded railroad construction.

It appears from this discussion that the principal source of volatility in the series of total loans is the category of loans collateraled by stock, the effects of which are not part of the credit story. The collateral for these loans was publicly priced and not in any way idiosyncratic to the individual loan contract. Nor do the characteristics of the borrower of such a loan enter into the pricing and loan contract in any obvious way. Instead, it is the business loans represented by "other loans" that more faithfully relate to the credit view. This

54. See Jaffee and Stiglitz, "Credit Rationing," and Mishkin, "Asymmetric Information."

55. Sprague argues the former in *History of Crises,* while G. William Schwert takes the latter view in "Stock Returns and Real Activity: A Century of Evidence," *Journal of Finance* 45 (Sept. 1990), pp. 1237–57.

56. See J. Bradford De Long, "'Liquidation' Cycles: Old-Fashioned Real Business Cycle Theory and the Great Depression," NBER Working Paper no. 3546 (Dec. 1990), p. 29.

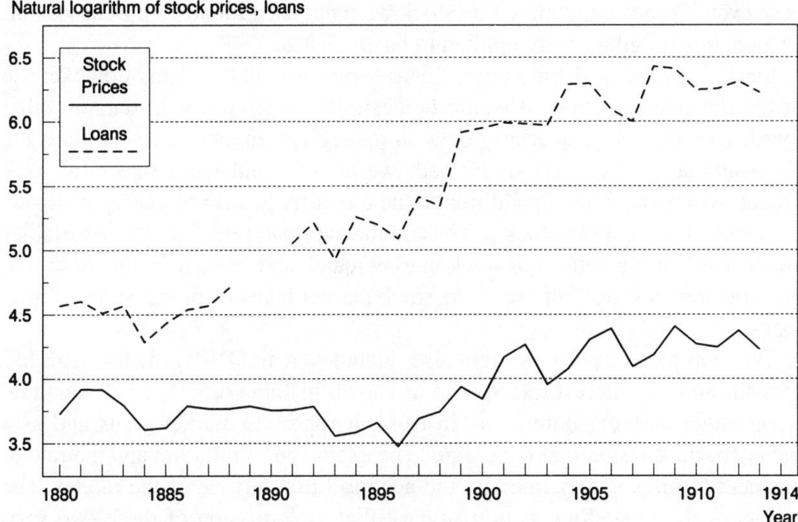

Fig. 6.7 Stock Prices and New York City National Bank Loans Secured by Stocks, 1880–1914
Source: See Appendix.

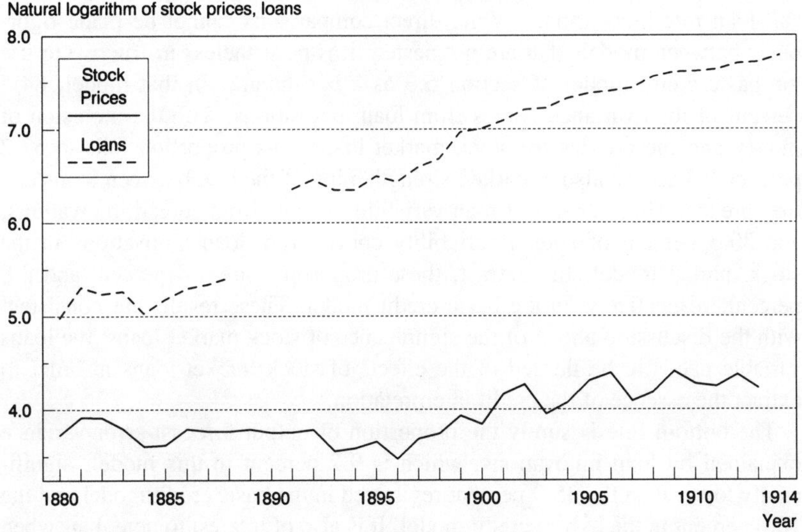

Fig. 6.8 Stock Prices and U.S. National Bank Loans Secured by Stocks, 1880–1914
Source: See Appendix.

is so even if loans collateraled by stock were not used for stock purchases but, as money is fungible, were applied to business use.

Ideally, instead of the aggregate loans series used in the estimation exercise of the preceding section, it would be desirable to rerun it with data on other loans. Unfortunately, quarterly data on disaggregated categories of loans are not available for this period. Instead, we have formulated a structural VAR model, which includes, in addition to the quarterly growth of aggregate loans, the quarterly change in stock prices and the call loan rate. The latter variables are proxies for the pattern of stock market loans, and so their inclusion should go some way toward "filtering" the stock market loans from the series of total loans.

The complete model, which also includes real GNP growth, real M2 growth, and the interest rate spread, is shown in Table 6.5. The call loan rate is, in effect, serving both as an instrument for stock market loans and as a proxy for the commercial paper rate. The exclusion of inflation and the rate of business failures is explained by the need to limit the size of the model. The results of the preceding section suggest that the omission of these two variables is of little consequence.

As Figure 6.9 shows, the response of output to real money shocks does not wash out in the long run, while the output response to loan innovations is more muted and transitory. The variance decomposition shows that 15.7 percent of the real loan forecast-error variance is accounted for by stock price and call loan rate innovations. While direct comparisons cannot be made rigorously between models that are not nested, it is nevertheless instructive to use the basic credit model of section 6.3 as a benchmark. In that model, 84.5 percent of loan variance comes from loan innovations; with the inclusion of money and the proxies for stock market loans, this proportion falls to 52.2 percent.[57] There is also a marked strengthening of the link between loans and the spread—19.1 percent of loan variability comes from spread innovations, and 30.3 percent of spread variability comes from loan innovations in the stock market model. In contrast, these proportions are 4.4 percent and 8.8 percent, respectively, in the basic credit model. These results are consistent with the discussion above of the significance of stock market loans: the loans variable needs to be purged of the effects of stock market loans in order to extract the essence of the credit interpretation.

The bottom line is surely the proportion of output forecast-error variance explained by loan innovations, which is 9.2 percent in this model, significantly lower than the 35.9 percent registered in the basic credit model and the 16.0 percent in the hybrid credit model. It is also of interest to note that, when the stock market model is run with loans by New York City banks—a series similar to that used by Calomiris and Hubbard (as noted above, with a far

57. Note that this also happens in the hybrid credit model, when money alone is included.

Table 6.5 **Stock Market Model**

Interactions among Contemporaneous Variables[a]

Equation	Real Loans	Stock Price	Real GNP	Real M2	Spread	Call Rate
Real loans		0.15^{+}		-0.063^{+}	24.8^{-}	-0.20^{-}
Stock price			0.70^{+}			
Real GNP	0.317^{+}			-0.158^{+}	0.17^{-}	0.683^{-}
Real M2	0.564^{+}					-0.028^{-}
Spread	-0.019^{-}	-0.003^{-}				0.003^{+}
Call rate		0.029^{+}				

Variance Decomposition (percent)

	Source of Innovation					
Equation	Real Loans	Stock Price	Real GNP	Real M2	Spread	Call Rate
Real loans	52.2	9.5	1.6	11.3	19.1	6.2
Stock price	4.9	70.3	5.8	11.4	2.5	5.0
Real GNP	9.2	14.0	54.1	16.8	1.7	4.1
Real M2	30.6	6.8	5.4	43.0	10.4	3.7
Spread	30.3	24.8	2.6	3.2	36.2	2.8
Call rate	6.3	12.3	2.2	8.2	2.7	66.3
Addendum: Model Using Real NYC Loans						
Real GNP	4.5	13.1	57.0	16.0	4.2	5.1

Notes: See Table 6.1.

[a]While a number of starting values converged to those reported in the table, which corresponded to the maximum found for the likelihood function, numerical computation of standard errors proved infeasible, as it was not possible to invert the Hessian.

greater proportion of their loan volume in the call loan market than was the case for total U.S. loans)—the contribution of loan innovations to the output forecast-error variance drops to 4.5 percent.[58] Indeed a substantial fraction of the variability in total U.S. loans is accounted for by movements in New York City loans, which in turn are largely composed of stock market loans. While accounting for only one-sixth of total loans, the variance of New York City loans accounts for one-fourth of the variance of U.S. loans.

In summary, an examination of the breakdown of loans into their various categories reveals that loans other than stock market loans are not closely related to output fluctuations during the national banking period. In contrast, the contribution of money to output variability is consistently in the range of 12 to 18 percent, and the combined contribution of money and the base is about 25 percent.

58. In this specification, the spread and loans variables once again explain minimal proportions of each other's forecast-error variance.

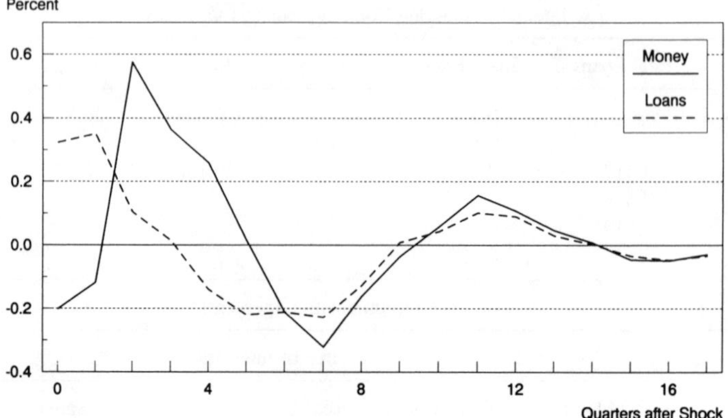

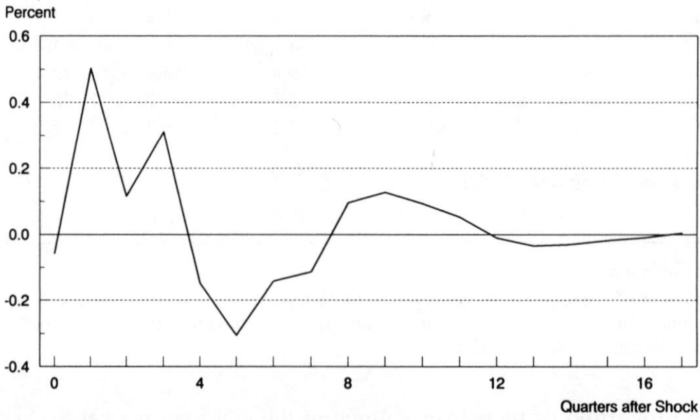

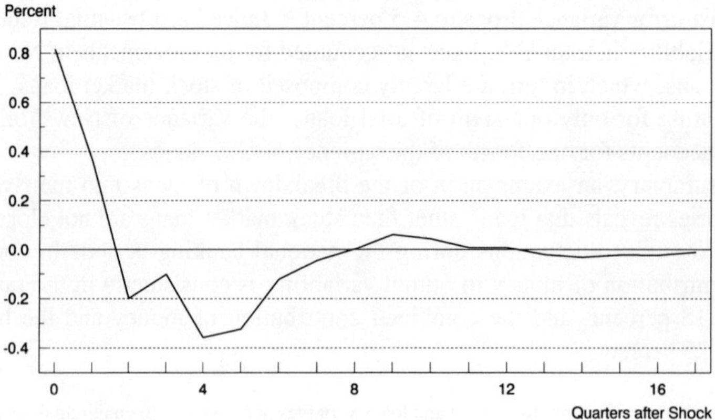

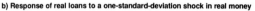

Fig. 6.9 Impulse Response Functions: Stock Market Model
Source: See text.

6.5 Conclusion

A growing theoretical literature of the past decade assigns a major role to credit rationing by banks, defined as a reduction in bank lending with little change in interest rates, in influencing the course of the real economy. The theory, elaborated in the context of existing banking and monetary arrangements, is far more developed than empirical verification of its propositions. The most advanced efforts at empirical verification apply the method of structural VARs to a limited number of variables designed to show that credit variables account for a preponderance of output forecast-error variance. Our point of departure is the application of the method by Calomiris and Hubbard to the national banking period.

We broaden the inquiry to encompass not only credit but also money variables, and apply the structural VAR methodology to assess the relative merits of money and credit explanations of real activity during the national banking period. This approach requires identification assumptions to be made concerning the contemporaneous interactions among variables. Since this approach also implies that the resulting system of simultaneous equations contains no substantive misspecification, it is well to test the robustness of the conclusions drawn from any one model by changing the identification assumptions. Experience with the models used in this paper counsels that one place stock only in those conclusions that are consistent with all models.

Table 6.6 summarizes our findings by showing the decomposition of the output forecast-error variance attributable to each model. The salient feature of the estimation results is that the explanatory power of money and the base is moderate and robust to changes in that specification of the underlying model. Similarly, we repeatedly fail to find a sizeable output effect of the spread and business failures variables. Last, the effect of loan variability on output fluctuations is highly sensitive to changes in specification, and declines dramatically when money is introduced into the model and stock market loans are controlled for.

These results motivate the conclusion that there is little support during the national banking era for the "credit-rationing" view of the transmission mechanism, that the asset side of banks' balance sheets is a significant determinant of output fluctuations. This inference, drawn from the variance decomposition of our structural VAR exercises, is supported by direct examination of the course of "other loans" (which we take to represent business loans) over the national banking period. Other loans exhibit little, if any, volatility, and so they cannot explain output fluctuations.

Our findings raise a number of issues that cannot be addressed within the confines of the present study. We have not examined whether interest rates flatten out instead of continuing to rise as output growth reaches a peak, which is a critical implication of the credit story. The VAR methodology is limited to an examination of short-run interactions among macroeconomic time series. The basis of the equilibrium credit-rationing story is microeconomic in

Table 6.6 **Money versus Credit: Contributions to the Forecast-Error Variance of Real GNP (%)**

Model	Real GNP	Monetary Base	M2	Loans	Commercial Paper Rate	GNP Deflator	Interest Rate Spread	Business Failures	Stock Price	Call Rate
Monetarist	52.2	8.5	18.3		12.1	8.9				
Credit	37.2			35.9	3.4	16.8	3.3	3.2		
Hybrid monetarist	52.2	12.3	12.7		4.2	8.9	5.5	4.1		
Hybrid Credit	47.1		14.3	16.0	5.2	7.5	7.0	2.8		
Stock Market (U.S. loans)	54.1		16.8	9.2			1.7		14.0	4.1
Stock Market (NYC loans)	57.0		16.0	4.5			4.2		13.1	5.1

Note: Estimated from structural VAR models using quarterly data from 1880 to 1914. A forecast horizon of three years is used.

nature, and our data provide little that can directly address the question whether banks refrain from lending, beyond a certain point, irrespective of their reserve positions.

Similarly, we find striking the lack of fluctuation in "other loans," a series that seems to grow with GNP. This may reflect an extreme form of customer relations between lenders and borrowers, or it may be a consequence of the relative ease of acquiring loans in a growing economy whose banking sector more than quadrupled over the period of our study. It appears that these issues would most fruitfully be addressed by a study of banks' historical records.

Finally, we can ask whether it was the asset or the liability side of bank balance sheets that contemporaries during the national banking period regarded as problematical. For them, it was unquestionably the liability side, in particular, the inflexibility during financial crises of the banks' bond-secured note issues.

The policy conclusion that contemporaries reached was embodied in the Federal Reserve Act of 1913. That legislation provided for the issue of asset-backed Federal Reserve notes that were expected to vary with changes in demand. Credit rationing by banks was neither a concern nor a policy issue.[59] In the new regime, the prescription was once again for loans to be based on short-term self-liquidating bills. No essential change was made in the regulations prevailing under the national banking system with regard to credit.

59. Calomiris and Hubbard quote examples of "credit rationing and credit market segmentation" which they state "appear frequently in Sprague" ("Price Flexibility," p. 437); see his *History of Crises*. However, we interpret the relevance of these quotations somewhat less broadly than do Calomiris and Hubbard. All are drawn from Sprague's chapter on the panic of 1907 and are intended to illustrate the inability of reserve-constrained banks to lend freely.

Appendix
Data Sources

Annual Series

U.S. and New York City Loan Classification for one call date (usually September). U.S. Comptroller of the Currency, *Annual Report,* 1880–1914.

Quarterly Series

GNP, real and nominal; GNP deflator. N. S. Balke and R. J. Gordon, "Historical Data," in R. J. Gordon, ed., *The American Business Cycle: Continuity and Change* (Chicago, 1986), app. B., app. table 2, pp. 790–93. *U.S. loans.* NBER Business Cycle tape, series 14,15, call dates interpolated to 3d month of the quarter. *New York City loans.* NBER Business Cycle tape, series 14,20, call dates interpolated to 3d month of the quarter. *M2.* M. Friedman and A. J. Schwartz, *Monetary Statistics of the United States: Estimates, Sources, Methods* (New York, 1970), table 2, pp. 61–66. *Base.* Friedman and Schwartz, *Monetary Statistics,* table 21, pp. 346–50; table 26, pp. 396–97, call dates interpolated to 3d month of quarter. *Net gold flows.* NBER Business Cycle tape, series 14,112, monthly, every third month. *Commercial paper rates in New York City.* F. R. Macaulay, *Some Theoretical Problems Suggested by the Movements of Interest Rates, Bond Yields and Stock Prices in the United States Since 1856* (New York, 1938), app. table 10, pp. A147–A156, monthly, every third month. *Call loan rates at the New York Stock Exchange.* NBER Business Cycle tape, series 13,01, monthly, every third month. *Spread.* Unpublished quarterly data from F. S. Mishkin underlying his paper, "Asymmetric Information and Financial Crises: A Historical Perspective," in R. Glenn Hubbard, ed., *Financial Crises and Financial Markets* (Chicago, 1991). *Liabilities of business failures.* NBER Business Cycle tape, series 9,32, monthly, every third month. *Stock price index.* J. W. Wilson, R. E. Sylla, and C. P. Jones, "Financial Market Panics and Volatility in the Long Run, 1830–1988," in Eugene N. White, ed., *Crashes and Panics: The Lessons from History* (New York, 1990).

7 Precedence and Wealth
Evidence from Nineteenth-Century Utah

David W. Galenson and Clayne L. Pope

7.1 Introduction

Persistence rates have been widely used by social historians to study geographic and social mobility.[1] A closely related measure, the precedence rate, has not received as much attention and may prove to be extremely useful for a variety of purposes. We explore here one important application of the precedence rate for economic history.[2]

To illustrate the relationship between the persistence rate and the proposed new rate, consider two samples of households drawn from the census manuscripts of 1860 and 1870 for some county or city. In each sample, the households that were present in the other census have been identified. The calculation of the persistence rate would be made using only the households of the 1860 sample by dividing households from that sample present in 1870 by the total number of households in the 1860 sample. In other words, a persistence rate is measured through forward linkage and has generally been used to consider the mobility or turnover of the population.

Alternatively, one could reverse the process and measure the percentage of households in the 1870 sample present ten years earlier. We will designate this new related measure as the "precedence rate" which is calculated by dividing

The authors are grateful to Stanley Engerman for his suggestions for improvement of the paper. The collection of the Utah data represents the joint effort of Dwight Israelsen, J. R. Kearl, Clayne L. Pope, and Larry T. Wimmer.

1. Stephan Thernstrom, *The Other Bostonians: Poverty and Progress in the American Metropolis, 1880–1970* (Cambridge, Mass., 1973), pp. 221–32, summarizes most of the persistence studies up to that time. For other studies, see David W. Galenson and Clayne L. Pope, "Economic and Geographic Mobility on the Farming Frontier: Evidence from Appanoose County, Iowa, 1850–1870," *Journal of Economic History*, 49 (Sept. 1989), pp. 635–56.

2. Precedence plays a central role in Kenneth J. Winkle's study of voting behavior and office holding in Ohio. See Winkle, *The Politics of Community: Migration and Politics in Antebellum Ohio* (Cambridge, Mass., 1988).

the households from the 1870 sample present in 1860 by the total number of households in the 1870 sample. The two rates are related since the persistence rate multiplied by the reciprocal of population growth (number of households in the population in 1860/number of households in the population in 1870) yields the precedence rate.[3] Rapid population growth, which often occurred during initial settlement of an area, reduces the precedence rate as does low persistence.

A number of investigations of the correlates of wealth in nineteenth-century America have considered duration of residence in a community as a possible determinant of a household's wealth. Several studies have now found a correlation between a household's duration in a community and household wealth.[4] Cross-sectional regressions indicate that increased duration of one year in mid-nineteenth-century Utah, holding age, birthplace, occupation, and rural/urban residence constant, was associated with over a 6 percent increase in wealth in 1860 and over 3 percent in 1870. In Chicago, duration had an even stronger relationship to wealth with a year's duration being associated with an increase of more than 7 percent in a household's wealth in 1860, controlling for nativity, occupation, and age.[5] The reward for duration suggested by these strong correlations between wealth and time in a community is probably the result of a number of factors including capital gains on real estate and information on local economic conditions.

As yet, there has been no systematic investigation of the determinants of the relationship between wealth and duration. We propose the hypothesis that the magnitude of the association between wealth and duration will be inversely related to the level of precedence, and will be positively related to the size of the community. That is, low precedence rates and large local markets will tend to produce a strong positive correlation between duration and wealth. We will present evidence from nineteenth-century Utah on the relationship between the precedence rate and the importance of precedence in

3. The relationship between the precedence rate and the persistence rate is useful when cross-checking the validity of different samples. A linkage of households sampled from the 1860 census to the 1870 census gives a direct estimate of a persistence rate, just as a linkage of a sample from the 1870 census backward to the 1860 census gives a direct measure of the precedence rate. The persistence rate calculated from the forward linkage may be combined with the population growth rate to calculate an independent estimate of the precedence rate, and the precedence rate calculated from the backward linkage may be used to calculate an independent estimate of persistence. For an example see David W. Galenson, "Economic Opportunity on the Urban Frontier: Nativity, Work and Wealth in Early Chicago," *Journal of Economic History,* 51 (Sept. 1991), pp. 581–603.

4. See Merle Curti, *The Making of an American Community: A Case Study of Democracy in a Frontier County* (Stanford, 1959) p. 141ff.; J. R. Kearl, Clayne L. Pope, and Larry T. Wimmer, "Household Wealth in a Settlement Economy," *Journal of Economic History,* 40 (Sept. 1980), pp. 477–96; Donald F. Schaefer, "A Model of Migration and Wealth Accumulation: Farmers at the Antebellum Southern Frontier," *Explorations in Economic History,* 24 (Apr. 1987), pp. 130–57; Galenson and Pope, "Economic and Geographic Mobility on the Farming Frontier."

5. J. R. Kearl and Clayne L. Pope, "Choices, Rents and Luck: Economic Mobility of Nineteenth-Century Utah Households," in Stanley L. Engerman and Robert E. Gallman, eds., *Long-Term Factors in American Economic Growth,* Studies in Income and Wealth, vol. 51 (Chicago, 1986), pp. 215–55; Galenson, "Economic Opportunity on the Urban Frontier."

wealth accumulation. For the counties of Utah, we find the importance of the relationship between early arrival and wealth was strongly associated with both rate of precedence and population size. We also find that the strength of the association between wealth and early arrival had a significant effect on the level of inequality in the various Utah counties.

7.2 Data Set

The information on wealth, household size, nativity, residence, age, and occupation has been retrieved from the census manuscripts for all households in Utah in 1860 and 1870. Wealth, self-reported in the census, was the household's own estimate of gross, rather than net, wealth, with holdings below $100 going unrecorded. The wealth figures in the census manuscripts appear to be reasonably accurate estimates of household wealth, even though they may not typically have been based on detailed calculations of household wealth.[6] Individual households that appeared in censuses of Utah in both 1860 and 1870 have been linked together. These linkages have been aided and corroborated by other available records, such as church and genealogy records used in the creation of the Utah panel data.[7] Consequently, the linkages should be fairly complete and accurate.

Table 7.1 gives basic data for Utah households with a male adult present for 1860 and 1870.[8] Household size fell slightly between 1860 and 1870, while the mean age of the male head rose by a little more than a year. The foreign born represented a larger proportion of the household heads in 1870 because of the large migration from England and Scandinavia during the 1860s. There was increased specialization in the 1860s, with a substantial increase in the percentage of the work force who designated themselves as craftsmen and a small increase in the proportion categorized as white collar. Few individuals considered themselves out of the labor force. A 25 percent increase in the

6. A comparison of wealth reported in the census to wealth reported in local tax rolls for a sample of households in 1870 shows a high simple correlation (.66) between wealth estimates from the two sources. That is, ln(census wealth) = 1.77 + 0.79 (tax roll wealth) with an R^2 of 0.44 and N = 1,568. The mean of the natural logarithm is 6.7 for wealth from the tax rolls and 7.04 from the census manuscripts. In Utah, the census marshals followed the instruction to leave wealth below $100 unrecorded. In 1870, only three households out of 19,187 were recorded with wealth below $100.

7. The Utah data consists of linked observations on household heads used to create a panel of households that are followed for as long as they are in Utah for the period from 1850 to 1900. For a fuller discussion of the panel data see J. R. Kearl and Clayne L. Pope, "Unobservable Family and Individual Contributions to the Distributions of Income and Wealth," *Journal of Labor Economics,* 4 (July 1986), pp. S53–S56.

8. Households headed by females have been excluded from the analysis since many of these households were actually part of polygynous households, in which case the households and wealth have been combined with other recorded households of the husband, or they were households with a husband who was absent for a year or two doing missionary or other service for the Latter-Day Saints Church. There were few households in Utah in this period that were headed by females without husbands.

Table 7.1 Characteristics of Utah Households with Husband Present

	1860	1870
Population	36,417	74,638
Households	6,975	16,064
Mean household size	5.2	4.6
Household heads		
Foreign born	57%	65%
Farmers	53%	43%
White collar	5%	6%
Craftsmen	18%	25%
Laborers	24%	26%
Not in labor force	< 1%	< 1%
Mean real estate wealth	$510	$636
Mean personal wealth	$471	$391
Mean total wealth	$982	$1,027

Source: Census manuscripts of 1860 and 1870.

mean value of real estate per household was largely offset by a fall in the mean value of personal wealth so that the mean of total gross wealth increased by less than 5 percent. This stagnation in mean total wealth over the decade was largely a result of the in-migration of poor families rather than lack of growth of the wealth of families already established in Utah in 1860.

The analysis here is conducted primarily at the county level, so some attention must be paid to the economic importance of county boundaries. If the counties of Utah represented different markets, then those differences may be exploited to test the hypotheses concerning the effect of size of an economy and the precedence rate on the correlation between wealth and early arrival.[9] We believe that the counties of Utah were sufficiently isolated from each other that they may be treated as separate economic entities. As seen in Table 7.2, most of the counties were quite large in area although much of the land was desert or mountains and unsuitable for farming. Water for irrigation and household use was the most important constraining resource in the settlement of Utah. Consequently, early settlement was confined in valleys, often quite far apart, with sufficient arable land that could be irrigated by rivers or mountain streams.[10] For example, the earliest settlements in Utah were in Salt Lake County irrigated by the Jordan river and several large canyon streams, Weber County with the Ogden river, Davis County between Ogden and Salt Lake irrigated by canyon streams, and Utah County irrigated by three small riv-

9. The use of county-level data here is similar to the use by Butler, Heckman, and Payner in their study of the effect of government regulation on discrimination in South Carolina. See Richard J. Butler, James J. Heckman, and Brook Payner, "The Impact of the Economy and the State on the Economic Status of Blacks: A Study of South Carolina," in David W. Galenson, ed., *Markets in History: Economic Studies of the Past* (Cambridge, 1989) p. 306ff.

10. For an overview of the settlement of Utah see Leonard J. Arrington, *Great Basin Kingdom: Economic History of the Latter-Day Saints, 1830–1900* (Cambridge, Mass., 1958).

Table 7.2 **Characteristics of Primary Utah Counties of 1870**

County[a]	Square Miles[b]	Households	Occupations: Farmers	Craftsmen	White Collar[c]	Laborers	Mean Wealth
Beaver	2,586	308	51%	26%	4%	19%	$ 915
Box Elder	5,614	1,157	24	33	14	29	754
Cache	1,171	1,387	64	16	4	15	624
Davis	299	722	42	19	3	36	1,210
Iron	3,302	390	43	26	2	29	777
Juab	3,396	359	40	11	2	47	908
Millard	6,818	512	68	12	3	16	916
Salt Lake	756	3,553	19	39	12	30	1,735
Sanpete	1,586	1,165	54	18	3	26	937
Summit	1,865	509	33	23	5	39	566
Tooele	6,919	411	58	20	2	20	968
Utah	2,018	2,146	47	16	3	33	742
Washington	2,422	573	50	25	3	22	1,126
Weber	566	1,582	43	20	10	26	854

Sources: Statistical Abstract of Utah, Bureau of Economics and Business Research, University of Utah (June, 1987); Census manuscript of Utah for 1870.

[a]Only the counties with significant population in 1860 are listed in the table.

[b]As a frame of reference for the size of the counties, Rhode Island has a land area of 1,055 square miles and Connecticut, 4,872 square miles.

[c]Includes merchants and proprietors.

ers—the Provo, Spanish Fork, and American Fork. Each of these counties was about one day's journey from the contiguous county with rather well-defined physical boundaries, except in the case of Davis and Weber counties. Within two years, two more counties were created in central and southern Utah, several days' journey from the nearest county. Once again communities were organized around available water sources. Counties or communities settled still later in the period were generally distinct from other counties.[11] Since local railroads were not built in Utah until after completion of the transcontinental railroad in 1869, transportation between counties was by wagon. Transportation over mountain passes was arduous and expensive and contributed to the isolation of some of the early counties.

The percentages of the labor force in different occupations given in Table 7.2 provide evidence that the counties differed from one another in economic structure. Some of the counties, such as Cache, Millard, and Tooele, were predominantly agricultural. Other counties, such as Salt Lake and Box Elder, had relatively few farmers. Yet each county had a significant number of crafts-

11. The dates of formation of counties may be found in George B. Everton, Sr., *The Handy Book for Genealogists* (Logan, Utah, 1962), pp. 170–72, while information on early settlements of Utah and changes in county boundaries may be found in David E. Miller, *Utah History Atlas* (Salt Lake City, 1968).

men and at least some white-collar workers (including merchants and proprietors), evidence that each county provided services and simple manufactured goods locally.

Early Utah Mormon leaders advocated settlement in villages or communities rather than random settlement on individual farms. Most settlement followed the village pattern of residence, with even farmers living in the village and traveling to their farms during the day.[12] As new land within an existing county was brought into cultivation, new villages or towns were created, but county division normally took place only when a somewhat distant area was settled. New counties were generally formed around newly settled valleys. Consequently, very few settled areas were shifted from one county to another as new counties were formed. In a few cases, communities in southern Utah were shifted from one county to another between 1860 and 1870. In these instances, adjustments were made in the data set so that persons living in such communities would be treated as if they had not shifted residence from one county to another.

In most cases, the county forms a reasonably good unit of analysis. All of the counties were connected to some degree economically, but their geographic separation was generally sufficient to distinguish their economies. Land rents differed across counties. Each county tended to have its own water resources and transportation links to the rest of Utah.

One cannot automatically assume, however, that a county is an appropriate unit for analysis, for one county might include several local economies. Washington County in the southwest corner of Utah illustrates the point. In 1860, Washington County contained some small, rather unsuccessful, settlements in the northeast corner of the county that were shifted to Kane County when it was created in 1864. In 1861, motivated by concerns over the availability of cotton goods from the South, Brigham Young "called" about 300 families to leave Salt Lake and Utah counties and settle entirely new areas in the southwestern part of Washington County to attempt cotton production.[13] Some of these households were quite wealthy by Utah standards. Virtually none of the households present in Washington County in the 1860 census moved to these new settlements, which became one of the economic centers of southern Utah even though cotton production failed. Of the 573 families in Washington County in 1870, 105 had been in either Salt Lake or Utah County in 1860. Consequently, a variable measuring presence in Washington County in 1860 would not measure early arrival into the economy that existed in 1870 in Washington County. Indeed, the Washington County of 1870 was not really started until 1861.

Although the issue of identifying local economies is critical, cases like Washington County were exceptional. The normal pattern was one in which

12. See Lowry Nelson, *The Mormon Village: A Pattern and Technique of Land Settlement* (Salt Lake City, 1952).

13. Arrington, *Great Basin Kingdom*, p. 216.

the economy of a county grew up around a center, typically located at the point of initial settlement.[14]

7.3 Migration to and within Utah

As Table 7.1 shows there were 6,975 households with male heads in 1860 and 16,064 in 1870. This obviously high rate of population growth of almost 9 percent per year was not unusual for frontier settlements. Many states experienced very rapid population growth during peak settlement periods.[15] Of the 6,975 households in Utah in 1860, 2,849 were still there in 1870, giving a persistence rate of 40.9 percent and a precedence rate of 17.7 percent for the state as a whole.[16] Thus, 13,215 of the 16,064 households of 1870 were either migrants to the state or had been formed by couples married since 1860. The preponderance of households were migrants to Utah since less than 25 percent of the households heads of 1870 were under age thirty and less than 2 percent born in Utah.[17]

Migrants to Utah between 1860 and 1870 were drawn from a wide variety of origins because of the proselytizing activity of the Latter-Day Saints Church. Converts to the church from the United Kingdom and Scandinavia accounted for approximately 70 percent of households enumerated in the 1870 census of Utah that had not appeared in the 1860 census. Other parts of Europe accounted for roughly 5 percent of the new households, with the balance coming from other states within the United States. There was relatively little movement within Utah by households already settled there. Slightly over 66 percent of the households present in both censuses did not change their county of residence between 1860 and 1870. The movement that did occur was drawn proportionately from the settled counties according to their population. Consequently, most of the movement of households within Utah occurred as households shifted from the earliest settled and larger counties to outlying settlements. Salt Lake County and the three counties close to it (Davis, Utah,

14. The county that fits least well into the model of a county with a dominant town and surrounding villages is Sanpete County. Several small communities were started there within three years of each other. None achieved predominance, and the county, beset by Indian conflicts, poor weather, and unstable water supplies, languished after 1870.

15. Wisconsin increased its population more than tenfold between 1840 and 1850. Texas's population increased threefold between 1850 and 1860. Minnesota had a population of a little over 6,000 in 1850 and over 170,000 in 1860. It was not uncommon for counties to grow from a few hundred residents in one census to tens of thousands a decade later.

16. There are no other state persistence rates to compare with this rate. The county rates reported by Thernstrom, *The Other Bostonians*, p. 226, bracket this rate. One would expect the persistence rate for a state to be higher than that for most of the counties within that state because of intrastate migration. Winkle, *The Politics of Community*, p. 19, concludes that there was substantial migration within Ohio from the countryside to the cities. In Utah, the migration is out of Salt Lake City to the countryside for most of the nineteenth century.

17. Some of those born outside of Utah would be children of earlier migrants born in other states. We have been able to identify fewer than 800 household heads in the census of 1870 whose fathers were also in the 1870 census as household heads.

and Weber) constituted 65 percent of the 1860 population, and 68 percent of the households migrating within Utah between 1860 and 1870 came from these counties.

Persistence rates, reported in Table 7.3, do not appear to vary systematically by county size, period of settlement, or other characteristics. Some of the outlying counties such as Iron, Summit, and Sanpete had low rates of persistence, all above 10 percent, while other "frontier" counties such as Beaver, Juab, and Millard had higher rates of persistence, all above 30 percent. The larger and more developed counties had persistence rates ranging from 23 percent to 29 percent.[18]

Persistence rates have typically been found to have a limited range. The variation in population growth rates adds variance to precedence rates compared with the variation in the persistence rates. As shown in Table 7.3, the ratio of 1870 population to 1860 population varied across counties from 1.37 to 11.31. Precedence rates also had substantial variation, ranging from 1 percent in Summit County to 21 percent in Utah County. Of the three counties with lowest precedence rates, Box Elder and Summit had low rates because of rapid population growth, while the low precedence rate of Iron County was due to an unusually low persistence rate. Utah County, which had the highest precedence rate, also had a relatively high persistence rate (29 percent) combined with the lowest rate of population growth of any county.

7.4 Relationship of Duration to Wealth

As discussed earlier, a household's duration within a local economy was strongly correlated with household wealth in a variety of places and circumstances in nineteenth-century America. Table 7.4 presents a series of cross-sectional regressions for individual counties relating the natural logarithm of wealth reported by the household in the 1870 census to age and its square, foreign birth, occupational classes, and a binary variable that assumes the value of 1 if the household was present in the 1860 census of the county. The regressions, confined to households with a male adult present, are based on native farmers as the control group.

18. Frontier areas have relatively low persistence rates. James Malin, "The Turnover of Farm Population in Kansas," *Kansas Historical Quarterly*, 4 (1935), pp. 339–72, found high rates for farm operators in Kansas, 26 to 59 percent throughout the nineteenth century, but note that his sample did not include groups more likely to move. The rates for counties in Utah are quite similar to those in Trempealeau County, Wisconsin and Wapello County, Iowa, and below those of east central Kansas. Curti, *The Making of an American Community*, found rates of 25 percent (1860–70) and 29 percent (1870–80) for Trempealeau County, Wisconsin. Mildred Throne, "A Population Study of an Iowa County in 1850," *Iowa Journal of History*, 57 (1959), p. 310, found a rate of 30 percent for Wapello County, Iowa. Peter J. Coleman, "Restless Grant County: Americans on the Move," *Wisconsin Magazine of History*, 66 (Autumn 1966), pp. 16–20, found a rate of 21 percent for Grant County, Wisconsin. William G. Robbins, "Opportunity and Persistence in the Pacific Northwest: A Quantitative Study of Early Roseburg, Oregon," *Pacific Historical Review*, 39 (1970), pp. 279–96, found a persistence rate of 34 percent between 1870 and 1880.

Table 7.3 Persistence, Precedence, and Wealth by County

County	Persistence Rate	Precedence Rate	Population Growth[a]
Beaver	31%	14%	2.28
Box Elder	20	4	4.63
Cache	32	11	2.91
Davis	23	14	1.69
Iron	14	6	2.34
Juab	42	15	2.92
Millard	48	11	4.41
Salt Lake	29	16	1.80
Sanpete	19	12	1.59
Summit	10	1	11.31
Tooele	29	11	2.67
Utah	29	21	1.37
Weber	28	11	2.52

Source: Utah Income and Wealth Project.
[a]Ratio of 1870 population to 1860 population.

The peaks in the age-wealth profiles for the individual counties were quite similar, ranging from age 43 in Cache County to age 52 in Salt Lake County. The slopes of county age-wealth profiles display considerable variation. The disadvantage of the foreign born varied widely by county, and the correlation was not always statistically significant. In two counties, Box Elder and Juab, there was actually positive correlation between foreign birth and wealth.

Laborers, which includes farm laborers and semi-skilled service workers as well as laborers, held very little wealth. Craftsmen were slightly richer than the unskilled, but less wealthy than farmers. The wealth of individuals classified as white collar (including low white collar, such as bookkeepers and bank clerks, as well as proprietors and higher white collar) was similar to that of farmers with both positive and negative coefficients usually not statistically significant.

Presence in the county in 1860 was positively correlated with wealth in all of the counties except Sanpete. The association was statistically significant at the 0.05 level in eight of the counties. The relationship was not statistically significant in Davis or Tooele counties and was marginally significant in Iron, Juab, and Summit counties. Disregarding Sanpete County, the coefficient for presence in the county ten years earlier varies from 0.43 in Davis County to 3.10 in Summit County.[19] The ratio of the wealth of preceders to that of non-

19. The equations in Table 7.4 are of the form wealth $= e^{\beta X + \delta P}$ where $P = 1$ if the household was present in the county in 1860 and 0 if not present, and X represents a vector of the other characteristics. The ratio of the wealth of households present in the county in 1860 to the wealth of households not present then is equal to $e^{\beta X + \delta P}/e^{\beta X}$ or e^{δ}. For example, the coefficient of 2.00 on the dummy for presence in 1860 in Salt Lake County implies that the ratio of the wealth of preceders to the wealth of nonpreceders is equal to $e^{2.00}$ or 7.39 for Salt Lake County, holding the other characteristics fixed.

Table 7.4 Regressions Explaining Household Wealth

County	Intercept	Age	Age^2	Foreign Birth	White Collar	Craftsmen	Laborers	Present in 1860	R^2
Beaver	.72	.26	−.0026	−.70	−.50	−.93	−.81	.90	.15
	(.63)	(4.61)	(4.09)	(2.81)	(.66)	(3.12)	(2.57)	(2.28)	
Box Elder	.10	.26	−.0027	.28	−.02	−3.15	−3.60	1.98	.33
	(.13)	(6.68)	(5.88)	(1.72)	(.05)	(13.59)	(17.14)	(3.99)	
Cache	2.74	.18	−.0021	−.41	.29	−1.25	−2.50	.66	.27
	(5.41)	(7.60)	(7.96)	(3.57)	(.99)	(8.74)	(17.70)	(3.54)	
Davis	2.17	.22	−.0022	−.93	−.26	−.80	−3.08	.43	.28
	(2.59)	(5.78)	(5.57)	(4.44)	(.38)	(2.88)	(13.01)	(1.11)	
Iron	−.75	.32	−.0034	−.20	−3.67	−.27	−1.20	.85	.24
	(.71)	(6.31)	(6.23)	(.64)	(2.97)	(.70)	(3.21)	(1.62)	
Juab	−1.55	.35	−.0036	.05	.79	−.49	−.61	.48	.32
	(2.11)	(10.83)	(10.36)	(.24)	(1.09)	(1.49)	(2.88)	(1.60)	
Millard	3.67	.13	−.0015	−.09	.83	−1.35	−4.29	1.25	.55
	(5.73)	(4.29)	(4.35)	(.58)	(1.72)	(5.71)	(21.39)	(4.77)	
Salt Lake	−1.58	.30	−.0029	−.31	.16	−1.13	−1.72	2.00	.18
	(3.41)	(13.81)	(12.14)	(2.69)	(.77)	(8.07)	(11.67)	(12.04)	
Sanpete	5.42	.065	−.0007	−.17	.19	−.18	−.56	−.04	.13
	(24.2)	(6.25)	(5.91)	(3.02)	(1.08)	(2.88)	(10.34)	(.50)	
Summit	3.53	.13	−.0013	−.69	−1.56	−4.37	−4.79	3.10	.49
	(3.27)	(2.44)	(2.14)	(2.95)	(2.53)	(13.61)	(18.65)	(1.84)	
Tooele	−1.63	.35	−.0038	−.31	.25	−1.89	−2.29	.57	.23
	(1.31)	(5.94)	(5.65)	(1.05)	(.19)	(5.58)	(6.57)	(1.17)	
Utah	1.35	.23	−.0024	−.32	−1.11	−1.61	−3.67	.84	.42
	(2.97)	(10.74)	(10.26)	(3.17)	(3.41)	(10.92)	(31.12)	(5.80)	
Weber	.48	.24	−.0024	−.26	−.52	−1.34	−3.23	1.42	.29
	(.79)	(8.43)	(7.76)	(1.76)	(1.89)	(6.54)	(18.33)	(5.24)	

Source: Utah Income and Wealth Project.

Notes: The dependent variable is the natural logarithm of total wealth. The number of observations is given in column 2 of Table 6.2. The absolute t-values are given in parentheses. The control group is native farmers.

preceders varies from 1.54 in Juab County to 22.2 in Summit County. Clearly, precedence is strongly, though variably, associated with higher wealth in most of the counties.

It might appear tempting to interpret the coefficient relating a measure of duration or precedence to wealth (such as the coefficient in col. 8 of Table 7.4) as a return to duration. However, such an interpretation presents difficulties, and the coefficients for duration should not be interpreted as an adequate measure of the return to duration in that particular county.

One potentially important bias would suggest that the coefficients estimated by the regressions in Table 7.4 are an overestimate of the actual return to duration. The higher propensity of poorer people to leave a county created the bias. Wealthier people constitute a higher proportion of households with longer duration (here, presence in the county in 1860) not necessarily because time in the county increased wealth, but because wealth enabled people to stay in the county. Thus, a sample selection bias may create the illusion that there is a return to early arrival in a county when there may not be one in fact. The strength of this bias will depend on the extent to which wealth influences the propensity to remain in a county.

Table 7.5 reports logit regressions that measure the effect of wealth on the likelihood that households will persist in the same county over the ten years from 1860 to 1870. Once again, the effects of age, foreign birth, and occupational class are controlled in these county-specific regressions. The final column of Table 7.5 gives the marginal effect of changes in wealth on county persistence holding age and birthplace constant. In all cases, wealth has a positive effect on the probability that a household will still be in the county in 1870; this effect is statistically significant at the 0.10 level in six of the thirteen counties. In Salt Lake County, the effect of wealth on persistence is moderate. The estimated probability of persistence for a 40-year-old native farmer with $500 of wealth is 0.25 compared with a probability of 0.30 for a 40-year-old native with $2,000. The log specification of wealth combined with a positive coefficient on that variable ensures that the effects of moving from no wealth to some wealth (say $500) will have a larger estimated effect on the probability of persistence than moving from some wealth to substantial wealth.[20] The size of the wealth correlation with persistence is almost nonexistent in four counties—Beaver, Box Elder, Davis, and Utah. In each of these counties, an increase in wealth from $500 to $2,000 increases the probability of persistence by less than 1.4 percentage points compared with mean persistence in those counties of 26 percent. The effect of wealth on persistence is relatively large in Cache and Juab counties. An increase in wealth from $500 to $2,000 in each of these areas will increase the probability of persistence by 9.6 and

20. The natural log of $1 is 0, of $500 is 6.2, and of $5,000 is 8.5. Consequently, the logit regressions with ln of wealth as a independent variable will show bigger changes in the probability of persisting for households with zero wealth compared to wealth of $500 than for households with $500 in wealth compared to those with $5,000.

Table 7.5 **Logit Regressions on the Probability of County-Level Persistence**

County	Intercept	Age	Age^2	Foreign Birth	White Collar	Craftsmen	Laborers	Log(Wealth)	Marginal Effect of Wealth
Beaver	−11.67	.10	−.0009	.05	7.60	.66	−.08	.002	.000
	(.99)	(.37)	(.49)	(.79)	(.99)	(.23)	(.80)	(.98)	
Box Elder	−12.97	.25	.003	.41	5.44	.42	.43	.04	.004
	(.98)	(.003)	(.06)	(.05)	(.99)	(.28)	(.22)	(.84)	
Cache	−4.26	.04	−.0006	−.05		−.19	−.10	.39	.069
	(.01)	(.54)	(.57)	(.69)		(.45)	(.56)	(.03)	
Davis	−12.50	.14	−.0016	.33	7.13	.14	.05	.07	.008
	(.97)	(.15)	(.17)	(.03)	(.98)	(.59)	(.80)	(.59)	
Iron	−10.79	.02	−.0003	.21	−.56	8.07	−.27	.20	.019
	(.99)	(.88)	(.86)	(.42)	(.38)	(.99)	(.56)	(.22)	
Juab	−10.4	−.01	−.00002	−.13	.21	.12	8.75	.19	.043
	(.99)	(.94)	(.99)	(.55)	(.74)	(.68)	(.99)	(.25)	
Millard	−6.40	−.21	.003	−.30	8.18	.68	.93	.09	.021
	(.99)	(.12)	(.11)	(.17)	(.99)	(.22)	(.02)	(.28)	
Salt Lake	−2.92	.03	−.0003	−.20	−.12	−.07	.03	.18	.030
	(.01)	(.30)	(.38)	(.01)	(.22)	(.29)	(.69)	(.01)	
Sanpete	−4.30	.07	−.001	−.22	−.04	.25	.01	.20	.026
	(.01)	(.26)	(.16)	(.06)	(.93)	(.14)	(.95)	(.01)	
Tooele	−3.48	−.004	−.002	−.19		.14	−.44	.44	.073
	(.18)	(.97)	(.90)	(.37)		(.73)	(.22)	(.04)	
Utah	−3.63	.10	−.001	−.17	.03	−.07	.19	.06	.010
	(.01)	(.01)	(.01)	(.01)	(.85)	(.43)	(.04)	(.06)	
Weber	−4.85	.10	−.001	.15	.02	−.08	.50	.24	.038
	(.01)	(.13)	(.08)	(.17)	(.96)	(.65)	(.01)	(.03)	

Source: Utah Income and Wealth Project.

Notes: The regression for Summit County did not converge to a solution. Values in parentheses are the significance levels. White-collar occupation created singularities in Tooele and Cache counties.

6.0 percentage points, respectively, compared with persistence rates of 32 percent in Cache and 42 percent in Juab.

The logit equations of Table 7.5 indicate that wealth did have an effect on persistence but its effect was not dramatic. The moderate impact of wealth on persistence is not particularly surprising, for migration to the state was the result of religious belief in most cases. Since about two-thirds of households in Utah in 1860 and 1870 did not change counties, most decisions to move were decisions to stay in Utah or exit the state. It seems likely that the decision to leave Utah was often connected to a change in religious belief rather than a decision to migrate for economic benefit. If wealth played a marginal role in persistence, this source of bias in the estimation of the relationship between duration and wealth would also be marginal.

There are other potential sources of bias that should be investigated and removed before one would have an acceptable measure of the return to duration. It is possible that different immigrants over time are of different quality, so the measured duration effect is confounded with changes in the quality of the in-migrants.[21] To measure these returns more accurately would require observation of wealth at the point of entry into and exit from the county.

7.5 Influences upon the Correlation between Precedence and Wealth

The correlation between wealth and duration in the local economy reported in Table 7.4 shows considerable variation across the thirteen counties. The hypothesis offered here proposes that there is an inverse relationship between the precedence rate and the coefficient relating wealth and duration, and a positive association between county population and that coefficient.

The reasoning behind the hypothesis is straightforward. If lengthy duration in a place were in short supply, duration would potentially command a premium.[22] If long duration were commonplace, it should receive a relatively small return. The size of the return should also depend on the size of the community. A favorable niche in a large economy is expected to have greater value than a comparable advantage in a small community.

The relationship between wealth and duration is the product of a variety of economic mechanisms. Early arrival may give access to the best locations. In Utah, locational advantage was tightly connected to good and certain access to water. In other situations, locational advantage would be linked to proxim-

21. George J. Borjas, "Self-Selection and the Earnings of Immigrants," *American Economic Review*, 77 (Sept. 1987), pp. 531–53, discusses the possibilities of changes in the quality of immigrants over time.

22. Note that the proposed hypothesis need not be true by definition, because early arrival could be a mistake. The case of Iron County illustrates the important influence of population growth on the return to duration. In Iron County, the precedence rate is low because of low persistence. Other households migrated into the county at a modest rate, but the correlation between wealth and early arrival is not very high. The Iron County example illustrates the important influence of population growth on the return to duration.

ity to the center of economic activity. As more and more people enter an economy, wealth based on locational advantages secured by early arrivers may grow faster than the wealth of those at the periphery. Differential capital gains on land may be an important source of the return to duration. Equally, early arrivers may use time and experience to gain valuable information about the local economy that they ultimately translate into higher wealth. They may also develop economic relationships with other people that confer an advantage. The precedence rate is a direct measure of the fraction of the population that has any or all of these advantages and is an indirect measure of the value of such advantages.

A first test of our hypothesis is made by relating the coefficients on early arrival in Table 7.4 to the precedence rates in Table 7.3 for the thirteen counties and to the population of those counties. A regression with the coefficient relating early arrival to wealth as the dependent variable and the precedence rate and the number of male-headed households in the county in 1870 as independent variables produces the following result:

$$\underset{}{\text{Coefficient}} = \underset{(5.45)}{1.99} + \underset{(2.78)}{.00051}\ \text{County Size} - \underset{(3.91)}{12.69}\ \text{Precedence Rate}$$

N = 13; $R^2 = 0.47$; absolute t-values are in parentheses.

Coefficients of the independent variables are significant at levels better than 0.05. Addition of a quadratic term on size does not materially improve the estimated equation. Elimination of the size variable reduces the coefficient on the precedence rate by about a third but does not change the sign or eliminate statistical significance.

The regression shows that the effect of the precedence rate on the correlation between wealth and early arrival was important in early Utah. A decline in the precedence rate of 1.0 percentage point increases the ratio of the wealth of early arrivers to that of others by 13.5 percent.[23] Consequently, a substantial difference in precedence rates results in a substantial difference in wealth of early arrivers relative to others.[24] For the Utah counties, an increase of 500 households in a county increases the ratio of the wealth of early arrivers to the wealth of others by about 30 percent. The estimated equation provides support for the hypothesis that the magnitude of the relation between duration and wealth depended on both the precedence rate and the size of the community.

23. The ratio changes by $e^{.1269} = 1.1353$.

24. Box Elder and Cache, contiguous counties in northern Utah of nearly the same size, provide a good example of the effect of the precedence rate on the wealth of early arrivers relative to others. Box Elder had an influx of migrants between 1860 and 1870, partially in response to the building of the transcontinental railroad. (The golden spike joining the railroad from the east with the railroad from the west was driven in Box Elder County.) There was less growth in Cache County though the persistence rate was higher. Consequently, Cache had a precedence rate of 11 percent and Box Elder a rate of 4 percent. The ratio of the wealth of those present in 1860 to those not present ceteris paribus was 1.93 for Cache and 7.24 for Box Elder.

7.6 Precedence and Inequality

When one considers the whole state of Utah in 1870, 12 percent of the households were present in the same county ten years earlier. Moreover, the ratio of the mean wealth of those early-arriving households to the mean wealth of households that migrated into the county since 1860 (holding other characteristics constant) is 3.16. The substantial difference between the wealth of these two types of households could be an important source of inequality. But, if the posited relationship between the early arrival–wealth correlation and the precedence rate holds true, then the contribution of precedence to inequality is somewhat mitigated by the interplay between the precedence rate and the strength of the wealth-duration relationship. That is, low precedence rates (meaning few households contain the characteristic of value) would imply a higher wealth effect associated with early arrival. A high precedence rate implies that more people have the advantageous characteristic of early arrival, but the size of the advantage would be smaller. Nevertheless, duration or early arrival would contribute some inequality to the distribution of wealth.

Table 7.6 summarizes the wealth distributions in 1860 and 1870 for the Utah counties. Inequality rose in every county except Sanpete between 1860 and 1870, with the largest increases in inequality coming in two counties (Box Elder and Summit) with very strong correlations between wealth and early entry into the economy.

The extent of inequality appears to be related to the strength of the association between wealth and duration. Considering either the Gini coefficients for 1870 wealth or the percentages of wealth held by the richest 5 or 10 percent, counties with high inequality—Salt Lake, Summit, and Box Elder—were counties with high coefficients for the regression of wealth on presence in 1860.[25] Alternatively, Sanpete and Juab counties had low levels of inequality and low or negligible associations between wealth and early arrival. A regression with the Gini coefficient as the dependent variable and the magnitude of the estimated relationship between wealth and presence in 1860 (col. 8 of Table 7.4) as the independent variable produces the following results:

$$\begin{array}{l} \text{Gini Coefficient} = 0.54 + 0.12 \times \text{Wealth–Early Arrival Coefficient} \\ \qquad\qquad\qquad\quad (17.16) \quad (5.15) \end{array}$$

N = 13; $R^2 = .62$; *t*-values are in parentheses.

25. For the United States as a whole, Lee Soltow, *Men and Wealth in the United States, 1850–1870* (New Haven, 1975), pp. 99–103, finds that the richest 5 percent of households owned 54 percent of the aggregate wealth in 1870 and the richest 10 percent owned 70 percent of the wealth. He estimates the Gini coefficient on total wealth to be 0.83 for the United States. Only Box Elder, Salt Lake, and Summit counties are near the U.S. level of inequality. Rural counties tend to have more equal distributions of wealth. Curti, *The Making of an American Community,* found that the richest 10 percent held 39.3 percent of the wealth in Trempealeau County, Wisconsin, and 37.6 percent of the wealth in a sample of eleven Vermont townships.

Table 7.6 **Wealth Inequality for Utah Counties**

	1860			1870		
County	Wealthiest 5 Percent	Wealthiest 10 Percent	Gini	Wealthiest 5 Percent	Wealthiest 10 Percent	Gini
Beaver	21%	32%	.46	42%	53%	.67
Box Elder	20	31	.41	53	67	.82
Cache	17	27	.37	28	40	.59
Davis	27	40	.57	31	43	.66
Iron	27	39	.52	32	51	.66
Juab	18	30	.44	35	45	.57
Millard	26	41	.58	43	54	.67
Salt Lake	45	59	.72	60	74	.85
Sanpete	34	43	.53	24	33	.39
Summit	20	32	.43	56	69	.83
Tooele	34	46	.56	42	56	.72
Utah	34	44	.58	35	50	.68
Weber	23	34	.48	30	43	.66
All	38	49	.62	46	59	.73

Source: Utah Income and Wealth Project.

Note: Gini is a common index of inequality which measures the ratio of the area between a Lorenz curve and the 45-degree line to the area under the 45-degree line. A Gini coefficient of 1 is absolute inequality while 0 is total inequality.

On average, a unit increase in the wealth–early arrival coefficient increased the Gini coefficient by 0.12 or about 18 percent for the mean value of the Gini coefficient in the Utah counties. The association between wealth and early arrival is clearly not the only important influence upon local inequality. Nevertheless, the results suggest that the association plays a role in the creation and maintenance of inequality.

The relationship between the apparent reward to early arrival and inequality provides one reason why equality on the frontier may have been nonexistent or at best short-lived. As any frontier community developed to the point of economic success, an influx of migrants pushed up the value of precedence or early arrival. The increase in the wealth–early arrival relationship, in turn, contributed to increasing inequality.[26]

7.7 Conclusion

We explored here the relationship between the precedence rate and the oft-observed relationship between high levels of wealth and early arrival. County-level data for Utah in the nineteenth century yield a clear relationship between

26. A comparison of the distributions for Trempealeau County for 1860 and 1870 shows a slight increase in inequality between 1860 and 1870 (Curti, *The Making of an American Community,* p. 78).

early arrival and higher wealth levels. The level of the correlation is inversely correlated with the precedence rate for the county and positively with the size of the county. Moreover, the level of these correlations is directly related to the extent of inequality in the county.

These results are a first step in understanding the connection between precedence and wealth accumulation. Research along these lines for other economies would be interesting and valuable for a firmer establishment of the relationship between the precedence rate and the correlates of wealth, as well as the resultant impact on inequality. The results for nineteenth- century Utah justify serious exploration of the role of the precedence rate in generating inequality in the course of economic development.

8 The Wealth of Women, 1774

Alice Hanson Jones
with the assistance of Boris Simkovich

8.1 The People of the Nation to Be

After 150 years of English settlement in the New World, the thirteen colonies that in 1774 were on the verge of declaring their independence were mostly rural and inhabited by a population in which more than one out of every two colonists was either a child or a young adult under 21 years of age. In New England, women outnumbered men; elsewhere, the reverse was true. Of the nearly two-and-a-half million non-Indian persons, about 77 percent were free whites, over 20 percent black slaves, and another 2 percent were indentured white servants.[1] The proportion of non-free persons varied sharply by region. The numerous slaves were located chiefly in the South, whereas indentured whites served relatively more often in the Middle Colonies. Most free women were housewives, and farming was by far the most frequent occupation for men. Slaves (women and children, as well as men) and indentured servants (including women) also labored in the fields. Substantial numbers of free farmers, particularly those with higher wealth, not only raised crops and livestock but also engaged in side activities more usually found in urban places. There were, for example, farmer-blacksmiths, farmer-millers,

Editors' note: This essay was prepared by Boris Simkovich, working from several manuscript versions of a paper by this title written by Alice Hanson Jones in 1980. The original manuscripts were found by Hugh Rockoff among the Alice Hanson Jones Papers owned by the Rare Book and Manuscript Library at Columbia University. Jones, it appears, began the paper with the intention of writing about all women, but at some point switched her emphasis to urban women. Because her sample of 919 inventories contains those of 81 women but only 18 urban women, the emphasis of this, the final, paper was changed back to all women. Urban women, however, play a special role in the discussion. Although various portions of the essay were rewritten, we believe that Jones's style and intent have been preserved. We would like to thank Stanley Engerman, Gloria Main, and Carole Shammas for helpful comments.

1. Tables 2.4 to 2.7 of Alice Hanson Jones, *Wealth of a Nation to Be: The American Colonies on the Eve of the Revolution* (New York, 1980), contain a summary of population estimates for the colonies.

farmer-carpenters, farmer-wheelwrights, and farmer-merchants. Some male slaves were taught artisan skills, and some black women and indentured white women were trained as seamstresses or, even more frequently, to cook, serve, launder, clean, and, in some wealthy southern households, serve as nursemaids for white children.

In this preindustrial era, navigation was by sail and towns had grown at natural trading points, principally at good harbors and at river junctions. Less than 10 percent of the colonists lived in places that might be called urban, and these areas were small by twentieth-century standards. Some county-seat towns had only a few hundred inhabitants yet maintained a courthouse, an inn or tavern, and a marketplace. The five major seaport cities with populations greater than 10,000 were Philadelphia, New York, Boston, Charleston, and Newport, Rhode Island. Male occupations in these cities suggest a slow pace of urban living and a limited range of available consumer goods and services, even in the few metropolises. The male occupation list includes merchant, sea captain, attorney, government official, teacher, shopkeeper, inn- or tavern-keeper, various artisan and chandler trades such as baker, blacksmith, brewer, carpenter, carriage maker, caulker, clockmaker, cooper, cordwainer (shoemaker), fuller, hatter, harness maker, hosier, joiner, mason, miller, painter, printer, ropemaker, saddler, sailmaker, shipwright, tailor, tallow chandler, tanner, watchmaker, weaver, and wheelwright. There were also laborers, porters, mariners, and ordinary seamen. Merchants in these large cities imported fine cloth, manufactured goods, tea, coffee, and wine from English and European ports, as well as sugar, molasses, and rum from the West Indies. They exported in exchange the tobacco, rice, indigo, grains, meat, fish, furs, and lumber produced chiefly in the rural areas of the colonies.

The largest seaport, Philadelphia, had approximately 25,000 inhabitants, which placed it close in size to such secondary British cities as Liverpool and Glasgow and at about half the size of Bristol. In Philadelphia, where Quakers predominated, black slaves were less than 3 percent of the inhabitants and were outnumbered by the nearly 4 percent who were indentured servants. New York, the second largest metropolis in 1774, had many slaves—some 14 percent of its population—but a smaller proportion of indentured servants (perhaps 2.5 percent). Boston ranked third in size, with some 16,000 people, nearly all free. Newport had 11,000 inhabitants and relatively more slaves than Boston. Charleston, the largest city of the South and fourth largest in the colonies, had some 12,000 persons, more than half of whom were slaves. Indeed, slaves there vastly outnumbered the white indentured servants, the latter accounting for less than 3 percent of the white, and nearer to 1 percent of the total, population.[2]

2. Exact populations of colonial cities are hard to determine before the federal census of 1790. Scholars have made estimates, however, based on tax lists, militia counts in governors' reports, and the like. The population figure for Philadelphia is from Sam Bass Warner, Jr., *The Private City: Philadelphia in Three Periods of Its Growth* (Philadelphia, 1968). Figures for the other cities are from Carl Bridenbaugh, *Cities in Revolt: Urban Life in America, 1743–1776* (New York, 1955).

8.2 Women and Colonial America

8.2.1 Women's Activities

Aside from attendance at church, activities open to free white women, whether they lived in towns or on farms, were almost exclusively limited to the family and household. This reflected English attitudes toward women and marriage that had evolved during and after the Middle Ages under the influence of various forces, including the church. These attitudes had been embodied in English law, including common law, where legal status was determined on the basis of sex, not personal qualifications. To marry and have a family and home was accepted without question as the proper destiny of a free colonial woman, whatever her social class. She was to be obedient to her husband, and her status, not only legally but also in terms of authority within the family, was inferior to his. The occupation and wealth of her father before her marriage, and of her husband after marriage, determined in large part her social status and how comfortably she lived. Men were also the predominant wealthholders, although their wealth was substantially supplemented by the efforts of their wives and children and by the wealth women sometimes brought to a marriage.

A multitude of the household tasks performed by free white women—in addition to the very important ones of bearing and rearing children—directly contributed to the creation of real income and wealth. Urban women frequently helped in their husbands' shops or businesses, which were often located in the largest room on the ground floor of the family dwelling. Despite lack of much training in arithmetic, some probably helped keep the "book accounts," a colonial way of doing business on credit which developed as a result of the shortage of coin and paper money. At times, the wives of merchants, innkeepers, or shopkeepers completely managed the business during protracted absences of their husbands, and they sometimes successfully ran such businesses on their own after the death of their husbands.[3] Nevertheless, the proportion of all urban women who performed functions that can be clearly labeled *business* was undoubtedly quite small. Many more did productive work within the household which contributed to family supplies of food, cloth, and equipment. Even in urban places there were often cows, poultry, and vegetable gardens to be tended, and butter and cheese to be made. There was also the shelling, cutting, drying, salting, pickling, and other preserving of foods purchased at farmers' markets or obtained from orchards or neighboring farms. In many urban households there were spinning wheels—small ones for flax, large ones for wool—which meant many hours of carding, combing, and spinning. The homespun thread would be woven or knitted into cloth, either at home or by a weaver or hosier, and the final cloth cut and sewn

3. See Lisa Wilson Waciega, "A 'Man of Business': The Widow of Means in Southeastern Pennsylvania, 1750–1850," *William and Mary Quarterly,* 44 (Jan., 1987), pp. 40–64, for accounts of colonial wives who, after their husbands' deaths, took over the management of family businesses.

into outerwear, underwear, table or bed linen, or sometimes curtains. Most northern women (except the most well-to-do) cut and made their own and their children's clothing as well as the shirts and undergarments of their husbands. Most floors were either bare or covered with homemade floor cloths or rugs made from woolen or linen strips. Only the very wealthy had Scotch or Wilton carpets. Urban women also equipped their households by making feather beds, pillows, and bolsters from goosefeathers usually obtained from farmers, but sometimes from geese raised in the backyard. Some bought candles from the tallow chandler, but others procured tallow and made their own. They or (if they were relatively rich) their slaves or servants prepared the family meals at open hearths. For this they used preserved or dried foods on hand in their cellars or cupboards plus such fresh foods as they could buy either at farmers' markets held weekly, in season, in cities such as Philadelphia, or from occasional hucksters who pulled carts through the streets and called out their wares. Many Philadelphia women had no ovens and bought their bread daily from bakers.

The only colonial hospital was located in Philadelphia and was considered a place for the indigent and sick poor. Women cared for their families in the home in times of injury or illness, frequently with homemade remedies and often without help from a doctor. Among the richer families, a doctor was likely to be consulted for serious matters, and perhaps a woman hired to give nursing care. Childbirth took place at home, with assistance from women. When a woman was able to sit up after childbirth, her women friends paid her a "sitting-up" call. Though infant and maternal mortality was high, it was lower than in contemporary Europe, perhaps due to the greater abundance of food.[4]

For women who did not marry, job opportunities were bleak. They could spin and help in household tasks in the homes of parents or relatives. The fact that the term spinster came to mean an unmarried woman (as it had earlier in England) suggests that many women, especially in New England, where women outnumbered men from a rather early date, made their livings in that fashion. Alternatively, unmarried women could be waitresses or servants in taverns or inns or in well-to-do families. They might occasionally be called on for nursing care in a last illness or when pestilence such as the yellow fever struck. A very few, if they had been educated by a minister father or had special lessons, might teach music, embroidery, or reading.

4. There is a growing body of evidence that life expectation was higher and *overall* mortality lower in the American colonies than in Europe. See, for example, Clayne L. Pope, chap. 9 in this volume, and Robert W. Fogel, "Nutrition and the Decline in Mortality since 1700: Some Additional Preliminary Findings," in Stanley L. Engerman and Robert E. Gallman, eds., *Long-Term Factors in American Economic Growth* (Chicago, 1986). Data are currently too sparse, however, to draw any firm conclusions regarding comparative rates of *infant* mortality. Nevertheless, results presented in such geographically focused works as John Demos, *A Little Commonwealth: Family Life in Plymouth Colony* (New York, 1970), and Philip J. Greven, *Four Generations: Population, Land, and Family in Colonial Andover, Massachusetts* (Ithaca, NY, 1970), corroborate the traditional view that colonial infant and child mortality rates were significantly lower—particularly in rural areas—than in England and the rest of Europe.

Most girls did not go to school and picked up in the home their training in domestic arts and, on rare occasions, reading. Though there were public schools in some towns in New England, education even for boys was limited to a few months or years of training in reading, writing, and arithmetic. A very small number of boys' academies taught Latin and grammar. A few daughters of well-to-do families, such as the Norris family in Philadelphia, were sent to private tutors for a year or so.[5] The few colleges that existed—Harvard, Yale, Philadelphia College (later the University of Pennsylvania), King's College in New York (later Columbia University), Queen's College (later Rutgers, the State University of New Jersey), and the College of William and Mary—admitted only men and were principally designed to prepare them for the ministry.

A very important part of women's lives, whether they lived in town or country, was taken up by pregnancies and child raising. As noted by Benjamin Franklin and worried over by Thomas Malthus, the colonial population had grown, principally by natural increase, at the fastest rate then known in the western world. However, studies of colonial demography suggest that by 1774, family size was smaller than it had been in the earlier years of colonization. The average completed family included perhaps three children, not counting several who might have died in infancy or in their early years.[6] Evidence suggests that urban families in the older settled areas tended to be smaller, and that the largest families were found in newer settlements in the west, particularly in frontier areas where much of the farming was for family subsistence rather than for the market or export.[7] The black population was more than reproducing itself, in contrast to the situation in the West Indies where a more unhealthy climate and severe work demands resulted in more deaths than births. The very high rate of overall population increase in the thirteen colonies from 1710 to 1770—more than 3 percent a year—slowed to 2.6 percent during the decade 1770–80. It fell to its lowest level, 1.5 percent, in New England, where the scarcity of land for new families was most severe.[8]

Some students of family history are concluding that women's attitudes toward themselves and men's perceptions of women had begun to change by the mid eighteenth century, even before industrialization. Women were coming to see themselves more as individuals rather than chiefly as bearers of children

5. *Editors' note:* Notes in the author's manuscript indicate that her information about the Norris family is based on the contents of various microfilms at the Pennsylvania Historical Society in Philadelphia.

6. Daniel Scott Smith discusses the size of families in early New England in "The Demographic History of Colonial New England," *Journal of Economic History,* 32 (March, 1972), pp. 165–83.

7. For example, in 1800 the number of children under 5 years of age per 1,000 women 20 to 44 years old was 1,098 in New England, 1,279 in the Middle Atlantic, and 1,840 in the East North Central census division. Separate urban and rural figures for the first two regions are 827 (urban) and 1,126 (rural) for New England, and 852 (urban) and 1,339 (rural) for the Middle Atlantic. See series B67–98 in U.S. Bureau of the Census, *Historical Statistics of the United States, Colonial Times to 1970, Part 1* (Washington, D.C., 1975), for more details.

8. Jones, *Wealth of a Nation to Be,* table 2.1, summarizes regional population growth rates in the colonies from 1650 to 1770.

and servants of their families and husbands. Choice of marriage partners became more romantic and less dominated by parental choice and economic considerations. Familial love was beginning to replace the pattern of patriarchal authority within the family. And the care and nurture of children was becoming more loving and more concerned with the development of the child as a person. Nevertheless, in matters of property ownership, the pattern remained one of male dominance.[9]

8.2.2 Women's Property Rights

In the American colonies at the eve of the Revolution, most of the wealth, in a legal sense, was held by men. The extent to which men controlled wealth in the colonies can be seen in the composition of probate inventories compiled at the time. In *Wealth of a Nation to Be,* I describe and analyze a set of 919 probate inventories drawn by random sampling principles from all inventories of estates probated in the colonies in 1774. In this sample of 919 probate inventories, fully 838 are men's and only 81 women's. Not surprisingly, none of the 81 women's inventories belongs to a married woman: when a married woman died before her husband, no probate inventory was taken, since her property belonged to the surviving husband without any action of the probate court. We do find, however, probate inventories for widows, usually for considerably smaller amounts of wealth than were originally left by their husbands. We also find probate inventories for a few single women wealthholders in New England and in the South (but not in the Middle Colonies).

The *Wealth of a Nation to Be* inventory sample, supplemented with data on land ownership and estimates of the wealth of estates which were not probated, suggests that in New England in 1774, 97 percent of all wealth was held by men. The corresponding percentage in both the Middle Colonies and the South was 95 (Table 8.1). That women had legal title to so little property in early America is hardly surprising given their status in colonial society. One aspect of this status which directly affected the ability of women to own property was the set of colonial laws and traditions concerning inheritance. When a man died during the colonial period, he often willed his real estate to his sons but granted his widow use of some or all of the property for the rest of her life or until she remarried. As a result, the widow acquired a right to a

9. For descriptions of society's changing attitudes toward women, see Eileen Power, *Medieval Women* (New York, 1975), and Carl Degler, *At Odds: Women and the Family in America from the Revolution to the Present* (New York, 1980). Although there is an early literature which argues that the colonial period was a relative "golden age" in terms of women's freedoms, a number of recent studies have been highly critical of this perspective. The traditional view has its origins in works such as Elisabeth Anthony Dexter, *Colonial Women of Affairs* (Boston, 1931), and Richard B. Morris, *Studies in the History of American Law: With Special Reference to the Seventeenth and Eighteenth Centuries* (New York, 1959), whereas recent criticisms can be found in works such as Lyle Koehler, *A Search for Power: The "Weaker Sex" in Seventeenth-Century New England* (Urbana, Ill., 1980), Mary Beth Norton, *Liberty's Daughters: The Revolutionary Experience of American Women, 1750–1800* (Boston, 1980), and Laurel Thatcher Ulrich, *Good Wives: Image and Reality in the Lives of Women in Northern New England, 1650–1750* (New York, 1982).

Table 8.1 **Wealth of Men and Women in 1774**

	Thirteen Colonies	New England	Middle Colonies	South
Aggregate physical wealth (1,000's of £ sterling)	£109,570	£22,238	£26,814	£60,518
Percentage held by men	95.8%	97.4%	95.5%	95.4%
Percentage held by women	4.2	2.6	4.5	4.6

Source: Estimates of aggregate physical wealth are from Alice Hanson Jones, *Wealth of a Nation to Be* (New York, 1980), table 3.1. Percentages of wealth held by either men or women are calculated from the figures in Table 8.2*a* as well as the population estimates in Jones, *Wealth of a Nation to Be*, tables 2.4 to 2.7, and Jones, *American Colonial Wealth: Documents and Methods* (New York, 1977), tables 4.23 and 4.25.

Note: Total physical wealth includes wealth in slaves, servants, real estate (land, buildings, and improvements), and movable wealth. It excludes financial assets.

portion of the real estate's flow of services but did not actually have title to the asset, and therefore her access to the property was not mentioned in her probate inventory. Such was also the result in cases where a man died intestate (without a will) or a widow was dissatisfied with the assets willed her by her husband. In such situations, common law granted a widow a dower's share—generally one-third or, if the couple had no children, one-half—of her husband's real estate. The dower's share was, however, a life interest only. A widow was entitled to use of the dower property and any income it produced, but she could not sell or will the real estate to someone else, and after her death it became the possession of her husband's heirs and/or creditors. Thus, although dower rights granted a widow many of the benefits commonly associated with property ownership, she still did not have actual title to the assets.[10]

In Massachusetts, Connecticut, and Pennsylvania, partible inheritance prevailed in cases where there was no will. That is, the law divided the remainder of the estate, after the widow's share, equally among all children regardless of sex, except that the eldest son received a double portion.[11] In cases of intestacy in New York, Virginia, Maryland, and South Carolina, primogeniture with respect to land prevailed until the time of the Revolution. However, fathers in these colonies frequently made wills specifically dividing their land equally among their sons.[12] They often also specified that their daughters re-

10. A husband could always will his wife more than the common law minimum, but he could not deprive her of her one-third or one-half. However, a widow could not claim both the assets granted her in her husband's will as well as the dower's share of her husband's real estate. If she opted for her dower's share, she simultaneously relinquished claim to any other assets granted her in her husband's will. See Marylynn Salmon, *Women and the Law of Property in Early America* (Chapel Hill, 1986), for more details on the subject of women and colonial inheritance practices.

11. For further details on partible inheritance, see George L. Haskins, "The Beginnings of Partible Inheritance in the American Colonies," *Yale Law Journal*, 51 (June, 1942), pp. 1280–1315, and Salmon, *Women and the Law of Property in Early America*, p. 227, note 5.

12. Salmon, *Women and the Law of Property in Early America*, p. 142 and p. 227, note 8.

ceive money or slaves, or that the sons should pay their sisters fair sums of money. Wills sometimes stipulated that the sons were to receive the father's land but were to permit their widowed mother to live in a certain designated room or rooms of the house, and that she was to be furnished with an annual supply of firewood and a designated number of bushels of wheat, corn, or apples, and was to be permitted to store lumber in the cellar, use water from the well, cook with the family oven, or carry out other similar activities in the house.[13]

Probate inventories in New England included land (i.e., real estate) and its value. Those in the Middle Colonies and the South did not. In all three regions the inventories listed in detail the personal estate (or movable wealth) of the decedent, giving the appraised value of each item and the financial credits owed to the estate; they did not show, however, the debts the decedent owed to others.[14] The purpose of the inventories was to prevent fraud, protect the claims of creditors, and provide for orderly distribution of the assets to heirs after payment of debts owed. A probate inventory of a man would list (in addition to land in New England) the slaves owned, if any, and their values, the livestock, crops standing in the field or stored in the barn, the farm or business tools and equipment, all the household furniture and furnishings, apparel, stored food, cider, hard liquor, and materials such as yarn, tallow, or boards. Among the apparel items on a man's inventory there often appeared articles of women's clothing; indeed, a man's will sometimes specifically stated that his wife was to be allowed to keep her wardrobe. In women's inventories, items similar to those found in men's inventories appear, except that articles of men's clothing are rarely listed. Another difference is that the women, who were mostly widows, much less frequently had crops, livestock, or implements of production or business. Often their inventories were limited to a list of household furnishings and apparel. In the inventories found for single women, some in New England owned land and some in the South owned slaves.

Later in this paper, I will examine in detail the contents of some of the women's inventories. One should bear in mind, however, that the economic status of, and access to use of wealth by, women can best be described by

13. There is an extensive literature on the treatment of widows in colonial wills. Examples of recent works on the subject can be found in part one of Ronald Hoffman and Peter J. Albert, eds., *Women in the Age of the American Revolution* (Charlottesville, Va., 1989). Sections of *Inheritance in America from Colonial Times to the Present* (New Brunswick, N.J., 1987), by Carole Shammas, Marylynn Salmon, and Michel Dahlin, also deal extensively with the subject, and Alexander Keyssar's essay, "Widowhood in Eighteenth-Century Massachusetts: A Problem in the History of the Family," *Perspectives in American History,* 8 (1974), pp. 83–119, is of related interest—it challenges the traditional view that widowhood generated few problems in American colonial society.

14. "Lists of debts" could be found, however, for 343 of the 919 probated estates. For those estates for which debt information could not be found, statistical procedures were used to estimate financial liabilities. See Jones, *Wealth of a Nation to Be,* pp. xxxi–xxxiii, 6, for more details on the subject.

considering the wealth of their families. Thus, the reader should interpret with caution the comparisons I make of the wealth of women with the wealth of men. The data I present are perhaps best understood as shedding light on differences in the wealth held by *families* in the American colonies in 1774 and the wealth held by *widowed* or *single women*. Descriptions of the wealth of men, most of whom were family heads, give us at least an idea of the wealth of which *married women* made use, even though they did not have legal title to it.

8.3 Measuring Wealth

8.3.1 Valuing Colonial Wealth

The wealth items listed in the probate inventories of colonial households were valued by contemporary appraisers appointed by the probate court.[15] The values were stated in local pounds, shillings, and pence of the particular colony or province where the decedent had lived—that is, in Massachusetts money, or in Pennsylvania money, or in South Carolina money, as the case may be. These local monies did not have the same value from province to province. They have been converted in both *Wealth of a Nation to Be* and this essay to the common denominator of pounds sterling and fractions of a pound by use of exchange rates prevailing at the time. To a modern reader, it is still hard to grasp the significance of 10 or 10.5 pounds worth of something in 1774. To get a rough equivalence in terms of the more recent purchasing power of money, I have constructed a price index from 1774 to the 1980s using linkages of prices collected by other scholars. I conclude it fair to say that what could be purchased for one pound sterling in 1774 would cost on the average about $76 in 1982. All dollar values in this essay have been calculated in terms of 1982 prices.[16]

15. The usually two or three appraisers, often friends or relatives, were appointed for this task by the probate court. They visited the home fairly soon after the death and itemized the contents both within and without the house. (In the Middle Colonies and the South, however, land and real estate were not inventoried. For the *Wealth of a Nation to Be* data set analyzed in this paper, estimates of the value of these missing assets were constructed from information in tax lists, deeds, and land grants.) There were no estate or inheritance taxes to encourage understatement or avoidance of probate, although there were small costs of probate administration that had to be met from the assets of the estate. The appraisers listed in the inventory the value of each item, or group of items, and swore an oath before the court that the inventory was "true and correct to the best of our knowledge and belief." Rather frequently there were sales or public auctions of estate assets, and preserved accounts of these events indicate that inventory valuations were close to actual market values.

16. My estimate of the value of a pre-Revolutionary pound sterling is based both on calculations presented in Jones, *Wealth of a Nation to Be,* table 1.2, as well the values of the implicit price deflator for gross national product presented in table B–3 of the *Economic Report of the President* (Washington, D.C., 1991). Of course, the components of wealth are very different at the beginning and end of a two-hundred-year span, and thus the price index I have constructed to value the pound sterling should be considered only approximate.

8.3.2 Who Were Wealthholders?

Slaves and indentured servants in the American colonies had claim to virtually no wealth except the clothing on their backs and a few household utensils. Although they constituted nearly one-fourth (23 percent) of the population, I did not count them as wealthholders. Free children form another very sizable group not counted as wealthholders. They accounted for over half (57 percent) of the population, compared with a much smaller proportion in the twentieth century (32 percent in the decennial census of 1980).[17] Women, as suggested earlier, were seldom holders of wealth in their own right until widowhood. If a woman remarried after being widowed, her new husband acquired legal right to her personal property as well the income from any real estate that she owned (unless specific provisions to the contrary were made in a prenuptial agreement). In *Wealth of a Nation to Be,* I estimate that about 10 percent of the 389,000 free women in 1774 were single or widowed, and thus likely wealthholders.[18] I also assume that virtually all 396,000 free men were wealthholders. Hence, of a total population of 2.4 million colonists, I estimate that approximately 435,000 (396,000 men and 39,000 women) were wealthholders.

8.4 Women's Wealth, 1774

8.4.1 The Wealth of Men Compared with Women

The data in the *Wealth of a Nation to Be* probate sample allow one to construct estimates of the average wealth of both male and female colonial wealthholders. These calculations indicate that the average male colonial wealthholder had more than twice as much wealth as the average female wealthholder (Table 8.2*a*). The figures measured in total physical wealth (including the value of slaves and servants but not of financial assets) are £262 ($20,000) for men and £117 ($8,900) for women. The discrepancy between the sexes was the most extreme in New England, where men held an average of four times the £42 ($3,200) of women. In the richer South, the men averaged almost double the women's figure of £215 ($16,000); similarly, in the Middle Colonies, their average was also almost double the women's £97 ($7,300).[19]

17. It is not strictly correct to argue that there were no child wealthholders, since there were orphans for whom guardians managed inherited wealth until the children reached their majorities. However, such cases were rare, and children therefore are not included as wealthholders in this study.

18. See Jones, *Wealth of a Nation to Be,* p. 410, note 15, for a description of the procedure used to estimate the number of women wealthholders.

19. In this study (as in *Wealth of a Nation to Be*), all estimates of average wealth per wealthholder are constructed not as simple means of the data in the *Wealth of a Nation to Be* sample, but rather as weighted averages. The weighting scheme used to construct the averages takes into account the different demographic structures of the probate sample and the colonial population as a whole, and is described in detail in Alice Hanson Jones, *American Colonial Wealth: Documents and Methods* (New York, 1977), and Jones, *Wealth of a Nation to Be,* Appendix A.

Table 8.2 **Average Physical Wealth of Free Men and Women Wealthholders, 1774 (in £ Sterling)**

	Thirteen Colonies	New England	Middle Colonies	South
(a) Total Physical Wealth				
Men	£262.1	£168.9	£191.9	£410.5
Women	117.1	42.4	96.7	214.8
(b) Total Physical Wealth Less Holdings of Real Estate				
Men	116.4	48.1	71.8	218.6
Women	77.4	16.7	60.4	157.6

Sources: **New England and the South**—Estimates of total physical wealth are from Alice Hanson Jones, *Wealth of a Nation to Be* (New York, 1980), table 7.5. Estimates of movable physical wealth (total physical wealth less holdings of real estate) are derived from the values in part (a) and the estimates of real estate holdings presented in *Wealth of a Nation to Be*, table 7.7. **Middle Colonies**—Values in parts (a) and (b) are population-weighted averages of estimates for New York and the rest of the Middle Colonies (Pennsylvania, New Jersey, and Delaware). Figures (not shown) for the rest of the Middle Colonies were calculated from the data in *Wealth of a Nation to Be*, tables 7.5 and 7.7. Estimates for New York (also not shown) were constructed according to the "hybrid" procedure discussed in Jones, *American Colonial Wealth: Documents and Methods* (New York, 1977), pp. 1903–7. This procedure derives estimates of mean New York wealth by weighting averages calculated from both the small set of New York inventories as well as those in the New England and other Middle Colonies regional samples. The New York data used for the hybrid estimate of male New York wealth are from *American Colonial Wealth*, table 7.10. Because no women's inventories appear in the New York sample, the hybrid procedure was modified when estimating the average wealth held by female New York wealthholders. In particular, the average total physical wealth of New York women was calculated as a weighted mean of the average total physical wealth of New England women and the average total physical wealth of women in the other Middle Colonies. A completely analogous procedure was used when calculating average movable physical wealth. In both cases, the weights used were one-third for the New England mean and two-thirds for the average of the other Middle Colonies. **Thirteen Colonies**—Estimates in parts (a) and (b) are simply population-weighted averages of the regional figures. Coefficients for population-weighted averages are based on estimates of the number of male and female wealthholders in each region. These estimates are summarized in *Wealth of a Nation to Be*, tables 2.4 to 2.7, and *American Colonial Wealth*, tables 4.23 and 4.25.

Editors' Note: The original manuscript of this paper contained a version of the above table based solely on values from Jones, *Wealth of a Nation to Be,* tables 7.5 and 7.5. The Middle Colonies data in those tables, however, do not incorporate Jones's estimates of New York wealth, and the values for the entire thirteen colonies appear to overstate the average level of female wealthholding. To remedy these problems, it was decided to reconstruct the estimates using the procedures outlined above. These procedures duplicate as faithfully as we feel possible the steps Jones herself would have taken had she had the opportunity to analyze more closely the results summarized in the *Wealth of a Nation to Be* tables.

If one ignores holdings of real estate, the difference in the average wealth held by male and female wealthholders declines markedly. Indeed, the figures in Table 8.2*b* indicate that—on the basis of such a restricted measure of wealth—female wealthholders possessed on average more than 65 percent of the wealth held by male wealthholders (£77, or $5,900, versus £116, or $8,800). Although there is generally little justification for using a restricted set of assets when comparing the wealth of two different groups of wealthholders, the peculiarities of early American inheritance practices suggest that such a procedure may be valid when contrasting the wealth of colonial men and women. As mentioned earlier, colonial widows often received use, or a life interest, in a portion of their late husband's real estate, even though they did not actually acquire ownership of the property. Because they did not actually receive title to the property, however, mention of their access to it would not be made in their probate inventories, even though such access was clearly of relevance to a widow's standard of living. Thus, to the extent that wealth comparisons are carried out to shed light on relative standard of livings, comparing the average, "unadjusted" total physical wealth of colonial male and female wealthholders may lead to misleading conclusions. Instead, it seems advisable to make two comparisons—one based on movable physical wealth (total physical wealth minus real estate), the other on total physical wealth without any adjustments—to establish bounds on the relative levels of wealth to which male and female colonial wealthholders had access.[20]

Separate figures for urban women's average wealth compared with that of urban men's are not available, but a tabulation for all urban wealthholders in the sample, men and women combined, shows somewhat higher urban than rural wealth in every region.[21] The higher urban wealth is most striking in the South. The urban cases in that sample are all from Charleston, except for one or two from Annapolis. For the Middle Colonies, the urban cases are all from Philadelphia, including its suburbs of Northern Liberties, Germantown, and Southwark. For New England, sample cases were found in Boston, Salem, and such secondary Massachusetts urban centers as Gloucester, Marblehead, Ipswich, Newburyport, Bridgewater, Middleborough, and Scituate.

Some interesting facts emerge from a comparison of the cases of the richest women wealthholders with the richest men in the sample.[22] For both sexes, the richest cases were all in the South, the region where 85 percent of the slaves and indentured servants of the colonies were located. The richest man in the entire colonial sample was Peter Manigault, Esq., a planter and attorney from Goose Creek, South Carolina, who also resided part of the year in Charleston. He had £28,000 ($2.1 million) in total physical wealth and £33,000 ($2.5 million) of net worth. His slaves were valued at £11,852 ($900,000). The second richest man was Elizah Postele, Esq., a planter from Dorchester, near Charleston. His total physical wealth was £15,561 ($1.2 million), his net worth £12,705 ($970,000), and his slaves valued at £11,384 ($870,000). Gauged by net worth, one New England esquire from Boston, William White, crowded out Postele for second place. His net worth was £15,303 ($1.2 million), although his total physical wealth was only £3,793 ($290,000). Based on physical wealth, he ranked behind Thomas Gerry, a

20. This last statement implicitly makes the assumption that the value of the real estate to which female colonial wealthholders had access, but not actual title, was no larger than the difference between their average holdings of real estate and those of colonial men. This seems a reasonable assumption given the large size of the difference at the time.

21. Jones, *Wealth of a Nation to Be*, table 7.5.

22. Ibid., tables 6.3 to 6.10, 7.32, and Jones, *American Colonial Wealth*, table 8.1.

merchant of Marblehead and father of Elbridge Gerry, who was subsequently a signer of the Declaration of Independence. Thomas Gerry's £4,188 ($320,000) made him the richest in total physical wealth in the New England sample. White owned no slaves; Gerry had £37.5 ($2,800) worth, the value of "a Negro man Cato." By total physical wealth, the third richest man in the southern sample was John Ainslie, Esq., a planter with a residence in Charleston who had nearly £12,000 (£11,796, or $900,000) in physical assets. His net worth was £9,625 ($730,000), and his slaves were valued at £8,489 ($650,000). The richest man in the Middle Colonies sample was Philadelphia merchant Samuel Neave, with £8,336 ($630,000) of physical wealth and £6,647 ($500,000) of net worth. Second in physical wealth was Lynford Lardner of Philadelphia, a provincial officer and large landholder. His physical wealth was £7,601 ($580,000) and his net worth £4,981 ($380,000). Neither Neave nor Lardner had slaves or indentured servants.

The richest women in the 1774 sample of wealthholders had nowhere near the quantities of wealth just described, yet the value of their holdings was substantial nonetheless. Gauged by total physical wealth, the richest woman was the widow Abigail Townsend of Wadmellow Island in the Charleston District, with £2,559 ($190,000) of such assets. Her net worth, however, was only £1,993 ($150,000), and the bulk of her physical wealth—£2,350 ($180,000)—consisted of slaves, although she also owned boats, plantation equipment, horses, and consumer goods of distinction. The second richest woman in terms of total physical wealth was Sarah Baker, a widow who lived in a rural part of the Charleston District. She owned slaves valued at £1,051 ($80,000), her total physical wealth was £1,618 ($120,000), and she had a net worth of £1,360 ($100,000). The richest urban woman in the sample—based on total physical wealth—was Miriam Potts, a widowed Philadelphia shopkeeper who also had shop goods in New Jersey. Her physical wealth totaled £690 ($52,000), including business inventory of £335.6 ($26,000) and real estate worth £287 ($22,000). She had no slaves. Her net worth was £475 ($36,000). The richest urban woman in the sample in terms of net worth was Elizabeth Smith, a Charleston widow. Her net worth of £2,439 ($190,000) was heavily dominated by financial assets valued at £2,229 ($170,000). Her total physical wealth alone was £269 ($20,000). The slaves she owned were worth £86 ($6,500) and consisted of two Negro women, one worth £50 sterling ($3,800) and one worth £36 ($2,700). Her consumer durables—items such as house furnishings and apparel—were valued at £169 ($13,000). I was unable to locate any evidence that she owned land or real estate. The second richest urban woman measured by net worth was Elizabeth Vanderspeigle, a Philadelphia widow. Her financial assets of £1,292 ($98,000) contributed significantly to her total net worth of £1,544 ($120,000). Her total physical wealth was only £252 ($19,000). She had no slaves or indentured servants. She did have £39 ($3,000) in real estate, and most of her physical assets—£210 ($16,000) worth—were consumer durables.

At the poor end of the wealthholder scale, the distinctions between the wealth of men and women were much less pronounced. In the list of the ten poorest wealthholders (based on total physical wealth) in the entire sample, the range was from the £3.9 ($300) of a Boston tailor, Isaac Herault, to the £2.6 ($200) of Daniel Carter, a farmer in Halifax County, North Carolina.[23] The list included Anne Haskell, a widow from Brookfield, Worcester County, Massachusetts, with £3.6 ($270), Sarah Cole, a single woman from Waterbury, New Haven County, Connecticut, with like wealth, and Ann King, a widow from Kent County, Delaware, with £3.2 ($240). There were no urban women among the lowest ten. In tables listing the poorest ten wealthholders in each regional sample, we find in New England three widows (one from Springfield, Massachusetts) and two single women; in New Jersey, Pennsylvania and Delaware, three widows (one from Philadelphia); and, in the South, no women at all.[24]

8.4.2 The Wealth of Urban Women

For the women in the *Wealth of a Nation to Be* sample whose estates were probated in colonial cities, the median wealth in consumer goods was about £30.4 ($2,300) for those who lived in Massachusetts, £15.3 ($1,200) for those in Philadelphia, and £61.0 ($4,600) for those in Charleston, South Carolina (Table 8.3, row 11). These were the median values of the principal contents of these women's dwellings. The figures include apparel, which was worth £4.8 ($365) at the median in Massachusetts, £3.9 ($300) in Philadelphia, and almost £7 (£6.7, or $500) in Charleston. Addition of the value of real estate (land and improvements, including buildings), livestock (chiefly horses), and producer goods such as spinning wheels, axes, plows, harnesses, grindstones, scales, pistols, yarn, cloth, and lumber, bring the median total physical wealth (Table 8.3, row 1) to £53.6 ($4,100) in Massachusetts, £95.6 ($7,300) in Philadelphia, and £186.6 ($14,000) in Charleston.

This regional relationship in the comparative size of total physical wealth follows the pattern within the overall sample of wealthholders. In the national sample, New England (including Massachusetts) was generally the poorest region, the Middle Colonies (including Philadelphia) was second, and the South (including Charleston) was the richest.[25] When the women in the overall sample were considered separately from men, the same relative ranking of regions occurred (although New England women were relatively poorer, compared with other regions, than were New England men).[26] This same relative regional pattern—poorest New England and richest South—was also found in the national sample when one subtracts the value of slaves and considers only nonhuman physical wealth.[27] For the few cases of urban women, how-

23. Jones, *Wealth of a Nation to Be*, table 6.7.
24. Ibid., tables 6.8 to 6.10.
25. Ibid., table 4.5.
26. Ibid., table 7.5.
27. Ibid., table 7.5, rows 7 and 8, minus table 7.10, rows 7 and 8.

Table 8.3 **Wealth of Urban Women in the *Wealth of a Nation to Be* Sample, 1774: Massachusetts, Philaelphia, Charleston (in £ Sterling)**

Category of Wealth	Massachusetts Mean	Massachusetts Median	Philadelphia Mean	Philadelphia Median	Charleston Mean	Charleston Median
1. Total physical wealth (4+5+6+7+11)	£103.4	£53.6	£176.3	£95.6	£154.9	£186.6
2. Nonhuman physical wealth (4+6+7+11)	103.4	22.6	176.3	95.6	84.9	62.2
3. Net worth (1+15+16−17)	36.2	22.6	371.5	217.7	974.6	339.5
4. Real estate	14.2	0.0	73.2[a]	19.7[a]	0.0[a]	0.0[a]
5. Slaves and indentured servants	0.0	0.0	0.0	0.0	70.0	85.7
6. Livestock[b]	6.3	0.0	2.8	0.0	4.8	0.1
7. Producer goods, total (8+9+10)	3.1	1.6	54.0	1.0	0.3	0.0
8. Equipment[c]	3.1	1.6	0.6	0.3	0.1	—[d]
9. Materials[e]	0.0	0.0	1.8	0.2	0.3	0.0
10. Business equipment and inventory	0.0	0.0	51.6	0.0	0.0	0.0
11. Consumer goods, total (12+13+14)	79.8	30.4	46.2	15.3	79.7	61.0
12. Furniture[f]	71.5	11.9	36.2	11.5	72.6	53.7
13. Apparel	7.3	4.8	9.9	3.9	6.9	6.7
14. Perishables[g]	0.9	0.0	0.1	0.0	0.2	0.0
15. Cash	0.8	0.0	7.3	3.8	164.9	132.2
16. Other financial assets	2.7	0.0	234.5	45.0	688.9	188.9
17. Financial liabilities	(70.6)[a]	(24.9)[a]	(46.6)[a]	(18.3)[a]	(34.2)[a]	(41.2)[a]

Source: Probate inventories for seven women in Massachusetts, two of whom were from Boston, and one each from Gloucester, Ipswich, Marblehead, Salem, and Springfield; eight women from Philadelphia, of which two were from Northern Liberties and one from Germantown; and three women from Charleston. These are all the cases of urban women—all widows except one single woman in Boston—that occurred in the overall sample of 919 randomly drawn inventories. See Alice Hanson Jones, *Wealth of a Nation to Be* (New York, 1980), for a more detailed description of the larger sample.

Note: Means for subitems may not sum to totals, due to rounding. Medians, by definition, are not addable.

[a]Estimates. See Jones, *Wealth of a Nation to Be*, pp. xxix–xxxiv.

[b]Mostly horses. None of these women had wealth in crops.

[c]For example, spinning wheels, axes, plows, harnesses, grindstones, or pistols.

[d]Less than 0.05.

[e]For example, yarn, cloth, lumber, etc.

[f]Includes bedding, pots, dishes, silverware, tablecloths, and the like.

[g]For example, dried and salted foods, liquor, tea, coffee, sugar, and firewood.

ever, this pattern was broken: the median nonhuman physical wealth of Charleston widows was exceeded by that of both the Philadelphia and the Massachusetts women (Table 8.3, row 2).

Though some of the women in both the New England cities and Philadelphia owned real estate, I was unable to find any evidence of such holdings for the three widows in Charleston. These three women did, however, own slaves of substantial value, in contrast to the women in the northern cities who neither owned slaves nor had any claims on indentured servants. The Charleston widow Elizabeth Smith, aged at least 45 at her death, had two Negro women listed in her estate inventory: Hannah, appraised at £50 ($3,800) sterling, and Nanny, at £35.7 ($2,700). Their combined value was the median slave figure among the three Charleston widows. That value was topped by the holdings of Sarah Johnston, who was 84 years old in 1774. She owned slaves worth £124 ($9,400): a Negro man and his wife (named Charleston and Venus, respectively), together worth £24.3 ($1,800), and two daughters, "one with sucking child, Ruth," all three appraised at another £100 sterling ($7,600). The third Charleston widow had no slaves or servants and a total physical wealth of only £9.4 ($710).

Besides physical wealth in consumer goods, real estate, livestock, producer goods, and slaves, urban women whose estates were probated in 1774 rather frequently held wealth in the form of cash or other financial assets (Table 8.3, rows 15 and 16). The cash sometimes consisted of gold and silver coins from England, but also included coins from other European countries, the latter reaching the colonists chiefly by way of their trade with the West Indies. More frequently the cash consisted of the paper currency of the province, issued by the provincial legislatures in the form of promissory notes to be redeemed from tax revenues (the colonists were forbidden by England to strike their own coins). These women also held financial assets in other forms, such as a note signed by an individual, promising to pay a stated principal plus interest at a specific rate, often 6 percent. Similarly, bonds and mortgages issued by individuals, bearing a stated interest, could also be found itemized on the probate inventories. (There were no colonial banks in our modern sense of the institution, although in some areas there were in the 1770s official loan offices of the particular province, and these advanced credit in provincial currency on the security of land mortgages.) Very frequently, financial transactions between individuals were handled, in view of the shortage of coins and currency, by "book account" or "book debt." This practice may be considered an early form of the charge account, cleared not by check or cash, but often by the barter of some return commodity—for example, tobacco, or corn, or wheat—or service. From time to time (sometimes as infrequently as once a year, or even longer), the two parties would reckon their accounts, agree on a new balance owed at the stated date, and carry the accounts forward or, on occasion, settle the accounts with the issuance of a bond or note in the amount of the balance due.

Except among the women in Massachusetts, financial assets held by urban women with estates probated in 1774 were substantial (Table 8.3, rows 15 and 16). They were the greatest among the three widows who lived in Charleston. The high level of financial assets in the South and the relatively low level of such wealth in New England follows the pattern found among all urban wealthholders (men and women combined) documented in tables 5.11, 5.12, and 5.13 of *Wealth of a Nation to Be*. But the pattern is not identical to that observed in the same tables for either all women (urban and rural combined) or all men (urban and rural combined). For both of these two groups, wealthholders in Pennsylvania, New Jersey, and Delaware were far ahead of those in the South in terms of the size of their financial assets. Women in New England had on average the fewest financial assets of the women in all three regions, but New England men had financial assets on average slightly greater than those of southern men.

When allowance is made for estimates of debts owed—which were very large in New England—the combination of total physical wealth with all financial assets and liabilities leads to the net worth figures of row 3 in Table 8.3. Here, Charleston widows were by far the richest, and Massachusetts ones by far the poorest. This pattern is duplicated in a regional comparison of net worth for the larger sample of all men and women wealthholders.[28]

We have not mentioned thus far one form of wealth held by only two women in the overall sample, the only two in it with specified occupations. Both happen to be Philadelphia widows, and the data for both were used in a number of the calculations for Table 8.3. The particular category of wealth which both of these women possessed was business equipment and inventory. Miriam Potts, shopkeeper, and Ann Stricker, innkeeper, were these two women, and they held £337.3 ($26,000) and £75.6 ($5,700), respectively, in business equipment and inventory. Potts was the richer in total wealth. Aged only 34 when she died, she owned real estate valued by the Philadelphia tax authorities at £286.9 ($22,000), and her total physical wealth was £690.1 ($52,000). The only financial asset listed in her probate inventory was cash of £23.4 ($1,800) in sterling. I estimated her financial liabilities at £238.6 ($18,000), which brings her net worth down to £474.9 ($36,000). Her financial assets were exceeded in size by four of the seven Philadelphia widows, including Ann Stricker, who had £90 ($6,800) in monies and credit. Financial assets for these others were £1,292 ($98,000) for Elizabeth Vanderspeigle, £360 ($27,000) for Catherine Reiff (who lived in Germantown), and £152 ($12,000) for Sarah Couch.

Miriam Potts's business assets included £1.7 ($130) worth of scales and other equipment and £335.6 ($26,000) of goods in both her Philadelphia shop as well as in storage "in the Jerseys." The shop goods were of very much the same sort, though somewhat less in total quantity, than those present in the inventories of several male Philadelphia merchants in the wider 1774 sample. Her goods included many pieces of cloth such as broadcloth, coating, serge, stamped linen, stamped Holland cloth, India calico, black velvet, fustian, dowlas, sagatha, muslin, cambric, black Persian cloth, shalloon, damask, mohair, taffeta, satin, silk camblet, bird's eye, striped silk and cotton, canvas, and poplin. There were also many pieces of lace, ribbons, tapes, garters, and thread. There were worsted stockings, silk hose, felt hats, buckles, sleeve buttons, coat and vest buttons, men's gloves, mourning bands, women's gloves, half-fingered mitts, silk bonnets, silk handkerchiefs, spectacles and

28. Ibid., table 5.2.

cases, pocket looking glasses, ivory fans, candle snuffers, watch keys, trowels, door locks, thirty-five gallons of vinegar, scales, and weights. Her personal apparel and watch were appraised at £5.4 ($410). Items judged to be her personal furniture and household equipment were worth a total of £58.2 ($4,400). They included a walnut chest of drawers, various pictures, looking glasses, a black walnut table, a black walnut tea table, a tea server, pewter plates and dishes, pewter basons, and brass candlesticks. There were six leather-bottom chairs worth together £2.6 ($200), and six "worked bottom" chairs valued the same as the leather-bottom ones. By contrast, six "old chairs" were appraised at £0.6 ($46). All of these items indicate that Miriam Potts led a comparatively comfortable life. She had no livestock, however, and no slaves, indentured servants, or vehicles were shown on her inventory. There were several beds and bedsteads with curtains, bolsters, and pillows. Among other miscellaneous items, she owned a spinning wheel and reel, two old guns, and two old pistols.

8.4.3 The Personal Belongings of Urban Women

Of the seven Philadelphia widows, Miriam Potts's £690 ($52,000) of physical assets—to which her shop inventory contributed substantially—made her the richest when gauged according to that measure of wealth. She was exceeded in net worth, however, by Elizabeth Vanderspeigle, aged 52, whose very large financial wealth of £252 ($19,000) brought her net worth to £1,544.2 ($120,000). Of Vanderspeigle's financial assets, only £12.8 ($970) were in cash. The rest of her very substantial financial claims consisted of 14 "bonds" or "bond and mortgage and interest," four of which were listed by the estate appraisers as "doubtful," indicating that there was some question as to whether payment could be collected. Elizabeth Vanderspeigle had no slaves or livestock, and her physical wealth was almost all in consumer goods. Her apparel was worth £46.3 ($3,500), and her other consumer goods £164 ($12,000). The latter included more status items than owned by Miriam Potts. One tea table and her dining table were mahogany. She had several walnut chests of drawers, chamber tables, a walnut tea table, a painted landscape, eighteen pictures painted on glass, and two pieces of needlework. She had cushions, chair bottoms and book covers of needlework, a spinet, an eight-day clock, china and delft dishes and plates, several beds and bedsteads with curtains and valances, a silver watch, a gold locket and chain, a gold-headed cane, a substantial amount of silverware, pewter plates, basons and mugs, a safe, thirty-six books, copper tea kettles and sauce pans, a silk umbrella, and other items suggesting a comfortably furnished house and a graceful way of living.

In contrast with the several women of substantial wealth in Philadelphia, the richest widow in New England was Mary Hubbard, who owned physical assets worth £460.2 ($35,000), had no financial assets, but did have financial liabilities estimated at £343.5 ($26,000), so that her estimated net worth was

£116.7 ($8,900). The lone single woman in the sample of urban women, Mary Grice, aged 60, of Boston, had £53.6 ($4,100) in total physical wealth, no financial assets, and estimated financial liabilities of £44.1 ($3,400), which brought her net worth to £9.5 ($720).

The richest of the three Charleston widows was Elizabeth Smith, aged at least 45, with total physical wealth of only £268.8 ($20,000), but financial assets of £2,229.4 ($170,000, of which £362.6, or $28,000, was cash). Her estimated financial liabilities of £59.4 ($4,500) brought her net worth to £2,438.8 ($190,000). The £85.7 ($6,500) value of her slaves constituted over a third of her physical wealth, but she also had £158.7 ($12,000) in consumer goods other than her apparel, which itself was valued at only £10 ($760). She had a bay horse worth £14.1 ($1,100) and a post chaise and harness appraised at £150 of South Carolina money, equivalent to £21.4 sterling ($1,600). She had a Wilton carpet and a Scotch carpet, both of which were luxury items, as well as silverware appraised at £33 sterling ($2,500). A gold watch, gold trinkets, a pair of gold shoe buckles, and one pair of gold sleeve buttons were worth a total of £1.2 ($91). She also had a set of books, numerous table cloths, napkins, towels, sheets, quilts, bolster and pillow cases, bedsteads with "curtains, pavilion and counterpane," and items of furniture suggesting a comfortable, even affluent, lifestyle.

In contrast, the poorest (in terms of physical wealth) of the three Charleston widows, Ann Timberly, had only £9.4 sterling ($710) worth of consumer goods, including apparel appraised at £3.9 ($300). She had no other physical wealth, no slaves or livestock, but financial assets described in South Carolina money as "cash found in her chests £925" and "five bonds making together £1,400," giving her financial claims worth a total of £2,325 in South Carolina money, equivalent to £332.1 sterling ($25,000). Her apparel and jewelry, valued at £3.9 ($300), included "a very thin and small plain gold ring" worth £0.2 sterling ($15). The inventory of apparel enumerated "6 calico and gingham gowns, 2 coarse quilted coats, and a red cardinal, 2 black hats, 30 old coarse caps, 4 old quilted coats and 5 coarse linen coats, 10 coarse old white linen aprons and 5 checked aprons, 10 coarse shirts, much worn, a pair of old woman's stays, 4 coarse white handkerchiefs, and three speckled linen" ones. She had an "old pine bedstead, a small feather bed and one bolster, two pillows and 3 old blankets," "8 coarse pillow cases and 4 old window curtains," "an old bedquilt and old gauze pavilion," "3 small cups and saucers of white stone ware, one old tea pot, a small old copper coffee pot," and "a small mahogany stand."

The smallest total physical wealth of a Philadelphia widow was the £7.6 sterling ($580) of Mary Catherine Richerts, aged 36. All of her physical assets consisted of household equipment, furniture, and clothing; yet, included in her inventories were two pairs of silver shoe buckles, a pair of silver knee buckles, and a silver snuff box. She had an "Indian blanket and carpet" valued at only 10 shillings Pennsylvania money, or £0.3 sterling ($23). She also had two feather beds, bolsters and pillows, another pillow, three pillow cases, one old bedstead and cord, one looking glass, some lumber, a few plates and utensils, some pewter, and a brass stew pan.

Sarah Leonard, the 84-year-old Springfield, Massachusetts, widow with the smallest total physical wealth of all urban women, had only apparel and a few consumer durable goods in the way of furniture and household equipment. She had a "bed, bedstead and cloathing thereto," a blue quilt and a striped quilt, a chest, a chair, a warming pan, one brass kettle, a trammel, and a little pewter. The entire list of clothing recorded in her inventory was as follows: one russet gown, a silk crepe gown, a drugget gown and coat, a crepe gown and coat, a silk hood, a serge cloak, two checked aprons, three shirts, stockings, handkerchiefs, and a pair of shoes. The total value of this apparel was £1.9 ($145).

8.5 Conclusions

Although attitudes toward women, and women's perceptions of themselves, may have begun to change during the colonial period, an examination of wealthholding by women in 1774 reveals a pattern of male dominance. Many women, of course, shared in the benefits produced by the wealth of their families, but few owned great wealth in their own right. In a random sample of 919 probate inventories for 1774, only 81 were of estates owned by women. The estates of women in the sample, moreover, were on average less than half as large as those of men. Overall I estimate that women in their own name owned only about 4.2 percent of the total physical wealth in 1774.

The relatively small number of women in the sample reflected the laws of inheritance and perhaps even more the limited opportunities for employment outside the home and the home workshop. The law protected the widow, to some extent, by establishing a dower's right to a minimum of one-third of her husband's real estate. In cases in which no will was left, partible inheritance (a double share to the eldest son) prevailed in some colonies and primogeniture with respect to land in others. But maintaining or adding to the wealth left to widows was difficult. Pregnancy, childrearing, and home production occupied the lives of most women. Unmarried women might spin, be waitresses or servants in taverns or inns or in the homes of the well-to-do, care for the sick, or in a few cases might teach music, embroidery, or reading. Many urban women undoubtedly helped in the family business and some continued the business after the death of their husbands.

A comparison of the wealth of men and women by region reveals similar patterns. The richest women, like the richest men, were in the South, the poorest in New England, with those from the Middle Colonies in between. The richest woman in the sample, gauged by physical wealth, was the widow Abigail Townsend of Wadmellow Island in the Charleston District. The bulk of her wealth was in slaves. The richest urban woman, by the same standard, was Miriam Potts, a widowed Philadelphia shopkeeper. If slaves are excluded, however, the pattern for urban women is somewhat different, with the widows of Charleston holding less nonhuman physical wealth than those from urban areas in Pennsylvania or Massachusetts.

One of the benefits of the probate data is that they contain inventories of household goods. From these we can derive a better appreciation for the standard of living that can be ascertained merely from an examination of numerical data on wealth or income at such early dates. It is apparent that, while a few women in the sample had lives of affluence and grace, the material possessions of most reflected the less prosperous lives of widows and unmarried women in a society in which women were expected to make their major contribution within their own homes.

III The Demography of Free and Slave Populations

9 Adult Mortality in America before 1900

A View from Family Histories

Clayne L. Pope

Economists and, to a lesser degree, economic historians have measured progress in the standard of living solely in terms of income per capita. Yet, there is a general belief that measurement of other elements, including the distribution of income, leisure, morbidity, and mortality, are needed for an accurate assessment of living standards.

Decreases in mortality rates have played a major role in the improvement of life in the twentieth century. The decrease in infant mortality from above 100 per thousand at the turn of the century to the current level of about 10 per thousand has contributed significantly to improved life expectation and the psychological comfort of families. The increase in adult life expectation, roughly a 35 percent improvement at ages twenty and sixty, has also materially enhanced the level of living.[1] Certainly, no one would argue that our assessment of progress in the standard of living would remain unchanged if life expectation had not improved.

Our knowledge of trends in mortality for the eighteenth and nineteenth centuries is considerably more fragmentary than our knowledge of the trend in

The data set used here was created by joint efforts of the Center for Population Economics, University of Chicago, and the College of Social Science, Brigham Young University. Donna Breckenridge supervised data collection, and Mark Showalter and Danelle Boothe provided programming. Nathan Sheets and Brigitte Condie Madrian provided research assistance. A very early draft of this work was presented at the Ninth Congress of the International Economic History Association in Bern and at the American Economic Association Meetings in 1986. Suggestions received at workshops at the University of Chicago, Brigham Young University, and University of California, Los Angeles, were very helpful. Richard Butler, Stanley Engerman, Robert Fogel, David Galenson, Claudia Goldin, Michael Haines, Dan Levy, Rulon Pope, Kenneth Sokoloff, and Larry Wimmer generously read drafts of this paper and provided useful suggestions for improvement.

1. U.S. Bureau of the Census, *The Statistical History of the United States from Colonial Times to the Present* (Stamford, 1964) Series B 76–112; and *Statistical Abstract of the United States, 1989,* 109th edn., U.S. Department of Commerce, pp. 73–77.

income per capita. Adequate death registration procedures did not exist for all states until 1933. Until 1910, death registration coverage was concentrated in the more industrialized and urbanized states of the Northeast.[2] Consequently, the oft-cited life tables from 1890 to 1920 based on the death registration area cannot be representative of the nation as a whole unless regional variation in mortality was unimportant by the turn of the century.[3] Life tables constructed for periods before the development of a significant death registration area (before 1900) are limited in geographical coverage and do not, in most cases, provide evidence on mortality for long time periods.

This essay adds to our knowledge of the trend in mortality before 1900, with particular emphasis on the antebellum period. The findings reinforce the importance of extending measurement of the standard of living beyond income per capita. The downturn in life expectation noted by Robert W. Fogel and others for the antebellum period is reconfirmed. The sizeable sex differential in mortality favoring women appears to be a twentieth-century phenomenon. Westward migration appears to have increased mortality rates modestly, especially for women, and regional differences in mortality narrowed in the nineteenth century.

9.1 Mortality Before the Twentieth Century

Scholars studying the trends in mortality have not yet reached a consensus on the period before 1900. Mortality studies of the colonial period have usually focused on counties or communities such as Andover or Salem, Massachusetts, or Charles County, Maryland, and are usually based on small samples of males. Most of the estimates have been confined to the seventeenth

2. The growth of the death registration area may be summarized as follows with the percentage of the population covered by that year:

Year	*%*	*States Added By That Year*
1880	6.2	District of Columbia, Massachusetts, New Jersey
1890	18.6	Connecticut, New Hampshire, New York, Rhode Island, Vermont
1900	26.2	Indiana, Maine, Michigan
1910	51.4	California, Colorado, Maryland, Minnesota, Montana, Ohio, Pennsylvania, Utah, Washington, Wisconsin
1920	80.9	Delaware, Florida, Illinois, Kansas, Kentucky, Louisiana, Mississippi, Missouri, Nebraska, North Carolina, Oregon, South Carolina, Tennessee, Virginia
1930	95.3	Alabama, Arizona, Arkansas, Georgia, Idaho, Iowa, Nevada, New Mexico, North Dakota, Oklahoma, South Dakota, West Virginia, Wyoming
1933	100.0	Texas

Sources: U.S. Bureau of the Census, *Historical Statistics of the United States: Colonial Times to 1970,* bicentennial edn. (Washington, D.C., 1975), part 1, p. 44; *Measures Relating to Vital Records and Vital Statistics* (Washington, D.C., 1943).

3. Preston and Haines find that the death registration, upon which the life tables of 1901 are based, somewhat misrepresents U.S. mortality, especially for blacks. See Samuel H. Preston and Michael R. Haines, "New Estimates of Child Mortality in the United States at the Turn of the Century," *Journal of the American Statistical Association,* 79 (June 1984), pp. 233–54.

and early eighteenth century and suggest that life expectation did not improve in New England over the colonial period.[4] Scholars do find, however, some improvement in life expectation in the Chesapeake where death rates were initially far worse.[5] Colonial evidence is thin because larger reliable samples are difficult to create. There is almost no evidence on mortality in the middle colonies.

The views of the trend in life expectation for the antebellum period are especially diverse because very few life tables (outside of Massachusetts) have been constructed for the antebellum period.[6] One group of scholars sees continuous, but uneven, improvement in life expectancy after the colonial period. Warren Thompson and P. K. Whelpton use life tables constructed by others to extrapolate a modest upward trend in life expectation from 1790 to 1890 with a sharp increase thereafter. Richard Easterlin also suggests an improvement in life expectation throughout the nineteenth century. Both depend heavily on the Wigglesworth life table for 1789 which Maris Vinovskis has

4. Phillip Greven, Jr., "Historical Demography and Colonial America," *William and Mary Quarterly,* 24 (July 1967) pp. 438–54; Daniel Scott Smith, "The Demographic History of Colonial New England," *Journal of Economic History,* 32 (Mar. 1972), pp. 165–83; John Demos, "Notes on Life in Plymouth," *William and Mary Quarterly,* 22 (Apr. 1965), pp. 264–86; Susan Norton, "Population Growth in Colonial America: A Study of Ipswich, Massachusetts," *Population Studies,* 25 (Nov. 1971), pp. 433–52; James K. Somerville, "A Demographic Profile of the Salem Family, 1660–1770," (manuscript, 1969). The New England estimates are summarized in Maris Vinovskis, *Fertility in Massachusetts from the Revolution to the Civil War* (New York, 1981), chap. 2.

5. Daniel S. Levy, "The Economic Demography of the Colonial South" (Ph.D. dissertation, University of Chicago, 1989); Daniel S. Levy, "The Life Expectancies of Colonial Maryland Legislators," *Historical Methods,* 20 (Winter 1987), pp. 17–27; Lorena S. Walsh and Russell Menard, "Death in the Chesapeake: Two Life Tables for Men in Early Colonial Maryland," *Maryland Historical Society,* 69 (Summer 1974), pp. 211–27; Daniel Blake Smith, "Mortality and Family in Colonial Chesapeake," *Journal of Interdisciplinary History,* 8 (Winter 1978), pp. 404–27; Darrett B. Rutman and Anita H. Rutman, *A Place in Time: Explicatus* (New York, 1984); James M. Gallman, "Mortality Among White Males: Colonial North Carolina," *Social Science History,* 4 (Summer 1980), pp. 295–316.

6. Paul H. Jacobson, "An Estimate of the Expectation of Life in the United States in 1850," *The Milbank Memorial Fund Quarterly,* 35 (Apr. 1957), pp. 197–201, is based on averages of the data on Massachusetts and Maryland published by Joseph C. G. Kennedy for the census of 1850 (Kennedy, *The Seventh Census: Report of the Superintendent of the Census for December 1, 1852* [Washington D.C., 1853]). For an evaluation of Jacobson's life table, see Maris Vinovskis, "The Jacobson Life Table of 1850: A Critical Reexamination from a Massachusetts Perspective," *The Journal of Interdisciplinary History,* 8 (Spring 1978), pp. 703–24; Michael R. Haines, "The Use of Model Life Tables to Estimate Mortality for the United States in the Late Nineteenth Century," *Demography,* 16 (May 1979), pp. 289–312, follows William Brass, "On the Scale of Mortality," in *Biological Aspects of Demography,* William Brass, ed., vol. 10 of the *Symposia of the Society for the Study of Human Biology* (London, 1971), to fit a two-parameter logit system to a set of life tables for parts of the United States from 1850 to 1910 and use the resulting system to examine the trend in U.S. mortality from 1850 to 1900; Maris Vinovskis, "Mortality Rates and Trends in Massachusetts before 1860," *Journal of Economic History,* 32 (March 1972), pp. 184–213; Levi Meech, *Systems and Tables of Life Insurance* (New York, 1898). For an appraisal of the Meech life table, see Michael R. Haines and Roger C. Avery, "The American Life Table of 1830–1860: An Evaluation," *Journal of Interdisciplinary History,* 11 (Summer 1980), pp. 73–95; A. J. Jaffee and W. I. Laurie, "An Abridged Life Table for the White Population of the United States in 1830," *Human Biology,* 14 (Sept. 1942).

criticized as being too low. Conrad and Irene Taeuber conclude that there was little upward movement in life expectation for the first half of the nineteenth century, but rather steady improvement thereafter. Edward Meeker examines the trend from 1850 to 1915 and concludes that life expectation improved very slowly before 1880, more thereafter. Paul Jacobson examines the increase in cohort life expectancy for cohorts born between 1840 and 1960. He shows modest increases in life expectation for males born in the 1850s and 1860s compared with the previous decade and larger increases for the later cohorts. The female pattern is similar, but the decadal increases begin earlier. Robert Higgs finds increasing life expectation in both the countryside and urban areas after 1870.[7]

Other scholars find little improvement in life expectation in the nineteenth century or actual declines. Vinovskis finds little evidence of an upward trend in life expectancy in the small agricultural towns of Massachusetts before 1860. Yasukichi Yasuba uses an examination of the census populations adjusted for immigration to argue for a fall in life expectation in the three decades before the Civil War. Fogel and Kent Kunze, both using genealogical samples, find a downturn in life expectancy in the antebellum period. Michael Haines's study combines sophisticated demographic techniques with the death rates in the census mortality schedules to produce life expectations for the last half of the nineteenth century. His estimates, lower than most for the period, show improved life expectation from 1850 to 1870, then a decline from 1870 to 1880 with improvement to 1900.[8] There seems to be a consensus that mortality diminished in the late nineteenth century—certainly after 1880. But no consensus has emerged on the trend in mortality from the late eighteenth century to the Civil War.

The large gaps in measurement of mortality are sometimes filled with a combination of fragmentary evidence and model life tables such as those of

7. Warren S. Thompson and P. K. Whelpton, *Population Trends in the United States* (New York, 1933), p. 230ff.; Richard A. Easterlin, "Population Issues in American Economic History: A Survey and Critique," in *Recent Developments in the Study of Business and Economic History: Essays in Memory of Herman E. Krooss,* Robert E. Gallman, ed., (Greenwich, 1977); Maris Vinovskis, "The 1789 Life Table of Edward Wigglesworth," *Journal of Economic History,* 31 (Sept. 1971), pp. 570–90; Conrad Taeuber and Irene B. Taeuber, *The Changing Population of the United States* (New York, 1958), p. 269ff.; Edward Meeker, "The Improving Health of the United States, 1850–1915," *Explorations in Economic History,* 9 (Summer 1972), p. 358; Paul H. Jacobson, "Cohort Survival for Generations Since 1840," *Milbank Memorial Fund Quarterly* (July 1964), p. 48; Robert Higgs, "Mortality in Rural America, 1870–1920: Estimates and Conjectures," *Explorations in Economic History,* 10 (Winter 1973), pp. 177–95; and "Cycles and Trends of Mortality in 18 Large American Cities, 1871–1900," *Explorations in Economic History,* 16 (Oct. 1979), pp. 381–408.

8. Vinovskis, *Fertility in Massachusetts,* chap. 2; Yasukichi Yasuba, *Birth Rates of the White Population in the United States, 1800–1860* (Baltimore, 1962), pp. 86–96; Robert W. Fogel, "Nutrition and the Decline in Mortality since 1700: Some Preliminary Findings," in *Long-Term Factors in American Economic Growth,* Stanley L. Engerman and Robert E. Gallman, eds., Studies in Income and Wealth, vol. 51 (Chicago, 1986); Kent Kunze, "The Effects of Age Composition and Changes in Vital Rates on Nineteenth Century Population Estimates from New Data" (Ph.D. dissertation, University of Utah, 1979); Haines, "The Use of Model Life Tables."

Ansley Coale and Paul Demeny.[9] The model life table provides estimated relationships between age, sex, and mortality based on life tables calculated from reliable data, which are usually based on twentieth-century experience in more developed countries.[10] Of course, the result of these sophisticated and useful efforts is dependent on the validity of these model tables for the particular time period and geographical area. After all, model tables are simply smoothings or averages of observed life tables.[11] These fundamental relationships for age, sex, and mortality that are the essence of model life tables are unlikely to be invariant through ime and across space.[12]

Since life expectancy is a basic measure of the material performance of a society, it is surprising how little we know about the course of mortality before the systematic development of death registration at the start of the twentieth century. The problem has not been lack of interest in mortality, but rather the lack of data sources that could generate evidence on a broad front concerning the trends in mortality, regional variation in mortality, and the relative experience of men and women. Scholars will necessarily have to depart from the familiar environs of death registrations and census data if they wish to create useful series on life expectation or mortality for the United States before 1900 or 1880 at best. The suggestion here is that data culled from printed family histories can be used to construct long-term series on mortality and life expectation for the native-born white population.

9.2 Family Histories as a Source of Demographic Data

There are at least 60,000 printed histories of families that have resided in the United States. Large collections are in the Library of Congress, Allen

9. For model tables, see Ansley J. Coale and Paul Demeny, *Regional Model Life Tables and Stable Populations* (Princeton, 1966); or United Nations, *Age and Sex Patterns of Mortality: Model Life-Tables for Under-Developed Countries*, Population Studies 22 (New York, 1955).

10. For example, Coale and Demeny use 326 life tables for their classic study. Twenty-three of the life tables are before 1870, all from Europe. About a third (113) are before 1918 with 76 percent of those coming from Europe. Sixty-three percent of all the tables used come from Europe and less than 6 percent from North America. Only three North American life tables are used before 1918. They group the life tables into four "regions" with the U.S. life tables of the twentieth century put in the "west" region.

11. Coale and Demeny found that e_{10} (life expectation at age ten) correlates best with the death probabilities at various ages. Those correlations are quite high for the tables used to construct model west. Indeed the average correlation between e_{10} and the five-year death probabilities is 0.955 for females and somewhat lower for males (0.921). However, for the pre–1870 tables of Europe, the correlations are much lower, 0.666 for females and 0.663 for males.

12. The categorization by Coale and Demeny of the life tables into four regions illustrates the variability of the basic patterns. At level five, male life expectation at birth ranges from 90.6 percent of female life expectation to 97.8 percent in the four area models. At higher levels of life expectation there is less variance, but male life expectation varies from 93.3 percent in model east to 94.6 percent in model north. For a discussion of issues regarding gender and life expectation, see Jacques Vallin, "Sex Patterns of Mortality: A Comparative Study of Model Life Tables and Actual Situations with Special Reference to the Case of Algeria and France," in *Sex Differentials in Mortality: Trends, Determinants and Consequences*, Alan D. Lopez and Lado T. Ruzicka, eds., Miscellaneous Series no. 4, Department of Demography (Canberra, 1983), pp. 443–76.

County Public Library in Fort Wayne, Indiana, New York Public Library, Newberry Library, and the LDS Genealogical Society Library in Salt Lake City.[13] In addition, there are collections with a regional emphasis in many libraries throughout the country. Many of these histories are small and of poor quality, while others are significant books that represents thousands of hours of detailed genealogical research.

A typical U.S. or Canadian family history begins with a brief discussion of European forbears of an immigrant couple who migrated to North America. Most of the book is then devoted to a history of this immigrant couple and their descendants. Table 9.1 illustrates the typical structure of a printed family history. Normally the number of individuals per generation increases for a few generations, then declines because the last generations of a book are incomplete in the sense that not all the individuals of those generations had been born when the book was published. Birth years of a particular generation may span as much as a century because of the time disparity between the birth of the first-born of the first-born and so on compared to that of the last-born of the last-born and so forth. Although the number of people in each completed generation increases, the rate of increase is below the expected rate for most families because some individuals in each generation are not followed in the basic genealogical records, which eliminates their descendants from the book. Because of this attrition, the cross-sectional age distribution within a book will be skewed toward older ages. This attrition, however, will not bias the calculation of the age-specific fertility or mortality rates.

Although family histories or genealogies have been used for some time by historians and demographers, they have not been widely accepted as a good source for mortality analysis for the United States during the pre-registration period.[14] There are concerns that the use of genealogies may generate mislead-

13. Marion J. Kaminkow, *Genealogies in the Library of Congress: A Bibliography,* 2 vols. (Baltimore, 1972), lists the collection of family histories in the Library of Congress through 1971. Two supplements have since been published bringing the listing through 1986. These four volumes survey about 33,500 family histories. In addition, Kaminkow, *A Complement to Genealogies in the Library of Congress* (Baltimore, 1981), reports the results of a survey of twenty-four other libraries to obtain listings of their family histories that were not in the Library of Congress. This volume has 20,000 entries. The largest collections are in the New York Public Library (6,100 books not in the Library of Congress) and the Allen County Public Library, Fort Wayne, Indiana (8,600 volumes of its collection of 26,000 were not in the Library of Congress). The LDS Genealogical Library in Salt Lake City has a very large collection of family histories, many of which would also be in the Library of Congress.

14. Genealogical sources have been used quite widely by historical demographers, especially in Europe. See T. H. Hollingsworth, *Historical Demography* (Ithaca, 1969), for a discussion. J. Dennis Willigan and Katherine A. Lynch, *Sources and Methods of Historical Demography* (New York, 1982), also has a discussion of the uses of genealogical data. Adams and Kasakoff have used a sample of New England genealogies to study patterns of migration. See John W. Adams and Alice Bee Kasakoff, "Migration and the Family in Colonial New England: The View from Genealogies," *Journal of Family History* (Spring 1984), pp. 24–42. Wahl has used a sample of family histories linked to mid-nineteenth-century census records to study fertility and its covariates. See Jenny Bourne Wahl, "New Results on the Decline in Household Fertility in the United States from 1750–1900," in *Long-Term Factors in American Economic Growth,* Stanley L. Engerman and Robert E. Gallman, eds., Studies in Income and Wealth, vol. 51 (Chicago, 1986). Fogel

Table 9.1 Structure of a Typical Family History

Gen	#M	MBY	MDY	MBPL	MDPL	#F	FBY	FDY	FBPL	FDPL
1	1	100%	100%	100%	100%	1	0%	100%	0%	0%
2	1	100	0	100	0	1	100	100	100	100
3	3	100	100	100	100	0	n.a.	n.a.	n.a.	n.a.
4	12	67	83	67	75	9	67	22	11	11
5	24	50	46	46	54	18	44	11	6	0
6	38	74	71	58	58	26	62	35	15	15
7	56	88	66	48	52	55	73	18	9	5
8	76	92	42	67	39	72	90	33	54	28
9	160	94	59	57	44	116	90	41	50	27
10	116	96	60	55	35	131	93	46	47	32
11	15	100	7	53	7	15	73	20	60	13

Notes: Gen is the generation with the immigrants to the United States considered as generation 1, their children as generation 2, and so forth. #M is the percentage of males in that generation. MBY is the percentage with a birth year recorded; MDY is the percentage with a death year recorded. MBPL is the percentage of males with birthplace recorded; MDPL with a deathplace recorded. #F, FBY, FDY, FBPL, and FDPL are the analogous variables for females. n.a. = not applicable.

Source: Eddis Johnson and Hugh B. Johnston, *The Johnsons and Johnstons of Corrowaugh in Isle of Wight County, Virginia,* vol. 1 (Martinsville, IN, 1979).

ing inferences because of selection bias although empirical evidence of bias among the large body of family histories mentioned above is meager.[15] Susan Norton compared reconstructed families with the general population of three communities of Massachusetts between 1790 and 1840 and found that the families in the reconstructed genealogies were slightly larger, more agricultural, and persisted through censuses more often. John Knodel and Edward Shorter found the German village genealogies to be accurate representations of the available data.[16] Examination of family histories suggests that their

found a downturn in life expectation calculated for age ten that correlated closely with the decline in stature for cohorts born before the Civil War. See Fogel, "Nutrition and the Decline in Mortality since 1700." Bettie C. Freemen, "Fertility and Longevity in Married Women Dying after the End of the Reproductive Period," *Human Biology* 7 (1935), pp. 392–418, used genealogies to study the effect of child-bearing on mortality of women. A group of sociologists, historians, and geneticists have used the genealogies of Utah to study genetic links for particular diseases as well as fertility of Mormon families. See L. L. Bean, D. L. May, and M. Skolnick, "The Mormon Historical Demography Project," *Historical Methods,* 11 (Winter 1978), pp. 45–53; L. L. Bean, G. P. Mineau, K. A. Lynch, and J. D. Willigan, "The Genealogical Society of Utah as a Data Resource for Historical Demography," *Population Index,* 46 (Spring 1980), pp. 6–19. There have been other applications. Louis Henry, *Ancienne Familles Genevoises: Etude Demographique, IVIe–XXe Siecle* (Paris, 1956); Bennett Dyke and Warren T. Morrill, eds., *Genealogical Demography* (New York, 1980).

15. For an example, see Vinovskis, "Mortality Rates and Trends in Massachusetts before 1860," pp. 191–92.

16. Susan L. Norton, "The Vital Question: Are Reconstructed Families Representative of the General Population?" in *Genealogical Demography,* Bennett Dyke and Warren T. Morrill, eds. (New York, 1980) pp. 11–22; John Knodel and Edward Shorter, "The Reliability of Family Reconstitution Data in German Village Genealogies (*Ortssippenbucher*)," *Annales de Demographie Historique* (Paris, 1976), pp. 115–54.

compilers made every attempt to include all descendants of an immigrant couple with as much data on births, marriages, and deaths as could be reasonably gathered.[17]

9.2.1 General Biases in Family Histories

Demographic data drawn from U.S. family histories underrepresents blacks because their genealogies are so difficult to reconstitute. Immigrants are also underrepresented in the sample used here, which is based on very few books and has not been designed to sample the foreign born in proportion to the population.[18] Even if a sampling scheme had been carefully designed to maintain balance between immigrants and natives, family histories could be a biased source of demographic data on immigrants because an immigrant without a descendant would not generate a family history. (Natives without descendants are well represented in family histories.) Because those immigrants who left descendants may have lived longer than those who did not, family histories may be a biased sample for immigrants.[19]

Biases in family histories reflect weaknesses in the underlying sources of data available to the compilers, such as vital registers, burial records, church records, probates, censuses, or family records. For example, infant and childhood deaths, underrecorded in the underlying sources, are necessarily underrecorded in family histories. This appears to be especially true before 1850. For cohorts born between 1760 and 1799 in the sample studied here, only 4.5 percent of males and 9.7 percent of females die before reaching age ten. From 1800 to 1849 the death rates below age ten for males (females) rises to 8.4 percent (10.1 percent). From 1850 to 1889, deaths below age ten were 15.0 percent for males and 17.7 percent for females. The recorded rise in infant deaths largely reflects improved record keeping.

Death dates are about half as common in family histories as are birth dates because parish registers, census schedules, and other sources allow the compiler to give at least a birth year for an individual. Dispersal of families and married women's name changes make death years harder to find. Fertility patterns, birth intervals, and the low recorded infant mortality rates in family histories suggest that individuals who died in infancy were generally included in the family history—most often with a birth year, but no death year, re-

17. The information on the ancestors of the compiler of a book is not unusually complete compared with information on other family lines—a fact of some comfort to those who want to use the book for demographic history. Individuals within the histories who do not marry are recorded in the book with their vital dates included. In other words, genealogists who compile such books are careful about the completeness and accuracy of their work.

18. For a sample design that does bring in the foreign born in the appropriate proportion see Robert W. Fogel, Stanley L. Engerman, James Trussell, Roderick Floud, Clayne L. Pope, and Larry T. Wimmer, "The Economics of Mortality in North America, 1650–1910: A Description of a Research Project," *Historical Methods,* 11 (Spring 1978), p. 102.

19. Many family histories start with immigrant couples who have children born in Europe who migrate with them to the United States. It may be possible to study the mortality experience of immigrants through these children, not all of whom survive to have descendants.

corded. Consequently, family histories are probably not very useful for the study of infant or child mortality, but they are a suitable source for study of mortality of native-born white adults.[20]

9.2.2 A Sample of Family Histories

Each history begins with an individual or couple who migrated from Europe to the colonies or the United States. This sample was drawn with a primary objective of understanding the structure and biases of family histories. Consequently, nearly the complete book was recorded.[21] From each book, the vital dates and places for each individual were recorded along with information about occupation, religion, and military service where available. Quality codes were attached to the dates that were imprecise such as "about 1825." The most troublesome categories of "before or after a particular year" have been eliminated from the analysis. In some cases, place information not included by the compiler was easily inferred and added. An algorithm using birthplaces of children and death place of a spouse was employed to impute missing death places. The relationships among individuals within the book were also recorded. For analysis of mortality, it was important to distinguish between two groups of individuals—those included by virtue of their birth and those included by virtue of their marriage. That is, individuals may be included because they are bloodline descendants of the immigrant or they may be in the book because they married one of these descendants. All individuals are designated as either "bloodline" or "non-bloodline."

9.2.3 Definition of Group at Risk

Mortality studies in family histories must be confined to a carefully defined subset of the individuals listed in the family history to ensure that an individual was actually at risk of death at the age entered into the life table. The two key considerations concern the way an individual enters the family history and missing evidence on the date of death.

Life tables used here assume that bloodline children, those whose parents are in the family history, are at risk of death from birth. Any child whose parents were recorded in the history would be included in the book, whether they died on the day of their birth or survived to old age. From the vantage of the family history, spouses who entered the family history by marrying direct descendants of the immigrants were not at risk of dying before marriage. If the individuals marrying into the family (non-bloodline) were included from birth, calculated life expectations would be biased upward. Therefore, these individuals are only included in the mortality calculations after marriage.

20. An appendix exploring the potential biases in the family histories that affect their use for mortality estimates is available from the author upon request.

21. Individuals at the very end of the book seemed to be of little use. Obviously, we have better sources than family histories to study twentieth-century demography. Consequently, we adopted a rule of not collecting data on the children of any woman who would not have reached age 45 by the publication date of the family history.

Individuals born near the completion of the book present a different problem. They are at risk of dying up until the compiler stopped collecting data. If there were death information for all deceased individuals in a family history, then all individuals without death dates could be presumed to be alive at publication of the book and their years of exposure could be used in the calculation of life expectancy. But, many death dates are missing, and one cannot distinguish between individuals still living at the time of publication and those whose actual death date has not been included. This deficiency seriously biases death rates upward near the end of a book if individuals with both birth and death years born near the date of the compilation of the book are included. Alternatively, this deficiency would significantly bias death rates downward if all persons without death dates were presumed alive at the compilation of the book. The approach used here is to eliminate all individuals born within ninety years of the latest vital date (not necessarily the publication date) listed in the book.[22]

The sample used here starts with 49,419 individuals taken from twenty-three different family histories. The majority of these individuals, however, had to be eliminated from the data used for mortality analysis.[23]

9.3 Trends in Mortality, 1760 to 1880

Mortality can be analyzed by cohort or by time period. Both approaches are useful and offer different perspectives. The current sample of family histories may be used to examine the trend in mortality for cohorts born between 1760 and 1880. Since the focus here is adult mortality beyond age twenty, period mortality may be analyzed from 1780 onward. It should be noted that the cohort experience is over the whole lifespan. That is, the cohort life expectancy of 44.4 years at age twenty for males born between 1800 and 1809 found in Table 9.2 is a measure of mortality beginning as early as 1820 and continuing until the last person in that cohort dies. A period mortality value for e_{20} (e_i refers to life expectation at age i) of 41.5 years reported in Table 9.4 for the decade 1840–49 reflects the experience for everyone older than age twenty who lived in that decade.

22. The absence of death dates for some individuals in the histories also means that increment/decrement life tables cannot be used. For example, one might consider using individuals with known intervals between birth and the birth of a child and then eliminating them from the life table calculations. Use of such individuals would bias the life tables upward because the individuals selected in this way would add years lived to the denominator but could not contribute deaths.

23. This procedure of collecting all individuals within a book greatly enhanced our understanding of complete histories, but has the disadvantage that book-specific effects could be a factor in the results. There may be particular effects of an extended family on location, economic status, or longevity that constitute a book-effect of mortality. Further work with family histories should increase the number of family histories studied to dilute these effects. Fortunately, most of the books have a wide geographical distribution of births and deaths.

Table 9.2 **Life Expectations for Ten-Year Cohorts (in years)**

		Male Life Expectation at Ages:				Female Life Expectation at Ages:		
Cohorts	N(30)	Twenty	Thirty	Fifty	N(30)	Twenty	Thirty	Fifty
1760–69	117	46.0	38.0	22.8	75	45.1	37.5	24.8
1770–79	135	44.3	37.2	21.8	77	47.9	39.4	24.8
1780–89	174	42.9	35.8	21.3	127	44.5	37.4	24.1
1790–99	208	42.9	35.1	20.8	163	40.7	33.4	20.4
1800–1809	267	44.4	37.3	23.1	205	45.3	38.1	23.6
1810–19	307	44.9	37.0	22.3	254	40.5	34.5	23.6
1820–29	353	41.1	34.9	22.1	314	38.2	33.4	21.8
1830–39	329	40.9	35.4	22.1	284	41.8	36.0	23.2
1840–49	418	42.8	36.8	21.7	372	42.3	36.8	23.5
1850–59	457	44.6	36.6	22.4	384	43.1	36.7	22.9
1860–69	404	43.3	35.9	22.6	360	44.7	38.7	24.0
1870–79	256	44.8	38.7	23.6	216	42.7	38.4	25.0
1880–89	131	46.5	39.9	23.1	133	48.9	41.6	25.8

Notes: N(30) is the number of individuals alive at age 30, which is generally larger than the number alive at age 20 because non-bloodline individuals only enter the life table after marriage.
Source: Family History Sample.

9.3.1 Cohort Life Expectation

Table 9.2 gives estimates based on the family history sample of life expectation at ages twenty, thirty, and fifty by ten-year birth cohorts for males and females. Sample sizes are small but reasonably representative of the geographic distribution of the population.[24] Sample sizes are even smaller for women because books contain less death information for them, probably because of name changes for married women.

The most striking feature of Table 9.2 is the similarity between the life expectancy of cohorts born at the end of the eighteenth century and those born a century later. A comparison of 1760–69 with 1880–89 reveals little improvement for males and only modest improvement for females. For males, life expectation at age twenty is 46.0 years for the 1760 cohort and 46.5 years for the 1880 cohort. Life expectation improves somewhat at ages thirty and fifty. Even comparisons of the 1770 cohort, which had lower life expectation for males than the 1760 cohort, with the cohort of 1880 show less than 8 percent improvement at all three ages. The fact that a century marked by a high rate of economic growth did not significantly raise the life expectation of the most economically favored segment of the population (native-born white

24. It should be noted that the experience is at least twenty years after the birth period in the case of e_{20} and beyond that for life expectations at older ages. Thus, most of the experience recorded in Table 9.4 occurs in the nineteenth and early twentieth centuries.

adults) is worthy of notice and is in marked contrast to the experience of the twentieth century.

The similarity in life expectations in the late eighteenth and late nineteenth centuries hides cyclical movements within the 120 years from 1760 to 1880. Table 9.2 suggests that there were significant periods of decline and improvement in adult life expectancy. Life expectation appears to have fallen for successive cohorts born in the 1760 to 1799 period, with a recovery in the first decade or two of the nineteenth century. Life expectancy then continued its downward trend, reaching a trough in the 1820s for women and the 1830s for men. The later trough for men was probably generated by the higher mortality of younger men in the Civil War. In spite of the effect of war on male mortality, the downturn in cohort life expectancy started earlier and was more severe for women.[25] For women born in the 1820s, life expectation at age twenty was only 78 percent of the expectation for women born in the 1880s. For men, life expectation for the highest mortality cohort (1830) was 88 percent of the value for the 1880s.

Cohorts born after the 1840s experienced modest and sporadic improvement in mortality conditions so that life expectancy for cohorts born in the 1880s was higher than for cohorts born in the revolutionary period. The pattern of decline in life expectation was less pronounced, but present, for ages thirty and fifty. Most of the cyclical movement in death rates appears to have been associated with what are normally the ages of low age-specific mortality between twenty and fifty.

The central finding of an antebellum decline in life expectation for native-born white adults, in spite of a growing economy, is sufficiently disturbing to warrant further exploration and testing. Could the cycle in life expectation be an artifact of the data set or a result of the selection procedures for family histories? It is easier to imagine a bias that would affect the level than one that would generate a spurious cycle.

A spurious cycle in life expectation could be generated by a cycle in the ability of the family historian to gather mortality data. Death years of long-lived individuals might be easier to find (they had a longer paper trail) than those of individuals dying at younger ages. Therefore, a lower proportion of death years to birth years for a particular time period in the histories could generate a higher life expectation. If the ratio of death years to birth years varied systematically over time, a spurious cycle could be generated.

But the cycle in life expectation in this data set is not generated by changing proportions of death recorded. The proportion of those born in a given year, who also have a death year in the family history, does not suggest a cyclical pattern in the ratio of death years to birth years. Early decades show more

25. The period estimates for the Civil War years suggest that the war had an impact on the mortality of both younger men and younger women. The effect goes beyond the war deaths. Perhaps the movement of so many men throughout the country, some with short periods of service who then returned home, increased the deaths from infectious disease.

yearly variance, but most decadal birth cohorts have just over 50 percent of the individuals with recorded death years.[26] The cycles in life expectation are not replicated by the cycles in the ratio of death years to birth years.

A spurious cycle in life expectation could also be produced by shifting regional weights, because this sample was not designed as a random sample of the native-born white adult population. The Northeast is overrepresented for cohorts born in the late eighteenth century and underrepresented for cohorts born in the mid-nineteenth century. Otherwise, the sample is reasonably representative of the regional distribution of native-born white adults. Still, the effect of proper weighting of the four main regions of the country on the antebellum decline remains unmeasured. Regional weights are difficult to calculate for two reasons. The weights should be based only on the geographical distribution of native-born whites who reach adulthood. In census tables before 1850, the foreign born were not separated from natives in census tables and tabulations for early censuses use broad age intervals. In addition, the life expectations are for cohorts with mortality experience that span several decades. Consequently, weights based on any single year inaccurately reflect the shifting weights that should be applied as cohorts age and migrate between regions.

Table 9.3 compares cohort life expectations for the unweighted sample with those of a weighted sample. The weights are calculated for the census year closest to the year of death for each birth grouping. For example, the regional weights for those born between 1800 and 1819 are based on the distribution of native-born white adults in the 1870 census, the census closest to their average year of death. The time periods of Table 9.3 reflect the major turning points in the trend in cohort life expectation. The differences between the expectations in the unweighted sample and those of the weighted sample are not large, and the pattern of the antebellum decline is maintained with nearly the same magnitudes of decline and increase. The weighted estimates show slightly higher female life expectation for cohorts born between 1820 and 1849, but a reduced e_{20} for females born between 1850 and 1869. The amplitude of the female cycle in life expectation is reduced in the weighted sample while, for males, the amplitude of the cycle is increased. But in both cases the changes are small.

9.3.2 Period Effects on the Trend in Mortality

Tables 9.2 and 9.3 show changes in cohort life expectation, but do not isolate the exact period of mortality decline or improvement. It is possible that successive cohorts born in the antebellum period simply suffered higher mortality rates at every age throughout their lives. Adverse changes in the nutri-

26. Surprisingly, the cohort born in the 1830s, a cohort with low life expectancy, is an exception since only 46 percent of that cohort have death years. While the 1830s is one of the decades of low life expectancy, the downturn in life expectation starts earlier and is sustained for more than this decade.

Table 9.3 Comparisons of Life Expectations at Age Twenty (in years)

	Males		Females	
	Unweighted Sample	Weighted Sample	Unweighted Sample	Weighted Sample
Birth Periods:				
1760–99	43.5	43.7	44.2	44.0
1800–1819	43.4	43.0	42.5	42.8
1820–49	41.3	41.4	40.2	40.6
1850–69	43.4	44.1	42.6	42.1

	1760–99		1800–1819		1820–49		1850–69	
	Sample %	Weight Used to Re-weight	Sample %	Weight Used to Re-weight	Sample %	Weight Used to Re-weight	Sample %	Weight Used to Re-weight
Region:								
Northeast	53%	.55	33%	.44	24%	.37	14%	.31
South Atlantic	17	.23	20	.15	16	.12	21	.12
North Central	19	.14	36	.26	45	.36	45	.41
South Central	10	.08	11	.15	15	.15	20	.16

Note: Weights are based on the adult white natives in each region in the census nearest to the expected year of death for that cohort. The census of 1840 was used for the groups born between 1760 and 1799; 1870 for the 1800–1819 cohort; 1900 for the 1820–49 cohort; and 1920 for the 1850–69 cohort. The regional life expectations are reported in Table 9.6.

Source: Family History Sample.

tional practices during pregnancy or in early childhood as well as shortages of food might have had this kind of an effect.[27] An alternative explanation for the cohort pattern could be an intense increase in mortality rates for a shorter period of time that adversely affected life expectancy of several cohorts in a differential manner. To illustrate: A severe epidemic in 1860 would not affect cohort life expectation, measured at age twenty, of the cohort born in 1800 as much as it would affect the cohort born in 1840, because the person-years lost would be significantly higher for the cohort that was younger at the time of the epidemic.[28] Consequently, a cycle in life expectations could be caused by

27. J. M. Tanner, *A History of the Study of Human Growth* (Cambridge, 1981).

28. This example assumes that the period impact on death rates is independent of age. There is always the possibility of differential effects by age. Older age groups could have an immunity because of previous exposure to infectious disease such as smallpox, or older people could be more susceptible to death from certain diseases such as influenza. The point here is that a period-specific increase in mortality that causes deaths proportionally in all age categories will lower life expectation more for younger cohorts.

a sharp increase in mortality for a brief period or by a cycle in mortality rates experienced by particular cohorts over their whole lives.

The period estimates in Table 9.4 suggest that the antebellum decline in life expectation was largely the result of high mortality rates from 1840 through the Civil War. The period mortality rate for ages twenty to forty-nine rose from 22 percent and 25 percent for men and women, respectively, for the first four decades of the nineteenth century to 28 percent and 35 percent for the period 1840 to 1859.[29] Clearly, such high period mortality rates experienced by adults in their most productive years drove most of the decline in adult life expectation. Period measures of e_{20} fell from 44.6 years in the 1830s to 40.8 years in the 1850s for males. The decline is steeper for women, whose period life expectation fell from 44.6 years in the 1830s to 37.1 years in the 1840s (39.5 in the 1850s). After the Civil War, life expectations rose, though not substantially. Estimates of period life expectation (e_{20}) are only 45.8 years for men and 42.9 years for women at age twenty in 1880. Thus, the decline in life expectation reported in Table 9.4 for individuals born from 1810 to 1849 was mainly the consequence of high mortality for a short period (1840–69) rather than higher mortality rates throughout their lives.

The Civil War years were marked by very high mortality rates for both men and women. For the period 1860–64, e_{20} for men (not shown in Table 9.4) was 34.9 years with the probability of dying between age twenty and twenty-four of 0.14, which is over three times the rate in earlier decades. The same values for women are 41.5 and 0.08. War casualties could account for some of the decline in life expectation for men, but would not have a measurable effect on women. War deaths including battle deaths and deaths from disease are estimated to be about 8 percent of males ages 15 to 50 in 1860–64.[30] If one assumes that the 1860–64 period without the war would have experienced the same period mortality as an average of the decades 1850 to 1859 and 1865 to 1874, cohort life expectations would increase significantly for males born between 1835 and 1844, but would increase only marginally for other cohorts. But such an adjustment to the 1860–64 rates does not seem warranted since war-related deaths appear to be only part of the story. The effect of moving large numbers of men throughout the country and the stress of the war increased the mortality of adults generally. But, the high mortality in the 1840s and 1850s had a larger effect on the antebellum cycle of life expectation than did the large effect of the Civil War.

Period death rates for the postwar period are lower than the rates for 1840–65, but they are not as low as the period rates at the end of the eighteenth

29. The first four decades would represent level 13 for women and level 14 for men in the model west tables of Coale and Demeny. The 1840s and 1850s would represent levels between 11 and 12 for men and 7 and 8 for women. Obviously these harsh conditions did not persist for very long. Kunze, "The Effects of Age Composition and Changes in Vital Rates," finds a similar downturn but it is not quite as severe in his data.

30. Claudia Goldin and Frank D. Lewis, "The Economic Cost of the American Civil War: Estimates and Implications," *Journal of Economic History*, 34 (June 1975), pp. 299–326.

Table 9.4 **Period Life Expectations (in years)**

Period	N(20)	Male Life Expectation At Age: Twenty	Thirty	Fifty	N(20)	Female Life Expectation At Age: Twenty	Thirty	Fifty
1750–79	174	44.4	35.8	20.0	—	—	—	—
1780–99	214	47.4	40.1	24.3	115	45.6	37.4	21.7
1800–1809	169	46.4	39.5	24.8	115	47.9	41.1	26.5
1810–19	204	44.6	38.0	24.4	141	44.4	37.4	24.5
1820–29	236	43.3	36.1	21.1	169	44.9	37.7	24.7
1830–39	280	44.6	36.7	22.7	228	44.6	39.1	25.0
1840–49	346	41.5	35.3	20.6	288	37.1	32.1	19.8
1850–59	328	40.8	35.2	22.0	263	39.5	33.4	22.3
1860–69	412	41.2	35.1	22.1	342	42.2	36.7	24.6
1870–79	428	44.3	36.4	22.3	341	42.2	35.7	22.8
1880–89	375	45.8	38.6	22.9	336	42.9	36.8	22.8

Note: N(20) is the number of individuals used to calculate the probability of dying between 20 and 29. A dash indicates that there were too few observations at older ages to calculate life tables.
Source: Family History Sample.

century. Hence, the long-run improvement was gradual. It appears that much of the rise in life expectation for cohorts born after 1850 came from improvements in the 1890s and early twentieth century.

9.3.3 Comparisons of Family History Life Tables with Other Evidence

Table 9.5 compares period life tables constructed from this family history sample with period tables drawn from other sources. The comparisons are with life tables for whites and native-born whites where possible. These comparisons suggest that life tables based on family histories are very similar to those based on other sources. Period estimates from the family histories for the antebellum era are compared with the life tables of Levi Meech for 1830 to 1860, Jacobson for Massachusetts and Maryland in 1850, and Vinovskis for Massachusetts in 1860. For most values, the life expectation based on the family histories is bracketed by the other estimates. The estimated female life expectation at ages twenty and thirty are slightly lower for the family histories compared with the other three estimates. In the comparison with Meech's life table, estimates from the family histories never deviate by more than 5 percent. The Jacobson life table for 1850, an average of experience in Massachusetts and Maryland, gives a slightly lower value of life expectation for males and a higher value for females than the family histories. Vinovskis has suggested that the Jacobson table understates life expectancy for Massachusetts because an outbreak of cholera in 1849–50 increased mortality. Vinovskis's estimates for Massachusetts are uniformly higher than the family history average for 1830–60, which is drawn from all regions of the country.

Table 9.5 **Comparison of Life Expectations from Family Histories and Other Sources**

		Males				Females			
Source	Years	e_{20}	e_{30}	e_{50}	e_{60}	e_{20}	e_{30}	e_{50}	e_{60}
Meech	1830–60	40.9	34.5	21.2	14.9	41.4	35.4	22.4	15.7
Family Histories	1830–60	42.8	36.0	21.6	15.3	40.8	35.1	22.5	16.2
Jacobson	1850	40.1	33.6	21.2	15.3	41.7	35.8	23.3	16.7
Haines	1850	37.6	31.0	17.8	11.4	38.8	32.2	18.6	11.9
Vinovskis/Massachusetts	1860	44.0	37.4	22.9	16.0	43.0	37.2	24.1	16.9
Family Histories	1878–82	43.6	35.9	22.7	15.8	41.1	35.6	24.4	17.5
Billings/Massachusetts	1878–82	43.5	36.4	22.5	16.0	43.4	37.3	23.9	17.3
Billings/New Jersey	1880	43.3	36.3	22.3	16.1	44.5	37.8	23.7	16.9
Haines	1880	38.7	31.9	18.3	11.7	39.3	32.7	18.9	12.1
Glover	1901	43.2	36.1	21.9	15.0	45.0	37.8	23.2	16.2
Family Histories Relevant Cohort Values		46.5	38.7	22.4	15.3	42.7	38.4	22.9	16.8

Notes: e_i is life expectation at age i. In the comparison with Glover, cohort values have been taken from cohort life tables. For example, e_{50} = 22.4 is taken from the life table for males born between 1850 and 1859. If life expectations are increasing through time, cohort values will exceed period values.

Sources: See footnotes of text. For Billings see the 1880 census, vol. 12.

Family histories also appear to be quite representative of the population for the period following the Civil War. The comparison of Billings's life tables for whites in Massachusetts and New Jersey around 1880 with the family histories is also reassuring. The family histories yield lower life expectation for women at younger ages, but fit closely at other ages. The family history expectations for males in the same period used by Billings, 1878 to 1882, deviate from his calculations by less than 5 percent. James Glover's life table for 1901 is based on the original death registration states concentrated in the Northeast. In Table 9.5, cohort estimates drawn from the relevant birth years are compared with Glover's period estimates. For example, the e_{20} value for males of 46.5 years is the value for the 1880 cohort while the e_{50} value of 22.4 years is the value for the 1850s birth cohort. The estimates are quite close, especially for the older ages of fifty and sixty where the cohort value and the period value should not be significantly different.

There are other comparisons that do not corroborate the genealogical findings as clearly. For example, the Haines estimates for the white population for 1850 and 1880 are uniformly and significantly lower than the family history estimates. The differences are partially explained by the lower life expectation of immigrants, who are not represented in the family histories but are included in the Haines data set. All told, however, the comparisons of family history data with other possible sources are reassuring. The differences between the family history estimates and estimates from other sources are often accounted for by the differences in the group being studied (all whites vs. native whites or Massachusetts vs. the United States). The difference between the results from the family histories and other estimates is never large enough to require acceptance or rejection of one source or the other.

The three samples based on genealogical records consistently find a decline in life expectation in the antebellum period. Fogel used earlier data drawn from a different sample of family histories and found that cohort life expectation measured by e_{10} declined from the late eighteenth century to the mid-nineteenth century. He estimated a twenty-five-year moving average of e_{10} that peaked for cohorts born around 1790 and hit a trough in 1860.[31] Kunze argued that mortality declined in the period from 1835 to 1860.[32] The sample used by Kunze was not drawn from family histories. Rather, it was taken from genealogical records known as family group sheets that have been filed in the LDS Genealogical Library. These records, each of which contains demographic information on a single family, have been compiled by members of the Latter-Day Saints Church who have searched the same basic record sources used by compilers of family histories. The family history sample reported in Tables 9.2–9.4 yields somewhat higher period life expectation in the first fifteen years of the nineteenth century than Kunze's sample, but very close correspondence thereafter even though Kunze smoothed his results using model life tables.

Taken together, then, evidence from these three family history sources supports the same pattern—decline in period life expectation in the antebellum period, followed by sporadic improvement for at least the two decades after the war, then more consistent improvement. The antebellum decline was especially severe in the two decades before the Civil War, but there was added mortality because of the Civil War. This period pattern of mortality is consistent with cohort life expectations peaking sometime around 1800, containing low values in the 1820s and 1830s, and having the greatest improvement for cohorts whose adult mortality experience was entirely within the twentieth century.

9.4 Regional Variations in Mortality

Studies of colonial mortality present a picture of considerable regional variation in adult mortality, with New Englanders enjoying life expectations well above those for individuals living in the Chesapeake and further south.[33]

31. Fogel, "Nutrition and the Decline in Mortality since 1700," p. 465. Because Fogel used a twenty-five-year moving average and Table 9.2 is simply ten-year cohorts without smoothing, the timing of the peaks and troughs will be somewhat different.

32. Kunze, "The Effects of Age Composition and Changes in Vital Rates," chap. 4. He reports period estimates rather than cohort values. The downturn will come later in the period values as compared with the cohorts.

33. Vinovskis, *Fertility in Massachusetts;* Levy, "The Economic Demography of the Colonial South"; Levy, "The Life Expectancies of Colonial Maryland Legislators"; Greven, "Historical Demography and Colonial America"; Smith, "The Demographic History of Colonial New England"; Demos, "Notes on Life in Plymouth"; Norton, "Population Growth in Colonial America";

There is evidence of the beginning of convergence in adult mortality rates during the colonial period. At age twenty, the life expectation for both men and women appears to have been more than 50 percent higher in New England than the Chesapeake in the seventeenth century. For the early eighteenth century, a comparison of the estimates of Phillip Greven, James Somerville, and Susan Norton for New England with Daniel Levy's for Maryland and South Carolina suggests that the New England advantage had fallen to about 25 percent. The New England studies generally show a slight fall in life expectancy between the seventeenth and eighteenth century, whereas Levy finds substantial improvement in life expectancy in Maryland.[34]

Table 9.6, which gives life expectations by region of residence at death, shows less regional variation in adult mortality in the nineteenth century than the colonial period.[35] No regional value differs from the national mean by more than 12 percent. Comparisons by region also reveal a diminishing southern disadvantage in life expectancy. There was sufficient relative improvement in the South Atlantic region to the point that life expectations for individuals born between 1850–69 who died in the region were actually above the national averages. Furthermore, life expectations of the 1850–69 cohort who died in the South Central region compare favorably with those of the North Central region.

The westward migration from the Atlantic regions to the central regions presents a problem in interpreting Table 9.6. The difficulty is illustrated by the high life expectation for individuals born before 1820 who died in the North Central and South Central regions. The majority of these individuals, born in the late eighteenth or early nineteenth century, were migrants.

Migrants should be treated separately for they generally are a self-selected group of stronger, healthier, or more robust individuals compared to the population from which they came. Alternatively they may experience higher mortality rates because of the stress of migration and migrants' exposure to two different disease environments. In addition to biological factors, migrants are likely to live longer on average than non-migrants simply because the cumulative probability of migration increases with age. That is, persons living long enough to migrate will, on average, have a longer life expectation than non-migrants. Indeed, if migration rates were extraordinarily high, the sending

---

Somerville, "A Demographic Profile of the Salem Family"; Walsh and Menard, "Death in the Chesapeake"; Smith, "Mortality and Family in Colonial Chesapeake"; and Rutman and Rutman, *A Place in Time*.

34. Compare Levy, "The Economic Demography of the Colonial South" and "The Life Expectancies of Colonial Maryland Legislators" with Greven, "Historical Demography and Colonial America," Smith, "The Demographic History of Colonial New England," Demos, "Notes on Life in Plymouth," Norton, "Population Growth in Colonial America," and Somerville, "A Demographic Profile of the Salem Family."

35. The colonial comparisons are for small populations or communities while the regional comparisons in Table 9.6 are for a more disperse population. Therefore, one might expect more variance in the colonial estimates.

Table 9.6 **Regional Variations in Life Expectation by Sex and Region of Death**

	Northeast		South Atlantic		North Central		South Central	
	Male	Female	Male	Female	Male	Female	Male	Female
Life Expectation at Age 20 by Birth Years:								
1760–99								
N(20)	276	151	89	47	97	44	52	26
e(20)	43.3	45.8	38.9	40.4	46.8	43.1	46.4	43.7
1800–1819								
N(20)	134	115	83	47	149	71	44	33
e(20)	43.1	43.5	40.9	38.1	46.1	43.7	40.1	42.5
1820–49								
N(20)	212	168	146	117	399	296	130	112
e(20)	41.3	44.4	38.1	39.8	42.4	39.9	41.3	35.4
1850–69								
N(20)	94	79	137	110	303	222	134	108
e(20)	47.2	40.9	44.4	46.6	42.2	40.7	42.2	43.5
Life Expectation at Later Ages by Birth Years:								
1760–99								
e(30)	36.1	39.1	33.2	34.9	38.1	35.9	37.6	36.6
e(40)	28.8	31.5	26.6	29.6	29.6	27.3	29.8	27.2
1800–1819								
e(30)	36.4	38.5	33.0	33.5	37.5	35.4	33.3	33.0
e(40)	29.5	31.6	26.0	30.9	29.4	26.7	26.3	23.0
1820–49								
e(30)	34.9	37.9	32.0	35.4	36.1	34.9	35.4	30.4
e(40)	27.1	31.0	28.0	30.5	29.7	29.5	30.4	27.3
1850–69								
e(30)	38.7	37.4	36.4	39.2	35.8	35.4	33.5	38.0
e(40)	30.5	30.7	31.2	32.6	30.1	30.3	27.3	30.2

Notes: N(20) is the sample size at age 20; *e*(20) is life expectation at age 20 and so on.
Source: Family History Sample.

region would have very low life expectations in contrast to the very high life expectancy in the receiving region. This would be especially true for life expectations at birth and at younger ages. After the age by which most migration had occurred, the differences between migrants and non-migrants would tend to reflect differences in true risks of mortality rather than measurement bias.

There is another bias that could persist even in measurement of regional life expectation at older ages. When migration is predominantly westward, the greater life expectation of individuals born in the eighteenth century and dying in the central regions was, in part, a reflection of the later settlement dates for most of the central regions.[36] Suppose someone born in Massachusetts in 1780

36. States are listed according to the decade in which they first experienced very rapid population growth (the year of statehood is given in parentheses): *1790s*, Tennessee (1796); *1800s*, Ohio (1803); *1810s*, Indiana (1816), Louisiana (1812); *1820s*, Alabama (1819), Illinois (1818), Missouri (1821); *1830s*, Arkansas (1836), Michigan (1837), Mississippi (1817), Texas (1845); *1840s*, Iowa (1846), Wisconsin (1848); *1850s*, Minnesota (1858); and *1860s*, Kansas (1861), Nebraska (1867).

died in Minnesota. Such a person is likely to have migrated at an old age since Minnesota had only 6,000 inhabitants in 1850 but more than 170,000 by 1860. Obviously, migration distorts the regional comparisons of Table 9.6 in several ways.

Regional life tables based on years of exposure in each region would be ideal. Dates of migration would be needed to create such regional life tables, but migration in the family histories is ordinarily inferred from the place information given on births, deaths, and marriages of individuals and their children. This inference of date of migration would impart a bias to life expectation in one of the two regions. Consider an individual born in Virginia in 1800, who migrated to Mississippi in 1810 (but this date is unknown), married in Mississippi in 1822, and died in Mississippi in 1858. One could reasonably allocate the last thirty-six years of life to the South Central region, but the allocation of the first twenty-two years of life between the South Atlantic and South Central regions would be arbitrary without further information. Allocation of all twenty-two years to the South Atlantic would lead to an overestimate of life expectation there and an underestimate of life expectancy in the South Central region. Some sharing of the twenty-two years of exposure would certainly be a reasonable, though arbitrary, procedure. The approach taken here, for simplicity and because of small regional samples, is to separate migrants from non-migrants, where non-migrants are defined as those who live and die in the same region and migrants are those who die in a region other than their birth region.

9.4.1 Regional Life Expectations of Non-migrants

Table 9.7 reports regional mortality relative to the national average. Comparisons on both axes seem useful—North compared with South and the newly settled West with the East. North-South comparisons of non-migrant males show diminishing excess mortality in the South. Comparisons of the South Atlantic with the Northeast and the South Central with the North Central reveal that life expectation for southern males was lower for all periods with the exception of e_{40} in 1820–49 and 1850–69. The largest differences were for the cohorts born in the eighteenth century. For those males born between 1850 and 1869, excess mortality in the South Atlantic region compared with that of the Northeast was negligible, but the differences between the two central regions still persisted.

The North-South comparisons for females do not favor the North as completely. Life expectation in the South Atlantic region was higher than in the Northeast for e_{40} in 1820–49 and at all ages in 1850–69. Life expectation in the South Central region exceeded that of the North Central for e_{20} and e_{30} in 1800–1819 and 1850–69. It would seem that excess mortality for females living in the South had disappeared by mid-century.

The East-West comparisons can be made only for those born in the nineteenth century. For males, the differences were not often large and tended to favor the East in 1800–1819 and 1850–69 and the West during the 1820–49

Table 9.7 **Regional Indices of Life Expectation for Non-migrants (national *e*(*i*) = 100)**

	Males				Females			
Birth Years	Northeast	North Central	South Atlantic	South Central	Northeast	North Central	South Atlantic	South Central
1760–99								
e(20)	100	n.a.	89	n.a.	104	n.a.	91	n.a.
e(30)	100	n.a.	90	n.a.	104	n.a.	91	n.a.
e(40)	100	n.a.	92	n.a.	105	n.a.	99	n.a.
1800–1819								
e(20)	100	102	94	91	102	102	89	106
e(30)	102	99	92	91	106	93	92	97
e(40)	105	98	92	91	108	93	105	86
1820–49								
e(20)	100	101	95	100	109	100	103	86
e(30)	100	103	92	99	108	99	103	86
e(40)	94	104	97	104	104	100	106	95
1850–69								
e(20)	110	99	103	93	92	96	111	103
e(30)	108	101	103	88	99	96	106	103
e(40)	102	103	105	88	99	100	107	99

n.a. = Less than twenty observations.
Source: Family History Sample.

downturn in life expectancy. For females, life expectations in the East tended to be higher with a few exceptions.

9.4.2 Life Expectations of Migrants

Table 9.8 compares the life expectations of migrants with non-migrants in the sending region (the region of birth for the migrant) and the receiving region (the death region of the migrant). Although sample sizes are small, some patterns are revealed. At age twenty, life expectations were almost always higher for the migrant (16 out of 20 instances). This result is simply a reflection of the biases discussed above. By age forty, migrants were about as likely (9 out of 20 instances) to have a lower life expectation than non-migrants. Since the biases appear to favor longer observed life expectation for migrants, any value below 100 in the table suggests that migrants were facing adverse mortality conditions.

For persons born during the years 1760 to 1799, migrants lived longer than non-migrants who stayed along the Atlantic seaboard. The later settlement of the North Central and South Central regions combined with the bias for older deaths of migrants outweighs any harsh frontier conditions, with the exception of e_{40} for women who migrated from the South Atlantic to the South Central region. For all three birth periods, male migrants tended to live longer than non-migrants from the sending regions, but the advantage declined at

Table 9.8 The Relative Life Expectations of Migrants by Sending and Receiving Regions

	Sending Regions				Receiving Regions			
	Northeast		South Atlantic		North Central		South Central	
Birth Years	Males (1)	Females (2)	Males (3)	Females (4)	Males (5)	Females (6)	Males (7)	Females (8)
1760–99								
e(20)	110	122	125	112	n.a.	n.a.	n.a.	n.a.
e(30)	104	123	117	113	n.a.	n.a.	n.a.	n.a.
e(40)	100	121	110	96	n.a.	n.a.	n.a.	n.a.
1800–1819								
e(20)	104	99	103	108	105	100	107	91
e(30)	104	109	98	98	108	113	100	93
e(40)	101	97	95	74	108	103	96	90
1820–49								
e(20)	108	108	119	77	106	103	113	89
e(30)	108	117	118	77	99	104	110	92
e(40)	105	108	111	73	96	97	104	81

Notes: Column (1) is the ratio (× 100) of life expectation for migrants from the Northeast to the North Central region to that of non-migrants of the Northeast. Columns (2), (3), and (4) are computed similarly. Column (5) is the simple mean of migrants from either Northeast or South to the North Central Region divided by the life expectation of non-migrants of the North Central region. The result is multiplied by 100. Column (6) is computed similarly. Column (7) is the ratio (× 100) of the life expectation of migrants to the South Central region to non-migrants of the South Central region. Column (8) is computed similarly. n.a. = Less than twenty observations.
Source: Family History Sample.

older ages. The advantage for e_{20} was about 10 percent, for e_{30} about 8 percent, and for e_{40} about 4 percent. Female migrants from the Northeast to the North Central region also tended to live longer than non-migrants. However, women who migrated from the South Atlantic region to the South Central region in the antebellum period had a much lower life expectation than their non-migrant counterparts. Migration evidently had a different effect on men and women.

The comparison between migrants and non-migrants of the receiving region is also of interest because migrants encountered a new disease environment.[37] Male migrants lived longer than their non-migrant neighbors, although the advantage was not large and largely disappeared by age forty. Such was not the case for female migrants who tended to have lower life expectations than the non-migrant women in the settlement region. The comparisons of migrants with non-migrants in both the sending and receiving regions suggest that migration extracted a small mortality cost for women and an even smaller

37. The bias in measurement exists for the receiving region just as it does for the sending region. If the mean age of migration were 30, then e_{20} for the migrants would be biased upward.

cost for men. The mortality cost of migration was evidently higher in the South than the North.

9.5 Sex Differentials in Mortality

Tables 9.2 and 9.4 indicate that sex differentials in mortality were not large before the twentieth century. Trends and levels were similar for males and females at age twenty, with women's life expectancy lower than men's for cohorts born between 1810 and 1830 and slightly higher after 1870. Women had a higher life expectation at age fifty, although the gap was small until after the Civil War. Thus, the lower life expectation in early adulthood for women was the result of the higher probability women faced of dying during their child-bearing years. The lack of a significant positive differential or the existence, at times, of a lower life expectation for women differs from the twentieth-century experience in developed economies where women live longer than men, although women in some poorer countries experience higher mortality.[38] Almost all studies document a positive relationship between the magnitude of the excess mortality of men and the level of life expectation.[39] That is, the gap between the life expectation of women and that of men widens as the overall level of life expectancy improves.

Colonial and other antebellum studies that include life expectations for women are consistent with the view that excess mortality of males was not apparent until after the Civil War. The studies of Greven, Demos, and Rutman

38. Samuel Preston, *Mortality Patterns in National Populations* (New York, 1976), finds that the increasing sex differential from cardiovascular diseases accounts for over 80 percent of the increase in the differential in the twentieth century. See also Ingrid Waldron, "What Do We know about Causes of Sex Differences in Mortality?: A Review of the Literature," *Population Bulletin of the United Nations,* No. 18 (1986). Many of the causes she cites should have been important in earlier times. Higher consumption of tobacco and alcohol by men probably extends back into the earlier centuries. However, the mortality impact of this consumption may be greater in the twentieth century. She suggests that ischaemic heart disease has a strong male bias, in part because female sex hormones reduce the risk of heart disease for women. Excess female mortality is associated with maternal mortality, obviously, and tuberculosis. Excess male mortality from accidents was probably not as important in the nineteenth century as in the twentieth century. Alan D. Lopez, "The Sex Mortality Differential in Developed Countries," in *Sex Differentials in Mortality: Trends, Determinants and Consequences,* Alan D. Lopez and Lado T. Ruzicka, eds., Miscellaneous Series no. 4, Department of Demography (Canberra, 1983), pp. 53–120, points to the widening differential indicating that most of the differential is due to trends after age forty-five. He finds that "this situation has arisen due to a widening disparity in death rates from the cardiovascular diseases, cancers, and motor vehicle accidents and the virtual elimination of maternal deaths for women.

39. Larry Heligman, "Patterns of Sex Differentials in Mortality in Less Developed Countries," and Jacques Vallin, "Sex Patterns of Mortality," in *Sex Differentials in Mortality: Trends, Determinants and Consequences,* Alan D. Lopez and Lado T. Ruzicka, eds., Miscellaneous Series no. 4, Department of Demography (Canberra, 1983); M. A. El-Badry,, "Higher Female than Male Mortality in Some Countries of South Asia: A Digest," *American Statistical Association Journal* (Dec. 1969), pp. 1234–44; Amartya Sen and Sunil Sengupta, "Malnutrition of Rural Children and the Sex Bias," *Economic and Political Weekly,* 18 (May 1983), pp. 855–64.

and Rutman found excess female mortality in the seventeenth century. But, in the eighteenth and early nineteenth centuries, there was no consistent sex differential in mortality. In Massachusetts, Greven and Somerville find a slight differential favoring females while Norton finds excess female mortality in Ipswich. Vinovskis finds excess mortality for females in 1840–42 and 1859–61 in Massachusetts, excess mortality for males in other years. Meech estimates a lower life expectation for females aged twenty or thirty compared with males and virtually the same expectation for both sexes at age fifty. Jacobson, on the other hand, estimates a slightly higher expectation at age twenty for females.[40] Taken together, the evidence from family histories and other studies is consistent with similar life expectation for males and females at early adulthood until the latter part of the nineteenth century.

The absence of a sex differential in mortality is supported by the sex ratios [(males/females) × 100] found in census summaries. Table 9.9 reports these ratios for the white population and the native-born white population. Because at birth there are slightly more males than females, it is only superior life expectancy of females that shifts the sex ratio below 100. The sex ratio for native-born whites of all ages remained above 100 from 1850 to 1940. This finding supports the view that life expectations for men and women were nearly equal. The sex ratio for individuals ages 20 to 49 first falls below 100 in 1930.[41] Before 1840, the sex ratio for all whites is near that of native-born whites due to the small immigration flow. From 1800 to 1840, the sex ratio for whites was above 100 except for groups older than seventy. Assuming census data provide reasonably accurate estimates of the sex ratios, there could not have been significant excess male mortality in the nineteenth century.[42] Both the direct evidence from the family history sample and other samples and the indirect evidence from the census sex ratios indicate that the systematic mortality sex differential in favor of females is primarily a twentieth-century phenomenon.

The regional breakdowns display an interesting pattern of sex differentials in mortality. In the more settled eastern regions, female life expectation tended to be higher than male life expectation. This is true for the South Atlantic region in all periods and all life expectations except e_{20} for the 1800–1819 cohort. For the Northeast, female life expectation is higher until the last

40. Greven, "Historical Demography and Colonial America"; Demos, "Notes on the Life of Plymouth"; and Rutman and Rutman, *A Place in Time;* Norton, "Population Growth in Colonial America"; Somerville, "A Demographic Profile of the Salem Family"; Vinovskis, "Mortality Trends in Massachusetts"; Meech, *Systems and Tables of Life Insurance;* Jacobson, "Expectation of Life in the United States in 1850."

41. The sharp drop in the sex ratio in 1870 is presumably due to the differential effect of the Civil War on mortality of males and females.

42. Ansley Coale and Melvin Zelnick, *New Estimates of Fertility and Population in the United States: A Study of Annual White Births from 1855 to 1960 and of Completeness of Enumeration in the Censuses from 1880 to 1960* (Princeton, 1963), suggest that there is a differential undercount in the census that would bias the sex ratio slightly upward. See pp. 179–82.

Table 9.9 **Long-term Change in the Sex Ratio**

Census Year	All Whites								Native Whites			
	All Ages	25–44	20–49	≥45	50–64	50–69	≥65	≥70	All Ages	20–49	50–64	≥65
1790	103.8											
1800	105.0	104.8		105.8								
1810	103.9	105.1		107.8								
1820	103.3	104.0		107.0								
1830	103.1		104.7			102.7		96.7				
1840	104.5		107.5			102.2		96.9				
1850		105.2				110.0		106.6	96.5			
1860	105.3	109.3				109.8		95.5	103.7			
1870	102.8		101.8		115.3		101.1		100.6	96.7	109.2	98.5
1880	104.0		105.1		111.6		101.5		102.1	101.5	106.1	98.7
1890	105.2		108.2		107.6		104.3		102.7	103.4	103.8	100.1
1900	104.7		107.5		108.2		101.8		102.6	103.6	104.6	98.7
1910	106.5		109.8		113.7		100.6		102.6	102.2	110.4	98.3
1920	104.3		105.3		112.2		100.6		101.7	100.4	108.0	99.0
1930	102.9		102.4		107.7		100.2		101.1	99.4	104.5	97.5
1940	101.2		99.7		105.3		95.0		100.2	99.1	99.9	92.0
1950	99.0		97.3		99.9		89.1		98.8	97.7	97.1	85.6

Source: U.S. Bureau of the Census, *Historical Statistics of the United States from Colonial Times to 1970* (Washington, D.C., 1975).

period (1850–69) when male life expectation is significantly higher.[43] For those living to the west, however, life expectation for men was quite often higher than for women, especially for the cohorts born between 1800 and 1849. Perhaps migration or living in less densely settled regions had a stronger adverse effect on women than men. It is also possible that male, but not female, migrants were self-selected by their vigor and health.

The cohorts born between about 1770 and 1850 contained the men and women who settled most of the central regions and brought the areas into economic and social maturity. It is within these cohorts that the mortality differential favored men most often. For cohorts born after the Civil War, the mortality differential shifted in favor of women and increased substantially in the twentieth century.

9.6 Summary of Mortality Trends

The results of the small sample from family histories presented here raise interesting questions and provide a point of departure for future studies of mortality before 1900. Caveats have been included in nearly every paragraph because of small sample sizes and the newness of family histories as a data source for the study of mortality. Nevertheless, the consistencies within the family history samples as well as comparisons with other sources are encouraging.

The results may be summarized as follows:

1. Adult life expectation for male and female cohorts declined in the antebellum period and rose sporadically after the Civil War to leave the nineteenth century as a whole with little overall improvement in mortality. The decline in antebellum life expectation reported here confirms the earlier findings of Fogel and Kunze, also based on genealogical sources.
2. The antebellum downturn in cohort life expectation was generated largely by period effects concentrated in the two decades before the war and the broad-ranging impact of the war period. But, the rebound in life expectation after this period was slow and sporadic.
3. The convergence of regional life expectations started during the colonial period and continued into the nineteenth century. Cohorts born in the South at mid-nineteenth century did not have significantly lower life expectations than those born in the North. In fact, female life expectation by 1860 was highest in the South Atlantic region.
4. Migrants generally lived longer than non-migrants, but most of the differential appears to be attributable to measurement bias rather than biological

43. I have no explanation for this anomaly except to note the e_{20} is exceptionally high for males and may be a statistical artifact. The values for e_{30} are closer and the expectations at age forty are equal.

factors. Migration, when measurement bias is controlled, may have increased mortality.

5. Female life expectancy was, at times, lower than that of males at early ages, but was consistently higher after age fifty. Excess female mortality appears to be associated with, but not limited to, the migration and settlement of areas to the west.

9.7 Historical Implications

There is, perhaps, a presumption that the economic growth which increased aggregate economic activity and appears to have increased the average standard of living substantially must also have increased life expectancy over the long run. Data are too fragmentary for the period from 1770 to 1839 to construct firm estimates of GNP and GNP per capita, but the available evidence suggests the economy was growing in both per capita and aggregate terms. More conclusive data from 1839 to 1860 indicate that GNP was growing at a vigorous rate of 4.8 percent and that GNP per capita advanced at an annual rate of 1.7 percent, at a time when the economy was also absorbing larger immigration flows.[44] Agricultural production grew rapidly as new land was brought into cultivation. It is not a large step to assume that food supplies were growing and improving nutrition and nutritional status which, in turn, reduced mortality and morbidity. The evidence presented here suggests that an optimistic assessment of the effects of antebellum economic growth on mortality is not accurate. The puzzle raised by Fogel of rapid growth in output per capita at the same time that height and life expectancy were declining is reinforced by the results presented here.[45] This puzzle still awaits successful resolution.

Yasuba suggested that industrialization and urbanization during the period in question generated the decline in life expectancy.[46] He also cited similar cycles in England, France, Sweden, and Norway. Urbanization would most certainly retard an upward trend in life expectancy. The urban-rural differential noted in colonial Massachusetts persisted well into the twentieth century. At the turn of the century, Glover estimated e_{20} to be 46.0 years for white males and 46.1 for white females in rural areas compared with 39.1 and 43.5 for their counterparts in cities.[47] Urbanization moved people from lower to higher mortality regimes, exacting a price for the increased economic opportunity of the city. Stephen Kunitz, who emphasized the effects of urbanization

44. Stanley L. Engerman and Robert E. Gallman, "U.S. Economic Growth, 1783–1860," in *Research in Economic History,* Paul Uselding, ed., vol. 8, (Greenwich, 1983), pp. 1–46.

45. Fogel, "Nutrition and the Decline in Mortality since 1700," and *Without Consent or Contract: The Rise and Fall of American Slavery* (New York, 1989), pp. 354–62.

46. Yasuba, *Birth Rates of the White Population*, pp. 86–96.

47. James W. Glover, *United States Life Tables: 1890, 1901, 1910, and 1901–1910* (Washington, D.C., 1921), pp. 104–17. These estimates include foreign born, but the differences for nativity are smaller than the urban-rural differences.

in the antebellum period, also pointed to the continuing importance of diseases such as malaria and dysentery that do not confer lifelong immunity.[48] The large increase in immigration from Ireland and Germany during the 1840s and 1850s, as well as the steady migration westward could have increased the exposure of the population to these endemic diseases. Furthermore, harsher conditions and lower population densities in the central regions, settled during the antebellum period, could well have increased infant and maternal mortality.

Fogel, in a series of papers, has also emphasized the importance of nutritional status as an explanation for changes in morbidity and mortality, while Komlos has emphasized reductions in per capita food supplies as the source of decline in heights in the antebellum period.[49] The pattern of cohort life expectation appears to coincide roughly with the recently discovered cycle in stature for the period. Fogel places the start of the downturn in heights with males born around 1830.[50] Komlos places the decline in the heights of West Point cadets slightly earlier. Life expectations for males in Table 9.4 show a downturn starting in the 1820s and continuing for cohorts born in the next two decades, although the sample is too small to pinpoint precise years of the decline.[51]

Explanations of the decline in life expectation for antebellum cohorts should take account of the sharp increase in period mortality between 1840 and 1865. Explanations that rely on a lifelong cohort effect would not be consistent with this sharp period effect. For example, urbanization accelerates after the Civil War when life expectation is also increasing. On the surface,

48. Stephen J. Kunitz, "Mortality Change in American, 1620–1920," *Human Biology*, 56 (Sept. 1984), pp. 559–82.

49. Robert W. Fogel, "Second Thoughts on the European Escape from Hunger: Famines, Price Elasticities, Entitlements, Chronic Malnutrition and Mortality Rates," NBER-DAE Working Paper no. 1 (May 1989); Fogel, "The Conquest of High Mortality and Hunger in Europe and American: Timing and Mechanisms," NBER-DAE Working Paper no. 16 (Sept. 1990); John Komlos, "The Height and Weight of West Point Cadets: Dietary Change in Antebellum America," *Journal of Economic History*, 47 (Dec. 1987), pp. 897–927.

50. Fogel, "Nutrition and the Decline of Mortality since 1700." See also Robert A. Margo and Richard H. Steckel, "Heights of Native-Born Whites during the Antebellum Period," *Journal of Economic History*, 43 (Mar. 1983), pp. 167–74.

51. The time pattern between the height decline and the decline in life expectation could vary. If the height decline is simply a result of a drop in food consumption as a child with no change in the disease environment, then one might expect the downturn in life expectation to occur simultaneously with the downturn in heights, with mortality increases at every age due to the lower nutritional status caused by lower food consumption. However, a decline in heights might be the product of an interaction between marginal diet and an increased level of disease during childhood and adolescence. See Nevin Scrimshaw, Carl E. Taylor, and John E. Gordon, *Interactions of Nutrition and Infection* (Geneva, 1968). If such were the case, the decline in life expectation might precede the decline in heights because of the effect of the increased level of disease on adults whose height had not been affected by disease. The fact that heights seem to reach their lowest point for individuals born in the 1850s or even 1860s, while adult life expectations reached their lowest ebb in the 1820s or 1830s, supports the view that the height decline was, in part, due to an increase in infectious disease rates. Komlos, "The Height and Weight of West Point Cadets," argues against an increase in infectious disease as an explanation for the observed height decline.

the large period effect on mortality between 1840 and 1865 appears to be consistent with a change in the disease environment, starting as early as the 1820s but reaching a peak in the 1840s and 1850s, that affected both height and life expectation.

There is no definitive evidence, at present, on the causes of antebellum decline in stature or life expectancy. The explanation will probably be found in effects and interactions of nutritional status, urbanization, immigration, and westward expansion. A viable explanation must also account for the ineffectiveness of general economic growth to produce increasing life expectation. The specific contributions of different elements to the decline in life expectation will require extensive analysis with large data sets. Family histories, especially when combined with census data for households and counties, should be a significant resource in the search for causes.

Whatever the causes, it appears that the middle of the nineteenth century had its darker side. The period from 1840 to 1860, praised by economic historians as a period of high economic growth, was not the best of times for native-born whites. They faced the startling prospect of significantly higher mortality rates than their parents. These decades were then followed by a war that took the lives of many soldiers and continued the pattern of high mortality rates for civilians. Perhaps economic historians and historical demographers should look more closely at these middle years, as they represent an important and costly episode in American social history.

10 Toward an Anthropometric History of African-Americans

The Case of the Free Blacks in Antebellum Maryland

John Komlos

Economic historians have been increasingly interested in the interaction between economic and biological processes, particularly as it relates to economic development.[1] Indicators such as height, weight, body-mass, age at menarche, and morbidity are all related to nutritional status and consequently to demographic variables such as life expectancy, with a feedback effect on the economy through their impact on labor productivity.[2] Within this context, the importance of the anthropometric history of African-Americans is accentuated by the debate over their material standard of living, especially their food consumption while in bondage. Calculations based on agricultural censuses indicate that the calorie and protein content of the slave diet was adequate on average. For example, slaves are said to have consumed circa 1,000

The author is greatly indebted to Peter Coclanis, Timothy Cuff, Seymour Drescher, Stanley Engerman, Claudia Goldin, Richard Steckel, and James Tanner for commenting on the manuscript. Data collection was supported in part by a grant from the University of Pittsburgh's Office of Research and Development and was processed by Philip Sidel of the university's Social Science Computer Research Institute.

1. The notion of using heights to gain insights into the biological maturation of human beings and its socio-economic implications was stimulated by the debate over the diet, health, and age at menarche of American slaves. For early papers see James Trussell and Richard H. Steckel, "The Age of Slaves at Menarche and Their First Birth," *Journal of Interdisciplinary History,* 8 (Winter 1978), pp. 477–505; Richard H. Steckel, "Slave Height Profiles from Coastwise Manifests," *Explorations in Economic History,* 16 (Oct. 1979), pp. 363–80. For a recollection of the inception of the nutrition project see "An interview with Robert W. Fogel," *The Newsletter of The Cliometric Society,* 5 (July 1990), p. 3ff.

2. Robert W. Fogel, "Nutrition and the Decline in Mortality since 1700: Some Preliminary Findings," in Stanley L. Engerman and Robert E. Gallman, eds., *Long-Term Factors in American Economic Growth* (Chicago, 1986), pp. 439–555; Roderick Floud, Kenneth Wachter, and Annabel Gregory, *Height, Health and History: Nutritional Status in the United Kingdom, 1750–1980* (Cambridge, 1990). For a theory of anthropometric history see John Komlos, *Nutrition and Economic Development in the Eighteenth-Century Habsburg Monarchy: An Anthropometric History* (Princeton, 1989), chap. 1.

calories more daily than European peasants.[3] The disadvantage of these estimates is that they cannot be decomposed by sex and by age, and, moreover, do not reveal temporal changes.

Anthropometric indexes were developed to overcome the limitations of these approaches. The method has become standard in assessing nutritional adequacy in third-world countries.[4] Several studies have explored the age-by-height profile of slaves to quantify their nutritional status and material well-being using two major sources of data, slave manifests and Civil War muster rolls.[5] The system of manifests was designed to discourage smuggling after the prohibition of slave imports in 1807. These shipping documents included physical descriptions used to identify slaves transported along the coast. The muster rolls pertain to black soldiers in the Union Army in the early 1860s. Both sources provide valuable information on the physical characteristics of African-Americans, but both have limitations.

Slaves, whose heights appear on the manifests, were transported in inter-regional trade, and thus they may not be representative of all slaves. Similarly, the military source contains information only on soldiers. Because it excludes females and youths, it cannot corroborate some of the results obtained from the manifest sample. Even with regard to males, the Civil War sample has no information on birth cohorts of the early nineteenth century and, consequently, provides only a limited trend in slave stature.[6] Moreover, the trend

3. On slave consumption see Robert W. Fogel and Stanley L. Engerman, *Time on the Cross: The Economics of American Negro Slavery* (Boston, 1974), p. 109; and for corroboration see Roger Ransom and Richard Sutch, *One Kind of Freedom: The Economic Consequences of Emancipation* (Cambridge, 1977), p. 244; for consumption of European peasants see Komlos, *Nutrition and Economic Development,* p. 101. The extent to which the diet was adequate in terms of vitamins and minerals, given the genetic make-up of slaves, is more controversial. See, for instance, Kenneth F. Kiple, "A Survey of Recent Literature on the Biological Past of the Black," *Social Science History,* 10 (Winter 1986), pp. 343–68.

4. Phyllis B. Eveleth and James M. Tanner, *Worldwide Variation in Human Growth* (2d edn., Cambridge, 1990).

5. Stanley Engerman, "The Height of U.S. Slaves," *Local Population Studies,* 16 (Spring 1976), pp. 45–50; Robert W. Fogel, Stanley L. Engerman, James Trussell, Roderick Floud, Clayne L. Pope, and Larry T. Wimmer, "The Economics of Mortality in North America, 1650–1910: A Description of a Research Project," *Historical Methods,* 11 (Spring 1978), pp. 75–108; Robert Margo and Richard H. Steckel, "The Heights of American Slaves: New Evidence on Slave Nutrition and Health," *Social Science History,* 6 (Fall 192), pp. 516–38; Richard H. Steckel, "A Peculiar Population: The Nutrition, Health, and Mortality of American Slaves from Childhood to Maturity," *Journal of Economic History,* 46 (Sept. 1986), pp. 721–41; Richard H. Steckel, "Birth Weights and Infant Mortality among American Slaves," *Explorations in Economic History,* 23 (Apr. 1986), pp. 173–98; Richard H. Steckel, "Growth Depression and Recovery: The Remarkable Case of American Slaves," *Annals of Human Biology,* 14 (Mar.–Apr. 1987), pp. 111–32; Robert W. Fogel, *Without Consent or Contract: The Rise and Fall of American Slavery* (New York, 1989), pp. 138–47.

6. In addition, the Civil War sample is not representative of the whole South because 43 percent of the black recruits were born in Tennessee and Kentucky; see Margo and Steckel, "The Heights of American Slaves." These two states had the tallest white men in the United States at that time. Therefore, the nutritional status of the black population born in the Upper South could have been above average.

obtained from the military sample differs from that of slaves shipped in interregional trade.

The trend for African-Americans obtained from Civil War military records essentially follows that of the whites. The results of the manifest sample, however, are more difficult to interpret. An early result actually resembled the one obtained from white soldiers.[7] Subsequent estimates, however, do not show a downward tendency prior to the Civil War.[8] If anything, they show the opposite.[9] The result is suspect, however, because African-born slaves, who were shorter than American-born slaves, might have been included in the early part of the sample, and the positive trend in height could be indicative of their changing share in the sample, instead of an improvement in nutritional status.

These limitations notwithstanding, major findings have emerged from the anthropometric evidence. The stature of slaves in nineteenth-century America indicates that they were well nourished as young adults, although not as children. In spite of their early nutritional deprivation, male slaves reached a terminal height exceeding 67 inches—within an inch of northern-born whites and well above contemporary African and European norms. In fact, their physical stature was closer to that of European aristocrats than to that of peasants.[10]

The evidence on slave children's nutritional status is more controversial than that on adults. Data in the manifests indicate that slave children were even shorter than children in the poorest third-world countries today.[11] They were below the first centile of modern height standards for industrialized countries. By comparison, the average slum child of Lagos, Nigeria, attains the twelfth centile. Although short children in developing countries grow into short adults, small slave children in America, according to the existing evidence, apparently grew up to be relatively tall adults, reaching the 25th centile of modern standards. The slaves' remarkable growth pattern has been attributed to a rise in food intake after a period of severe deprivation.[12] Previously, this pattern of "catch-up" growth has been observed only for shorter periods of deprivation than alleged for slaves.[13]

7. Steckel, "Slave Height Profiles," p. 377.

8. Margo and Steckel, "The Heights of American Slaves," p. 523.

9. This later result is the trend being accepted by the profession. See, for example, David Eltis, "Welfare Trends among the Yoruba in the Early Nineteenth Century: The Anthropometric Evidence," *Journal of Economic History,* 50 (Sept. 1990), pp. 521–40.

10. John Komlos, "Height and Social Status in Eighteenth-Century Germany," *Journal of Interdisciplinary History,* 20 (Spring 1990), pp. 607–21.

11. Eveleth and Tanner, *Worldwide Variation in Human Growth.*

12. Steckel refers to the degree of catch-up growth as "remarkable" in Steckel, "Growth Depression and Recovery," pp. 115, 129.

13. Technically it is incorrect to speak of catch-up growth here because the term usually is reserved for cases in which the nutritional deprivation is temporary. Slaves, in contrast, suffered prolonged deprivation. It is perhaps better to describe the pattern as moving through the centiles

Richard Steckel, using the manifest data, observed that slave children showed the first signs of improvement in height prior to adolescence, when they began to enter the labor force. As workers, Steckel reasons, they must have received greater allotments of food.[14] A weakness in this interpretation is that the initial signs of recovery among the children were fairly weak. Not much catch-up growth took place at the ages of ten and eleven, when many slaves entered the labor force and before the modern reference population experiences the adolescent growth spurt. At age eleven, slave children were still in the second or third centile of the modern height standards (Table 10.2).[15] During the early teenage years, they fall back through the centiles because the modern reference population reaches the adolescent growth spurt earlier than did slaves. But even after the adolescent growth spurt, at age seventeen the slave boys were still below the fifth centile (Figures 10.1 and 10.2). Hence the acceleration in the rate of growth appears to have been confined to a few years in the late teens.[16] Consequently, the juncture between the timing of the children's entrance into the labor force and their becoming taller relative to the modern reference population seems tentative. Why significant catch-up growth occurred earlier among females than among males is another unaddressed issue.[17] Because the degree of catch-up growth appears extraordinarily large, one might ask whether the results are a consequence of some peculiarity of the manifest sample as much as of the children's labor force participation rates. The military sample cannot illuminate the issue because it contains no evidence on slave children. Hence, the nature of the available data restricts our knowledge of slave nutritional experience in two respects: the nutritional experience of slave children and the secular trend in slave stature. It is fortunate that new data, such as the Certificates of Good Character of Louisiana and the Maryland manumission records, have been found.[18]

---

of the modern standard. See James Tanner, *Foetus into Man: Physical Growth from Conception to Maturity* (2d. edn., Cambridge, Mass., 1990), p. 161.

14. Steckel, "Growth Depression and Recovery," p. 130. Short stature is also indicative of deprivation in utero, brought about by women working in the cotton fields until close to delivery. Labor force participation of pregnant females could have varied by crop specialization, and thus could have been different in the tobacco fields of Maryland. Slave children older than twelve were more easily separated from their parents. Some states forbade the importation of children under ten years of age without their mothers unless they were orphans. Perhaps these factors had an impact on which slave children ended up in the manifest sample. See Frederic Bancroft, *Slave Trading in the Old South* ([1931]; New York, 1959), pp. 197, 202, 212.

15. This means that 97 or 98 percent of today's youth are taller than the average slave child.

16. Slaves in the tobacco fields of Maryland, at least, were working full time by the age of ten (Allan Kulikoff, *Tobacco and Slaves: The Development of Southern Cultures in the Chesapeake, 1680–1800* [Chapel Hill, 1986], pp. 373, 377).

17. Children were reared by their families. It is possible that parents (and kin) supplemented children's rations from their own, particularly since slaves did produce some of their own food, cooked it mostly themselves, and often consumed it together (Kenneth M. Stampp, *The Peculiar Institution: Slavery in the Ante-Bellum South* [New York, 1967], p. 287). Some slave owners discouraged maternal neglect; see Bancroft, *Slave Trading in the Old South,* p. 86.

18. The system of certifying the good character of imported slaves was in effect between 1829 and 1831 in an attempt to keep troublemakers out of Louisiana (Herman Freudenberger and Jona-

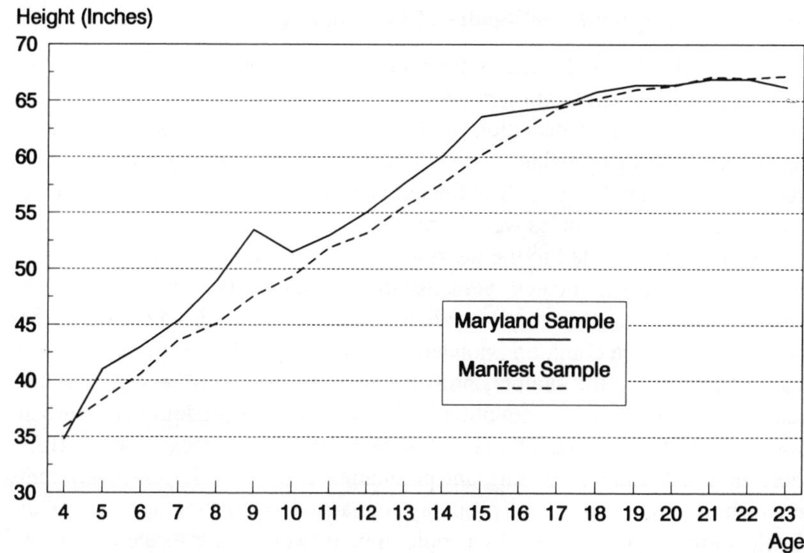

Fig. 10.1 Heights of Male African-American Youth
Source: Table 10.2.

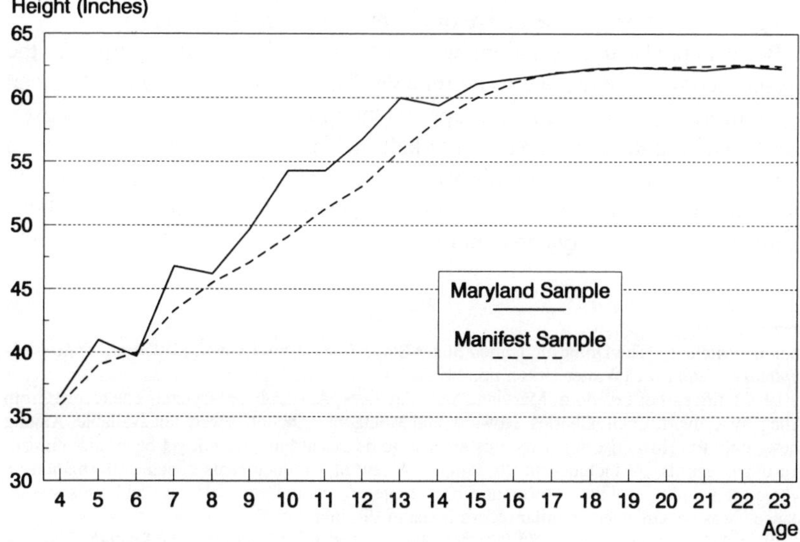

Fig. 10.2 Height of Female African-American Youth
Source: Table 10.2.

10.1 The Maryland Certificates of Freedom

The Maryland Certificates of Freedom were compiled between 1806 and 1864 to provide identification papers for blacks no longer bound to a master. The records contain information on the individual's height, age, sex, date of birth, color, county of residence and of birth, and whether the person was born free.[19] The number of records collected is 14,665; 35 percent of the females and 24 percent of the males were born free (Table 10.1).[20]

Current age, recorded to the nearest year, is not indicative of age at manumission because certificates were usually obtained when the former slave wanted to travel outside the immediate vicinity to an area where his or her status would not be common knowledge.[21] Although all ages are represented, few children are in the sample, probably because they were less mobile than adults (Table 10.1). The destination of the migrants was predominantly urban, evidenced by the fact that 39 percent of Maryland's free blacks lived in Baltimore in 1850. Like other migrant populations, most of the black migrants would have been young and probably unmarried when they applied for the certification. This explains why people in their twenties constitute nearly half of the sample and why there are so few children in the sample. There are more observations for teenage girls than boys. This could indicate that girls left home to marry or to work as domestics at a younger age than boys. Because adult migrants are frequently the more enterprising and possibly healthier, the sample may not be representative of all free blacks in Maryland.

Because physical descriptions were crucial for identification purposes, the height records are expected to be reliable. That heights were generally given to the nearest quarter of an inch supports their reliability. There was, however, some rounding to the nearest inch or half inch as indicated by the distribution of the height observations (Table 10.1). Unless otherwise stated, references to time indicate date of birth, not date of measurement, and references to Baltimore mean both the city and county.

---

than B. Pritchett, "The Domestic United States Slave Trade: New Evidence," *Journal of Interdisciplinary History,* 21 [Winter 1991], pp. 447–78).

19. Certificates of Freedom, Maryland State Archives, Annapolis, Maryland. The records from Allegany, Calvert, Cecil, Charles, Howard, and Montgomery counties were not available. Among these, only the Howard County records are said to be extant but have not yet been microfilmed. All other records are included in the sample. A few of the documents contain information on where the person grew up. Information on the age of manumission, also available in some instances, was not collected. Similar records exist in Virginia.

20. In 1850 there were about 75,000 free blacks in the state (*Abstract of the Seventh Census of the United States: 1850* [Washington, D.C., 1853], p. 150). Females may outnumber males in this sample because females may have been more likely to migrate either to work or to marry.

21. Jeffrey R. Brackett, *The Negro in Maryland: A Study of the Institution of Slavery* (Baltimore, 1889), pp. 89, 163. Only 1.7 percent of the sample pertains to those under the age of fifteen. Authorities feared that the manumission of children would burden public relief, and in 1858 it was forbidden in Maryland. See James M. Wright, *The Free Negro in Maryland, 1634–1860* (New York, 1921), p. 65.

Table 10.1 Characteristics of the Sample of Maryland Certificates of Freedom

Part A: By County

County	Certificate[a]	Birthplace	Grew Up[b]
Anne Arundel	13.7%	13.4%	
Baltimore City	4.2	7.7	
Baltimore County	16.4	7.1	
Caroline	7.6	6.7	5.5%
Cecil	0.2	0.2	
Charles	0.3	0.0	
Dorchester	11.6	11.0	
Frederick	7.9	2.9	
Harford	2.5	2.0	
Kent	3.1	3.0	
Prince George	5.1	1.8	1.2
Queen Ann	3.2	0.4	0.3
St. Mary's	6.5	6.5	
Somerset	7.3	7.5	
Talbot	8.7	7.1	2.7
Washington	1.4	0.8	
Other		1.0	0.5
Unknown		20.2	89.7

Part B: By Legal Status at Birth

	Male	Female	Total
Born free	1,591 (24%)	2,802 (35%)	4,393 (30%)
Not born free	6,107 (76%)	5,165 (65%)	10,272 (70%)
Total	6,698	7,667	14,665

Part C: By Decade of Birth, Age, and Color

Decade of Birth		Age		Color	
1750	0.5%	1–9 years	0.6%	Black	14.8%
1760	1.7	10–14	1.1	Brown	5.6
1770	5.0	15–19	11.8	Dark	23.4
1780	10.4	20–24	28.9	Light	12.7
1790	15.0	25–29	19.4	Yellow	7.1
1800	18.0	30–34	14.2	Copper	1.3
1810	18.7	35–39	10.0	Chestnut	11.4
1820	15.1	40–49	10.6	Mulatto	10.0
1830	13.0	50–59	2.6	Bright	1.6
1840	2.3	≥60	0.6	Unknown	12.0
1850	0.0				
Unknown	0.1				

(*continued*)

Table 10.1 (continued)

Part D: By Precision of Height Measurement in Fractions of an Inch	
0.0 inch	46.6
0.25	11.6
0.50	30.0
0.75	11.0
Other	0.7

Source: Certificates of Freedom, Maryland State Archives, Annapolis, Maryland.
[a]County in which certificate was obtained.
[b]County in which person grew up.

10.2 Anthropometric Evidence from the Maryland Sample

10.2.1 Children

Although the Maryland sample corroborates the notion that slave children of both sexes were undernourished, they were, however, less malnourished than the manifest sample indicates (Table 10.2).[22] Free black children were several inches (about 3.5 percent) taller than the slave children transported on water to the Lower South (Table 10.3, rows 5 and 13; Figures 10.1 and 10.2 above). After age seventeen the distinction between the two results diminishes or even vanishes, even when the number of observations remains small, as in the case of seventeen-year-old boys. There is considerable variation in the centile of modern standards reached until the late teens because the number of observations in the free black sample is small. On average, children reached about the tenth centile of modern heights. Catch-up growth is evident and begins at about the same age as in the manifest sample, but it is less abrupt, and thus resembles more closely conventional growth profiles. Relative to their modern counterparts, free black girls were somewhat taller than boys (Table 10.2). Children born enslaved tended to be taller than those who were born free (Tables 10.3 and 10.4).

10.2.2 Time Trend

The time trend in stature is analyzed in three age categories for both sexes. Turning first to males, sample sizes are insufficient to explore the trend for those under age sixteen. Regression analysis on youth (ages 16 to 20) indicates that their height increased until approximately the birth cohorts of the 1820s and subsequently declined (Tables 10.5 and 10.6; Figure 10.3). Among

22. Here and elsewhere comparison is made with the hitherto published results of the manifest sample. Richard Steckel has now enlarged the sample to about 28,000 manifests, including all those housed in the National Archives. His preliminary investigation seems to indicate that slave children in Maryland and Virginia reached about the fifth centile of modern standards and were taller than those born in the Lower South. Hence, the yet unpublished results seem to be closer to the height of the free black children of Maryland.

Table 10.2 Height by Age Profile of African-American Youth

Part A: Height (in inches)

	Male				Female			
	Free		Slave Manifests		Free		Slave Manifests	
Age	N	Height	N	Height	N	Height	N	Height
1					1	27.0		
2	1	33.5			7	30.1		
3					7	34.7		
4	2	34.8	195	35.9	6	36.5	206	35.9
5	1	41.0	169	38.3	8	41.0	200	39.0
6	2	43.0	218	40.6	5	39.7	262	40.0
7	4	45.4	200	43.6	14	46.8	241	43.3
8	4	48.9	281	45.1	8	46.2	337	45.5
9	3	53.5	266	47.6	11	49.7	306	47.1
10	1	51.5	557	49.3	11	54.3	528	49.1
11	5	53.0	347	51.9	10	54.3	443	51.3
12	6	55.1	751	53.2	23	56.8	736	53.1
13	6	57.7	470	55.6	30	60.0	556	55.9
14	18	60.1	732	57.7	54	59.4	765	58.3
15	12	63.6	571	60.2	89	61.1	812	60.0
16	30	64.1	709	62.2	245	61.5	113	61.2
17	42	64.5	655	64.3	352	61.9	871	62.0
18	61	65.8	1,142	65.2	439	62.3	1,268	62.2
19	96	66.4	900	66.0	375	62.4	594	62.4
20	168	66.4	1,527	66.3	412	62.3	1,764	62.4
21	746	66.9	944	67.1	367	62.2	337	62.5
22	685	66.9	1,374	67.0	439	62.5	664	62.6
23	466	66.2	795	67.2	339	62.3	404	62.5
Total	2,359		12,806		3,253		11,807	

Part B: Standard Deviations and Centiles of Modern Height

	Standard Deviations of Heights				Centiles of Modern Height			
	Male		Female		Male		Female	
Age	Free	Slave Manifests	Free	Slave Manifests	Free	Slave Manifests	Free	Slave Manifests
2			2.2		7.6		0.02	
3			3.5				1.7	
4	6.7	5.5	2.5	5.5	0.01	0.3	0.7	0.5
5	0.0	5.3	1.8	5.2	6.8	0.3	10.6	1.6
6	2.1	5.3	1.9	5.7	5.7	0.5	0.2	0.4
7	1.1	5.0	3.6	5.5	7.5	1.5	27.8	1.8
8	2.8	5.0	1.7	5.4	21.2	0.9	3.8	2.2
9	1.6	5.1	2.7	5.0	60.3	1.7	11.9	1.4
10	0.0	5.8	3.9	5.7	9.3	1.6	40.5	1.4

(continued)

Table 10.2 (continued)

Part B: Standard Deviations and Centiles of Modern Height

	Standard Deviations of Heights				Centiles of Modern Height			
	Male		Female		Male		Female	
Age	Free	Slave Manifests	Free	Slave Manifests	Free	Slave Manifests	Free	Slave Manifests
11	3.4	4.7	4.3	4.9	7.4	3.6	13.8	2.1
12	3.3	5.0	3.1	4.7	8.4	2.4	12.7	0.9
13	3.3	4.8	2.5	4.7	10.8	3.0	20.3	0.9
14	3.4	4.5	2.6	4.1	8.5	2.1	5.0	1.7
15	3.7	3.9	2.3	3.4	12.9	1.3	12.9	5.6
16	2.6	3.7	2.6	3.1	5.7	1.2	16.6	13.3
17	3.0	3.1	2.3	2.8	5.5	4.6	21.2	21.5
18	3.0	3.0	2.4	3.4	12.7	8.9	26.4	24.5
19	2.7	3.2	2.5	3.1	18.1	14.5	28.1	27.4
20	2.8	3.0	2.3	3.0	18.1	17.6	26.4	26.8
21	2.6	2.9	2.7	2.8	23.6	26.1	25.1	28.4
22	2.6	3.0	2.7	3.0	23.6	24.8	29.5	29.5
23	2.6	3.0	2.5	3.4	23.6	26.8	26.4	28.4

Note: N = number of observations.

Sources: See Table 10.1. Slave heights are derived from the manifest sample, see Richard H. Steckel, "Growth Depression and Recovery: The Remarkable Case of American Slaves," *Annals of Human Biology,* 14 (Mar.–Apr. 1987), pp. 111–32. Modern height standards are from J. M. Tanner, R. H. Whitehouse, and M. Takaishi, "Standards from Birth to Maturity for Height, Weight, Height Velocity, and Weight Velocity: British Children, 1965, Part II," *Archives of Disease in Childhood,* 41 (Dec. 1966), pp. 613–35.

adults the trend is flatter prior to the 1820s, the coefficients being either small or insignificant. The increase of the 1820s and the decline in height among the birth cohorts of the 1830s is as evident as among the youth (Tables 10.6 to 10.8). The decline of the 1830s is more pronounced among the urban than the rural population. In spite of the decline in physical stature, adults of the 1830s were only marginally shorter than those of the late eighteenth and early nineteenth centuries. The few observations available for the 1840s suggest that the downward trend continued.

Regional differences in the extent of the decline are noteworthy as well. In Baltimore the birth cohorts of the 1830s were 0.87 inches shorter than those of the 1820s, while those for the rest of Maryland were only 0.22 inches shorter (Table 10.8). Only among those born in Baltimore was mean height in the 1830s markedly below the level that prevailed at the turn of the century. This might indicate that the decline in nutritional status among the males was initially, at least, an urban phenomenon.

If the notion of "urban" is expanded to include Anne Arundel County, be-

Table 10.3 **Height Indexes of Black Children in Antebellum America[a]**

		Male		Female		Total	
Sample	Characteristics	N	Height	N	Height	N	Height
1) Maryland	Rural, born slave	81	101.0	336	100.5	417	100.6
2) Maryland	All, born slave	91	100.7	373	100.4	464	100.5
3) Maryland	Rural, all	120	100.7	592	100.3	712	100.4
4) Maryland	Rural, free	39	100.0	256	100.0	295	100.0
5) Maryland	All, free	163	100.0	860	100.0	1,025	100.0
6) Maryland	All, free	72	99.3	487	99.7	559	99.6
7) Louisiana	Imported	365	98.8	350	100.3	715	99.5
8) Maryland	Urban, born slave	10	98.5	37	99.6	47	99.4
9) Maryland	Urban, free	33	98.4	231	99.4	264	99.3
10) Maryland	Urban, all	43	98.4	268	99.4	311	99.3
11) Manifests	New Orleans	866	98.9	999	98.9	1,865	98.9
12) Manifests	New Orleans	1,603	97.9	1,558	98.7	3,161	98.3
13) Manifests	Shipped	7,263	96.6	7,366	96.3	14,639	96.5
14) Manifests	Shipped	383	96.1	313	94.2	696	95.2

Notes: 1) manumitted, not born free, rural; 2) manumitted, not born free, rural and urban; 3) manumitted, free born, rural and urban; 4) free born, rural; 5) manumitted, free born, rural and urban; 6) free born, rural and urban; 7) transported to Louisiana overland and by ship; 8) manumitted, urban; 9) free born, urban; 10) manumitted, free born, urban; 11) shipped to New Orleans and sold there; 12) all slaves disembarked at New Orleans; 13) all slaves shipped in interregional trade; 14) slaves disembarked at New Orleans but not sold there.

Sources: See Tables 10.2 and 10.4; Jonathan Pritchett and Herman Freudenberger, "A Peculiar Sample: The Selection of Slaves for the New Orleans Market" (manuscript, Tulane University, 1990).

[a]Males include children between the ages of 4 and 18; females, between the ages of 4 and 17. The index is standardized for age. The calculation is made by setting the heights in the Maryland sample (row 5) equal to 100.

cause of its proximity to Baltimore, the case is strengthened. If the state is divided in this manner, one finds that urban heights began to decline in the 1820s, that is, a decade before rural areas (Table 10.8). In sum, the small number of observations, as well as the considerable regional variation in height, make it difficult to determine the turning point in the trend of the men's physical stature. It is probable that the urban population suffered a decline in height, and thus in nutritional status, earlier than the rural population (Figure 10.3). Moreover, regressions (3) and (4) in Table 10.7 indicate that the antebellum decline in nutritional status could have been greater among those who were not born free than among those who were, even though those born free tended to be shorter prior to the 1840s.

Among females the number of observations is sufficient to ascertain the trend for youth, adults, and children. The trends for all three strongly support the inference of a decline in nutritional status in the antebellum period (Tables 10.6 and 10.9; Figure 10.3). The change in average height among females after the 1820s is quite similar to that experienced by men. The decrease for females born in bondage was not greater than that of the free born. The female

Table 10.4 **Height of African-American Children by Status and Place of Birth, Antebellum Maryland**

	Males										
	Born in Baltimore					Born Outside Baltimore					
	Born Free		Born Slave			Born Free		Born Slave			
Age	(1) N	(2) Height	(3) N	(4) Height	(2) − (4)	(5) N	(6) Height	(7) N	(8) Height	(6) − (8)	ΔH
5											
6											
7											
8											
9											
10											
11											
12											
13											
14	5	60.5				2	58.4	11	60.2	−1.8	−0.3
15	1	60.5	2	61.1	−0.6	4	64.4	5	64.6	−0.2	0.0
16	3	64.9	1	63.0	+1.9	8	63.6	18	64.2	−0.6	−0.2
17	10	63.2	2	63.1	+0.1	8	63.9	22	65.5	−1.6	−1.8
18	14	64.1	5	65.6	−1.5	17	66.3	25	66.6	−0.3	−1.1
19	20	66.2	5	66.4	−0.2	21	66.7	50	66.4	+0.3	0.0
20	15	65.9	7	63.8	+2.1	51	67.1	95	66.2	+0.9	+0.8

	Females											
	Born in Baltimore					Born Outside Baltimore						
	Born Free		Born Slave			Born Free		Born Slave				
Age	(9) N	(10) Height	(11) N	(12) Height	(10) − (12)	(13) N	(14) Height	(15) N	(16) Height	(14) − (16)	ΔH	Percent Urban[a]
5	3	40.7	2	39.6				3	42.3		−0.6	55%
6	5	39.7										
7	7	46.0	1	42.0		3	47.8	3	49.0		−0.7	44
8	4	46.0				2	47.8	2	45.0		−0.4	33
9	4	48.9	2	47.0		1	49.8	4	51.8		−1.1	43
10	7	54.9				2	53.5	2	53.3		+1.3	67
11	6	54.8				1	51.8	3	54.1		+0.3	53
12	13	56.6				3	56.3	7	57.5		−0.9	52
13	12	59.4	2	60.9		5	62.1	11	59.7		+0.3	42
14	24	58.4	1	57.0		10	60.1	19	60.6	0.5	−1.5	42
15	27	60.6	5	60.1	+0.5	33	61.3	24	61.6	−0.3	−0.4	35
16	48	61.6	11	62.2	−0.6	84	61.6	102	61.3	−0.3	+0.2	23
17	71	61.4	13	62.4	−1.0	112	61.6	156	62.4	−0.8	−0.9	24
18	84	62.3	31	62.2	+0.1	153	62.0	171	62.6	−0.6	−0.5	27
19	65	62.1	21	61.3	+0.8	153	62.3	136	62.8	−0.5	−0.4	24
20	83	61.9	21	62.4	−0.5	128	61.9	180	62.7	−0.8	−0.8	22

Notes: N = number of observations. ΔH = height of all those born free minus the height of all those born enslaved.

Source: See Table 10.1.

[a]Percentage of children (male and female) born in Baltimore City and County.

Table 10.5 Regressions on the Height of Free Black Youth

	Females (1)	Males (2)
Constant	61.92*	65.79*
Age		
19	0.17	0.00
18	0.15	−0.31
17	−0.34**	−1.68
16	−0.80*	−2.76*
Birth decade		
1790s	0.92*	0.40
1800s	0.80*	0.65
1810s	1.06*	0.91**
1820s	0.40	1.32
Birthplace: Baltimore	−0.60*	−1.46*
Born free	−0.50*	0.32
N	1,603	346
R^2	.06	.09
F	9.6*	.46*

Note: The constants refer to a twenty-year-old born as a slave outside Baltimore in the 1830s.
Source: See Table 10.1.
*Significant at the 5 percent level.
**Significant at the 10 percent level.

regional trend is similar to the male pattern as the decline in height (between 1800 and 1830) was greater among those born in Baltimore than in the rest of the state, 0.77 versus 0.50 inches (Table 10.10).

An important difference between the trend in the height of males and that of females is that the decline in height among the latter group began earlier. The pattern does not change much if Anne Arundel County is included in the urban group. Baltimore women began to experience a decline in height in the 1810s, while those born in the rest of the state experienced the decline in the 1820s, that is, about a decade before men. As among men, the deterioration in nutritional status of women began earlier in urban areas. In the 1830s, rural women were between 0.5 and 0.8 inches shorter than birth cohorts of the 1800s, while rural men were about equally tall. In other words, in rural areas women appear to have fared worse in nutritional terms than did men, but in the city perhaps about the same.

Regressions on the height of female youth confirm the pattern obtained for adult women (Table 10.5). The fall in nutritional status among females between the ages of sixteen and twenty also started earlier than it did among males and was greater. By the 1830s the decline in the height of female youth appears to have been close to an inch. This is not unreasonable if one notes that the height of youth is more sensitive to nutritional stress than is terminal height because growth can cease at later ages.

Table 10.6 Indexes of the Trend in the Height of the Free Black Population

			Adults[c]	
	Girls[a]	Youths[b]	Born in Baltimore	Born Oustide Baltimore
		Females (1810 = 100.0)		
1760				99.7
1770				100.4
1780			100.5	99.8
1790	98.1	99.9	99.9	100.2
1800	99.2	99.7	100.5	100.0
1810	100.0	100.0	100.0	100.0
1820	99.7	99.1	99.4	99.6
1830	98.5	98.4	99.2	99.2
1840	98.1			98.6
		Males (1820 = 100.0)		
1760				99.0
1770			99.8	99.2
1780			99.0	99.8
1790		98.6	99.8	99.4
1800		99.0	99.9	99.8
1810		99.4	99.5	99.7
1820		100.0	100.0	100.0
1830		98.0	98.7	99.7
1840				99.3

Sources: Tables 10.5, 10.8, and 10.10

[a]Between the ages of 5 and 15.

[b]Between the ages of 16 and 20.

[c]For females, between the ages of 18 and 50; for males, between the ages of 21 and 50.

In sum, the downward tendency in nutritional status is evident among both males and females, and among all age brackets for which evidence exists. It is stronger and began earlier among females and in areas experiencing urbanization. These results are consistent with the trend obtained from the Civil War sample. Between the birth cohorts of the 1820s and the 1840s, the estimated diminution in the height of adult black recruits into the Union army is 0.4 inches.[23] This is practically identical to the decline found among West Point cadets, among white Union soldiers, and also among the free blacks of Maryland (Table 10.8).[24] Another similarity between the Union Army and Maryland samples is that the men born in the second half of the 1830s were

23. Margo and Steckel, "The Heights of American Slaves," pp. 526–27; Fogel, *Without Consent or Contract,* p. 361; John Komlos, "The Height and Weight of West Point Cadets: Dietary Change in Antebellum America, 1820–1880," *Journal of Economic History,* 47 (Dec. 1987), pp. 897–927.

24. No evidence has been collected on the height of white females in the antebellum period.

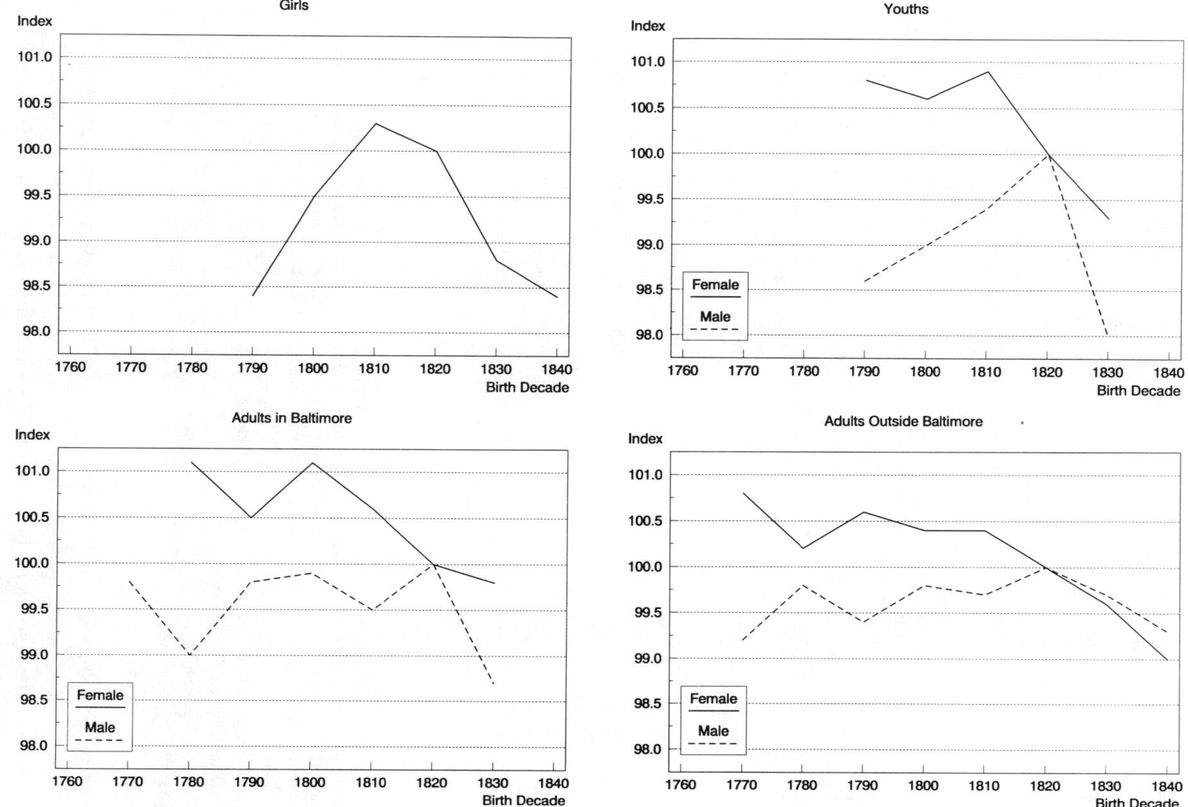

Fig. 10.3 Secular Trends in the Heights of African-Americans by Birth Decade, 1760–1840
Source: See Table 10.1.

Table 10.7 **Regressions on the Height of Free Adult Black Males**

	Entire Sample		Born Enslaved	Born Free	Entire Sample
	(1)	(2)	(3)	(4)	(5)
Constant	66.99*	67.02*	67.02*	66.77*	66.95*
Age, 20–22	−0.21*	−0.20*	−2.6*	−0.12*	0.22*
Birth decade					
1750	0.14	0.13			
1760	−0.35	−0.37	−0.32		−0.31
1770	−0.11	−0.14	−0.11		−0.04
1780	0.10	0.08	0.16	−0.36	−0.12
1790	−0.07	−0.08	−0.08	0.10	−0.06
1800	0.16	0.16	0.19	0.22	0.17
1810	0.10	0.10	0.16	−0.08	0.11
1820	0.30*	0.29*	0.35*	0.22	0.31*
1840	−0.16	−0.19	−0.50	0.02	−0.18
Region of birth[a]					
Eastern Shore	−0.08	−0.07	−0.18	0.41*	
Baltimore City	−0.83*	−0.84*	0.72*	} −0.65*	−0.62*
Baltimore County	−0.52*	−0.51*	−0.50*	}	−0.55*
North[b]	−0.18	−0.20	−0.22		−0.17
South	−0.17*	0.14	−0.18	0.08	−0.05
Color					
Brown	−0.09		0.01	−0.12	−0.11
Dark	−0.06		−0.07	−0.03	−0.03
Light	0.09		0.00	0.23	0.15
Yellow	0.07		−0.01	0.47	0.05
Copper	0.60*		0.59*	0.85	0.56*
Chestnut	0.07		0.08	0.40	0.03
Mulatto	0.05		0.04	0.12	0.10
Bright	0.54**		0.58**	0.16	0.49**
Born free	0.19*	0.16**			0.17*
N	6,251	6,251	4,780	1,461	6,242
R^2	.04	.04	.04	.04	.04
F	2.8*	3.5*	2.3*	1.8*	2.9*

Notes: Dependent variable is the height of adult black males. All values are in inches. Constants refer to a male between the ages of 23 and 50, born in the 1830s; in equations (1) and (3) they refer, in addition, to a man whose place of birth was unknown and who was born a slave, with black skin color; in equation (2), to a man whose place of birth was unknown and who was born a slave; equation (4) is the same as (3), but the constant refers to a man born free instead of as a slave; equation (5) is the same as (1), but region of birth is replaced by region of residence.

Source: See Table 10.1

[a]In equation (5), region of birth is replaced by region of residence.

[b]Does not include Baltimore City or County.

*Significant at the 5 percent level.

**Significant at the 10 percent level.

unusually short in both. The terminal height of the Maryland men was identical to the one estimated from the manifest sample, almost the same as that of the Civil War black soldiers, but somewhat shorter than that of the freed slaves of Virginia (Table 10.11).[25]

25. The preliminary (Coopersmith-Steckel) sample of manifests appears to be more homogeneous than its enlarged counterpart, as the standard deviations of its height estimates are within

Table 10.8 **Height of Adult Black Men by Region of Birth**

Decade of Birth	Eastern Shore		Baltimore		North		South		Total		Outside Baltimore		Urban		Rural	
	Height	N	Height	N	Height	N	Height	N	Height	N	Height	N	Height	N	Height	N
1760	66.80	70	66.15	13	65.96	13	66.32	31	66.53	127	66.57	114			66.7	101
1770	66.93	218	66.76	61	66.58	53	66.38	72	66.73	404	66.76	343	66.7	102	66.8	300
1780	67.04	410	66.19	117	67.13	86	67.27	159	66.97	772	67.11	655	66.2	145	67.1	556
1790	66.87	555	66.73	75	66.80	119	66.93	197	66.86	946	66.87	871	66.9	82	67.0	631
1800	67.18	527	66.79	96	67.08	125	67.02	202	67.09	950	67.12	854	66.7	120	67.1	595
1810	67.10	628	66.52	60	66.64	111	67.34	171	67.05	970	67.09	910	67.3	94	67.0	579
1820	67.38	544	66.88	93	67.20	123	67.08	264	67.24	1,024	67.27	931	66.9	234	67.4	541
1830	67.09	468	66.01	93	66.78	125	67.08	303	66.95	989	67.05	896	66.7	181	67.2	352
1840	66.91	24	66.30	5	66.90	5	66.72	26	66.77	60	66.82	55				

Notes: Adult includes those between the ages of 21 and 50. Baltimore includes Baltimore City and County. Urban includes Baltimore City and County, and Anne Arundel County. N = number of observations.

Source: See Table 101.1

Table 10.9 Regressions on the Height of Adult Black Females

	Entire Sample (1)	Born Enslaved (2)	Born Free (3)
Constant	62.00*	61.92*	61.73*
Age, 20–22	0.04	0.23*	−0.21
Birth Decade			
1760	0.31	0.52	
1770	0.76*	0.92*	
1780	0.46*	0.62*	0.56* (1770–1790)
1790	0.57*	0.70*	
1800	0.57*	0.62*	0.78*
1810	0.43*	0.57*	0.53*
1820	0.22*	0.37*	0.20
1840	−0.46		
Region of birth			
Eastern Shore	−0.16**	0.08	0.46**
Baltimore City	−0.28*	−0.31*	−0.10
Baltimore County	−0.26	−0.18	−0.18
North	0.06	0.00	2.17
South	−0.17	0.21**	−0.05
Color			
Brown	−0.28*	−0.35*	−0.07
Dark	0.01*	−0.01	0.03
Light	0.05	−0.02*	0.12
Yellow	0.15**	0.01	0.65
Copper	0.25	0.22	0.81
Chestnut	0.03	−0.05	0.13
Mulatto	0.20	0.22	0.18
Bright	0.38	0.33	0.46
Born free	0.02		
N	6,061	4,247	1,812
R^2	.01	.01	.01
F	3.8*	2.5*	2.7*

Notes: Dependent variable is the height of adult black females. All values are in inches. For definition of constants see Table 10.7.

Source: See Table 10.1

*Significant at the 5 percent level.

**Significant at the 10 percent level.

---

the acceptable range (Steckel, "Slave Height Profiles," pp. 364, 368). The trend in heights from the initial sample agrees with the trend outlined above, and also with that of the Civil War sample in many respects: a) male stature increased in the 1820s and decreased in the 1830s; b) the decline in female adult stature began earlier than among males and continued into the antebellum period; and c) the decline among female youth was larger than among adults in the 1840s (Steckel, "Slave Height Profiles," p. 377). The only noteworthy difference between the first manifest sample and the Maryland results is that, according to the former, the height of female youth rose until the 1830s instead of declining monotonically as in the Maryland sample. Apparently, something important happened in the expansion of the manifest sample that influenced the estimated trends.

Table 10.10 **Height of Adult Black Women By Region of Birth**

Decade of Birth	Eastern Shore		Baltimore		North		South		Total		Outside Baltimore		Urban		Rural	
	Height	N	Height	N	Height	N	Height	N	Height	N	Height	N	Height	N	Height	N
1760	62.65	35	61.77	9	61.75	3	62.20	25	62.35	72	62.42	63			61.7	45
1770	62.93	139	67.81	28	62.70	19	62.53	77	62.78	263	62.78	235	62.7	76	62.8	187
1780	62.56	326	62.78	91	62.80	45	62.19	221	62.49	683	62.44	592	62.4	232	62.5	460
1790	62.91	434	62.15	156	62.91	76	62.32	342	62.59	1,008	62.67	852	62.3	409	62.8	664
1800	62.68	515	62.48	386	62.53	72	62.45	384	62.55	1,357	62.58	971	62.4	755	62.8	715
1810	62.73	429	62.20	374	62.11	81	62.42	267	62.44	1,151	62.56	777	62.3	791	62.7	593
1820	62.35	342	61.81	160	62.33	98	62.32	248	62.24	848	62.33	648	61.9	457	62.4	519
1830	62.07	257	61.71	77	61.92	98	62.17	208	62.04	640	62.08	563	61.9	310	62.0	479
1840	61.37	15	61.26	5	62.38	4	61.79	26	61.66	50	61.70	45	61.2	71	62.2	96

Notes: Adult includes women between the ages of 18 and 50. Baltimore includes Baltimore City and County. Urban includes Baltimore City and County, and Ann Arundel County. N = number of observations.

Source: See Table 10.1.

Table 10.11 Various Estimates of Heights of Adult African-Americans

			Male		Female		
Status	Birthplace	Period[a]	N	Height	N	Height	Source
1) Free[b]	Virginia	1782–1861	433	67.9	400	63.0	
2) Soldiers	Atlantic[c]	1820s	3,651	67.1			Army
3) Slaves	Baltimore[d]	1820s[e]	9,726	67.3	6,745	62.8	Manifests
5) Free	Maryland	1820s	6,251	67.3	6,048	62.2	Certificates[f]
6) Slaves[g]	Upper South	1780–1835	743	67.2	256	63.1	Manifests
7) Slaves[h]	Upper South	1780–1835	359	67.2	260	62.4	Manifests
8) Slaves[i]	Upper South	1780–1815	313	67.1	87	63.0	Certificates[j]

Sources: See Tables 10.6 and 10.8; Robert Margo and Richard H. Steckel, "Heights of American Slaves: New Evidence on Slave Nutrition and Health," *Social Science History,* 6 (Fall 1982), pp. 519, 520, 526, 533; Jonathan Pritchett and Herman Freudenberger, "A Peculiar Sample: The Selection of Slaves for the New Orleans Market" (manuscript, Tulane University, 1990).

[a]Periods, except row 1, refer to years of measurement.

[b]Numbers of males and females are approximate. Total number of observations is 833.

[c]Upper South Atlantic.

[d]Transported on ships departing from Baltimore.

[e]For women, 1780–1840.

[f]Maryland Certificates of Freedom.

[g]Sold in New Orleans.

[h]Disembarked but not sold in New Orleans.

[i]Transported to Louisiana overland and by ship.

[j]Certificates of Good Character.

10.2.3 Regional Pattern

The variation in height between urban and rural regions accords with practically all samples studied thus far. Until improvements in agricultural technology and food distribution toward the end of the nineteenth century, when the urban epidemiological environment also became healthier, the nutritional status and physical stature of urban dwellers were consistently lower than for the rural population. The relative price of nutrients was also higher in towns, and the urban population was less likely to produce even part of its food requirement.

Thus, the free adult male blacks of Baltimore were as much as 0.5 to 0.8 inches shorter than those born in rural areas (Tables 10.7 and 10.8). Among females the difference was somewhat smaller, but it was significant (Tables 10.3, 10.5, 10.9 and 10.10). The rural advantage increased over time. Before 1810, Baltimore men in the sample were about 0.36 inches shorter than rural men, while those born thereafter were 0.67 inches shorter. The pattern is similar among women: the rural-urban difference increased from 0.17 to 0.33 inches during the same period.

Nineteenth-century Maryland had three distinct economic regions. Industrial activity was located in the northern counties of the state. According to the census of 1850, manufacturing output per capita in Northern Maryland, where 90 percent of the industrial workers were located, was about seven times as large as in the rest of the state. Baltimore held a dominant position in manufacturing. In the other parts of the northern region, truck farming, animal husbandry, and grain-growing were important agricultural pursuits. Just two of the counties produced one-third of the state's wheat crop. The value of an improved acre of farmland was almost twice that of the other counties. Slavery was tangential to this economic system; blacks were not more than one-sixth of the population.[26]

In contrast, the counties of Southern Maryland remained economically less developed. This was a relatively backward agricultural region, with the exception of areas around Washington, D.C., and Annapolis, the state capital with a population of 3,000 in 1850. Tobacco remained the primary crop, but wheat production did make some inroads. Here, the number of whites declined during the antebellum decades, and blacks constituted more than half of the population by the end of the period under consideration.

The third main region, the Eastern Shore, occupied an intermediate economic position. Less industrialized and urbanized than northern Maryland and not as dependent on tobacco as the southern counties, farmers of the Eastern Shore cultivated cereal. Blacks represented two-fifths of the population by 1850. In the rural economy, free blacks generally earned a living as hired agricultural laborers; in Baltimore they were concentrated in menial occupations.

Although heights did not vary much among the three main regions of Maryland, they did so at the county level (Tables 10.7 to 10.10). The rank order of the mean height by counties was ascertained in two ways. First, simple averages of adult heights in the entire sample were considered (Table 10.12). As these were quite similar for both sexes, more precise estimates were made using regression analysis, holding the decade of birth constant. Rank orders are similar to those based on the raw means. The final rank was calculated by averaging the rank orders of both sexes as obtained through the regressions.

Baltimore was excluded from further spatial analysis because, as noted above, it is obvious why it had the shortest population in the state. The remainder of the available sample was divided into the three main regions of Maryland, the industrially and economically developed North, the more backward tobacco-producing South, and the grain-producing Eastern Shore. Within each region the county with the tallest population (G1) was compared with the other counties (G3). The counties of the Eastern Shore were divided into three groups, instead of two, as there were enough counties represented in the sample to create a middle category, G2. Heights in the G1 counties all ranked in the top half of the fourteen counties represented in the sample. Av-

26. Blacks constituted a somewhat higher proportion of the labor force; see Barbara J. Fields, *Slavery and Freedom on the Middle Ground: Maryland during the Nineteenth Century* (New Haven, 1985).

Table 10.12 Heights of Maryland Free Blacks by County

			Raw Means[a]						Regression Results[b]					
			Male			Female			Male		Female[c]		Final Rank[d]	
		County	N	Rank	Height	N	Rank	Height	Rank	Height	Rank	Height	A	B
No	G1	Harford	164	1	68.09	148	1	63.41	1	1.74*	1	1.22*	1	1
ES	G1	Dorchester	890	4	67.26	598	2	62.81	5	.76*	3	0.72*	2	2
So	G1	Prince George	346	5	67.16	244	5	62.68	4	.81*	4	0.52*	3	4
No	G1	Washington	118	3	67.42	77	6	62.63	3	.83*	6	0.45	4	5
So	G1	St. Mary's	497	6	67.08	268	4	62.76	7	.58*	2	0.82*	5	3
ES	G1	Talbot	618	6	67.10	513	3	62.78	6	.59*	5	0.47*	6	6
ES	G1	Kent	250	2	67.52	153	12	62.16	2	.88*	10	0.17	7	7
ES	G2	Queen Ann	264	10	66.93	195	9	62.35	10	.37*	8	0.19	8	8
ES	G2	Caroline	601	9	66.98	360	11	62.24	8	.38*	11	0.12	9	9
No	G3	Frederick	641	11	66.81	408	10	62.31	11	.31*	9	0.22	10	10
ES	G3	Somerset	561	12	66.56	344	7	62.38	13	−.00	7	0.36*	11	12
So	G3	Anne Arundel	486	8	67.02	1,146	13	62.15	9	.37*	13	0.02	12	11
No		Baltimore County	525	14	66.52	1,347	8	62.37	14	−.02	12	0.12	13	13
No		Baltimore City	260	13	66.59	247	14	61.96	12	66.47	14	61.68	14	14

Notes: N = number of observations. No = North; So = South; ES = Eastern Shore. G1 = counties that had the tallest populations in their respective regions; G2 = counties whose population had intermediate physical stature within the region; G3 = counties with the shortest population.

[a]Adults only.

[b]Other coefficients of the regression are not reported. The variables included were: decade of birth, born free, and age 20–22. Results for Baltimore City are given for the birth cohorts of the 1830s. The results for the other counties are the average for the whole period by which heights exceeded that of Baltimore.

[c]Between the ages of 16 and 50; hence, in addition to the variables included in the male regression, dummy variables were included for age below 20.

[d]Final rank: A) Average rank of the two sexes. B) The rank according to the mean of the two regression coefficients.

*Significant at the 5 percent level.

eraged across the two sexes, heights in the G1 group were more than half an inch greater than those of the free black population of Baltimore City. In contrast, heights in the other counties were at most about a quarter inch above those of Baltimore. In other words, in nutritional terms there was a noticeable gap between G1 and the other counties.[27]

The black populations of Anne Arundel, Somerset, and Frederick counties (referred to as the G3 counties) were the shortest (Table 10.12).[28] These counties also tended to experience faster population growth (or slower population decline) than the G1 counties (Table 10.13). This is also true if the population is divided into three components, whites, free blacks, and slaves. Thus, the biological standard of living was higher in counties where demographic expansion did not excessively strain the resource base and did not unduly increase competition in the labor market.[29] An exception is found among the white population of Northern Maryland, which grew faster in G1 counties than in G3 counties. Yet, despite the more rapid population growth in Washington and Harford counties (G1), the per capita output of nutrients remained close to that of Frederick County. For Southern Maryland and the Eastern Shore, without exception per capita nutrient production was considerably higher in G1 and G2 than in G3 counties for both 1840 and 1850 (Table 10.13). This confirms the pattern found in other data sets, namely, that during the early stages of industrialization propinquity to nutrients improved nutritional status.

Increased money income from manufacturing employment was, by itself, not inimical to nutritional status, that is, as long as it did not displace agricultural production. Thus, in the G1 counties of Northern Maryland, per capita industrial output was higher than in the G3 county, without having a deleterious effect on nutritional status.[30] Yet manufacturing income did not compensate for, or was not as good as, agricultural income for the maintenance of nutritional status. The slightly higher per capita industrial output of Somerset County did not compensate for its lower per capita output of nutrients. The

27. In other studies, skin color has been found to be a significant correlate of slave heights, inasmuch as light-skinned slaves were born in the New World. Thus, in the Civil War sample, light-skinned slaves were 0.17 inches (and significantly) taller than average (Margo and Steckel, "The Heights of American Slaves," p. 520). This result is not found in the Maryland data, perhaps because in this sample most blacks were born in America.

28. The eighteenth-century residents of Somerset County were among the poorest of the region. Tobacco was a staple, but its land was less fertile than other areas of the Chesapeake. See Russell R. Menard and Lorena S. Walsh, "The Demography of Somerset County, Maryland: A Progress Report," *The Newberry Papers in Family and Community History* (July 1981). The discussion of food consumption based on census records should include the caveat that there is no available evidence on some items, such as game and seafood production.

29. On competition between white and free black labor, see Wright, *The Free Negro in Maryland*, pp. 159, 172. Free blacks also had to compete with slaves who were hired out and accepted smaller wages than whites; see John H. Russell, *The Free Negro in Virginia, 1619–1865* (New York, 1913), pp. 146–47.

30. The regional pattern in northern Maryland must be considered tentative because sample sizes are very small and are mostly for the early part of the century, before nutritional status declined. In addition, evidence is not available for several counties of the region.

Table 10.13 Demographic and Economic Correlates of Regional Variation in Height within Maryland

Demographic Indicators

Region	% Change in Population, 1790–1850			
	White	Black		Total
		Free	Slave	
Eastern Shore				
G1	−2%	324%	−29%	5%
G2	14	484	−42	−3
G3	62	1,200	−21	44
North				
G1	64	448	−10	63
G3	24	1,665	8	33
Southern Shore				
G1	−17	446	−4	−4
G3	42	472	11	43

Economic Indicators, Per Capita

	Output							
	Wheat	Corn	Tobacco	Cattle	Swine	Improved Acres	Animals Slaughtered	Industrial Output
1840								
Eastern Shore								
G1	10.6	35.9	0	0.77	1.3			
G2	6.8	37.9	0	0.72	1.1			
G3	3.5	13.1	0	0.52	0.9			
North								
G1	17.8	21.3	0	0.62	1.3			
G3	20.2	19.4	9	0.58	1.4			
South								
G1	4.5	23.3	370	0.63	1.3			
G3	7.0	19.1	136	0.47	1.1			
1850								
Eastern Shore								
G1	13.7	40.3	0	0.68	1.0	8.0	5.5	5.8
G2	10.2	49.7	0	0.71	1.0	13.0	5.5	5.8
G3	7.0	16.9	0	0.44	0.7	5.7	5.0	6.9
North								
G1	9.8	17.6	0	0.47	0.8	5.6	4.8	47.9
G3	17.9	19.9	4	0.45	0.9	6.2	5.9	39.1
South								
G1	11.0	30.4	288	0.60	1.0	8.3	5.4	13.7
G3	11.1	28.6	140	0.43	0.9	6.9	1.9	28.9

Notes: For region and group designations see Table 10.12. Grain output is measured in bushels, animal stock in heads, tobacco in pounds, industrial output in dollars.

Sources: U.S. Census Office, Seventh Census, 1850, *Statistical View of the United States . . . Being a Compendium of the Seventh Census, etc.*, J. D. B. DeBow, ed. (Washington, D.C., 1854), p. 178.

pattern is particularly revealing in Southern Maryland. There, the per capita output of industrial products was twice as high in Anne Arundel (the G3 county) as in the G1 counties (St. Mary's and Prince George). If one were to add the value of tobacco output to the value of manufactured products, the G1 and G3 counties would have about the same amount of non-nutrient output by value. Nonetheless, the population in the G1 counties was taller, even though their per capita output of nutrients was not much greater (with the exception of livestock slaughtered) than that of Anne Arundel County (Table 10.13).[31] This suggests, once again, that being close to the source of nutrients confers nutritional advantages. While tobacco and industrial goods were both inedible, tobacco was complementary to nutrient production while industrial goods were not to the same extent. Farmers who produced tobacco and raised foodstuffs did not have to pay the cost of transporting food and could supplement their earnings by gardening, which might not be reflected in the census figures. In addition, manufacturing was connected with commerce, and consequently with the movement of people, thereby increasing the exposure to childhood diseases which may have increased nutritional stress among the young.

10.3 The Maryland and Manifest Samples

As far as the adult parts of the two samples are concerned, the results are practically identical (Table 10.11), but the children's components differ. A careful comparison of the two samples is warranted, because nutritional evidence on black children is quite rare. It is difficult to determine which sample is closer to reproducing the nutritional reality of the average slave child, because both samples have weaknesses and neither was randomly drawn from the African-American population.

The Maryland sample size is small for the young. Yet the consistency with which the height of free children exceeds that of the transported children suggests that it is not the small number of observations that is causing the results to diverge (Figures 10.1 and 10.2). If sample size were the crucial factor, one would expect much more variation in height about the manifest estimates. Yet, it is possible that the free black children were taller than the slave children whose heights were recorded in the manifests on account of their legal status. To be included in the Maryland sample would require a child to have had a free mother or to have been set free by his or her master.[32] In the latter case, manumission probably depended on the religious, ethical, and political con-

31. The propinquity to Baltimore was an additional drain on nutrients for Anne Arundel County.

32. If the mother was a slave, the child became a slave even if the father was free. Manumissions were most often effective either upon the death of the owner or at some specified age of the slave (Wright, *The Free Negro in Maryland*, p. 43). In addition, a free black could purchase the freedom of slaves, and a slave could redeem him or herself as well.

victions of the owner rather than on the physical attributes of the child.[33] If masters with such convictions also treated their slaves better than was typical, then one would expect that manumitted children would have higher nutritional status than those belonging to less benevolent masters.

However, children who were born free would not have benefited from such largess. Their parents were probably common laborers whose work in rural areas complemented that of the slaves. To be sure, there was some social differentiation among free blacks, as among the slaves themselves. Some free blacks occupied skilled positions, a few accumulated property, and fewer still even became well-to-do. While the level of per capita income among free blacks is not known precisely, their average socio-economic position was probably no better than that of slaves: "the environment seemed to foster the preservation of conditions existing before they became free," and in the agricultural sector they were "offered arrangements which were strikingly like those of involuntary servitude."[34]

Slaves had certain advantages over free blacks, since they had a more secure access to medical attention, even if rudimentary, and they were not

33. Kulikoff, *Tobacco and Slaves,* p. 419. The restrictions on manumissions were eased in 1790. The Quakers and Methodists became particularly devoted to the abolitionist cause. See Wright, *The Free Negro in Maryland,* pp. 39, 44–46.

34. Wright, *The Free Negro in Maryland,* pp. 43, 152–53, 157, 160, 171, 239, 243, 247. A bushel of meal and 15–20 pounds of meat allotment for contract laborers was on the order of slave rations, but below that of white men (p. 164). "The allowances for the slaves thus became a sort of standard to which free negroes aimed to attain when providing for themselves. The majority fared apparently about as well as did the slaves excepting sometimes in the winter season" (p. 241). In 1860 about 10 percent of the free black families owned some property, but the average amounted to no more than $13 per capita, or 2.5 percent of white wealth (p. 185). "They seemed in many cases to have believed that their material condition would have been just as good in slavery as in freedom" (p. 258). "The two classes shared . . . the same standards of living . . . it seems certain that the average slave was better provided for than was many a free negro. Had the 83,942 free negroes exchanged places with the 87,189 slave negroes in 1860, but little difference in the material welfare of the majority of either class would probably have resulted" (p. 259). Also see Russell, *The Free Negro in Virginia, 1619–1865,* pp. 130, 145. "The free negro was not infrequently a better 'slave' than his kinsman in bondage" (p. 148). "The occupations of persons of this class [free blacks] are nearly the same as those of slaves" (George Tucker, *Progress of the United States in Population and Wealth in Fifty Years, as exhibited by the Decennial Census from 1790 to 1840* [New York, 1855], p. 139, as cited in Russell, p. 150). Barbers were supposedly the most prosperous occupational group among free blacks, see Russell, p. 151. See also Ira Berlin, *Slaves without Masters: The Free Negro in the Antebellum South* (New York, 1974), p. 218; and Leonard P. Curry, *The Free Black in Urban America, 1800–1850: The Shadow of the Dream* (Chicago, 1981). The poverty of free blacks exposed them to a higher incidence of cholera: "In Philadelphia, the case rate among Negroes was almost twice as great as that among whites—probably a reliable, if informal, index to the poverty in which the North's free Negroes lived" (Charles E. Rosenberg, *The Cholera Years: The United States in 1832, 1849, and 1866*[(2d edn., Chicago, 1987], pp. 59–60). Moreover, children who were born free could have had a slave father, blurring further the material significance of the legal distinction. In addition, some free children were neglected sufficiently to become wards of the county, and some were apprenticed out by county authorities. For a contemporary debate over the mental health of free blacks compared to that of slaves see William Stanton, *The Leopard's Spots: Scientific Attitudes Toward Race in America, 1815–1859* (Chicago, 1959), p. 58.

threatened by cyclical unemployment to the same extent as free blacks.[35] Hence, free-born black children probably did not fare better than their slave counterparts. Consequently their heights should approximate the overall slave average.[36] If, however, manumitted children came from benevolent owners, their nutritional status could have been higher than that of children who were born free. Perhaps this is why children in the Maryland sample who were born free tended to be shorter than those who were born enslaved (Tables 10.3 and 10.4). The pattern is most vivid among female youth, whose height difference is close to half an inch in favor of those born into slavery (Table 10.5). The pattern does not hold among adults; with more time to reach terminal height, adults' nutritional status affected mainly the tempo of growth. The nutritional advantage of having been born a slave is clearer and more consistent among rural children than among urban ones (Tables 10.3 and 10.4). Higher urban food prices may have induced urban slave owners to be more stringent than their rural counterparts. Alternatively, urban slaves, who were hired out more frequently than rural slaves, may have been fed more frequently by employers.

The comparison of the two results is confounded by the fact that the slaves in the manifests were more diverse in regional origin than in the free sample, which is limited to blacks born in Maryland. A shortcoming of the manifests is that they do not contain information on the provenance of the slaves, only on the port of embarkation.[37] This is a problem because there was considerable regional variation in stature for which we cannot control. With such a heterogeneous composition of the manifest sample of slave children it would, indeed, be possible to obtain both a small average height for a particular age and a large variance in heights. If all slave children were malnourished, one would not expect the standard deviations to be as high as the records in the manifests indicate.[38] Because height varied considerably by place of birth, it is possible that the Maryland children were taller than those in the manifests on account of their geographic distribution.

35. Wright, *The Free Negro in Maryland*, pp. 131, 133, 246; Russell, *The Free Negro in Virginia*, p. 155. Another factor to consider is that, after their emancipation, the labor force participation rates of blacks declined considerably, and it is conceivable that a similar pattern obtained among free blacks in the antebellum period.

36. From this it also follows that children imported into Louisiana would have been about as well nourished as the average, but children whose heights appear on the manifests would be shorter than the average slave child by as much as 3.4 percent (Table 10.3, rows 6, 7 and 13). This inference requires further substantiation.

37. Margo and Steckel, "The Heights of American Slaves," p. 521. Hence African-born slaves could be in the early part of the sample. See Bancroft, *Slave Trading in the Old South*, p. 22.

38. Habsburg children enrolled in schools run by the military at the turn of the nineteenth century were about two inches shorter than slave children reported in the manifest sample. Yet the standard deviation of Habsburg children's height is well within the normal range. In other words, the distribution of height is generally not affected by nutritional deprivation, as long as that deprivation is evenly distributed; see Komlos, *Nutrition and Economic Development*, p. 91.

An unpublished analysis of the manifest sample by Richard Steckel reveals a North-South gradient in children's stature along the Atlantic seaboard, with children in Virginia and Maryland being taller than those in the Carolinas. Consequently, the difference between the height of the free black children of Maryland and that of the slave children entering interregional trade from the Chesapeake region is likely to be less than between the entire samples.[39] Part of the disparity shown in Figures 10.1 and 10.2 might, therefore, be accounted for by the regional divergence between the Maryland and manifest samples. Another reason the results may differ is that neither height profile has been standardized for year of birth.[40] Because stature declined over the course of the antebellum decades, a greater share of children born in the latter part of the period could also make the manifest children appear shorter than those in Maryland.[41]

Although one might argue that freedom conferred nutritional advantages on children, this hypothesis is called into question by the fact that children in the Maryland sample who were born free were shorter on average than those born into slavery. The pattern holds for both sexes and also among those born in urban and in rural areas (Tables 10.3 and 10.4).[42] Admittedly, we do not know how long children born as slaves spent in bondage before they were freed, but it was clearly more time than for children of the same age who were born free. Thus, if freedom guaranteed a better diet, one would expect those children who gained their freedom earlier to have been taller. Since this is not the case, it is improbable that the free black children of the Maryland sample were taller on account of their legal status than those who ended up in the manifest sample.[43]

Another aspect of the manifest sample to consider is that the very high

39. Personal communication from Richard Steckel.

40. Although both samples cover the same period, the distribution within the period may vary somewhat. The number of children in the Maryland sample is too small to do a statistically adequate job of standardization. The distribution of the children under the age of seventeen by birth cohorts was: 1790s, 8.8 percent; 1800s, 15.2 percent; 1810s, 31.0 percent; 1820s, 21.0 percent; 1830s, 13.9 percent; 1840s, 9.9 percent.

41. Height tended to be greater inland, that is, in newly settled regions. But children in the Maryland sample and children in the manifests originated largely from the Atlantic seaboard. (Those who lived farther inland were more likely to have been taken South overland.) Consequently, from the perspective of the East-West height gradient, the Maryland-born children were not at a nutritional advantage compared with the slaves represented on the manifests. It might also be mentioned that urbanites tended to be shorter than those born in rural areas, but it is improbable that urban slaves appeared on the manifests more frequently than in the freedom certificates. In fact, even urban free black children were taller than the children of the manifests (Table 10.3, rows 9 and 13). It is, therefore, improbable that the urban-rural mix in the two samples accounts for the differences in stature.

42. The effect is more pronounced among the rural than among the urban born (Table 10.3). While the difference among the former is between 0.5 and 1.0 percent, among the latter it is 0.1–0.2 percent.

43. Having been born free did not necessarily confer privileges since the father could still have been a slave. See Kulikoff, *Tobacco and Slaves*, p. 375; Russell, *The Free Negro in Virginia*, p. 131.

standard deviations of children's height throughout childhood and adolescence indicate a high level of diversity in the composition of the sample over time and space and perhaps nutritional experience. Yet, the standard deviation of heights in a population is generally in the neighborhood of 2.7 inches.[44] While deviations from this standard of a few tenths of an inch are not extraordinary, the ones found in the manifests are often twice their expected value (Table 10.2). Such a large variance about the mean has never been documented in homogeneous populations, and consequently is an indication that the manifest records contain observations from several distinct segments of the slave child population. This possibility is underscored by the fact that in the preliminary version of the manifest sample, confined to just two ports of disembarkation, standard deviations were close to the normal range and the height of the children was consistently above that in the enlarged sample.[45] Moreover, a recent decomposition of the height of the slave children who disembarked at New Orleans by those who were sold there and those who were not, had variances well within the normal range, as did the heights found in the recently discovered Louisiana Certificates of Good Character.[46] In contrast, it is reassuring that standard deviations in the Maryland sample lie within the normal range.[47] Moreover, the differences between the standard deviations of height at a particular age in the two samples and the differences in heights have an almost perfectly linear relationship.[48] This means that as the standard deviations of the manifest sample approach the normal range, the average heights of the transported children approach those found in the certificates of freedom.

44. The variance in height does depend to some extent on the distribution of income, but in the case of the manifest sample all observations refer to the same class of subjects. One might expect to obtain large variances if the height observations of lower-class London paupers and upper-class gentry boys of the same age were mixed into the same sample. Note that although Trinidad slave children were even shorter than American slaves, the standard deviations of their height are much smaller than those of the heights in the manifest sample, even though they were often still somewhat above the normal range. See Barry W. Higman, "Growth in Afro-Caribbean Slave Populations," *American Journal of Physical Anthropology,* 50 (Mar. 1979), pp. 373–85. The standard deviation increases with age until adolescence and then levels off. At the time of the adolescent growth spurt the standard deviation can reach as high as 3.3 inches. See J. M. Tanner, R. H. Whitehouse, and M. Takaishi, "Standards from Birth to Maturity for Height, Weight, Height Velocity, and Weight Velocity: British Children, 1965, Part II," *Archives of Disease in Childhood,* 41 (1966), pp. 613–35.

45. Steckel, "Slave Height Profiles," pp. 364, 368. The Coopersmith-Steckel sample of slave manifests appears to be more homogeneous than its enlarged version, perhaps because it was limited to two ports of disembarkation, Mobile and New Orleans. The height of the children in that sample was also consistently greater than in its enlarged version.

46. Jonathan B. Pritchett and Herman Freudenberger, "A Peculiar Sample: The Selection of Slaves for the New Orleans Market" (manuscript, Tulane University, 1990).

47. The extraordinarily high variances found in the manifest sample need not necessarily bias the estimated mean heights, but they have that potential. The variances indicate that the sample consists of observations from different segments of the slave children population, and it is impossible to verify whether the number of observations collected from each stratum is appropriate relative to the size of the population in that stratum.

48. That is, a regression of the differences in standard deviations on the differences in height is linear.

10.4 Conclusion

The physical stature of free blacks in Maryland declined in the antebellum decades in close agreement with the trend found for other segments of the American population, both black and white. This suggests that the decline in nutritional status was widespread.[49] The cumulative decline in the height of free black males between the 1820s and the 1840s of about half an inch is similar to that experienced by whites.

The widespread decline in height among whites and blacks appears to have been caused by an acceleration in the growth of the urban population and the industrial sector. The relatively slow expansion of the agricultural labor force and the absence of technological breakthroughs in food production, coupled with the increased demand for food, meant that the price of nutrients increased both absolutely and relative to industrial products in the antebellum decades. Although incomes rose, they did not rise fast enough for many workers to compensate fully for the rise in food prices. Hence, per capita calorie and protein consumption (particularly animal protein) declined. Yet, because of out-migration, the population of Maryland was growing at a slower rate than the average for the entire United States prior to 1840. Compared with the norm of about 30 percent per decade, Maryland's growth was only about 8 percent. In the subsequent decade, however, its demographic expansion was very close to the national average. Perhaps this is why the height of men declined slowly in rural Maryland. In contrast, Baltimore's population expanded from 13,500 in 1790 to 169,000 in 1850, and that rapid growth could very well account for the deterioration in nutritional status among both its free black men and women.[50]

Relative to modern standards, free black girls were taller than boys in both the manifest and the Maryland samples, as were adult women prior to the deterioration in nutritional status. Females born in the first decade of the new century reached the 29th centile, while males reached the 27th centile of modern standards. By the 1830s, however, the rank order was reversed, 21st for women and 25th for men. The early female nutritional advantage might be attributed to two factors. Female youth may have been more likely to be engaged in domestic service, thereby gaining access to nutrients within the white household.[51] Furthermore, the sex ratio favored women. Among both

49. The relationship among the rapid economic growth of the antebellum decades, the increase in the relative price of food, and the concomitant decline in the consumption of nutrients is outlined in Komlos, "The Height and Weight of West Point Cadets," p. 919. Among free blacks, the highest per capita property holdings were in Caroline, Kent, and Queen Anne's counties, in that order. These counties were in the middle of the rank order by height, occupying the seventh, eighth, and ninth place (Table 10.12). See Wright, *The Free Negro in Maryland,* p. 185.

50. The growth of the nearby Philadelphia market would also have served as a source of demand for foodstuffs; see Diane Lindstrom, *Economic Development in the Philadelphia Region, 1810–1850* (New York, 1978), p. 62.

51. For the nutritional advantages of domestic service in Vienna see W. Peter Ward, "Weight at Birth in Vienna, 1865–1930," *Annals of Human Biology,* 14 (Nov.–Dec. 1987), pp. 495–506. Servants owned by wealthy planters had a higher social status in the black community than poor free blacks; see Russell, *The Free Negro in Virginia,* p. 133.

races, females were scarce in the eighteenth century, as there were 12 percent more men than women in the population (Table 10.14).[52] The advantage diminished over time, however, and by 1840 it had vanished altogether. The decline in the sex ratio was greatest among free blacks. Compared with the 8 percentage point decline among slaves and a 10 point decline among whites, the diminution in the sex ratio among the free blacks was 33 points. The demand for the services of black women, therefore, including those who were free, would not have been growing as fast as the supply, possibly explaining why their nutritional status began to decline earlier than it did for black men.

To the extent that the evidence above corroborates earlier findings, the following aspects of the anthropometric history of African-Americans now appear beyond debate. 1) All samples consistently indicate that heights of adult slaves, whether manumitted, born free, transported in interregional trade, or recruited into the Union Army, fell within a narrow range: about 67 inches for males and a little over 62 inches for females. By both African and European standards of the time, American blacks were quite tall, as were whites. The attainment of such physical stature is indicative of the nutritional advantages of the New World. But by modern standards, African-Americans appear to have been less well nourished. The average adult slave reached between the 20th and 25th centile of the height distribution of today's industrialized nations. Even compared with their white American contemporaries, blacks fared less well, reaching, on average, about the 35th centile of the antebellum white height distribution. 2) The nutritional status of all groups studied in the American population declined in the antebellum period. 3) Black children were shorter for their age than were black adults. Undernutrition meant that the tempo of slave growth was slower than that of whites.[53] 4) The lower and upper bounds of the black children's growth profile have now been identified as lying between about the first and tenth centile of modern standards. The height of children transported from the Upper to the Lower South on water might be considered the lower bound of all slave children. In contrast, the height of the manumitted slave children could very well constitute the upper bound. 5) Steckel's suggestion of an acceleration of growth in the late teenage years is confirmed by the Maryland sample, but seems to have been somewhat smaller than previously thought. This means that malnutrition among blacks was perhaps less severe and less widespread than the manifest sample indicates. This finding is corroborated by a number of samples recently analyzed.[54] 6) Proximity to the source of nutrients had biological advantages in

52. Earlier in the eighteenth century the sex imbalance was much greater among both races, reaching as high as 40 percent (Russell R. Menard, *Economy and Society in Early Colonial Maryland* [New York, 1985], p. 265).

53. On anthropological evidence on slave undernutrition see Ted A. Rathbun, "Health and Disease at a South Carolina Plantation: 1840–1870," *American Journal of Physical Anthropology*, 74 (Oct. 1987), pp. 239–53.

54. Pritchett and Freudenberger, "A Peculiar Sample." An intense catch-up growth during late adolescence has now been found among runaway slaves as well as among runaway white apprentices in eighteenth-century America. This pattern suggests that a late adolescent growth spurt was

Table 10.14 **Sex Ratios in Maryland, 1755–1840**

	White	Black		
		Slave	Free	Total
1755	1.10	1.14	1.22	1.12
1790	1.06			
1820	1.03	1.10	0.89	1.03
1840	1.00	1.06	0.89	0.99

Note: The sex ratio is the ratio of males to females in the population.
Sources: Various federal population censuses: James M. Wright, *The Free Negro in Maryland, 1634–1860* (New York, 1921), p. 85.

the early industrial period. Rural populations were taller than urban ones. Higher per capita output of food was more important in determining nutritional status than was money income.

Some findings need further confirmation on the basis of other data sets to broaden their applicability beyond the Maryland free black population. Among these are: 1) In the antebellum United States the nutritional status of black females began to decline earlier than it did among males, possibly because of a decline in the relative market value of their labor. 2) The nutritional status of females relative to males depended on the population's sex ratio. When the sex ratio favored women their nutritional status, too, was greater. 3) The decline in nutritional status affected urban black populations before it affected rural populations. 4) Owners who set their slaves free may have been especially benevolent, and consequently may have provided a better-than-average diet for their young slaves prior to manumission. If so, this part of the sample should not be considered representative of all slave children. Because black children who were born free would not have benefited from such largess, their height is probably a better proxy for the slave average than that of either the manumitted children or the children in the manifests. 5) The exact beginning of the decline in nutritional status is difficult to determine because it was region, age, and gender specific. In this regard even place of residence begins to play a role. But once one divides the sample in so many ways, the number of observations becomes insufficient to determine accurately the turning point at the county level. It appears, however, that in rural areas of Maryland the nutritional status of black men improved for those born in the 1820s, and then fell among those born in the latter half of the 1830s. Urban men were less likely to benefit from the improvements of the 1820s; on the contrary, in some cases a decline was already evident, as was the case among men living

an integral part of the human experience of the New World, probably until the end of the nineteenth century; see John Komlos, "A Malthusian Episode Revisited: The Height of Indentured Servants in Colonial America," and "The Height of Runaway Slaves in Colonial America" (manuscripts, University of Pittsburgh, 1991).

in Baltimore and in the bordering Anne Arundel County, home of the state capital, Annapolis. 6) Although the catch-up growth of the late teenage years is now beyond question, the degree of malnourishment among children prior to puberty needs further exploration.

Female height did not increase among the birth cohorts of the 1820s. The deterioration in female nutritional status began at least a decade earlier than it did for men. Like men, urban women were more likely to suffer from nutritional stress earlier than their rural counterparts. Because changes in the epidemiological environment probably would have affected men and women equally, it is unlikely to have caused the earlier onset of the decline in stature among women. The pattern, therefore, supports the notion that the decline in nutritional status was related more to a fall in nutritional intake than to an increase in the claims on the nutrients.

11 The Slave Family
A View from the Slave Narratives

Stephen Crawford

The slave narrative collections of the Work Projects Administration and Fisk University contain over 2,200 interviews with aged ex-slaves taken primarily in the late 1930s. Although the interviews were largely unstructured and vary greatly in quality, they have rightly come to be accepted as important sources for the study of slavery.[1] There has been a growing realization during the past fifteen years that the narratives can provide quantitative evidence for research on slave historiography.[2] These quantitative uses must take into account the considerable biases inherent in a source that consists entirely of the memories of aged ex-slaves. But, if these biases are reported and corrected for, the resulting quantitative measures are extremely useful summaries of this vast body of information.

One of the most important issues that can be quantitatively studied with the narrative source is slave family structure. The vast majority of the ex-slaves talked about their family experience under slavery, providing a snapshot of slave family structure in the immediate antebellum period. By examining the data and cross-tabulating family type with relevant variables, such as plantation size and location, it is possible to observe how slave family structure was altered by both slaves and masters.

The nature of the ex-slave interviews makes the narrative sample a unique data source. Because few of the ex-slaves reached adulthood before emancipation, the sample consists of children reared under various family types. More important, each ex-slave did not provide information for just a single

1. See Eugene D. Genovese, *Roll, Jordan, Roll: The World the Slaves Made* (New York, 1974), Herbert G. Gutman, *The Black Family in Slavery and Freedom* (New York, 1976), and George P. Rawick, *From Sundown to Sunup: The Making of the Black Community* (Westport, 1972).

2. Paul D. Escott, *Slavery Remembered: A Record of Twentieth Century Slave Narratives* (Chapel Hill, 1979).

cross section but, rather, a chronological history of his or her family. To illustrate, consider the case of a slave child born into a family containing both parents but whose father was subsequently sold away. The informant was then sold from his mother and on the eve of emancipation was living without family, alone in the slave quarters. To quantify this information requires two family distributions. The first is given here by the family at the time the informant was taken away from the family (or at the time of emancipation, if the slave were not separated from the family of origin). It is a history of the marriage, in all but legal terms, of the slave's parents. The example given would be coded as a female-headed family created through sale of the father. The second distribution focuses on the informant at the time of emancipation. The example would be coded as a child living alone in the quarters without family owing to sale or transfer.

I term the first distribution the "Family of Origin." It summarizes all the information in the narratives about the marriages of the informant's parents. The second distribution I term the "Slave Household Type." This distribution is a snapshot of slave households that contained children just prior to emancipation.

Developing the two distributions requires accurate coding of often sketchy qualitative information. The narratives did not come from structured question-and-answer sessions designed to generate easily quantifiable data. Interviewers were encouraged to cover important topics, such as family life under slavery, but, more often than not, the aged informants simply reminisced about their experience as slaves. Thus, the family-type categories have been created out of numerous individual coding decisions, the possible biases of which will be discussed.

Table 11.1 presents the Family of Origin distribution. This distribution focuses on slave marriages by categorizing the ex-slave's family type either when he or she was separated from the family of origin or at the time of emancipation. Roughly two-thirds of the ex-slaves grew up in families defined as "two-parent consolidated," meaning the family lived together on the same plantation, or "two-parent divided residence," meaning the father lived on a different plantation from his wife and children.[3] The remaining third were raised for at least part of their childhood in a single-parent family, almost exclusively female headed. To understand this distribution requires an examination of the individual family types.

Half of the ex-slaves who provided information belonged to two-parent consolidated families. These families were easy to categorize because ex-slaves often reminisced about mothers and fathers and their relationships during slavery. In general, these were enduring relationships that began under slavery and extended into the post-emancipation period. Less than 2 percent

3. I will use words like "wife," "husband," and "marriage" throughout to describe relationships in the terms the ex-slaves did.

Table 11.1 Distribution of Family Type for Slave's Family of Origin

Family Type	Absolute Frequency	Percentage within Sample
Two-parent, consolidated	694	51.1%
Two-parent, divided residence	168	12.4
One-parent, female headed	451	33.2
One-parent, male headed	24	1.8
Orphan	20	1.5
Total	1,357	100.0%

Note: Family of Origin is given by the structure at the time the slave was sold from the family or at emancipation.

of these two-parent consolidated families were voluntarily broken when slavery ended.[4]

A surprising feature of the two-parent consolidated households is the virtual absence of stepparents, especially stepfathers. Only 2 percent of the category identified the fathers as a step, as opposed to a biological, parent. Apparently, once a slave marriage was broken by death or sale it was rarely reformed, at least not in the eyes of the slave child. Thus one explanation for the high percentage of female-headed families is the lack of *re*marriage, rather than an absence of marriage altogether. For some reason, be it the availability of potential new spouses or reluctance on the part of the slaves, few women re-established two-parent households through remarriage.[5]

The second category in Table 11.1 comprises families defined as two-parent, divided residence. Such families are inferred when the slave said that his or her father lived on a nearby plantation but visited often enough to maintain the family bond. More often than not, the father spent Saturday afternoon through Sunday night with his family. In a minority of cases, a weekday visit was allowed. A small minority of less fortunate fathers were allowed only irregular, infrequent, or merely seasonal visits.

The separation of divided-residence families undoubtedly placed strains on the marriage and the family. For instance, Jane Sutton's parents lived on farms that were geographically near, but the father's absence seriously endangered the relationship between the father and his children.

> My pappy's name was Steve Hutchins. He b'lon to de Hutchins what live down near Silver Creek. He jus' come on Satu'day night an' us don' see

4. The low level of voluntary disruption suggests that slave marriages were largely by choice. If slaveowners forced slaves together, I would expect higher levels of separation when there was no longer a slaveowner to require that parents stay together.

5. An alternative explanation is that the reforming of families by stepparentage was so easy that the new parent was completely accepted. This seems unlikely given both the explicit mention of stepparents by ex-slaves and the lack of any discussion of the loss of parents by death or sale among those in two-parent families. Even if the new parent were completely accepted, I would expect that there would be some discussion of the loss of the natural parent.

> much of 'im. Us call him 'dat man'. Mammy tol' us to be more 'spectful to 'im 'cause he was us daddy, but us aint care nothin' 'bout 'im. He aint never bring us no candy or nothin'.[6]

More often, however, the ex-slaves' stories demonstrate the strength of the family bond. Charly Davis's parents lived on adjoining plantations and Charly's father avoided patrollers during extra visits with his wife and family.

> My mammy and pappy got married after freedom, 'cause they didn't git de time for a weddin' befo'. They called deirselves man and wife a long time befo' they was really married, and dat is de reason dat I's as old as I is now. I reackon they was right, in de fust place 'cause they never did want nobody else 'cept each other, no how.[7]

That fathers and husbands clandestinely, and under threat of punishment, made extra family visits demonstrates the cohesiveness of these families. Samuel Boulvware remembered that his father came to see the family even though he faced a whipping if caught.

> My daddy was a slave on Reuban Bouwave's plantation, 'bout two miles from Marster Hunter's place. He would git a pass to come to see mammy once every week. If he come more than dat he would have to skeedaddle through de woods and fields from de patrollers. If they ketched him widout a pass, he was sho' in for a skin cracklin' whippin. He knowed all dat but he would slip to see mammy anyhow, whippin' or not.[8]

The most important quantitative measure of the strength of divided-residence families is the extent to which they voluntarily reunited after freedom. Information on the post-emancipation history is available for half of the families. In 80 percent of this subsample, the family reunited. The importance of the father's role in these divided families is revealed by where the family reunited after emancipation. The sample is very small, but, in the twelve cases with information, eleven reported the family reuniting on the father's plantation and, in the other, on neither the mother's nor the father's plantation.

Given all the indications of cohesiveness in the two-parent divided-residence families, it seems correct to group these families together with the two-parent consolidated families to obtain a measure of families with strong, unbroken bonds between the parents. Fully 62 percent of the ex-slaves were raised by parents who had an unbroken marriage. What of the remaining ex-slaves?

The single-parent-family category is more difficult to code than either of the two-parent categories. When the family was never formed because the father was unknown or when it was broken due to parental death or sale,

6. Rawick, vol. 7, *Mississippi Narratives*, p. 151. Note that all references are cited by abbreviated reference to George P. Rawick, editor, *The American Slave: A Composite Autobiography*, 19 vols. (Westport, 1972).

7. Rawick, vol. 2 (1), *South Carolina Narratives*, p. 252.

8. Ibid., p. 68.

coding was straightforward. It was also straightforward when the ex-slave talked about the father not being present. In roughly 20 percent of the cases, however, the father was mentioned as having a different owner from the rest of the family, but the father did not visit. Although it might be argued that some of these families were really two-parent divided residence, I have chosen to code them as single parent. These families clearly exhibit a weaker or possibly nonexistent bond between the mother and children and the absent father. To include them in the divided-residence category could call into question the aggregation of two-parent consolidated and divided residence into an overall two-parent category.

Single-parent families were created by four factors, two of which were unique to slavery. The general causes were parental death and bastardy. The causes unique to slavery were the sale of a parent and the existence of a white father.[9]

Nine percent of the female-headed families resulted from death of the father. If we add orphans to this figure, the total percentage of the ex-slaves providing family information who reported their fathers as dead is 4.5 percent. Most of the father-headed families were created by the death of the mother. Taking these together with the orphans leaves a total percentage of dead mothers of 3 percent. Parental death was not a major cause of single-parent families in the slave narrative collection.

The number of children with unknown fathers is difficult to investigate using the narratives. A two-parent family could well have been composed of children with different fathers who were simply accepted into the family. If "illegitimacy" is defined as ex-slaves who said that they did not know the identity of their father, 9 percent of the children in the mother-headed category could be defined as illegitimate. This group can be further divided in two segments: one in which the child was clearly illegitimate and another in which the parents were separated before the child knew his or her father. Henderson Perkins fell into the former category: "In dem days, 'twarnt so particular 'bout gettin married, and my mammy warn't before I'se born, so I'se don' know my father."[10] John Finely told a somewhat different story but one that also indicates his mother and father were never "married": "My pappy an on dat plantation but I don't know him 'cause mammy never talks 'bout him 'cept to say. He am here."[11] In the other group were children such as Easter Wells who was very young when she was separated from her father.

> I never saw my father; in fact, I never heard my mammy say anything about him and I don't guess I ever asked her anything about him for I never thought anything about not having a father. I guess he belonged to another

9. White parentage is treated as a separate category from bastardy because of legal issues regarding slavery. Whites could not form a legal family with blacks even if they chose to.

10. Rawick, vol. 5 (3), *Texas Narratives*, p. 180.

11. Rawick, vol. 4 (2), *Texas Narratives*, p. 35.

family and when we moved away he was left behind and he didn't try to find us after de War.[12]

Parental death and unknown fathers were common to both slave and free populations. But the reasons for the absence of fathers in slave families also includes sale and the fact that some fathers were white. Six percent of the ex-slaves in the white-interviewer sample and 10 percent of the ex-slaves in the black-interviewer sample claimed to have had white fathers. Put another way, between 15 percent and 25 percent of the mother-headed households were formed because the father was white.

The narratives are an important source for exploring sexual relations between female slaves and white men. Table 11.2 cross-tabulates the incidence of white fathers on large and small plantations. A slave child was twice as likely to have a white father if the child's mother lived on a small plantation than if she lived on a large plantation. The increased risk was undoubtedly due to the increased contact between master and slave on the smaller plantations.

The risk from close contact is confirmed by the cross-tabulation of white parentage by the mother's job in Table 11.3. Slave children whose mothers worked in a house-related occupation were twice as likely to have a white father than those whose mothers worked in the field. The risk of interracial sex was strongly related to the level of day-to-day interaction between white men and black women, and slave women working as domestics and on small slave holdings faced the highest risk. While the size of the plantation can be treated as exogenous, a master may have brought a female slave who attracted his attention into his house.

Roughly half the ex-slaves who were children of white fathers did not comment on their mothers' experiences. The remainder told of events ranging from brutal rape to a long-term relationship with obvious affection. Mary Peters related that her mother was raped at fifteen by all three of the master's sons.

> My mothers mistress had three boys, one twenty-one, one nineteen, and one seventeen. . . . While she was alone, the boys came in and threw her down on the floor and tied her down so she couldn't struggle, and one after the other used her as long as they wanted for the whole afternoon . . . that's the way I came to be here.[13]

Victor Duhan's mother was also forced to have sex with the master's son.

> I didn't have brothers or sisters, except half ones. It is like this, my mama was a houseservant in the Duhon family. She was a hairdresser. One day she barbered master's son, who was Lucien. He says that he'll shave her head if she won't do what he likes. After that she his woman till he marries a white lady.[14]

12. Rawick, vol. 7, *Oklahoma Narratives*, p. 316.
13. Rawick, vol. 10 (5), *Arkansas Narratives*, pp. 328–29.
14. Rawick, vol. 4 (1), *Texas Narratives*, p. 307.

Table 11.2 **The Race of the Ex-slave's Father Cross-tabulated by the Size of the Plantation**

Race of Father	Plantation Size (in number of slaves) 1–49	50 or More
Black	196 (92.5%)	188 (96.7%)
White	16 (7.5%)	7 (3.6%)
Total	212	195

Table 11.3 **Cross-tabulation of the Race of the Ex-slave's Father by the Job of the Ex-slave's Mother**

Race of Father	Mother's Job House-Related	Fieldwork
Black	261 (92.9%)	135 (96.4%)
White	(7.1%)	5 (3.6%)
Total	281	140

Entirely different are cases where there was a lasting affection between the white father and the ex-slave's mother. Thomas Ruffin reported that his father was his master: "He never married. Carried my mother around everywhere he went. Out of all the niggers, he didn't have but one with him. That was in slavery time and he was a fool about her."[15] Betty Brown's white father and black mother also clearly cared for each other.

> Our daddy; he wuz an Irishman, name Millan, an' he had de bigges' still in Arkansas. Yes'm, he had a white wife, an' five chillern at home, but mah mammy says he like her an' she like him.[16]

About 8 percent of the slave families were broken by the sale of one of the parents. But the 8 percent figure is probably a lower bound estimate, because the sample is weighted toward ex-slaves who were very young when slavery ended, and thus may have been spared the sale of a parent. Looking only at the group who reached age 15 before emancipation, the proportion who experienced the sale of a parent rises to 11 percent. It is also likely that parental sales are disguised by such responses as "my father had a different master."

15. Rawick, vol. 10 (6), *Arkansas Narratives,* p. 97.
16. Rawick, vol. 11, *Missouri Narratives,* p. 52.

Adding this factor puts an upper limit on the proportion of slave children who saw their parents' marriage broken through sale at 23 percent.

To assess the disruptive forces working on the slave marriage, having a white father must be grouped with parental sale. Using the black-interviewer sample, 10 percent of the ex-slaves had white fathers and 11 percent of those age 15 or under experienced the sale of a parent. Thus at minimum 21 percent of slave children in the narratives lived in families that were broken because of forces peculiar to slavery. Slavery strongly affected the permanence of slave marriage, creating a dual family structure with roughly two-thirds of the slave children experiencing two-parent families and one-third experiencing single-parent families.

The number of siblings might be expected to vary across the three main family types presented in the Family of Origin distribution. Although the ex-slaves were not directly asked about the size of the family, they often mentioned the number of siblings. Since ex-slaves may not have known about siblings who died or were sold, the family-size information is potentially measured with error but probably not systematically so across family types.

The average number of children in different family types is presented in Table 11.4. As might be expected, the number of children was larger in two-parent than in single-parent families. The difference, however, is smaller than one might anticipate. Female-headed families still averaged almost six children. This large family size could indicate either that the father was separated from the family after a considerable time or that the ex-slave's mother continued to have sexual relations with other slave men after the father left.

Some ex-slaves reported that when their father left, their mother stopped having children. Other ex-slaves were just as clear that the loss of their father was not the end of the mother's sexual activity and childbearing. As Emma Watson related in her story of life under slavery:

> My paw, I don't know nothin' bout. My sister Anna and me, us have de same paw, but my mammy's sold out of Miss'sippi 'way from my paw 'fore my birthin'. My maw kept de name of Lucindy Lane, but Martha and Jennie, my other sisters, had different paws.[17]

Continued sexual activity was part of the explanation for large female-headed families, and only infrequently did new two-parent families form. Female-headed families lacked an adult male on a continuing basis. Thus for continued sexual activity to explain most of the family size, the ex-slave's mother would have had to raise children whose father did not become a continuing part of the family.

The second explanation for the relatively large number of children in female-headed families is that fathers were sold away from already large families. The narratives include many profoundly sad descriptions of fathers being sold away which, by virtue of their detail, could only have come from

17. Rawick, vol. 5 (4), *Texas Narratives*, p. 147.

Table 11.4 The Average Number of Children Per Slave Family

Family Type	Number of Children
Two-parent, consolidated	7.2
Two-parent, divided residence	8.0
One-parent, female headed	5.7

children old enough probably to have younger brothers and sisters. Thus both continued sexual activity and the sale of fathers with numerous children help explain the relatively large size of female-headed families. Nonetheless, these families were smaller than their two-parent counterparts, so slaveowners who interrupted a union forfeited some of their female slave's fertility.

Family size was even smaller when the ex-slave claimed to have had a white father. Although the sample size is small, the average number of children in these families is approximately 4.5. This smaller family size, compared with regular female-headed families, indicates that black women who bore a child by a white man tended to bear fewer children.

Two-parent consolidated-residence families tended to be somewhat smaller than their divided counterparts. This finding confirms the regularity of visits between the divided husband and wife. Overall, the comparison of family size among the three major family types shows that female-headed families were one-to-two-children smaller than either consolidated or divided-residence two-parent families. On average, breaking up a slave family had a real economic cost to the slaveowner. Slave women separated from their husbands often continued sexual activity, but the absence of a husband led to smaller families.

The Family of Origin distribution focuses on the slave marriage and how slaves came to reside in a dual- or single-parent family. The narratives have, however, much more information on the slave family. The Family of Origin distribution has limited relevance because it does not allow for one of the most disruptive influences of slavery, the sale or transfer of slave children from their parents. The importance of the slave family can only begin to be understood if we know the age at which slave children were taken from their families. And the overall effect of slavery can only be known by understanding the conditions under which children lived away from their families.

Table 11.5 presents a complete distribution of the households in which slave children lived just prior to emancipation. At the time the snapshot was taken the ex-slaves varied in age from small children to young adults. The distribution includes the family types already discussed plus three new categories: living in the master's house or in the quarters without parents, and married in own household.

Roughly 5 percent of the ex-slaves were raised for at least part of their childhood in the master's house away from their parents. These slave children were largely, but not exclusively, female. They ended up in the master's house

Table 11.5 Slave Household Types

Household Type	Absolute Frequency	Percentage within Sample
Two-parent, consolidated	624	42.9%
Two-parent, divided residence	151	10.4
One-parent, female headed	328	22.5
One-parent, male headed	16	1.1
Living in master's house	69	4.7
Living in quarters without parents	186	12.8
Married in own household	82	5.6
Total	1,456	100.0

Note: Based on the ex-slaves' actual living situation at emancipation.

primarily because they were transferred to a relative of the slaveowner or because they lost their natural parents through sale or death. The distinction between sale and transfer within the slaveowner's family is important. Rarely were slave husband and wife separated by transfer. Children were transferred from their families but, unlike children sold from their families, rarely ended up alone in slave quarters. For example, Eliza Scantling told the following story about being given to her master's daughter as a wedding present.

> Both my missus wuz good to me. De last missus I own treat me jes' de same as her own child. I stayed right dere in de house wid her, an' if I wuz sick or anything she'd take care of me same as her own chillun. I nurse one of her chillun. An dat child would rather be wid me than wid her own mother.[18]

Many of the ex-slaves who grew up in the master's house were separated from their parents by such an intrafamily transfer. Other children were taken into the slaveowner's home when their parents were sold away or died. Lola Chambers, who grew up in Kentucky, had such an experience.

> I ain't never seen my mother enough to really know her, cause she was sold off the plantation where I was raised, when I was too young to remember her, and I just growed up in the house with the white folks dat owned me, . . . I fared right well with my white masters. I done all de sewing in de house, wait on de table, clean up de house, knit and pick wool, and my old miss used to carry me to church with her whenever she went.[19]

While most of the children who lived in the big house were permanently separated from their parents, some had family members on the farm. In certain cases the slave child performed household chores and slept in the master's house until he or she was old enough to work in the field. In other cases the split with the slave family was more permanent.

18. Rawick, vol. 3 (4), *South Carolina Narratives*, p. 80.
19. Rawick, vol. 11, *Missouri Narratives*, pp. 79–80.

> My young marster married a Miss Nannie Long, and then he give me to her for a maid. They taken me from mother on Christmas, and I was not six years old until March. I never lived with my mother; I lived right in the house with the white folks. I carried a white child on my arm most of the time. Of course I had company, but at nine o'clock I had to go into the house.[20]

The narratives suggest that slave children in the master's house experienced an improved standard of living. In contrast, the 13 percent of the ex-slaves who lived without their parents in slave quarters experienced a harsher life-style. The distinguishing characteristic of these children is the lack of narrative information about their day-to-day living arrangements. The information on the family of origin and the tales of separation are extensive. After the separation, however, the information stops. This suggests that rather than joining a new family, the slave had to fend for her- or himself in the slave quarters. The narratives do not indicate that slaves moved easily from their biological family to a new protective family.

The risk a slave child faced of being sold from his or her family can be calculated from the narrative sample. Looking at the narrative collection as a whole, somewhat more than one hundred, or roughly 5 percent, of the slaves said they were sold away from their family at some time in their lives. The 5 percent is a lower bound since many narratives did not touch on family history. Restricting the sample to only those who provide family information increases to 7.5 percent the estimate of children sold from their family. Either figure, however, is significantly biased by the age distribution of the narrative sample at the time of emancipation. What is needed to evaluate the risk of sale away from the family is the probability at different ages.

The probability of sale at different ages for slave children can be estimated by using the exact ages at sale provided by 42 of the 109 ex-slaves who reported being sold. Table 11.6 outlines the computation of the probability of sale for slave children, with the results reported in column 5. Through age sixteen, the slave child faced roughly a 20 percent chance of being sold away from the family. Basing these calculations on the subsample of people who spoke of their family history would raise this probability to about 26 percent. The table also shows the relatively low probability of sale before age nine. Through age nine the cumulative probability of sale was just 5 to 7 percent. From age ten to sixteen the probability increased to 20 to 26 percent.

The probability of sale indicates that a significant number of slave children were sold from their families, a finding that may indicate the tendency of some slaveowners to break up slave families. There are indications, however, that slaveowners did not completely disregard the slave family when making decisions on slave sales. If a slaveowner desired to sell a slave, he had the option of choosing from a group. If the decision were random, we would

20. Rawick, vol. 18, *Fisk University Narratives,* pp. 226–27.

Table 11.6 Probability of a Child's Sale from the Family of Origin, by Age

Age	% Sold[a] (1)	Expected Number Sold[b] (2)	Cumulative Number Sold (3)	Slaves at Given Age or Older[c] (4)	Cumulative Probability of Sale[d] (5)
3	4.8%	5.23	5.23	1,833.6	.0028
4	7.1	7.74	12.97	1,764.6	.0073
5	7.1	7.74	20.71	1,695.6	.0122
6	7.1	7.74	28.45	1,599.9	.0178
7	14.3	15.59	44.04	1,519.4	.0290
8	14.3	15.59	59.63	1,423.6	.0419
9	2.4	2.62	62.25	1,308.6	.0476
10	9.5	10.36	72.61	1,222.4	.0594
11	11.9	12.97	85.58	1,118.9	.0765
12	2.4	2.62	88.20	1,021.2	.0864
13	4.8	5.23	93.43	915.8	.1020
14	4.8	5.23	98.66	785.6	.1256
15	4.8	5.23	103.89	705.1	.1473
16+	4.8	5.23	109.12	561.4	.1944
Total	100.0	109.0			

[a]Derived from the percentage of ex-slaves who reported being sold at that age among all who gave age at sale.

[b]Derived by multiplying the percentages in column 1 by 109, the total number of ex-slaves in the entire sample sold from their families.

[c]Derived by applying the age distribution of the subsample of ex-slaves who gave their exact age, 1,167, to the entire sample, 1,916.

[d]Column 3 divided by column 4.

expect the probability of sale to be equal for all slave children. A detailed look at the 109 ex-slaves sold from their families shows that 41 of them, or 38 percent, were subsequently sold at least once. Since the probability of sale within the entire sample was 5 to 7 percent, the probability of being resold once the slave child was initially separated from his or her family increased substantially. Correcting for the age distributions of the different samples would bring these probabilities somewhat closer together, but the fact remains that slaveowners showed a preference for selling slave children already separated from their families.[21]

Sale, transfer, and, to some extent, the marriage of the ex-slave are the added information that converts the Family of Origin distribution into the household distribution. The probability that a slave experienced any of these events increased with age. Table 11.7 cross-tabulates this household distribu-

21. An alternative explanation is that disobedient or naughty slaves were sold. If so, it would suggest that young slaves who were separated by sale from their parents did not become effectively socialized into the slave system.

Table 11.7 **Cross-tabulation of Ex-slaves by Household Type and Age in 1865**

	Age in 1865						
Household Type	0–3	4–7	8–11	12–15	16–19	20–25	25+
Two-parent, consolidated	66.2%	55.8%	47.1%	42.2%	34.5%	31.5%	16.9%
Two-parent, divided residence	14.1	10.9	16.0	10.0	10.0	5.6	1.5
One-parent, female headed	18.3	24.2	23.5	26.5	20.0	12.4	14.9
One-parent, male headed	0.0	0.0	1.6	0.0	2.7	1.1	0.0
Living in master's house	0.0	2.4	3.7	6.6	10.0	9.0	3.0
Living in quarters without parents	1.4	6.1	8.0	12.8	14.5	27.0	25.4
Married in own household	0.0	0.0	0.0	1.9	8.1	13.5	28.4
Subsample size	71	165	187	211	110	89	67

tion by the ex-slave's age at the end of slavery. Roughly 80 percent of the ex-slaves were born into either a two-parent consolidated or a two-parent divided-residence family. The proportion of two-parent families steadily decreases as the age of the ex-slave increases. The decrease is due to the breakup of slave marriages through death or sale and the sale or transfer of the slave children. These two factors reduce the percentage of children living in two-parent families to 52 percent by age 12 to 15, and to 40 percent by age 20 and over.

The bottom three rows of Table 11.7 show the movement of slave children away from their families into the three special household situations: alone in the quarters or in the master's house, and married in their own household. The three categories increase steadily across the age distributions from only 1.4 percent who lived separately by age 0 to 3, to 33 percent living separately by age 16 to 29. The incidence of the three household types is best examined by looking at separate household-by-age cross-tabulations for male and female ex-slaves. These cross-tabulations are presented in Tables 11.8 and 11.9.

As the age of the ex-slave increases, the pattern of children leaving the family differs significantly. Female slave children were more likely to be separated from their families and more likely to live in the master's house than were male slave children. For instance, in the 12–15 age group, 12.5 percent of the males compared with 30 percent of the females were alone either in the quarters or the master's house. This substantial difference was due to the larger number of females living in the master's house, with close to 15 percent of females 12 to 15 years of age in the master's house compared with almost none of the males. The percentage for males and females in the master's house and quarters does not become the same until the 20–25 age group when roughly 35 percent of both the males and females were apart from their families. The proportion of male slaves in the master's house increased dramatically for slaves aged 16 to 25. For the female slaves, the proportion in the

Table 11.8 Cross-tabulation of Male Ex-slaves by Household Type and Age in 1865

	Males, Age in 1865						
Household Type	0–3	4–7	8–11	12–15	16–19	20–25	25+
Two-parent, consolidated	61.5%	61.4%	49.5%	47.1%	35.6%	39.0%	26.8%
Two-parent, divided residence	15.4	9.6	14.7	9.9	11.9	3.4	0.0
One-parent, female headed	23.1	18.1	22.0	28.1	28.8	15.3	9.8
One-parent, male headed	0.0	0.0	1.8	0.0	3.4	1.7	0.0
Living in master's house	0.0	1.2	2.8	0.8	6.8	8.5	2.4
Living in quarters without parents	0.0	9.6	9.2	11.6	11.9	25.4	36.5
Married in own household	0.0	0.0	0.0	2.5	1.7	6.8	24.4
Subsample size	39	83	109	121	59	59	41

Table 11.9 Cross-tabulation of Female Ex-slaves by Household Type and Age in 1865

	Females, Age in 1865						
Household Type	0–3	4–7	8–11	12–15	16–19	20–25	25+
Two-parent, consolidated	73.3%	51.3%	43.6%	34.8%	33.3%	14.8%	23.1%
Two-parent, divided residence	13.3	12.5	17.9	10.1	7.8	11.1	3.8
One-parent, female headed	10.0	31.3	25.6	24.7	9.8	7.4	23.1
One-parent, male headed	0.0	0.0	1.3	0.0	2.0	0.0	0.0
Living in master's house	0.0	3.8	5.1	14.6	13.7	11.1	3.8
Living in quarters without parents	3.3	1.3	6.4	14.6	17.7	25.9	11.5
Married in own household	0.0	0.0	0.0	1.1	15.7	29.6	34.6
Subsample size	30	80	78	89	51	27	26

master's house peaks among the 12–15 age group and then falls off steadily. Slave girls who nursed, cooked, and cleaned were useful at a younger age than were slave boys who acted as personal servants and coachmen.

Tables 11.8 and 11.9 include information from the narratives regarding the age at which slaves married. The sample is small because few of the ex-slaves interviewed had reached marriageable age during slavery. After all, a slave twenty years old in 1865 would have been a 92-year-old ex-slave informant in 1937. The reported incidence of marriage among the ex-slaves who did reach marriageable age was low in the narratives. This might reflect the lack of interviewer interest in the subject or the ex-slave's focus on initial family life. Even if the absolute levels are suspect, the movement in the percentage-married at different ages provides information on the age at which males and females tended to get married.

Female slaves were married at a significantly earlier age than males, although very few females were married before fifteen years of age. The first large group of female slaves to marry was in the 16–19 age group where 16 percent reported being married. The percentage married doubles between the 16–19 and the 20-and-older age groups. Slave girls began marrying after age 16, but the largest percentage waited until they were 20 or older. The first jump in the percentage of male slaves married does not come until the 20-and-older category. In fact, the small number who said they were married suggests that many male slaves probably waited until their mid to late twenties before getting married.

The household information together with the previously discussed estimates of sale can be used to provide a view of the permanence of slave families. Roughly 75 to 80 percent of the slaves in the narratives were born into two-parent (consolidated and divided-residence) families. By age nineteen, close to 50 percent of the slaves were still members of such families. Thus roughly 40 percent of the slave children born into two-parent families experienced the loss of a parent by death or sale or were themselves sold or transferred from the family. Roughly 20 percent of slave children never experienced life in a two-parent household—because they had a white father or a slave father whom they never knew, their family was never fully formed. To grossly simplify the slave family structure, 80 percent of the children were born into two-parent households and 40 percent of these would experience a disruption from death, sale, or transfer, by age twenty. Twenty percent of the slave children never experienced life in a two-parent family.

The analysis of the family thus far groups all ex-slaves together regardless of location, plantation size, or job of their parents. By cross-tabulating either the family of origin or household distribution with these important factors, subgroups in the slave population can be examined in detail.

Arguments about the families of fieldhands and houseservants have existed since the pioneering work of W. E. B. Du Bois. Du Bois thought that it was only among the houseservants that a strong family existed. Although it is difficult to determine whether Du Bois believed that the relationships within families were weak or that no nuclear family structure existed among fieldhands, his statement implies different family distributions among houseservants and fieldhands. Table 11.10 presents a cross-tabulation of family type

Table 11.10 **Cross-tabulation of the Family of Origin by the Job of the Ex-slave's Mother**

	Mother's Job	
Family Type	House-Related	Fieldwork
Two-parent, consolidated	56.1%	58.1%
Two-parent, divided residence	14.1	14.1
One-parent, female headed	29.8	27.7
Sample size	326	191

by the job of the ex-slave's mother (given the low percentage of male-headed families, a comparable analysis is not possible for the job of the father). Quite clearly there was no difference between the family structure of houseservants and fieldhands. It is possible that the family relationship differed in other ways, but there was no significant difference in the proportion of two-parent and one-parent families.

The two most important factors affecting the household distribution were the size and location of the ex-slave's plantation. The plantation-size cross-tabulation is presented in Table 11.11. The percentage of children in two-parent, consolidated households was lower on farms with one to fifteen slaves than on those with sixteen or more slaves. The lower percentage is offset in part by the higher incidence of two-parent divided-residence households on small farms. Taking all of the two-parent households together, however, only 35 percent of the children on farms with one to five slaves and 52 percent of those on farms with six to fifteen slaves were in two-parent households. On slaveholdings of sixteen or more slaves, 67 to 73 percent were in two-parent households. The smaller slaveholdings had a higher incidence of one-parent households and of children separated from their parents. Twenty-eight to thirty-five percent of the households on small farms were one-parent compared with only 14 to 19 percent on the larger units. There was also a higher percentage of children living apart from their parents on the smallest farms. There thus appear to be two household distributions, with the separation coming at roughly fifteen slaves. Below that level, the slave farm may have been too small to provide marriage partners. More likely, small farms had grown or decreased through purchase or sale with resulting breakup of marriages and the separation of children from their parents. On plantations with sixteen or more slaves the two-parent family predominated, although even on these plantations the percentage of slave children living apart from their parents averaged 10 to 20 percent.

Table 11.11 Cross-tabulation of Ex-slaves by Household Type and Size of the Plantation

	Plantation Size (in number of slaves)				
Household Type	1–5	6–15	16–49	50–99	100+
Two-parent, consolidated	16.3	27.5	59.4	52.8	55.6
Two-parent, divided residence	10.2	19.6	8.5	11.1	6.8
One-parent, female headed	28.6	26.5	16.0	13.9	18.5
One-parent, male headed	6.1	2.0	0.9	0.0	0.6
Living in master's house	6.1	6.9	3.8	4.2	5.6
Living in quarters without parents	24.4	12.7	6.6	15.3	6.8
Married in own household	8.2	4.9	4.7	2.8	6.2
Subsample size	49	102	106	72	162

After plantation size, it has been assumed that the most important factor affecting the distribution of slave households was location. The story of the movement of the locus of slavery from East to West is well known. This movement separated the South into slave-importing states (Deep South and Southwest) and slave-exporting states (Southeast).

This movement did not, however, create two distinct household distributions. Table 11.12 shows that in both regions, 55 to 60 percent of slave children lived in two-parent consolidated or divided-residence households. The only real difference is the split between these two household types. In the slave-exporting states roughly 15 percent of the slave children grew up in two-parent divided-residence households compared with only 5 percent in the importing regions. The percentages in all other categories are similar.

The differences in the divided-residence household percentages in exporting and importing states could in large part be due to the effect of plantation size. Tables 11.13 and 11.14 present cross-tabulations of household type by plantation size within the two slave regions. Some of the differences already noted in the discussion of plantation size are again present. The proportion of two-parent consolidated households in both regions is much higher on slaveholdings of more than fifteen slaves. Two-parent divided-residence and one-parent residence show significant differences in the two regions. The divided-residence households were more prevalent in the longer settled exporting states and within the region on small farms. Divided-residence households were comparatively rare in the importing region, owing, at least in part, to the greater geographical distance between slave farms in the new regions.

The higher percentage of female-headed households raises some questions about family formation on small farms in the importing region. These households were the result of fathers unknown to the slave child or, more probably, breakup by sale or transfer. Slaves on small farms in the importing region either migrated with their masters from the exporting states or were purchased

Table 11.12 **Cross-tabulation of Ex-slaves by Household Type and Location of Plantation**

	Plantation Location	
Household Type	Slave-exporting States	Slave-importing States
Two-parent, consolidated	39.4%	46.5%
Two-parent, divided residence	14.7	5.2
One-parent, female headed	22.3	23.2
One-parent, male headed	0.8	1.3
Living in master's house	5.3	4.4
Living in quarters without parent	11.8	13.9
Married in own household	5.6	5.3
Subsample size	620	640

Note: Based on the ex-slaves' actual living situation at emancipation.

Table 11.13 Cross-tabulation of Ex-slaves by Household Type and Size of the Plantation for Ex-slaves from Slave-exporting States

	Plantation Size (in number of slaves)				
Household Type	1–5	6–15	16–49	50–99	100+
Two-parent, consolidated	23.1%	25.0%	54.4%	51.6%	45.5%
Two-parent, divided residence	38.5	23.1	15.8	9.7	10.6
One-parent, female headed	15.4	25.0	14.0	22.6	18.2
One-parent, male headed	0.0	1.9	0.0	0.0	1.5
Living in master's house	7.7	7.7	5.3	6.5	9.1
Living in quarters without parents	15.4	13.4	5.3	9.7	7.6
Married in own household	0.0	3.8	5.3	0.0	7.6
Subsample size	13	52	57	31	66

Note: Based on the ex-slaves' actual living situation at emancipation.

Table 11.14 Cross-tabulation of Ex-slaves by Household Type and Size of the Plantation for Ex-slaves from Slave-importing States

	Plantation Size (in number of slaves)				
Household Type	1–5	6–15	16–49	50–99	100+
Two-parent, consolidated	14.8%	27.5%	81.5%	59.4%	66.3%
Two-parent, divided residence	0.0	12.5	0.0	9.4	2.5
One-parent, mother headed	37.0	32.5	23.1	6.3	18.8
One-parent, father headed	7.4	0.0	0.0	0.0	0.0
Living in master's house	3.7	12.5	7.7	15.5	5.0
Living in quarters without parents	29.6	12.5	7.7	15.5	5.0
Married in own household	7.4	7.5	5.1	6.3	5.0
Subsample size	27	40	39	32	80

Note: Based on the ex-slaves' actual living situation at emancipation.

after the move. The uprooting of a small slave farm was much more likely to break up a slave family because of the higher incidence of divided-residence families on small farms in the slave-exporting regions. As Josephine Howard who grew up in Texas related, "One mornin' we is all herded up and mammy am cryin' and say de gwine to Texas, but can't take papa. He don't 'long to dem. Dat de lastes' time we ever seed papa."[22]

The second factor affecting the level of one-parent families was the extent to which owners of small farms, especially in the importing states, purchased slaves. The higher level of slave purchase and transfer is suggested by the 25

22. Rawick, vol. 4 (2), *Texas Narratives,* p. 164.

to 30 percent of slave children on the small farms in importing states who resided alone in the quarters or the master's house. The tendency to acquire slaves by sale or transfer undoubtedly led to the purchase of slave mothers and some or all of her children. These purchases, along with the breakup of divided-residence families when small farms moved, fueled the growth of one-parent households in the slave-importing region.

Analysis of the factors affecting slave household structure shows that the integrity of the family was most secure on large plantations in both importing and exporting regions. Because small farms grew by slave purchase and, if they moved, were more likely to disrupt divided-residence families, the slave child was much more likely to face family disruption if he or she lived on a small farm.

It has been widely accepted that the slave family was characterized by a dual structure of two-parent and female-headed families. The narrative sample suggests a two-to-one ratio of these types. While there has not been as much discussion of the importance of the divided-residence family, its existence does not alter the accepted interpretation of a strong slave family.

The narratives also provide some quantitative measures of the permanence of slave families. Slavery disrupted the family through the separation of husband and wife and the sale of slave children. On the latter issue, it is important to note the existence of a group of slave children separated from their families who were repeatedly sold. The disproportionate sale of these slave children could indicate that owners tended to avoid disrupting families if possible.

It is in the controversy over how a stable dual family structure came into existence that the narratives have been less helpful. Because of the nature of the source, it can support many interpretations. And even the quantitative data are open to numerous interpretations when combined with other primary and secondary sources on slavery.

The study of the slave family shows that slave owners benefited from encouraging the family through increased fertility. It is also possible, but unsupported by the narratives, that stable family life encouraged higher productivity. The effect could operate through the positive incentives associated with families or the negative incentive of the threat of selling family members. The role of strong, viable, and effective family life has been inadequately studied. It is key to what I believe is the proper interpretation of the development of the slave family structure. Stable families grew out of the economic interaction of the slaveowner's desire for the growth and productive use of his labor force and the slave's desire to improve the living conditions for kin.

Elsewhere I have examined the effect of family type on diet, housing, clothing, and the probabilities of sale and punishment to show that slave children fared differently across family types.[23] The differences are most pronounced

23. See Stephen Crawford, "Quantified Memory: A Study of the WPA and Fisk University Slave Narrative Collections" (Ph.D. dissertation, University of Chicago, 1980), chap. 6.

when comparing children alone in the quarters to all other children. A slave child living separately from his family and alone in the quarters faced the greatest risk of harsh treatment. And a slave child was less likely to be sold away from a family that had two parents, even if the parents resided on different plantations.

The two-parent family, whether consolidated or divided-residence, also tended to provide the basic necessities of life more effectively than did one-parent families. While the differences are not always large or statistically significant, two-parent families have lower levels of inadequate treatment. The similarity among the three family types is, however, more surprising than the differences. The slave narratives suggest that slave women effectively provided for their families. The quality of life in their families might have been marginally below that of a comparable family with two parents, but their children lived at levels far above those of children alone in the quarters.

Both slaveowner and slave had incentives to create and maintain the family structure identified in this study. The master may have encouraged two-parent families because of their higher fertility or, possibly, because their members were more productive in the field. The slave's incentive was the higher living standard obtained by those in two-parent families. Slaveowners did sell husbands from wives, but they did so, I believe, only after weighing the penalty of such actions. Slaves chose not to create or maintain two-parent families but, again, they may have done so knowing the consequences. This essentially economic interaction created a dual family structure of two-parent and single-parent families. The sheer volume of information about the family in the narratives attests to the importance ex-slaves placed on family in recalling and defining their slave experience. The reader of the narratives cannot help but recognize the bonds of many slaves to their families and the horrible emotional loss slaves endured in trying to hold family together. Quantifying the narrative information brings solid measure to both sides of this equation. One facet of slavery's inhumanity was that it added to the normal strains of family through the fear—and often reality—of family breakup and through sexual relations between white men and black women. While slaveowners, we may presume, were inclined to maintain slave families because of increased fertility and productivity, there were other conflicting incentives that often rendered the slave family vulnerable and fragile. A history of the slave family reveals the struggle between the slave's desire and need for a viable family with the too-often-present economic necessity of slavery to ignore the family.

12 The Fertility Transition in the United States

Tests of Alternative Hypotheses

Richard H. Steckel

12.1 Introduction

The secular decline of fertility in the United States and its East-West gradient have intrigued several generations of economists, historians, and demographers. The fertility transition was well underway before substantial industrial or urban development, which has led to explanations that feature a rural setting. A prominent model emphasizes land availability, while alternative, yet complementary, explanations rely on changes in education, wealth, occupational structure, ethnic composition, saving behavior, family-limitation techniques, and child wages.

The average age at first birth, the average age at last birth, the average spacing interval, and the share of women who eventually have children determine average completed family size.[1] While a comprehensive study would examine all four aspects, nearly all explanations of nineteenth-century fertility patterns accept, or at least do not deny, that decisions made within marriage partly influenced completed family size. Specifically, decisions on birth control, the frequency of intercourse, and breastfeeding practices may have influenced the number of births within marriage. Despite the importance of these types of decisions for completed family size, there has been little research on marital fertility per se for the early part of the transition.

This essay has two major objectives. The first is to describe regional and temporal patterns of fertility for the white population in the United States

The author has benefited from comments or discussions with Lee Alston, Charles Calomiris, Colin Cameron, Paul Evans, David Galenson, Patrick Galloway, Claudia Goldin, Marvin McInnis, Clayne Pope, Patricia Reagan, Richard Sutch, Jenny Wahl, Eugene White, and seminar participants at Berkeley, Illinois, Ohio State, the Research Triangle Economic History Workshop, and Stanford. Financial support was provided by the National Science Foundation (SES–8410660) and by Ohio State University.

1. Richard H. Steckel, *The Economics of U.S. Slave and Southern White Fertility* (New York, 1985) discusses an equation for completed family size in terms of these components.

during the nineteenth century and to assess the extent to which variations in marital fertility contributed to fertility patterns in the United States at mid-century.[2] The second is to describe and evaluate empirically the major alternative hypotheses for variations in marital fertility.

Early work on the formulation of hypotheses was guided heavily by analysis of group data, principally evidence at the regional and state levels.[3] Difficulties of identifying operative mechanisms in highly aggregate data led to subsequent work at the county or township level and more recently to study of individual and household data in cross-sectional or longitudinal form.[4] The cross-sectional samples from the federal censuses have the advantage (beginning in 1850) of including substantial socioeconomic information about the household but are silent on adaptations to changing circumstances. Longitudinal data from genealogies have the advantage of tracking fertility over the life cycle but may require tedious matching with other sources as a prelude to socioeconomic analysis.

The empirical research here rests on longitudinal data assembled from the manuscript schedules of the federal censuses of 1850 and 1860. By using a child's reported state of birth to track changes in residence, I have assembled a national sample of 638 rural families that contained wives of childbearing age and that had husbands and wives who survived through the decade of the 1850s.[5] I measure fertility by surviving additions to the family that occurred from 1850 to 1860 as indicated by the number of children aged 10 or less listed on the 1860 census manuscripts. The fertility measure, combined with information from the manuscript schedules on household features and with data from the published census on county-of-residence characteristics, enables the estimation of models on the determinants of marital fertility.

2. As used in this paper the term "marital fertility" refers to the behavior from 1850 to 1860 of the subset of married women who had at least one child by 1850.

3. Richard A. Easterlin, "Does Human Fertility Adjust to the Environment?" *American Economic Review,* 61 (May 1971), pp. 399–407; Colin Forster and G. S. L. Tucker, *Economic Opportunity and White American Fertility Ratios, 1800–1860* (New Haven, 1972); Maris A. Vinovskis, "Socioeconomic Determinants of Interstate Fertility Differentials in the United States in 1850 and 1860," *Journal of Interdisciplinary History,* 6 (Winter 1976), pp. 375–96; Yasukichi Yasuba, *Birth Rates of the White Population in the United States, 1800–1860* (Baltimore, 1961).

4. Don R. Leet, "The Determinants of the Fertility Transition in Antebellum Ohio," *Journal of Economic History,* 36 (June 1976), pp. 359–78; Maris A. Vinovskis, "A Multivariate Regression Analysis of Fertility Differentials among Massachusetts Regions and Towns in 1860," in *Historical Studies of Changing Fertility,* Charles Tilly, ed. (Princeton, 1978), pp. 225–56; Michael R. Haines, "Fertility and Marriage in a Nineteenth-Century Industrial City: Philadelphia, 1850–1880," *Journal of Economic History,* 40 (Mar. 1980), pp. 151–58; Richard H. Steckel, "Antebellum Southern White Fertility: A Demographic and Economic Analysis," *Journal of Economic History,* 40 (June 1980), pp. 331–50; Jenny Bourne Wahl, "New Results on the Decline in Household Fertility in the United States, 1750–1900," in *Long-Term Factors in American Economic Growth,* Stanley L. Engerman and Robert E. Gallman, eds. (Chicago, 1986), pp. 391–437.

5. See Richard H. Steckel, "Census Matching and Migration: A Research Strategy," *Historical Methods,* 21 (Spring 1988), pp. 52–60, for discussion of details and limitations of the matching process.

12.2 Child-Woman Ratios

Because the system of vital registration was substantially incomplete in the United States during the nineteenth century, studies of childbearing for this era often use an indirect measure of fertility such as the child-woman ratio. Usually tabulated from census age distributions, the numerator of this ratio consists of the number of young children, while the denominator is the number of women of childbearing age. Because the numerator includes only surviving children, variations in the ratios may reflect differential mortality rather than genuine differences in fertility. Moreover, the fertility history captured by the numerator may include children born outside the region or state under study. Despite these shortcomings, this measure of fertility has been shown to be highly correlated with direct measures such as total fertility and the refined birth rate.[6]

Table 12.1 presents evidence on long-term trends and regional differences in the number of white children under age 10 per thousand white women aged 15 to 49. During the nineteenth century the ratio diminished by varying magnitudes within each region and by 41 percent in the nation as a whole. Roughly one-half of the national decline in the century had occurred by 1850. Regions within the North had the largest rates of decline, especially the East North Central region (60 percent), while southern regions, particularly the West South Central (24 percent), experienced lesser reductions.[7] In any year the ratio was usually higher in western compared with eastern states. In 1830, for example, the ratio in the East North Central states exceeded that in the Northeast by 43 percent, while it was 12 percent below that in the West North Central region. A similar pattern prevailed in most of the South. An exception is found in the western states in the early decades of the century, but the anomaly may be explained by the numerical dominance of the city of New Orleans, which probably had low fertility and high childhood mortality rates.[8] The re-

6. Donald J. Bogue and James A. Palmore, "Some Empirical and Analytic Relations Among Demographic Fertility Measures, with Regression Models for Fertility Estimation," *Demography,* 1 (1964), pp. 316–38.

7. The possible influence of mortality differences and trends on the child-woman ratios is substantially unknown because information is scanty before the end of the nineteenth century. A time series on human stature indicates, however, that cohorts of the late 1700s and early 1800s experienced improving levels of net nutrition while those born after 1830 witnessed declines. See Robert William Fogel, "Nutrition and the Decline in Mortality since 1700: Some Preliminary Findings," in *Long-Term Factors in American Economic Growth,* Stanley L. Engerman and Robert E. Gallman, eds. (Chicago, 1986), pp. 439–555. Since adult stature is sensitive to environmental conditions in childhood, one may argue that childhood mortality rates followed the cycle in heights. If so, the child-woman ratios may understate the extent of fertility decline in the early part of the century but exaggerate the decline after the 1830s.

8. The West South Central region consisted exclusively of Louisiana before 1840, and in 1850 the state represented about 45 percent of the population in the region. About 25.9 percent of the population in Louisiana resided in urban areas (towns or cities having a population of 2,500 or more) in 1850 compared with 8.3 percent in the South as a whole. It is well established that urban areas traditionally have relatively low fertility rates. The warm climate and high concentration of

Table 12.1 Number of White Children under Age 10 Per Thousand White Women Aged 15 to 49 by Census Year and Region

Year	NE	ENC	WNC	SA	ESC	WSC	WEST	U.S.
1800	1,462	2,143		1,580	2,065			1,541
1810	1,448	1,998		1,542	1,961	1,632		1,542
1820	1,321	1,870		1,480	1,820	1,582		1,465
1830	1,226	1,755	2,000	1,430	1,783	1,562		1,413
1840	1,138	1,579	1,761	1,405	1,711	1,604		1,348
1850	984	1,366	1,478	1,261	1,563	1,404		1,186
1860	973	1,280	1,411	1,211	1,350	1,432	1,285	1,164
1870	878	1,156	1,311	1,047	1,161	1,171	1,260	1,056
1880	833	1,037	1,220	1,167	1,266	1,421	1,044	1,042
1890	739	926	1,082	1,080	1,160	1,308	937	939
1900	762	864	1,001	1,059	1,126	1,240	885	914

Notes: Interpolation of the age categories, based on the distribution of exact ages in a random sample of households drawn from the 1860 census manuscript schedules (see Richard H. Steckel, *The Economics of U.S. Slave and Southern White Fertility* [New York, 1985], pp. 660–74), was required for women in the census years of 1800 to 1820. NE = Northeast, ENC = East North Central, WNC = West North Central, SA = South Atlantic, ESC = East South Central, WSC = West South Central, WEST = Mountain and Pacific.

Sources: Published federal population censuses, 1800–1900.

gional contrasts tended to diminish during the course of the century. By 1900 the excess of the ratio in the West North Central states over that in the Northeast, for example, was 31 percent compared with 63 percent in 1830.

The net additions of children to families from 1850 to 1860, shown in Table 12.2, are consistent with the regional gradient of child-woman ratios given in Table 12.1, but the contrasts, although substantial, are less than those observed for child-woman ratios. Regional differences existed for women of all ages and ranged from a high of nearly one child between the Northeast and the frontier for women aged 20 to 24 to a low of 0.64 children among those aged 25 to 29. In an era when the total fertility rate was approximately 5.2 for white women in the country as a whole, these regional differences in the number of surviving children aged 10 or less were important relative to average fertility behavior.[9] If all ages are combined, a married woman on the frontier had about one-third more children than a married woman in the Northeast, while the child-woman ratio in the West North Central and the West South Central states (an approximation of the frontier) was about 46 percent above

population living near waterways or swamps suggests that children had high rates of exposure to disease. Data on adult stature are consistent with the argument of poor health. According to union army records, enlisters from Louisiana were shorter than those from the other southern states that furnished significant numbers of troops (Kentucky, Tennessee, Maryland, and Missouri). See Benjamin Apthrop Gould, *Investigations in the Military and Anthropological Statistics of American Soldiers* (New York, 1869), pp. 94–95.

9. Estimates of total fertility are available in Ansley J. Coale and Melvin Zelnik, *New Estimates of Fertility and Population in the United States* (Princeton, 1963), p. 36.

Table 12.2 **Average Number of Children Aged 10 or Less among Rural Families in 1860 by Region of Residence in 1850**

	Wife's Age in 1850								
	20–24			25–29			30–34		
Region	Mean	Stand. Dev.	N	Mean	Stand. Dev.	N	Mean	Stand. Dev.	N
Northeast	2.76	1.23	25	2.79	1.65	81	2.10	1.54	63
North Central	3.23	1.54	35	3.12	1.42	52	2.58	1.19	52
South	3.42	1.47	84	3.33	1.53	110	2.85	1.60	80
Frontier[a]	3.71	1.45	17	3.43	1.80	23	2.94	1.48	16
Total	3.30	1.46	161	3.13	1.58	266	2.56	1.51	211

Sources: Manuscript schedules of the 1850 and 1860 federal population censuses.
[a]Includes Minnesota, Iowa, Kansas, Texas, and states farther west.

that in the Northeast. Therefore variations in other determinants of child-woman ratios, such as the age at first birth and the share of women who ever had children, must have been important influences on regional fertility patterns.

12.3 Alternative Hypotheses

Alternative hypotheses of long-term declines and regional differences in fertility differ considerably in the details of their operative mechanisms. Newcomers to this literature may find these distinctive features—land availability, bargaining between parents and children, literacy, occupation, and ethnicity—unrelated and not elements of an integrated model of fertility. Yet, all these hypotheses have underpinnings in the standard framework of household choice. From this common starting point explanations differ in the emphasis given to the components of choice and in their selection of proxies for determining variables.

Land-availability models follow a Malthusian tradition that views the couple's ability to support children as crucial to fertility decisions.[10] Proponents argue that opportunities for financial independence depended heavily on the cost of acquiring new land in the agricultural setting of the early nineteenth century. When land was expensive, the present value of future income was small and many prospective couples could not afford to marry.[11] The desired number of births was attained by regulating the age at marriage or, if effective

10. See, for example, Yasuba, *Birth Rates;* and Forster and Tucker, *Economic Opportunity.* According to Forster and Tucker (p. 4), opportunities for the establishment of new households could have affected the incentives of married people to restrict family size.

11. If credit markets were poorly developed, then cash was required to buy land. If credit was available, then couples needed to amass a downpayment. In either case, higher land prices, other things being equal, discouraged family formation.

knowledge was available, by control of births within marriage. A central tenet of the land availability–Malthusian reasoning is that couples desired children; births would increase if parents could afford to support a larger family. Adherents claim this reasoning explains the high child-woman ratios in western relative to eastern states and that the growth in population density led to the long-term fertility decline.

Richard Easterlin developed a variant of the land-availability thesis, called the target-bequest model, that empowered farmers with motives to establish children on nearby land.[12] Couples in an area of land scarcity, such as New England in the early nineteenth century, anticipated the cost of providing land for their children and took steps to limit family size. Higher prices for land increased the cost of children, effectively shrinking the couple's opportunity set. This variant has the same implications as the general land-availability model for regional patterns and the long-term decline in fertility.

High correlations between child-woman ratios and measures of population density at the state or county level have supported the land-availability thesis. But the results of research using household-level data have been mixed.[13] Nancy Landale, for example, found that men at the end of the nineteenth century delayed marriage when agricultural opportunity (measured by the average value of a farm in the county of residence) diminished. Marvin McInnis, however, has questioned the strength of the mechanism using Canadian data.[14] In addition, I note that long-term declines in child-woman ratios in frontier areas are troublesome for the hypothesis.[15] Roger Ransom and Richard Sutch observe that the land-scarcity model does poorly in the South, a region that began its fertility decline later than the North and that experienced a more gradual decline despite a settlement history similar to that of the Midwest.[16]

William Sundstrom and Paul David have developed a model of bargaining between parents and children to explain the fertility decline.[17] The traditional

12. Richard A. Easterlin, "Population Change and Farm Settlement in the Northern United States," *Journal of Economic History,* 36 (Mar. 1976), pp. 45–75. See also Richard A. Easterlin, George Alter, and Gretchen A. Condran, "Farms and Farm Families in Old and New Areas: The Northern States in 1860," in *Family and Population in Nineteenth-Century America,* Tamara K. Hareven and Maris A. Vinovskis, eds. (Princeton, 1978), p. 72.

13. Yasuba, *Birth Rates;* Leet, "Determinants of the Fertility Transition"; Morton Owen Schapiro, "Land Availability and Fertility in the United States, 1760–1870," *Journal of Economic History,* 42 (Sept. 1982), pp. 577–600.

14. Nancy S. Landale, "Agricultural Opportunity and Marriage: The United States at the Turn of the Century," *Demography,* 26 (May 1989), pp. 203–18; R. M. McInnis, "Childbearing and Land Availability: Some Evidence from Individual Household Data," in *Population Patterns in the Past,* Ronald Demos Lee, ed. (New York, 1977), pp. 201–27.

15. Steckel, *The Economics of U.S. Slave and Southern White Fertility,* pp. 132–33.

16. Roger L. Ransom and Richard Sutch, "Did Rising Out-Migration Cause Fertility to Decline in Antebellum New England? A Life-Cycle Perspective on Old-Age Security Motives, Child Default, and Farm-Family Fertility," Working Papers on the History of Saving no. 5 (University of California, Apr. 1986).

17. William A. Sundstrom and Paul A. David, "Old-Age Security Motives, Labor Markets, and Farm Family Fertility in Antebellum America," *Explorations in Economic History,* 25 (Apr. 1988), pp. 164–97.

family structure on farms of the colonial and early national periods placed old-age care for parents in the hands of their grown children, a system that was enforced through inheritance and inter vivos transfers. Sundstrom and David maintain that the terms of intergenerational exchange of parental wealth for old-age support were arrived at through a process of intrafamily bargaining. Their analysis concludes that the bargaining power of the young was enhanced, and the marginal value of children to nonaltruistic parents was diminished, by improved labor market opportunities for children and young adults outside agriculture. From the parents' perspective these new labor market opportunities effectively increased the net cost of raising children. The implications of this model regarding changes in the economy for parental choice are identical to those of Easterlin's bequest motive but the operative mechanism differs in its reliance on events beyond agriculture.

Roger Ransom and Richard Sutch also link the long-term decline in fertility to the demise of the old-age security motive for having children.[18] Like Sundstrom and David they emphasize family structure, but connect the beginning of the fertility decline to westward migration. In their view the Sundstrom-David mechanism (job market opportunities outside agriculture) played only a supporting role. The opening of western lands after 1815 triggered out-migration of young people who, they argue, effectively defaulted on implicit obligations to care for their parents in old age. Child default led prospective parents to curtail childbearing and accumulate financial assets that would later be spent for old-age care, a process that Ransom and Sutch call the "life-cycle transition."

Analysts have suggested several possible explanations for the inverse relationship often observed between fertility and the education or literacy of the parents.[19] Those who emphasize a connection between education and knowledge of family-limitation methods recognize that children are not acquired in the manner of market products such as apples and oranges, but are produced by a biological process over which couples have only partial control. Thus, parents may have difficulty implementing desired family size. Biological constraints may generate less than the optimum in some cases, but it is likely that a significant share of couples produced more than the desired number. Higher levels of education might have led to greater awareness of effective birth control methods. The regional patterns and time trends in fertility can be explained by noting that additional schooling and greater exposure to reading materials and ideas characterized the eastern compared with western states

18. Ransom and Sutch, "Rising Out-Migration"; Roger L. Ransom and Richard Sutch, "Two Strategies for a More Secure Old Age: Life-cycle Saving by Late-Nineteenth Century American Workers," Paper presented at the NBER Summer Institute on the Development of the American Economy, Cambridge, Mass. (July 1989).

19. The connection may be bi-directional and complex. For a discussion of issues see Harvey J. Graff, "Literacy, Education, and Fertility, Past and Present: A Critical Review," *Population and Development Review,* 5 (Mar. 1979), pp. 105–40.

and that levels of schooling improved during the century.[20] Survey information on family limitation is scanty, but that which has been analyzed as well as indirect evidence on spacing and age patterns of fertility, suggest that by the mid to late 1800s some couples, particularly those who resided in the North, effectively limited conception.[21]

Parental goals or social norms for educating children may have influenced desired family size. Industrialization during the nineteenth century increased the returns to human capital for some workers and much of the burden of financing skill accumulation fell on parents in the form of direct costs of education and foregone earnings of child labor. The net rise in child costs noted by John Caldwell and others can be represented by a diminished opportunity set for prospective parents.[22] The human capital approach associated with Gary Becker and others emphasizes the value of mother's time in child-rearing costs.[23] If market opportunities for women improved with industrialization, child costs rose correspondingly and couples were led in Becker's analysis to reduce births but not child "services" by substituting child "quality" for "quantity."[24] Although it often has been taken for granted that married women's market opportunities improve with industrialization, Claudia Goldin's recent study of women in the labor market reports that factual support for this view is lacking before 1920.[25] Despite the increased employment of single women during industrialization, Goldin notes that married women did not experience increased employment outside the home until the second decade of the twentieth century.

Richard Easterlin argues that education may have adversely affected tastes and preferences for children.[26] Growth in literacy and wider distribution of books, periodicals, and magazines could have changed the preference functions of couples away from children and toward travel, entertainment, and the consumer goods of the Industrial Revolution.

The effect of wealth on the desired number of children depends upon the

20. Lee Soltow and Edward Stevens, *The Rise of Literacy and the Common School in the United States: A Socioeconomic Analysis to 1870* (Chicago, 1981). Soltow and Stevens note the East (high literacy)–West (low literacy) gradient (p. 195) and on the time (p. 201) trend report that: "By 1800 the level of illiteracy was between 30 and 40 percent for those who occupied the lower half of the wealth distribution. This rate probably declined moderately until 1830, at which point it began to decline rapidly, especially between 1840 and 1860."

21. Paul A. David and Warren C. Sanderson, "Rudimentary Contraceptive Methods and the American Transition to Marital Fertility Control, 1855–1915," in *Long-Term Factors in American Economic Growth,* Stanley L. Engerman and Robert E. Gallman, eds. (Chicago, 1986), pp. 307–79; Warren C. Sanderson, "Quantitative Aspects of Marriage, Fertility and Family Limitation in Nineteenth Century America: Another Application of the Coale Specifications," *Demography,* 16 (Aug. 1979), pp. 339–58; Wahl, "New Results."

22. John C. Caldwell, *Theory of Fertility Decline* (New York, 1982).

23. Gary S. Becker, *A Treatise on the Family* (Cambridge, Mass., 1981).

24. Using intergenerational household-level data, Jenny Bourne Wahl finds that the nineteenth-century fertility decline is consistent with the quantity-quality model. See Wahl, chapter 13 in this volume.

25. Claudia Goldin, *Understanding the Gender Gap: An Economic History of American Women* (New York, 1990).

26. Easterlin, "Does Human Fertility Adjust to the Environment?"

relative strength of two opposing influences, a true wealth effect and a price effect. Under Malthusian assumptions the positive wealth dominates the negative price effect. Earlier empirical studies are mixed on the question of the net effect of wealth on family size. Marvin McInnis and I, for example, find a direct relationship between wealth and fertility for predominantly rural populations of Canada and the American South in the mid-nineteenth century. On the other hand, Gary Becker and H. Gregg Lewis report that fertility was lower among the wealthier in twentieth-century America. In a study of nineteenth-century families that uses genealogies, Jenny Wahl reports that the relationship between family size and wealth is complex. The number of children first declines, then increases, and eventually declines as wealth moves from low to high levels.[27]

The possible persistence of habits or cultural traditions adapted to environments of the country of birth suggests that ethnicity may have influenced the demand for children. This phenomenon could be represented in the model of choice by the persistence of Old World tastes among New World residents or that it took time for newcomers to accurately perceive and respond to their new economic surroundings. Consistent with these notions, several studies report that fertility was higher among immigrants compared with the native born in the late nineteenth century. There is some controversy, however, whether the same ethnic differences in fertility existed during the antebellum period. Studies by Maris Vinovskis, Jeremy Atack and Fred Bateman, and Colin Forster and G. S. L. Tucker report that differences were small, while Jenny Wahl found that the foreign born had higher fertility that was attributable to tighter spacing intervals.[28]

Numerous studies report systematic occupational patterns of fertility. These patterns might be attributable to differences in income or wealth, levels of education, differential bequest motives, or the value of children in home production. Birth rates in modern data tend to be higher among populations of manual compared with white-collar or professional occupations.[29] Fertility in the nineteenth century tended to be higher among farmers compared with nonfarm occupations.[30] In a sample of genealogies for the eighteenth and nineteenth centuries the number of children was lower among professionals, proprietors, and craftsmen compared with unskilled workers.[31]

27. McInnis, "Childbearing and Land Availability"; Steckel, *The Economics of U.S. Slave and Southern White Fertility;* Gary S. Becker and H. Gregg Lewis, "Interaction between Quantity and Quality of Children," in *Economics of the Family,* T. W. Schultz, ed. (Chicago, 1974); Wahl, "New Results."

28. Maris A. Vinovskis, *Fertility in Massachusetts from the Revolution to the Civil War* (New York, 1982), pp. 108–11; Jeremy Atack and Fred Bateman, *To Their Own Soil: Agriculture in the Antebellum North* (Ames, 1987); Forster and Tucker, *Economic Opportunity;* Wahl, "New Results."

29. United Nations, *The Determinants and Consequences of Population Trends: New Summary of Findings on Interaction of Demographic, Economic, and Social Factors* (New York, 1973).

30. Atack and Bateman, *To Their Own Soil;* Wahl, "New Results."

31. Wahl, "New Results."

12.4 Selection of Proxies

In designing tests of alternative hypotheses it is important to recognize that variables constructed from empirical evidence seldom correspond precisely to theoretical concepts of economic models. The lack of data often forces empirical researchers to use constructions that approximate desired variables. Therefore empirical tests are usually tests of two joint hypotheses: that the proxies adequately represent theoretical concepts and that theoretical concepts are potent explanations of behavior. In tests of the hypotheses outlined above I generally use proxies of conceptual variables favored by their proponents. For land availability there are two: the ratio of improved acres in the county of residence to the maximum acres ever improved and the ratio of the rural population in the county to the maximum rural population.[32] Because some families changed county (or state) of residence between 1850 and 1860, the choice widens, and I chose the average of the values in 1850 and 1860. Thus, the improved-acres measure is the average of the values that existed in the county of residence in 1850 and that in 1860. The use of average values of variables extends beyond density measures and includes most of the explanatory variables in the statistical analysis.

In their test of the parent-child bargaining model, Sundstrom and David measure the relative bargaining power of children and parents by off-farm employment opportunities.[33] Their proxies are the ratio of the nonagricultural to the agricultural labor force in the state and the ratio of the daily wage of common labor to the monthly wage of farm labor in the state. Using state-level census data for 1840 they find that the child-woman ratio is negatively related to each proxy. My tests of their model are limited to household heads who were farmers.

Ransom and Sutch use five proxies to identify the change in behavior they term the "life-cycle transition."[34] The variables they employ to explain child-woman ratios at the state level in the 1840 census are: 1) the rate of growth of the rural population from 1830 to 1840, a measure of out-migration that is a rough index of the chances of child default; 2) the proportion of children under age 10 who were male, which is used as a measure of selective family migration and as a measure of differential care given to children; 3) the ratio of children who attended school to the number of children aged 5 to 19; 4) the ratio of the nonagricultural to the agricultural labor force; and 5) the ratio of the daily wage of common labor to the monthly wage of farm labor. The last two variables, which are measures of the risk of child default, are identical to those used by Sundstrom and David. Data limitations of the 1840 census forced Ransom and Sutch to use ad hoc measures of migration and education.

32. The maximum was determined for the period from 1850 to 1920. See discussions of land-availability measures in Easterlin, Alter, and Condran, "Farms and Farm Families," and Schapiro, "Land Availability."

33. Sundstrom and David, "Old-Age Security Motives."

34. Ransom and Sutch, "Rising Out-Migration."

In place of their proxies I am able to substitute the percentage of the population born in the state that was living outside the state for their measure of migration and a household-specific measure of children's education—the proportion of children aged 10 to 15 in the family who attended school—for their school enrollment ratio.[35]

Ransom and Sutch briefly mention the existence and reliability of markets for financial assets in their discussion of the life-cycle transition, but proxies for the condition of these markets are completely absent from their empirical work and from their discussion of research needs.[36] Yet, the condition of financial institutions could have influenced desired family size. Well-developed financial markets give prospective parents the option of accumulating financial assets instead of investing in children as a means of providing old-age care. Indeed, an intergenerational model of parental choice under conditions of financial development predicts the substitution of financial instruments for children.[37] Consistent with this argument, John Knodel reports that fertility in administrative areas of Germany was inversely correlated with the number of bank accounts per capita.[38] Alternatively, the condition of financial institutions could be viewed as an indicator of the pace of the life-cycle transition. Which view is appropriate depends upon the importance of life-cycle savings in overall savings. If the emergence of savings for old age was relatively important in boosting banks and other financial institutions, then financial development should be viewed as an indicator of the extent of the transition. If banks and financial institutions arose primarily for other reasons, then the lack of financial development could be viewed as a constraint on the evolution of life-cycle economic processes. In either case, fertility should have been positively correlated with the condition of financial markets. For these reasons I investigate what I term the "financial-institutions hypothesis" by examining measures of the extent of financial development for their possible influence on fertility behavior. Accordingly, the regression analysis incorporates the number of banks (and branches) per 100,000 white population in the state of residence as an explanatory variable.

Years of schooling are unavailable for the early and mid-nineteenth century. I adopt the often used, but crude, proxy of the husband's and the wife's literacy as reported by the 1850 census enumerators. Information on wealth is also meager for 1850. The census of that year recorded only the value of real estate. I employ the household's value of real estate as a measure of wealth.[39]

35. I confine the measure to the ages at least as old as 10 because there was little opportunity cost of education at younger ages. Above age 15, children left home at increasing rates, leaving behind a group more likely to have been selected for attending school.

36. See Ransom and Sutch, "Two Strategies," p. 5.

37. Philip A. Neher, "Peasants, Procreation, and Pensions," *American Economic Review,* 61 (June 1971), pp. 380–89.

38. John E. Knodel, *The Decline of Fertility in Germany, 1871–1939* (Princeton, 1974), pp. 232–36.

39. A sample of 1,581 male-headed households from the 1860 census indicates that the value of real estate was an excellent predictor of total wealth (real and personal estate) beyond low levels

Occupations of the household head reported by the 1850 census are grouped into white collar, blue collar, unskilled, farmers, and other and unknown categories. The white-collar group consists of clerks, clergymen, doctors and physicians, lawyers and attorneys, merchants, and teachers, among others. Blue-collar workers are composed primarily of blacksmiths, bricklayers and masons, carpenters, coopers, shoemakers, tailors, and wagon makers. About 89 percent of the unskilled were laborers.

12.5 Tests of Hypotheses

The previous section discussed several socioeconomic variables that may have influenced marital fertility. A statistical methodology is required to measure the independent effects of these possible influences on family size, to test for their statistical significance, and to assess their practical importance. This section views the number of children aged 10 or less in 1860 as the outcome of a decision process governed by household, county, and state characteristics in 1850 and 1860. Because none of the models placed constraints on the estimating procedures, the objective is to discover which variables are correlated with fertility.

Econometric models of qualitative response are designed to portray situations in which decision outcomes assume discrete values. The number of surviving children is an example suitable for this class of models. The analysis uses a basic model in this class, the Poisson.[40] In particular, it is assumed that the number of surviving children Y_i, born in the decade of the 1850s, in the ith of N families is distributed according to the probability density

$$Pr(Y_i = y_i) = e^{-\lambda_i} \lambda_i^{y_i}/y_i\,!, \quad y_i = 0, 1, 2, \ldots; i = 1, 2, \ldots, N$$

where y_i is the realized value of the random variable and λ_i is both the mean and variance of Y_i. To incorporate exogenous variables X_{ij} $(j = 1, \ldots, K)$, including a constant, the parameter λ_i is specified to be a nonnegative function of the exogenous variables

$$\lambda_i = exp\,(X_i\beta)$$

The results below were estimated using the method of maximum likelihood.

Because simultaneous tests of these hypotheses increase the chance of multicollinearity, which biases estimated standard errors, I proceed with a series

of total wealth. See Richard H. Steckel, "Poverty and Prosperity: A Longitudinal Study of Wealth Accumulation, 1850–1860," *Review of Economics and Statistics,* 72 (May 1990), pp. 275–85.

40. Colin A. Cameron and Pravin K. Trivedi, "Econometric Models Based on Count Data: Comparisons and Applications of Some Estimators and Tests," *Journal of Applied Econometrics,* 1 (Jan. 1986), pp. 29–53. Specifically, I used the model they call Negbin I (see p. 33). Because the variance of the number of surviving children was significantly below the mean, I used the formula on page 46 to estimate a, which led to an upward adjustment of t-values by approximately 15 percent.

of pair-wise tests. The land-availability model has been widely discussed in the historical fertility literature of the past three decades and several studies show that its implications are consistent with aggregate data for several regions in the United States. On this basis I test the land-availability model against alternative hypotheses that emphasize wealth, ethnicity, occupations, education (of parents), intrafamily bargaining, life-cycle processes, and financial institutions.[41] The findings reported are based on the land-density measure chosen by Easterlin et al., but the results are similar if the rural-population measure, preferred by Morton Schapiro, is used.[42] Several tables present two specifications, the second of which differs from the first only by the inclusion of a dummy variable for the South as a way of assessing the capability of the models to explain the higher fertility observed in that region. Biological considerations justify the inclusion of dummy variables for the wife's age in all equations.

The results in Tables 12.3 through 12.9 fail to support the wealth and the education hypotheses. Supporters of these arguments may claim, however, that the relevant variables are simply measured inadequately. The value of real estate may be a poor proxy for total wealth, and literacy has obvious shortcomings as a measure of education. The findings are mixed for the bargaining and the life-cycle approaches; the negative and statistically significant coefficient on the agricultural labor force variable favors these hypotheses, but the positive and sometimes significant coefficient on the wage variable is contrary to the arguments. In the case of the life-cycle hypothesis, the migration and the school variables also have the wrong sign. The size of the t-value on the variable for southern residence indicates that separate explanations for higher fertility in the South are required when wealth, ethnicity, occupations, and literacy are used, but not in cases involving intrafamily bargaining, life-cycle transition, and financial institutions. The land-availability measure is significant in all equations with the exception of cases involving variables for intrafamily bargaining and financial institutions.

Table 12.9 shows that the measure of financial development is the only statistically significant variable in a regression that also includes population density and a dummy variable for the South. Moreover, the bank variable is reasonably potent in explaining regional differences in fertility. The marginal effect on the number of surviving children of a one-unit increase in banks per

41. The occupational classifications follow those outlined in the appendix of Stephan Thernstrom, *The Other Bostonians* (Cambridge, Mass., 1973). For additional discussion see Steckel, "Census Matching." Given the debate over appropriate classifications, the vagueness of descriptions employed by the census, and the possibilities of multiple employment, the results merely approximate the actual underlying relationships.

I have conducted some experiments on functional forms and the results are insensitive to choice of linear or semi-log specifications. Because foreign-born husband and foreign-born wife are highly correlated, I use only one (the husband) to represent ethnicity.

42. See Easterlin, Alter, and Condran, "Farms and Farm Families"; and Schapiro, "Land Availability." The correlation between these measures is about 0.73 in this sample.

Table 12.3 Explaining the Number of Children Aged 10 or Less among Rural Families by Wife's Age, Density, Wealth, and Region of Residence

Variable	Coefficient	$\partial y/\partial x_i$	*t*-value	Coefficient	$\partial y/\partial x_i$	*t*-value
Age 25–29	−0.0333	−0.099	−0.69	−0.0183	−0.054	−0.38
Age 30–34	−0.223	−0.662	−4.17	−0.200	−0.594	−3.75
Density (improved acres)	−0.199	−0.591	−2.78	−0.193	−0.573	−2.73
Wealth (real estate)						
$ 1–499	0.0399	0.118	0.65	0.0604	0.179	0.99
500–1,499	−0.0180	−0.053	−0.30	−0.00713	−0.021	−0.12
1,500–4,999	−0.0451	−0.134	−0.69	−0.0330	−0.098	−0.51
5,000+	−0.0775	−0.230	−0.93	−0.0935	−0.278	−1.13
South				0.135	0.400	3.39
Constant	1.292		19.59	1.202		17.02
N = 638		−2 log(λ) = 29.06			−2 log(λ) = 36.88	

Notes: The omitted variables are Age 20–24 and Wealth = 0.

Table 12.4 Explaining the Number of Children Aged 10 or Less among Rural Families by Wife's Age, Density, Nativity of the Husband, and Region of Residence

Variable	Coefficient	$\partial Y/\partial x_i$	*t*-value	Coefficient	$\partial Y/\partial x_i$	*t*-value
Age 25–29	−0.0439	−0.130	−0.92	−0.0260	−0.077	−0.55
Age 30–34	−0.235	−0.697	−4.45	−0.207	−0.611	−3.92
Density (improved acres)	−0.189	−0.561	−2.68	−0.176	−0.519	−2.52
Foreign-born husband[a]	0.171	0.506	2.49	0.0231	0.682	3.32
South				0.155	0.459	3.84
Constant	1.268		25.06	1.163		17.23
N = 638		−2 log(λ) = 31.50			−2 log(λ) = 42.18	

Notes: The omitted variables are Age 20–24 and Born in the United States.
Sources: Manuscript schedules of the 1850 and 1860 federal population censuses and published federal population censuses, 1850–1920.
[a]Because foreign-born husband and foreign-born wife are highly correlated, I use only one (the husband) to represent ethnicity.

100,000 of population is approximately − 0.07, but the interstate difference in this variable exceeds 20 and the interregional difference is as large as 14. Therefore, differences in financial development are capable of explaining a substantial portion of differences in regional fertility behavior.

The favorable results for the financial-institutions hypothesis warrant a second series of tests against others that could not be rejected in round one, namely the ethnicity, occupations, intrafamily bargaining, and life-cycle explanations. Tables 12.10 through 12.13 give these results. The banking variable is statistically significant in all regressions and the occupations and ethnicity variables also perform well, but the intrafamily bargaining and life-cycle models are less powerful predictors. With the exception of the first comparison (Table 12.10) the variable for the South is statistically insignificant.

Table 12.5 **Explaining the Number of Children Aged 10 or Less among Rural Families by Wife's Age, Density, Occupation, and Region of Residence**

Variable	Coefficient	$\partial Y/\partial x_i$	*t*-value	Coefficient	$\partial Y/\partial x_i$	*t*-value
Age 25–29	−0.0310	−0.091	−0.64	−0.0197	−0.058	−0.41
Age 30–34	−0.237	−0.700	−4.49	−0.218	−0.643	−4.11
Density (improved acres)	−0.170	−0.501	−2.39	−0.172	−0.508	−2.44
Husband's occupation (1850)						
White collar	−0.191	−0.565	−2.43	−0.183	−0.541	−2.34
Blue collar	−0.184	−0.545	−3.26	−0.155	−0.457	−2.70
Unskilled	−0.459	−0.136	−0.63	−0.0212	−0.062	−0.29
Other and unknown	0.0560	0.166	0.52	−0.0666	0.197	0.62
South				0.105	0.311	2.61
Constant	1.314		26.25	1.244		21.92
N = 638		−2 log(λ) = 38.78			−2 log(λ) = 43.72	

Notes: The omitted variables are Age 20–24 and Farmer.

Sources: Manuscript schedules of the 1850 and 1860 federal population censuses and published federal population censuses, 1850–1920.

Table 12.6 **Explaining the Number of Children Aged 10 or Less among Rural Families by Wife's Age, Density, Literacy, and Region of Residence**

Variable	Coefficient	$\partial Y/\partial x_i$	*t*-value	Coefficient	$\partial Y/\partial x_i$	*t*-value
Age 25–29	−0.0475	−0.141	−0.99	−0.0281	−0.083	−0.58
Age 30–34	−0.244	−0.724	−4.61	−0.217	−0.641	−4.07
Density (improved acres)	−0.195	−0.581	−2.74	−0.194	−0.574	−2.73
Husband illiterate	−0.0321	−0.095	−0.40	−0.756	−0.224	−0.93
Wife illiterate	0.101	0.300	1.60	0.861	0.255	1.37
South				0.126	0.373	3.14
Constant	1.281		24.60	1.204		21.14
N = 638		−2 log(λ) = 28.70			−2 log(λ) = 36.08	

Note: The omitted variable is Age 20–24.

Sources: Manuscript schedules of the 1850 and 1860 federal population census and published federal population censuses, 1850–1920.

Table 12.14 contains regressions testing those hypotheses that could not be rejected in round two, namely the financial-institutions, ethnicity, and occupations arguments. In addition, the life-cycle model, though a weak performer, is also tested. The financial-institutions, ethnicity, and occupations hypotheses all emerge as contenders and constitute a package that does not require separate arguments for higher southern fertility.[43] Indeed, data in Table 12.15 on regional characteristics of the white population and the partial deriv-

43. If the life-cycle variables are dropped from the regression reported in Table 12.14, the coefficient for the South remains insignificant at the conventional level of 0.05.

Table 12.7 Explaining the Number of Children Aged 10 or Less among Rural Families by Wife's Age, Density, the Ratio of the Nonagricultural to the Agricultural Labor Force, the Ratio of the Wage of Common Labor to that of Farm Labor, and Region of Residence

Variable	Coefficient	$\partial Y/\partial x_i$	*t*-value	Coefficient	$\partial Y/\partial x_i$	*t*-value
Age 25–29	−0.00194	−0.006	−0.03	−0.00106	−0.003	−0.12
Age 30–34	−0.174	−0.541	−2.76	−0.175	−0.544	−2.78
Density (improved acres)	−0.137	−0.426	−1.48	−0.131	−0.408	−1.37
Log (labor force ratio)	−0.102	−0.318	−2.49	−0.105	−0.328	−1.76
Log (relative wage)	0.366	1.138	1.39	4.001	12.451	1.11
South				0.0275	0.086	0.42
Constant	2.133		3.07	1.005		3.86
N = 401	−2 log(λ) = 19.478			−2 log(λ) = 19.716		

Note: The omitted variable is Age 20–24.

Sources: Manuscript schedules of the 1850 and 1860 federal population censuses and published federal population censuses, 1850–1920.

Table 12.8 Explaining the Number of Children Aged 10 or Less among Rural Families by Wife's Age, Density, the Ratio of the Nonagricultural to the Agricultural Labor Force, the Ratio of the Wage of Common Labor to that of Farm Labor, the Percentage of those Born in State Who Resided Out of State, the Proportion of Children Aged 10–15 in the Family Who Attended School, and Region of Residence

Variable	Coefficient	$\partial Y/\partial x_i$	*t*-value	Coefficient	$\partial Y/\partial x_i$	*t*-value
Age 25–29	−0.0357	−0.105	−0.74	−0.0347	−0.103	−0.72
Age 30–34	−0.220	−0.651	−4.16	−0.219	−0.647	−4.12
Density (improved acres)	−0.252	−0.745	−2.75	−0.257	−0.759	−2.73
Log (labor force ratio)	−0.0900	−0.266	−2.94	−0.0831	−0.245	−1.91
Log (relative wage)	0.539	1.593	2.40	0.519	1.532	2.13
Log (migration)	0.0707	0.209	1.58	0.0712	0.210	1.59
School	0.0376	0.111	0.86	0.0394	0.116	0.89
South				0.139	0.041	0.22
Constant	2.406		4.07	2.349		3.65
N = 638	−2 log(λ) = 42.96			−2 log(λ) = 42.98		

Note: The omitted variable is Age 20–24.

Sources: Manuscript schedules of the 1850 and 1860 federal population census and published federal population censuses, 1850–1920.

atives in Table 12.14 suggest that fertility was lower in the North despite a greater presence of the foreign born largely because the South had a poorly developed banking system and secondarily because the region had a higher concentration of farmers and laborers.[44] Comparison of the regional age dis-

44. Essentially the same conclusion is reached if characteristics of the sample of matched households are used in place of characteristics of the population.

Table 12.9 Explaining the Number of Children Aged 10 or Less among Rural Families by Wife's Age, Density, Banks Per 100,000 White Population, and Region of Residence

Variable	Coefficient	$\partial Y/\partial x_i$	t-value	Coefficient	$\partial Y/\partial x_i$	t-value
Age 25–29	−0.0343	−0.101	−0.72	−0.0262	−0.077	−0.55
Age 30–34	−0.222	−0.654	−4.21	−0.210	−0.620	−3.98
Density (improved acres)	−0.0104	−0.031	−0.13	−0.0358	−0.105	−0.43
Banks	−0.0242	−0.071	−4.30	−0.0209	−0.062	−3.62
South				0.0777	0.229	1.87
Constant	1.282		25.83	1.236		22.31
N = 638		−2 log(λ) = 43.16			−2 log(λ) = 45.74	

Note: The omitted variable is Age 20–24.

Sources: Manuscript schedules of the 1850 and 1860 federal population censuses; published federal population censuses, 1850–1920; and U.S. Census Office, *Statistics of the United States in 1860* (Washington, D.C., 1866), p. 292.

Table 12.10 Explaining the Number of Children Aged 10 or Less among Rural Families by Wife's Age, Banks Per 100,000 White Population, Nativity of the Husband, and Region of Residence

Variable	Coefficient	$\partial Y/\partial x_i$	t-value	Coefficient	$\partial Y/\partial x_i$	t-value
Age 25–29	−0.0354	−0.104	0.61	−0.0245	−0.072	−0.42
Age 30–34	−0.217	−0.640	−3.48	−0.201	−0.591	−3.21
Banks	−0.0241	−0.071	−4.76	−0.0207	−0.601	−3.97
Foreign-born husband	0.183	0.540	1.86	0.225	0.661	2.24
South				0.106	0.311	2.18
Constant	1.260		25.13	1.181		19.15
N = 638		−2 log(λ) = 48.26			−2 log(λ) = 52.86	

Note: The omitted variable is Age 20–24.

Sources: Manuscript schedules of the 1850 and 1860 federal population censuses; published federal population censuses, 1850–1920; and U.S. Census Office, *Statistics of the United States in 1860* (Washington, 1866), p. 292.

tributions in the sample indicates that a lower proportion in the age group 30 to 34 was also a minor factor in the South's higher rate of marital fertility. These data also suggest that higher fertility on the frontier compared with the Northeast was largely the consequence of differences in the development of the banking system and to some extent the result of differences in occupational structure.

12.6 Implications

While there are risks in using a model estimated for the 1850s to understand long-term trends, the estimated relationships and the changes in the American economy after 1810 point to development of the banking system and the

Table 12.11 Explaining the Number of Children Aged 10 or Less among Rural Families by Wife's Age, Banks Per 100,000 White Population, Occupation, and Region of Residence

Variable	Coefficient	$\partial Y/\partial x_i$	t-value	Coefficient	$\partial Y/\partial x_i$	t-value
Age 25–29	−0.0229	−0.067	−0.48	−0.0173	−0.051	−0.36
Age 30–34	−0.218	−0.643	−4.17	−0.210	−0.617	−3.99
Banks	−0.0221	−0.065	−4.58	−0.0205	−0.060	−4.18
Husband's occupation (1850)						
White collar	−0.183	−0.539	−2.35	−0.180	−0.530	−2.32
Blue collar	−0.148	−0.435	−2.62	−0.135	−0.396	−2.36
Unskilled	−0.00301	−0.009	−0.04	−0.0788	0.023	0.11
Other and unknown	0.0736	0.217	0.68	0.0790	0.233	0.74
South				0.0616	0.181	1.49
Constant	1.298		31.49	1.253		24.39
N = 638		−2 log(λ) = 52.24			−2 log(λ) = 53.84	

Notes: The omitted variables are Age 20–24 and Farmer.

Sources: Manuscript schedules of the 1850 and 1860 federal population censuses; published federal population censuses, 1850–1920; and U.S. Census Office, *Statistics of the United States in 1860* (Washington, D.C., 1866), p. 292.

Table 12.12 Explaining the Number of Children Aged 10 or Less among Rural Farm Families by Wife's Age, Banks Per 100,000 White Population, the Ratio of the Nonagricultural to the Agricultural Labor Force, the Ratio of the Wage of Common Labor to that of Farm Labor, and Region of Residence

Variable	Coefficient	$\partial Y/\partial x_i$	t-value
Age 25–29	0.0123	0.032	0.18
Age 30–34	−0.160	−0.498	−2.55
Banks	−0.0242	−0.075	−2.99
Log (labor force ratio)	−0.0458	−0.142	−0.74
Log (relative wage)	0.307	0.953	1.07
South	0.00546	0.017	0.07
Constant	2.025		2.70
N = 401		−2 log(λ) = 24.9546	

Note: The omitted variable is Age 20–24.

Sources: Manuscript schedules of the 1850 and 1860 federal population censuses; published federal population censuses, 1850–1920 and U.S. Census Office, *Statistics of the United States in 1860* (Washington, 1866), p. 292.

changing occupational structure, particularly after the War of 1812, as important ingredients in the decline of antebellum fertility. In 1811 there were only eighty-eight banks for a population of about six million free Americans, or 1.45 banks per 100,000.[45] The ratio more than doubled by 1820 and by 1840

45. Calculated from U.S. Bureau of the Census, *Historical Statistics of the United States, Colonial Times to 1970* (Washington, D.C., 1975), series X 561–579, X 580–587, and A 91–104.

Table 12.13 **Explaining the Number of Children Aged 10 or Less among Rural Families by Wife's Age, Density, the Ratio of the Nonagricultural to the Agricultural Labor force, the Ratio of the Wage of Common Labor to that of Farm Labor, the Percentage of those born in State Who Resided Out of State, the Proportion of Children Aged 10–15 in the Family Who Attended School, and Region of Residence**

Variable	Coefficient	$\partial Y/\partial x_i$	*t*-value
Age 25–29	−0.0358	−0.105	0.74
Age 30–34	−0.218	−0.640	−4.10
Banks	−0.0237	−0.070	−3.91
Log (labor force ratio)	−0.0443	−0.130	−0.99
Log (relative wage)	0.356	1.049	1.47
Log (migration)	0.0639	0.188	1.58
School	0.0271	0.080	0.61
South	0.00464	0.005	0.08
Constant	1.954		3.02
N = 638	−2 log(λ) = 50.14		

Note: The omitted variable is Age 20–24.

Sources: Manuscript schedules of the 1850 and 1860 federal population censuses and published federal population censuses, 1850–1920.

Table 12.14 **Explaining the Number of Children Aged 10 or Less among Rural Families by Wife's Age, Banks Per 100,000 of White Population, the Ratio of the Nonagricultural to the Agricultural Labor Force, the Ratio of the Wage of Common Labor to that of Farm Labor, the Percentage of those Born in State Who Resided Out of State, the Proportion of Children Aged 10–15 in the Family Who Attended School, Nativity of the Husband, and Occupation**

Variable	Coefficient	$\partial Y/\partial x_i$	*t*-value
Age 25–29	−0.0234	−0.069	−0.39
Age 30–34	−0.206	−0.604	−3.20
Banks	−0.0208	−0.061	−3.33
Log (labor force ratio)	−0.0329	−0.096	−0.64
Log (relative wage)	0.283	0.830	0.99
Log (migration)	0.0736	0.216	1.48
School	0.0212	0.062	0.41
Foreign-born husband	0.250	0.734	2.42
Husband's occupation (1850)			
White collar	−0.192	−0.563	−2.37
Blue collar	−0.136	−0.399	−2.05
Unskilled	−0.0109	−0.032	−0.13
Other and unknown	0.0782	0.229	0.54
South	0.0372	0.109	0.52
Constant	1.725		2.24
N = 638		−2 log(λ) = 66.44	

Notes: The omitted variables are Age 20–24 and Farmer.

Sources: Manuscript schedules of the 1850 and 1860 federal population censuses; published federal population censuses, 1850–1920 and U.S. Census Office, *Statistics of the United States in 1860* (Washington, 1866), p. 292.

Table 12.15 Regional Characteristics of the Population

Variable	Northeast	North Central	North[a]	South	Frontier[b]	Total
Banks	9.07	4.89	7.41	4.52	0.01	6.08
Proportion foreign-born	0.194	0.175	0.186	0.066	0.202	0.153
Proportion farmer or laborer	0.393	0.633	0.475	0.618	0.509	0.514

Sources: U.S. Census Office, *Statistics of the United States in 1860* (Washington, D.C., 1866), p. 292; and U.S. Census Office, *Population of the United States in 1860* (Washington, D.C., 1864), pp. xxix, 656–79.

[a]Includes Northeast and North Central.

[b]Includes Minnesota, Iowa, Kansas, Texas, and states farther west.

had more than quadrupled. If the partial derivative for the banks coefficient (− 0.06) in Table 12.14 is applied to this change in the ratio of banks to population of 4.90, then the number of surviving children that married women had per decade would have declined by approximately 0.3. This is, then, a moderately important factor when compared with the fall in the total fertility rate of 0.78 between 1810 and 1840.[46] But one should recognize that this calculation underestimates the impact of financial development on total fertility because most married women had children over an interval that was considerably longer than ten years and because total fertility measures actual births rather than survivors. Moreover, it is possible that the economic changes that led to lower marital fertility also contributed to lower total fertility through other routes, such as a rise in the age at marriage or a decline in the share of women who married. One should also recognize that the ratio of banks to population actually declined slightly from 1840 to 1860, which suggests that other explanations are required for the continuation of the fertility decline through the late antebellum period.

Labor force data are sparse for the early 1800s, but the evidence points to a changing occupational structure that would have reduced fertility. The share of the labor force engaged in farming declined by approximately 16.5 percentage points between 1810 and 1860.[47] How the decline of farming was apportioned among the rise of white-collar, blue-collar, and other occupations is unknown, but some rough calculations suggest changes in occupational structure contributed modestly to diminished fertility. For example, if the decline in the share of farmers of 16.5 percentage points resulted in an 8-percentage-point rise in each share of white-collar and blue-collar workers, then, given the marginal effects reported in Table 12.14, the number of surviving children per decade would have fallen by approximately 0.08. This mag-

46. According to Coale and Zelnik, *New Estimates* (p. 36), the total fertility rate of white women was 6.92 in 1810 and 6.14 in 1820.

47. Thomas Weiss, "U.S. Labor Force Estimates, 1800 to 1860" (manuscript, University of Kansas, 1990), table 1.

nitude (and others that are likely to emerge from other plausible assumptions) is relatively small compared with the decline of 1.71 in total fertility between 1810 and 1860.[48]

Fertility declined despite a growth in immigration rates over the antebellum period. Inflows represented a trivial share of the population in the early decades of the century but rose thereafter. By the 1820s, for example, the annual rate of immigration reported by the U.S. Immigration and Naturalization Service was about 12,850 compared with a mid-decade white population of slightly over nine million, or a ratio of about 0.14 percent. By the 1850s the ratio of annual immigration to the white population was about 1.2 percent.[49] The regression coefficient estimate reported in Table 12.14 and the magnitude of change in immigration suggest that the total impact on the long-term trend in fertility rates was small. The share of the white population that was foreign born was only 15.3 percent as late as 1860. Even if the share was zero at the beginning of the century, the number of surviving children per married woman would have declined by only 0.11 before 1860. Nevertheless, the rapid increase in immigration rates during the late antebellum period adds to the need for other explanations of the fertility decline in the late antebellum period.

12.7 Child Mortality

It is important to ask whether observed differences in the number of surviving children were simply an artifact of different rates of child mortality. Unfortunately, I cannot address the issue directly; the system of vital registration was poorly developed in this era, leaving modern researchers with inadequate resources to trace the fate of those born during the decade of the 1850s. Some help is available, however, by studying the fate of children born before 1850 who survived to be recorded in the 1850 census.

In a separate study I examined the influence of household and regional characteristics on the survival of young children from 1850 to 1860.[50] In a logistic regression framework I employed several of the regressors included in this study, namely, occupation of the head, wealth (value of real estate), literacy, foreign birth, and region of residence. Losses for children aged 1 to 4 did not vary systematically by wealth, literacy, or foreign birth, but were about 8 percentage points higher on the frontier compared with the Northeast. Therefore, use of surviving children underestimates the East-West gradient in the actual number of births. Among children under age 1 in 1850 the chances of nonsur-

48. The estimates of total fertility are from Coale and Zelnik, *New Estimates*, p. 36.

49. Calculated from U.S. Bureau of the Census, *Historical Statistics*, series C 89–119 and A 91–104.

50. Richard H. Steckel, "The Health and Mortality of Women and Children, 1850–1860," *Journal of Economic History*, 48 (June 1988), pp. 333–45. Because some children may have left home as early as age 15 or 16, the study was confined to those aged 0 to 4 in 1850.

vival were about 18 percentage points higher among the unskilled compared with farmers. This occupational pattern, though large, had little impact on spatial differences in the number of births because the share of laborers in the work force varied by only a few percentage points across regions.[51] Little is known about the trend in the share of laborers in the work force in the early 1800s. A large share were probably employed in farming, however, and the relative decline of this industry suggests that the overall share of these people in the work force may have declined. If correct, the number of surviving births declined despite the diminished importance of a group that had relatively higher child mortality. I did not test the hypothesis that mortality rates were higher in places where banks were relatively more numerous compared with the population; such a test may be warranted, but to my knowledge this idea has not been discussed in the health literature.[52] In conclusion, the study of child survival suggests that systematic differences in mortality rates probably introduces mild to moderate distortions into the number of surviving children as an index of actual births in regional (East-West) and occupational comparisons.

12.8 Conclusions

A national sample of married women from the 1850 and 1860 manuscript censuses is used to test hypotheses that have been developed to explain the East-West gradient and the decline in fertility in the United States during the nineteenth century. Financial institutions and, to a lesser extent, occupational structure emerge as important explanations in a series of pair-wise tests. The number of banks per capita was highly correlated with marital fertility, and the East-West gradient in the density of banks had an important influence on the corresponding pattern of marital fertility, which suggests that the rise of the banking system, or other factors correlated with the spread of financial institutions, contributed substantially to the decline in fertility before 1840. The number of surviving children was systematically lower among white-collar and blue-collar workers compared with farmers and the unskilled. Differences in occupational structure played a supporting role in explaining regional and temporal patterns of marital fertility.

It should be noted that I do not attempt to formulate a comprehensive explanation of fertility patterns. Hypotheses that were rejected in these tests on marital fertility may perform successfully in understanding other aspects of childbearing, such as when and whether women married. Yet, variations in marital fertility did make important contributions to overall variations in fertility.

51. According to the 1860 census, for example, laborers as a percentage of the labor force were 19.9 in the Northeast, 24.4 in the North Central, 21.8 in the South, and 18.4 on the frontier.

52. It is conceivable that the banks variable was positively correlated with knowledge of birth control practices but it is not one of the standard proxies for this type of information.

The findings here suggest several research needs. One is to understand precisely how financial institutions may have influenced fertility behavior. The results are congenial to life-cycle ideas that prospective parents substituted financial instruments for children in their portfolios, but questions about the efficacy of the mechanism are raised by the finding that other variables associated with this framework, such as schooling for children, were not statistically significant. It would be important to study the possible joint nature of decisions on births and schooling and to explore alternative specifications that would appropriately capture this interdependence.

Second, skeptics may wonder whether these early banks had the confidence of the public as safe places for old-age savings. Therefore, additional evidence on life-cycle behavior should be assembled by studying the evolution of household portfolios. If the life-cycle model is substantially correct, then families that reduced births should have been accumulating liquid or semiliquid assets relatively rapidly during the typical childbearing years for depletion in old age. Savings for old age could have taken many forms, including not only deposits but also stocks, bonds, life insurance, and land. If banks were important to the process, then researchers should find a strong relationship between fertility and the volume of deposits, something that might be done by examining the balance sheets of banks and child-woman ratios.

A third line of work would explore whether the measure of financial institutions (banks per capita) is merely a proxy for a different variable that directly influenced fertility, such as economic or commercial development. For example, areas that lacked banks may have been poorly integrated into the market system, which resulted in high prices for manufactured goods but relatively low prices for children who were produced locally. A casual examination of correlations between explanatory variables within the sample does not suggest that this was the case. For example, the correlation between banks per capita and the percent of a county's population residing in an urban area ($\geq$2,500 population) was only 0.215. The correlation was 0.493 with the measure of population density (improved acres), but results in Table 12.9 show that when both variables are included as regressors only the banks variable was statistically significant. This finding suggests that population density may be a proxy for financial development in explaining high correlations between measures of land availability and child-woman ratios reported in other studies.

Access to sound financial institutions also requires further study. We need more information on the proximity of depositors to banks, which is important for knowing the level of geographic analysis appropriate for testing the financial-institutions hypothesis. The rapid growth in numbers of banks during the 1830s may have overstated the use of banks to house life-cycle savings if some of these banks were financially unsound or were remote from large population centers. The estimation of time-series models based on county- or state-level data may help to clarify this issue. Study of the financial development and fertility patterns in other countries is also desirable.

Further study of the relationship between fertility and mortality is warranted; if child mortality rates were higher on the frontier, for example, parents may have had relatively more births in anticipation of excess losses. It is also important to understand why the number of surviving births was lower among white-collar and blue-collar workers compared with farmers and the unskilled. One argument would place the explanation on differential costs and benefits of children. Yet it is also possible that occupation was merely a better proxy for education than literacy or that occupation was a proxy for income.

The most important contribution of this research is the empirical identification of a mechanism that contributed substantially to the early (preindustrial) decline of fertility in the United States. The data analyzed here suggest that growth of financial institutions was important for the decline in marital fertility before 1840. Yet, many questions about the financial-institutions hypothesis remain unanswered and the findings point to the complexity of the process. No single explanation accounts for most of the change in fertility observed before 1860, and the explanatory power of financial institutions seems to diminish in the late antebellum period. Study of when and whether women married will help to find answers to these important questions.

13 Trading Quantity for Quality

Explaining the Decline in American Fertility in the Nineteenth Century

Jenny Bourne Wahl

> The economic transformation [that accompanied the industrial revolution] coincided with—and in part caused—a change in the quality of family life as well as the quantity of children. As the family became less an economic unit it ripened into a covenant of love and nurturance of children. . . . Families became more child-centered. . . . And as parents lavished more love on their children, they had fewer of them and devoted more resources to [them]. . . . This helps explain the . . . decline of the birth rate . . . in the nineteenth century.
>
> James McPherson, *Battle Cry of Freedom*[1]

The fertility of Americans fell throughout the nineteenth century, beginning in the northeastern states. Economic historians have attempted to explain these patterns with microeconomic models, but they have had to rely on aggregate data, principally census records, for empirical testing. The character of the available data has circumscribed inquiry about the decline of fertility and has limited scholars to speculations rooted in broad macroeconomic movements in land and labor markets.

Civil War historian James McPherson suggests a different approach: families shrank as parents focused on the quality of home life. His comments parallel a model of fertility that Gary Becker, among others, pioneered to explain the negative correlation between the quantity and quality of children per family in both cross-sectional and time-series data for the twentieth century.[2] Can this quantity-quality model help us understand shrinking family size in nine-

The author acknowledges the helpful suggestions made by Claudia Goldin and Edward Wahl. Special thanks also go to Robert Fogel, Gary Becker, and Thomas Mroz.

1. James McPherson, *Battle Cry of Freedom* (New York, 1988), pp. 34–35.

2. See particularly Gary Becker and H. Gregg Lewis, "On the Interaction between Quantity and Quality of Children," *Journal of Political Economy,* 81 (Mar./Apr. 1973), pp. S279–88; and Gary Becker and Nigel Tomes, "Child Endowments and the Quantity and Quality of Children," *Journal of Political Economy,* 84 (Aug. 1976), pp. S143–62.

teenth-century America? I conclude here that it can. Decreased infant and child mortality, more available schooling, and the separation of home and work places increased the relative price of a child, encouraging parents to have fewer children and to spend more on each child. Empirical testing with a unique, intergenerationally linked, household-level data set collected from pre-twentieth-century sources bolsters this conclusion. The quantity-quality model, supported by microeconomic data, thus offers a fresh view on declining fertility in the United States before 1900.

13.1 Evidence of the Fertility Decline in America

Demographic evidence suggests that the size of American families fell persistently after 1800. Most studies of the fertility decline rely on statistics that do not distinguish marital fertility changes from variations in nuptiality, mortality, and the age structure of the population. Yasukichi Yasuba and Richard Easterlin, for instance, point to regional differences in the child-woman ratio for nineteenth-century cross-sectional data; Easterlin speculates that the fertility decline swept westward across America as the population moved away from the Atlantic coast.[3] Warren Thompson and P. K. Whelpton, and Ansley Coale and Melvin Zelnik, establish a decrease in the period total fertility rate through the century.[4]

In a 1986 paper, I analyzed shifts in marital fertility separately from other demographic shifts.[5] The major proximate determinants of decreased fertility before 1850 were increases over time in the proportion of women who never married, in the average marriage age, and in the mortality rate.[6] But after

3. The child-woman ratio is the ratio of the number of children in a given age group to every thousand women in a given age group. The numerator includes children ages 0 to 9 or ages 0 to 4; the denominator includes women ages 15 to 44, 15 to 49, 20 to 44, or 20 to 49. Easterlin further refines his child-woman ratio to include only the children had by married farm wives aged 30 to 39. See Yasukichi Yasuba, *Birth Rates of the White Population in the United States, 1800–1860* (Baltimore, 1962); and Richard Easterlin, "Population Change and Farm Settlement in the Northern United States," *Journal of Economic History,* 36 (Mar. 1976), pp. 45–75.

4. The period total fertility rate is the sum of age-specific fertility rates for women alive at a given time multiplied by the length of the interval over which each age-specific rate was calculated. An age-specific fertility rate equals the number of children born to women in a given age interval divided by the number of woman-years lived during the interval. The interval length is usually five years. See Warren Thompson and P. K. Whelpton, *Population Trends in the United States* (New York, 1933); and Ansley Coale and Melvin Zelnik, *New Estimates of Fertility and Population in the United States* (Princeton, 1963).

5. Jenny Wahl, "New Results on the Decline in Household Fertility in the United States from 1750 to 1900," in *Long-Term Factors in American Economic Growth,* Stanley Engerman and Robert Gallman, eds. (Chicago, 1986), pp. 391–438. A couple's fertility refers to their actual childbearing experience rather than to their potential to have children.

6. For evidence on mortality, see also Robert Fogel, "Nutrition and the Decline in Mortality Since 1700: Some Preliminary Findings," in *Long-Term Factors in American Economic Growth,* Stanley L. Engerman and Robert E. Gallman, eds. (Chicago, 1986), pp. 439–556. For a discussion of average marriage age, see Michael Haines and Barbara Anderson, "New Demographic History of the Late 19th-Century United States," *Explorations in Economic History,* 25 (Oct. 1988), pp. 341–65. For additional evidence on declining marital fertility and increasing marriage ages during this period, see Warren Sanderson, "New Interpretations of the Decline in the Fertility of White Women in the United States, 1800–1920" (manuscript, Stanford University, undated).

1850, married couples began to limit the number of children they had by ending their childbearing before the wife's menopause occurred. Married couples' control of their fertility began earliest in the northeastern United States. Evidence of contraception within marriage sets the stage for analyzing the determinants of a couple's demand for children and for deciphering the connection between household fertility decisions and the aggregate fertility decline.[7]

13.2 Explanations for the Decline in Fertility

In a series of papers, Becker and others consider decisions about the number and "quality" of children as jointly determined and interactive.[8] Most empirical analyses of the quantity-quality model have focused on cross-sectional relations of fertility and wealth, yet the model is useful for examining fertility behavior over time as well. Thus far, the testing ground for the quantity-quality model has been twentieth-century data. McPherson's comments—which echo the work of John Demos and Nancy Cott, among others—suggest that an investigation of nineteenth-century data might also prove fruitful.[9]

13.2.1 A General Description of the Quantity-Quality Model

The chief characteristic of the quantity-quality model is that the cost of an additional child, holding the quality of each child constant, is greater for higher-quality children. Similarly, the cost of increasing the quality of each child, holding the number of children constant, is greater for larger families. These interactions imply that an increase in wealth would initially tend to increase the desired number of children and their quality, which in turn would raise the "prices" of each good and blunt the impact of the wealth increase. If the induced price effect exceeds the initial wealth effect on fertility, one might observe a negative relationship between family size and wealth in some wealth ranges.[10] In Becker's model and my own, the downward bias observed

7. The lack of evidence of marital fertility control for pre–1850 families does not preclude viewing their decisions to have children as economic ones. The constraints on the supply of children caused by early parental death could have been binding, for instance, so the demand for children coincided with (or fell short of) the available supply.

8. Becker and Lewis, "On the Interaction between Quantity and Quality"; Becker and Tomes, "Child Endowments"; Gary Becker, *A Treatise on the Family* (Cambridge, Mass., 1981); and Jenny Wahl, "Fertility in America: Historical Patterns and Wealth Effects on the Quantity and Quality of Children" (Ph.D. dissertation, University of Chicago, 1985), esp.chap. 3.

9. John Demos, *Past, Present, and Personal* (New York, 1986); Nancy Cott, *The Bonds of Womanhood* (New Haven, 1977).

10. For primarily twentieth-century results, see Robert Michael, "Dimensions of Household Fertility: An Economic Analysis," a paper given at the annual meeting of the American Statistical Association (New York, 1971); Warren Sanderson and Robert Willis, "Economic Models of Fertility: Some Explanations and Implications," *Annual Report of the National Bureau of Economic Research* (Cambridge, Mass., 1971); Robert Willis, "Economic Theory of Fertility Behavior," in *Economics of the Family,* Theodore W. Schultz, ed. (Chicago, 1974), pp. 25–75; and Becker and Tomes, "Child Endowments."

on the wealth effect approaches zero as wealth increases.[11] One would therefore expect to see a positive relation between fertility and wealth at the highest wealth levels.

The general quantity-quality model is formulated as follows. Children partly inherit their parents' intrinsic ability (PABLTY), so $0<c_1<1$ in equation (1). Although parents are assumed to know their children's ability (CHABLTY), ability is not perfectly observable by an outsider, so an error term σ appears in equation (1).

$$\text{(1)} \qquad \text{CHABLTY} = c_0 + c_1\text{PABLTY} + \sigma$$

Parents derive pleasure from children and from the quality of their children. Parents' demands for a particular number of children (PNUMKID) and for the quality of each child (measured by the child's wealth as an adult, or

11. Becker and Tomes in "Child Endowments," pp. S144–47, formulate a child's quality (measured as child's wealth, or CHWEALTH) as a linear function of the child's ability (CHABLTY) and parental contributions to the child's wealth (PCONTRIB):

$$\text{CHWEALTH} = \text{CHABLTY} + \text{PCONTRIB}$$

As a result, the elasticity of quality associated with parental contributions (OBSELST) exceeds the true quality elasticity (TRUELST) at lower levels of wealth, but the two converge as parental wealth (PWEALTH) increases if parental contributions to their children increase with parental wealth. That is,

$$\text{OBSELST} = (\text{CHWEALTH/PCONTRIB}) \times (\text{TRUELST}) > \text{TRUELST}$$

$$\partial(\text{CHWEALTH/PCONTRIB})/\partial\text{PWEALTH} = [(\text{PCONTRIB} - \text{CHWEALTH})\cdot(\partial\text{PCONTRIB}/\partial\text{PWEALTH})]/\text{PCONTRIB}^2 < 0, \text{ if } (\partial\text{PCONTRIB}/\partial\text{PWEALTH}) > 0$$

By the adding-up rule, the observed wealth elasticity of quantity is biased downward (and could be negative) for lower levels of parental wealth; the bias becomes smaller as parental wealth increases.

My model presumes that parents contribute to children's human capital and may leave bequests (BEQUEST) (Wahl, "Fertility in America," pp. 65–66). Human-capital investments interact with a child's ability to generate the child's lifetime earnings:

$$\text{CHWEALTH} = \text{BEQUEST} + \text{PCONTRIB}^x\text{CHABLY}^y$$
$$0 < x < 1; 0 < y < 1$$

Parents allocate expenditures on children so that the marginal dollar spent on bequests and on human-capital investments yields the same increment to a child's wealth. I assume that the marginal return to human-capital investment exceeds 1 at low levels of investment and is less than 1 at high levels. The marginal return to bequests is 1. As a result, parents of low wealth leave no bequest and the observed wealth elasticity of quality exceeds the true elasticity of quality by a constant ($1/x$) greater than 1. The observed wealth elasticity of quantity could therefore be negative in this wealth range. Where bequests exceed zero, an increase in parental wealth—with no change in child's ability—increases bequests but leaves parental contributions to human capital unchanged. The observed quality elasticity therefore exceeds the true elasticity by a fraction that approaches zero as parental wealth increases if bequests increase with parental wealth:

$$\text{OBSELST} = (\text{CHWEALTH/BEQUEST}) \times (\text{TRUELST}) > \text{TRUELST}$$

$$\partial(\text{CHWEALTH/BEQUEST})/\partial\ \text{PWEALTH} = [(\text{BEQUEST} - \text{CHWEALTH})(\partial\text{BEQUEST}/\partial\text{PWEALTH})]/\text{BEQUEST}^2 < 0, \text{ if } (\partial\text{BEQUEST}/\partial\text{PWEALTH}) > 0.$$

As in Becker and Tomes's model, the adding-up rule implies that the observed wealth elasticity of quantity will approach the true elasticity as parental wealth increases.

CHWEALTH) are thus functions of the exogenous variables, children's ability (CHABLTY) and parental wealth (PWEALTH). Equations (2) and (3) represent linear reduced-form demand equations for PNUMKID and CHWEALTH. Higher-order wealth terms in equation (2) allow one to test for a varying observed relationship between fertility and wealth in different wealth ranges.

$$\text{(2)} \quad \text{PNUMKID} = a_0 + a_1\text{CHABLTY} + a_2\text{PWEALTH} + a_3\text{PWEALTH}^2 + a_4\ \text{PWEALTH}^3$$

$$\text{(3)} \quad \text{CHWEALTH} = b_0 + b_1\text{CHABLTY} + b_2\text{PWEALTH}$$

Because ability is not directly observable, empirical work must use proxies for children's ability. Testable equations are obtained by lagging equations (2) and (3) and substituting in equation (1):

$$\text{(2}'\text{)} \quad \text{PNUMKID} = \alpha_0 + c_1\text{GPNUMKID} + a_2(\text{PWEALTH} - c_1\text{GPWEALTH}) + a_3(\text{PWEALTH}^2 - c_1\text{GPWEALTH}^2) + a_4(\text{PWEALTH}^3 - c_1\text{GPWEALTH}^3) + \varepsilon$$

$$\text{(3}'\text{)} \quad \text{CHWEALTH} = \beta_0 + (c_1 + b_2)\text{PWEALTH} - c_1 b_2\text{GPWEALTH} + \mu$$

where $\alpha_0 = a_0(1 - c_1) + a_1c_0$; $\beta_0 = b_0(1 - c_1) + b_1c_0$; $\varepsilon = a_1\sigma$; $\mu = b_1\sigma$; GPNUMKID = PNUMKID_{-1}; and GPWEALTH = PWEALTH_{-1}. Equations (2′) and (3′) show that grandparental wealth (GPWEALTH) and fertility (GPNUMKID) serve as proxies for children's ability.

Because the interaction of the quantity and quality of children implies that wealth and fertility might appear negatively related, the quantity-quality model makes no predictions on the signs of the wealth coefficients in equation (2′). The model does, however, generate coefficient restrictions. The coefficient on each grandparental wealth term equals the negative of the coefficient on the corresponding parental wealth term multiplied by that on GPNUMKID. Grandparental fertility has a positive coefficient, equaling the degree to which ability is inherited.

The coefficients in equation (3′) are also constrained by the quantity-quality model. The coefficient on PWEALTH is positive, equaling the sum of two positive fractions: (a) the degree to which ability is inherited and (b) parents' propensity to invest in children's wealth out of an increment in their own wealth. The coefficient on GPWEALTH is negative, equaling the negative of the product of the two fractions. The absolute value of the estimated coefficient on GPWEALTH in equation (3′) should therefore be smaller than the estimated coefficient on PWEALTH.

Empirical analyses of the relation between fertility and parental wealth often exclude grandparental variables because data are not available. How would this omission affect the coefficients on parental wealth in equation (2′)? Suppose that one's ability interacts with parental contributions to one's human capital to affect one's wealth positively. Then wealth and ability are positively related within a generation and ability is positively related across generations, implying that the covariance between CHABLTY and PWEALTH is likely to be positive. The bias from omitting grandparental variables (which stand in for CHABLTY) from equation (2′) therefore depends on the sign of a_1, the effect of CHABLTY on PNUMKID.

Two effects influence the sign of a_1. Greater ability lowers the cost to parents of providing a given amount of quality to each child, which would tend to increase PNUMKID and make a_1 positive. Greater ability also increases the productivity of investing in children, however, because ability and parental contributions interact to determine a child's wealth. This tends to increase quality, decrease PNUMKID, and make a_1 negative. If a_1 is positive, omitting the proxies for ability biases the true wealth effect upward. If a_1 is negative, the omission biases the wealth effect downward.[12]

Omitting child's ability from equation (3′) alters observed parental wealth effects on child quality. Becker shows that excluding the ability proxy (GPWEALTH) from equation (3′) biases downward the coefficient on PWEALTH.[13]

13.2.2 The Quantity-Quality Model and the Nineteeth-Century American Family

Economists have neglected the quantity-quality model as a depiction of nineteenth-century American fertility, partly because household data have been unavailable to test it. Additionally, many economists believe that nineteenth-century parents regarded their children as investment goods, begotten for their capacity to work on the family farm and to support their parents in old age.[14] Historians and sociologists have been more amenable to the idea that children had non-pecuniary value before this century; economic data explored here corroborate this view.

The quantity-quality model helps illuminate the decline in American fertility through its focus on the prices of quality and quantity and on the interaction of the two. The price of quality fell through the nineteenth century be-

12. If CHABLTY or proxies for it are omitted from equation (2′), the expected value of each coefficient on a parental wealth variable equals the following: the true coefficient, plus the product of a_1 and the ratio of the covariance of CHABLTY and the parental wealth variable to the variance of the parental wealth variable. In "Fertility in America," I assume that one's ability interacts with parents' contributions to human capital to produce one's wealth. In the linear model used by Becker and Tomes in "Child Endowments"—where a child's ability is separate from human capital investments made in him or her—an increase in CHABLTY unambiguously causes the relative price of quantity to fall, thus increasing the number of children. Because the coefficient on CHABLTY is positive, omitting grandparents' variables would bias observed wealth coefficients upward in their model.

13. Becker, *A Treatise*, pp. 168–69.

14. Roger Ransom and Richard Sutch, "Did Rising Out-Migration Cause Fertility to Decline in Rural New England?", Working Papers on the History of Saving no. 5 (University of California, Apr. 1986); and William Sundstrom and Paul David, "Old-Age Security Motives, Labor Markets, and Farm Family Fertility in Antebellum America," *Explorations in Economic History*, 25 (Apr. 1988), pp. 164–97.

cause children survived longer and public schooling became increasingly available. As Lawrence Stone notes, "very high infant and child mortality rates . . . made it folly to invest too much . . . in such ephemeral beings."[15] Better public health procedures in the latter half of the nineteenth century reduced infant and child mortality.[16] More attention to personal cleanliness and improvements in water carriage and city planning, for example, boosted the health of the population.[17] At the same time, public education became more prevalent as greater population density reduced costs of providing schools and as literacy generated urban opportunities for many, particularly those who had little hope of ever owning a farm.[18] While longer life spans raised the payoff from investing in children, cheaper access to schooling lowered the cost.[19] These effects decreased the price of child quality, inducing parents to substitute toward quality and away from the quantity of children.

While the price of quality fell, the price of the quantity of children rose through the nineteenth century. Several factors were responsible. Historians, sociologists, and economists have commented on the separation of the home from the work place that accompanied the Industrial Revolution.[20] Nancy Cott points out that the nineteenth century heralded the separation of job from

15. Lawrence Stone, *The Family, Sex, and Marriage* (New York, 1979), p. 82. Stone was referring to emotional capital invested by English parents in an earlier era; the reasoning is the same for American parents investing in a child's human capital in the first part of the 1800s. Clayne Pope, Robert Fogel, and I trace the decline in mortality through the nineteenth century. See Clayne L. Pope, chap. 9 in this volume; Fogel, "Nutrition and the Decline in Mortality"; and Wahl, "Fertility in America."

16. See Daniel Scott Smith, "Differential Mortality in the United States Before 1900," *Journal of Interdisciplinary History,* 13 (Spring 1983), pp. 735–59.

17. Richard Bushman and Claudia Bushman, "The Early History of Cleanliness in America," *Journal of American History,* 74 (Mar. 1988), pp. 1213–38; Jon Peterson, "The Impact of Sanitary Reform upon American Urban Planning, 1840–1890," *Journal of Social History,* 13 (Fall 1979), pp. 83–104. Harvey Levenstein suggests that the mid–1800s signaled an end to the practice of feeding infants cows' milk directly from the udder. ("'Best for Babies' or 'Preventable Infanticide'? The Controversy over Artificial Feeding of Infants in America, 1880–1920," *Journal of American History,* 70 [June 1983], pp. 75–94).

18. Robert Gallman reviews the relation between literacy and population density in a North Carolina county in "Changes in the Level of Literacy in a New Community of Early America," *Journal of Economic History,* 48 (Sept. 1988), pp. 567–82. Avery Guest and Stewart Tolnay, and Maris Vinovskis, note the concomitant decline in fertility, rise in schooling, and move out of agriculture. See Avery Guest and Stewart Tolnay, "Urban Industrial Structure and Fertility, The Case of Large American Cities," *Journal of Interdisciplinary History,* 13 (Winter 1983), pp. 387–409; Maris Vinovskis, "Historical Perspectives on Rural Development and Human Fertility in Nineteenth Century America," in *Rural Development and Human Fertility,* Wayne Schutjer and C. Shannon Stokes, eds. (New York, 1984), pp. 77–96.

19. Peter Lindert found that expenditures on public elementary and secondary schooling and on education in general for children aged 5 to 19 rose steadily from 1840 to 1930, with the sharpest increase taking place before 1900 (*Fertility and Scarcity in America* [Princeton, 1978]).

20. Claudia Goldin surmises that the decline in women's labor force participation with the advent of industrialization was caused in part by this separation, which removed the convenience and increased the costs of being in the labor force, especially for women with preadolescent children ("The Economic Status of Women in the Early Republic: Quantitative Methods," *Journal of Interdisciplinary History,* 16 [Winter 1986], pp. 375–404).

home, man's world from woman's world: "To render *home* happy, is woman's peculiar province; home is *her* world."[21] Carl Degler maintains that this dichotomy gave women more control over household decisions, including sex and reproduction; increasing domesticity went hand-in-hand with the notion that the individual child was a precious commodity. Nancy Dye and Daniel Blake Smith note that mothers seemed more devoted to their children in the 1800s; they illuminate the role of costs in decision-making and highlight the quantity-quality interaction. They believe that mothers had fewer children and emphasized each child's quality because mothers saw that their efforts to nurture their children paid off as babies increasingly survived infancy. Children were no longer trusted to the hands of God; their mothers' capable hands could protect them.[22] As well as watching over their children more, nineteenth-century women spent more time in religious, social, and educational activities than their mothers and grandmothers.[23] Additional children detracted from the caliber of family life, the amount of time spent nurturing each child, and the time mothers could spend in other activities. As a result, the price of the quantity of children rose through the 1800s, inducing parents to have smaller families.

Increasing real wealth over time might also have generated lower fertility because observed wealth effects do not control for the interaction between quantity and quality. If the price effect dominated the true wealth effect on quantity over some range of wealth, the desired number of children could have fallen over time as observed wealth increased. Alternatively, decreasing wealth would imply lower fertility for families in the wealth range where fertility and wealth were positively related. The increasing dispersion of wealth in the nineteenth century therefore could have produced lower fertility if those getting richer and those getting poorer reduced their family sizes.[24]

13.2.3 An Alternative Model—Richard Easterlin's Target-Bequest Model

The leading model proposed to explain the fertility decline in nineteenth-century America is that of Richard Easterlin.[25] He argues that the greater pop-

21. Cott, *The Bonds*, p. 74.

22. Carl Degler, *At Odds: Women and the Family in America from the Revolution to the Present* (New York, 1980); Nancy Dye and Daniel Blake Smith, "Mother Love and Infant Death, 1750–1920," *Journal of American History*, 73 (September 1986), pp. 329–53. Linda Pollock cites evidence that parents may have cherished children as early as the 1500s, while Philippe Ariès claims that the notion of childhood flowered during the seventeenth century. See Linda Pollock, *Forgotten Children: Parent-Child Relations from 1500–1900* (New York, 1983); Philippe Ariès, *Centuries of Childhood* (New York, 1962).

23. For a discussion of the early history of women's groups, see Anne Boylan, "Women in Groups: An Analysis of Women's Benevolent Organizations in New York and Boston," *Journal of American History*, 71 (Dec. 1984), pp. 497–523.

24. In *Fertility and Scarcity*, Lindert notes the drift toward greater wealth inequality from 1770 to 1860 and the high plateau of inequality from 1860 to 1929.

25. Easterlin, "Population Change." Other economic historians suggest that nineteenth-century children ensured old-age support for their parents. Ransom and Sutch, "Rising Out-Migration," argue that American fertility might have fallen as children migrated westward and parents realized

ulation density in the Northeast in the 1800s led northeasterners to have fewer children than frontier families. Like the quantity-quality model, Easterlin's model suggests that, all else equal, more wealth would lead to higher fertility because children are a normal good. Easterlin surmises that another instinct motivated nineteenth-century parents: parents wanted their children to have as good a start in life as they had. The prospective increase in parental wealth was the key factor indicating parents' ability to provide their children with a proper start in life. The smaller the growth in wealth expected by parents, the fewer children they would have had. Because greater population density implied lower expected growth in wealth, according to Easterlin, fertility was lower in the Northeast. As population density increased across the country, one might expect overall American fertility to fall.

Easterlin's target-bequest model resembles the quantity-quality model in important ways. Both view children as consumption goods that give parents non-monetary pleasures. Both shape parents' utility as a function of not only children but also the children's quality of life. Both conjecture that a couple's fertility is related to their wealth and to the previous generation's wealth and fertility. Yet the two models imply disparate empirical results and assign a fundamentally different role to the grandparental variables.

Because the variables each model emphasizes are the same, equations (2′) and (3′) can be used for Easterlin's target-bequest model, as well as for the quantity-quality one. The target-bequest model implies a positive parental wealth effect, a positive coefficient on GPNUMKID, and a negative grandparental wealth effect in equation (2′). The reasoning is as follows. Consider two couples having the same wealth, but different childhood living standards. The couple with the more prosperous childhood (greater GPWEALTH and smaller GPNUMKID, all else equal) will have fewer children and give more to each child. The predictions on coefficient signs in equation (2′) from the target-bequest model are therefore more restrictive than those from the quantity-quality model, which merely requires opposite signs on parental and grandparental wealth variables. Easterlin's framework also suggests a positive coefficient on GPWEALTH in equation (3′), unlike the quantity-quality model. The couple with a more prosperous childhood (greater GPWEALTH, all else equal) would provide a better lifestyle for each child.[26] According to Easter-

---

that their children would increasingly default on "old-age security" payments. Sundstrom and David, "Old-Age Security Motives," take a different tack. They speculate that better labor market conditions through the nineteenth century gave the young more bargaining power with their parents, which enabled youths to extract additional family wealth in exchange for providing old-age support to parents. As a result, couples began to have fewer children. The old-age security model is consistent with a panoply of signs on coefficients in equation (2′) and is empirically indistinguishable from the quantity-quality model.

26. The strength of this effect depends on the number of siblings in the family of origin. If grandparents of higher wealth had more children, the coefficient on GPWEALTH will be positive in equation (3′) as long as wealthier grandparents also provided higher living standards for each

lin, parents with greater wealth would tend to give more to their children as well. Thus, like the quantity-quality model, Easterlin's implies a positive coefficient on PWEALTH in equation (3′).

Grandparental wealth and fertility are causally related to the endogenous variables PNUMKID and CHWEALTH in Easterlin's model. In contrast, grandparental variables serve only as proxies for children's ability in the quantity-quality model.

As in the quantity-quality model, omission of grandparental variables from the target-bequest model would bias the coefficients on parental wealth variables in equations (2′) and (3′). A more prosperous childhood (greater GPWEALTH and smaller GPNUMKID) implies greater PWEALTH and smaller PNUMKID. Omission of grandparental wealth and fertility in equation (2′) would thus bias downward the coefficients on parental wealth variables. Again, this prediction is more restrictive than that of the quantity-quality model, which allows either a positive or a negative bias. A more prosperous childhood for parents causes them to contribute more to CHWEALTH as well as increasing PWEALTH. Elimination of GPWEALTH in equation (3′) would therefore bias the coefficient on PWEALTH upward in Easterlin's model, contrasting with the downward bias in the quantity-quality model.

13.3 Empirical Analysis

13.3.1 The Data Sample

Fertility data for two consecutive generations of households and wealth data for three consecutive generations are needed to estimate equations (2′) and (3′). The sample used here consists of sets of families connected by marriage through several generations. Demographic and socioeconomic characteristics are taken from a data source that links, on an individual basis, genealogical records to the decennial federal manuscript census schedules for the years 1850 to 1880.[27] Not only is the structure of the sample appropriate for estimating equations (2′) and (3′), it is also a unique, large, micro-level data set with longitudinal information antedating the twentieth century.

Each sample observation has demographic and socioeconomic data for all individuals from three generations of a single family. Genealogical data include each individual's dates and places of birth, marriage, and death, and the total number of children born to the individual and his or her spouse. Census data include wealth, occupation, literacy, school attendence, relation to the

child. Given Easterlin's assumptions about wealth effects on fertility and on bequests, this is likely to be true.

27. For a complete data description, see Jenny Bourne, Robert Fogel, Clayne Pope, and Larry Wimmer, "A Description and Analysis of the Data in the DAE/CPE Pilot Sample of Genealogies" (manuscript, University of Chicago, 1984); and Fogel, "Nutrition and the Decline in Mortality."

head of household, and residence by county, at the time of the census. By assigning personal and marriage identification numbers to individuals, the individuals are aggregated into families and families aggregated across generations. Appendix A gives more detail on the process by which data were collected.

Genealogies tend to be produced by relatively wealthy families, and average wealth is greater for this census sample than for other census samples collected. Households in my sample held an average of $4,184 in 1860 census wealth and $8,823 in 1870 census wealth. But household heads in this sample were also richer because they were older on average at the time of the census than those in other samples.[28] Fortunately, a wide range of wealth values are reported, including a good representation of families with no reported wealth.[29]

Several potential biases can be overcome by restricting the sample.[30] Only families in which childbearing was complete when the genealogy was published are included. As a result, information about fertility for a sample family is incomplete only if records are incomplete, not because children were born after the genealogy's publication date. In addition, analysis concentrates on once-married couples who had at least one child and who were at risk to bear children until the mother was age 45.[31] These constraints buttress the notion that the number of children ever born is a good proxy for the number of children demanded in the observed families. Including only once-married couples generally ensures that each child recorded is matched to its natural mother and father.[32] Omitting families with no children excludes couples in which at least

28. Households in the Vedder and Gallaway 1860 Ohio census sample held average wealth of $2,900, and those in Lee Soltow's 1860 national sample held $3,027. Households in Soltow's 1870 national sample held $3,035 on average, and those in the Hershberg and Dockhorn 1870 Philadelphia sample held $3,257 on average. Soltow's 1860 census sample of older men (aged 40 to 99 years) held average wealth of $5,264, while his older-men 1870 sample averaged $5,323. See Richard Vedder and Lowell Gallaway, "Migration in the Old Northwest," in *Essays in Nineteenth Century Economic History: The Old Northwest,* David Klingamen and Richard Vedder, eds. (Athens, Ohio, 1975); Lee Soltow, *Men and Wealth in the United States, 1850–1870* (New Haven, 1975); Theodore Hershberg and Robert Dockhorn, "Occupation Classification," *Historical Methods*, 9 (Spring/Summer 1976), pp. 59–97.

29. Soltow reports 38 percent of his overall sample in each year with zero wealth; the sample used here has 51 percent of households with zero wealth for 1860 and 43 percent for 1870.

30. Some sampling biases inherent in the sample remain in the constrained subsample. Genealogies are produced by families with higher-than-average fertility and nuptiality and lower-than-average mortality because such families are more likely to have a surviving heir compile the family's history. Moreover, the regression sample consists solely of whites, with 98 percent of adults reporting themselves as literate.

31. To ensure completed childbearing, only families in which the mother was born at least 45 years before the publication date of the genealogy are included. By age 45, secondary sterility sets in for most women. Couples in which both partners survived to the mother's forty-fifth birthday were assumed to be at risk to bear children up to that date.

32. This constraint excludes stepchildren but not adopted children. Adopted children reflect parents' inability to bear the children they want, which reinforces viewing the recorded number of children as a good proxy for the desired number.

one spouse suffered from primary sterility.[33] Eliminating families in which one parent died before the mother went through menopause helps ensure that childbearing was not curtailed before couples had the family they desired.[34]

Equations (2′) and (3′) are analyzed separately for families recorded in 1860 and for those recorded in 1870.[35] These results, contained in the following two sections, support the quantity-quality model. Equation (2′) is the focal point of the analysis; equation (3′) further demonstrates the validity of the quantity-quality model. Table 13.1 reports descriptive statistics for the variables used in the regression analyses.

13.3.2 Estimating the Fertility Equation (2′)

The Unconstrained Model

Table 13.2 compares coefficients and standard errors for two fertility regressions using the number of children ever born as the dependent variable.[36]

33. Excluding no-child families cuts out couples who could have had children but chose not to. One would like to include such couples in the regression, but they are indistinguishable from primary-sterility couples. The percentage of families with no children in the sample (4 percent) is close to the estimated primary sterility rate for the period and slightly higher than the estimated twentieth-century rate of 1.7 percent. See W. Henry Mosley, "Reproductive Impairments in the United States, 1965–1982," *Demography,* 22 (Aug. 1985), pp. 415–30. If one assumes that all childless couples suffered from primary sterility, the probability of a Type II error is small relative to the probability of a Type I error. Therefore, all childless couples are excluded from the regression analysis. I am grateful to Robert Fogel for this discussion.

34. Did parents have more children than they wanted? Available contraceptive methods certainly were fallible, yet the sample exhibited fertility control within marriage. Modeling fertility as a choice variable is therefore consistent with empirical evidence. See Wahl, "Fertility in America," esp. table 6. For analyzing equation (2′), the important question is whether knowledge of contraception was correlated with wealth; wealthier families may have been more aware of how to prevent having children. As a result, omitting contraceptive knowledge from equation (2′) could bias wealth coefficients downward because wealthy parents would have had relatively fewer children they did not want. John d'Emilio and Estelle Freedman, *Intimate Matters* (New York, 1988), pp. 59–64, note, however, that accurate information about contraception began to circulate widely by the 1830s.

Other excluded variables had little effect on the number of children. Although mother's age at marriage is omitted, women marrying later had significantly higher fertility rates within given age groups, indicating that fertility for these women might have caught up with fertility for younger brides. See Jenny Bourne, "Preliminary Analysis of Mortality and Fertility in the United States, 1650–1899" (manuscript, University of Chicago, 1983). Although infant mortality is excluded, parents attempted to "replace" dead children by increasing their fertility rates, which suggests that the number of children ever born is closely related to the number of surviving children. See Anne Williams, "Measuring the Impact of Child Mortality on Fertility: A Methodological Note," *Demography,* 14 (Nov. 1977) pp. 581–90; and Bourne, "Preliminary Analysis." Fecundity variables were not included, but studies indicate that only extreme malnutrition affects a woman's ability to conceive. See Jane Menken, James Trussell, and Susan Watkins, "The Nutrition Fertility Link: An Evaluation of the Evidence," *Journal of Interdisciplinary History,* 11 (Winter 1981), pp. 425–41. Adding these demographic variables to equation (2′) reduces the variance of the disturbance term but does not substantially affect wealth coefficients.

35. The 1850 and 1880 censuses are not used here because the former recorded only the value of real estate, while the latter recorded no wealth data. The 1860 and 1870 censuses recorded the values of both real estate and personal property.

36. The next section reports results for a nonlinear regression. Alternatively, a Poisson model could be used. See Richard Steckel's paper, chap. 12 in this volume.

Table 13.1 **Descriptive Statistics for Regressions: The Linked Genealogy-Census Sample**

	1860			1870		
	Mean	Standard Deviation	%	Mean	Standard Deviation	%
Quantity of Children Regression, Equation 2′: Tables 13.2 and 13.3						
Parental variables						
Total children	5.6	3.0		5.1	2.0	
Wealth instrument	$6,753.0	$2,874.0		$10,088.0	$5,710.0	
Father's age	44.0	14.0		42.0	14.0	
Grandparental variables						
Total children	8.6	3.0		8.0	3.0	
Wealth instrument	$4,645.0	$2,741.0		$12,512.0	$6,322.0	
Grandfather's age	76.0	14.0		74.0	15.0	
Quality of Children Regression, Equation 3′: Table 13.4						
Child's wealth	$2,753.0	$1,943.0		$4,730.0	$2,449.0	
Parents' wealth	$6,547.0	$2,178.0		$8,185.0	$4,283.0	
Grandparents' wealth	$7,653.0	$3,512.0		$10,363.0	$6,514.0	
Child's age	31.0	5.0		34.0	4.0	
Father's age	55.0	9.0		59.0	8.0	
Grandfather's age	87.0	6.0		87.0	6.0	
Regression to Create Parental Wealth Instrument: Table 13B.1						
Wealth	$4,507.0	$9,009.0		$9,593.0	$19,080.0	
Father's age	51.0	18.0		51.0	18.0	
Farm resident			56%			59%
Father's occupation						
Craftsman			8%			11%
None			4			1
Professional			5			6
Proprietor			5			9
Unknown			11			18
Laborer			67			55
Region of residence						
Unknown			36%			45%
Pacific			0			1
Mountain			0			0
Midwest			3			4
South			3			5
Mid-Atlantic			2			1
North-Atlantic			48			36
New England			8			8

Source: Linked geneaology-census sample.

Table 13.2 **Estimating Equation 2′: Number of Children Ever Born Regressed on Parental Wealth, Grandparental Wealth, and Grandparental Fertility**

Independent Variable	Including Grandparental Variables: Coefficient	Including Grandparental Variables: Standard Error	Excluding Grandparental Variables: Coefficient	Excluding Grandparental Variables: Standard Error
1860 Sample				
Parental variables				
Wealth/10^3	1.00	0.50	1.20	0.48
Wealth^2/10^8	−5.06	3.35	−4.41	3.44
Wealth^3/10^{13}	5.72	4.61	4.56	4.75
Grandparental variables				
Wealth/10^3	−0.20	0.54		
Wealth^2/10^8	1.42	3.02		
Wealth^3/10^{13}	−2.69	4.34		
Number of children	0.15	0.31		
Number of observations	104		104	
R^2	0.34		0.20	
F-test[a]			1.81	
1870 Sample				
Parental variables				
Wealth/10^3	0.22	0.11	0.30	0.14
Wealth^2/10^8	−0.44	0.47	−0.77	0.45
Wealth^3/10^{13}	0.16	0.17	0.31	0.16
Grandparental variables				
Wealth/10^3	−0.10	0.05		
Wealth^2/10^8	0.33	0.16		
Wealth^3/10^{13}	−0.09	0.05		
Number of children	0.23	0.27		
Number of observations	96		96	
R^2	0.30		0.13	
F-test[a]			1.90	

Sources: Linked genealogy-census sample and Table 13B.1

[a]The F-statistic tests the significance of the omission of the intergenerational variables. Its degrees of freedom are (10,83) for the 1860 regression and (10,75) for the 1870 regression.

The first regression includes grandparents' fertility and instruments for parental and grandparental wealth as independent variables, while the second omits grandparental variables.[37] Appendix B discusses how the wealth instruments were obtained.

37. The standard errors for regressions that use instrumental variables are not exact. This is caused by the failure to control for the estimation error in the predictions derived from the first-stage regressions that create the instruments (Peter Schmidt, *Econometrics* [New York, 1976], p. 160). Absence of direct measures of lifetime wealth precludes their inclusion in the regressions,

Fertility is positively related to parental wealth for most of the sample's wealth range. The relationship (displayed in Figure 13.1) is negative for the mid- to upper-wealth range, then turns positive at the highest estimated wealth levels. The pattern is congruent with the interaction between quantity and quality of children.[38] It is not consistent with Easterlin's model, which suggests a uniformly positive relationship of fertility to wealth. Additionally, empirical relationships among coefficients approximate the quantity-quality model's predictions. The coefficients on grandparental wealth terms are close to the negatives of the products of the coefficient on GPNUMKID and the respective coefficients on parental wealth terms. Only the coefficients on linear wealth terms are significant.

Omission of the grandparental variables has significant consequences for observed wealth effects on fertility. The omission biases the linear parental wealth term and increases its apparent significance.[39] The overall bias on the parental wealth effect is positive for the 1860 sample, though small. A positive bias is consistent with the quantity-quality model but not with Easterlin's model. For the 1870 sample, the bias is positive at most wealth levels but negative at the highest levels of lifetime wealth estimated for the sample.[40] Omission of grandparental variables is significant at the 90 to 95 percent level.

The Constrained Model

The quantity-quality model implies several restrictions that were not incorporated in the estimating procedure used in Table 13.2. The parameters of the constrained model are therefore estimated by nonlinear least squares (Table 13.3). If the constraints are appropriate, the estimated coefficients of the un-

---

so true standard errors cannot be derived. Dummy variables for farm residence for both generations were not significant.

38. The positive relation at high wealth comports with the shrinking bias in the observed elasticities discussed in the text and in footnote 11. The initial positive relation coupled with the mid-range negative relation suggests that the interaction between quantity and quality was weak at low levels of wealth and became stronger as wealth increased.

39. The bias is expected in the quantity-quality model because the instrumental wealth variables are correlated with ability. The instruments are constructed in part from occupational variables, which are related to earnings; one would expect earnings to be correlated with ability (Wahl, "Fertility in America," p. 55). Omission of the proxies for ability therefore biases the coefficients on wealth instruments. If instruments were constructed from variables uncorrelated with ability, the omission would affect standard errors but not coefficients (Schmidt, *Econometrics*, p. 40).

40. One reason for the high-end negative bias within the framework of the quantity-quality model could be that the return to investing in human capital increasingly varied through time over families of different wealths. The most likely explanation is, however, that 1870 wealth variables are not as reliable as 1860 variables. The distortion to land markets caused by the 1862 Homestead Act and the wealth transfers caused by the emancipation of slaves imply that 1870 census wealth may not be as accurate a basis for lifetime-wealth estimation as 1860 census wealth. The sample drawn here from the 1870 census also may not be representative, as it recorded a higher average wealth than other collected census samples.

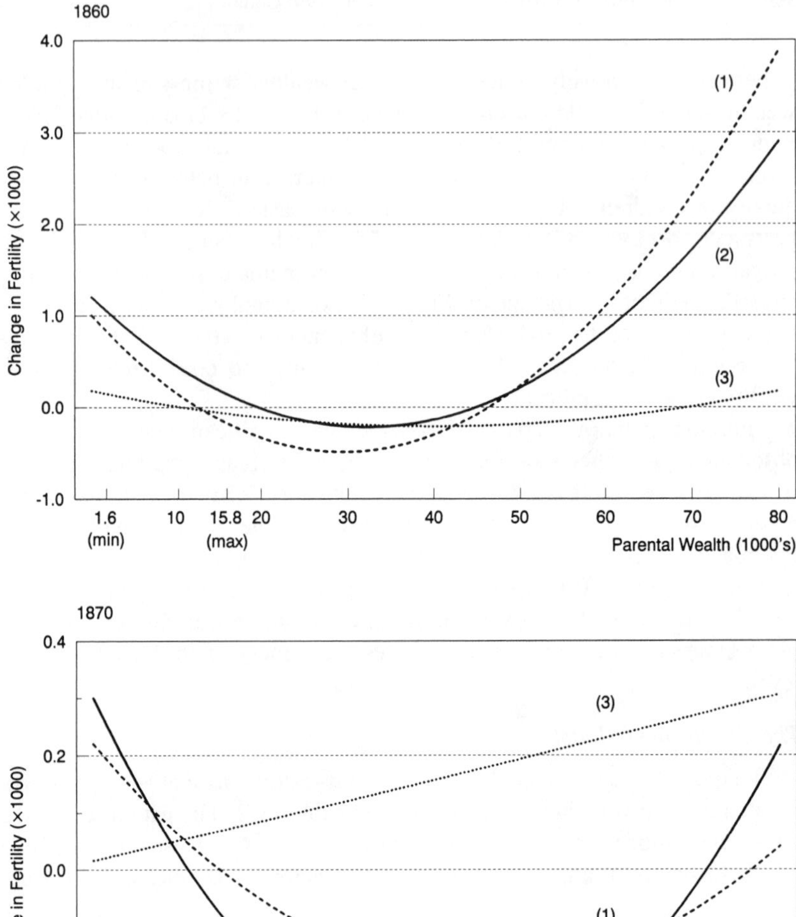

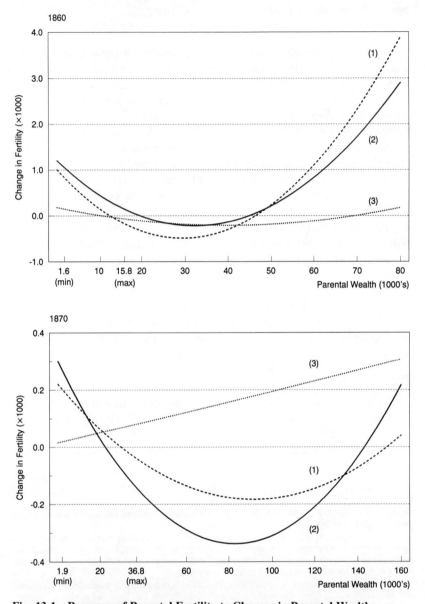

Fig. 13.1 Response of Parental Fertility to Changes in Parental Wealth

Note: This figure represents the change in the quantity of children with respect to a change in parental wealth graphed against the level of parental wealth in thousands of 1860 or 1870 dollars. Line (1) graphs the change in quantity with respect to a change in parental wealth when the number of children ever born is regressed on parental wealth, grandparental wealth, and grandparental fertility. Line (2) graphs the same derivative when the number of children ever born is regressed only on parental wealth. Both are derived from Table 13.2. Line (3) is derived from Table 13.3 and represents the derivative from a regression of the number of children ever born on parental wealth, grandparental wealth, and grandparental fertility, using the constraints on coefficients specified by the quantity-quality model. Min is the minimum wealth estimated for the sample, and max gives the maximum.

Sources: Tables 13.2 and 13.3.

Table 13.3 **Estimating Equation (2′) with Quantity-Quality Coefficient Constraints: Number of Children Ever Born Regressed on Parental Wealth, Grandparental Wealth, and Grandparental Fertility**

	1860		1870	
Independent Variable	Coefficient	Asymptotic Standard Error	Coefficient	Asymptotic Standard Error
Parental Wealth/10^3	0.179	0.325	0.016	0.058
Parental Wealth^2/10^8	−0.980	2.111	0.086	0.068
Parental Wealth^3/10^{13}	0.815	2.580	0.002	0.026
Grandparental fertility	0.025	0.098	0.113	0.075
Number of observations	104		96	
Chi-square test for constrained versus unconstrained model (4 degrees of freedom)	2.91		6.41	

Note: The constraints of the quantity-quality model indicate that the coefficient on each grandparental wealth variable (linear, quadratic, and cubic) equals the negative of the product of the coefficient on the corresponding parental wealth variable and the coefficient on grandparental fertility.

Sources: Linked genealogy-census sample and Table 13B.1

constrained model provide consistent initial estimates for the constrained procedure.[41]

Although the coefficients are not the same for the constrained and unconstrained regressions, they are not significantly different. A chi-square test reveals that the difference is significant only at the 40 percent level for the 1860 sample and at the 80 percent level for the 1870 sample. As in the unconstrained regression, Figure 13.1 shows that wealth affects fertility positively for most of the relevant range of lifetime wealth, although the effect is negative in the middle-wealth range for constrained regressions using 1860 wealth. In constrained regressions using 1870 wealth, the wealth effect appears positive throughout.

13.3.3 Estimating the Wealth Equation (3′)

Table 13.4 reports the estimation of equation (3′) to show that the coefficients and the bias from omitting grandparental variables correspond to the quantity-quality model's predictions.[42] In regressions including grandparental wealth, the coefficients accord with the quantity-quality model: the parental wealth coefficient is positive, and it is opposite in sign to and larger in absolute

41. Various initial estimates result in unique coefficient estimates for 1860 data. For regressions using 1870 wealth, a second local optimum results if large starting values (0.45 to 0.75) are used to estimate the degree to which ability is inherited (coefficient c_1).

42. As in equation (2′), farm residence variables are not significant.

Table 13.4 Estimating Equation 3′: Child's Wealth Regressed on Parental Wealth and Grandparental Wealth

Independent Variable	Including Grandparental Variables: Coefficient	Including Grandparental Variables: Standard Error	Excluding Grandparental Variables: Coefficient	Excluding Grandparental Variables: Standard Error
1860 Sample				
Parental wealth	0.260	0.124	0.153	0.065
Grandparental wealth	−0.008	0.005		
Number of observations	106		106	
R^2	0.14		0.09	
1870 Sample				
Parental wealth	0.462	0.215	0.333	0.150
Grandparental wealth	−0.030	0.019		
Number of observations	125		125	
R^2	0.10		0.07	

Sources: Linked genealogy-census sample and Table 13B.1

magnitude than the grandparental wealth coefficient. These results are inconsistent with Easterlin's model, which predicts positive coefficients on both wealth variables.

Omission of grandparental wealth has effects congruent with the quantity-quality model's predictions. The omission of GPWEALTH is significant at the 70 percent level for both census years. Furthermore, the observed coefficient on PWEALTH in regressions that use three generations of wealth data is higher than the wealth coefficient found in many studies, including this one, that use only two.[43] The downward bias on the PWEALTH coefficient caused by the omission of GPWEALTH is consistent with the quantity-quality model, but not with Easterlin's model.

43. For a review of two-generation studies, see Gary Becker and Nigel Tomes, "The Rise and Fall of Families," Working Paper no. 84–10, National Opinion Research Center (Chicago, Oct. 1984). Two-generation studies using probate data find larger wealth effects. See Paul Menchik, "Inter-Generational Transmission of Inequality: An Empirical Study of Wealth Mobility," *Economica,* 46 (Nov. 1979), pp. 349–62. The size of the wealth effect in probate samples may, however, result from a selection bias. Many probate samples include only families in which fathers and sons made wills, and individuals who make wills are generally wealthy. Wealth is probably more highly correlated across generations for these families: a higher percentage of their wealth is bequeathed and bequests are not as variable as earnings. Michael Hurd and B. Gabriela Mundaca, for example, find that inherited wealth is 15 to 20 percent of wealthy individuals' total wealth, and gifts are 5 to 10 percent. ("The Importance of Gifts and Inheritances Among the Very Wealthy," a paper given at the National Bureau of Economic Research Conference on Research in Income and Wealth [Baltimore, 1987]).

13.4 Conclusion

Many scholars have modeled how nineteenth-century American families made life-cycle decisions, with an emphasis on explaining decreasing family sizes. Easterlin's target-bequest model has been the most influential for economic historians, although old-age security models and various biological and sociological models have also been proposed. Explanations of the fertility decline focus on household responses to macroeconomic phenomena, such as increasing population density and improving labor markets for youth. My work, like that of others, suggests that nineteenth-century household fertility decisions were influenced by movements in macroeconomic variables. Thus far, proposed fertility models have remained untested or have had to rely on imperfect, aggregate measures of fertility and wealth. Mine is the first to examine and test a microeconomic fertility model using wealth and fertility data for three generations of families.

The empirical analysis presented here indicates that the tradeoff between the quantity and quality of children offers a new view of the nineteenth-century American family and a promising explanation for the fertility decline through the 1800s. The quantity-quality model performs better on nineteenth-century household-level data than the leading alternative, Easterlin's model. Coefficient signs comport with the predictions of the quantity-quality model; coefficient restrictions of the quantity-quality model are not rejected at any conventional significance level; and the omission of grandparental variables from regressions is significant and biases parental wealth effects in the direction predicted by the quantity-quality model. Neither coefficient signs nor observed biases from omitting grandparental variables harmonize with the predictions of Easterlin's model.

How does the quantity-quality model help account for the decline in nineteenth-century American fertility? The model implies that fertility would have fallen if the relative price of quantity rose, either because the interaction of quantity and quality affected the prices of the two goods when wealth changed or the relative price itself initially increased. Changes in the prices of the quantity and quality of children and in the degree of dispersion of wealth, rather than increasing average wealth or changing attitudes toward offspring, provide the key.

Table 13.1 shows an increase in average lifetime wealth from the 1860 to the 1870 census.[44] Figure 13.1 shows that this increment is in the range of wealth where fertility moved with wealth, so the growth in wealth would have tended to increase rather than decrease family sizes. The distribution of wealth was, however, also more spread out for the sample in 1870—hinting

44. This results partly from inflation: the Warren-Pearson price index reveals that prices over the decade rose by 45 percent. See U.S. Bureau of the Census, *Historical Statistics of the United States from Colonial Times to 1970* (Washington, 1975).

that families, though wealthier on average, may have been in wealth ranges of lower fertility.[45] Greater dispersion of wealth implies that some families moved into higher wealth ranges, where fertility decreased as wealth increased, while some moved into lower wealth ranges, where fertility decreased as wealth decreased.

Changes in the prices of quality and quantity furnish the most likely explanation for the fertility decline. The price of quality fell over time as lifespans increased and as public education became more available, causing investment in children to become more productive. The price of quantity rose as home life became a separate entity, more children survived infancy, and women participated more in activities outside the home. Both effects increased the relative price of quantity, encouraging nineteenth-century parents to have smaller families than their ancestors.

Appendix A
Creation of the Data Sample

Step 1

Each of nine genealogies is structured as follows. The first male immigrant to the United States with a recorded departure and destination place begins the genealogy. Within the genealogies, 25 percent of individuals were born in the period 1650–1799, 50 percent were born in the period 1800–1849, and 25 percent were born in the period 1850–99.[46] A family was included in the sample only if the mother was born at least forty-five years before the publication date.[47] Publication dates include 1877 to 1970.[48]

Step 2

Each individual in the genealogies born between 1750 and 1880 was potentially matched to him- or herself in the federal census manuscript schedules

45. Figure 13.1 demonstrates the relatively narrow band within which family size fluctuated. For instance, a $1,000 increment in a family's 1860 lifetime wealth with all else constant would have increased the number of children by only half a child if initial family wealth were zero, and by only one-tenth a child if initial wealth were $1,000. The same increment would have decreased the number of children by only about one-twentieth if initial wealth were $30,000. Although one might hope to observe larger wealth effects, these results are not terribly surprising—the range of family sizes is small relative to the range of wealth for the sample.

46. The large proportion of the genealogical sample born in the nineteenth century means a high degree of potential matches with census data.

47. By including only families in which the mother was born at least forty-five years before the publication date of the genealogy, the sample includes only families that are observed for their entire potential childbearing years.

48. Publication at a fairly recent date increases a genealogy's legibility and accuracy relative to unpublished or pre-nineteenth-century genealogies.

for 1850 to 1880. Matching characteristics included name, age, region of residence, and knowledge of family structure. For successful matches, each person had both genealogical information (date and place of birth, death, and marriage; number of offspring; name of and other information on spouse; and identification numbers for own marriage and parents' marriage if present) and census information (residence, occupation, literacy, school attendence, relationship to household head, and wealth).

Step 3

Individuals (each carrying the information described in step 2) were linked to their siblings through their parents' marriage identification number, so that a single observation was formed for generation $t + 1$. Two generations were then linked together by matching the parents' marriage identification number for the generation $t + 1$ sibling group to the own-marriage identification number for generation t individuals. A nuclear family observation with information on parents and children resulted from this step.

```
   0      Generation t (parents)
  //∧\\
000 00    Generation t + 1 (children)
```

The genealogical file contains 16,820 individuals from 5,632 nuclear families. Nuclear families at risk to be found in one of the censuses must have had at least one family member alive during the census year. The number of families at risk to be found in at least one census year is about 2,500; the number actually located is 2,042. The numbers of families found in each census year are 782 in 1850, 649 in 1860, 661 in 1870, and 706 in 1880.

Step 4

Nuclear families were linked through marriage identification numbers to grandparents of generation $t - 1$. The parents' marriage identification number corresponding to generation t was matched to the own-marriage identification number for generation $t - 1$. The resultant observation constitutes all census and genealogical information on one generation t individual (and his or her spouse), on one or two generation $t - 1$ individuals (and their spouses), and on all generation $t + 1$ individuals (and their spouses) born to the generation t couple. The analysis of the paper is based on the fertility and wealth of generation t.

```
  0 0     Generation t − 1 (grandparents)
  \ /
   0      Generation t (parents)
  //∧\\
000 00    Generation t + 1 (children)
```

Appendix B
Creation of the Wealth Instruments

The estimation of equations (2′) and (3′) uses instruments for all wealth variables. Table 13B.1 shows coefficients and standard errors for the regression producing the instrument for parental wealth.[49] Census family wealth is regressed on the age and age squared of the father and on three dummy variables: the occupation of the father, the family's residence on a farm, and the family's region of residence. The age variables are included to account for life-cycle effects in wealth accumulation and are statistically significant.[50] Other variables are included to correct for differences in earnings and wealth profiles and to act as proxies for the number and wealth of children.

Instrumental wealth variables are created because cross-sectional wealth suffers as an independent measure of resources available to "purchase" the quantity and wealth of children. Parental wealth is directly related to the product of the number of children born and the amount already spent on each (which influences children's wealth) before the census date. Moreover, the use of cross-sectional wealth could generate a selection bias. Cross-sectional parental wealth in families with deceased grandparents at the time of observation may include a bequest, while cross-sectional wealth in families with living grandparents would not. If most sample families had living grandparents when observed, grandparental wealth and fertility could serve as components of lifetime parental wealth—that is, bequests. A regression coefficient on cross-sectional parental wealth would thus be biased. The lack of independence and the bias associated with cross-sectional wealth point to the need for an instrumental variable for lifetime parental wealth.[51]

The use of wealth instruments is critical in evaluating wealth effects. Regressions using parental wealth instruments yield very different results from those using cross-sectional parental wealth. In contrast to the generally positive relationship of fertility to estimated lifetime parental wealth, fertility is negatively related to cross-sectional wealth in all but the uppermost wealth range. Coefficients on estimated lifetime parental wealth are large compared with those on cross-sectional wealth, similar to results found by others for

49. Because parental wealth squared and wealth cubed and grandparental wealth variables are included in the fertility regression, these variables are also instrumented (Wahl, "Fertility in America").

50. Wealth increases to age 50.5 in the 1860 sample and to age 62.3 in the 1870 sample, and then falls, similar to the results of Jeremy Atack and Fred Bateman, "Egalitarianism, Inequality, and Age: The Rural North in 1860," *Journal of Economic History,* 41 (Mar. 1981), pp. 85–93; and Soltow, *Men and Wealth.*

51. Another selection bias could arise if cross-sectional grandparental wealth were used as a proxy for their lifetime wealth. Families would be included in regressions only if the grandparents were living (and thus had not made a bequest) at the time of the observation. Because even an instrument for parental wealth controls imperfectly for bequests, cross-sectional grandparental wealth could act as a proxy for a component of parental wealth. Therefore, an instrumental variable for grandparental wealth is also necessary.

Table 13B.1 Creation of Parental Wealth Instrument for Regressions of Equations (2′) and (3′)

	1860		1870	
Independent Variable	Coefficient	Standard Error	Coefficient	Standard Error
Father's age	404	157	872	318
Father's age squared	−4	2	−7	3
Nonfarm resident (dummy)	2,596	1,937	−2,588	3,697
Father's occupation (dummy)				
Craftsman	−4,369	2,362	3,176	4,603
None	−3,586	5,433	1,434	13,036
Professional	1,771	2,643	20,827	5,207
Proprietor	−297	2,285	8,142	3,555
Unknown	119	1,983	7,468	4,243
Laborer (omitted)				
Region of residence (dummy)				
Unknown	−471	1,884	5,899	4,125
Pacific	−6,068	6,596	−1,570	9,812
Mountain	−122	1,220		
Midwest	264	2,933	3,407	5,162
South	3,563	13,393	1,345	6,405
Mid-Atlantic	1,709	3,798	8,730	9,809
North-Atlantic	2,225	11,870	8,022	4,093
New England (omitted)				
Mean wealth	$4,507		$9,593	
Number of observations	408		417	
R^2	0.12		0.13	

Source: Linked genealogy-census sample.

Note: The table gives coefficients and standard errors from a regression that creates the parental wealth instrument used in regressions of equations (2′) and (3′). Similar regressions derive instrumental variables for wealth squared and wealth cubed and for grandparental wealth variables. See Jenny Wahl, "Fertility in America: Historical Patterns and Wealth Effects on the Quantity and Quality of Children" (Ph.D. dissertation, University of Chicago, 1985).

twentieth-century data.[52] Furthermore, coefficients on the estimated lifetime parental wealth linear terms are significant at the 95 percent level; coefficients on cross-sectional wealth are not significant.[53]

52. Bruce Gardner, "Economics of the Size of North Carolina Rural Families," *Journal of Political Economy,* 81 (Mar./Apr. 1973), pp. S99–122; Dennis De Tray, "Child Quality and the Demand for Children," *Journal of Political Economy,* 81 (Mar./Apr. 1973), pp. S570–95; Willis, "Economic Theory"; and Becker and Tomes, "Rise and Fall."

53. Instruments for grandparental wealth are equally important. Lifetime parental wealth had a positive effect on fertility throughout much of the range, lifetime grandparental wealth a negative effect, and grandparental fertility a positive effect. In contrast, coefficients on cross-sectional grandparental wealth terms are of the same sign as those on parental wealth terms, while the coefficient on grandparental fertility is negative. In estimating equation (3′), grandparental cross-sectional wealth suffers from the selection problem discussed in footnote 51: only families with grandparents living at the time of the observation are included. Cross-sectional grandparental wealth serves partly as a measure of the bequest expected by parents, so it is not surprising that the coefficients on parental and grandparental wealth are both positive when cross-sectional grandparental wealth is used. For all these results, see Wahl, "Fertility in America," pp. 81–87.

IV Political Economy

14 The Profitability of Early Canadian Railroads

Evidence from the Grand Trunk and Great Western Railway Companies

Ann M. Carlos and Frank Lewis

14.1 Introduction

It was not until the middle of the nineteenth century that Canada moved into the railroad era. Although railroads had been built in the United States some twenty years earlier, it was during the decade of the 1850s that Canadian construction began in earnest. With only sixty-six miles of track in 1850, Central Canada had, within ten years, nearly 2,000 miles of track, or three quarters of a mile per thousand inhabitants.[1] But far from bringing the shareholders the 11 to 15 percent rates of return anticipated, these early railroads teetered on the brink of bankruptcy for most of their lives and were nationalized in 1917.

Yet when it comes to discussions of Canadian railroads, economists have shown far greater interest in the transcontinental or post-Confederation (1867) phase.[2] This is not to say the earlier railroad boom went unnoticed. Economic

The authors thank Merv Daub, Peter George, Knick Harley, Marvin McInnis, Angela Redish, and Anna Schwartz for helpful comments; and the Social Sciences and Humanities Research Council of Canada for supporting various parts of this project (grants 410–84–1189 and 410–85–0159, respectively). They also are grateful to the late Noel Butlin, who provided them with microfilmed accounts of early Canadian railroads, and this paper is dedicated to his memory.

1. The Dominion of Canada grew out of the confederation, in 1867, of most of the existing British North American colonies. To help the reader, we use post-Confederation names for the provinces of Central Canada: Ontario and Quebec. From 1797 to 1841 these provinces were known as Upper and Lower Canada, and each had its own legislature. In 1841, the two colonies were merged to form the Province of Canada, which differentiated the two areas by calling them Canada West and Canada East. With Confederation, the Province of Canada was divided into the two existing provinces. The total railway mileage for Ontario and Quebec in 1861 was 1,856 miles, and the population of the region was 2.5 million, most of whom lived in rural areas. See J. M. Trout and Edward Trout, *The Railways of Canada for 1870–71* (Toronto, 1871), pp. 35–36; and *Historical Statistics of Canada* (2d edn., Ottawa, 1983), pp. A2–14.

2. The following represents some of the research on the transcontinental phase. Harold A. Innis, *A History of the Canadian Pacific Railway* (Toronto, 1971); Peter J. George, "Rates of Return in Railway Investment and Implication for Government Subsidization of the Canadian

historians have extolled the ability of the Province of Canada to build an extensive and unified rail system, while telling the usual railroad story of corruption, greed, and government scandal. A. W. Currie begins his history of the longest line built, the Grand Trunk Railway, by stating that although this company has been "characterized as the world's worst commercial failure . . . it was, in fact, a pioneer—in design and management, in finance and in the economic interrelations of Britain, the United States and Canada."[3] O. D. Skelton makes the same assessment: "there had been waste and mismanagement, . . . but the railways had brought indirect gain that more than offset the direct loss."[4] A more directly economic perspective is given by William Marr and Donald Paterson who write: "examining only Canadian trade, the railways' contribution to social savings and indirect benefits are clearly positive and large," but "the railways of Central Canada were, on the other hand, not an unqualified success."[5]

The generally accepted view is that this first railroad boom, although financially unsuccessful, contributed greatly to the general development of the region. This is clearly an ex post assessment of the pre-Confederation construction phase. The ex ante expectation, on the other hand, was not only that the railroads would contribute to the general development of the region but also that private investors would enjoy large financial rewards. It was this combination of expected profitability and large social benefits that led the provincial government to promote railway building. The Grand Trunk Railway Company, for example, received over £3 million in government loan guarantees during its early construction phase.

Although the motivation for government involvement differs, there are striking parallels between the history of the Grand Trunk Railway Company of Canada and the Union Pacific Railroad.[6] As Robert Fogel documents, every history of the Union Pacific praises the joining of the country from coast to coast while at the same time decrying the political maneuvering, bribery, and corruption. This is also the history of the Grand Trunk Railway (a line that linked the Province of Canada from Sarnia to Montreal and from Montreal to Portland on the Atlantic seaboard) since coloring this achievement have been claims that the British construction company of Peto, Brassey, Jackson, and

---

Pacific Railway: Some Preliminary Results," *Canadian Journal of Economics*, 1 (Nov. 1968), pp. 740–62; Lloyd J. Mercer, "Rates of Return and Government Subsidization of the Canadian Pacific Railway: An Alternate View," *Canadian Journal of Economics*, 6 (Aug. 1973), pp. 428–37; and T. D. Regehr, *The Canadian Northern Railway: Pioneer Road of the Northern Prairies, 1895–1917* (Toronto, 1976).

3. A. W. Currie, *The Grand Trunk Railway of Canada* (Toronto, 1957), p. 31.

4. O. D. Skelton, *The Railroad Builders: A Chronicle of Overland Highways* (Toronto, 1916), p. 94.

5. William L. Marr and Donald G. Paterson, *Canada: An Economic History* (Toronto, 1980), pp. 318–19.

6. Robert W. Fogel, *The Union Pacific Railroad: A Case in Premature Enterprise* (Baltimore, 1960).

Betts "foisted a 'job' on the Grand Trunk and then quietly withdrew, leaving the company to work out its own salvation." In addition, Sir Francis Hincks, premier of the province, and some members of his cabinet were allegedly corrupt in their dealings with the railroad. These allegations led to the formation of special legislative committees of investigation, first in 1857 and then in 1861.[7]

Given the vast literature on railways, it is surprising that no one has examined the widely held view that lines built during the first Canadian railroad boom were privately unprofitable but socially desirable. Here we address this issue by examining two of the lines, the Grand Trunk Railway Company of Canada and the Great Western Railway Company. Together they accounted for 70 percent of the track built during the 1850s and one, the Grand Trunk, received a large amount of government aid. We find that for each line both the ex post unaided and ex post aided private rates of return lie below the market rate. The ex post social rate of return lies below the market rate for the Grand Trunk and above that rate for the Great Western. Our findings on private profitability are consistent with the historical literature, but our estimate of the Grand Trunk's social profitability suggests that the £3 million subsidy it received might have been used more efficiently elsewhere in the economy.[8] Indeed, if some of this aid had been given to the Great Western, it would have been in a far more stable financial position. We also argue that the form of the government aid, guaranteed bonds, may have contributed to the Grand Trunk Railway's financial difficulties.

14.2 The Central Canadian Environment and Government Legislation

The timing and pattern of railroad construction in Canada differed from its southern neighbor. Not only did the first period of major construction occur later than in the United States, but government was more directly involved. The provincial government granted financial aid, legislated a uniform gauge, specified those companies composing the main trunk line, and helped determine the location of that line. This occurred while state governments in the United States were moving away from direct involvement with railroads.[9]

Whatever the lag in actual construction, Canadian railroad companies began to emerge almost as early as in the United States. The first railroad was chartered in Central Canada in 1832, and many more were chartered in subsequent years, but they were unable to proceed with actual construction. The capital market in Canada was small; Ontario, the province with the largest

7. Currie, *Grand Trunk*, pp. 35, 67–68.

8. As noted below, we must be equivocal about this finding because of the downward biases associated with our social return calculation.

9. For a detailed discussion of American railroad construction and the role of government, see Albert Fishlow, *American Railroads and the Transformation of the Ante-Bellum Economy* (Cambridge, Mass., 1965).

number of companies chartered, was only partially settled; and the government had no independent source of funds.[10] With the union of Ontario and Quebec in 1841 and the rapid growth of Ontario's population, some of these problems were solved. However, the newly unified province immediately became involved in canal construction on the St. Lawrence River rather than in railroads. As a result, Ontario and Quebec had, by 1848, a well-developed water route from the Upper Lakes to Montreal with a canal capacity that far outstripped its shipping requirements.[11]

The St. Lawrence canal system was intended to channel the products of the Great Lakes drainage basin to Montreal and then on to England. As early as 1825, the Erie Canal threatened the primacy of the St. Lawrence, but the Canadian route was protected, at least early on, by the Corn Laws, Navigation Acts, and high American tariffs. In 1846 with the end of colonial privilege and with the drawback legislation in the United States, which allowed products for reexport to move through that country in bond, the dominance of the St. Lawrence route was again put at risk. These events caused a crisis within the province and, in spite of the well-developed water route, led to a call for a more modern mode of transportation that would allow the province to compete for the midwestern trade and reestablish Montreal as a leading entrepôt.

Vocal demand for railroads elicited a government response, but the government's intention was to help the railways acquire funds on capital markets rather than to build lines themselves. The first general railroad act, the Guarantee Act of 1849, guaranteed the interest on loans of companies chartered by the legislature of the province.[12] The guarantee, which was available to any company building a line at least 75 miles long that was at least half completed, provided for the interest on a sum up to half the company's expenditure. But the rate was to be no greater than 6 percent; the government was to have first charge on the tolls and profits of the company; and no dividends could be paid unless a sinking fund equal to 3 percent of the loans outstanding was set aside annually. Despite these constraints, it was believed that such aid would make it easier for companies to float shares and bonds, and because the railroads would be profitable ventures, the guarantees would cost the government nothing. In fact most guarantees were eventually converted into cash subsidies.

In 1851 the government altered the terms of the Guarantee Act with an "Act

10. The main source of funds for the British North American colonies at this time was tariff revenue. Unfortunately for Ontario, it was upriver from Montreal. Thus all imports were landed at Montreal and assessed duty at that port even if the final destination was Ontario. Although a formula for the division of the import duties existed, the share going to Ontario was a continual source of conflict. Ontario argued that it was not receiving its due share. Ontario was also growing faster than Quebec, and most of the canal construction that Ontario wanted was on the Quebec section of the St. Lawrence. To overcome these problems the two provinces united in 1840–41. As part of the union agreement, the British government guaranteed the interest payments on a £1.5 million loan to be used for improvements to infrastructure.

11. Thomas F. McIlwraith, "Freight Capacity and Utilization of the Erie and Great Lakes Canals before 1850," *Journal of Economic History,* 36 (Dec. 1976), pp. 852–75.

12. Province of Canada, Legislative Assembly, 1849, 12 Victoriae c. 29.

to Make Provision for the Construction of a Main Trunk Line" (or Main Line Act). Now the guarantee was "restricted and confined to those railroads which may form part of the said Main Trunk Line."[13] In essence the government was trying to ensure that assisted lines would form part of a unified system that would move commodities and people along the St. Lawrence route. The act defined the main trunk line to include those lines that would run from Detroit/Windsor to Montreal and then on to Portland (see Map). The government also mandated a gauge, and although restricting the number of lines that could apply for the guarantee, it relaxed the mileage provision. Now any company whose line was longer than 100 miles could divide it into sections of not less than 50 miles, each section being viewed as a distinct railroad for the purposes of the act. The act also extended the guarantee provisions to principal as well as to interest. A second act was passed in 1851. "An Act to Consolidate and Regulate the General Clauses relating to Railways," otherwise known as "The Railway Clauses Consolidation Act," covered all railroads unless the individual acts of incorporation specifically exempted them.[14] This legislation specified various conditions companies had to meet with respect to capital stock, shareholders, bridges, fences, rights-of-way, and so on.

The provincial government quickly recognized that individual municipalities would not be able to provide funds on their own, especially for branch and feeder lines now disqualified by the Main Line Act. Thus in 1852, the legislature passed an "Act to Establish a Consolidated Municipal Loan Fund for Upper Canada" (or Municipal Loan Fund Act). The preamble stated that such a fund "would greatly facilitate the borrowing upon advantageous terms of such sums as may be required . . . for effecting or aiding in effecting important works."[15] This fund allowed individual municipalities to borrow from the fund rather than on the open capital market. In return for their debentures, municipalities received cash or provincial debentures which would be given to railroad companies in return for stock. These debentures stated that "the Provincial Government undertakes to pay the principal sum mentioned in them and the interest thereon, out of monies forming part of the Consolidated Municipal Loan Fund, and out of no other monies or funds whatsoever."[16] Although the Municipal Loan Fund Act was intended to be self-financing, the provincial government became liable for all monies lent to railroad companies by municipalities in the event that the railroads were not successful. In 1859 the government dissolved the fund and acquired a debt of almost £2 million.[17]

13. Ibid., 1851, 14 and 15 Vic. c. 73. The railroads specified as part of the main trunk line were the Great Western (main line only), the St. Lawrence and Atlantic (Montreal to the Maine border), and the Ontario Simcoe and Huron (from Goderich to Buffalo). The Grand Trunk was formed as part of the main trunk route through the province.

14. Ibid., c. 51.

15. Ibid., 1852, 16 Vic. c. 22.

16. Ibid.

17. Although the Municipal Loan Fund Act was designed to aid in the building of branch and feeder lines, some of the municipalities used the fund to purchase stock in the main trunk line

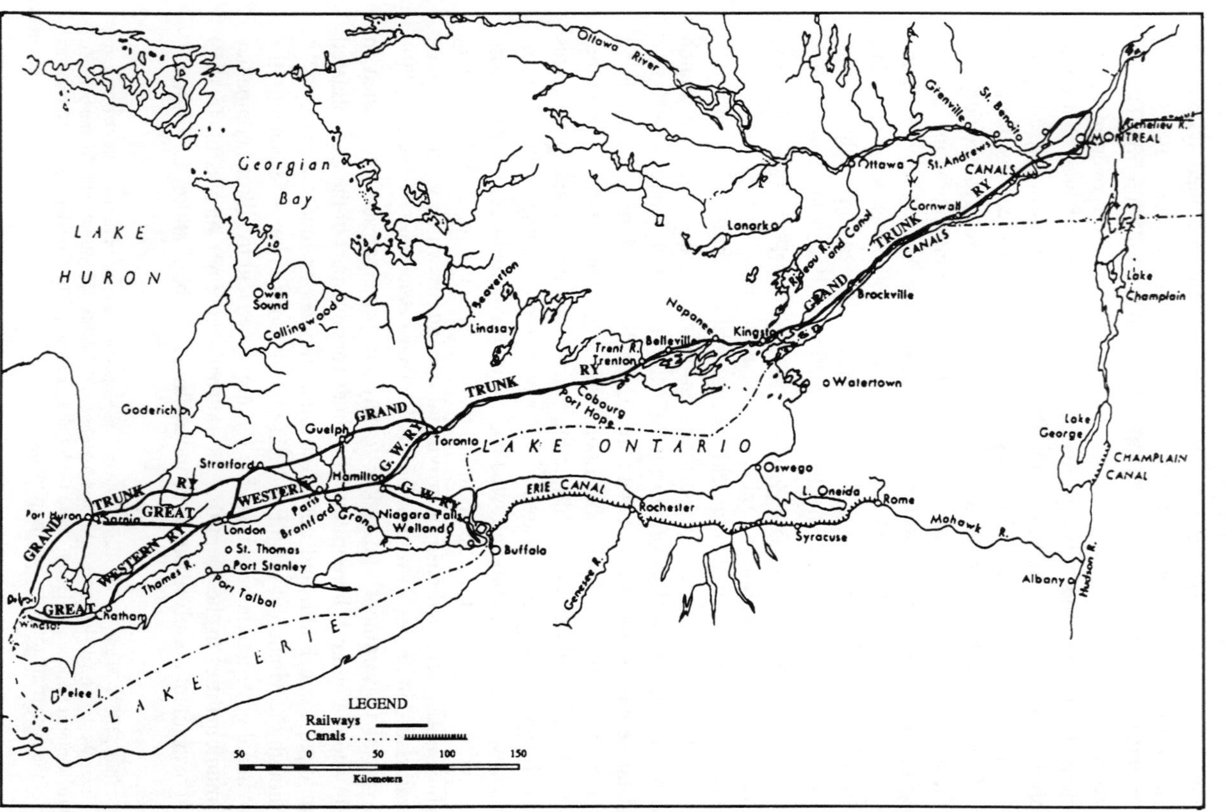

Location of Grand Trunk and Great Western Railway Companies
Source: D. G. G. Kerr, *Historical Atlas of Canada* (Toronto, 1975), p. 51.

14.3 Economic Issues in Canadian Railroad Construction

The literature on Canadian railroads, summarized briefly above, argues that the railroads were necessary for the continuing development of the country, especially in light of railroad development in the United States. The possibility that American lines would divert traffic from the existing Canadian infrastructure as well as the presumed benefits from having a rail system put pressure on the government to aid railroad construction. The contemporary view was that railroads would be financially profitable but the small size of the Canadian capital market made it impossible for them to raise sufficient funds locally. Funds could be obtained on the London market, but here Canadian companies were hurt by English investors' ignorance of the region. This was where government bond guarantees could increase accessibility.

There is a strong element of boosterism in the contemporary view that, once constructed, railroads would be privately profitable, but one might have expected that the early railroads built through the developed areas of southwestern Ontario would be successful. Historians, however, see these lines as financial failures even with the government subsidies. The issue of unaided and aided private profitability has been asked of the land-grant American lines by Lloyd Mercer and of the Canadian Pacific Railroad by both Mercer and Peter George.[18] Mercer finds great variability in the unaided and aided private rates of return across the lines studied. Here we follow Mercer's methodology, which allows us to measure the ex post private rates of return to the Grand Trunk and Great Western Railways and to compare these lines with the U.S. land-grant railroads and the Canadian Pacific Railway.

Contemporaries not only argued that the early Canadian railroads would be successful, they also convinced the provincial government to aid these companies on the grounds that the lines would protect the existing trading network and encourage further development within the region. The commitment to railroad development was, in fact, a commitment to a policy of "defensive expansionism."[19] The current view seems to be that the lines were socially profitable and on these grounds government aid was justified. Yet no assessment has been made of the social profitability of the early Canadian lines and in particular of the Grand Trunk line which received the lion's share of government help. The question of the social profitability of a line is also not new. Fogel addressed the issue in his study of the Union Pacific as did Lloyd Mercer in his study of the land-grant railroads. The methodology of studying so-

companies. For a full listing of the monies borrowed by the municipalities see the *Monetary Times* (Toronto, 1871).

18. Lloyd L. Mercer, *Railroads and Land Grant Policy* (New York, 1982); George, "Rates of Return."

19. Hugh G. J. Aitken, "Defensive Expansionism: The State and Economic Growth in Canada," in *The State and Economic Growth,* Hugh G. J. Aitken, ed. (New York, 1959).

cial profitability has itself generated much controversy, a point we will return to later.[20]

One justification for governmental involvement in the building of infrastructure is that such projects promote faster growth in a region and, without government help, these projects might be delayed. But as Fogel points out, inherent in such "premature" enterprises is "a real dichotomy between sound private investment principles and public or national necessity."[21] Railroads face the additional problem that a market for their services often does not develop until after the line is completed. This may require what is sometimes described as building ahead of demand, which in turn can create a financial obstacle for railroad companies.[22] They must secure the financing necessary to build the line before they earn any revenue. Government loan guarantees can alleviate the problem by improving access to capital markets, but such aid may have serious consequences for a company's financial viability: bond guarantees encourage firms to issue more debt, thereby increasing the likelihood of bankruptcy.[23] We suggest the Grand Trunk Railway may be a case in point. Encouraged by legislation, it acquired a large bonded debt which put the company in a precarious financial position. To make matters worse, it also was a line for which the private rate of return was far below the market rate.

14.4 Private Rates of Return: The Grand Trunk Railway and the Great Western Railway Companies

The Great Western Railway was initially incorporated in 1834 as the London [Ontario] and Gore Railroad Company. The act of incorporation gave the company until 1845 to build a line, but nothing was done. Due to lapse, the act was amended and the name of the company changed to the Great Western Railway. It was now authorized to build from some point on the Niagara River to Windsor and was to service the southern part of Ontario, linking with American lines in New York and Michigan. Options on 55,000 shares were quickly taken in Britain and 5,000 in Canada, but the railroad boom in Britain collapsed before any money was paid. The company then took advantage of

20. Fogel, *Union Pacific;* Mercer, *Railroads and Land Grant Policy;* Stanley Engerman, "Some Economic Issues Relating to Railroad Subsidies and the Evaluation of Land Grants," *Journal of Economic History,* 32 (Sept. 1972), pp. 443–63.

21. Fogel, *Union Pacific*, pp. 23, 165–71.

22. On the question of building ahead of demand, see Fishlow, *American Railroads,* pp. 165–71; C. Knick Harley, "Oligopoly Strategy and the Timing of American Railroad Construction," *Journal of Economic History,* 42 (Nov. 1982), pp. 797–824; and Engerman, "Some Economic Issues."

23. Fogel, *Union Pacific,* p. 55; Frank Lewis and Mary MacKinnon, "Government Loan Guarantees and the Failure of the Canadian Northern Railway," *Journal of Economic History,* 47 (Mar. 1987), pp. 175–96.

the Guarantee Act to sell stock and bonds. Construction commenced in 1851, and the line was open for traffic in late 1853.[24]

The history of the Grand Trunk Railway is more complex.[25] This railway grew out of a desire on the part of the British North American colonies for an all-weather link. By 1850, it was believed that the Imperial Parliament in Britain would subsidize an intercolonial line, and the British construction firm of Peto, Brassey, Jackson, and Betts showed interest in building it. But with the decision of Lord Derby and the English government not to help with financing, the Premier of Canada, Sir Francis Hincks, opened direct discussions with Peto and associates. The line was initially intended to run from Montreal to Toronto where it would join the Great Western, but through a series of particular circumstances, the Grand Trunk was extended from Montreal to Quebec City and from Toronto to Sarnia on Lake Huron. The Grand Trunk also leased the St. Lawrence and Atlantic which ran from Montreal to Portland. Once completed, the Grand Trunk, at over 1,000 miles, was one of the longest railways in existence. Because of its length and because of the direct involvement of Hincks, the company was allowed to use the Guarantee Act up to only £616 ($3,000) per mile rather than for fully half of the cost of construction.

The first question addressed here is the extent to which the Grand Trunk and Great Western Railways, which accounted for over 70 percent of track in the province, were privately profitable. We derive ex post private rates of return using the same approach as Lloyd Mercer in his analysis of six American land-grant railroads and the Canadian Pacific Railway mentioned above.[26] The internal rate of return is the solution to:

$$\sum_{t=1}^{T} \frac{R_t - C_t - I_t}{(1 + r)^t} + \frac{A}{(1 + r)^T} = 0 , \tag{1}$$

where R is the operating revenue, C is the operating cost, I is gross investment expenditures, A is the estimated value of the firm in the terminal year, and r is the internal rate of return. Like Mercer we adjust for the cost of leased lines and also base our estimates on actual construction cost rather than on the book value of each railway's securities. Actual construction costs and the book value of a railway's securities will diverge if the stocks and bonds of the company are discounted. In this latter regard the Grand Trunk did issue discounted securities. All too often in the railroad literature discounting has been taken as evidence of stock manipulation, but this is only one reason why securities

24. The most accessible histories of the Great Western Railway Company are in Currie, *Grand Trunk,* chaps. 8 and 9; and in Norman Thompson and Major J. H. Edgar, *Canadian Railway Development from the Earliest Times* (Toronto, 1933), chap. 2.

25. The standard history of this company is Currie, *Grand Trunk.*

26. Mercer, *Land Grant,* chap. 4.

might sell at a discount. As Fogel points out in his analysis of the Union Pacific, railroad companies might be forced to sell securities at a discount to obtain sufficient funding to allow them to commence construction or to finish construction already started. The existence of laws limiting the interest rate payable on the securities could also result in a security selling at a discount. We argue below, however, that the discounted bonds that Grand Trunk issued may have had more to do with the type of aid the railway received than with any usury laws or even the inherent riskiness of the project.

The rate of return to the Grand Trunk is derived for the period from 1853, the year in which it was formed, to 1882, the year in which it amalgamated with the Great Western. Figure 14.1 shows the path of revenue, expenses, and net revenue from 1853 to 1882. Our estimates are based on the company's semi-annual reports, which offer a complete series of revenues and costs, including capital costs.[27] The Grand Trunk was grossly over-capitalized. Bonds, and especially shares, sold at large discounts, and the company often issued securities in lieu of interest or dividend payments. As a result, the reported capitalization exceeded the true cost of the line, the rolling stock, and other physical assets. To allow for this, we include in gross investment only reported expenditures, excluding interest, discounts, and other components that entered the company's capital account. Indeed, even reported investment outlays must be adjusted downward. As Currie notes, Peto and Company, the chief contractor for the Grand Trunk, received some payments in company bonds and shares.[28] These were valued at par for the purpose of recording expenditure by the railroad even though their market values were much less. To compensate, Peto and Company inflated its reported costs. In deriving our estimates we, therefore, have used the market value of securities to adjust reported capital expenditures downward.[29]

Table 14.1 presents the book value, reported capital cost, and adjusted capital cost for selected periods. The book value of the Grand Trunk approximated its construction cost in 1853 and 1854; and in 1855 its book value exceeded true expenditures by only 5 percent, but by 1857 book value was nearly 25 percent above expenditures. During the 1860s and 1870s, the book value of the Grand Trunk continued to grow rapidly despite a sharp decline in

27. Grand Trunk Railway Company of Canada, Half Yearly Reports of the Directors, 1853–82.

28. Currie, *Grand Trunk*, pp. 41–46.

29. A complete breakdown of payments made to Peto and Co. over the period 1853–56 is given in Canada, Parliamentary Legislative Assembly, *Report of the Special Committee Appointed to Enquire and Report as to the Condition, Management and Prospects of the Grand Trunk Railway* (Toronto, 1857), p. 180. Peto and Co. received payment in Grand Trunk "B" shares, "B" bonds, and the shares and debentures of the Atlantic and St. Lawrence Railway. All were selling at a discount. Our estimated construction cost is based on the market values rather than the face values of the railway securities at the time they were received by the contractor. We allow for the fact that Peto and Co. paid £12.5 for each "B" share it received. See Currie, *The Grand Trunk Railway*, p. 41.

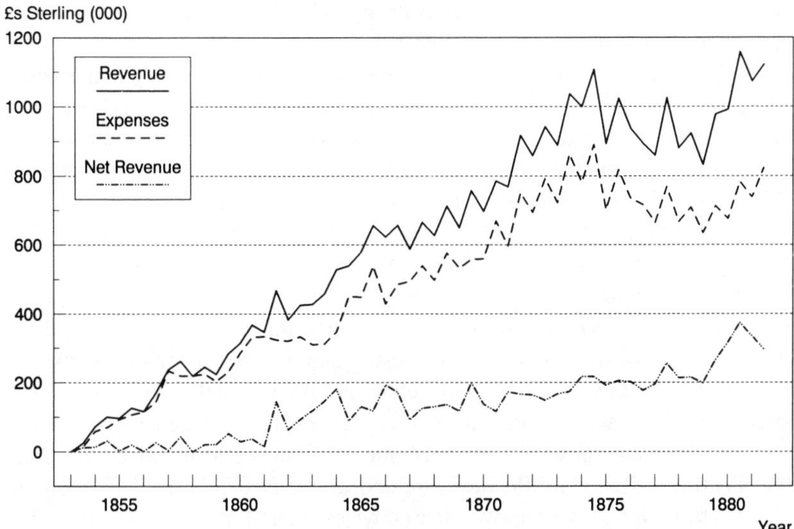

Fig. 14.1 Grand Trunk Railway Revenues and Expenses
Source: Appendix Table 14A.1.

Table 14.1 Capital Cost of the Grand Trunk Railway for Selected Dates (in thousands of £ sterling)

Accumulated to:	Book Value	Reported Expenditures	Adjusted Expenditures
15 July 1853	£1,068	£1,068	£1,068
30 June 1854	2,981	2,827	2,827
30 June 1855	5,505	5,201	5,201
30 June 1856	7,316	6,966	6,299
30 June 1857	8,207	7,627	6,605
30 June 1860	12,388	11,560	10,536
30 June 1865	17,210	12,330	11,306
30 June 1870	18,999	12,643	11,619
30 June 1875	30,633	15,362	14,338
30 June 1880	30,988	15,540	14,516

Sources: Grand Trunk Railway Company of Canada; Report of the Directors to the Bond and Stockholders, and Statement of the Revenue and Capital Accounts for the Half-Years ending 30 June and 31 December, 1853–82; The *London Times,* Railway Intelligence Column, 1853 to 1882; and A. W. Currie, *The Grand Trunk Railway of Canada* (Toronto, 1957).

the rate of gross investment. As a result, by 1880 the railway's book value was more than double its true capital cost.[30]

Much of the negative assessment of the Grand Trunk, both by contemporaries and historians, may be due in part to a comparison of the railway's net returns to its book value. Certainly on the basis of such a comparison, the railway did very poorly. We estimate an ex post (unaided) private return of −3.7 percent. As a reflection of the return to the project, this rate is far too low. In Table 14.2, we present ex post private rates of return using our best estimates of the railway's actual cost. We estimate that, unaided, the railway would have provided private investors a return of 1.7 percent. This is much lower than the normal rate for the period, which was about 6 percent, and also lower than any of the equivalent rates estimated by Mercer for the railroads in his sample.[31] Although the private return is low, it is not unusually so compared with the Canadian Pacific Railway, generally regarded as the success story of Canadian railway history. Mercer estimates that unaided, the Canadian Pacific Railway would have yielded an ex post return of 2.4 percent, which is only 0.7 percent above the rate we estimate for the Grand Trunk.[32]

The Grand Trunk Railway, like the Canadian Pacific, was subsidized, al-

30. In 1880 the book value of the Grand Trunk was 2.15 times its estimated capital cost. Of Mercer's railroads, only the Northern Pacific and Central Pacific had higher ratios, 2.36 and 3.17, respectively (Mercer, *Land Grant,* Table A-15, pp. 176–77).

31. This estimate is based on the assumption that the Grand Trunk was a fully maintained system. The railway made large outlays for maintenance and renewal of track and rolling stock, and these expenditures were charged to its operating account. In fact, the renewals in some cases led to the upgrading of old capital. We therefore base our rate-of-return estimates on a zero depreciation rate, but to the extent rolling stock and track were upgraded, our estimates would be biased downward. Another possible source of bias is our failure to deflate any of the railway's costs or revenues. This is dictated by the lack of a good general price index for Canada. If, however, the U.S. experience and the available Canadian data can be taken as a guide, the period 1853–80 appears to have been one of general price stability (note: Canada was not subject to as much of the U.S. Civil War inflation). If anything, by 1880 prices likely trended downward, implying that as measures of the real rate of return our estimates are biased downward. Finally, it should be noted that the (nominal) rate of return on riskless securities remained fairly stable at about 6 percent. Government of Canada bonds, sold on the London market, carried a coupon rate of 6 percent.

32. This is based on the comparison using Mercer's "C" adjustment. Mercer assumes a depreciation rate of 1.97 percent which appears to have been appropriate given that it implies a terminal adjustment roughly equal to the market value of the firm's securities (*Land Grant,* chap. 4). The unaided and aided rates of return (using terminal adjustment C) are:

Railroad	*Unaided*	*Aided*
Central Pacific	10.6	11.6
Union Pacific	11.6	13.1
Great Northern	8.7	10.0
Texas and Pacific	2.2	4.3
Atchison, Topeka & Santa Fe	6.1	7.1
Northern Pacific	6.3	9.2
Canadian Pacific	2.4	8.4

Thus the Grand Trunk performed more poorly than any of the lines in Mercer's study, including the most studied of the Canadian railways, the Canadian Pacific Railway.

Table 14.2 Private and Social Rates of Return, Grand Trunk and Great Western Railways (in percentages)

	Grand Trunk		Great Western
	Actual Starting Date	1 January 1861	Actual Starting Date
Private rate of return			
Unaided	1.71%	2.25%	4.06%
Aided	3.00	4.79	5.20
Social rate of return	2.77	3.57	6.10

Notes: The present value of leased lines for the Grand Trunk is £1,538,000 based on the actual starting date, and £1,142,000 assuming a starting date of 1 January 1961. The social rates of return are based on the estimated value of c/p^*, which is 0.77 for the Grand Trunk and 0.69 for the Great Western. In deriving the estimate of c/p^* for the Grand Trunk, the decade of the 1850s was excluded.

Sources: Grand Trunk Railway Company of Canada; Report of the Directors to the Bond and Stockholders, and Statement of the Revenue and Capital Accounts for the Half-Years ending 30 June and 31 December, 1853–82. Great Western Railway of Canada; Report of the Directors of the Great Western Railway of Canada for the Half-Years ending 31 July and 31 January, 1852–80. A detailed account of the derivation of these numbers is given in the text and footnotes 29 through 35.

though the subsidy came in a different form. The Canadian Pacific received direct aid: cash grants, land grants, and aid to construction; whereas the Grand Trunk was provided guaranteed provincial debentures under the Guarantee Act. When issued, these debentures were given first priority on the firm's assets, but as the financial position of the firm worsened, the priority was reduced and eventually both interest and principal were forgiven. The railway received these debentures between 1853 and 1858, by which time they totaled £3,115,000 sterling. Incorporating this subsidy in our calculations gives an aided private rate of return of 3.0 percent.[33] This rate is far below the 8.4 percent ex post aided rate of return estimated by Mercer for the Canadian Pacific. The small gap in unaided rates and the large gap in aided rates of return suggests that differences in the ex post profitability of the projects to the private investors had more to do with the size and type of subsidy each railway received than to differences in their intrinsic profitability.

The Grand Trunk is sometimes criticized in the historical literature for having been, in Fogel's terms, a premature enterprise. Certainly the railway's net returns during the 1850s were very low. Early problems with construction may account for part of the poor performance, but more fundamental may have been the lack of demand for rail services in the early years. To test the proposition that the 1853 starting date was too early, we have recomputed rates of return starting in 1861 but otherwise apply the same aggregate investment

33. This rate is computed as above, deducting from investment expenditures the (face) value of the government loan guarantees.

expenditures.[34] Our estimates provide some support for the view that the enterprise was premature. Had construction of the Grand Trunk lines been delayed to 1861, the unaided rate of return would have increased by 0.5 percent, which would have made the railway comparable to the Canadian Pacific in intrinsic profitability. More importantly, with the delay in construction, the same government subsidy would have provided a rate of return to private investors only about one percent below the normal rate of 6 percent.[35]

The Great Western was one of the first railway companies to operate in Canada, commencing operations in late 1853. It ran through some of the most populated areas of southwestern Ontario and provided an important link to the U.S. Midwest. It also was viewed ex ante as profitable and successful. Company bonds and shares sold quickly and at a premium in the London market. Yet this line, like the Grand Trunk, has been viewed as a commercial failure. As Currie puts it: "From first to last it was badly managed."[36] While Currie's view of the management may be valid, the ex post rates of return implied by the revenue and cost data suggest that the Great Western was significantly more profitable than either the Grand Trunk or the Canadian Pacific (see Figure 14.2 and Table 14.2). We estimate the unaided private rate of return to be 4.1 percent. Although this is below the normal rate, it exceeds the rates of return on the Canadian Pacific and Grand Trunk by 1.7 and 2.4 percentage points, respectively.[37]

The provincial government offered loan guarantees to the Great Western as it did to the Grand Trunk, but these guarantees were, in total, much smaller, £700,000 rather than £3,115,000. In July 1860 the loan guarantees were only 13 percent of the company's book value (£5,204,000) and only 15 percent of the estimated capital cost (£4,568,000). The latter figure for the Grand Trunk was roughly 30 percent. In addition, since the loans to the Great Western were almost fully repaid, almost no subsidy was granted ex post. Had the loan guarantees been converted into a subsidy, investors in the Great Western

34. For this calculation, investment expenditures in the hypothetical initial year (1861) are the cumulated investment expenditures over the period 1853–61. The capital value of leased lines is the discounted (at 6 percent) sum of all payments for leased lines from 1861 to 1881. Our estimates assume no lag between completion of a line and demand for rail services. Although this clearly is inappropriate in cases where a rail link is a prerequisite to settlement, the Grand Trunk, like the Great Western, was built through an already settled area. Indeed, the Great Western enjoyed high operating revenues as soon as the line was completed. The year 1861 also marks the start of the U.S. Civil War, which may have adversely affected earnings. Both companies reported large losses due to discounts on revenues received in U.S. dollars. However, to the extent that U.S. freight rates rose, this compensated for the change in exchange rates. Also the volume of through-freight increased as trade was diverted from the Mississippi.

35. This calculation is based on the assumption that the present value of the government subsidy would have been the same. The actual subsidy payments are compounded at 6 percent to 1861.

36. Currie, *Grand Trunk,* p. 218.

37. As with the Grand Trunk, we assume expenditures on maintenance and renewals were sufficient to assure no depreciation of the Great Western's capital stock. The assumption of a zero depreciation rate implies a terminal capital stock in 1880 of £7,838,000, which is very close to the market value of the firm's securities in that year.

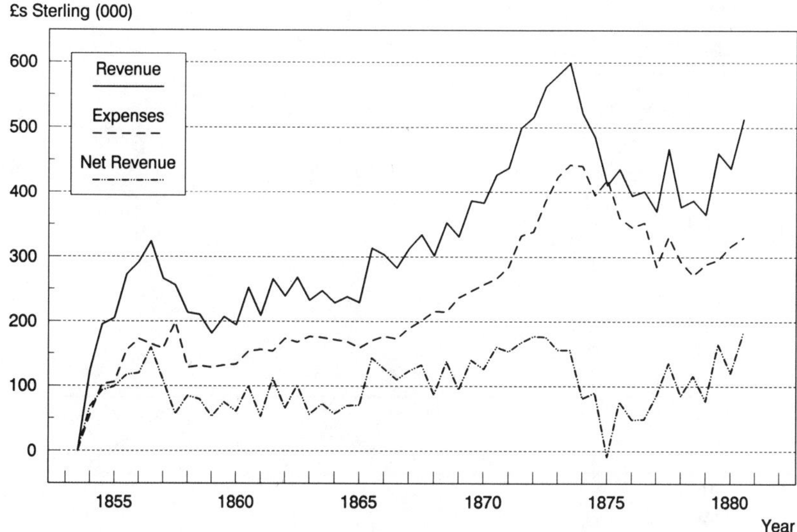

Fig. 14.2 Great Western Railway Revenues and Expenses
Source: Appendix Table 14A.2.

would have earned a rate of return of 5.2 percent, suggesting that a relatively small subsidy would have made the Great Western a privately profitable venture.

14.5 Social Rates of Return: The Grand Trunk Railway and Great Western Railway

More important than the issue of private profitability, at least from a policy perspective, is the question of whether the government decision to encourage the railways to proceed was appropriate. To help answer this question we have derived social rates of return based on estimates of the consumers' surplus for those who demanded railroad services. This approach is conceptually the same as social savings, since social savings also measures the net benefit of using railroads rather than a higher cost alternative; however, because we must choose a somewhat arbitrary demand elasticity, our estimates are necessarily less accurate. The demand elasticities we select are based on the assumption that the Grand Trunk and Great Western priced as profit-maximizing monopolists.[38] This allows us to generate what we regard as plausible, downwardly biased estimates of the true social rate of return. In Figure 14.3, we represent

38. Since the railways had monopoly power and appeared able to set their own freight and passenger rates, assuming monopoly pricing seems reasonable. To the extent, however, that the railways priced below the monopoly level, our estimates of the social rate of return would be biased downward.

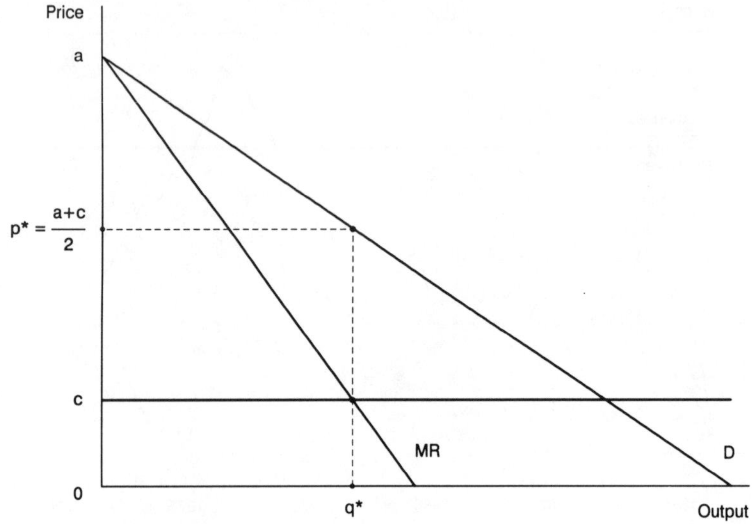

Fig. 14.3 Estimating the Social Return to Railways

consumers' surplus assuming a linear demand and a constant marginal cost.[39] Under these assumptions the per-period social return is given by

$$(2)\qquad SR = pq + \frac{(a - p)q}{2} - cq,$$

where p is price, q is output, c is marginal cost, and a is price where demand is zero. Substituting the profit-maximizing condition:

$$(3)\qquad p^* = \frac{a + c}{2},$$

we derive the social return to be

$$(4)\qquad SR^* = \frac{p^*q^*}{2}\left\{3 - \frac{c}{p^*}\right\} - cq^*,$$

where an asterisk indicates the profit-maximizing value. From equation (4) it follows that the private return is converted to the social return by multiplying

39. A linear demand is consistent with a location model in which the intensity of activity is independent of distance to the market. To the extent that intensity declines with distance, our estimate of the social return would be biased downward. See Frank D. Lewis and David R. Robinson, "The Timing of Railway Construction on the Canadian Prairies," *Canadian Journal of Economics,* 17 (May 1984), pp. 344–45; Ann M. Carlos, "Land Use, Supply, and Welfare Distortions Induced by Inefficient Freight Rates," *Canadian Journal of Economics,* 21 (Nov. 1988), pp. 835–45. Assuming constant marginal cost may bias our social return estimates upward since, with upward-sloping marginal cost, marginal cost exceeds average variable cost. This potential bias, however, is likely very small since neither the Grand Trunk nor the Great Western were operating near capacity, the implication being that marginal cost was not rising steeply if at all.

total revenue by a factor that depends on the ratio of marginal cost to price. Note that if $c = p^*$, the firm, as a profit-maximizer, must face a perfectly elastic demand, in which case the social and private return would be the same. The ratio, c/p^*, is central to the social return calculation. For both railways we base it on the ratio of all costs, excluding capital costs, to total revenue. It should be noted that expenditures on maintenance and renewals are included in operating costs. To the extent that these are more appropriately treated as part of capital, we are overstating the ratio, c/p^*, and hence understating the social return.[40] Recognizing that our estimates are biased downward, we estimate that the Great Western Railway generated a social rate of return of 6.1 percent, which is just above the normal rate of 6 percent. Therefore, even though the Great Western was not a privately profitable project, our social return estimate suggests it was a socially desirable one.

Our estimate for the Grand Trunk Railway has a very different implication. We estimate that the social rate of return was 2.8 percent, well below the normal rate. Had the project been delayed, though, the social rate of return would have been higher. If an 1861 starting date is assumed, the social rate of return is estimated to be 3.6 percent. This suggests that the problem with the Grand Trunk was partly one of timing. Perhaps the government was overly optimistic about the early demand for rail services or overly optimistic about the ability of the operators during the early years to run a socially desirable if not privately profitable line. Finally, given the biases associated with our procedure, we can conclude only that the Grand Trunk may have been a socially undesirable investment.

14.6 Financing the Grand Trunk Railway

As shown in Table 14.1 and also noted by Currie, the Grand Trunk was financed with discounted stocks and bonds. The use of discounted bonds—in modern parlance, junk bonds—may appear inconsistent with the insights of Modigliani-Miller. According to the simplest version of their model, the value of a firm does not depend on the proportions of the firm's investment which are financed with debt and equity. That model, however, assumes no bankruptcy costs. Where bankruptcy costs are significant, the optimal strategy is to avoid these costs completely by issuing debt with a face value no greater than the liquidation value of the firm. Since such debt will be fully secured by the firm's assets, it follows that the optimal strategy is inconsistent with the

40. Mercer derives his social rate of return by adding estimates of intraregional benefits and passenger external benefits to total revenue. Intraregional benefits are inconsistent with the linear demand we have assumed. Mercer's estimates of the passenger external benefits are generally between 30 and 40 percent of total revenue. This is more than double the external benefit we derive. Part of the difference may be due to the availability of good substitutes for the Canadian railways, but part is likely due as well to our attempt to understate benefits. Our estimated elasticities of demand at equilibrium are 3.2 for the Great Western and 4.3 for the Grand Trunk. See Mercer, *Land Grant*, app. B and C.

issuing of discounted or junk bonds. This result extends to very risky projects, which should be financed almost entirely with equity.

In their analysis of a post-Confederation prairie railroad, the Canadian Northern Railway, Frank Lewis and Mary MacKinnon have shown that the optimal debt condition changes if the government offers to guarantee some of the firm's debt.[41] The firm now maximizes its ex ante present value by issuing debt with a face value equal to the sum of its liquidation value and the full amount of the guarantees. This implies a positive bankruptcy probability because the firm's assets may not be sufficient to cover all debts. Whether or not the firm's bonds sell at a discount, however, also depends on how certain investors are of a government bailout in the event of bankruptcy. In the case of the Canadian Northern, for example, bonds were not discounted despite a high bankruptcy probability, because the railway's debt was fully secured by a combination of the firm's assets and the government guarantees.

The same was not true of the Grand Trunk, and the difference, we argue, was in the nature of the government commitment. The Grand Trunk, Great Western, and Canadian Northern received loan guarantees, but in the case of the Grand Trunk, the status of the loan guarantee was unclear. At the outset the loan guarantees had first priority on the firm's assets, but once the Grand Trunk got into serious financial difficulty, the status of the government loans was reduced. Now company bonds had first call on the assets of the company. Since ex post the status of the guarantee changed, we argue that ex ante the value of the government loan guarantee was uncertain. Indeed, as we discuss later, although the government made a definite commitment initially, the view of the investors was of a much more open-ended government policy.[42]

We model this arrangement by assuming that the government offers a loan guarantee that is uncertain; that is, will be honored with a probability less than one. Bonds with first claim on the firm's assets are secure, but those backed by the uncertain loan guarantee have an ex ante value of:

$$V_G = [1 - (1 - p)\pi]G, \tag{5}$$

where G is the face value of the loan guarantee, π is the probability of bankruptcy, and p is the probability the guarantee will be honored in the event of bankruptcy. In this formulation, the larger the (potential) loan guarantee, G, the higher the probability of bankruptcy (since the firm will take on more debt), and hence the greater the discount on the unsecured bonds.

The provincial loan guarantees to the Grand Trunk Railway, which totalled

41. Lewis and MacKinnon, "Government Loan Guarantees."

42. The government commitment to the Great Western was far less strong. This was made clear with the formation of the Grand Trunk. With the Main Line Act of 1851, the government incorporated the main line of the Great Western as part of the main trunk line. But once the Grand Trunk was extended from Toronto to Sarnia, the government sought to have that section as the trunk link instead of the Great Western. This would have disallowed the Great Western from any loan guarantees. Although the government was not successful, the incident showed its commitment to the two companies.

£3,111,500 by 30 June 1858, were given priority over the railway's assets. This reduced the effective guarantee. However, the status of the provincial debentures was reduced in the late 1850s, suggesting the government commitment to the Grand Trunk extended beyond the initial value of the early loans. Provincial support for the Grand Trunk was less certain than in the case of the Canadian Northern Railway; nevertheless, the guarantees still allowed the Grand Trunk to raise substantial amounts on the bond market. It should be noted, however, that because the support from the government was uncertain, these bonds sold at a discount.[43]

Government subsidies mattered. In its review of 1852, the *London Times* reported:

> During the concluding portion of the year, various loans and enterprises of all descriptions, home and foreign were introduced, the chief temptation employed being that of state guarantees . . . a system mainly traceable to the want of self-reliance, which, since the railway Mania has led people to prefer any undertaking backed with even as indifferent guarantee to the noblest enterprises dependent upon their own judgement.[44]

Subsequent to the sale of the Grand Trunk shares, the *Times* laid out the level and the type of government involvement. At the same time, the public was given a somewhat wider interpretation of this aid package, one that implied a more open-ended commitment. Columnists talked about the line being "supported by the government" and that "in Canada the Board comprises some of the principal members of Parliament." Potential investors were told that in matters relating to the Grand Trunk that they "had to deal with Messrs. Glyn and Baring as the financial agents of the Canadian Government."[45] In addition, when the prospectus for the line was issued, appended to it was a report on the growth potential of the province from Lord Elgin, the Governor General, to Sir John Pakington, the Colonial Secretary. Although the report says nothing about the Grand Trunk, by using it in this manner the company "sought to convey the impression that Lord Elgin was endorsing the Railway."[46] Thus, while investors were informed of the actual nature of the aid, the packaging in which this information was placed suggested the possibility of a greater government role.

Certainly complaints of the shareholders in early 1861, when the company was once again in serious financial difficulty, suggest that some had a wider interpretation of the level of government support. Investors wrote:

43. When the company introduced its 6 percent bond in July 1854, it sold at 93 to 95 on a 100 face value. Two years later, it was selling for 84 to 86. By 1858 the discount had risen yet again, and the bond sold for 72 to 77.

44. *London Times*, 1 January 1852, Money Markets and City Intelligence column.

45. Ibid.

46. Currie, *Grand Trunk*, p. 21. Lord Elgin's report was not appended to the prospectus when it was issued in Canada.

> it was in *bona fide* reliance upon the representations put forward as from the Canadian Government in this [GTR] prospectus that, in 1853, the petitioners and other persons became subscribers to the Grand Trunk Railway, and in the full persuasion that a Colonial Government which had sought assistance in England in a form so public and conspicuous would at all times be ready to extend to the obligations thus incurred.[47]

Herapath's *Railway and Commercial Journal* summed up the views of the ordinary bond holders in a similar manner. It traced

> the whole of the misfortunes of the company to the conduct of the Canadian Government, since the Government knowing the quantity of traffic the line would have, must have been aware that it was not just to ask English people for their capital for such an enterprise unsupported and unprotected by a guarantee.[48]

Although both quotations describe only after the fact what people believed, they do suggest that at least some of the investors saw the government commitment as being more open-ended than laid out in the Guarantee Act. This would, in turn, affect the quantity of bonds which the company could sell and, because of the uncertain nature of the commitment, these bonds would have to sell at a discount. Indeed, the debt-equity ratio was far in excess of what is considered appropriate for a non-subsidized firm.[49] In 1854 the ratio was high but still a fairly reasonable 1.7, but by 1858 the ratio was 3.0 (see Table 14.3).[50] Moreover, because much of this debt had been sold at a discount, the face value of the firm's debt on 30 June 1858 was 82 percent of actual capital expenditures. This meant that an ex post return just slightly below the normal rate of return would have been enough, in the absence of government support, to drive the firm into bankruptcy. Of course the actual ex post return was far below the normal rate. Despite this the railway's bonds, while discounted, still sold at prices substantially higher than the company's shares.[51] These prices, then, must have reflected not investor confidence in the viability of the Grand Trunk but rather the view, eventually borne out, that the government would bail investors out should the railway get into more serious trouble.

47. Trout and Trout, *The Railways of Canada*, p. 78.

48. Currie, *Grand Trunk*, p. 74.

49. In the twentieth century, debt-equity ratios for railroads that did not go bankrupt were close to one. See Lewis and MacKinnon, "Government Loan Guarantees," p. 184.

50. This effect of government loan guarantees on the debt-equity ratios of railroads is also consistent with the U.S. experience. In the antebellum period, before government became heavily involved with railroad building, the debt-equity ratios of U.S. railroads averaged only 0.8. See Fishlow, *American Railroads*, p. 187. This was in contrast to the postbellum experience of Mercer's land-grant railroads, which all received loan guarantees. In the mid 1890s, their debt-equity ratios averaged 1.8. In fact, of the railroads in Mercer's study only the Canadian Pacific Railway received no loan guarantees, and its debt-equity ratio was just 0.6. See *Poor's Manual of Railroads*, 1896 (New York, 1896) pp. 354, 553, 555, 696, 893, 913, 922, 996.

51. In late June 1858, Grand Trunk shares were selling at a discount of 55 percent from par, while company bonds were selling at only a 20 percent discount (London, *Times*, Railway Intelligence column).

Table 14.3 **Capital Structure of the Grand Trunk Railway Company, 1854–1858 (in thousands of £ sterling)**

	Bonds (Face Value)			Shares		
Year	Provincial Debentures	Other Debentures	Total	Face Value	Market Value	Debt/ Equity
1854	£ 467.5	£1,260.5	£1,728.0	£1,253.1	£1,026.1	1.68
1855	1,776.3	1,929.1	3,705.5	1,860.0	1,326.7	2.79
1856	2,793.8	1,768.7	4,562.5	2,753.9	1,931.4	2.36
1857	3,044.8	1,943.7	4,988.5	3,097.6	2,101.3	2.37
1858	3,111.5	3,330.5	6,442.0	3,206.1	2,172.6	2.97

Sources: Grand Trunk Railway Company of Canada; Report of the Directors to the Bond and Stockholders, and Statement of the Revenue and Capital Accounts for the Half-Years ending 30 June and 31 December, 1853–82.

The financing of the Great Western is also consistent with our view of implicit and explicit government loan guarantees. In contrast to the Grand Trunk, the Great Western received little support ex ante and almost none ex post.[52] This comparative lack of government involvement was reflected in the way the railway was financed. The debt-equity ratio remained well below 1 throughout its history and, unlike the Grand Trunk, the Great Western sold no junk bonds. Even when its shares were selling at significant discounts, its bonds sold very close to par or, typically, at a premium.

The experience of the Grand Trunk may have implications for the financial problems currently facing U.S. firms and banks that became involved in the junk bond market. Some savings and loan associations were among the heaviest purchasers of junk bonds, and many are threatened with bankruptcy or have gone bankrupt. Most of their losses though, will be covered by the U.S. federal government which by law insures these banks' deposits.[53] This, of course, was known when the risky investments were undertaken. Thus deposit insurance, which is a form of government loan guarantee, may explain why some savings and loan associations became big players in the junk bond market and made other very risky investments, mainly in real estate.

14.7 Conclusion

The Great Western and the Grand Trunk Railways were two of the earliest lines built in the Province of Canada. Together they constituted over 70 per-

52. Under the Guarantee Act, the Great Western received £700,000 in bond guarantees over the period 1852 to 1854 and some interest payments were deferred. Eventually the company repaid more than 90 percent of the face value of the loan. See Currie, *Grand Trunk,* pp. 191–92.

53. As of December 1990, savings and loan institutions as a group owned only 5 percent of U.S. high-yield bonds. This was in part because the U.S. government, through the Resolution Trust Corporation, had already acquired a large portfolio of junk bonds from failed S&L's, and in part because only a small segment of the industry had purchased these securities. See *The Economist,* 30 March–5 April 1991, p. 73.

cent of the rail line constructed during the decade of the 1850s. The historical literature on these two companies argues that, although they turned out to be privately unprofitable, they were socially necessary for the development of the area. For this latter reason the government was correct in subsidizing them. We attempted here to assess the historical view by measuring the degree to which these two lines were privately or socially profitable.

We began by estimating the unaided and aided private rates of return to the Great Western and the Grand Trunk. Our unaided private rates of return show that the current historical literature is correct in its assessment. Both lines had ex post private rates of return below the market rate. At the same time the Great Western performed better than the Canadian Pacific, which is considered to be a "successful" line in Canadian historiography, and the Grand Trunk performed just marginally worse than the Canadian Pacific. The government subsidized the Grand Trunk and, to a much lesser degree, the Great Western, but our estimates of the aided private rates of return show that the subsidies were not large enough to make either railway privately profitable.

Our examination of the social rates of return for these two companies shows that although the Great Western was a socially profitable venture, the same cannot be said for the Grand Trunk; but we cannot state that the Grand Trunk was a socially unprofitable venture either because of the downward-biased nature of our calculation. It is possible that with a more complete accounting of all benefits, the Grand Trunk could be shown to have been a socially desirable line as well.

The aid given to Canadian railroad companies came in the form of bond guarantees. In the case of the Grand Trunk, we argue that the form of the subsidy and the market perception of government actions resulted in a very high debt-to-equity ratio. It also resulted, down the road, in a situation where the government was forced to "bail out" the Grand Trunk to preserve the stability of the market for Canadian bonds.

Appendix

Table 14A.1 Grand Trunk Railway Revenues and Expenses (in thousands of £ sterling)

Year	Operating Revenue	Operating Expenses	Net Revenue	Investment Expenses
1853a	£ 0	£ 0	£ 0	£1,068.3
1853b	24.9	13.6	11.3	1,024.2
1854a	72.5	58.8	13.8	734.0
1854b	100.6	69.8	30.8	1,659.0
1855a	97.0	93.3	3.7	715.8
1855b	126.1	106.6	19.5	709.3
1856a	116.3	114.7	1.6	388.1
1856b	170.8	143.9	27.0	21.8
1857a	237.9	234.0	3.9	284.9
1857b	262.0	219.1	42.9	535.0
1858a	218.8	218.9	−0.1	778.4
1858b	244.8	224.2	20.7	783.2
1859a	223.9	203.1	20.9	435.5
1859b	282.9	230.4	52.5	1,114.1
1860a	314.8	285.6	29.2	284.1
1860b	367.8	330.8	37.1	131.4
1861a	347.1	333.1	14.0	15.5
1861b	468.5	323.8	144.7	137.2
1862a	383.0	319.6	63.4	32.4
1862b	425.7	332.6	93.1	167.1
1863a	427.8	310.2	117.6	6.2
1863b	457.8	312.1	145.7	59.8
1864a	528.3	346.5	181.1	65.2
1864b	539.8	450.5	89.3	116.7
1865a	579.0	448.6	130.5	39.2
1865b	655.9	538.3	117.6	37.9
1866a	623.2	429.7	193.5	10.4
1866b	657.5	486.0	171.5	52.9
1867a	587.6	495.0	92.5	12.5
1867b	665.0	539.3	125.7	25.8
1868a	627.9	498.0	129.9	3.9
1868b	712.8	576.3	136.6	0.4
1869a	649.8	533.0	116.8	38.8
1869b	758.3	558.3	200.0	67.5
1870a	697.4	559.7	137.7	62.3
1870b	785.5	668.9	116.6	93.0
1871a	768.8	596.4	172.3	31.6
1871b	917.2	751.0	166.2	22.6
1872a	858.8	694.0	164.8	83.0
1872b	942.5	793.3	149.2	227.7
1873a	888.8	721.6	167.1	136.6
1873b	1,036.6	863.1	173.5	1,022.1

(continued)

Table 14A.1 (continued)

Year	Operating Revenue	Operating Expenses	Net Revenue	Investment Expenses
1874a	999.5	782.0	217.5	230.0
1874b	1,107.2	890.5	216.8	707.5
1875a	893.1	701.5	191.7	164.8
1875b	1,023.9	818.4	205.4	99.4
1876a	936.4	773.9	202.4	8.4
1876b	893.9	716.6	177.2	170.6
1877a	860.4	664.5	195.9	12.4
1877b	1,025.3	769.2	256.1	36.1
1878a	881.0	667.3	213.8	12.7
1878b	924.0	708.8	215.3	21.4
1879a	832.9	634.4	198.4	10.7
1879b	978.2	712.8	265.4	27.5
1880a	992.0	675.3	316.6	−221.4
1880b	1,158.4	783.9	374.5	65.7
1881a	1,073.4	738.5	334.9	62.3
1881b	1,121.2	824.3	296.9	99.1

Source: Grand Trunk Railway Company of Canada; Report of the Directors to the Bond and Stockholders, and Statement of the Revenue and Capital Accounts for the Half-Years ending (a) 30 June and (b) December, 1853–82.

Table 14A.2 **Great Western Railway Revenues and Expenses (in thousands of £ sterling)**

Year	Operating Revenue	Operating Expenses	Net Revenue	Investment Expenses
1852a	£ 0	£ 0	£ 0	£433.9
1852b	0	0	0	397.2
1853a	0	0	0	444.8
1853b	0	0	0	492.3
1854a	123.4	55.3	68.1	494.0
1854b	195.5	102.5	93.1	403.7
1855a	205.2	106.0	99.1	302.6
1855b	272.7	155.4	117.2	223.9
1856a	292.4	172.4	120.0	588.4
1856b	323.7	164.5	159.3	303.3
1857a	266.4	157.8	108.6	125.0
1857b	256.1	199.2	57.0	164.3
1858a	213.7	128.6	85.1	37.8
1858b	211.0	131.2	79.8	83.3
1859a	181.5	128.5	52.9	35.5
1859b	207.5	132.2	75.3	11.7
1860a	194.5	133.7	60.8	25.8
1860b	252.8	153.3	99.5	11.1
1861a	209.3	156.2	53.1	4.1
1861b	266.0	153.8	112.2	16.7
1862a	239.3	173.3	65.9	7.9
1862b	268.4	167.4	101.0	12.4
1863a	233.0	176.6	56.4	5.1
1863b	247.6	175.1	72.5	21.1
1864a	229.0	171.5	57.6	16.2
1864b	238.2	168.6	69.7	18.2
1865a	229.6	158.8	70.8	27.2
1865b	313.7	170.0	143.7	32.5
1866a	303.4	176.7	126.7	55.7
1866b	283.3	173.0	110.3	137.7
1867a	312.9	189.6	123.3	18.8
1867b	334.2	201.6	132.6	21.3
1868a	301.9	215.6	86.3	20.8
1868b	352.9	215.2	137.8	5.5
1869a	331.3	237.2	94.1	4.5
1869b	387.0	247.0	140.0	98.8
1870a	383.6	257.3	126.3	20.5
1870b	427.0	266.6	160.4	71.6
1871a	438.2	284.9	153.3	121.6
1871b	499.5	332.7	166.9	225.6
1872a	516.0	339.4	176.7	163.2
1872b	562.7	386.7	175.9	626.4
1873a	580.3	424.4	155.9	453.1
1873b	598.7	443.0	155.7	695.9
1874a	521.6	440.8	80.8	109.6
1874b	485.4	395.3	90.1	105.0
1875a	411.2	420.3	−9.1	44.3

(*continued*)

Table 14A.2 (continued)

Year	Operating Revenue	Operating Expenses	Net Revenue	Investment Expenses
1875b	436.1	360.1	76.0	21.2
1876a	394.8	346.2	48.5	10.6
1876b	401.6	352.9	48.8	−13.3
1877a	370.5	284.9	85.6	5.7
1877b	467.2	331.5	135.8	16.2
1878a	377.5	292.7	84.8	12.7
1878b	387.3	271.5	115.8	7.3
1879a	365.8	288.8	77.0	4.1
1879b	461.1	296.1	165.0	6.4
1880a	437.4	317.0	120.5	19.4
1880b	513.0	330.3	182.8	11.1

Sources: Great Western Railway of Canada; Report of the Directors of the Great Western Railway of Canada for the Half-Years ending (a) 31 July and (b) 31 January, 1852–80.

15 The Rise and Fall of Urban Political Patronage Machines

Joseph D. Reid, Jr., and Michael M. Kurth

15.1 Urban Patronage: Its Common History

One of the most notable political changes of the past hundred years is the rise and fall of urban patronage machines. In most years between 1865 and 1930, patronage machines ruled many large cities—St. Louis, New Orleans, Los Angeles, Minneapolis, Pittsburgh, Philadelphia, New York, Chicago, and Detroit—and many smaller cities and towns, too. Patronage increased from affecting half of the thirty cities surveyed by M. Craig Brown and Charles N. Halaby in 1870 to affecting over 70 percent between 1890 and 1910. Thereafter it declined to affecting 65 percent in 1930, and declined further, affecting half after 1940. But machines controlled few urban governments before 1850 or after 1975.[1]

The common explanation ties the rise and fall of patronage machines to the rise and fall of immigrant urban electorates. Patronage commonly is defined as "a political currency with which to 'purchase' political activity and political responses" from "voters whose loyalty was ensured by an organizationally created web of jobs, favors, and payoffs" "distributed at the discretion of political leaders."[2] Patronage jobs bought the votes of immigrants, who were

Earlier versions of the paper benefited from presentations to the Washington Area Economic History Society, the Public Choice Society, and the Cliometrics session at the 1988 Allied Social Sciences Association meeting in New York; seminars at the University of Montreal, Columbia University, Dartmouth College, and the University of Chicago; and comments by Morris P. Fiorina, Hugh Rockoff, Gordon Tullock, John Wallis, and James Q. Wilson.

1. M. Craig Brown and Charles N. Halaby, "Machine Politics in America, 1870–1945," *Journal of Interdisciplinary History,* 17 (Winter 1987), p. 598; the thirty cities are listed in fn. 3, pp. 588–89. See also Bradley Robert Rice, *Progressive Cities* (Austin, 1977); Lincoln Steffens, *The Shame of the Cities* (New York, 1904).

2. Quotes are from Frank J. Sorauf, "The Silent Revolution in Patronage," *Public Administration Review,* 20 (Winter 1960), p. 28; Brown and Halaby, "Machine Politics," p. 596; and James Q. Wilson, "The Economy of Patronage," *Journal of Political Economy,* 69 (Aug. 1961), p. 370. See also V. O. Key, Jr., "The Techniques of Political Graft in the United States" (Ph.D. Disserta-

"ignorant and pliable voters" or "primitive people, such as the South Italian peasants,"[3] who were accustomed to and wanted "quasi-feudal relationships" with their machine and were not accustomed "to seek the good of the community."[4] Entrenched with bought votes, the patronage machine sold "city jobs, business opportunities, easements from city regulations, and gifts" to businessmen, so that "the boss, rich with graft, . . . and having doled out many a favor to businessmen, . . . could draw upon the world of private business as well as the public payroll to provide jobs for his constituents."[5]

Nonetheless, many historians call patronage good in its time: "city machines . . . have generally been viewed positively as integrators of the poor and providers of social welfare services to immigrant populations."[6] At the same time, most historians agree that patronage was wasteful, because patronage workers loafed between elections and patronage bosses accepted shoddy or overbilled construction of public works.[7] Some, however, argue that "the practice of distributing patronage to voters in exchange for political support was less costly . . . and less inconsistent with the [desired] principles of *laissez faire* than would [have been alternative governmental responses] . . . to certain [redistributive] demands" of voters or, in other words, that the largesse of patronage machines absorbed or deflated revolutionary impulses of immigrants, much as today's food subsidies immobilize the urban poor of less developed countries.[8]

Finally, most historians believe that patronage waxed as Protestant morality and self-reliance waned, so that patronage flourished during the massive immigrations of southern and eastern Europeans around 1900, and died out after war and the reforms of the Progressives—slowing immigration, increasing access to education, replacing patronage with merit appointment to political

---

tion, University of Chicago, 1934), p. 68; and Stephen Skowronek, *Building a New American State* (Cambridge, Mass., 1982), p. 48.

3. James Bryce, "Setting the Stereotype," in *Urban Bosses, Machines, and Progressive Reformers,* Bruce M. Stave, ed. (Lexington, 1972), p. 9. Jane Addams, "Why the Ward Boss Rules," in *Bosses, Machines, and Reformers,* Bruce M. Stave, ed., p. 11.

4. Robert Merton, "The Latent Functions of the Machine," in *Urban Bosses, Machines, and Progressive Reformers,* Bruce M. Stave, ed. (Lexington, 1972), p. 30. Edward C. Banfield and James Q. Wilson, *City Politics* (Cambridge, Mass., 1967), p. 41.

5. The first quote is from Aaron A. Rhodes, "Material and Nonmaterial Incentives in Political Machines," *European Journal of Sociology,* 25 (May 1984), p. 28. He documents that this is the traditional view of patronage—votes for jobs and bent laws for money—but argues that closeness to power and charisma of politicians also motivate voters and political workers (pp. 28–53). The second quote is from Richard Hofstadter, *The Age of Reform* (New York, 1955), p. 184. For a confirming account of the Tweed Ring's methods, see Seymour J. Mandelbaum, *Boss Tweed's New York* (New York, 1965), pp. 46–104.

6. James C. Scott, "Political Clientelism: A Bibliographical Essay," in *Friends, Followers, and Factions,* Steffen W. Schmidt, Laura Guasti, Carl H. Lande, and James C. Scott, eds. (Berkeley, 1977), p. 494; Arthur S. Link and Richard L. McCormick, *Progressivism* (Arlington Heights, 1983), pp. 9–17.

7. Banfield and Wilson, *City Politics,* p. 41, write that "the pay for [patronage jobs] . . . is greater than the value of the public services performed."

8. Martin Shefter, *Political Crisis/Fiscal Crisis* (New York, 1985), p. 16, writing about Boss William Marcy Tweed's New York.

jobs, and making ballots simpler and voting secret—reduced the influence of culturally divergent voters. The common understanding of patronage, in sum, is that political machines were "supported by continuing immigration, sustained by patronage, fattened by loot," and in the end were felled by determined Progressive virtue.[9] Historians of patronage view its demise as progress.[10]

But the common understanding of patronage rests upon false theories and facts. In theory, voters generally are seeking private rather than public betterment: private betterment accrues to oneself, but public betterment accrues to all. Because public betterment is a public good, too few citizens will cast their votes for the common good because they expect others to do so. They expect to reap the rewards of public betterment without their private sacrifice. Thus, voters, in a rational manner, must be ignorant about politics, because politics by definition is about public goods which accrue to individuals with or without their participation or about minuscule negative transfers each too small to justify fighting.[11] Only large transfers shared with few others are worth learning about and getting in politics. Thus, the Progressive explanation of political change, which relies upon the mass of voters becoming more sophisticated and a large elite devoting effort to public betterment, is suspect in theory.[12]

9. Quote from Arthur Mann, "When Tammany was Supreme: Introduction," in William L. Riordon, *Plunkitt of Tammany Hall* (New York, 1963), p. xv. In addition to the references above, for the traditional view that "attributes the rise in [political machines] . . . to the social and political disarray accompanying urbanization, industrialization, and immigration; and the decline . . . to Progressive reforms and the gradual assimilation of the foreign born," see M. Craig Brown and Charles N. Halaby, "Machine Politics," p. 610, and references at pp. 588, fn. 2, and 589, fn. 4; and (in chronological order): M. I. Ostrogorski, *Democracy and the Party System in the United States* (New York, 1910); Sorauf, "The Silent Revolution," p. 31; Hofstadter, *Age of Reform*, pp. 9, 179–86, 257–71; Elmer E. Cornwell, Jr., "Bosses, Machines, and Ethnic Groups," *Annals of the American Academy of Political and Social Science: City Bosses and Political Machines*, 18 (May 1964), pp. 27–39; Banfield and Wilson, *City Politics*, pp. 40–41, 123, 330–46; L. E. Fredman, *The Australian Ballot* (East Lansing, 1968); Sam Bass Warner, Jr., *The Private City: Philadelphia in Three Stages of its Growth* (Philadelphia, 1968), pp. 54–56; Nathan Glazer and Daniel P. Moynihan, *Beyond the Melting Pot* (Cambridge, Mass., 1970), pp. 221–29; Barry D. Karl, *The Uneasy State* (Chicago, 1983), pp. 16–33. Raymond E. Wolfinger, "Why Political Machines Have Not Withered Away," *The Journal of Politics*, 34 (May 1972), pp. 365–98, agrees that this is the traditional view, but feels it is "inadequate" (p. 386). Amy Bridges, *A City in the Republic: Antebellum New York and the Origins of Machine Politics*, (Cambridge, Mass., 1984), p. 4, summarizes the traditional view, but argues against its post–Civil War dating. Nathaniel H. Leff articulates the common identification of corruption with culture: "Corruption is deeply rooted in the psychological and social structure of the countries where it exists. . . . Corruption will persist until universalistic norms predominate over particularistic attitudes," in "Economic Development Through Bureaucratic Corruption," *American Behavioral Scientist*, 8 (Dec. 1964), p. 13.

10. Daniel P. Moynihan, "When the Irish Ran New York," *The Reporter* (8 June 1961), pp. 32–44. See also Ari Hoogenboom, *Outlawing the Spoils: A History of the Civil Service Reform Movement, 1865–83* (Urbana, 1961), p. 257; Mann, "When Tammany was Supreme."

11. See Mancur Olson, *The Logic of Collective Action* (Cambridge, Mass., 1965); and Joseph D. Reid, Jr., "Understanding Political Events in the New Economic History," *Journal of Economic History*, 37 (June 1977), pp. 302–28.

12. Might one argue that the fact that voting currently is more prevalent among those more educated offers support for the Progressive explanation that the best of the electorate shouldered their responsibility to improve elections? We think not. Today participation is heaviest in national and least in local elections, while outcomes' differential impacts on voters are least in national and

The Progressive explanation is suspect in fact, as well. The Progressives identified patronage machines with the uneducated and unprincipled immigrants clustered in growing cities: "a great city is the best soil for the growth of a Boss, because it contains the largest masses of manageable voters as well as numerous offices and plentiful opportunities for jobbing."[13] But the Progressives were mistaken. Patronage and political machines did not arise first in response to post–Civil War immigrants. Amy Bridges reports that the Federalists appointed 1,500 faithful workers to positions in New York City in the 1780s and 1790s, or one patronage appointment for every three voters.[14] Under Tammany's Boss Tweed in the 1860s, only one in eight voters would be patronage appointments.[15] Furthermore, credit for the first political machine generally is given to Martin Van Buren, who created and managed the "Albany Regency" to trade votes at the federal level for largesse for his state and largesse at the local level for votes to the Regency after 1820.[16] Thus, patronage antedates large cities filled with recent immigrants.

Because attribution of patronage machines to post–Civil War immigrants and cities is questionable in theory and fact, we propose a new understanding. We think that the rise and fall of patronage machines mirrors a fall and rise in the incomes and homogeneity of voters that made patronage more, then less, efficient. Our first step is to build an appropriate model of government.

15.2 A Model of Government

We start from agreement with the Chicago machine boss who said that a political organization is "just like any sales organization trying to sell its product."[17] It wants to produce cheaply while reaping maximum reward from the difference between sales value and production cost. Therefore, we model a political organization as any other business, as an association of inputs in hope of profit. Our political firm, like a business firm, is an institution defined by a set of transactions, rather than a set of specific functions. As with a business firm, which transactions are accomplished in the political firm and

greatest in local elections (federal taxes and expenditures vary less than local taxes and expenditures in response to elections). So even though the educated are more likely to vote, they are not voting where their votes count most. This suggests that voting involves motives other than a means of enacting preferred platforms.

13. James Bryce, "Setting the Stereotype," in *Urban Bosses, Machines, and Progressive Reformers,* Bruce M. Stave, ed. (Lexington, 1972), p. 4.

14. Amy Bridges, *City in the Republic,* p. 132.

15. Morton Keller, *Affairs of State* (Cambridge, Mass., 1977), p. 239, cited in Shefter, *Political Crisis,* p. 16.

16. Although, Van Buren may have just grasped and elaborated at the state level what was commonplace at "a 'grass roots' level in almost every locality"; see Alvin Kass, *Politics in New York State, 1800–1830* (Syracuse, 1965), pp. 9, 55–56, and passim. Also see Skowronek, *New American State,* pp. 24–26, who argues that patronage parties were the efficient means to present diverse local interests to state and federal legislators before the Civil War.

17. Quoted in Banfield and Wilson, *City Politics,* p. 115.

which are conducted in the marketplace depends upon the costs of internal metering and monitoring versus the costs of search and negotiation in the market. The only constraint is that whatever a political firm does must maximize political profit, or ultimately it will be defeated or deserted in electoral competition.[18] Accepting the metaphor that a political firm is an optimizing entity devoted to the profitable supply of political outcomes, then if political firms differ from private firms, it is because of difference in the transactions undertaken, products provided, technologies used, or environments. We need to evaluate each in turn.

Political transactions are more complex and costly than private market transactions. In private market transactions, payment of precisely so many dollars secures immediately some (comparatively) well-defined good or service for the purchaser. But politicians trade promises and ambiguous outcomes for cash or votes of uncertain worth and not delivered simultaneously.[19] Accordingly, it is hard for voters to know what politicians have done and it is hard for politicians to know what voters have and want done. Thus, successful political exchange requires extensive metering and monitoring of the exchange itself, as well as of the design and production processes. Since the function of a firm is to reduce transaction costs, it follows that transacting bulks larger for a political firm than for a market firm.[20]

18. Admittedly, our terms here are imprecisely defined. Political profit is some mix of votes and cash (which in turn can be spent on comforts for politicians or on benefits for voters). Political competition will drive politicians to buy votes from the minimum winning coalition expected to be most profitable, served with the most efficient political organization. A likely coalition would be those whose votes were cheap and who would not be upset by favors sold to big spenders: poor employees for votes and big employers for big spenders, say. For the transactions theory of the firm, see R. H. Coase, "The Nature of the Firm," *Economica,* new series 4 (1937), pp. 386–405; Armen Alchian and Harold Demsetz, "Production, Information Costs and Economic Organization," *American Economic Review,* 62 (Dec. 1972), pp. 777–95; M. Jensen and W. Meckling, "Theory of the Firm: Managerial Behavior, Agency Costs, and Ownership Structure," *Journal of Financial Economics,* 3 (1976), pp. 305–60. For an enlightening survey, see Beth V. Yarbrough and Robert M. Yarbrough, "The Transactional Structure of the Firm: A Comparative Survey," *Journal of Economic Behavior and Organization,* 10 (July 1988), pp. 1–28. Gary Becker, "A Theory of Competition Among Pressure Groups for Political Influence," *Quarterly Journal of Economics,* 98 (1983), pp. 371–400, presents a formally complete model of a legislature as a profit-maximizing institution with a minimum votes constraint. Barry Weingast and William Marshall, "The Industrial Organization of Congress," *Journal of Political Economy,* 96 (Feb. 1988), pp. 132–61, explicitly discuss a legislature (Congress) as a multi-task firm.

19. Too few or too many votes purchase little for a political firm, just the right amount of votes gives optimal control of taxing, spending, and regulation. William F. Riker, *The Theory of Political Coalitions* (New Haven, 1962), as modified by George J. Stigler, "Economic Competition and Political Competition," *Public Choice,* 13 (Fall 1972), pp. 91–106, implies that political control increases and average benefit declines as coalition size rises. Frequently politicians make it harder to determine if promises have been honored. For instance, members of Congress often gut a law so that the outcome diverges from its title and then vote the title. See Morris P. Fiorina, *Congress, Keystone of the Washington Establishment* (New Haven, 1977). See also Reid, "Understanding Political Events."

20. This is not to say that private market transactions are not complex, uncertain, ambiguous, and open-ended, as argued forcefully by Oliver Williamson, Jr., in *Markets and Hierarchies* (New York, 1975), only that they are simpler than political market transactions.

For a better illumination of the issues, we classify political exchanges into two types, direct and general. In direct exchanges goods go from the political firm directly to the constituent in individual units. General exchanges provide goods and services that benefit all who qualify and avail themselves of them. Consider a political exchange of apples for (past or future) votes. In a direct exchange the voter requests and receives an apple from a politician or a public employee. In a general exchange some quantity of apples are available to all qualified claimants (say, all registered voters) at some location (the courthouse) for some time (the week before elections). General exchanges usually are produced by large capital-intensive units that permit many simultaneous general exchanges—thus, the exchange (improved transport) is provided by a source (highway) that accommodates many travelers at once, and flood control typically is provided by a dam that protects all who live downstream.

In an efficient production of votes the ratio of marginal production costs of direct and general exchanges must equal the ratio of perceived sale values. Political changes can occur in the form of products provided or in how they are provided. Political changes can be prompted by alterations in voters' values, by shifts in perceived or collectible values, and by shifts in the costs of possible exchanges. As the output of a political firm changes, organization and types of employees might change. For instance, a political firm organized to collect cash from government contractors might need different form and people than one organized to deliver quality education. A political firm adept at trash removal might not be adept at obtaining intergovernmental subsidies.[21]

15.3 The Model Applied to Patronage

Our model helps explain the rise and fall of patronage. In our vision, the principal jobs of patronage employees were to: 1) search out voters, identify their preferences, and communicate an offer to them (patronage workers had to work in the many languages of illiterate voters); 2) make politicians' promises credible by befriending voters; 3) monitor votes; and 4) distribute largesse to those deserving "in the different ways they need help . . . quarters . . . clothes . . . a job."[22] Plunkitt of Tammany Hall said that to accomplish these tasks "you have to go among the people, see them and be seen. I know every man, woman, and child in the . . . District. . . . I know what they like and what they don't like, what they are strong at and what they are weak in, and French them by approachin' at the right side."[23] The Chicago machine of the 1960s resembles the Tammany machine of a century earlier; in it a "good

21. For further discussion and graphical analysis, see Joseph D. Reid, Jr., and Michael M. Kurth, "Public Employees in Political Firms: Part A. The Patronage Era," *Public Choice*, 59 (Dec. 1988), pp. 253–62.

22. Riordon, *Plunkitt of Tammany Hall*, pp. 27–28.

23. Ibid., p. 25.

precinct captain spends his evenings visiting his neighbors, doing chores at ward headquarters, traveling to and from city hall on errands, and talking politics."[24]

The patronage machine worked well because the poor, polyglot voters in machine wards were served efficiently by patronage workers. Poor voters mostly needed help coping: insurance against unemployment, bad health, and scrapes with the law; direction to housing; assistance with forms; and the like. However, many of these needs are subject to self-serving misrepresentations: "I am too sick to work," "I cannot find suitable work," or "I am still hungry" may not be reported truthfully. Therefore, reliefs may be oversupplied unless closely monitored and adjusted.

The decision to monitor depends upon the cost of monitoring versus the cost of oversupply. Close monitoring is more likely if voters' wants can be supplied discriminatorily, because the profits from discrimination underwrite the costs of monitoring. Among the poor, profit from discrimination is usually plausible. For instance, supplying health care requested or needed by a voter depends upon the degree of sickness and the ability of family to care for the sick. For any degree of relief, the income, food, and housing needed depend upon family size and standards. Discrimination requires policing the resale of remedies, which a close monitor can do.

When providing direct relief, patronage workers need to be able to assure the poor that relief will be delivered when wanted, because direct relief cannot be stockpiled. The means employed is trust. In getting close enough to monitor his voters and profitably discriminate among them, the patronage monitor becomes known well enough to be trusted. Finally, close monitoring is more likely if political talk must be carried out in different languages. For, if the politician must talk Italian on one block and Polish on another, he needs many spokespersons who can monitor as they communicate door to door.

Considering together moral hazard, discrimination in supply, assurance of supporters, and neighborhood scale economies in political discourse and delivery, it is plausible that direct supply of political payoffs could accomplish efficiently all of the transactions required for political exchange in poor, polyglot wards. The ward heeler who lived in the neighborhood and continually made its rounds, attended its churches and funerals, brought a turkey to the injured and found a job for the recovered—in sum, who spoke his neighbors' language and shared their ways—could thereby discern their wants and gain their trust.[25]

Because he knew his voters well, he needed to pay them no more than needed for their votes, and he knew he could count on their repaying votes at elections. Because he was required to carry communications between politi-

24. Banfield and Wilson, *City Politics*, p. 119.

25. Cornwell, "Bosses, Machines, and Ethnic Groups," p. 31. See also Banfield and Wilson, *City Politics*, pp. 117–19; John Petrocik, "Voting in a Machine City, Chicago, 1975," *Ethnicity*, 8 (1981), pp. 320–40; and Riordon, *Plunkitt of Tammany Hall*, pp. 90–93.

cians and voters, the patronage worker could efficiently carry political products to voters. Not surprisingly, machines won elections by giving the poor new immigrants to urban areas not just jobs but a broader "security from the uncertainties of their existence" directly.[26] Thus, our translation of Plunkitt's description of a patronage worker's work is talk to every voter individually (because each speaks a different language), learn how to buy each vote most cheaply, buy votes by promising and, when pressed, delivering payment, and collect repayments from voters.

But direct intermediaries are not efficient with all voters. Rich voters save to provide for their own needy days. Rich voters want income-elastic services from government. Even today, clean parks and speedy transport are the demands of the wealthy, not the poor.[27] Although these demands could be met directly—trails could be swept ahead of rich hikers and bearers could carry rich travelers over rough terrain—scale economies favor the general provision of such wants from a source prepared in advance and consumed as wanted, especially since the user-furnished complements to consumption (a vacation or an auto) successfully discriminate between rich and poor. The way to riches generally requires literacy and articulateness, so the rich can be reached through mass media and can make their wants known without intermediaries. In the patronage era, the rich were a homogeneous group of white Anglo-Saxon Protestants who could be communicated with generally and surveyed statistically. Thus, a patronage worker was not an efficient means to find, assure, monitor, and distribute political payoffs to the rich.

15.4 The Historical Record

15.4.1 State and Federal Governments

History amply supports the distinction between the heterogeneous, inarticulate poor and the homogeneous rich as determining the extent of patronage. Before its postbellum urban flowering, patronage arose in the New York state government. Patronage suited New York in the early 1800s, because many of the state's western cities and hamlets were sufficiently isolated to preclude general communication and sufficiently heterogeneous economically to make specific and discriminatory provision of political assistance worthwhile. Patronage came to the federal government as the westward migration isolated, made heterogeneous, and dispersed the national electorate.[28] The heteroge-

26. Fred Greenstein, "The Changing Pattern of Urban Party Politics," *Annals of the American Academy of Political and Social Science: City Bosses and Political Machines*, 353 (May 1964), pp. 1–13.

27. Thomas E. Borcherding and Robert T. Deacon, "The Demand for the Services of Non-Federal Governments," *American Economic Review*, 62 (Dec. 1972), pp. 897–98, calculate an income elasticity for parks of 2.7.

28. For the facts of federal patronage see Lee Benson, *The Concept of Jacksonian Democracy* (Princeton, 1961); and Kass, *Politics in New York*. For the heterogeneity of population, consider the increasing percentage of the population living outside of old coastal areas (the New England,

neous communities and regions of New York, and then of the United States, were analogous to the neighborhoods of the patronage cities. Votes could be bought cheaply with specific remedies (dam this river, remove these Indians, provide transport links to this entrepôt) that had to be made known (difficult in the cities because of language, and in the countryside because of distance), satisfied efficiently (difficult because of voters' self-serving requests for more), and collected for (beforehand, which required voters' to trust the political firm, or after, which required the firm to present its bills and watch their payment—but in either case required some political intermediary and monitor on the spot).

The decline of federal patronage was prompted by changing (increasing) homogeneity among those who demanded governmental services and spurred by falls in the cost of communicating with voters and interest groups with new technologies. The exclusion of the South from national political importance after the Civil War made the national electorate much more homogeneous. The desire of the North and West to develop the trans-Mississippi Midwest was fulfilled with railroads, land-grant colleges, agricultural research stations, and so forth. At the federal level, regional economic interests evolved into national line-of-business interests: shipping and entrepôt interests, financial interests, mercantile interests, and others. The ported rim of the country reorganized from regional interests into clustered lines of specialized commercial interests that spilled over congressional district lines. The agricultural interiors reorganized from locational interests to crop interests that similarly outgrew congressional district limits: the old and new Souths became more completely the cotton interest, and the newly franchised trans-Mississippi Midwest became the grains interest. Thus, political outcomes demanded from the federal government increasingly became transregional demands for protection from specific ruinous imports, or subsidization of specific products, or alleviation of broadly impacting ills, such as price instabilities newly introduced by interlinked and internationalized markets.[29]

Political outcomes that crossed district lines could be supplied more efficiently through general rather than direct means. A general tariff was cheaper than direct reliefs. Direct reliefs had to reach specific producers in specific congressional districts. They might take the form of the purchase of the

Middle Atlantic, and South Atlantic census regions) an estimate of heterogeneity. It is a lower bound estimate, in light of our attribution of Middle Atlantic New York's patronage under Van Buren to its within-state heterogeneity. But this lower bound estimate, percentage of population outside old areas, increases steadily while patronage comes to the federal government; the percentage of population outside old coastal areas is 5.8 in 1800, 22.7 in 1820, 37.2 in 1840, and 49.0 in 1860 (calculated from Jonathan Hughes, *American Economic History* [Glenview, Ill., 1987], table 5.1, p. 96).

29. For discussions of the rising demand from the middle class for protection from change and exploitation, see Link and McCormick, *Progressivism;* Robert A. McGuire, "Economic Causes of Late Nineteenth Century Agrarian Unrest," *Journal of Economic History,* 41 (Dec. 1981), pp. 835–52; and Anne Mayhew, "A Reappraisal of the Causes of Farm Protest in the United States, 1870–1900," *Journal of Economic History,* 32 (June 1972), pp. 464–75.

import-competing good for federal stores. A producer with plants in several congressional districts could easily claim hardship in one district by hiding his prosperity in another. Lacking the proper reference comparisons and expertise, a district patronage worker probably could not gauge the needs of manufacturers as well as those of voters. More efficiently, the prosperity of the industry would monitor the adequacy of general relief, and competition within the industry would stretch relief as far as possible. Likewise, midwestern farmers could be protected from fluctuating costs and prices by regulations and laws enacted in Washington; general means, rather than through direct remunerations which would be more costly. Trade associations and cartels that developed after the Civil War allowed distant politicians to identify and to communicate with urban commercial interests without the help of intermediaries.[30]

New communications technology further favored the substitution of general for direct political exchanges particularly at the state and federal levels of government. The advent of the telegraph and telephone and increased newspaper circulation lowered the cost of communicating with the government. The federal and state government were relatively more affected than local governments, and richer, more educated voters were more affected than poorer, less educated voters. Between 1869 and 1899, telegraph messages increased sevenfold. They increased another threefold by 1929. Telephones per thousand population increased elevenfold between 1880 and 1899, and another elevenfold between 1899 and 1929. Illiteracy among native whites fell from 8.7 percent (or 3.2 million) in 1880 to 4.6 percent (2.6 million) in 1900, and to 1.6 percent (1.5 million) in 1930. Newspaper circulation per household rose fourfold over the period.[31]

Accordingly, federal and state governments substituted general political outcomes for direct outcomes, and broad economic outcomes for specific and local outcomes. Establishment of the Interstate Commerce Commission in 1887 was one manifestation of the move from direct and local political outcomes to broad and general political outcomes. Reform of federal customs houses and post offices was another. The new jousting between the president and Congress to control federal employment was a third. With the spread of steam and then electricity, manufacturing firms tended to locate in urban areas. With improved transport, management techniques, and synergistic urban growth, retail sales and general commercial activities centered in larger

30. Olson, *Logic of Collective Action,* argues convincingly that trade groups that can withhold private benefits to secure payments for association-public benefits will secure such benefits more successfully. The increasing ease of communicating with commercial interests generally (from a distance) is evidenced by their growth in size: production employees per manufacturing establishment increased from 8.1 in 1869 to 10, counting all manufacturing establishments; to 22, excluding hand and neighborhood industries in 1899; and to 40 in 1929 (calculated from Bureau of the Census, *Historical Statistics of the United States* [Washington, D.C., 1960], series P4 divided by P1, p. 409).

31. Calculated from Bureau of the Census, *Historical Statistics of the United States* (Washington, D.C.,1960), series R2 and R7, pp. 480–81; R45 and R53, pp. 484–85; H409, p. 214; R176, p. 500; A51 and A55, p. 9; and A255, p. 16.

urban locations. Managers of these dispersed enterprises came to depend more and more on speedy mail and customs clearings. Spanning many congressional districts and even states, merchants and manufacturers effectively communicated to the federal government that they wanted speedier service. Because speedier service would also raise the vote-payoff from richer and more literate consumers, the federal government began to separate production of these services from kickbacks by patronage appointees in large cities. That is, the federal government turned from direct to general political exchange to secure the votes and cash of a growing constituency, the rich and the newly insistent commercial interests.

The movement from direct toward general political exchange was accelerated by scale economies that became possible as the homogeneity of voters increased and became affordable as ease of communicating with voters improved. The disappearing frontier and the spread of literacy and media outside of the largest (more immigrant) cities played a role. Economic changes, moreover, led middle class voters to place more weight on securing their wealth. On the demand side, then, rising incomes led more voters to prefer self-insurance and income-elastic political payoffs. Where interests were united, reliefs could be provided most cheaply through regulatory agencies and laws enacted in Washington and distributed generally through a uniform nationwide system of justice. So federal (and later state) politicians began to disengage from the hierarchical arrangement of party patronage that had linked cities to higher governments since Jackson.

Presidents became spokesmen for the federal government in discussions with special interests with nationwide constituencies. Urban congressmen began to deal with urban interests through trade groups and media without the aid of state and local intermediaries. Rural representatives experienced the least change in communicating and collecting from constituents, because farmers stayed put. The coalescence of district interests into crop interests did move rural congressmen away from patronage exchange with rural constituents, but efficiency did not dictate that rural congressmen replace direct with general political exchange as rapidly. In consequence, the president, allied with urban senators and members of Congress, pushed federal reform against recalcitrant rural interests.[32] In response to rising homogeneity and falling communication costs, federal patronage began to give way to merit evaluation in the 1880s in urban activities directed at those who were richer and more literate. Merit employees represented 10.5 percent of all federal employees in 1884, 25.5 percent in 1894, 53.0 percent in 1904, 60.6 percent in 1914, and 79.7 percent in 1924.[33] Federal patronage first shrank from tasks that served a

32. For example, members of Congress representing urban entrepôts were significantly more likely to support the Pendleton Act initiating civil service. See regression results of Ronald N. Johnson and Gary D. Libecap, "Patronage to Merit: Political Change in the Federal Government Labor Force" (manuscript, University of Arizona, Mar. 1990), table 1, p. 27.

33. Federal employment grew fourfold over this time, so that the absolute number of federal patronage employees did not decline until after 1914. See Extension of Competitive Civil Service, Committee on Post Office and Civil Service, *History of Civil Service Merit Systems of the United*

newly insistent clientele, as when larger post offices and customs houses were put under civil service as members of the business community pressured for prompt and secure service.[34] Some reform reflected rivalries within the federal government, but rivalries produced by the waxing and waning importance of components of the constitutionally constrained government in political supply, rather than rivalries between reform and corrupt political antagonists.[35]

More slowly, but for similar reasons, patronage also began to shrink in the states. State patronage workers were withdrawn first from tasks that served nonvoters. In 1883, for instance, the state of New York passed a civil service bill which "applied to officers employed in connection with canals, public works, prisons, asylums, and reformatories."[36]

15.4.2 Urban Patronage

In contrast, urban patronage grew fastest between 1884 and 1900. Brown and Halaby's study of thirty large cities indicates that urban patronage takeovers grew 200 percent between 1884 and 1892, and competition among contending patronage machines rose 50 percent. Patronage politics prevailed in 80 percent of their cities in 1892 and 73 percent in 1900.[37] From aggregate data it is arguable that cities filled with polyglot poor voters and jostling and growing commerce found it efficient to move toward direct political exchanges. Voters poured into cities. As Table 15.1 reports, cities boomed. Between 1870 and 1900, the U.S. population increased 97 percent, with the foreign-born population increasing 86 percent, while total and foreign-born population in the thirty sample cities increased 179 percent and 104 percent, respectively. Between 1880 and 1900, the number of manufacturing establishments in the United States rose 102 percent, manufacturing capital rose 252 percent, population rose 51 percent, and the manufacturing work force rose 94 percent. In the one hundred principal cities, manufacturing establishments rose 138 percent, capital rose 261 percent, population rose 89 percent, and the work force rose 84 percent. In the thirty sample cities, establishments rose 144 percent, capital rose 279 percent, population rose 89 percent, and the work force grew 73 percent. Population of the one hundred principal cities was 18 percent of U.S. population in 1880 and 23 percent in 1900. Work force per establishment averaged 69 percent greater in cities than in the nation in 1880 and 38 percent larger in 1900. In cities, manufacturing capital per

---

States and Selected Foreign Countries, 94th Cong., S.S. (Washington, D.C., 1976), table 1, p. 305. For details of the Pendleton Act, see *Congressional Record,* 47th Cong., 2d sess., 1883, pp. 403–7.

34. Skowronek, *New American State,* pp. 69, 72–74, passim; Mandelbaum, *Tweed's New York,* pp. 155–57.

35. Skowronek, *New American State,* pp. 62–74.

36. Hoogenboom, *Outlawing the Spoils,* p. 257.

37. Brown and Halaby, "Machine Politics," fig. 1, p. 598. We identify competition among contending machines with "a factional pattern, where several ward-level machines compete with each other and 'regular' political groups for city power" (ibid., p. 590).

Table 15.1 **Statistics for Selected Cities and the United States: 1870, 1880, 1890, and 1900**

Item	Year				Percentage Increase		
	1870	1880	1890	1900	1870–1900	1880–90	1880–1900
Thirty Cities							
Patronage (%)	52	67	70	73	40	4	4
Population (000)	4,575	6,753	9,117	12,754	179	35	40
Foreign born (000)	1,779	2,312	3,102	3,647	105	34	58
Manufacturing establishments (000)	—	58	126	140	—	118	144
Manufacturing capital ($000,000)	—	981	2,581	3,714	—	163	279
Work force (000)	—	1,063	1,650	1,844	—	55	73
One Hundred Cities							
Population (000)	6,683	9,131	13,139	17,233	158	44	89
Manufacturing establishments (000)	—	78	168	186	—	115	139
Manufacturing capital ($000,000)	—	1,385	3,524	5,001	—	155	261
Work force (000)	—	1,431	2,310	2,639	—	61	84
United States							
Population (000)	38,558	50,156	62,662	75,995	97	25	52
Foreign born (000)	5,567	6,680	9,250	10,341	86	38	55
Manufacturing establishments (000)	252	254	355	512	103	40	102
Manufacturing capital ($000,000)	—	2,790	6,525	9,814	—	134	252
Work force (000)	2,046	2,733	4,252	5,306	159	56	94

Sources: Percentage of cities with patronage machines is calculated from M. Craig Brown and Charles N. Halaby, "Machine Politics in America, 1870–1945," *Journal of Interdisciplinary History,* 17 (Winter 1987), fig. 1, p. 598. The thirty cities are identified in Brown and Halaby, "Machine Politics," fn. 3, pp. 588–89. The thirty cities population and foreign born are from Bureau of the Census, *Ninth Census: Statistics of Population of the United States* (Washington, D.C., 1872), vol. 1, table 8, p. 380; Bureau of the Census, *Compendium of the Tenth Census: 1880* (Washington, D.C., 1883), part 1, pp. 452–63, 542; Bureau of the Census, *Compendium of the Eleventh Census: 1890* (Washington, D.C., 1894), part 1, pp. 44–51, 540–79; and Bureau of the Census, *Twelfth Census: Report on Population of the United States* (Washington, D.C., 1902), vol. 1, part 1, pp. 609–46. The thirty cities manufacturing data are from Bureau of the Census, *Compendium* (1880), pp. 379–80; Bureau of the Census, *Report on Manufacturing Industries in the United States, Eleventh Census* (Washington, D.C., 1895), part 2, pp. 8–13; and Bureau of the Census, *Report on Manufactures, Twelfth Census* (Washington, D.C., 1902), vol. 7, part 1, pp. 992–1003. One hundred cities population for 1870 is the population of fifty-two principal cities plus half of the population of the next 116 cities from Bureau of the Census, *Historical Statistics of the United States* (Washington, D.C., 1975), series A 58-64 and A 44-50, pp. 11–12. The remainder of the one hundred cities data are from Bureau of the Census, *Manufactures* (1902), p. ccxix. U.S. total population is calculated from Bureau of the Census, *Historical Statistics,* series A 119, p. 15; series A 105, 112, p. 14. The numbers of manufacturing establishments for 1870 are from ibid., series P 1, p. 666. The size of the work force is calculated from discussion in ibid., p. 653, series P 3-5, wage earners estimate, multiplied by the average ratio of Bureau of the Census, *Manufactures* (1902), wage earners, p. ccxix, to *Historical Statistics* discussion estimate, 1880–1900. Remaining data are from Bureau of the Census, *Manufactures* (1902), p. ccxix.

worker doubled, while in the nation it increased only 85 percent between 1880 and 1900.

The 1880 to 1900 comparisons understate the political impacts of the growth rates. The urban centers' gain in poorer and foreign residents, and the centers' expansion of bigger manufacturers which employed these new residents, was dramatically higher in the earlier decades. Also, the proportion of foreign born or native born of foreign parents (arguably a better measure of heterogeneity) was dramatically higher than the proportion of foreign born alone. In 1890 in the thirty sample cities, 31 percent were foreign born but 71 percent had at least one foreign-born parent. Finally, the flow of manufacturing capital and jobs to the cities was at its relative peak in the 1880s. Thus, urban patronage grew in cities that became most heterogeneous and accommodated most rapidly to changed economic circumstances.

Later, gradual withdrawal of patronage and the rise of general political outcomes was observed in municipalities where the interests of voters and business overlapped. Commission government and at-large elections, well-known instruments of political reform, were adopted in midwestern farm entrepôts which focused on transshipment of a main crop and servicing of surrounding farmers. The homogeneity of their citizens, of their economic interests, and of alternative towns meant that voters and commercial interests could be addressed and responded to generally, or could move Tiebout-style away from inefficiency. Therefore legislation rather than corruption predominated in facilitating farm-town commerce.[38]

In older and heterogeneous cities the most profitable way to accommodate business remained having patronage workers who sold variances individually and bought votes with political favors.[39] In these cases blanket accommodation of industrial modernization was blocked by established voting groups or by the influence of unique resources (such as a port, railhead, or an agglomeration of people) where locational rents retarded the flight of voters and taxpayers from political inefficiencies and inequities.

Even in the heyday of municipal patronage, "no city [was] . . . composed exclusively of wards filled with voters responsive to . . . the dispensation of favors. In addition to the 'river wards' there are others, called in Chicago 'newspaper wards' and in New York 'silk-stocking' districts, which . . . respond[ed] much less, if at all, to the infusion of patronage."[40] In rich and homogeneous wards, political machines ran low-key operations or acquiesced to a reform representative, so long as the reformer did not strive to expand his

38. To see the focus of municipal reform among homogeneous farm entrepôts, see Rice, *Progressive Cities,* pp. 52–71, especially table 4, pp. 54–55. For choice of flight or reform as remedy to unwanted government, see Charles M. Tiebout, "A Pure Theory of Local Expenditures," *Journal of Political Economy,* 64 (Oct. 1956), pp. 416–24.

39. See table 6, "Social Characteristics of Cities of 25,000 or More by Adoption of Commission Form of Government, 1913," in Rice, *Progressive Cities,* p. 89.

40. Wilson, "Patronage," p. 374. See also Leonard White, reported in Paul P. Van Riper, *History of the United States Civil Service* (White Plains, NY, 1958), p. 27.

representation or to curtail the activities of the machine in its wards.[41] Machines or reformers won richer and more literate neighborhoods with income-elastic general exchanges: reform opponents of Tweed's Tammany Hall wanted "'a good police force, good pavements, substantial docks, a well-lighted and healthy city, a good fire department, economic expenditure and honest and efficient administration,'"[42] so Tweed, to disarm them, supplied the high-income wards of upper Manhattan with "new streets, water mains, sewers, parks, and streetcar lines."[43] The poor neighborhoods difficult to communicate with or to monitor except individually were won with direct exchanges. Tweed supplied poor and immigrant wards welfare—housing, jobs, and protection from catastrophe, as well as beer for voters. In the 1960s, patronage Mayor Richard J. Daley placated reformers in Chicago by inaugurating "street cleaning, street lighting, road building, a new airport, and a convention hall." For businesses he made Chicago the city that worked. Daley won votes from poor wards with "turkeys and hods of coal" and other direct helps to make the neighborhoods livable.[44]

In sum, urban history supports our prediction that if economic outcomes are shared, competitive political firms will provide them generally, but if they are contested, political firms will sell economic outcomes directly and individually. In fact, a sizable portion of the electorate wanted the same things (cheap incarceration of inmates, fast passage through customs, speedy mail, good roads) and could be trusted not to abuse their provision, and communication with that electorate became cheap (by media) and sure (because wants were homogeneous and spokespersons were identified), so employees who specialized in performing tasks replaced patronage employees who specialized in representing specific neighborhoods. Patronage declined as the relative value of general exchanges rose and the cost declined.[45]

15.5 Other Explanations

The decline of patronage is not usually attributed to changes in the efficiency of various political transactions. The main explanation is the disap-

41. Banfield and Wilson, *City Politics*, pp. 116–21.

42. From newspaper quote by Mandelbaum, *Tweed's New York*, p. 179, of the son of the reform Public Works Commissioner, 1878.

43. Shefter, *Political Crisis*, p. 16.

44. Banfield and Wilson, *City Politics*, pp. 124, 118–19.

45. In a seminar discussion, Gary Becker asked why, given the increased incomes of governments, is there not more direct welfare in poor areas and more general welfare in rich areas? It is a good question. Although the answer is not critical to our thesis, we think Becker is incorrect. The minimum winning coalition gets the bulk of payoffs from governments. Currently that coalition consists of middle-class voters and, for cash payers, small producers such as farmers in the countryside and contractors in cities. Therefore, what looks like payoffs to the poor—food stamps, in-kind relief, housing developments, and the like—are principally payoffs to the farmers and contractors who make and replace the payoffs. Indeed, even payoffs to the middle class are twisted further than technology dictates toward being general so that they can be contracted out as capital construction, to win contractors' votes and to insulate the payoff from repeal. See Kenneth

pearance of foreign stock in the population (produced by the stoppage of immigration during World War I and subsequent immigration reforms) and the assimilation of immigrants' progeny. This explanation is often supplemented by lesser, supporting reasons for the rise of the civil service.

One supplemental explanation for the end of patronage is that civil service arose to protect faithful political employees from hostile successor administrations. Some growth did occur this way.[46] But not much because the plan would encourage patronage employees to work for the quick defeat of their patron to gain their sinecures. If the affected employees were not expecting job gifts, then giving gifts would not influence their loyalty beforehand and would render their loyalty unusable and "unsalable" in the future.

A related explanation is that transformations from patronage to civil service represented a scorched earth policy by lame-duck administrations. By transferring its patronage workers to classified merit lists, an outgoing administration hindered its successor from rewarding its own workers and further reduced the efficiency of services provided by the new administration. The implicit contention is that the immediate value of scorched earth offsets the future loss from no subsequent patronage appointments. Even if there were inconvenience to the successor administration, there is little reason to think that lame-duck transfers to merit lists would survive. The incoming winner has no reason to honor such transfers and could repeal them. Repeals have happened. President Eisenhower, upon his inauguration, withdrew civil service protection from 134,000 federal incumbents blanketed in by President Truman. Earlier, congressional Democrats and Republicans were outraged when President Cleveland increased merit appointments by a third in 1896 in a "vengeful act of a President whose party support had dissolved."[47] Upon taking office, President McKinley restored a third (9,000) of these positions to patronage, then federal employment expansions relieved pressure for further restorations.[48] It has been suggested that civil service sinecures arose not to influence the efforts of public employees but to win their votes.[49] But econometrically modeling favors for votes in state legislatures, we find that governments with large pluralities do not further reward voting coalitions.[50] Thus,

Shepsle, Barry Weingast, and Christopher Johnson, "The Political Economy of Benefits and Costs: A Neoclassical Approach to Distributive Politics," *Journal of Political Economy,* 89 (Aug. 1981), pp. 642–64.

46. Committee on Post Office and Civil Service, *History of Civil Service*, pp. 181–85.

47. Skowronek, *New American State,* p. 73.

48. Committee on Post Office and Civil Service, *History of Civil Service,* pp. 268–69.

49. Argued by Gordon Tullock, "Dynamic Hypothesis on Bureaucracy," *Public Choice,* 19 (Fall 1974), pp. 127–31, and accepted by Amy H. Dalton, "A Theory of the Organization of State and Local Government Employees," *Journal of Labor Research,* 3 (Spring 1982), pp. 163–77.

50. We found that a dominant party rewards marginal (potentially swing) constituency members in inverse proportion to the margin of dominance. A barely dominant party pays its marginal voters a lot, while a hugely dominant party pays little. See Joseph D. Reid, Jr., and Michael M. Kurth, "The Organization of State and Local Government Employees: Comment," *Journal of Labor Research,* 5 (Spring 1984), pp. 191–200; and Joseph D. Reid, Jr., and Michael M. Kurth,

implied transfers of wealth from politicians to employees are too benevolent in theory and too rare in fact to explain the transformation of patronage workers to civil servants.

Another supplemental explanation for the end of patronage is that patronage employees left as their opportunity wages rose, while reform required scarce merit qualifications for all but the most unattractive jobs.[51] That rising opportunity wages reduced the supply of patronage workers implies that the supply of patronage workers shrank relative to demand, so that the number of people available to register voters and canvass neighborhoods fell. But, typically, such patronage workers were uneducated. Furthermore, their jobs today are easily filled by volunteers.[52] Thus, it is unlikely that opportunity wages of rank-and-file patronage workers rose in the period. The more likely explanation is that demand for patronage workers rather than their supply shifted back.

Now let us directly address the traditional explanation for reform, that reform "was the effort to restore a type of economic individualism and political democracy that was widely believed . . . to have been destroyed by the great corporation and the corrupt political machine."[53] We do not disagree that agitation against electoral corruption and advocacy linking corruption with immigration policy existed. It is plausible that public pressure for reform began to build after the Civil War. The demise of slavery freed the intelligentsia to fulminate against other national shortfalls, and the fires of repeated scandals illuminated patronage governments as prominent shortfalls. When President Garfield was shot by a would-be spoilsman, it is possible that reformers' zeal became so frenzied that reform became electorally irresistible, even if (as we argue) the mass of voters did not much care.[54] It is also possible that reform attracted political champions who saw it as a vehicle of successful advocacy, and thus as a career builder.[55]

But the essence of the traditional explanation is that the "better" or "more American" voters compelled reform. We have already questioned this. From public goods theory, we have argued that few voters would rationally press for

---

"The Contribution of Exclusive Representation to Union Strength," *Journal of Labor Research,* 5 (Fall 1984), pp. 391–412.

51. Sorauf, "Patronage," p. 30; Greenstein, "The Pattern of Urban Politics," pp. 8–9; Cornwell, "Bosses, Machines, and Ethnic Groups," p. 34; Committee on Post Office and Civil Service, *History of Civil Service,* chap. 4.

52. Rhodes, "Incentives in Political Machines," p. 37, documents that wages of contemporary machine employees are commonly below opportunity earnings.

53. Richard Hofstadter, *The Age of Reform,* p. 5.

54. Olson, *The Logic of Collective Action,* convincingly argues that a committed few can win political changes.

55. Reid, "Understanding Political Events," argues that leaders can forecast the evolution of support for and of acquiescence in political outcomes and will champion outcomes becoming popular in order to demonstrate leadership. Theodore Roosevelt is a likely example of a would-be leader championing reform to demonstrate leadership. Reid emphasizes that sustainable political outcomes, such as reform, generally are not unique.

reform. In fact, across and within governments reforms came piecemeal (first this bureau, then that, was transformed to merit employment), which is inconsistent with the idea that an irresistible notion swept the country. Indeed, a respectable theory argues that members of the business community led reform to block rather than to extend democracy, which questions the role of voters in stimulating reform.[56]

Attacks by reformers and displacement of patronage politicians do not gainsay our conclusion that reform represented the reorganization of governments to govern more profitably. Producers of political exchanges that did not adjust were displaced by more efficient rivals.[57] At different locations and times, supply efficiencies differed. Reorganizations and supplier substitutions were chaotic. Leonard White noted in 1933 that "most of the change [towards the merit system] has been, relatively speaking, undirected growth. Especially the extension of organized groups of public officials and employees, some with a highly professional point of view and others with interests primarily of an economic nature, has proceeded without much public notice and certainly without recognized leadership apart from that associated with each group."[58] Stephen Skowronek similarly concluded that "between 1877 and 1900, the [federal] merit service failed to attain internal coherence. . . . It remained inchoate."[59]

Ari Hoogenboom concluded that "the scope of the [Pendleton Act] was determined . . . by the political potential of the offices themselves."[60] For all reform, we conclude the same. We accept the supply-side argument made by the father of federal reform, Senator Jenckes, in 1867, "that by decreasing patronage obligations, Members of Congress could save countless hours now spent dealing with office seekers and then utilize the time for more important duties."[61] Sixteen years later, a majority of his congressional colleagues agreed. At different times, in different places, but for the same reason—changing costs and values of general relative to direct political exchanges—

56. See Samuel P. Hays, "Business Elite and the Centralization of Decision-Making," and James Weinstein, "Businessmen and the City Commission and Manager Movements," in *Urban Bosses, Machines, and Progressive Reformers*, Bruce M. Stave, ed. (Lexington, 1972), pp. 119–29, 129–43.

57. See the description of Carmen DeSapio's (failed) attempt to adapt Tammany Hall in Shefter, *Political Crisis*. Harvey Boulay and Alan DiGaetano, "Why Did Political Machines Disappear?" *Journal of Urban History*, 12 (Nov. 1985), p. 37, agreeably attribute the replacement of many machines to the inability to respond efficiently to newcomers. Also see Kevin T. Deno and Stephen L. Mehay, "Municipal Management Structure and Fiscal Performance: Do City Managers Make a Difference?" *Southern Economic Journal*, 54 (Jan. 1987), pp. 627–39, which reports that there is today no statistically significant difference in expenditures of reform (city manager) and unreformed (council-mayor) municipal governments, other things equal. This contradicts the reform assumptions (that structure matters or that reform indicates differences in the electorates), but is as our model predicts, that survivors in a competitive environment have the same supply cost.

58. Leonard D. White, *Trends in Public Administration* (New York, 1933), p. 5.

59. Skowronek, *New American State*, p. 78.

60. Hoogenboom, *Outlawing the Spoils*, p. 244.

61. Committee on Post Office and Civil Service, *History of Civil Service*, p. 127.

other politicians agreed. In sum, politicians walked rather than were pushed away from patronage.

15.6 Conclusion

Patronage is the efficient means to effect direct political exchanges. Direct political exchange is favored when public wants are heterogeneous and profitably provided discriminatorily, and when it is hard to determine indirectly how people voted. General political exchange is favored when public wants are sufficiently homogeneous to be learned and the necessary payment to be predicted by surveys or by communicating with special interest representatives, and when wants are satisfied efficiently by supply independent of receipt (as a park is built and available, independent of use).

Patronage gives way when and where government becomes responsible for providing continuing services to general users rather than for sporadic favors to individuals. To achieve a defensible level of competency at general production, appointment and promotion are entrusted to meritorious credentials: so much education, so much experience, and so on. Politicians are content to let "expert" civil servants design the details, with the benefit to the politicians that they are not accountable immediately, if ever, for civil servants' production of general services malfunctions.

Our analysis explains why the meritocracy of the founding fathers was replaced with "Jacksonian democracy," and why similar political machines later came to dominate the cities. Machines were successful because they exchanged services and favors directly for the votes of lower socioeconomic groups. Public employees earned their pay by "turning out" the vote. What many decried as encouraging governmental inefficiency actually promoted efficient service of myriad voters with diverse wants subject to moral hazard in representation. That is why machines were the rule only with diverse and needy voters.

Patronage fell because the political value of general services increased, not because of the efforts of reformers, even though reforms tended to reduce the cost of general services relative to direct services. To provide general services efficiently required a new structure of incentives. Public administration was professionalized, and civil service boards were established to promote professionalism. The civil service league replaced the political club, and the merit system dominated public-sector labor relations until the 1960s.[62]

62. Our argument even explains the recent rise of militant unionism among public employees. When the costs of distantly monitored communication fell in the late 1950s (with the advent of television, wide area telephone service, and computer-developed addresses), the federal government began to expand its domain at the expense of state and local governments. These governments either encouraged or tolerated militant job actions by their employees to slow and redirect the federal expansion. State and local public employees joined unions to get expert assistance with militancy. See Joseph D. Reid, Jr., and Michael M. Kurth, "Union Militancy Among Public Employees: A Public Choice Hypothesis, *Journal of Labor Research*, 5 (Winter 1990), pp. 1–23.

16 Dividing Labor

Urban Politics and Big-City Construction in Late-Nineteenth-Century America

Gerald Friedman

16.1 Labor Divided

American workers have never formed class-wide institutions like those found in the labor movements of other western countries. Instead, America's working class is fragmented, leading to wide wage differentials in different industries and occupations. Since at least 1900, wage differentials between skilled and unskilled workers have been significantly greater in the United States than in Europe.[1] Workers in construction crafts especially have enjoyed a wide premium over other workers. From their privileged position they formed the backbone of a conservative American trade union movement that fought hard to defend their privileges against the rest of the labor force as well as against their employers.

Some have attributed sharp divisions among American workers to exogenous conditions, including ethnic and racial distinctions.[2] Such an interpretation fails as a historical explanation, however, because it assumes unchanging characteristics and attitudes. It cannot, therefore, explain variations in working-class solidarity such as the rise and precipitous decline in organized labor solidarity in the 1880s.[3] I take a different approach. Instead of treating divisions as exogenously determined, I argue that divisions were fostered by

The author is grateful to Claudia Goldin, Stanley Engerman, Ken Fones-Wolf, Debra Jacobson, Sandy Jacoby, Robert Margo, Jeffrey Williamson, and seminar participants at the University of Pennsylvania and the 1988 ASSA meetings for comments. Research was supported by a grant from the German Marshall Fund of the United States.

1. Henry Phelps-Brown, *The Inequality of Pay* (Berkeley, 1977), p. 73.

2. See, for example, Seymour Martin Lipset, "Radicalism or Reformism: The Sources of Working Class Protest," *American Political Science Review,* 77 (Mar. 1983), pp. 1–18; Gwendolyn Mink, *Old Labor and New Immigrants in American Political Development* (Ithaca, 1986).

3. See, for example, Eric Foner, "Why Is There No Socialism in America?" *History Workshop,* 17 (Spring 1984), pp. 57–80; Richard J. Oestreicher, *Solidarity and Fragmentation: Working People and Class Consciousness in Detroit, 1875–1900* (Urbana, 1986).

politicians who sought to undermine working-class challenges to their power. Using the example of construction workers around 1900, I argue that the extraordinarily large wage differential they received in big cities was fueled by a strategy pursued by urban political machines to head off radical labor movements by promoting urban public works, thereby cultivating allies among construction craft unions.

16.2 Levels and Determinants of Wage Differentials

Big-city construction workers were paid wages far beyond those of workers in other industries or in smaller towns. To measure the effect of city size on wages, I have estimated regressions of the average wage paid to workers in different occupations in a locality using data from the 1904 Report of the Commissioner of Labor.[4] In addition to industry and regional dummy variables, I include variables designed to control for supply- and demand-side influences on wages: the proportion of immigrants and blacks in the population, the locality's rate of population growth, and a city cost of living index for 1890.[5]

In a labor market free of distortions, labor mobility should equalize real wages within an occupation across regions.[6] After controlling for industry, ethnicity, race, establishment size, and prices, city size should measure the residual impact of urban disamenities and political influences on wages. Assuming that a worker's industry and skill are not associated with preferences for city living, the interaction of city population with skill and industry variables tests whether the impact of urban politics on wages differed in the construction and manufacturing sectors, and for skilled and unskilled workers.

The regressions are all highly significant and demonstrate that even within an increasingly efficient national labor market, big-city construction had a special place in the American working class. As others have found, wages were higher in the West and lower in the South than in the Northeast or Midwest. Regional differentials, however, were largely due to the smaller size of

4. U.S. Department of Commerce and Labor, *Nineteenth Annual Report of the Commissioner of Labor, 1904: Wages and Hours of Labor* (Washington, D.C., 1905).

5. City population characteristics are from the U.S. Census Office, *Eleventh Census, 1890: Population* (Washington, D.C., 1895), vol. 1, part 1, pp. 524–58; U.S. Census Office, *Twelfth Census of the United States, 1900: Census of Population* (Washington, D.C., 1901), vol. 1, part 1, pp. 609–94. Price data are from Michael Haines, "A State and Local Consumer Price Index for the United States in 1890," National Bureau of Economic Research, Working Paper Series on Historical Factors in Long Run Growth, no. 2 (May 1989). Because price data are available for only about half of the cities, real wage regressions have only been estimated for a subset of the observations.

While not reported directly, establishment size can be calculated from the data and are included in the regressions to test the impact of different production technologies on wages.

6. Real wage differentials will persist in efficient markets to compensate workers for living in relatively undesirable localities.

southern and western cities and to higher prices in the West. After controlling for city size, nominal wages were only 10 percent lower in the South than in the Northeast in 1890, and southern wages almost reached northern levels in 1903. Wages were higher in the western states even after controlling for city size, but nearly half of the 30 percent nominal wage differential between the West and the Northeast was due to differences in the cost of living. Comparing the results for 1890 with those for 1903, wage differentials narrowed sharply for both the South and West. This may suggest the emergence of a national labor market.[7]

Other evidence also suggests that labor markets functioned efficiently. Apparently, laborers responded to fluctuations in regional labor demand by moving to high-wage localities. The highest wages were paid in the fastest growing cities, and there is little evidence that cultural or historical factors led immigrants or blacks to crowd into low-wage cities.[8] Every ten-percentage-point increase in the proportion of foreign-born residents is associated with an increase in both nominal and real wages of over 3 percent in both 1890 and 1903.

All workers received higher wages in big cities. The effect of city size on wages was much greater in construction than it was in manufacturing.[9] For skilled manufacturing workers, nominal wages increased by around 3 percent with every doubling in city size. Wages increased faster for unskilled manufacturing workers, rising by 6 to 7 percent with every doubling in city size. Going from a town of 4,000 to a city of a million reduced the manufacturing skill premium by twenty percentage points.

Construction workers in large cities enjoyed wages higher than those earned by workers in other industries or by small-town construction workers. Despite widespread labor migration, the wage structure of small cities and towns was significantly different from that in large cities, and the differences persisted from 1890 to 1903. Skilled construction workers' wages increased much faster with city size than did those of skilled manufacturing workers, rising by about 10 percent for every doubling in city size. As a result, they

7. Joshua L. Rosenbloom, "One Market or Many? Labor Market Integration in the Late Nineteenth-Century United States," *Journal of Economic History,* 50 (Mar. 1990), pp. 85–108; Lonny Wilson, "Intercity Wage and Cost of Living Differentials in the United States, 1889–1939" (Ph.D. dissertation, University of Iowa, 1973).

8. In these reduced-form wage equations, there is no separate control for labor mobility. As a result, the regression coefficients confound the depressing effect of immigration and increased labor supply on wages and the positive effect of high wages on labor mobility. The coefficients are the net result of these two effects. On balance, they indicate that the effect of wages on migration was greater than any depressing effect of exogenous migration on wages because wages were higher in cities with a high proportion of foreign-born residents. Wages also increased with the proportion of nonwhite residents in a city.

9. In his dissertation, Lonny Wilson finds that nominal earnings increased by 5 percent with every doubling in city size in 1890 and by over 4 percent in 1900. He also presents evidence suggesting that these differences were much greater than the price differentials between small and large cities; see Wilson, "Intercity Wage Differentials," pp. 103, 125.

earned 50 percent more in cities of a million than in towns of 4,000, gaining 30 percent on skilled manufacturing workers.[10]

Labor market distortions are even more striking in markets for common labor. Despite an absence of specialized skills, laborers employed in big-city construction earned much more than those employed in small cities, and they earned more than laborers in big-city manufacturing. While going from a city of 4,000 to one of a million raised unskilled manufacturing wages by 35 percent, day laborers and hod carriers working on construction jobs in cities of a million earned 50 percent more than their counterparts in towns of 4,000.[11] Skilled and unskilled construction workers in big cities apparently worked in a labor market separated both from their small town counterparts and from other unskilled workers in big cities.

It is unlikely that high urban construction wages reflect compensation for urban disamenities. Only disamenities specific to urban construction jobs could explain the wide premium urban construction workers earned over other urban workers.[12] Urban construction workers also enjoyed at least one particularly favorable nonwage job condition beyond their high wages: they led others in winning shorter hours.[13] Every doubling in city size was associated with a reduction in the construction workweek of nearly two hours in 1890 and of over thirty minutes in 1903.[14]

Urban construction workers may have been paid more to compensate for a relatively long trip to work. Unlike manufacturing, whose workers could move closer to a fixed work site, construction work is carried out at different sites over the year. The geographic spread of many large cities may have in-

10. This is in nominal terms; after adjusting for cost of living differentials, real wages for skilled construction workers rise by 60 to 70 percent while those of skilled manufacturing workers rise by 10 to 15 percent.

11. Hod carriers are laborers employed in carrying bricks and other materials to bricklayers and other craftsmen working on construction jobs.

12. Disamenities common to all workers, such as urban crowding and mortality, would raise all wages without producing an extra premia for construction workers.

13. American unions struggled for decades to reduce the workweek. In 1886 the AFL inaugurated the tradition of striking on May Day by calling a general strike for the eight-hour day. The AFL continued this campaign in 1890 with the carpenters' union taking the lead.

14. This is from a regression for the length of the workweek similar to the wage regressions in Table 16.1. Note that hours declined with city size even faster for skilled than for unskilled construction workers.

Urban construction workers probably suffered less unemployment than did other construction workers. In New York, for example, unemployment rates for union members in 1898 and 1899 are nearly identical for construction workers in New York City as those in the rest of the state. At a seasonal unemployment peak, in December 1898, 35.7 percent of New York City's unionized construction workers were unemployed compared with 33.4 percent in the rest of the state; while in September 1899, 4.3 percent of the city's unionized construction workers were unemployed compared with 5.2 percent elsewhere. See New York Bureau of Labor Statistics, *Seventeenth Annual Report, 1899* (Albany, 1900), pp. 32–36. In addition, as Alexander Keyssar observes, urban workers may have been more successful in finding alternative employments during construction downturns than their counterparts in smaller locales because cities' diverse economies insulate workers from the effects of downturns in individual industries. See Keyssar, *Out of Work: The First Century of Unemployment in Massachusetts* (Cambridge, Mass., 1986), p. 119.

Table 16.1 Explaining the (Log) Real Wage by Occupation and Locality, 1890 and 1903

	1890		1903	
Variable	Wage	Real Wage	Wage	Real Wage
Constant	4.902*	5.132*	5.175*	5.393*
Log of city population	0.032**	0.019	0.037*	0.025
Population growth rate, 1890–1900	0.149*	0.067	0.048	−0.012
% Nonwhite	0.170	0.451*	−0.039	0.241
% Foreign born	0.368*	0.313***	0.379*	0.361**
South	−0.069	−0.105	−0.025	−0.010
West	0.294*	0.171*	0.244*	0.161*
Midwest	−0.021	0.073*	0.014	0.122*
Unskilled	−0.958*	−1.073**	−1.039*	−1.221*
Log of population × unskilled in manufacturing	0.040	0.048	0.046***	0.060
Log of population × unskilled in construction	0.067*	0.063*	0.079*	0.086*
Log of population × skilled in construction	0.070*	0.089*	0.071*	0.108*
Construction	−0.172	0.003	−0.166	−0.035
Construction × skilled	−0.409	−0.847	−0.298	−0.918***
Wood and furniture	0.048	0.061	0.026	0.057
Printing	0.561*	0.569*	0.738*	0.761*
Log of establishment size	−0.029*	−0.029**	−0.054*	−0.072*
Number of observations	680	392	694	402
F-statistic	117.6	59.0	130.0	71.5
R^2	0.74	0.72	0.76	0.76
Mean of dependent variable	5.421	5.446	5.613	5.632

Notes: The regressions are ordinary least squares, weighted by the number of employees in the occupation and locality. There are fewer observations in the real wage than in the nominal wage regressions because price data are available only for a subset of cities.

Sources: The average wage in occupation in localities is reported in the U.S. Commissioner of Labor, *Nineteenth Annual Report: Wages and Hours of Labor* (Washington, D.C., 1905). City characteristics are from the U.S. Census Office, *Eleventh Census, 1890: Population* (Washington, D.C., 1895), vol. 1, part 1, pp. 524–58; U.S. Census Office, *Twelfth Census, 1900: Population* (Washington, D.C., 1901), vol. 1, part 1, pp. 609–94. Price data are from Michael Haines, "A State and Local Consumer Price Index for the United States in 1890," National Bureau of Economic Research, Working Paper Series on Historical Factors in Long Run Growth, no. 2 (May 1989).

*Significant at the 1% level.

**Significant at the 5% level.

***Significant at the 10% level.

creased construction workers' commuting time.[15] However, this effect is probably small. While workers may have changed job sites, most urban construction was carried out in relatively compact downtown business districts. In addition, intraurban transit improved substantially during the period. If the

15. Although the increase in commuting time would be balanced by urban construction workers' shorter workday.

wage premium urban construction workers received in 1890 reflected compensation for commuting, then transit improvements should have lowered the premium by 1903.

Differences in technology might have contributed to big-city construction workers' high wages. Entrepôts for continental and even world trade, big cities were relatively inhospitable to monopolies in manufacturing products. Competition pushed big-city manufacturers to use the most advanced technologies available, carrying out production in relatively large, modern establishments.[16] As David Gordon, Richard Edwards, and Michael Reich have argued, technological progress in urban manufacturers may have reduced the demand for skilled manufacturing workers, lowering their wage.[17] This is in contrast with construction where the slow pace of technological change protected traditional crafts from competition with the unskilled.

By itself, however, a demand-side, technology-driven account cannot explain the effect of city size on wages. Without barriers blocking the movement of labor into urban construction, a slow rate of technological progress does not explain the relative increase in wages for unskilled construction workers in large cities. Instead, with efficient labor markets, changing technologies should change economy-wide relative wages without having any lasting impact on local wage patterns. Certainly over the thirteen years considered here, the flow of labor out of low-demand and low-wage towns toward high-demand and high-wage big cities could be expected to equalize occupational wages between localities. To explain the persistence of regional wage differentials, a demand-side model of regional wage differentials must be complemented by an explanation for labor market rigidities.

Strong unions supported high urban construction wages, and their membership and apprenticeship restrictions provided one important barrier to entry into urban construction labor markets.[18] Big-city construction unions supported national union federations to spread organization to small towns to maintain high urban wages.[19] In addition to working to raise wages in small towns and cities, these unions discouraged workers from seeking urban jobs by publicizing news of strikes and any unfavorable labor market conditions in big cities.

Unions raised urban construction wages, but outside of the largest cities

16. Establishments in large cities were larger than their small-town counterparts. The number of workers per establishment increases by about 40 percent for every doubling in city size.

17. David Gordon, Richard Edwards, and Michael Reich, *Segmented Work, Divided Workers* (Cambridge, Mass., 1982), pp. 100–164.

18. Even unskilled urban construction workers would have benefited from unionization because they had among the few functioning unions of common laborers. Note that almost all of the unionized building laborers were in a few large cities. In New York, for example, 93 percent of the unionized building laborers in 1899 lived in New York City, compared with 70 percent of the nonlaborers (New York BLS, *Annual Report, 1899,* pp. 64–67).

19. See, for example, the United Brotherhood of Carpenters and Joiners, *The Carpenter* (Aug. 1881), p. 2.

their effect was probably small. Wages were only 3 to 5 percent higher in cities and trades with a union local. Including a dummy variable for the presence of a union does not significantly reduce the independent effect of city size.[20] Unions may have had a larger influence on wages in big-city construction, because there the unions were among the nation's strongest. Between 1881 and 1894, for example, strike success rates are significantly higher for construction workers in big cities than for workers in other industries or for construction workers in smaller towns and cities (see Table 16.2).[21] Perhaps reflecting their ability to conduct effective strikes, big-city construction unions enrolled a relatively large proportion of the potential workforce. The unionization rate of the entire labor force for the four largest construction trades in Chicago in 1902, for example, was 47 percent including 69 percent for carpenters and 68 percent for bricklayers.[22] In contrast, the unionization rate in the same four crafts in Illinois outside of Chicago was only 7 percent.[23]

Unions formed within the manufacturing sector were also stronger in big cities than in rural areas, but city size had less of an impact in manufacturing than in construction. In contrast with construction strikes, there is only a small, statistically insignificant positive relationship between strike success and city size in manufacturing. Perhaps as a result, there is only a weak relationship between city size and unionization rates. In Illinois in 1902, for example, unionization rates were higher in Chicago than in the rest of the state for all of eight large nonconstruction trades, but few workers belonged to unions even in Chicago, and the difference between Chicago and the rest of the state is often small.[24] Only 15 percent of Chicago machinists, for example, belonged to unions compared with 13 percent of those outside of Chicago. In

20. This is from regressions similar to those in Table 16.1 including only occupations for which I have local union information: bricklayers, carpenters, machinists, and molders. The estimate given is the coefficient on a dummy variable for the existence of a union local in the trade and locality.

21. Data are not available for individual strikes in other years. For a more detailed discussion of these data, see Gerald Friedman, "Strike Success and Union Ideology: The United States and France, 1880–1914," *Journal of Economic History,* 48 (Mar. 1988), pp. 1–25.

22. The unionization rate for the same crafts in New York City in 1900 is only 27 percent. Some of the difference in unionization rates between New York and Illinois reflects the rapid growth of unions in both states between 1900 and 1902. Note, however, that these rates are below the unionization rate of wage earners because the denominator, the entire labor force, includes employers. Also, the unions' reach exceeded their formal membership because many nonmembers would regularly support union strikes and wage demands without paying dues.

The labor force data are from the U.S. Census Office, *Twelfth Census of the United States, 1900: Census of Population* (Washington, D.C., 1901), v. 2, pt. 2, pp. 558–61, 578–81. New York union membership in September 1900 is from New York Bureau of Labor Statistics, *Eighteenth Annual Report, 1900* (Albany, 1901), pp. 505–44. Illinois membership in 1902 is from Illinois Bureau of Labor Statistics, *Twelfth Biennial Report, 1902* (Springfield, 1904), pp. 299–311.

23. The gap between the metropolitan and nonmetropolitan unionization rates in New York is smaller, 27 percent for New York City compared with 17 percent for the rest of the state. The number of nonmetropolitan union members and the size of the labor force are from the same sources as in fn. 22.

24. These crafts include machinists, printers, boot and shoe makers, tailors and garment workers, bakers, butchers, brewers, and coopers.

Table 16.2 Determinants of Strike Success in the United States: Strikes in 625 Cities, 1881–1894

Variable	Mean	Coefficient	*t*-statistic
Constant	1.00	−0.155	−0.25
Union strike, 1881–94	0.71	0.163	0.86
Union strike, 1887–94	0.41	0.490	1.83
Log of city population, 1880	12.21	0.056	1.36
Construction industry × log of city population	3.03	0.235	2.53
Construction industry × union strike	0.19	−1.050	−2.41
Construction industry × union strike, 1887–94	0.15	1.049	2.90
City percentage of foreign born, 1880	0.51	0.038	0.70
Strike participation rate	0.60	0.739	2.92
Log of strike size	3.54	0.001	0.18
Log of establishment size	3.99	−0.701	−1.02
Striker rate in industry and state	1.67	0.028	1.15
Number of issue dummy variables: 4			
Number of industry dummy variables: 3			
Number of year dummy variables: 13			
Chi-square statistic	161.06		
Mean of dependent variable	0.58		
Number of observations (individual strikes)	1,417		

Notes: The estimating procedure is a logit where the dependent variable is a dummy equal to 1 for strikes where the workers gain at least some of their demands and equal to 0 otherwise. The industry dummy variables include construction, transportation, and mining. The dummy variables for strike issues include dummy variables for strikes over work rules, strikes against wage cuts, strikes over the hours of work, and strikes over personnel policies.

Sources: Samples of individual strike records in U.S. Commissioner of Labor, *Third Annual Report: Strikes and Lockouts* (Washington, D.C., 1888); and *Tenth Annual Report: Strikes and Lockouts* (Washington, D.C., 1895). Only strikes in the 625 largest American cities are included. City characteristics are from U.S. Census Office, *Statistics of the Population of the U.S. at the Tenth Census, 1880* (Washington, D.C., 1886), vol. 1, pp. 447–56.

New York, any positive effect of city size on unionization is even smaller. In five of these same eight crafts, unionization rates are higher outside New York City than within, including machinists, boot and shoe makers, butchers, brewers, and coopers.[25]

The impact of city size on unionization in construction and in manufacturing can be explored further using data on the distribution of union locals for several American unions. Data have been collected on the location of union locals in December 1903 for four of the most important American unions: in construction, the United Brotherhood of Carpenters and Joiners and the United Bricklayers and Masons, and in the metal trades, the International As-

25. There is a substantially higher unionization rate in New York City among printers (51 percent vs. 32 percent outside the city) and among garment workers (16 percent vs. 8 percent). The unionization rate among bakers is nearly the same in the city (15 percent) as outside (14 percent).

sociation of Machinists and the International Iron Molders Union.[26] In Table 16.3, I report the results of logit regressions for the effect of city size on the probability that a union local will exist for each trade in the 1,884 largest American cities. In each case, city size is associated with a significant increase in the probability that there will be a union local in a city. But the effect of city size on the probability of having a union is significantly larger for the construction trades than for the others.[27] Big cities were the centers of craft organization around 1900, especially for construction workers.

The relative strength of urban unions might surprise both economic theorists and labor historians. Theorists might expect workers in smaller towns to be more successful in forming unions because it should be easier to mobilize a smaller number of workers for collective action and because a smaller town's relative isolation should insulate local monopolies from outside competition.[28] Prominent labor historians, such as Herbert Gutman, also argue that labor militancy was more effective in smaller locales. Gutman, for example, finds evidence that collective action by workers in smaller communities often succeeded because the workers were supported by many in the middle classes sympathetic to their struggles against outside corporations.[29]

These arguments underestimate, however, the importance of the political leverage enjoyed by big-city workers. Construction workers in several of America's largest cities especially benefited from alliances formed with political machines after 1886. These alliances allowed urban construction workers to use municipal police powers, including licensing and other regulatory authority, to isolate themselves from national labor markets. While such alliances were of little value to manufacturing workers facing national markets in products as well as in labor, they helped construction workers to gain higher wages. These gains came, however, at the expense of separating urban construction workers from the rest of the working class.

16.3 Big-City Politics and the Building Trades

By the late nineteenth century, political machines were the strongest political force in most large American cities.[30] Unlike working-class socialists or middle-class good government reformers, machines formed cross-class coali-

26. The distribution of union locals is available from the following union newspapers: United Brotherhood of Carpenters and Joiners, *The Carpenter* (Dec. 1903); the United Bricklayers and Masons, *The Bricklayer and Mason* (Dec. 1903); the International Iron Molders' Union, *The Iron Molders' Journal* (Dec. 1903); and the International Association of Machinists, *Machinists' Monthly Journal* (Dec. 1903).

27. The differences in the coefficients between the carpenters or masons and the machinists or molders are significant at 99 percent confidence with *t*-ratios of about 4.

28. See, for example, Mancur Olson, *The Logic of Collective Action: Public Goods and the Theory of Groups* (Cambridge, Mass., 1966).

29. See, for example, Herbert Gutman, *Work, Culture, and Society in Industrializing America* (New York, 1976).

30. M. Craig Brown and Charles N. Halaby, "Machine Politics in America, 1870–1945," *Journal of Interdisciplinary History,* 17 (Winter 1987), pp. 587–612.

Table 16.3 **Determinants of the Presence of a Union Local among the 1,884 Largest American Cities, 1903**

Variable	Carpenters	Bricklayers	Machinists	Molders
Constant	−18.63*	−19.56*	−17.03*	−16.89*
Log of city population	2.17*	2.19*	1.77*	
% Foreign born	−2.95*	−3.88*	−2.10*	−3.08*
% Black	0.03	−0.61	−2.00**	−4.33*
South	−0.08	−0.35	1.22*	0.11
Midwest	0.35*	0.20	0.83*	0.13
West	1.16*	0.72*	0.79*	−0.83**
Mean of the dependent variable	0.49	0.32	0.25	0.17
Log-likelihood ratio	−952.43	−795.31	−741.39	−583.45
Number of observations (cities)	1,884	1,884	1,884	1,884

Note: The estimating procedure is a logit where the dependent variable is a dummy equal to 1 for cities with a union local and equal to 0 otherwise.

Sources: Data on the location of union locals are from the United Brotherhood of Carpenters and Joiners, *The Carpenter* (Dec. 1903); the United Bricklayers and Masons, *The Bricklayer and Mason* (Dec. 1903); the International Iron Molders' Union, *The Iron Molders' Journal* (Dec. 1903); the International Association of Machinists, *Machinists' Monthly Journal* (Dec. 1903). Census characteristics of cities are from U.S. Census Office, *Twelfth Census, 1900: Population* (Washington, D.C., 1901), vol. 1, part 1, pp. 609–46.

*Significant at the 1% level.

**Significant at the 5% level.

tions using government resources to broker a deal among the classes.[31] Such alliances were necessary to govern successfully America's large cities. Machines needed working-class votes to win elections. But to govern effectively, they depended on the support, or at least the tolerance, of property holders.[32] In exchange for their votes, workers received individual benefits, patronage jobs, and relief. At the same time, machines wooed upper-class voters by nominating prestigious candidates for major offices and by holding down taxes and municipal debt.[33] Here, of course, was the rub. The spending restraint needed to appeal to property holders came at the expense of the machines' working-class supporters.

31. This discussion draws on the work of Martin Shefter, *Political Crisis/Fiscal Crisis* (New York, 1985); and Steven Erie, *Rainbow's End: Irish Americans and the Dilemmas of Urban Machine Politics, 1840–1985* (Berkeley, 1988).

32. Facing the nearly unanimous opposition of the city's property holders, with their control over investment and the banking system, even San Francisco's Union Labor Party (ULP) government was forced "to continuously straddle the line between corporate wishes and a forthright defense of the needs of its core constituency. Straining not to cross that line led to inaction, and that won the ULP no friends on *either* side of the class divide" (Michael Kazin, *Barons of Labor: The San Francisco Building Trades and Union Power in the Progressive Era* [Urbana, 1987], p. 192).

33. Jon Teaford, *The Unheralded Triumph: City Government in America, 1870–1900* (Baltimore, 1984), pp. 15–82, 204–5, 208–10, 283–306.

Ethnic ties, especially among the Irish, helped political machines navigate these difficult shoals. But such ties could not substitute for a program attractive to voters in different economic circumstance.[34] Most late-nineteenth-century machines were led by Irish-Americans. But constituting less than 20 percent of the adult male population in most large cities, the Irish lacked the numbers to dominate municipal elections. Further, because they were predominantly working class, the Irish controlled little private capital.[35] And even among the Irish, political appeals based on ethnicity failed when they clashed with workers' economic interests. In New York in 1886, for example, Tammany Hall's working-class Irish supporters protested the machine's policy of fiscal restraint and opposition to labor militancy by abandoning Tammany to support Henry George's campaign for mayor as the candidate of the radical Union Labor Party.

Neither wage workers nor property holders were able to use machine-dominated city governments to advance their interests. Both workers and property holders accepted machine rule only from fear that the alternative would be open rule by their class enemy. Workers preferred machines to the alternative of elite domination, even though machines made significant concessions to property owners. Property owners tolerated machines because they impeded worker militancy and provided protection against socialism.

Machines like Tammany, therefore, were a big-city phenomenon because city property owners feared militant labor enough to tolerate machines. Their fear was realistic because in a democratic regime, working-class majorities could make cities dangerous places to hold property. In 1882, for example, the *New York Times* warned that "we are in this City over the crust of a volcano, with a powerful dangerous class who cares nothing for our property or civilization, . . . who burrow at the roots of society, and only come forth . . . in times of disturbance to plunder and prey."[36] Historian Francis Parkman agreed that in big cities, "the dangerous classes are most numerous and strong, and the effects of flinging the suffrage to the mob are most disastrous. . . . Democracy hands over great municipal corporations, the property of those who hold stock in them, to the keeping of greedy and irresponsible crowds . . . whose object is nothing but plunder."[37] Because of their high proportion of propertyless voters, a Harvard professor warned that big cities

34. Elmer J. Cornwell, Jr., "Bosses, Machines, and Ethnic Groups," *Annals of the American Academy of Political and Social Science: City Bosses and Political Machines,* 353 (May 1964), pp. 27–39; Nathan Glazer and Daniel Patrick Moynihan, *Beyond the Melting Pot* (Cambridge, Mass., 1964); W. B. Munro, *The Government of American Cities* (New York, 1916). Erie's *Rainbow's End* provides an alternative view.

35. Amy Bridges, *A City in the Republic: Antebellum New York and the Origins of Machine Politics* (New York, 1984), discusses the origins of New York's political machines.

36. Quoted in David Scobey, "The Class Politics of City-Building in Gilded Age New York" (manuscript, Brandeis University, Nov. 1988), p. 9.

37. Francis Parkman, "The Failure of Universal Suffrage," *North American Review,* 126 (1878), p. 20.

promoted radicalism: "Urban concentration means . . . that the landless man rises to supremacy in the voting-lists, that the property-owning element dwindles in relative importance."[38]

Not only were there more workers in larger cities, but their concentration facilitated collective action. John Mitchell, head of the United Mine Workers of America, argued that unions in small towns were relatively weak because workers in these communities were integrated into the broader community. Small-town workers then were easily influenced by the hostility of their property-owning neighbors to labor organization. "The wage earners of the industrial centers," by contrast, formed "a society of their own." Their neighborhoods bolstered independent values, incubating and supporting working-class militancy.[39] As a result, collective action by workers was much more common in bigger cities. Not only was union membership more common in big cities, but so was strike activity. Strike rates rose with city size; in 1881–86, the share of the population striking was nearly four times as high in cities of over 100,000 than in cities of under 25,000.[40] Over the 1881–1900 period, the nation's four largest cities, with less than 10 percent of the population of the United States, accounted for over half the nation's strikers and struck establishments.[41]

Property holders in small towns had less to fear from labor. The smaller scale of production produced a relatively smaller working class. The social structure of many smaller American cities and towns was little changed by industrialization. With few large establishments, their industrial proletariat was relatively small, too small to pose a significant political threat. In Massachusetts towns of under 2,500 in 1885, for example, the average industrial establishment had eight workers and only 20 percent of the potential voters were wage earners. In cities of over 5,000 residents, in contrast, the average industrial establishment employed 31 wage workers and 64 percent of all voters were wage earners. Political patterns reflected these differences in social structure. Parties supported by the economic elite were strongest in smaller communities. In Massachusetts, for example, Republicans dominated small towns but their vote declined with city size. Independent labor candidates, in contrast, increased their vote with city size. In 1884, for example, the Green-

38. Munro, *Government,* p. 48.

39. John Mitchell, *The Wage Earner and His Problems* (Washington, D.C., 1913), p. 152. Also note Frank Parkin, "Working-Class Conservatives: A Theory of Political Deviance," *British Journal of Sociology,* 18 (Sept. 1967), pp. 278–90.

40. The number of strikers in each of 625 cities with a population over 4,000 is from the U.S. Commissioner of Labor, *Third Annual Report, 1887* (Washington, D.C., 1888). City population characteristics for these cities are from the U.S. Census Office, *Tenth Census, 1880: Population* (Washington, D.C., 1883), vol. 1, part 1, pp. 447–56.

41. U.S. Commissioner of Labor, *Sixteenth Annual Report, 1901* (Washington, D.C., 1902), pp. 28–29. Also see the discussion in Sari J. Bennett and Carville V. Earle, "Labour Power and Locality in the Gilded Age: The Northeastern United States, 1881–1894," *Social History,* 15 (Nov. 1982), pp. 383–405.

back-Labor Party gained only 4 percent of the vote in the smallest cities compared with more than 9 percent in cities of over 5,000.

It was in the mid–1880s, the period entitled the "Great Upheaval" by labor historians, that the potential threat posed by urban labor came closest to realization. At the peak of the period's labor turmoil in 1886, as much as 5 percent of the nation's total labor force was on strike. Conflicts between strikers and municipal police combined with anger at fiscal retrenchment to turn these industrial actions into political challenges. In 1885 and 1886, independent working-class political movements contested elections in 18 percent of cities with populations of over 4,000, including most with more than 100,000.[42] In New York, for example, repressive court decisions against strikes and boycotts and working-class anger at Tammany leader "Honest John" Kelly's fiscal prudence made the city in 1886 "ripe for independent political action."[43] Swollen with new recruits, the city's unions organized the United Labor Party to run Henry George for mayor on a radical labor platform.

To defeat George, Tammany was forced to seek allies on its right and among the propertied classes. Nominating the manufacturer Abram Hewitt, the candidate of its long-time rivals organized as the County Democracy, Tammany defeated George with a fusion campaign, appealing to conservative voters "for the saving of society."[44] The George candidacy in New York attracted the most attention, but in the same year candidates supported by trade unions and the Knights of Labor also ran strong races in other large cities, including Milwaukee and Chicago. As in New York, these challenges were blocked by a united front of bourgeois defense, organized "to save the city government from capture by the 'Reds'."[45]

The Great Upheaval demonstrated anew to urban politicians the need for a strategy to accommodate property owners without alienating labor voters. Machines like Tammany developed tighter, more centralized organizations to restrain popular revolts.[46] Organization gave the machine's central leadership the tools to punish grass-root revolts. But even the best organization depended on policies that gave both workers and property holders a stake in the machine's success. Machines provided these with public works.

42. This is from a coding of the cities in Leon Fink, *Workingmen's Democracy: The Knights of Labor and American Politics* (Urbana, 1983), pp. 28–29, matched with population data for 625 cities with a population of over 4,000. The population data are from the U.S. Census Office, *Tenth Census, 1880: Population*, vol. 1, part 1, pp. 447–56.

43. Gustavus Myers, *The History of Tammany Hall* (New York, 1917), p. 269. Also see Martin Shefter, "The Electoral Foundations of the Political Machine," in *History of American Electoral Behavior*, Joel Silbey, Allan Bogue, and William Flanigan, eds. (Princeton, 1978), p. 290.

44. Hewitt won only with the support of many Republican voters who deserted their own candidate, future president Theodore Roosevelt. Tammany did not depend on such support but also used frauds "so glaring and so tremendous in the aggregate" that most supporters of George believed their candidate won only to be "counted out" (Myers, *History of Tammany Hall*, p. 270).

45. Ralph Scharnau, "Thomas J. Morgan and the United Labor Party of Chicago," *Journal of the Illinois State Historical Society*, 66 (Spring 1974), pp. 51–54.

46. This is emphasized by Martin Shefter in *Political Crisis/Fiscal Crisis*, p. 21.

The American tradition of using public works to reward supporters has a long history. As early as the 1830s, Democrats and Whigs solicited votes with jobs on canal and highway projects.[47] Public works spending can be the ideal cement for a cross-class political coalition. Such spending provides working-class jobs, which in turn enhances property values and rents of landowners, and it creates educational, recreational, transportation, and health facilities for middle-class use.[48] As a result, and in contrast with welfare measures benefiting exclusively workers and the unemployed, support for capital improvements spans the class divide. Even in San Francisco, where middle-class and working-class voters between 1899 and 1910 agreed on little else, both approved ten bond issues to build schools, hospitals, parks, sewers, and railroad and water systems by nearly identical three-to-one margins.[49]

Late-nineteenth-century political machines embarked on a jamboree of city building. Because of the economies of scale that come with a relatively dense population, per capita expenditures on road, waterworks, sewer, park, and public building construction should decline with city size. Instead, around 1890, cities of over 100,000 spent 55 percent more per capita on these facilities than did those of 10,000 to 15,000. Built by workers but used almost exclusively by the upper classes, park improvements demonstrate most clearly how political machines established cross-class coalitions. By 1890, cities of more than 100,000 had spent over eight times the amount on park improvements than had the smallest cities and over four times as much as cities of 50,000 to 100,000.[50] Through public works, political machines supplied the propertied classes with public goods and gave workers jobs and wages without class struggle.

Big-city political machines did not rely exclusively on municipal Keynesianism to gain working-class support. They also consciously undermined working-class solidarity by favoring selected elements of organized labor. Craft unions were their preferred allies. Alliances with radical unions organized along working-class lines, such as the Knights of Labor or the International Workers of the World, would frighten all property holders because these unions challenged the system of private property, threatening all property holders regardless of industry. In contrast, an alliance with craft unions was

47. See, for example, Erie, *Rainbow's End,* p. 12.

48. While constituting only about 10 percent of the American labor force in 1900, Irish-born workers were 19 percent of the labor force in four construction trades in the ten largest cities; see U.S. Department of Commerce and Labor, Bureau of the Census, *Special Reports: Occupations at the Twelfth Census* (Washington, D.C., 1904), pp. 64, 488–715.

49. Erie, *Rainbow's End,* p. 82.

50. There is an interesting contrast between the relatively heavy per capita expenditures on public facilities in big cities with the relatively low expenditures on private business recreation. Theaters and other private recreational facilities were more available per capita in smaller cities. See the U.S. Department of the Interior, Census Office, *Report on the Social Statistics of Cities, at the Eleventh Census: 1890* (Washington, D.C., 1895), pp. 15–47.

less threatening because craft unions consciously rejected class alliances and restricted their concerns to a part of the working class without challenging the basic organization of society.

In Chicago, for example, municipal government favored construction craft unions while they used the police to repress broader working-class solidarity. Carter Harrison I, Chicago's mayor for most of the 1880s, was openly allied with the city's conservative craft unions. Through the early and mid–1880s, he hired Trades Assembly leaders for city positions and restrained the city's police force during strikes.[51] This alliance did not stop him from crushing the city's Knights of Labor and Central Labor Union after May Day 1886 and the Haymarket Affair. Drawing on contributions from Marshall Field and three hundred other prominent citizens, the city's police used the Haymarket Affair as an excuse to attack Chicago's radical labor movement. Union meetings were banned, halls closed, records confiscated, and leaders hauled off to police stations for questioning, or worse.

The post-Haymarket repression may have hurt all of Chicago's unions, but it was most damaging to the anarchist and radical industrial unions and the Knights of Labor, who were the focus of police repression. Once these unions were defeated, the city's Democratic politicians and conservative craft unions quickly renewed an alliance that both had found advantageous. On one side, the experience of police repression demonstrated forcefully to craft unions the importance of maintaining political support for their activities, and the surge of independent labor politics in 1886 and 1887 convinced Democratic politicians that they needed to cultivate alliances to hold onto elements of the working-class electorate. To preempt further independent labor politics, Chicago's Democratic machine consciously sought allies among construction craft unions. At the behest of these unions, the Democratically controlled City Council on 8 June 1889 adopted an eight-hour ordinance drafted by Clarence Darrow for city construction. The City Council's action was soon copied by the city's School Board and the Cook County Board of County Commissioners.[52] Construction unions responded to these overtures and the Carpenters Union quickly endorsed the Democratic candidate for reelection in 1889. The alliance gave the Democratic machine leverage to undermine independent political action by organized labor. To protect their alliance with the Democrats, the Carpenters sabotaged a campaign by other unions (including the city's machinists' union) to renew the city's Union Labor Party in 1890. Observers said the carpenters feared that independent political action by labor "would exasperate the Democratic city administration and bring on the active opposition of the City Hall officials and the police" right before the Carpenter's major

51. Bruce Nelson, *Beyond the Martyrs: A Social History of Chicago's Anarchists, 1870–1900* (New Brunswick, 1988), p. 43.

52. Richard Schneirov and Thomas J. Suhrbur, *Union Brotherhood, Union Town: The History of the Carpenters' Union of Chicago, 1863–1987* (Carbondale, 1988), p. 40.

eight-hour day campaign in 1890.[53] To maintain their alliance with the Democratic machine, Chicago's Carpenters abandoned working-class solidarity.

Chicago's construction unions profited from this alliance. By 1900, when Carter Harrison's son was mayor, there were twenty-two building trades union leaders on the city payroll, including the head of Chicago's Building Trades Council who also headed the city's Civil Service Board. Many union leaders served as city building inspectors and supervised the employers they dealt with over the bargaining table and during strikes. Chicago's city government openly favored unions during labor disputes. During a major construction lockout in 1900, for example, contractors and their strikebreakers were denied basic police protection and were forced to hire five hundred special detectives to guard their building sites.[54] One employer denounced the protection their plants received from police as a "farce" and blamed their troubles on city hall's twenty-two "laboring men."[55] His problem, however, was not the unionists in city hall, some of whom were there in 1886 as well, but the tight alliance that had been formed since the Great Upheaval between construction craft unions and the Democratic machine.

Political machines, like Chicago's, helped their construction union allies outside of strikes. Workers employed on public construction, including utilities and workers at the 1893 Chicago World's Fair, were shielded from labor market competition by municipal regulations setting wages and working conditions at union levels. State support made these "good jobs," preferred to other private employments and obtained only through personal influence. Control over such employment gave unions and political machines leverage over workers and voters. Personalized administration gave municipal officials, including building inspectors, opportunities to grant favor or "petty penalties and annoyances" to employers, discretion they used to harass anti-union businesses and building contractors with unfavorable tax assessments, building and safety inspections, or by withholding authorization to use public ways. In San Francisco, under Boss Reuf's rule, for example, open-shop contractors and employers battled repeated attempts by municipal departments to hamper their operations with petty citations and bureaucratic delays. Many agreed to operate union shops out of fear that a city inspector would close them down otherwise.[56]

With open city support, construction unions boomed in Chicago even while manufacturing-sector unions made little headway. Machines rarely formed alliances with unions outside of the building trades, partly because alliances the machines made with construction unions reduced their need for alliances with other unions. The machines also had more to offer unions in the construction

53. *Chicago Tribune* (1 June 1890), p. 6.

54. Royal Montgomery, *Industrial Relations in the Chicago Building Trades* (Chicago, 1927), p. 29. Schneirov and Suhrbur, *Union Brotherhood,* pp. 80–82.

55. David Montgomery, *The Fall of the House of Labor* (Cambridge, Mass., 1987), p. 272.

56. Michael Kazin, *Barons of Labor,* p. 188.

sector than in manufacturing. While manufacturing employers could shift location to avoid unfriendly local governments, construction was fixed to particular locations. Tied to particular locations and schedules, construction contractors were particularly vulnerable to local action by city governments and workers. As the Illinois governor and social reformer J. P. Altgeld observed, building trades unions could achieve gains that eluded others because construction "is always a local question."[57]

Regardless of location, technical conditions helped make construction workers throughout the United States, and the world, among the most unionized of workers.[58] But it was political support that made large cities American construction unionism's stronghold. The New York correspondent of the business-oriented *Boston Evening Transcript* reported in 1892 that "it is only in the building trades that the labor unions in New York have of late retained much power for evil. There they are a constant bane."[59] While probably exaggerating the weakness of other unions, this was an accurate assessment of the strength of unionism in the construction trades, both in New York and in other large American cities.

16.4 Conclusion: Wages and Politics in Large American Cities

Construction workers played a central role in American radical politics from the 1770s through the 1830s, the 1850s, and the 1880s.[60] Among the leaders of Philadelphia's Order of United American Mechanics, for example, were George F. Turner, carpenter, John Bottsford, bricklayer, and Matthew W. Robinson, carpenter.[61] Later building tradesmen joined workers from outside the building trades to support radical political action in the Great Upheaval of the 1880s.[62] Peter McGuire, carpenter, founder of the American Federation of Labor and of the United Brotherhood of Carpenters and Joiners, for example, was a Lassallian socialist and organizer for the Socialist Labor Party. Under his leadership, the Carpenters at their first national convention endorsed independent working-class political action and industrial unionism.[63] Radical building tradesmen joined alliances structured according to their relationship

57. John P. Altgeld, "The Eight Hour Movement: An Address Delivered before the Brotherhood of United Labor, at the Armory in Chicago, Feb. 22, 1890" (Chicago, 1890), p. 13. A similar point was made by the *New York Tribune* (2 May 1886), p. 12.

58. Montgomery, *Fall of the House of Labor,* pp. 298–99; Montgomery, *Industrial Relations,* pp. 4–6.

59. *Boston Evening Transcript* (16 July 1892), p. 6.

60. Eric Foner, *Tom Paine and Revolutionary America* (New York, 1976), pp. 57–63; Sean Wilentz, *Chants Democratic: New York City and the Rise of the American Working Class, 1788–1850* (New York, 1984), pp. 410, 414; Jonathan Garlock, "A Structural Analysis of the Knights of Labor" (Ph.D. dissertation, University of Rochester, 1974), pp. 42, 62.

61. Bruce Laurie, *Working People of Philadelphia, 1800–50* (Philadelphia, 1980), pp. 174, 182–83.

62. See, for example, the involvement of building tradesmen in Chicago's anarchist movement in the 1880s in Nelson, *Beyond the Martyrs,* p. 89.

63. United Brotherhood of Carpenters and Joiners, *The Carpenter* (Aug. 1881), p. 2.

to property rights, uniting all those whose only productive property was their labor.

As long as construction workers had the same relationship to the state and the legal system as did other workers, there were grounds for a broad, working-class alliance. The active role of local officials in construction and their support for construction unions and workers, however, made construction workers a privileged part of the working class. Treated differently by the state, construction workers had reason to distance themselves from the rest of the working class.

Focusing on national politics, scholars comparing American and European unions have stressed differences between politicized European central union federations and their relatively apolitical American counterparts. By neglecting local action, however, these studies overlook much of American craft unions' political action. Craft unions were generally uninterested in national legislation, but this did not preclude an active involvement in local politics.[64] American craft unions understood well the importance of government policy, but living in a decentralized regime they sought to influence local politics. Far from not being conscious of their position as wage earners, construction workers were extraordinarily active in defense of their interests against their employers. And far from being apolitical, they were intimately involved in politics.[65] But their militancy and their political action did not leadto alliances with other workers because they found they could advance their interests—at least their short-run interests—better through alliances with local political machines resting on cross-class coalitions.

In cross-class alliances with urban political machines, construction unions used America's political system to their advantage. But their cross-class alliances weakened any working-class challenge to capitalist domination. Allied with local Republican or Democratic machines, construction unions supported the AFL's voluntarist ideology because it required no commitment on political issues that might upset their local alliances.[66] Construction workers became the crucial missing component to any socialist political coalition. Without them America's big cities and its working class were lost to socialism.

Through alliances with political machines, construction unions carved a niche for themselves within the existing political and social order. Secure in their urban fortresses, construction workers were labor's aristocrats, able to stand on their own and for themselves.

64. Michael Rogin, "Voluntarism: The Political Functions of an Antipolitical Doctrine," *Industrial and Labor Relations Review,* 15 (July 1962), p. 534.

65. This separation of worker militancy and political action is at the core of Ira Katznelson's discussions of American exceptionalism. See his "Working-Class Formation and the State: Nineteenth-Century England in American Perspective," in *Bringing the State Back In,* Peter Evans, Dietrich Rueschemeyer, and Theda Skocpol, eds. (Cambridge, Mass., 1985), pp. 257–84.

66. Rogin, "Voluntarism," p. 535.

Dissertations Supervised by Robert W. Fogel

Adie, Douglas, University of Chicago, 1968
"Peel's Act Deposits and the Currency Banking School Controversy"

Albanese, Paul, Harvard University, 1982
"Toward a Methodology for Investigating the Formation of Preferences: A Case Study of Generational Changes in the Italian Family in the United States"

Betts, Diane, University of Texas at Austin, 1990
"The Pattern of Female Labor Force Participation in England and Wales: 1851–1901"

Blackhurst, Wallace G., University of Chicago, 1990
"Wealth, Polygamy, and Fertility in a Polygamous Society: Utah County Mormons, 1851–1870"

Bordo, Michael D., University of Chicago, 1972
"The Effects of the Sources of Change in the Money Supply on the Level of Economic Activity: An Historical Essay"

Brittain, Bruce, University of Chicago, 1975
"Monetary Factors in the French Balance of Payments: 1880–1913"

Cardell, N. Scott, Harvard University, 1989
"Extensions of Multinomial Logit: The Hedonic Demand Model, the Nonindependent Logit Model, and the Rank Logit Model"

Correa da Lago, Luiz Aranha, Harvard University, 1978
"The Transition from Slave to Free Labor in the Southern and Coffee Regions of Brazil: A Global and Theoretical Approach and Regional Case Studies"

Costa, Dora, University of Chicago, In progress
"Labor Force Participation of Older Men"

Crawford, Stephen, University of Chicago, 1988
"Quantified Memory: A Study of the WPA and Fisk University Slave Narrative Collections"

De Mello, Pedro Carvelho, University of Chicago, 1977
"The Economics of Labor in Brazilian Coffee Plantations, 1850–1888"

Della Paolera, Gerardo, University of Chicago, 1988
"How the Argentine Economy Performed during the International Gold Standard: A Reexamination"

Easton, Stephen T., University of Chicago, 1978
"Aggregate Aspects of the Poor Law, Unemployment Insurance and Unemployment in Britain from 1855–1910"

Evenson, Robert, University of Chicago, 1968
"The Contribution of Agricultural Research and Extension to Agricultural Production"

Ferrie, Joseph, University of Chicago, In progress
"Settlement Patterns, Occupational Mobility, and Wealth Accumulation Among European Immigrants to the United States: 1840–1860"

Friedman, Gerald, Harvard University, 1985
"Politics and Union Growth and the Labor Movement in France and the United States: 1880–1914"

Galantine, Ralph, University of Chicago, In progress
"Economic Factors in the Political Realignment between 1851 and 1860"

Galenson, David W., Harvard University, 1979
"The Indenture System and the Colonial Labor Market: An Economic History of White Servitude in British America"

Gardener, Bruce, University of Chicago, 1968
"An Analysis of U.S. Farm Family Income Inequality"

Goldin, Claudia D., University of Chicago, 1972
"The Economics of Urban Slavery: 1820–1860"

Green, Jerry, University of Rochester, 1970
"Some Aspects of the Use of the Core as a Solution Concept in Economic Theory"

Grubb, Farley, University of Chicago, 1984
"Immigration and Servitude in the Colony and Commonwealth of Pennsylvania: A Quantitative and Economic Analysis"

Harral, Clell, University of Rochester, 1969
"The Social Costs of Highway Transport in Eastern India"

Hill, Peter J., University of Chicago, 1970
"The Economic Impact of Immigration into the United States"

Honda, Gail, University of Chicago, In progress
"Social Costs of Japan's Industrial Revolution: 1868–1940"

Hopkins, Mark, Harvard University, ABD

Huertas, Thomas, University of Chicago, 1977
"Economic Growth and Economic Policy in a Multinational Setting: The Habsburg Monarchy, 1841–1865"

John, A. Meredith, Princeton University, 1984
"The Demography of Slavery in Nineteenth Century Trinidad"

Jones, Alice Hanson, University of Chicago, 1968
"Wealth Estimates for the American Middle Colonies, 1774"

Kahn, Charles, Harvard University, 1981
"Equilibrium Models of Illiquid Asset Pricing"

Klepper, Robert, University of Chicago, 1973
"The Economic Bases for Agrarian Protest Movements in the United States, 1870–1900"

Komlos, John, University of Chicago, 1990
"The Economic Development of the Eighteenth Century Habsburg Monarchy: An Anthropometric History"

Koshal, Rajindar K., University of Rochester, 1968
"Statistical Cost Analysis—Indian Railways"

Kulikoff, Allan, Brandeis University, 1976
"Labor and Slaves: Population, Economy, and Society in Eighteenth-Century Prince George's County, Maryland"

LaVeen, Phillip, University of Chicago, 1971
"British Slave Trade Suppression Policies, 1821–1865: Impact and Implications"

Levy, Daniel, University of Chicago, 1987
"The Economic Demography of the Colonial South: The Economic Determinants of Life-Cycle Events and Demographic Change in Maryland and South Carolina, 1635–1789"

Lewis, Frank, University of Rochester, 1977
"Explaining the Shift of Labor from Agriculture to Industry in the United States: 1869 to 1899"

Lindholm, Richard, University of Chicago, In progress
"Studies of the Renaissance Florentine Woollen Industry"

Manning, Richard, University of Chicago, 1989
"Consequences of Changing Product Liability Rules: Evidence from the Childhood Vaccine Market"

Margo, Robert A., Harvard University, 1982
"Disfranchisement, School Finance, and the Economics of Segregated Schools in the U.S. South, 1890–1910"

McMahon, Sarah, Brandeis University, 1981
"A Comfortable Subsistence: A History of Diet in New England, 1630–1850"

McMillan, John, University of Chicago, In progress
"Techniques and Technology in U.S. Agriculture"

Metzer, Jacob, University of Chicago, 1972
"Some Economic Aspects of Railroad Development in Tsarist Russia"

Moen, John, University of Chicago, 1987
"Essays on the Labor Force and Labor Participation Rates in the United States from 1860 through 1950"

Nelson, Forrest, University of Rochester, 1975
"Estimation of Economic Relationships with Censored, Truncated and Limited Dependent Variables"

Olson, John, University of Rochester, 1983
"The Occupational Structure of Plantation Slave Labor in the Late Antebellum Era"

Pope, Clayne L., University of Chicago, 1972
"The Impact of the Ante-Bellum Tariff on Income Distribution"

Pritchett, Jonathan, University of Chicago, 1986
"The Racial Division of Education Expenditure in the South, 1910"

Reid, Joseph D., Jr., University of Chicago, 1974
"Reconstruction in the American South, 1866–1890"

Rockoff, Hugh, University of Chicago, 1972
"American Free Banking before the Civil War: A Reexamination"

Rosen, Sherwin, University of Chicago, 1966
"Short-Run Employment Variations on Class-I Railroads in the United States, 1947–1963"

Rothenberg, Winifred, Brandeis University, 1984
"Markets and Massachusetts Farmers: A Paradigm of Economic Growth in Rural New England, 1750–1855"

Rutner, Jack, University of Chicago, 1974
"Money and the Gold Standard before the American Civil War"

Sanderson, Allen R., University of Chicago, ABD
"Child Labor Legislation"

Saraydar, Edward, University of Rochester, 1968
"An Exploration of Unresolved Problems in Bargaining Theory"

Shlomowitz, Ralph, University of Chicago, 1979
"The Transition from Slave to Freedman: Labor Arrangements in Southern Agriculture, 1865–1870"

Sokoloff, Kenneth L., Harvard University, 1982
"Industrialization and the Growth of the Manufacturing Sector in the Northeast, 1820–1850"

Solmon, Lewis C., University of Chicago, 1968
"Capital Formation by Expenditures on Formal Education, 1880 and 1890"

Steckel, Richard, University of Chicago, 1977
"The Economics of U.S. Slave and Southern White Fertility"

Surdam, David, University of Chicago, In progress
"A Case Study of Regicide—The Strange Demise of King Cotton"

Vickery, William Edward, University of Chicago, 1969
"The Economics of the Negro Migration, 1900 to 1960"

Villaflor, Georgia, Harvard University, In progress
"Essays on Labor Migration in Antebellum America"

Wahl, Jenny Bourne, University of Chicago, 1985
"Fertility in America: Historical Patterns and Wealth Effects on the Quantity and Quality of Children"

Walker, James, University of Chicago, 1986
"An Empirical Investigation of the Timing and Spacing of Births in Sweden: The Effects of Changing Economic Conditions and Public Policy"

Webb, Steve, University of Chicago, 1978
"The Economic Effects of Tariff Protection in Imperial Germany, 1878–1914"

Wimmer, Larry T., University of Chicago, 1968
"The Gold Crisis of 1869"

Yang, Donghyu, Harvard University, 1984
"Aspects of United States Agriculture circa 1860"

Zevin, Robert B., Harvard University, 1981
"Summary of the Growth of Manufacturing in Early Nineteenth Century New England"

The Writings of Robert W. Fogel

Books

The Union Pacific Railroad: A Case in Premature Enterprise (Johns Hopkins, 1960).

Railroads and American Economic Growth: Essays in Econometric History (Johns Hopkins, 1964); Spanish edition, 1972.

The Reinterpretation of American Economic History (Harper & Row, 1971; co-edited with S. L. Engerman); Italian edition, 1975.

The Dimensions of Quantitative Research in History (Princeton, 1972; co-edited with W. O. Aydelotte and A. G. Bogue).

Time on the Cross: The Economics of American Negro Slavery (Little, Brown, 1974; with S. L. Engerman); English edition, 1974; Braille transcription, 1974; Italian edition, 1978; Japanese edition, 1980; Spanish edition, 1981; University Press of America edition, 1984; Norton edition, 1989, with new Afterword.

Ten Lectures on the New Economic History [in Japanese] (Nan-un-do, 1977).

Aging: Stability and Change in the Family (Academic Press, 1981; co-edited with E. Hatfield, S. Kiesler, and E. Shanas).

Trends in Nutrition, Labor Welfare, and Labor Productivity (a special issue of *Social Science History,* Fall 1982; co-edited with S. L. Engerman).

Which Road to the Past? Two Views of History (Yale, 1983; with G. R. Elton); Fogel's essay translated into Hungarian and published in *Világtörténet* (1986).

Long-Term Changes in Nutrition and the Standard of Living (Ninth International Economic History Congress, 1986; R. W. Fogel, editor).

Without Consent or Contract: The Rise and Fall of American Slavery (W. W. Norton 1989).

Without Consent or Contract: The Rise and Fall of American Slavery; Evidence and Methods (W. W. Norton, 1991; co-edited with R. A. Galantine and R. L. Manning).

Without Consent or Contract: The Rise and Fall of American Slavery; Markets and Production: Technical Papers, Volume I (W. W. Norton, 1991; co-edited with S. L. Engerman).

Without Consent or Contract: The Rise and Fall of American Slavery; Conditions of Slave Life and the Transition to Freedom: Technical Papers, Volume II (W. W. Norton, 1991; co-edited with S. L. Engerman).

A Guide to Business Ethics in the 1990s (forthcoming).

The Escape from Hunger and Early Death: Europe, America, and the Third World: 1750–2050 (forthcoming).

Simon Kuznets and the Empirical Tradition in Economics (forthcoming; with Enid M. Fogel).

Papers

"A Quantitative Approach to the Study of Railroads in American Economic Growth: A Report of Some Preliminary Findings," *Journal of Economic History* (June 1962); reprinted in *Readings in United States Economic and Business History,* Ross M. Robertson and James L. Pate, eds. (Houghton Mifflin, 1966); *Essays in American Economic History,* A. W. Coats and R. M. Robertson, eds. (Arnold, 1969); *The West of the American People,* Allan G. Bogue, et al. (Peacock, 1970); *Quantification in American History*, Robert Swierenga, ed. (Atheneum, 1970); *The New Economic History*, Peter Temin, ed. (Penguin, 1973).

"A Provisional View of the 'New Economic History,'" *American Economic Review* (May 1964); reprinted in *New Views on American Economic Development,* Ralph Andreano, ed. (Schenkman, 1965).

"The Reunification of Economic History with Economic Theory," *American Economic Review* (May 1965); reprinted in *Essays in American Economic History,* A. W. Coats and Ross M. Robertson, eds. (Arnold, 1969); *Issues in American Economic History,* Gerald D. Nash, ed. (2d edn., Heath, 1972).

"American Interregional Trade in the Nineteenth Century," *New Views on American Economic Development,* Ralph Andreano, ed. (Schenkman, 1965).

"Railroads and the Axiom of Indispensability," *New Views on American Economic Development,* Ralph Andreano, ed. (Schenkman, 1965).

"Railroads as an Analogy to the Space Effort," *Economic Journal* (March 1966); reprinted in *The Railroad and the Space Program,* Bruce Mazlish, ed. (M.I.T., 1965); *The New Economic History,* Peter Temin, ed. (Penguin, 1973).

"The New Economic History: Its Findings and Methods," *Economic History Review* (Dec. 1966); reprinted in *Quantitative History,* K. D. Rowney and J. G. Graham, Jr., eds. (Dorsey, 1969); Kölner Vortrage zur Social- und Wirtschaftgeschichte, Heft 8 (Universität Köln, 1970); *The Reinterpretation of American Economic History,* R. W. Fogel and S. L. Engerman, eds. (Harper & Row, 1971).

"The Specification Problem in Economic History," *Journal of Economic History* (Sept. 1967); reprinted in *The New Economic History,* Peter Temin, ed. (Penguin, 1973).

"Econometrics and Southern Economic History: A Comment," *Explorations in Entrepreneurial History,* vol. 6, no. 1 (1968); reprinted in *The New Economic History,* Ralph Andreano, ed. (Wiley, 1970).

"A Model for the Explanation of Industrial Expansion During the Nineteenth Century: With an Application to the American Iron Industry" (with S. L. Engerman), *Journal of Political Economy* (June 1969); reprinted in *The Reinterpretation of American Economic History,* R. W. Fogel and S. L. Engerman, eds. (Harper & Row, 1971).

"History and Retrospective Econometrics," *History and Theory* (1970).

"The Relative Efficiency of Slavery: A Comparison of Northern and Southern Agriculture in the United States During 1860" (with S. L. Engerman), *Explorations in Economic History* (Winter 1971).

"Quantitative Economic History: An Interim Evaluation: Past Trends and Present Tendencies" (with Albert Fishlow), *Journal of Economic History* (March 1971).

"The Efficiency Effects of Federal Land Policy, 1850–1900: Some Provisional Findings" (with Jack L. Rutner), in *The Dimensions of Quantitative Research in History,* W. O. Aydelotte, Allan G. Bogue, and R. W. Fogel, eds. (Princeton University Press, 1972).

"New Directions in Black History" (with others), *Forum* (Spring 1972)

"A Comparison of the Efficiency of Slave and Free Agricultural Labor in the United States During 1860" (with S. L. Engerman), published in *Papers and Proceedings of the Fifth International Economic History Conference.*

"Current Directions in Economic History (a note)," *Journal of Economic History,* 32 (March 1972).

"Philanthropy at Bargain Prices: Notes on the Economics of Gradual Emancipation" (with S. L. Engerman), *Journal of Legal Studies,* vol. 3, no. 2 (June 1974).

"The Limits of Quantitative Methods in History," *American Historical Review* (May 1975).

"Three Phases of Cliometric Research on Slavery and Its Aftermath," *American Economic Review* (May 1975).

"From the Marxists to the Mormons," *The Times Literary Supplement* (13 June 1975).

"Explaining the Relative Efficiency of Slave Agriculture in the Antebellum South" (with S. L. Engerman), *American Economic Review* (June 1977).

"Cliometrics and Culture: Some Recent Developments in the Historiography of Slavery," *Journal of Social History* (Sept. 1977); reprinted in *Esclave = facteur de production; l'économie de l'esclavage,* S. Mintz, ed. (Paris, 1981).

"The Economics of Mortality in North America, 1650–1910: A Description of a Research Project" (with others), *Historical Methods* (Spring 1978).

"Notes on the Social Saving Controversy," *Journal of Economic History* (March 1979).

"Recent Findings on Slave Demography and Family Structure" (with S. L. Engerman), *Sociology and Social Research* (April 1979).

"Explaining the Relative Efficiency of Slave Agriculture in the Antebellum South: Reply" (with S. L. Engerman), *American Economic Review* (Sept. 1980).

"'Scientific' History and Traditional History," in L. J. Cohen, J. Los, H. Pfeiffer, and K. P. Podewski, eds., *Logic, Methodology, and Philosophy of Science,* vol. 6 (North-Holland, 1982).

"Circumstantial Evidence in 'Scientific' and Traditional History," in David Carr, William Dray, and Theodore Geraets, eds., *Philosophy and History and Contemporary Historiography* (University of Ottawa Press, 1982).

"Explaining the Uses of Data on Height" (with S. L. Engerman and J. Trussell), *Social Science History* (Nov. 1982).

"Secular Changes in American and British Stature and Nutrition" (with others), *Journal of Interdisciplinary History* (Autumn 1983).

"Physical Growth as a Measure of the Economic Well-Being of Populations: The Eighteenth and Nineteenth Centuries," in Frank Falkner and J. M. Tanner, eds., *Human Growth* (2d edn., Plenum Press, 1986).

"Nutrition and the Decline in Mortality Since 1700: Some Preliminary Findings," in S. L. Engerman and R. Gallman, eds., *Long-Term Factors in American Economic Growth,* Studies in Income and Wealth, vol. 51 (University of Chicago Press, 1986); a condensed version reprinted in *Society, Health, and Population During the Demographic Transition,* A. Brandstrom and Lars-Göran Tedebrand, eds. (Coronet Books, 1988).

"Some Notes on the Scientific Methods of Simon Kuznets," in Simon Kuznets, *Economic Development, the Family, and Income Distribution: Selected Essays* (Cambridge University Press, 1989).

"Afterword 1989" (with S. L. Engerman), in the Norton edition of *Time on the Cross* (W. W. Norton, 1989).

"Modeling Complex Dynamic Interactions: The Role of Intergenerational, Cohort, and Period Processes and of Conditional Events in the Political Realignment of the 1850s," NBER Working Paper Series on Historical Factors in Long Run Growth, no. 12 (1990).

"Second Thoughts on the European Escape from Hunger: Famines, Price Elasticities, Entitlements, Chronic Malnutrition, and Mortality Rates," in S. R. Osmani, ed., *Nutrition and Poverty* (Clarendon Press, Oxford, 1991).

"The Conquest of High Mortality and Hunger in Europe and America: Timing and Mechanisms," in Henry Rosovsky, David S. Landes, and Patrice Higgonet, eds., *Favorites of Fortune: Technology, Growth, and Economic Development since the Industrial Revolution* (Harvard University Press, 1991).

"Aging of the Union Army Men: A Longitudinal Study, 1830–1840" (with Larry T. Wimmer). Paper presented at the Joint Statistical Meetings in Atlanta, GA., August 19–22, 1991.

"New Findings on Secular Trends in Nutrition and Mortality: Some Implications for Population Theory," Nobel Jubilee Symposium, Population, Development, and Welfare. Lund, Sweden, December 5–7, 1991.

"Nutrition and Mortality in France, Britain, and the United States, 1700–1938" (with Roderick Floud), University of Chicago, 1991, typescript.

"New Sources and New Techniques for the Study of Secular Trends in Nutritional Status, Health, Mortality, and the Process of Aging," NBER Working Paper Series on Historical Factors in Long Run Growth, no. 26 (1991).

"Toward A New Synthesis on the Role of Economic Issues in the Political Realignment of the 1850s," in Donald Schaffer and Thomas Weiss, eds., *Economic Development in Historical Perspective* (Stanford University Press, forthcoming 1992).

Biographies

Howard Bodenhorn is assistant professor of economics at St. Lawrence University in New York State.

Michael D. Bordo is professor of economics at Rutgers University and was previously at the University of South Carolina. He is also a research associate of the National Bureau of Economic Research.

Ann M. Carlos is associate professor of economics at the University of Colorado at Boulder and has recently moved there from the University of Western Ontario.

Stephen Crawford is an advertising executive with Leo Burnett, Inc. in Chicago.

Stanley L. Engerman is the John H. Munro Professor of Economics and professor of history at the University of Rochester and a research associate of the National Bureau of Economic Research.

Gerald Friedman is assistant professor at the University of Massachusetts at Amherst.

David W. Galenson is professor of economics at the University of Chicago and a research associate of the National Bureau of Economic Research.

Claudia Goldin is professor of economics at Harvard University where she moved recently from the University of Pennsylvania. She is program director and research associate of the National Bureau of Economic Research and was the editor of the *Journal of Economic History* from 1984 to 1988.

Alice Hanson Jones was, until her death in 1985, professor emeritus of economics at Washington University in St. Louis. She served as president of the Economic History Association from 1982 to 1983.

John Komlos is associate professor of history and economics at the University of Pittsburgh.

Michael Kurth is associate professor of economics at McNeese State University in Louisiana.

Frank Lewis is professor of economics at Queen's University in Ontario.

Robert A. Margo is professor of economics at Vanderbilt University and was previously at Colgate University and the University of Pennsylvania. He is also a research associate of the National Bureau of Economic Research.

Donald N. McCloskey is the John F. Murray Professor of Economics and professor of history at the University of Iowa and is the director of the Project on the Rhetoric of Inquiry.

Clayne L. Pope is professor of economics at Brigham Young University and a research associate of the National Bureau of Economic Research.

Peter Rappoport is assistant professor of economics at Rutgers University.

Joseph D. Reid, Jr., is associate professor of economics at George Mason University.

Hugh Rockoff is professor of economics at Rutgers University and a research associate of the National Bureau of Economic Research.

Winifred B. Rothenberg is assistant professor of economics at Tufts University.

Anna J. Schwartz is research associate emerita of the National Bureau of Economic Research.

Boris Simkovich is a graduate student in economics at Harvard University.

Kenneth L. Sokoloff is associate professor of economics at the University of California at Los Angeles and a research associate of the National Bureau of Economic Research.

Richard H. Steckel is professor of economics at the Ohio State University and a research associate of the National Bureau of Economic Research.

Georgia C. Villaflor teaches economics at San Diego State University.

Jenny Bourne Wahl is assistant professor of economics at St. Olaf College in Minnesota.

Donghyu Yang is associate professor of economics at Seoul National University, Korea.

Contributors

Howard Bodenhorn
Department of Economics
Hepburn Hall
St. Lawrence University
Canton, NY 13617

Michael D. Bordo
Department of Economics
New Jersey Hall
Rutgers University
New Brunswick, NJ 08903

Ann M. Carlos
Department of Economics
Campus Box 256
University of Colorado
Boulder, CO 80309

Stephen Crawford
Leo Burnett, Inc.
35 West Wacker Drive
Chicago, IL 60601

Stanley L. Engerman
Department of Economics
University of Rochester
Rochester, NY 14627

Gerald Friedman
Department of Economics
Thompson Hall
University of Massachusetts
Amherst, MA 01003

David W. Galenson
Department of Economics
University of Chicago
1126 East 59th Street
Chicago, IL 60637

Claudia Goldin
Department of Economics
Harvard University
Cambridge, MA 02138

John Komlos
Department of History
University of Pittsburgh
Pittsburgh, PA 15260

Michael Kurth
Department of Economics and Finance
McNeese State University
Lake Charles, LA 70609

Frank Lewis
Department of Economics
Queen's University
Kingston, Ontario K7L 3N6
Canada

Robert A. Margo
Department of Economics
Calhoun 109
Vanderbilt University
Nashville, TN 37235

Donald N. McCloskey
Department of Economics
University of Iowa
Iowa City, IA 52242

Clayne L. Pope
Department of Economics
154 Faculty Office Building
Brigham Young University
Provo, UT 84602

Peter Rappoport
Department of Economics
New Jersey Hall
Rutgers University
New Brunswick, NJ 08903

Joseph D. Reid, Jr.
Department of Economics
4400 University Drive
George Mason University
Fairfax, VA 22030

Hugh Rockoff
Department of Economics
New Jersey Hall
Rutgers University
New Brunswick, NJ 08903

Winifred B. Rothenberg
Department of Economics
Tufts University
Medford, MA 02155

Anna J. Schwartz
National Bureau of Economic Research
269 Mercer Street, 8th floor
New York, NY 10003

Boris Simkovich
Department of Economics
Harvard University
Cambridge, MA 02138

Kenneth L. Sokoloff
Department of Economics
405 Hilgard Avenue
University of California
Los Angeles, CA 90024

Richard H. Steckel
Department of Economics
Ohio State University
410 Arps Hall
1945 North High Street
Columbus, OH 43210

Georgia C. Villaflor
3521 Columbia Street
San Diego, CA 92103

Jenny Bourne Wahl
St. Olaf College
1520 St. Olaf Avenue
Northfield, MN 55057

Donghyu Yang
Department of Economics
Seoul National University
Sillim-dong, Kwanak-gu
Seoul, Korea

Author Index

Subject Index